Study Guide

STUDY GUIDE

Richard O. Straub
University of Michigan, Dearborn

to accompany

Kathleen Stassen Berger

The Developing Person Through the Life Span
Fifth Edition

WORTH PUBLISHERS

Study Guide
by Richard O. Straub
to accompany
Berger: **The Developing Person Through the Life Span**, Fifth Edition

ISBN: 1-57259-944-8

Printing: 1 2 3 4 5
Year: 04 03 02 01

Cover credit: "On the Dock" by Christian Pierre.

Worth Publishers
41 Madison Avenue
New York, NY 10010
www.worthpublishers.com

Contents

Preface

This Study Guide is designed for use with *The Developing Person Through the Life Span*, Fifth Edition, by Kathleen Stassen Berger. It is intended to help you to evaluate your understanding of that material, and then to review any problem areas. "How to Manage Your Time Efficiently, Study More Effectively, and Think Critically" provides detailed instructions on how to use the textbook and this Study Guide for maximum benefit. It also offers additional study suggestions based on principles of time management, effective note-taking, evaluation of exam performance, and an effective program for improving your comprehension while studying from textbooks.

Each chapter of the Study Guide includes a Chapter Overview, a set of Guided Study questions to pace your reading of the text chapter, a Chapter Review section to be completed after you have read the text chapter, and three review tests. One chapter in each section of the text includes a crossword puzzle that provides an alternative way of testing your understanding of the terms and concepts. The review tests are of two types: Progress Tests that consist of questions focusing on facts and definitions and a Thinking Critically Test that evaluates your understanding of the text chapter's broader conceptual material and its application to real-world situations. For all three review tests, the correct answers are given, followed by textbook page references (so you can easily go back and reread the material), and complete explanations not only of why the answer is correct but also of why the other choices are incorrect.

I would like to thank Betty and Don Probert of The Special Projects Group for their exceptional work in all phases of this project. My thanks also to Graig Donini and Stacey Alexander for their skillful assistance in the preparation of this Study Guide. We hope that our work will help you to achieve your highest level of academic performance in this course and to acquire a keen appreciation of human development.

Richard O. Straub
July 2000

How to Manage Your Time Efficiently, Study More Effectively, and Think Critically

How effectively do you study? Good study habits make the job of being a college student much easier. Many students, who *could* succeed in college, fail or drop out because they have never learned to manage their time efficiently. Even the best students can usually benefit from an in-depth evaluation of their current study habits.

There are many ways to achieve academic success, of course, but your approach may not be the most effective or efficient. Are you sacrificing your social life or your physical or mental health in order to get A's on your exams? Good study habits result in better grades *and* more time for other activities.

Evaluate Your Current Study Habits

To improve your study habits, you must first have an accurate picture of how you currently spend your time. Begin by putting together a profile of your present living and studying habits. Answer the following questions by writing *yes* or *no* on each line.

_____ 1. Do you usually set up a schedule to budget your time for studying, recreation, and other activities?

_____ 2. Do you often put off studying until time pressures force you to cram?

_____ 3. Do other students seem to study less than you do, but get better grades?

_____ 4. Do you usually spend hours at a time studying one subject, rather than dividing that time between several subjects?

_____ 5. Do you often have trouble remembering what you have just read in a textbook?

_____ 6. Before reading a chapter in a textbook, do you skim through it and read the section headings?

_____ 7. Do you try to predict exam questions from your lecture notes and reading?

_____ 8. Do you usually attempt to paraphrase or summarize what you have just finished reading?

_____ 9. Do you find it difficult to concentrate very long when you study?

_____ 10. Do you often feel that you studied the wrong material for an exam?

Thousands of college students have participated in similar surveys. Students who are fully realizing their academic potential usually respond as follows: (1) yes, (2) no, (3) no, (4) no, (5) no, (6) yes, (7) yes, (8) yes, (9) no, (10) no.

Compare your responses to those of successful students. The greater the discrepancy, the more you could benefit from a program to improve your study habits. The questions are designed to identify areas of weakness. Once you have identified your weaknesses, you will be able to set specific goals for improvement and implement a program for reaching them.

Manage Your Time

Do you often feel frustrated because there isn't enough time to do all the things you must and want to do? Take heart. Even the most productive and successful people feel this way at times. But they establish priorities for their activities and they learn to budget time for each of them. There's much in the saying "If you want something done, ask a busy person to do it." A busy person knows how to get things done.

If you don't now have a system for budgeting your time, develop one. Not only will your academic accomplishments increase, but you will actually find more time in your schedule for other activities. And you won't have to feel guilty about "taking time off," because all your obligations will be covered.

Establish a Baseline

As a first step in preparing to budget your time, keep a diary for a few days to establish a summary, or baseline, of the time you spend in studying, socializing, working, and so on. If you are like many students, much of your "study" time is nonproductive; you may sit at your desk and leaf through a book, but the time is actually wasted. Or you may procrastinate. You are always getting ready to study, but you rarely do.

Besides revealing where you waste time, your diary will give you a realistic picture of how much time you need to allot for meals, commuting, and other fixed activities. In addition, careful records should indicate the times of the day when you are consistently most productive. A sample time-management diary is shown in Table 1.

Plan the Term

Having established and evaluated your baseline, you are ready to devise a more efficient schedule. Buy a calendar that covers the entire school term and has ample space for each day. Using the course outlines provided by your instructors, enter the dates of all exams, term paper deadlines, and other important academic obligations. If you have any long-range personal plans (concerts, weekend trips, etc.), enter the dates on the calendar as well. Keep your calendar up to date and refer to it often. I recommend carrying it with you at all times.

Develop a Weekly Calendar

Now that you have a general picture of the school term, develop a weekly schedule that includes all of your activities. Aim for a schedule that you can live with for the entire school term. A sample weekly schedule, incorporating the following guidelines, is shown in Table 2.

1. Enter your class times, work hours, and any other fixed obligations first. *Be thorough.* Using information from your time-management diary, allow plenty of time for such things as commuting, meals, laundry, and the like.

Table 1   Sample Time-Management Diary

Activity	Time Completed	Duration Hours: Minute
	Monday	
Sleep	7:00	7:30
Dressing	7:25	:25
Breakfast	7:45	:20
Commute	8:20	:35
Coffee	9:00	:40
French	10:00	1:00
Socialize	10:15	:15
Videogame	10:35	:20
Coffee	11:00	:25
Psychology	12:00	1:00
Lunch	12:25	:25
Study Lab	1:00	:35
Psych. Lab	4:00	3:00
Work	5:30	1:30
Commute	6:10	:40
Dinner	6:45	:35
TV	7:30	:45
Study Psych.	10:00	2:30
Socialize	11:30	1:30
Sleep		

Prepare a similar chart for each day of the week. When y finish an activity, note it on the chart and write down t time it was completed. Then determine its duration by su tracting the time the previous activity was finished from t newly entered time.

2. Set up a study schedule for each of your cours The study habits survey and your time-manageme diary will direct you. The following guidelir should also be useful.

(a) Establish regular study times for each course. T 4 hours needed to study one subject, for example, a most profitable when divided into shorter perio spaced over several days. If you cram your studyi into one 4-hour block, what you attempt to learn the third or fourth hour will interfere with what y studied in the first 2 hours. Newly acquired know edge is like wet cement. It needs some time to "ha en" to become memory.

(b) Alternate subjects. The type of interference j mentioned is greatest between similar topics. Set u schedule in which you spend time on several *differ* courses during each study session. Besides reduci the potential for interference, alternating subjects w help to prevent mental fatigue with one topic.

(c) Set weekly goals to determine the amount of stu time you need to do well in each course. This w

Table 2   Sample Weekly Schedule

Time	Mon.	Tues.	Wed.	Thurs.	Fri.	Sat.
7–8	Dress Eat	Dress Eat	Dress Eat	Dress Eat	Dress Eat	
8–9	Psych.	Study Psych.	Psych.	Study Psych.	Psych.	Dress Eat
9–10	Eng.	Study Eng.	Eng.	Study Eng.	Eng.	Study Eng.
10–11	Study French	Free	Study French	Open Study	Study French	Study Stats.
11–12	French	Study Psych. Lab	French	Open Study	French	Study Stats.
12–1	Lunch	Lunch	Lunch	Lunch	Lunch	Lunch
1–2	Stats.	Psych. Lab	Stats.	Study or Free	Stats.	Free
2–3	Bio.	Psych. Lab	Bio.	Free	Bio.	Free
3–4	Free	Psych.	Free	Free	Free	Free
4–5	Job	Job	Job	Job	Job	Free
5–6	Job	Job	Job	Job	Job	Free
6–7	Dinner	Dinner	Dinner	Dinner	Dinner	Dinner
7–8	Study Bio.	Study Bio.	Study Bio.	Study Bio.	Free	Free
8–9	Study Eng.	Study Stats.	Study Psych.	Open Study	Open Study	Free
9–10	Open Study	Open Study	Open Study	Open Study	Free	Free

This is a sample schedule for a student with a 16-credit load and a 10-hour-per-week part-time job. Using this chart as an illustration, make up a weekly schedule, following the guidelines outlined here.

epend on, among other things, the difficulty of your ourses and the effectiveness of your methods. Many rofessors recommend studying at least 1 to 2 hours or each hour in class. If your time-management diary ndicates that you presently study less time than that, o not plan to jump immediately to a much higher evel. Increase study time from your baseline by set- ng weekly goals [see (4)] that will gradually bring ou up to the desired level. As an initial schedule, for xample, you might set aside an amount of study me for each course that matches class time.

d) Schedule for maximum effectiveness. Tailor your chedule to meet the demands of each course. For the ourse that emphasizes lecture notes, schedule time or a daily review soon after the class. This will give ou a chance to revise your notes and clean up any ard-to-decipher shorthand while the material is still resh in your mind. If you are evaluated for class par- cipation (for example, in a language course), allow me for a review just before the class meets. Schedule udy time for your most difficult (or least motivat-

ing) courses during hours when you are the most alert and distractions are fewest.

(e) Schedule open study time. Emergencies, addition-al obligations, and the like could throw off your schedule. And you may simply need some extra time periodically for a project or for review in one of your courses. Schedule several hours each week for such purposes.

3. After you have budgeted time for studying, fill in slots for recreation, hobbies, relaxation, household errands, and the like.

4. Set specific goals. Before each study session, make a list of specific goals. The simple note "7–8 PM: study psychology" is too broad to ensure the most effective use of the time. Formulate your daily goals according to what you know you must accomplish during the term. If you have course outlines with advance assignments, set systematic daily goals that will allow you, for example, to cover fifteen chapters before the exam. And be realistic: Can you actually

expect to cover a 78-page chapter in one session? Divide large tasks into smaller units; stop at the most logical resting points. When you complete a specific goal, take a 5- or 10-minute break before tackling the next goal.

5. Evaluate how successful or unsuccessful your studying has been on a daily or weekly basis. Did you reach most of your goals? If so, reward yourself immediately. You might even make a list of five to ten rewards to choose from. If you have trouble studying regularly, you may be able to motivate yourself by making such rewards contingent on completing specific goals.

6. Finally, until you have lived with your schedule for several weeks, don't hesitate to revise it. You may need to allow more time for chemistry, for example, and less for some other course. If you are trying to study regularly for the first time and are feeling burned out, you probably have set your initial goals too high. Don't let failure cause you to despair and abandon the program. Accept your limitations and revise your schedule so that you are studying only 15 to 20 minutes more each evening than you are used to. The point is to identify a regular schedule with which you can achieve some success. Time management, like any skill, must be practiced to become effective.

Techniques for Effective Study

Knowing how to put study time to best use is, of course, as important as finding a place for it in your schedule. Here are some suggestions that should enable you to increase your reading comprehension and improve your note-taking. A few study tips are included as well.

Using SQ3R to Increase Reading Comprehension

How do you study from a textbook? If you are like many students, you simply read and reread in a *passive* manner. Studies have shown, however, that most students who simply read a textbook cannot remember more than half the material ten minutes after they have finished. Often, what is retained is the unessential material rather than the important points upon which exam questions will be based.

This *Study Guide* employs a program known as SQ3R (*S*urvey, *Q*uestion, *R*ead, *R*ecite, and *R*eview) to facilitate, and allow you to assess, your comprehension of the important facts and concepts in *The Developing Person Through the Life Span*, Fifth Edition, by Kathleen Stassen Berger.

Research has shown that students using SQ3R achieve significantly greater comprehension of textbooks than students reading in the more traditional passive manner. Once you have learned this program, you can improve your comprehension of any textbook.

Survey Before reading a chapter, determine whether the text or the study guide has an outline or list of objectives. Read this material and the summary at the end of the chapter. Next, read the textbook chapter fairly quickly, paying special attention to the major headings and subheadings. This survey will give you an idea of the chapter's contents and organization. You will then be able to divide the chapter into logical sections in order to formulate specific goals for more careful reading of the chapter.

In this Study Guide, the *Chapter Overview* summarizes the major topics of the textbook chapter. This section also provides a few suggestions for approaching topics you may find difficult.

Question You will retain material longer when you have a use for it. If you look up a word's definition in order to solve a crossword puzzle, for example, you will remember it longer than if you merely fill in the letters as a result of putting other words in. Surveying the chapter will allow you to generate important questions that the chapter will proceed to answer. These question correspond to "mental files" in which knowledge will be sorted for easy access.

As you survey, jot down several questions for each chapter section. One simple technique is to generate questions by rephrasing a section heading. For example, the "Preoperational Thought" head could be turned into "What is preoperational thought?" Good questions will allow you to focus on the important points in the text. Examples of good questions are those that begin as follows: "List two examples of . . .." "What is the function of . . .?" "What is the significance of . . .?" Such questions give a purpose to your reading. Similarly, you can formulate questions based on the chapter outline.

The *Guided Study* section of this Study Guide provides the types of questions you might formulate while surveying each chapter. This section is a detailed set of objectives covering the points made in the text.

Read When you have established "files" for each section of the chapter, review your first question, begin reading, and continue until you have discovered the answer. If you come to material that seems to answer an important question you don't have a file for, stop and write down the question.

Using this Study Guide, read the chapter one section at a time. First, preview the section by skimming it, noting headings and boldface items. Next, study the appropriate section objectives in the *Guided Study*. Then, as you read the chapter section, search for the answer to each objective.

Be sure to read everything. Don't skip photo or art captions, graphs, marginal notes. In some cases, what may seem vague in reading will be made clear by a simple graph. Keep in mind that test questions are sometimes drawn from illustrations and charts.

Recite When you have found the answer to a question, close your eyes and mentally recite the question and its answer. Then *write* the answer next to the question. It is important that you recite an answer in your own words rather than the author's. Don't rely on your short-term memory to repeat the author's words verbatim.

In responding to the objectives, pay close attention to what is called for. If you are asked to identify or list, do just that. If asked to compare, contrast, or do both, you should focus on the similarities (compare) and differences (contrast) between the concepts or theories. Answering the objectives carefully will not only help you to focus your attention on the important concepts of the text, but it will also provide excellent practice for essay exams.

Recitation is an extremely effective study technique, recommended by many learning experts. In addition to increasing reading comprehension, it is useful for review. Trying to explain something in your own words clarifies your knowledge, often by revealing aspects of your answer that are vague or incomplete. If you repeatedly rely upon "I know" in recitation, you really may not know.

Recitation has the additional advantage of simulating an exam, especially an essay exam; the same skills are required in both cases. Too often students study without ever putting the book and notes aside, which makes it easy for them to develop false confidence in their knowledge. When the material is in front of you, you may be able to recognize an answer, but will you be able to recall it later, when you take an exam that does not provide these retrieval cues?

After you have recited and written your answer, continue with your next question. Read, recite, and so on.

Review When you have answered the last question in the material you have designated as a study goal, go back and review. Read over each question and your written answer to it. Your review might also include a brief written summary that integrates all of your questions and answers. This review need not take longer than a few minutes, but it is important. It will help you retain the material longer and will greatly facilitate a final review of each chapter before the exam.

In this Study Guide, the *Chapter Review* section contains fill-in and one- or two-sentence essay questions for you to complete after you have finished reading the text and have written answers to the objectives. The correct answers are given at the end of the chapter. Generally, your answer to a fill-in question should match exactly (as in the case of important terms, theories, or people). In some cases, the answer is not a term or name, so a word close in meaning will suffice. You should go through the Chapter Review several times before taking an exam, so it is a good idea to mentally fill in the answers until you are ready for a final pretest review. Textbook page references are provided with each section title, in case you need to reread any of the material.

Also provided to facilitate your review are two *Progress Tests* that include multiple-choice questions and, where appropriate, matching or true–false questions. These tests are not to be taken until you have read the chapter, written answers to the objectives, and completed the *Chapter Review*. Correct answers, along with explanations of why each alternative is correct or incorrect, are provided at the end of the chapter. The relevant text page numbers for each question are also given. If you miss a question, read these explanations and, if necessary, review the text pages to further understand why. The *Progress Tests* do not test every aspect of a concept, so you should treat an incorrect answer as an indication that you need to review the concept.

Following the two Progress Tests is a *Thinking Critically Test*, which should be taken just prior to an exam. It includes questions that test your ability to analyze, integrate, and apply the concepts in the chapter. As with the *Progress Tests*, answers for the *Thinking Critically Test* are provided at the end of each chapter, along with relevant page numbers.

The chapter concludes with *Key Terms*, either in list form only or also in a crossword puzzle. In either form, as with the *Guided Study* objectives, it is important that the answers be written from memory, and in list form, in your own words. The *Answers* section at the end of the chapter gives a definition of each term, sometimes along with an example of its usage and/or a tip to help you remember its meaning.

One final suggestion: Incorporate SQ3R into your time-management calendar. Set specific goals for completing SQ3R with each assigned chapter. Keep a record of chapters completed, and reward yourself for being conscientious. Initially, it takes more time and effort to "read" using SQ3R, but with practice, the steps will become automatic. More importantly, you will comprehend significantly more material and retain what you have learned longer than passive readers do.

Taking Lecture Notes

Are your class notes as useful as they might be? One way to determine their worth is to compare them with those taken by other good students. Are yours as thorough? Do they provide you with a comprehensible outline of each lecture? If not, then the following suggestions might increase the effectiveness of your note-taking.

1. Keep a separate notebook for each course. Use 8 1/2 × 11-inch pages. Consider using a ring binder, which would allow you to revise and insert notes while still preserving lecture order.

2. Take notes in the format of a lecture outline. Use roman numerals for major points, letters for supporting arguments, and so on. Some instructors will make this easy by delivering organized lectures and, in some cases, by outlining their lectures on the board. If a lecture is disorganized, you will probably want to reorganize your notes soon after the class.

3. As you take notes in class, leave a wide margin on one side of each page. After the lecture, expand or clarify any shorthand notes while the material is fresh in your mind. Use this time to write important questions in the margin next to notes that answer them. This will facilitate later review and will allow you to anticipate similar exam questions.

Evaluate Your Exam Performance

How often have you received a grade on an exam that did not do justice to the effort you spent preparing for the exam? This is a common experience that can leave one feeling bewildered and abused. "What do I have to do to get an A?" "The test was unfair!" "I studied the wrong material!"

The chances of this happening are greatly reduced if you have an effective time-management schedule and use the study techniques described here. But it can happen to the best-prepared student and is most likely to occur on your first exam with a new professor.

Remember that there are two main reasons for studying. One is to learn for your own general academic development. Many people believe that such knowledge is all that really matters. Of course, it is possible, though unlikely, to be an expert on a topic witho[ut] achieving commensurate grades, just as one ca[n] occasionally, earn an excellent grade without tru[ly] mastering the course material. During a job intervie[w] or in the workplace, however, your A in Cobol wo[n't] mean much if you can't actually program a compute[r.]

In order to keep career options open after you grad[u]ate, you must know the material and maintain com[-] petitive grades. In the short run, this means perfor[m] ing well on exams, which is the second main objecti[ve] in studying.

Probably the single best piece of advice to keep [in] mind when studying for exams is to *try to predict exa[m] questions*. This means ignoring the trivia and focusi[ng] on the important questions and their answers (wi[th] your instructor's emphasis in mind).

A second point is obvious. How well you do [on] exams is determined by your mastery of both lectu[re] and textbook material. Many students (partly becau[se] of poor time management) concentrate too much [on] one at the expense of the other.

To evaluate how well you are learning lecture a[nd] textbook material, analyze the questions you miss[ed] on the first exam. If your instructor does not revie[w] exams during class, you can easily do it yourse[lf.] Divide the questions into two categories: those dra[wn] primarily from lectures and those drawn primari[ly] from the textbook. Determine the percentage of que[s-] tions you missed in each category. If your errors a[re] evenly distributed and you are satisfied with yo[ur] grade, you have no problem. If you are weaker in o[ne] area, you will need to set future goals for increasi[ng] and/or improving your study of that area.

Similarly, note the percentage of test questions dra[wn] from each category. Although exams in most cours[es] cover both lecture notes and the textbook, the relati[ve] emphasis of each may vary from instructor to instru[c] tor. While your instructors may not be entirely consi[s] tent in making up future exams, you may be able [to] tailor your studying for each course by placing add[i] tional emphasis on the appropriate area.

Exam evaluation will also point out the types of que[s] tions your instructor prefers. Does the exam cons[ist] primarily of multiple-choice, true–false, or ess[ay] questions? You may also discover that an instructor [is] fond of wording questions in certain ways. For exa[m] ple, an instructor may rely heavily on questions th[at] require you to draw an analogy between a theory [or] concept and a real-world example. Evaluate bo[th] your instructor's style and how well you do wi[th] each format. Use this information to guide yo[ur] future exam preparation.

important aids, not only in studying for exams but also in determining how well prepared you are, are the Progress and Thinking Critically Tests provided in this Study Guide. If these tests don't include all of the types of questions your instructor typically writes, make up your own practice exam questions. Spend extra time testing yourself with question formats that are most difficult for you. There is no better way to evaluate your preparation for an upcoming exam than by testing yourself under the conditions most likely to be in effect during the actual test.

A Few Practical Tips

Even the best intentions for studying sometimes fail. Some of these failures occur because students attempt to work under conditions that are simply not conducive to concentrated study. To help ensure the success of your time-management program, here are a few suggestions that should assist you in reducing the possibility of procrastination or distraction.

1. If you have set up a schedule for studying, make your roommate, family, and friends aware of this commitment, and ask them to honor your quiet study time. Close your door and post a "Do Not Disturb" sign.

2. Set up a place to study that minimizes potential distractions. Use a desk or table, not your bed or an extremely comfortable chair. Keep your desk and the walls around it free from clutter. If you need a place other than your room, find one that meets as many of the above requirements as possible—for example, in the library stacks.

3. Do nothing but study in this place. It should become associated with studying so that it "triggers" this activity, just as a mouth-watering aroma elicits an appetite.

4. Never study with the television on or with other distracting noises present. If you must have music in the background in order to mask outside noise, for example, play soft instrumental music. Don't pick vocal selections; your mind will be drawn to the lyrics.

5. Study by yourself. Other students can be distracting or can break the pace at which your learning is most efficient. In addition, there is always the possibility that group studying will become a social gathering. Reserve that for its own place in your schedule.

If you continue to have difficulty concentrating for very long, try the following suggestions.

6. Study your most difficult or most challenging subjects first, when you are most alert.

7. Start with relatively short periods of concentrated study, with breaks in between. If your attention starts to wander, get up immediately and take a break. It is better to study effectively for 15 minutes and then take a break than to fritter away 45 minutes out of an hour. Gradually increase the length of study periods, using your attention span as an indicator of successful pacing.

Critical Thinking

Having discussed a number of specific techniques for managing your time efficiently and studying effectively, let us now turn to a much broader topic: What exactly should you expect to learn as a student of developmental psychology?

Most developmental psychology courses have two major goals: (1) to help you acquire a basic understanding of the discipline's knowledge base, and (2) to help you learn to think like a psychologist. Many students devote all of their efforts to the first of these goals, concentrating on memorizing as much of the course's material as possible.

The second goal—learning to think like a psychologist—has to do with critical thinking. Critical thinking has many meanings. On one level, it refers to an attitude of healthy skepticism that should guide your study of psychology. As a critical thinker, you learn not to accept any explanation or conclusion about behavior as true until you have evaluated the evidence. On another level, critical thinking refers to a systematic process for examining the conclusions and arguments presented by others. In this regard, many of the features of the SQ3R technique for improving reading comprehension can be incorporated into an effective critical thinking system.

To learn to think critically, you must first recognize that psychological information is transmitted through the construction of persuasive arguments. An argument consists of three parts: an assertion, evidence, and an explanation (Mayer and Goodchild, 1990).

An assertion is a statement of relationship between some aspect of behavior, such as intelligence, and another factor, such as age. Learn to identify and evaluate the assertions about behavior and mental processes that you encounter as you read your textbook, listen to lectures, and engage in discussions with classmates. A good test of your understanding of an assertion is to try to restate it in your own words. As you do so, pay close attention to how important terms and concepts are defined. When a researcher asserts that "intelligence declines with age," for example, what does he or she mean by "intelligence"? Assertions such as this one may be true when a critical term ("intelligence") is defined one way (for example, "speed of thinking"), but not when defined in another way (for example, "general knowledge"). One of the strengths of psychology is the use of *operational* definitions that specify how key terms and concepts are measured, thus eliminating any ambiguity about their meaning. "Intelligence," for example, is often operationally defined as performance on a test measuring various cognitive skills. Whenever you encounter an assertion that is ambiguous, be skeptical of its accuracy.

When you have a clear understanding of an argument's assertion, evaluate its supporting evidence, the second component of an argument. Is it *empirical*? Does it, in fact, support the assertion? Psychologists accept only *empirical (observable) evidence* that is based on direct measurement of behavior. Hearsay, intuition, and personal experiences are not acceptable evidence. Chapter 1 discusses the various research methods used by developmental psychologists to gather empirical evidence. Some examples include surveys, observations of behavior in natural settings, and experiments.

As you study developmental psychology, you will become aware of another important issue in evaluating evidence—determining whether or not the research on which it is based is faulty. Research can be faulty for many reasons, including the use of an unrepresentative sample of subjects, experimenter bias, and inadequate control of unanticipated factors that might influence results. Evidence based on faulty research should be discounted.

The third component of an argument is the explanation provided for an assertion, which is based on the evidence that has been presented. While the argument's assertion merely *describes* how two things (such as intelligence and age) are related, the explanation tells *why*, often by proposing some theoretical mechanism that causes the relationship. Empirical evidence that thinking speed slows with age (the assertion), for example, may be explained as being caused by age-related changes in the activity of brain cells (a physiological explanation).

Be cautious in accepting explanations. In order to think critically about an argument's explanation, ask yourself three questions: (1) Can I restate the explanation in my own words?; (2) Does the explanation make sense based on the stated evidence?; and (3) Are there alternative explanations that adequately explain the assertion? Consider this last point in relation to our sample assertion: It is possible that slower thinking speed of older adults is due to their having less recent experience than younger people with tasks that require quick thinking (a disuse explanation).

Because psychology is a relatively young science, theoretical explanations are still emerging, and often change. For this reason, not all psychological arguments will offer explanations. Many arguments will only raise additional questions for further research to address.

Some Suggestions for Becoming a Critical Thinker

1. Adopt an attitude of healthy skepticism in evaluating psychological arguments.

2. Insist on unambiguous operational definitions of an argument's important concepts and terms.

3. Be cautious in accepting supporting evidence for an argument's assertion.

4. Refuse to accept evidence for an argument if it is based on faulty research.

5. Ask yourself if the theoretical explanation provided for an argument "makes sense" based on the empirical evidence.

6. Determine whether there are alternative explanations that adequately explain an assertion.

7. Use critical thinking to construct your own effective arguments when writing term papers, answering essay questions, and speaking.

8. Polish your critical-thinking skills by applying them to each of your college courses, and to other areas of life as well. Learn to think critically about advertising, political speeches, and the material presented in popular periodicals.

Some Closing Thoughts

I hope that these suggestions help make you more successful academically, and that they enhance the quality of your college life in general. Having the necessary skills makes any job a lot easier and more pleasant. Let me repeat my warning not to attempt to make too drastic a change in your life-style immediately. Good habits require time and self-discipline to develop. Once established they can last a lifetime.

Study Guide

CHAPTER 1

Introduction

Chapter Overview

The first chapter introduces the study of human development. The first section defines development, introduces the life-span perspective, and describes the three domains into which development is often divided.

The second section makes clear that development is influenced as much by external factors as by internal factors. Beginning with a discussion of the ecological model—Bronfenbrenner's description of how the individual is affected by, and affects, many other individuals, groups of individuals, and larger systems in the environment—this section describes different aspects of the overlapping contexts in which people develop. The story of David illustrates the effects of these contexts.

The next two sections discuss the strategies developmentalists use in their research, beginning with the scientific method and including scientific observation, correlational research, experiments, surveys, and case studies. To study people over time, developmentalists have created several research designs: cross-sectional, longitudinal, and cross-sequential.

The final section discusses the ethics of research with humans. In addition to ensuring confidentiality and safety, developmentalists who study children are especially concerned that the benefits of research outweigh the risks.

NOTE: Answer guidelines for all Chapter 1 questions begin on page 12.

Guided Study

The text chapter should be studied one section at a time. Before you read, preview each section by skimming it, noting headings and boldface items. Then read the appropriate section objectives from the following outline. Keep these objectives in mind and, as you read the chapter section, search for the information that will enable you to meet each objective. Once you have finished a section, write out answers for its objectives.

The Study of Human Development (pp. 3–6)

1. Define the study of human development, and identify five characteristics of development identified by the life-span perspective.

2. Identify and describe the three domains into which human development is often separated.

Contexts and Systems (pp. 6–15, 16–17)

3. Describe the ecological model of human development, and explain how this approach leads to an understanding of the overlapping contexts in which people develop.

4. Discuss the three broad, overlapping contexts that affect development throughout the life span.

9. Describe surveys and case studies, noting at le[ast] one advantage (or strength) and one disadva[n]tage (or weakness) of each.

Developmental Study as a Science (pp. 15, 18)

5. List and describe the basic steps of the scientific method.

10. Describe three basic research designs used [by] developmental psychologists.

6. Identify several controversies that echo throughout the study of development.

Ethics and Science (pp. 30–33)

11. Briefly summarize some of the ethical issu[es] involved in conducting research with human s[ub]jects.

Research Methods (pp. 18–30)

7. Describe scientific observation and correlation as research strategies, noting at least one advantage (or strength) and one disadvantage (or weakness) of each.

Chapter Review

When you have finished reading the chapter, wo[rk] through the material that follows to review [it]. Complete the sentences and answer the questions. [As] you proceed, evaluate your performance for each se[c]tion by consulting the answers on page 12. Do [not] continue with the next section until you understa[nd] each answer. If you need to, review or reread [the] appropriate section in the textbook before continuin[g].

The Study of Human Development (pp. 3–6)

1. The scientific study of human development ca[n] be defined as the science that seeks to understa[nd]

_____

_____

8. Describe the components of an experiment, and discuss the main advantage and some of the limitations of this research method.

Central to this science is the _____-_____ _____ , which recognizes the sources of continuity and discontinuity from the beginning of life to the end.

e five developmental characteristics embodied thin the life-span perspective are that development

a. _____

b. _____

c. _____

d. _____

e. _____

One of the most encouraging aspects of the life-span perspective is that development is characterized by _____ , or the capability of change.

The study of human development can be separated into three domains: _____ , _____ , and _____ .

The study of brain and body changes and the social influences that guide them falls within the _____ domain.

Thinking, perception, and language learning fall mainly in the _____ domain of development.

The study of emotions, personality, and interpersonal relationships falls within the _____ domain.

All three domains _____ (are/are not) important at every age. Each of the domains _____ (is/is not) affected by the other two. While development is organized into domains, each person is an integrated whole; that is, development is _____ .

texts and Systems (pp. 6–15, 16–17)

Forces outside the individual that influence development make up the _____ of development.

The approach that emphasizes the influence of the systems, or contexts, that support the devel-

oping person is called the _____ model of development. This approach was first emphasized by _____ .

10. According to this model, the family, the peer group, and other aspects of the immediate social setting constitute the _____ .

11. Systems that link one microsystem to another constitute the _____ .

12. Community structures and local educational, medical, employment, and communications systems make up the _____ .

13. Cultural values, political philosophies, economic patterns, and social conditions make up the _____ .

14. A recent addition to this model is the _____ , which emphasizes the importance of historical time on development.

15. The ecological model emphasizes the _____ (unidirectional/multidirectional) and _____ nature of social influences.

16. This idea is most clearly expressed in two theories from the natural sciences: _____ theory and _____ theory, which stress the unpredictability and dynamism of all natural systems.

17. The phenomenon of the _____ _____ refers to the fact that the ecosystems _____ (act/do not act) in isolation; even a tiny change in one system can have a profound effect on the other systems of development.

18. A group of people born within a few years of each other is called a _____ . These people tend to be affected by history in _____ (the same way/different ways).

19. One such group is the huge "_____ _____ " generation of children born just after World War II. The historical circumstances of their youth may have promoted greater _____ and _____ than did those of older and younger adults.

20. In addition to being influenced by the particular social contexts in which they develop, cohorts can be affected by differences in their relative _____ .

21. A widely shared idea about the way things are, or should be, is a _____ . An important point about such ideas is that they _____ (often change/are very stable) over time.

22. The life stage of _____ is also an example of a social construction.

23. A contextual influence that is determined by a person's income, education, place of residence, and occupation is called _____ _____ , which is often abbreviated _____ .

24. The values, assumptions, and customs as well as the physical objects that a group of people have adopted as a design for living constitute a _____ .

25. One example of the impact of cultural values on development is the greater tendency for children to be viewed as an economic asset in _____ _____ communities. In such communities, infant care is designed to maximize _____ and emphasize family _____ . By contrast, middle-class parents in _____ nations are less worried about infant mortality and thus focus care on fostering _____ growth and emotional _____ . For these reasons, most women in developed nations want _____ (how many?) children and most women in developing countries want _____ children.

26. (A Life-Span View) The minimum income needed to pay for a family's basic necessities is called the _____ _____ . Among the hazards and pressures of poverty are higher rates of _____ _____ ,

_____ _____ , inadequate _____ , and adolescen[t] _____ .

27. (A Life-Span View) Fifty years ago, the poorest age group in most nations of the world were th[e] _____ . Today, poverty rates are highest in the _____ _____ age group.

28. (A Life-Span View) Although poverty is a usef[ul] signal for severe problems throughout life, oth[er] variables, such as the presence of _____ _____ withi[n a] family, play a crucial role in determining indiv[id]ual development. For example, some children seem resilient to the hazards of poverty, especi[al]ly those whose parents are _____ and involved. As another example, there are li[ke]ly to be fewer social problems among poor peo[ple] who work to keep up their _____ .

29. A collection of people who share certain attributes, such as ancestry, national origin, religio[n,] and language and, as a result, tend to have sim[i]lar beliefs, values, and cultural experiences is called a(n) _____ _____ . In distinguishing racial identity, _____ traits are less important than are the _____ and _____ t[hat] arise from ethnic or racial consciousness. Thus race is actually a _____ .

30. (In Person) Because his mother contracted the disease _____ during her pregna[n]cy, David was born with a heart defect and cataracts over both eyes. Thus, his immediate problems centered on the _____ domain. However, because he was born at a p[ar]ticular time, he was already influenced by the larger _____ context. His physic[al] handicaps later produced _____ and _____ handicaps.

evelopmental Study as a Science (pp. 15, 18)

. In order, the basic steps of the scientific method are:

a. _____

b. _____

c. _____

d. _____

e. _____

. A specific, testable prediction that forms the basis of a research project is called a _____ .

. To repeat an experimental test procedure and obtain the same results is to _____ the test of the hypothesis.

. The people who are studied in a research project are called the _____ .

. Age, sex, education, and other quantities that may differ during an investigation are called _____ . Developmental researchers deal with both _____ variation, which occurs from day to day in each person, and _____ variation, which occurs between people or groups.

. The nature/nurture controversy concerns how much, and which aspects, of development are affected by _____ and how much by _____ . The _____/_____ controversy concerns whether development is largely gradual in nature or characterized by sudden transformations. The _____/_____ controversy focuses on when individual differences in development are celebrated or considered problems that need correcting.

search Methods (pp. 18–30)

. In designing research studies, scientists are concerned with four issues: _____ , or whether a study measures what it purports to measure; _____ , or whether its measurements are correct; _____ , or whether the study applies to other populations and situations; and _____ , or whether it solves real-life problems.

38. When researchers observe and record, in a systematic and unbiased manner, what research subjects do, they are using _____ _____ . People may be observed in a _____ setting or in a _____ .

39. A chief limitation of observation is that it does not indicate the _____ of the behavior being observed.

40. (Research Report) To be sure that trained observers are viewing the traits of interest, each trait has be described in a precise behavioral manner, that is, it has to be _____ _____ .

41. (Research Report) To determine whether a difference between two groups occurred purely by coincidence, or chance, researchers apply a mathematical test of _____ _____ . Generally, coincidence is ruled out if there is less than 1 possibility in _____ that the difference could have occurred by chance.

42. A statistic that indicates whether two variables are related to each other is a _____ . To say that two variables are related in this way _____ (does/does not) necessarily imply that one caused the other.

43. A correlation is _____ if the occurrence of one variable makes it more likely that the other will occur, and _____ if the occurrence of one makes it less likely that the other will occur.

44. The method that allows a scientist to test a hypothesis in a controlled environment, in which the variables can be manipulated, is the _____ . In this method, researchers manipulate a(n) _____ variable to determine its effect on a(n) _____ variable.

45. Although this research method enables researchers to uncover the links between _____ and _____ , it is sometimes criticized for studying behavior in a situation that is _____ .

46. Another limitation is that participants in this research technique (except very young children) who know they are research subjects may attempt to _____ _____ . A final limitation is that most research studies of this type are of very limited _____ .

47. In a(n) _____ , scientists collect information from a large group of people by personal interview, written questionnaire, or by some other means.

48. A potential problem with this research method is that respondents may give answers they think the researcher _____ .

49. An intensive study of one individual is called a(n) _____ . An advantage of this method is that it provides a rich _____ description of development, rather than relying only on _____ data. Another important use is that it provides a good _____ _____ for other research.

50. Research that involves the comparison of people of different ages is called a _____- _____ research design.

51. With cross-sectional research it is very difficult to ensure that the various groups differ only in their _____ . In addition, every cross-sectional study will, to some degree, reflect _____ .

52. Research that follows the same people over a relatively long period of time is called a _____ research design.

State three drawbacks of this type of research design.

53. The research method that combines the longitudinal and cross-sectional methods is the _____-_____ research method.

Ethics and Science (pp. 30–33)

54. Researchers who study humans must ensure that their subjects are not _____ and that their participation is _____ and _____ .

55. The most complex matter in research with humans is ensuring that the _____ of a proposed study outweigh its _____ . Complicating this issue is the fact that research with the greatest potential benefit often involves groups that are the most _____ .

56. A research study that is a compilation of data from many other sources is called a _____-_____ .

Progress Test 1

Multiple-Choice Questions

Circle your answers to the following questions and check them against the answers on page 13. If your answer is incorrect, read the explanation for why it is incorrect and then consult the appropriate pages of the text (in parentheses following the correct answer).

1. The scientific study of human development is defined as the study of:
   a. how and why people change or remain the same over time.
   b. psychosocial influences on aging.
   c. individual differences in learning over the life span.
   d. all of the above.

2. The cognitive domain of development includes:
   a. perception.
   b. thinking.
   c. language.
   d. all of the above.

3. Changes in height, weight, and bone thickness are part of the _____ domain.
   a. cognitive
   b. biosocial
   c. psychosocial
   d. physical

4. Psychosocial development focuses primarily on personality, emotions, and:
   a. intellectual development.
   b. sexual maturation.
   c. relationships with others.
   d. perception.

5. The ecological model of developmental psychology focuses on the:
   a. biochemistry of the body systems.
   b. cognitive domain only.
   c. internal thinking processes.
   d. overall environment of development.

6. Researchers who take a life-span perspective on development focus on:
   a. the sources of continuity from the beginning of life to the end.
   b. the sources of discontinuity throughout life.
   c. the "nonlinear" character of human development.
   d. all of the above.

7. During the 1960s, American society tilted toward a youth culture. This is a vivid example of the effect of _____ on society.
   a. the "baby boom" cohort
   b. the biosocial domain
   c. the cognitive domain
   d. the microsystem

8. A hypothesis is a:
   a. conclusion.
   b. prediction to be tested.
   c. statistical test.
   d. correlation.

9. A developmentalist who is interested in studying the influences of a person's immediate environment on his or her behavior is focusing on which system?
   a. mesosystem
   b. macrosystem
   c. microsystem
   d. exosystem

10. Socioeconomic status is determined by a combination of variables, including:
    a. age, education, and income.
    b. income, ethnicity, and occupation.
    c. income, education, and occupation.
    d. age, ethnicity, and occupation.

11. A disadvantage of experiments is that:
    a. people may behave differently in the artificial environment of the laboratory.
    b. control groups are too large to be accommodated in most laboratories.
    c. they are the method most vulnerable to bias on the part of the researcher.
    d. proponents of the ecological approach overuse them.

12. In an experiment testing the effects of group size on individual effort in a tug-of-war task, the number of people in each group is the:
    a. hypothesis.
    b. independent variable
    c. dependent variable.
    d. level of significance.

13. Which research method would be most appropriate for investigating the relationship between parents' religious beliefs and their attitudes toward middle school sex education?
    a. experimentation
    b. longitudinal research
    c. naturalistic observation
    d. the survey

14. In which type of community are children generally valued most highly as economic assets?
    a. developing agricultural communities
    b. developed postindustrial nations
    c. low-income families in developed countries
    d. middle-income families in developing nations

15. Developmentalists who carefully observe the behavior of schoolchildren during recess are using a research method known as:
    a. the case study.
    b. cross-sectional research.
    c. naturalistic observation.
    d. cross-sequential research.

True or False Items

Write T (*true*) or F (*false*) on the line in front of each statement.

_____ 1. Psychologists separate human development into three domains, or areas of study.

_____ 2. (A Life-Span View) The case study of David clearly demonstrates that for some children only nature (or heredity) is important.

_____ 3. Observation usually indicates a clear relationship between cause and effect.

_____ 4. Each developmental domain influences development independently.

_____ 5. Cohort differences are an example of the impact of the social context on development.

_____ 6. A study of history suggests that particularly well-defined periods of child and adult development have always existed.

_____ 7. Socioeconomic status is rarely measured solely by family income.

_____ 8. The influences between and within Bronfenbrenner's systems are unidirectional and independent.

_____ 9. People of different ethnic groups can all share one culture.

_____ 10. Longitudinal research is the design used by most psychologists working from the developmental perspective.

Progress Test 2

Progress Test 2 should be completed during a final chapter review. Answer the following questions after you thoroughly understand the correct answers for the Chapter Review and Progress Test 1.

Multiple-Choice Questions

1. An individual's context of development refers to his or her:
   a. microsystem and mesosystem.
   b. exosystem.
   c. macrosystem.
   d. microsystem, mesosystem, exosystem, and macrosystem.

2. The three domains of developmental psychology are:
   a. physical, cognitive, psychosocial.
   b. physical, biosocial, cognitive.
   c. biosocial, cognitive, psychosocial.
   d. biosocial, cognitive, emotional.

3. Which of the following is true of the three domains of development?
   a. They are important at every age.
   b. They interact in influencing development.
   c. They are more influential in some cultures than in others.
   d. a. and b. are true.

4. People often mistakenly believe that most developmental changes:
   a. originate within each individual.
   b. take place in a larger social context.

   c. are temporary.
   d. occur in the same way in all people.

5. According to the ecological model, the macrosystem would include:
   a. the peer group.   c. cultural values.
   b. the community.   d. the family.

6. The effects of a person's family life on his or her development would be classified as part of the:
   a. microsystem.   c. exosystem.
   b. mesosystem.   d. macrosystem.

7. Professor Cohen predicts that because "baby boomers" grew up in an era that promoted independence and assertiveness, people in their 40s and 50s will respond differently to a political survey than will people in their 20s and 30s. The professor's prediction regarding political attitudes is an example of a(n):
   a. meta-analysis.
   b. hypothesis.
   c. independent variable.
   d. dependent variable.

8. A cohort is defined as a group of people:
   a. of similar national origin.
   b. who share a common language.
   c. born within a few years of each other.
   d. who share the same religion.

9. (A Life-Span View) Five decades ago, _____ people were the poorest age group in the United States. Today, _____ are the poorest.
   a. young; old   c. young; young
   b. old; young   d. old; old

10. In differentiating ethnicity and culture, we note that:
    a. ethnicity is an exclusively biological phenomenon.
    b. an ethnic group is a group of people who were born within a few years of each other.
    c. people of many ethnic groups can share a culture, yet maintain their ethnic identities.
    d. racial identity is always an element of culture.

11. If developmentalists discovered that poor people are happier than wealthy people are, this would indicate that wealth and happiness are:
    a. unrelated.
    b. positively correlated.
    c. negatively correlated.
    d. causally related.

2. The plasticity of development refers to the fact that:

   a. development is not always linear.

   b. each human life must be understood as embedded in many contexts.

   c. there are many reciprocal connections between childhood and adulthood.

   d. human characteristics can be molded into different forms and shapes.

3. In an experiment testing the effects of noise level on mood, mood is the:

   a. hypothesis.

   b. independent variable.

   c. dependent variable.

   d. scientific observation.

14. (A Life-Span View) An important factor in the impact of living in poverty on development is:

   a. family size.

   b. the presence of supportive relationships within the family.

   c. the child's gender.

   d. the family's nationality.

15. Which of the following statements concerning ethnicity and culture is not true?

   a. Ethnicity is determined genetically.

   b. Race is a social construction.

   c. Racial identity is an element of ethnicity.

   d. Ethnic identity provides people with shared values and beliefs.

Matching Items

Match each definition or description with its corresponding term.

Terms

_____ **1.** independent variable
_____ **2.** dependent variable
_____ **3.** culture
_____ **4.** replicate
_____ **5.** biosocial domain
_____ **6.** cognitive domain
_____ **7.** psychosocial domain
_____ **8.** socioeconomic status
_____ **9.** cohort
_____ **10.** ethnic group
_____ **11.** cross-sectional research
_____ **12.** longitudinal research

Definitions or Descriptions

a. group of people born within a few years of each other

b. determined by a person's income, education, and occupation

c. research study comparing people of different ages at the same time

d. concerned with physical growth and development

e. collection of people who share certain attributes, such as national origin

f. shared values, attitudes, and customs maintained by people in a specific setting

g. concerned with thought processes

h. the variable manipulated in an experiment

i. concerned with emotions, personality traits, and relationships

j. to repeat a study and obtain the same findings

k. the variable measured in an experiment

l. research study retesting one group of people at several different times

Thinking Critically About Chapter 1

Answer these questions the day before an exam as a final check on your understanding of the chapter's terms and concepts.

1. Dr. Wong conducts research on the psychosocial domain of development. She is *most* likely to be interested in a child's:
   a. perceptual abilities.
   b. brain-wave patterns.
   c. emotions.
   d. use of language.

2. A psychologist who focuses on the connections between a child's home and school environments is interested primarily in the child's:
   a. microsystem.   c. exosystem.
   b. mesosystem.   d. macrosystem.

3. Jahmal is writing a paper on the role of the social context in development. He would do well to consult the writings of:
   a. Piaget.   c. Bronfenbrenner.
   b. Freud.   d. Skinner.

4. Dr. Ramirez looks at human development in terms of the individual's supporting ecosystems. Evidently, Dr. Ramirez subscribes to the _____ model.
   a. psychosocial   c. biosocial
   b. ecological   d. cognitive

5. For her class project, Shelly decides to write a paper on how neighborhood and community structures influence the family. She cleverly titles her paper:
   a. "The Microsystem in Action."
   b. "The Mesosystem in Action."
   c. "The Exosystem in Action."
   d. "The Macrosystem in Action."

6. (Research Report) When researchers find that the results of a study are statistically significant, this means that:
   a. they may have been caused purely by chance.
   b. it is unlikely they could be replicated.
   c. it is unlikely they could have occurred by chance.
   d. the sample population was representative of the general population.

7. When we say that the idea of old age as we know it is a "social construction," we are saying that:
   a. the idea is built on the shared perceptions members of society.
   b. old age has only recently been regarded as distinct period of life.
   c. old age cannot be defined.
   d. the idea is based on a well-tested hypothesis

8. As compared with parents in developing countries, middle-class American parents emphasi cognitive and social stimulation in their chil rearing efforts because:
   a. they are more likely to regard children as economic asset.
   b. their families are smaller.
   c. they do not have to be as concerned abo infant mortality.
   d. of all the above reasons.

9. Karen's mother is puzzled by the numerous d crepancies between the developmental psychol gy textbook she used in 1976 and her daughte contemporary text. Karen explains that the diffe ences are the result of:
   a. the lack of regard by earlier researchers for t scientific method.
   b. changing social conditions and cohort effects
   c. the widespread use of cross-sectional resear today.
   d. the widespread use of longitudinal resear today.

10. If height and body weight are positively correl ed, which of the following is true?
    a. There is a cause-and-effect relationship t tween height and weight.
    b. Knowing a person's height, one can pred his or her weight.
    c. As height increases, weight decreases.
    d. All of the above are true.

11. An example of longitudinal research would when an investigator compares the performar of:
    a. several different age groups on a memory te
    b. the same group of people, at different ages, a test of memory.
    c. an experimental group and a control group subjects on a test of memory.
    d. several different age groups on a test of me ory as each group is tested repeatedly ove period of years.

2. For her developmental psychology research project, Lakia decides she wants to focus primarily on qualitative data. You advise her to conduct:
   a. a survey.
   b. an experiment.
   c. a cross-sectional study.
   d. a case study.

3. Which of the following is *not* a major controversy in the study of development?
   a. nature vs. nurture
   b. difference vs. deficit
   c. continuity vs. discontinuity
   d. individual vs. society

4. Dr. Weston is comparing research findings for a group of 30-year-olds with findings for the same individuals at age 20, as well as with findings for groups who were 30 in 1990. Which research method is she using?
   a. longitudinal research
   b. cross-sectional research
   c. case study
   d. cross-sequential research

5. Professor Albertini wants to determine whether adopted children have personalities that are more similar to their biological parents or to their adoptive parents. In this instance, the professor is primarily concerned with the issue of:
   a. deficit/difference.
   b. continuity/discontinuity.
   c. nature/nurture.
   d. individual/society.

Key Terms

Writing Definitions

Using your own words, write a brief definition or explanation of each of the following terms on a separate piece of paper.

1. scientific study of human development
2. life-span perspective
3. plasticity
4. biosocial domain
5. cognitive domain
6. psychosocial domain
7. cohort
8. social construction
9. socioeconomic status (SES)
10. culture
11. ethnic group
12. race
13. scientific method
14. hypothesis
15. replicate
16. subjects
17. variable
18. scientific observation
19. statistical significance
20. correlation
21. experiment
22. independent variable
23. dependent variable
24. survey
25. case study
26. cross-sectional research
27. longitudinal research
28. cross-sequential research

Cross Check

After you have written the definitions of the key terms in this chapter, you should complete the crossword puzzle to ensure that you can reverse the process—recognize the term, given the definition.

ACROSS

1. To prevent bias, the experiment should be "_____ ."
2. Domain concerned with thinking.
7. Group of people born at about the same time.
9. A subset of a population.
11. A measure of status.
13. Research design involving the study of different age groups over time.
14. Set of values shared by a group.
15. Treatment-absent comparison group.

DOWN

1. Domain concerned with physical growth.
3. An _____ _____ shares certain characteristics such as national origin.
4. The treatment-present group.
5. A testable prediction.
6. Research design in which people in different age groups are compared.
7. A measure of a statistical relationship.
8. Research design that follows a group of people over time.
10. All the members of a certain group.
12. An in-depth study of one person.

ANSWERS

CHAPTER REVIEW

1. how and why people change as they grow older, as well as how and why they remain the same; life-span perspective
   a. multidirectional
   b. multicontextual
   c. multicultural
   d. multidisciplinary
   e. plastic
2. plasticity
3. biosocial; cognitive; psychosocial
4. biosocial
5. cognitive
6. psychosocial
7. are; is; holistic
8. contexts (or systems or environments)
9. ecological; Urie Bronfenbrenner
10. microsystem
11. mesosystem
12. exosystem
13. macrosystem
14. chronosystem
15. multidirectional; interactive
16. complexity; chaos
17. butterfly effect; do not act
18. cohort; the same way
19. baby boom; assertiveness; independence
20. sizes

1. social construction; often change
2. childhood
3. socioeconomic status; SES
4. culture
5. developing agricultural; survival; cooperation; postindustrial; cognitive; intellectual; independence, one or two; three to five
6. poverty level; child neglect; infant mortality; schools; violence
7. old; youngest
8. supportive relationships; nurturant; neighborhoods
9. ethnic group; biological; attitudes; experiences; social construction
10. rubella; biosocial; social; cognitive; psychosocial
11. a. formulate a research question;
    b. develop a hypothesis;
    c. test the hypothesis;
    d. draw conclusions;
    e. make the findings available.
12. hypothesis
13. replicate
14. subjects
15. variables; intrapersonal; interpersonal
16. genes; environment; continuity/discontinuity; difference/deficit
17. validity; accuracy; generalizability; usefulness
18. scientific observation; naturalistic; laboratory
19. cause
20. operationally defined
21. statistical significance; 20
22. correlation; does not
23. positive; negative
24. experiment; independent; dependent
25. cause; effect; artificial
26. produce the results they believe the experimenter is looking for; duration
27. scientific survey
28. expects
29. case study; qualitative; quantitative; starting point
30. cross-sectional
31. ages; cohort differences
32. longitudinal

over time, some subjects may leave the study. Some people may change simply because they are part of

the study. Longitudinal studies are time-consuming and expensive.
53. cross-sequential
54. harmed; confidential; voluntary
55. benefits; costs; vulnerable
56. meta-analysis

PROGRESS TEST 1

Multiple-Choice Questions

1. **a.** is the answer. (p. 4)

   b. & c. The study of development is concerned with a broader range of phenomena, including biosocial aspects of development, than these answers specify.

2. **d.** is the answer. (p. 5)

3. **b.** is the answer. (p. 5)

   a. This domain is concerned with thought processes.

   c. This domain is concerned with emotions, personality, and interpersonal relationships.

   d. This is not a domain of development.

4. **c.** is the answer. (p. 5)

   a. This falls within the cognitive and biosocial domains.

   b. This falls within the biosocial domain.

   d. This falls within the cognitive domain.

5. **d.** is the answer. This approach sees development as occurring within four interacting levels, or environments. (p. 7)

6. **d.** is the answer. (p. 23)

7. **a.** is the answer. (pp. 8–9)

   b. The biosocial domain is concerned with brain and body changes.

   c. The cognitive domain is concerned with thought processes in individuals and the factors that influence them.

   d. The microsystem is the immediate social setting that surrounds an individual.

8. **b.** is the answer. (p. 15)

9. **c.** is the answer. (p. 7)

   a. This refers to systems that link one microsystem to another.

   b. This refers to cultural values, political philosophies, economic patterns, and social conditions.

   d. This includes the community structures that affect the functioning of smaller systems.

10. c. is the answer. (p. 10)

11. a. is the answer. (p. 23)

12. b. is the answer. (p. 23)

a. A possible hypothesis for this experiment would be that the larger the group, the less hard a given individual will pull.

c. The dependent variable is the measure of individual effort.

d. Significance level refers to the numerical value specifying the possibility that the results of an experiment could have occurred by chance.

13. d. is the answer. (pp. 24–25)

a. Experimentation is appropriate when one is seeking to uncover cause-and-effect relationships; in this example the researcher is only interested in determining whether the parents' beliefs *predict* their attitudes.

b. Longitudinal research would be appropriate if the researcher sought to examine the development of these attitudes over a long period of time.

c. Mere observation would not allow the researcher to determine the attitudes of the subjects.

14. a. is the answer. (p. 11)

15. c. is the answer. (p. 19)

a. In this method, *one* subject is studied over a period of time.

b. & d. In these research methods, two or more *groups* of subjects are studied and compared.

True or False Items

1. T (p. 5)

2. F   The case study of David shows that both nature and nurture are important in affecting outcome. (pp. 16–17)

3. F   A disadvantage of observation is that the variables are numerous and uncontrolled, and therefore cause-and-effect relationships are difficult to pinpoint. (p. 20)

4. F   Each domain is affected by the other two. (p. 6)

5. T (p. 8)

6. F   Our ideas about the stages of childhood and adulthood are historical creations that have varied over the centuries. (p. 8)

7. F   In government statistics it often is. (p. 10)

8. F   Quite the reverse is true. (p. 7)

9. T (p. 14)

10. T (p. 29)

PROGRESS TEST 2

Multiple-Choice Questions

1. d. is the answer. (p. 7)

2. c. is the answer. (p. 5)

3. d. is the answer. (pp. 5–6)

c. Research has not revealed cultural variations the overall developmental influence of the thr domains.

4. a. is the answer. (p. 6)

b. This is the emphasis of the newer, ecologic perspective.

c. & d. The text does not suggest that people com monly make these assumptions.

5. c. is the answer. (p. 7)

a. & d. These are part of the microsystem.

b. This is part of the exosystem.

6. a. is the answer. (p. 7)

b. This refers to systems that link one microsy tem to another.

c. This refers to the community structures th affect the functioning of smaller systems.

d. This refers to the overarching traditions, b liefs, and values of the society.

7. b. is the answer. (p. 15)

a. In a meta-analysis, the results of a number separate research studies are combined.

c. & d. Variables are treatments (independent) behaviors (dependent) in *experiments*, which th situation clearly is not.

8. c. is the answer. (p. 8)

a., b., & d. These are attributes of an ethnic grou

9. b. is the answer. (p. 12)

10. c. is the answer. (p. 14)

a. & d. Ethnicity refers to shared attributes, su as ancestry, national origin, religion, and la guage.

b. This describes a cohort.

11. c. is the answer. (p. 22)

a. Wealth and happiness clearly *are* related.

b. This answer would be correct if wealthy pe ple were found to be happier than poor people.

d. Correlation does not imply causation.

12. d. is the answer. (p. 4)

13. c. is the answer. (p. 23)

a. Hypotheses make *specific*, testable prediction

b. Noise level is the independent variable.

d. Scientific observation is a research method in which subjects are watched, while their behavior is recorded unobtrusively.

4. **b.** is the answer. (p. 12)

   a., c., & d. The text does not suggest that these variables affect poverty's influence on development.

5. **a.** is the answer. Ethnic identity is a product of the social environment and the individual's consciousness. (p. 14)

Matching Items

1. h (p. 23)	**5.** d (p. 5)	**9.** a (p. 8)
2. k (p. 23)	**6.** g (p. 5)	**10.** e (p. 14)
3. f (p. 11)	**7.** i (p. 5)	**11.** c (p. 27)
4. j (p. 15)	**8.** b (p. 10)	**12.** l (p. 28)

THINKING CRITICALLY ABOUT CHAPTER 1

1. **c.** is the answer. (p. 5)

   a. & d. These pertain to the cognitive domain.

   b. This pertains to the biosocial domain.

2. **b.** is the answer. (p. 7)

3. **c.** is the answer. (p. 7)

   a. Piaget is notable in the area of cognitive development.

   b. Freud was a pioneer of psychoanalysis.

   b. Skinner is notable in the history of learning theory.

4. **b.** is the answer. (p. 7)

   a., c., & d. These are the three domains of development.

5. **c.** is the answer. (p. 7)

6. **c.** is the answer. (p. 21)

7. **a.** is the answer. (pp. 9–10)

8. **c.** is the answer. (pp. 12–13)

9. **b.** is the answer. (p. 8)

   a. Earlier developmentalists had no less regard for the scientific method.

   c. & d. Both cross-sectional and longitudinal research were widely used in the 1970s.

10. **b.** is the answer. (p. 22)

    a. Correlation does not imply causation.

    c. If height and body weight are positively correlated, as one increases so does the other.

11. **b.** is the answer. (pp. 28–29)

    a. This is an example of cross-sectional research.

c. This is an example of an experiment.

d. This type of study is not described in the text.

12. **d.** is the answer. (p. 26)

    a., b., & c. These research methods generally yield *quantitative*, rather than qualitative, data.

13. **d.** is the answer. On this issue, developmentalists are in agreement: individuals are inextricably involved with their social groups. (p. 18)

14. **d.** is the answer. (p. 30)

    a., & c. In these research methods only one group of subjects is studied.

    b. Dr. Weston's design includes comparison of groups of people of different ages *over time*.

15. **c.** is the answer. (p. 30)

    a. This issue concerns whether individual differences are considered problems that need correcting, or causes for celebration.

    b. This issue concerns whether development builds gradually, or occurs through sudden transformations.

    d. This issue concerns whether individual people can be studied apart from the social groups to which they belong.

KEY TERMS

Writing Definitions

1. The **scientific study of human development** is the science that seeks to understand how and why people change, and how and why they remain the same, as they grow older. (p. 4)

2. The **life-span perspective** on human development recognizes that human growth is lifelong and characterized by both continuity (as in personality) and discontinuity (as in the number of brain cells). (p. 4)

3. **Plasticity** is the capability of any human characteristics to be molded or reshaped by time and circumstances. (p. 4)

4. The **biosocial domain** is concerned with brain and body changes and the social influences that guide them. (p. 5)

5. The **cognitive domain** is concerned with thought processes, perceptual abilities, and language mastery, and the educational institutions that encourage these aspects of development. (p. 5)

6. The **psychosocial domain** is concerned with emotions, personality, interpersonal relationships with family, friends, and the wider community. (p. 5)

7. A **cohort** is a group of people who, because they were born within a few years of each other, experience many of the same historical and social emotions. (p. 88)

8. A **social construction** is an idea about the way things are, or should be, that is built more on the shared perceptions of members of a society than on objective reality. (p. 10)

9. An individual's **socioeconomic status (SES)** is determined by his or her income, education, place of residence, and occupation. (p. 10)

10. **Culture** refers to the set of shared values, assumptions, customs, and physical objects that a group of people have developed over the years as a design for living to structure their life together. (p. 11)

11. An **ethnic group** is a collection of people who share certain attributes, such as national origin, religion, ancestry, and/or language and who, as a result, tend to identify with each other and have similar daily encounters with the social world. (p. 14)

12. **Race** is a misleading social construction that was originally based on biological differences between people whose ancestors came from different regions of the world. (p. 14)

13. The **scientific method** is a general procedural model that helps researchers remain objective as they study behavior. The five basic steps of the scientific method are (1) formulate a research question; (2) develop a hypothesis; (3) test the hypothesis; (4) draw conclusions; and (5) make the findings available. (p. 15)

14. In the scientific method, a **hypothesis** is a specific, testable prediction regarding development. (p. 15)

15. To **replicate** a test of a research hypothesis is to repeat it and obtain the same results using a different but related set of subjects or procedures in order to test its validity. (p. 15)

16. In a research project, the **subjects** are the people who are being studied. (p. 15)

17. A **variable** is any quantity, characteristic, or action that can take on different values within a group of individuals or a single individual. (p. 18)

18. **Scientific observation** is the unobtrusive watching and recording of subjects' behavior in a situation that is being studied, either in the laboratory or in a natural setting. (p. 19)

19. **Statistical significance** means that an obtained result, such as a difference between two groups, very likely reflects a real difference rather than chance factors. (p. 21)

20. **Correlation** is a statistical term that merely indicates whether two variables are related to each other such that one is likely (or unlikely) to occur when the other occurs or one is likely to increase (or decrease) when the other increases (or decreases). (p. 21)

21. The **experiment** is the research method in which an investigator tests a hypothesis in a controlled situation in which the relevant variables are limited and can be manipulated by the experimenter. (p. 23)

22. The **independent variable** is the variable that is manipulated in an experiment. (p. 23)

23. The **dependent variable** is the variable that is being studied in an experiment. (p. 23)

    Example: In the study of the effects of a new drug on memory, the subjects' memory is the dependent variable.

24. The scientific **survey** is the research method in which information is collected from a large number of people, either through written questionnaires or through interviews. (p. 24)

25. The **case study** is the research method involving the intensive study of one person. (p. 26)

26. In **cross-sectional research**, groups of people who differ in age but share other important characteristics are compared with regard to the variable under investigation. (p. 27)

27. In **longitudinal research**, the same group of individuals is studied over a period of time to measure both change and stability as they age. (p. 28)

28. **Cross-sequential research** follows a group of people of different ages over time, thus combining the strengths of the cross-sectional and longitudinal methods. (p. 30)

Cross-Check

CROSS	DOWN
1. blind	**1.** biosocial
2. cognitive	**3.** ethnic group
7. cohort	**4.** experimental
9. sample	**5.** hypothesis
11. SES	**6.** cross-sectional
13. cross-sequential	**7.** correlation
14. culture	**8.** longitudinal
15. control	**10.** population
	12. case study

CHAPTER 2

Theories

Chapter Overview

Developmental theories are systematic statements of principles and generalizations that explain behavior and development and provide a framework for future research. Many such theories have influenced our understanding of human development. This chapter describes and evaluates five broad theories—psychoanalytic, learning, cognitive, sociocultural, and epigenetic systems—that will be used throughout the book to present information and to provide a framework for interpreting events and issues in human development. Each of the theories has developed a unique vocabulary with which to describe and explain events as well as to organize ideas into a cohesive system of thought.

Three of the theories presented—psychoanalytic, cognitive, and learning theory—are "grand theories" that are comprehensive in scope but inadequate in the face of recent research findings. Two of the theories—sociocultural and epigenetic systems—are considered "emergent theories" because they may become the comprehensive theories of the future. Rather than adopt any one theory exclusively, most developmentalists take an eclectic perspective and use many or all of them.

As you study this part of the chapter, consider what each of the theories has to say about your own development, as well as that of friends and relatives in other age groups. It is also a good idea to keep the following questions in mind as you study each theory: Which of the theory's principles are generally accepted by contemporary developmentalists? How has the theory been criticized? In what ways does this theory agree with the other theories? In what ways does it disagree?

NOTE: Answer guidelines for all Chapter 2 questions begin on page 30.

Guided Study

The text chapter should be studied one section at time. Before you read, preview each section by skimming it, noting headings and boldface items. The read the appropriate section objectives from the following outline. Keep these objectives in mind and, you read the chapter section, search for the information that will enable you to meet each objective. On you have finished a section, write out answers for objectives.

What Theories Do (pp. 37–38)

1. Define developmental theory, and describe how developmental theories help explain human behavior and development. In your answer, be sure to differentiate grand theories, minitheories, and emergent theories.

Grand Theories (pp. 38–51, 52–53)

2. Discuss the major focus of psychoanalytic theories, and describe the conflicts that occur during Freud's stages of psychosexual development.

3. Describe the crises of Erikson's theory of psychosocial development, and contrast them with Freud's stages.

7. Identify the primary focus of cognitive theory, and briefly describe Piaget's stages of cognitive development.

4. Discuss the major focus of learning theories, and explain the basic principles of classical and operant conditioning.

8. Discuss the process that, according to Piaget, guides cognitive development.

5. (Research Report) Discuss Harlow's research with infant monkeys, and explain how it contributed to revisions of psychoanalytic and learning theories.

9. Identify the major criticisms and contributions of each of the grand theories of development.

6. Discuss social learning theory as an extension of learning theory.

Emergent Theories (pp. 51, 54–64)

10. Discuss the basic ideas of Vygotsky and the sociocultural theory of development.

11. (Changing Policy) Explain the nature–nurture controversy, particularly as it pertains to sexual orientation.

12. Discuss the basic ideas of epigenetic systems theory.

13. (In Person) Discuss the ethology of infant social instincts and adult caregiving impulses.

The Theories Compared (pp. 64–65)

14. Summarize the contributions and criticisms of the major developmental theories, and explain the eclectic perspective of contemporary developmentalists.

Chapter Review

When you have finished reading the chapter, work through the material that follows to review it. Complete the sentences and answer the questions. As

you proceed, evaluate your performance for each section by consulting the answers on page 30. Do not continue with the next section until you understand each answer. If you need to, review or reread the appropriate section in the textbook before continuing.

What Theories Do (pp. 37–38)

1. A systematic set of principles and generalizations that explains behavior and development is called a(n) _____ _____ .

2. Developmental theories provide a broad and _____ view of the influences on development; they form the basis for educated guesses, or _____ , about behavior, and they provide a framework for future research.

3. Developmental theories fall into three categories: _____ theories, which offer a comprehensive view of development but have proved to be outdated; _____ theories, which explain a specific area of development; and _____ theories, which may be the comprehensive theories of the future.

Grand Theories (pp. 38–51, 52–53)

4. Psychoanalytic theories interpret human development in terms of intrinsic _____ and _____ , many of which are _____ (conscious/unconscious) and _____ .

5. According to Freud's _____ theory, children experience sexual pleasures and desires during the first six years as they pass through three _____ _____ . From infancy to early childhood to the preschool years, these stages are the _____ stage, the _____ stage, and the _____ stage. Finally, after a period of sexual _____ , which lasts for about _____ years, the individual enters the _____ stage, which begins at about age _____ and lasts throughout adulthood.

pecify the focus of sexual pleasure and the major evelopmental need associated with each of Freud's tages.

ral _____

_____

nal _____

_____

hallic _____

_____

enital _____

_____

6. Erik Erikson's theory of development, which focuses on social and cultural influences, is called a(n) _____ theory. In this theory, there are _____ (number) developmental stages, each characterized by a particular developmental _____ related to the person's relationship to the social environment. Unlike Freud, Erikson proposed stages of development that _____ (span/do not span) a person's lifetime.

Complete the following chart regarding Erikson's tages of psychosocial development.

Age Period	Stage
irth to 1 yr.	trust vs. _____
–3 yrs.	autonomy vs. _____
–6 yrs.	initiative vs. _____
–11 yrs.	_____ vs. inferiority
dolescence	identity vs. _____
oung adulthood	_____ vs. isolation
iddle adulthood	_____ vs. stagnation
lder adulthood	_____ vs. despair

7. A major theory in American psychology, which directly opposed psychoanalytic theory, was _____ . This theory, which emerged early in the twentieth century under the influence of _____ , forms the basis for contemporary _____ theory because of its emphasis on how we learn specific behaviors.

8. Learning theorists have formulated laws of behavior that are believed to apply

_____ (only at certain ages/at all ages). The basic principles of learning theory explore the relationship between an experience or event (called the _____) and the behavioral reaction associated with it (called the _____). The learning process, which is called _____ , takes two forms _____ _____ and

_____ _____ .

9. In classical conditioning, which was discovered by the Russian scientist _____ and is also called _____ conditioning, a person or an animal learns to associate a(n) _____ stimulus with a meaningful one.

10. According to _____ , the learning of more complex responses is the result of _____ conditioning, in which a person learns that a particular behavior produces a particular _____ , such as a reward. This type of learning is also called _____ conditioning.

11. The process of repeating a consequence to make it more likely that the behavior in question will recur is called _____ . The consequence that increases the likelihood that a behavior will be repeated is called the

_____ .

12. The extension of learning theory that emphasizes the ways that people learn new behaviors by observing others is called _____ _____ . The process whereby a child patterns his or her behavior after a parent or teacher, for example, is called

_____ .

13. This process is most likely to occur when an observer is _____ and when the model is _____ . This type of learning is also affected by the individual's

_____ .

14. (Research Report) The behavior of infant monkeys separated from their mothers led researcher _____ to investigate the origins of _____ in infant monkeys. These studies, which demonstrated that infant monkeys clung more often to "surrogate" mothers that provided _____ (food/contact comfort), disproved _____ theory's idea that infants seek to satisfy oral needs and _____ theory's view that reinforcement directs behavior.

15. The structure and development of the individual's thought processes and the way those thought processes affect the person's understanding of the world are the focus of _____ theory. A major pioneer of this theory is _____ .

16. In Piaget's first stage of development, the _____ stage, children experience the world through their senses and motor abilities. This stage occurs between birth and age _____ .

17. According to Piaget, during the preschool years (up to age _____), children are in the _____ stage. A hallmark of this stage is that children begin to think _____ . Another hallmark is that sometimes the child's thinking is _____ , or focused on seeing the world solely from his or her own perspective.

18. Piaget believed that children begin to think logically in a consistent way at about _____ years of age. At this time, they enter the _____ stage.

19. In Piaget's final stage, the _____ stage, reasoning expands from the purely concrete to encompass _____ thinking. Piaget believed most children enter this stage by age _____ .

20. According to Piaget, cognitive development is guided by the need to maintain a state of mental balance, called _____ _____ .

21. When new experiences challenge existing understanding, creating a kind of imbalance, the individual experiences _____ _____ , which eventually leads to mental growth.

22. According to Piaget, people adapt to new experiences either by reinterpreting them to fit into, or _____ with, old ideas. Some new experiences force people to revamp old ideas so that they can _____ new experiences.

Identify two psychoanalytic ideas that *are* widely accepted.

Identify one way in which the study of human development has benefited from learning theory.

Identify one way in which the study of human development has benefited from cognitive theory.

3. Today, hypotheses and concepts from _____ theory are more often the topic of research than those from the other two grand theories.

4. The idea that every person passes through fixed stages, as proposed by _____ , _____ , and _____ cannot account for the diversity of human development worldwide. Similarly, the idea that every person can be conditioned in the same way, as proposed by _____ , _____ , and _____ has also been refuted.

5. Research has demonstrated that the grand theories focus too much on the _____ context of development and underestimate the role of _____ and _____ influences.

6. (Changing Policy) The debate over the relative influence of heredity and environment in shaping personal traits and characteristics is called the _____-_____ controversy. Traits inherited at the moment of conception give evidence of the influence of _____ ; those that emerge in response to learning and environmental influences give evidence of the effect of _____ .

7. (Changing Policy) Developmentalists agree that, at every point, the _____ between nature and nurture is the crucial influence on any particular aspect of development.

8. (Changing Policy) All the grand theories tended to explain homosexuality in terms of _____ (nature/nurture). However, new research suggests that it is at least partly due to _____ (nature/nurture).

(Changing Policy) Briefly summarize two research findings concerning homosexuality and the nature-nurture controversy.

Emergent Theories (pp. 51, 54–64)

29. In contrast to the grand theories, the two emerging theories draw from the findings of _____ (one/many) discipline(s).

30. Sociocultural theory sees human development as the result of _____ _____ between developing persons and their surrounding _____ .

31. A major pioneer of this perspective was _____ , who was primarily interested in the development of _____ competencies.

32. Vygotsky believed that these competencies result from the interaction between _____ and more mature members of the society, acting as _____ , in a process that has been called an _____ _____ _____ .

33. In Vygotsky's view, the best way to accomplish the goals of apprenticeship is through _____ _____ , in which the tutor engages the learner in joint activities.

34. (A Life-Span View) According to Vygotsky, a mentor draws a child into the _____ _____ _____ , which is defined as the range of skills that the child can exercise with _____ but cannot perform independently.

Cite several contributions and several criticisms of sociocultural theory.

35. The newest of the theories, epigenetic systems theory emphasizes the interaction between _____ and the _____ .

36. In using the word *genetic*, this theory emphasizes that we have powerful _____ and abilities that arise from our _____ heritage.

37. The prefix "epi" refers to the various _____ factors that affect the expression of _____ . These include _____ factors such as injury, temperature, and crowding. Others are _____ factors such as nourishing food and freedom to play.

38. Some epigenetic factors are the result of the evolutionary process called _____ , in which, over generations, genes for useful traits that promote survival become more prevalent.

39. "Everything that seems to be genetic is actually epigenetic." This statement highlights the fact that _____ (some/most/all) genetic instructions are affected by the environment.

40. The "systems" aspect of this theory points out that changes in one part of the individual's system _____ _____ .

41. (In Person) The study of animal behavior as it is related to the evolution and survival of a species is called _____ . Newborn animals and human infants are genetically programmed for _____ _____ as a means of survival. Similarly, adult animals and humans are genetically programmed for _____ _____ .

The Theories Compared (pp. 64–65)

42. Which major theory of development emphasizes:
    a. the importance of culture in fostering development? _____
    b. the ways in which thought processes affect actions? _____
    c. environmental influences? _____
    d. the impact of "hidden dramas" on development? _____
    e. the interaction of genes and environment _____

43. Which major theory of development has been criticized for:
    a. being too mechanistic? _____
    b. undervaluing genetic differences? _____
    c. being too subjective? _____
    d. neglecting society? _____
    e. neglecting individuals? _____

44. Because no one theory can encompass all of human behavior, most developmentalists have a(n) _____ perspective, which capitalizes on the strengths of all the theories.

Progress Test 1

Multiple-Choice Questions

Circle your answers to the following questions and check them with the answers on page 31. If your answer is incorrect, read the explanation for why it is incorrect and then consult the appropriate pages of the text (in parentheses following the correct answer).

1. The purpose of a developmental theory is to:
   a. provide a broad and coherent view of the complex influences on human development.
   b. offer guidance for practical issues encountered by parents, teachers, and therapists.
   c. generate testable hypotheses about development.
   d. do all of the above.

2. Which developmental theory emphasizes the influence of unconscious drives and motives on behavior?
   a. psychoanalytic
   b. learning
   c. cognitive
   d. sociocultural

3. Which of the following is the correct order of the psychosexual stages proposed by Freud?
   a. oral stage; anal stage; phallic stage; latency; genital stage
   b. anal stage; oral stage; phallic stage; latency; genital stage
   c. oral stage; anal stage; genital stage; latency; phallic stage
   d. anal stage; oral stage; genital stage; latency; phallic stage

4. Erikson's psychosocial theory of human development describes:
   a. eight crises all people are thought to face.
   b. four psychosocial stages and a latency period.
   c. the same number of stages as Freud's, but with different names.
   d. a stage theory that is not psychoanalytic.

5. Which of the following theories does *not* belong with the others?
   a. psychoanalytic
   b. learning
   c. sociocultural
   d. cognitive

6. An American psychologist who explained complex human behaviors in terms of operant conditioning was:
   a. Lev Vygotsky.
   b. Ivan Pavlov.
   c. B. F. Skinner.
   d. Jean Piaget.

7. Pavlov's dogs learned to salivate at the sound of a bell because they associated the bell with food. Pavlov's experiment with dogs was an early demonstration of:
   a. classical conditioning.
   b. operant conditioning.
   c. positive reinforcement.
   d. social learning.

8. (Changing Policy) The nature-nurture controversy considers the degree to which traits, characteristics, and behaviors are the result of:
   a. early or lifelong learning.
   b. genes or heredity.
   c. heredity or experience.
   d. different historical concepts of childhood.

9. Modeling, an integral part of social learning theory, is so called because it:
   a. follows the scientific model of learning.
   b. molds character.
   c. follows the immediate reinforcement model developed by Bandura.
   d. involves people's patterning their behavior after that of others.

10. Which developmental theory suggests that each person is born with genetic possibilities that must be nurtured in order to grow?
    a. sociocultural
    b. cognitive
    c. learning
    d. epigenetic systems

11. Vygotsky's theory has been criticized for neglecting:
    a. the role of genes in guiding development.
    b. developmental processes that are not primarily biological.
    c. the importance of language in development.
    d. social factors in development.

12. Which is the correct sequence of stages in Piaget's theory of cognitive development?
    a. sensorimotor, preoperational, concrete operational, formal operational
    b. sensorimotor, preoperational, formal operational, concrete operational
    c. preoperational, sensorimotor, concrete operational, formal operational
    d. preoperational, sensorimotor, formal operational, concrete operational

13. When an individual's existing understanding no longer fits his or her present experiences, the result is called:
    a. a psychosocial crisis.
    b. equilibrium.
    c. disequilibrium.
    d. negative reinforcement.

14. (Changing Policy) In explaining the origins of homosexuality, the grand theories have traditionally emphasized:
    a. nature over nurture.
    b. nurture over nature.
    c. a warped mother-son or father-daughter relationship.
    d. the individual's voluntary choice.

15. (A Life-Span View) The zone of proximal development refers to:

    a. the control process by which information is transferred from the sensory register to working memory.

    b. the influence of a pleasurable stimulus on behavior.

    c. the range of skills a child can exercise with assistance but cannot perform independently.

    d. the mutual interaction of a person's internal characteristics, the environment, and the person's behavior.

True or False Items

Write T (*true*) or F (*false*) on the line in front of each statement.

_____ 1. Learning theorists study what people actually do, not what they might be thinking.

_____ 2. Erikson's eight developmental stages are centered not on a body part but on each person's relationship to the social environment.

_____ 3. Most developmentalists agree that the nature-nurture controversy has been laid to rest.

_____ 4. Few developmental theorists today believe that humans have instincts or abilities that arise from our species' biological heritage.

_____ 5. Of the major developmental theories, cognitive theory gives the most emphasis to the interaction of genes and experience in shaping development.

_____ 6. New research suggests that homosexuality is at least partly genetic.

_____ 7. According to Piaget, a state of cognitive equilibrium must be attained before cognitive growth can occur.

_____ 8. In part, cognitive theory examines how an individual's understandings and expectations affect his or her behavior.

_____ 9. According to Piaget, children begin to think only when they reach preschool age.

_____ 10. Most contemporary researchers have adopted an eclectic perspective on development.

Progress Test 2

Progress Test 2 should be completed during a final chapter review. Answer the following questions after you thoroughly understand the correct answers f the Chapter Review and Progress Test 1.

Multiple-Choice Questions

1. Which developmental theorist has been criticize for suggesting that every child, in every cultu in every nation, passes through certain fix stages?

   a. Freud   c. Piaget
   b. Erikson   d. all of the above.

2. Of the following terms, the one that does describe a stage of Freud's theory of childhoo sexuality is:

   a. phallic.
   b. oral.
   c. anal.
   d. sensorimotor.

3. We are more likely to imitate the behavior of ot ers if we particularly admire and identify w them. This belief finds expression in:

   a. stage theory.
   b. sociocultural theory.
   c. social learning theory.
   d. Pavlov's experiments.

4. How do minitheories differ from grand theori of development?

   a. Unlike the more comprehensive grand the ries, minitheories explain only a part of dev opment.

   b. Unlike grand theories, which usually refl the thinking of many researchers, minithe ries tend to stem from one person.

   c. Only the recency of the research on whi they are based keeps minitheories from ha ing the sweeping influence of grand theories

   d. They differ in all the above ways.

5. According to Erikson, an adult who has difficul establishing a secure, mutual relationship with life partner might never have resolved the cri of:

   a. initiative versus guilt
   b. autonomy versus shame
   c. intimacy versus isolation
   d. trust versus mistrust

6. Who would be most likely to agree with the sta ment, "anything can be learned"?

   a. Jean Piaget   c. John Watson
   b. Lev Vygotsky   d. Erik Erikson

7. Classical conditioning is to _____ as operant conditioning is to _____ .
   a. Skinner; Pavlov   c. Pavlov: Skinner
   b. Watson; Vygotsky   d. Vygotsky; Watson

8. Learning theorists have found that they can often solve a person's seemingly complex psychological problem by:
   a. analyzing the patient.
   b. admitting the existence of the unconscious.
   c. altering the environment.
   d. administering well-designed punishments.

9. According to Piaget, an infant first comes to know the world through:
   a. sucking and grasping.
   b. naming and counting.
   c. preoperational thought.
   d. instruction from parents.

10. According to Piaget, the stage of cognitive development that generally characterizes preschool children (2 to 6 years old) is the:
   a. preoperational stage.   c. oral stage.
   b. sensorimotor stage.   d. psychosocial stage.

11. In Piaget's theory, cognitive equilibrium refers to:
   a. a state of mental balance.
   b. a kind of imbalance that leads to cognitive growth.

   c. the ultimate stage of cognitive development.
   d. the first stage in the processing of information.

12. You teach your dog to "speak" by giving her a treat each time she does so. This is an example of:
   a. classical conditioning.   c. reinforcement.
   b. respondent conditioning. d. modeling.

13. A child who must modify an old idea in order to incorporate a new experience is using the process of:
   a. assimilation.
   b. accommodation.
   c. cognitive equilibrium.
   d. guided participation.

14. Which of the following is a common criticism of sociocultural theory?
   a. It places too great an emphasis on unconscious motives and childhood sexuality.
   b. Its mechanistic approach fails to explain many complex human behaviors.
   c. Development is more gradual than its stages imply.
   d. It neglects developmental processes that are not primarily social.

15. A major pioneer of the sociocultural perspective was:
   a. Jean Piaget.   c. Lev Vygotsky.
   b. Albert Bandura.   d. Ivan Pavlov.

Matching Items

Match each theory or term with its corresponding description or definition.

Theories or Terms

_____ 1. psychoanalytic theory
_____ 2. response
_____ 3. learning theory
_____ 4. social learning theory
_____ 5. cognitive theory
_____ 6. stimulus
_____ 7. sociocultural theory
_____ 8. conditioning
_____ 9. emergent theories
_____ 10. modeling
_____ 11. epigenetic systems theory

Descriptions or Definitions

   a. emphasizes the impact of the immediate environment on behavior
   b. relatively new, comprehensive theories
   c. emphasizes that people learn by observing others
   d. an action or event that triggers a behavioral response
   e. a process of learning, as described by Pavlov or Skinner
   f. emphasizes the "hidden dramas" that influence behavior
   g. emphasizes the cultural context in development
   h. emphasizes how our thoughts shape our actions
   i. the process whereby a person learns by imitating someone else's behavior
   j. emphasizes the interaction of genes and environmental forces
   k. a behavior triggered by an action or event

Thinking Critically About Chapter 2

Answer these questions the day before an exam as a final check on your understanding of the chapter's terms and concepts.

1. Many songbirds inherit a genetically pro-grammed species song that enhances their ability to mate and establish a territory. The evolution of such a trait is an example of:
   a. selective adaptation.
   b. epigenetic development.
   c. accommodation.
   d. assimilation.

2. When a pigeon is rewarded for producing a particular response, and so learns to produce that response to obtain rewards, psychologists describe this chain of events as:
   a. operant conditioning.   c. modeling.
   b. classical conditioning.   d. reflexive actions.

3. Research studies have shown that human handling of rat pups makes them smarter as adults. This is because handling:
   a. increases the mother's grooming of her pup.
   b. indirectly decreases the release of stress hormones.
   c. leads to less brain degeneration in the face of adult stresses.
   d. does all of the above.

4. Dr. Ivey's research focuses on the biological forces that shape each child's characteristic way of reacting to environmental experiences. Evidently, Dr. Ivey is working from a(n) _____ perspective.
   a. psychoanalytic   c. sociocultural
   b. cognitive   d. epigenetic systems

5. Which of the following is the best example of guided participation?
   a. After watching her mother change her baby sister's diaper, 4-year-old Brandy changes her doll's diaper.
   b. To help her son learn to pour liquids, Sandra engages him in a bathtub game involving pouring water from cups of different sizes.
   c. Seeing his father shaving, 3-year-old Kyle pretends to shave by rubbing whipped cream on his face.
   d. After reading a recipe in a magazine, Jack gathers ingredients from the cupboard.

6. A child who calls all furry animals "doggie" wi experience cognitive _____ whe she encounters a hairless breed for the first tim This may cause her to revamp her concept "dog" in order to _____ the ne experience.
   a. disequilibrium; accommodate
   b. disequilibrium; assimilate
   c. equilibrium; accommodate
   d. equilibrium; assimilate

7. A confirmed neo-Freudian, Dr. Thomas strong endorses the views of Erik Erikson. She would t most likely to disagree with Freud regarding tl importance of:
   a. unconscious forces in development.
   b. irrational forces in personality formation.
   c. early childhood experiences.
   d. sexual urges in development.

8. After watching several older children climbir around a new junglegym, 5-year-old Jenn decides to try it herself. Which of the followir best accounts for her behavior?
   a. classical conditioning
   b. modeling
   c. guided participation
   d. reinforcement

9. I am 8 years old, and although I understand son logical principles, I have trouble thinking abo hypothetical concepts. According to Piaget, I a in the _____ stage of development
   a. sensorimotor
   b. preoperational
   c. concrete operational
   d. formal operational

10. Two-year-old Jamail has a simple understandir for "dad," and so each time he encounters a m; with a child, he calls him "dad." When he lear that these other men are not "dad," Jamail exper ences:
    a. conservation.   c. equilibrium.
    b. cognition.   d. disequilibrium.

11. (In Person) Most adults become physiological aroused by the sound of an infant's laughte These interactive reactions, in which caregive and babies elicit responses in each other:
    a. help ensure the survival of the next gener tion.
    b. do not occur in all human cultures.
    c. are the result of conditioning very early in lif
    d. are more often found in females than in male

2. The school psychologist believes that each child's developmental needs can be understood only by taking into consideration the child's broader social and cultural background. Evidently, the school psychologist is working within the _____ perspective.
   a. psychoanalytic
   b. epigenetic systems
   c. social learning
   d. sociocultural

3. Four-year-old Bjorn takes great pride in successfully undertaking new activities. Erikson would probably say that Bjorn is capably meeting the psychosocial challenge of:
   a. trust vs. mistrust.
   b. initiative vs. guilt.
   c. industry vs. inferiority.
   d. identity vs. role confusion.

4. Dr. Cleaver's developmental research draws upon insights from several theoretical perspectives. Evidently, Dr. Cleaver is working from a(n) _____ perspective.
   a. cognitive
   b. learning
   c. eclectic
   d. sociocultural

5. Dr. Bazzi believes that development is a lifelong process of gradual and continuous growth. Based on this information, with which of the following theories would Dr. Bazzi most likely agree?
   a. Piaget's cognitive theory
   b. Erikson's psychosocial theory
   c. Freud's psychoanalytic theory
   d. learning theory

Key Terms

Writing Definitions

Using your own words, write a brief definition or explanation of each of the following terms on a separate piece of paper.

1. developmental theory
2. grand theories
3. minitheories
4. emergent theories
5. psychoanalytic theory
6. learning theory
7. stimulus
8. response
9. conditioning
10. reinforcement
11. social learning
12. modeling
13. cognitive theory
14. cognitive equilibrium
15. sociocultural theory
16. guided participation
17. epigenetic systems theory
18. zone of proximal development
19. ethology
20. selective adaptation
21. eclectic perspective

Cross Check

After you have written the definitions of the key terms in this chapter, you should complete the crossword puzzle to ensure that you can reverse the process—recognize the term, given the definition.

ACROSS

2. Theory that emphasizes the sequences and processes of conditioning.
8. An instinctive or learned behavior that is elicited by a specific stimulus.
11. All the genetic influences on development.
12. Developmental perspective that accepts elements from several theories.
14. Influential theorist who developed a stage theory of cognitive development.
16. Type of theory that brings together information from many disciplines into a comprehensive model of development.
18. All the environmental (non-genetic) influences on development.
19. An early and especially strong proponent of learning theory in America.

DOWN

1. Theory that focuses on some specific area of development.
3. Theory that emphasizes the interaction of genetic and environmental factors in development.
4. The process by which the consequences of a behavior make the behavior more likely to occur.
5. Comprehensive theory of development that has proven to be inadequate in explaining the full range of human development.
6. Theory of personality and development that emphasizes unconscious forces.
7. Learning process that occurs through the association of two stimuli or through the use of reinforcement.
9. Influential theorist who outlined the principles of operant conditioning.
10. The study of behavior as it relates to the evolution and survival of a species.
13. The process of learning by imitating another person's behavior.
14. Russian scientist who outlined the principles of classical conditioning.
15. Psychoanalytic theorist who viewed development as a series of psychosocial crises.
17. The developer of psychoanalytic theory.

ANSWERS

CHAPTER REVIEW

1. developmental theory
2. coherent; hypotheses
3. grand; mini; emergent
4. motives; drives; unconscious; irrational
5. psychoanalytic; psychosexual stages; oral; an phallic; latency; 5 or 6; genital; 12

Oral stage: The mouth is the focus of pleasurable se sations as the baby becomes emotionally attached the person who provides the oral gratificatio derived from sucking.

Anal stage: Pleasures related to control and self-co trol, initially in connection with defecation and toi training, are paramount.

Phallic stage: Pleasure is derived from genital stim lation; interest in physical differences between t sexes leads to the development of gender identi sexual orientation, and the child's development moral standards.

Genital stage: Mature sexual interests that l throughout adulthood emerge.

6. psychosocial; 8; crisis (challenge); span

Age Period	Stage
Birth to 1 yr.	trust vs. **mistrust**
–3 yrs.	autonomy vs. **shame and doubt**
–6 yrs.	initiative vs. **guilt**
–11 yrs.	**industry** vs. inferiority
Adolescence	identity vs. **role confusion**
Young adulthood	**intimacy** vs. isolation
Middle adulthood	**generativity** vs. stagnation
Older adulthood	**integrity** vs. despair

7. behaviorism; John B. Watson; learning
8. at all ages; stimulus; response; conditioning; classical conditioning; operant conditioning
9. Ivan Pavlov; respondent; neutral
10. B. F. Skinner; operant; consequence; instrumental
11. reinforcement; reinforcer
12. social learning; modeling
13. uncertain or inexperienced; admired, powerful, or similar to the observer; self-understanding
14. Harry Harlow; attachment; contact comfort; psychoanalytic; learning
15. cognitive; Jean Piaget
16. sensorimotor; 2
17. 6; preoperational; symbolically; egocentric
18. 7; concrete operational
19. formal operational; abstract (hypothetical); 12
20. cognitive equilibrium
21. cognitive disequilibrium
22. assimilate; accommodate

Two widely accepted psychoanalytic ideas are that (1) unconscious motives affect our behavior, and (2) the early years are a formative period of personality development.

Learning theory's emphasis on the causes and consequences of behavior has led researchers to see that many seemingly inborn problem behaviors may actually be the result of learning.

By focusing attention on active mental processes, cognitive theory has led to a greater understanding of the different types of thinking that are possible at various ages.

23. cognitive
24. Freud; Erikson; Piaget; Watson; Skinner; Pavlov
25. social; biological; genetic

26. nature-nurture; nature; nurture
27. interaction
28. nurture; nature

A man is more likely to be gay if his mother's brother or his own brother is gay. Most children who were raised by lesbian mothers are heterosexual.

29. many
30. dynamic interaction; culture
31. Lev Vygotsky; cognitive
32. novices; mentors (or tutors); apprenticeship in thinking
33. guided participation
34. zone of proximal developmental; assistance

Sociocultural theory has deepened our understanding of the diversity in the pathways of development. It has also emphasized the need to study development in the specific cultural context in which it occurs. The theory has been criticized for neglecting the importance of developmental processes that are not primarily social, such as the role of biological maturation in development.

35. genes; environment
36. instincts; biological
37. environmental; genetic instructions; stress; facilitating
38. selective adaptation
39. all
40. cause corresponding changes and adjustments in every other part
41. ethology; social contact; infant caregiving
42. a. sociocultural
    b. cognitive
    c. learning
    d. psychoanalytic
    e. epigenetic systems
43. a. learning
    b. cognitive
    c. psychoanalytic
    d. epigenetic systems
    e. sociocultural
44. eclectic

PROGRESS TEST 1

Multiple-Choice Questions

1. **d.** is the answer (p. 37)

2. **a.** is the answer. (p. 39)

   b. Learning theory emphasizes the influence of the immediate environment on behavior.

   c. Cognitive theory emphasizes the impact of *conscious* thought processes on behavior.

   d. Sociocultural theory emphasizes the influence on development of social interaction in a specific cultural context.

3. **a.** is the answer. (p. 39)

4. **a.** is the answer. (pp. 40–41)

   b. & c. Whereas Freud identified four stages of psychosexual development, Erikson proposed eight psychosocial stages.

   d. Although his theory places greater emphasis on social and cultural forces than Freud's did, Erikson's theory is nevertheless classified as a psychoanalytic theory.

5. **c.** is the answer. Sociocultural theory is an emergent theory. (p. 38)

   a., b., & d. Each of these is an example of a grand theory.

6. **c.** is the answer. (p. 43)

7. **a.** is the answer. In classical conditioning, a neutral stimulus—in this case, the bell—is associated with a meaningful stimulus—in this case, food. (p. 43)

   b. In operant conditioning, the consequences of a voluntary response determine the likelihood of its being repeated. Salivation is an involuntary response.

   c. & d. Positive reinforcement and social learning pertain to voluntary, or operant, responses.

8. **c.** is the answer. (p. 52)

   a. These are both examples of nurture.

   b. Both of these refer to nature.

   d. The impact of changing historical concepts of childhood on development is an example of how environmental forces (nurture) shape development.

9. **d.** is the answer. (p. 46)

   a. & c. These can be true in all types of learning.

   b. This was not discussed as an aspect of developmental theory.

10. **d.** is the answer. (p. 55)

    a. & c. Sociocultural and learning theories focus almost entirely on environmental factors (nurture) in development.

    b. Cognitive theory emphasizes the developing

person's own mental activity but ignores genet[ic] differences in individuals.

11. **a.** is the answer. (p. 55)

    b. Vygotsky's theory does not emphasize biolog[i]cal processes.

    c. & d. Vygotsky's theory places considerab[le] emphasis on language and social factors.

12. **a.** is the answer. (p. 48)

13. **c.** is the answer. (p. 49)

    a. This refers to the core of Erikson's psychosoci[al] stages, which deals with people's interactio[n] with the environment.

    b. Equilibrium occurs when existing schemes [c]fit a person's current experiences.

    d. Negative reinforcement is the removal of [a] stimulus as a consequence of a desired behavior[.]

14. **b.** is the answer. (p. 53)

    c. This is only true of psychoanalytic theory.

    d. Although the grand theories have emphasize[d] nurture over nature in this matter, no theory su[g]gests that sexual orientation is voluntarily chose[n.]

15. **c.** is the answer. (p. 56)

    a. This describes attention.

    b. This describes positive reinforcement.

    d. This describes reciprocal determinism.

True or False Items

1. T (p. 42)

2. T (p. 41)

3. F   Although most developmentalists believe th[at] nature and nurture interact in shaping develop[ment], the practical implications of wheth[er] nature or nurture plays a greater role in certa[in] abilities keep the controversy alive. (p. 52)

4. F   This assumption lies at the heart of epigene[tic] systems theory. (p. 55)

5. F   Epigenetic systems theory emphasizes t[he] interaction of genes and experience. (p. 55)

6. T (p. 53)

7. F   On the contrary, *dis*equilibrium often foste[rs] greater growth. (p. 49)

8. T (p. 47)

9. F   The hallmark of Piaget's theory is that, [at] every age, individuals think about the world [in] unique ways. (p. 47)

10. T (p. 65)

PROGRESS TEST 2

Multiple-Choice Questions

1. **d.** is the answer. (pp. 50–51)

2. **d.** is the answer. This is one of Piaget's stages of cognitive development. (pp. 39, 40)

3. **c.** is the answer. (p. 47)

4. **a.** is the answer. (p. 38)

   b. *Grand* theories, rather than minitheories, usually stem from one person.

   c. This describes emergent theories.

5. **d.** is the answer. (p. 40)

6. **c.** is the answer. (p. 42)

   a. Piaget formulated a cognitive theory of development.

   b. Vygotsky formulated a sociocultural theory of development.

   d. Erikson formulated a psychoanalytic theory of development.

7. **c.** is the answer. (p. 43)

8. **c.** is the answer. (p. 42)

   a. & b. These are psychoanalytic approaches to treating psychological problems.

   d. Learning theorists generally do not recommend the use of punishment.

9. **a.** is the answer. These behaviors are typical of infants in the sensorimotor stage. (p. 48)

   b., c., & d. These are typical of older children.

10. **a.** is the answer. (p. 48)

   b. The sensorimotor stage describes development from birth until 2 years of age.

   c. This is a psychoanalytic stage described by Freud.

   d. This is not the name of a stage; "psychosocial" refers to Erikson's stage theory.

11. **a.** is the answer. (p. 48)

   b. This describes *dis*equilibrium.

   c. This is formal operational thinking.

   d. Piaget's theory does not propose stages of information processing.

12. **c.** is the answer. (pp. 45–46)

   a. & b. Teaching your dog in this way is an example of operant, rather than classical (respondent), conditioning.

   d. Modeling involves learning by imitating others.

13. **b.** is the answer. (p. 49)

   a. Assimilation occurs when new experiences do *not* clash with existing ideas.

   c. Cognitive equilibrium is mental balance, which occurs when ideas and experiences do *not* clash.

   d. This is Vygotsky's term for the process by which a mentor engages a child in shared learning activities.

14. **d.** is the answer. (p. 55)

   a. This is a common criticism of psychoanalytic theory.

   b. This is a common criticism of learning theory.

   c. This is a common criticism of psychoanalytic and cognitive theories that describe development as occurring in a sequence of stages.

15. **c.** is the answer. (p. 54)

Matching Items

1. f (p. 39)
2. k (p. 42)
3. a (p. 42)
4. c (p. 46)
5. h (p. 47)
6. d (p. 42)
7. g (p. 51)
8. e (p. 42)
9. b (p. 38)
10. i (p. 46)
11. j (p. 55)

THINKING CRITICALLY ABOUT CHAPTER 2

1. **a.** is the answer. (p. 60)

   b. This term was not used to describe development.

   c. & d. These terms describe the processes by which cognitive concepts incorporate (assimilate) new experiences or are revamped (accommodated) by them.

2. **a.** is the answer. This is an example of operant conditioning because a response recurs due to its consequences. (p. 43)

   b. & d. In classical conditioning, the individual learns to associate a neutral stimulus with a meaningful stimulus.

   c. In modeling, learning occurs through the observation of others, rather than through direct exposure to reinforcing consequences, as in this example.

3. **d.** is the answer. (p. 62)

4. **d.** is the answer. (p. 55)

   a. Psychoanalytic theorists focus on the role of unconscious forces in development.

b. Cognitive theorists emphasize how the developing person actively seeks to understand experiences.

c. Sociocultural theorists focus on the social context, as expressed through people, language, and customs.

5. **b.** is the answer. (p. 54)

   a. & c. These are both examples of modeling.

   d. Guided participation involves the coaching of a mentor. In this example, Jack is simply following written directions.

6. **a.** is the answer. (p. 49)

   b. Because the dog is not furry, the child's concept of dog cannot incorporate (assimilate) the discrepant experience without being revamped.

   c. & d. Equilibrium exists when ideas (such as what a dog is) and experiences (such as seeing a hairless dog) do *not* clash.

7. **d.** is the answer. (p. 41)

8. **b.** is the answer. Evidently, Jennie has learned by observing the other children at play. (p. 46)

   a. Classical conditioning is concerned with the association of stimuli, not with complex responses, as in this example.

   c. Guided participation involves the interaction of a mentor and a child.

   d. Reinforcement is a process for getting a response to recur.

9. **c.** is the answer. (p. 48)

10. **d.** is the answer. When Jamail experiences something that conflicts with his existing understanding, he experiences disequilibrium. (p. 49)

   a. Conservation is the ability to recognize that objects do not change when their appearances change.

   b. Cognition refers to all mental activities associated with thinking.

   c. If Jamail's thinking were in equilibrium, all men would be "dad"!

11. **a.** is the answer. (pp. 58–59)

   b. & c. Infant social reflexes and adult caregiving impulses occur in all cultures (b), which indicates that they are the product of nature rather than nurture (c).

   d. The text does not address the issue of gender differences in infant reflexes or caregiving impulses.

12. **d.** is the answer. (p. 51)

13. **b.** is the answer. (pp. 40, 41)

   a. According to Erikson, this crisis concern younger children.

   c. & d. In Erikson's theory, these crises concer older children.

14. **c.** is the answer. (p. 65)

   a., b., & d. These are three of the many theoretic perspectives upon which someone working fro an eclectic perspective might draw.

15. **d.** is the answer. (p. 42)

   a., b., & c. Each of these theories emphasizes th development is a discontinuous process th occurs in stages.

KEY TERMS

Writing Definitions

1. A **developmental theory** is a systematic stat ment of principles and generalizations th explains behavior and development and provid a framework for future research. (p. 37)

2. **Grand theories** are comprehensive theories human development that have proven to be ina equate in the face of research evidence that deve opment is more diverse than the theories pr posed. Examples of grand theories are psychoa alytic, cognitive, and learning theories. (p. 38)

3. **Minitheories** are less general and comprehensi than grand theories, focusing instead on son specific area of development. (p. 38)

4. **Emergent theories**, such as sociocultural theo and epigenetic systems theory, are newer con prehensive theories that bring together inform tion from many disciplines but are not yet coherent, comprehensive whole. (p. 38)

5. **Psychoanalytic theory**, a grand theory, interpre human development in terms of intrinsic driv and motives, many of which are irrational a unconscious. (p. 39)

6. **Learning theory,** a grand theory based on beha iorism, emphasizes the sequences and process of conditioning that underlie most of human a animal behavior. (p. 42)

7. In learning theory, a **stimulus** is an action event that elicits a behavioral response. (p. 42)

8. In learning theory, a **response** is an instinctual, learned, behavior that is elicited by a certain sti ulus. (p. 42)

9. **Conditioning** is the learning process that occurs either through the association of two stimuli (classical conditioning) or through the use of positive or negative reinforcement or punishment (operant conditioning). (p. 42)

10. **Reinforcement** is the process by which the consequences of a particular behavior strengthen the behavior, making it more likely that the behavior will be repeated. (p. 46)

11. An extension of learning theory, **social learning theory** emphasizes that people often learn new behaviors through observation and imitation of other people. (p. 46)

12. **Modeling** refers to the process by which we observe other people's behavior and then pattern our own after it. (p. 46)

13. **Cognitive theory** emphasizes that the way people think and understand the world shapes their perceptions, attitudes, and actions. (p. 47)

14. In Piaget's theory, **cognitive equilibrium** is a state of mental balance, in which a person's thoughts about the world seem not to clash with each other or with his or her experiences. (p. 48)

15. **Sociocultural theory** seeks to explain development as the result of a dynamic interaction between developing persons and their surrounding culture. (p. 51)

16. **Guided participation** is a learning process in which the learner is tutored, or mentored, through social interaction with a skilled teacher. (p. 51)

17. The **epigenetic systems theory** emphasizes the genetic origins of behavior but also stresses that genes, over time, are directly and systematically affected by environmental forces. (p. 55)

18. According to Vygotsky, developmental growth occurs when mentors draw children into the **zone of proximal development**, which is the range of skills the child can exercise with assistance but cannot perform independently. (p. 56)

19. **Ethology** is the study of behavior as it relates to the evolution and survival of a species. (p. 58)

20. **Selective adaptation** is the evolutionary process through which useful genes that enhance survival become more frequent within individuals. (p. 60)

21. Developmentalists who work from an **eclectic perspective** accept elements from several theories, instead of adhering to only a single perspective. (p. 65)

Cross-Check

ACROSS

2. learning
8. response
11. nature
12. eclectic
14. Piaget
16. emergent
18. nurture
19. Watson

DOWN

1. minitheory
3. epigenetic systems
4. reinforcement
5. grand
6. psychoanalytic
7. conditioning
9. Skinner
10. ethology
13. modeling
14. Pavlov
15. Erikson
17. Freud

CHAPTER 3

Heredity and Environment

Chapter Overview

Conception occurs when the male and female reproductive cells—the sperm and ovum, respectively—come together to create a new, one-celled zygote with its own unique combination of genetic material. The genetic material furnishes the instructions for development—not only for obvious physical characteristics, such as sex, coloring, and body shape but also for certain psychological characteristics, such as bashfulness, moodiness, and vocational aptitude.

Every year scientists make new discoveries and reach new understandings about genes and their effects on the development of individuals. This chapter presents some of their findings, including that most human characteristics are polygenic and multifactorial, the result of the interaction of many genetic and environmental influences. Perhaps the most important findings have come from research into the causes of genetic and chromosomal abnormalities. The chapter discusses the most common of these abnormalities and concludes with a section on genetic counseling. Genetic testing before and after conception can help predict whether a couple will have a child with a genetic problem.

Many students find the technical material in this chapter difficult to master, but it *can* be done with a great deal of rehearsal. Working through the Chapter Review several times and mentally reciting terms are both useful techniques for rehearsing this type of material.

NOTE: Answer guidelines for all Chapter 3 questions begin on page 48.

Guided Study

The text chapter should be studied one section at a time. Before you read, preview each section by skimming it, noting headings and boldface items. Then read the appropriate section objectives from the following outline. Keep these objectives in mind and, as you read the chapter section, search for the informa-

tion that will enable you to meet each objective. Once you have finished a section, write out answers for it objectives.

Development Begins (pp. 69–76)

1. Describe the process of conception and the first hours of development of the zygote.

2. Identify the mechanisms of heredity, and explain how sex is determined.

3. Discuss genetic continuity and diversity, and distinguish between monozygotic and dizygotic twins.

4. (Changing Policy) Discuss age-related changes in the sex ratio and whether there should be a social policy to regulate sex selection of children.

8. Explain how scientists distinguish the effects of genes and environment on development, and explain the role of molecular genetics in this process.

Genotype to Phenotype (pp. 77–86)

5. Differentiate genotype from phenotype, and explain the polygenic and multifactorial nature of human traits.

9. Identify some environmental variables that affect genetic inheritance, and describe how a particular trait, such as shyness (inhibition) or schizophrenia, might be affected.

10. (A Life-Span View) Discuss the interaction of genes and environment in the development of alcoholism.

6. Explain the additive and nonadditive patterns of genetic interaction. Give examples of the traits that result from each type of interaction.

Inherited Abnormalities (pp. 86–93)

11. Describe the most common chromosomal abnormalities, focusing on abnormalities involving the sex chromosomes.

7. Discuss *X*-linked genes in terms of genotype and phenotype, and explain the concept of genetic imprinting.

12. (Research Report) Explain the major methods of prenatal diagnosis, noting the advantages of each.

13. Identify two common genetic disorders, and discuss reasons for their relatively low incidence of occurrence.

14. (In Person) Describe four situations in which couples should seek genetic testing and counseling.

Chapter Review

When you have finished reading the chapter, work through the material that follows to review it. Complete the sentences and answer the questions. As you proceed, evaluate your performance for each section by consulting the answers on page 48. Do not continue with the next section until you understand each answer. If you need to, review or reread the appropriate section in the textbook before continuing.

Development Begins (pp. 69–76)

1. The human reproductive cells, which are called _____ , include the male's _____ and the female's _____ .

2. When the gametes' genetic material combines, a living cell called a _____ is formed.

3. Before the zygote begins the process of cellular division that starts human development, the combined genetic material from both gametes is _____ to form two complete sets of genetic instructions. Soon after, following a genetic timetable, the cells start to _____ , with various cells beginning to specialize and reproduce at different rates.

4. A complete copy of the genetic instructions inherited by the zygote at the moment of conception is found in _____ (every/most/ only a few) cell(s) of the body.

5. The basic units of heredity are the _____ , which are discrete segments of a _____ , which is a molecule of _____ .

6. Genetic instructions are "written" in a chemical code, made up of four pairs of bases:

_____ , _____ ,
_____ , and _____ .

The precise nature of a gene's instructions is determined by this _____ _____ , that is, by the overall _____ in which base pairs appear along each segment of the DNA molecule.

7. The _____ _____  _____ is the ongoing international effort to map and interpret the complete genetic code. This task is complicated by the fact that some genes appear in several versions, called _____ , and that most genes have _____ (only one/several different) function(s).

8. Genes direct the synthesis of hundreds of different kinds of _____ , including _____ , which are the body's building blocks and regulators. Genes direct not only the form and location of cells, but also life itself, instructing cells to _____ _____ .

9. Each normal person inherits _____ chromosomes, _____ from each parent.

0. During cell division, the gametes each receive _____ (one/both) member(s) of each chromosome pair. Thus, in number each gamete has _____ chromosomes.

1. The developing person's sex is determined by the _____ pair of chromosomes. In the female, this pair is composed of two _____-shaped chromosomes and is designated _____ . In the male, this pair includes one _____ and one _____ chromosome and is therefore designated _____ .

2. The critical factor in the determination of a zygote's sex is which _____ (sperm/ovum) reaches the other gamete first.

3. Genes ensure both genetic _____ across the species and genetic _____ within it.

4. When the twenty-three chromosome pairs divide up during the formation of gametes, which of the two pair members will end up in a particular gamete is determined by _____ .

5. Genetic variability is also affected by the _____-_____ of genes, and by the interaction of genetic instructions in ways unique to the individual. This means that any given mother and father can form approximately _____ genetically different offspring.

6. Identical twins, which occur about once in every _____ pregnancies, are called _____ twins because they come from one zygote. Such twins _____ (are/are not) genetically identical.

7. Twins who begin life as two separate zygotes created by the fertilization of two ova, are called _____ twins. Such twins have approximately _____ percent of their genes in common.

18. Dizygotic births occur naturally about once in every _____ births. Women in their _____ (what age?) are three times as likely to have dizygotic twins than women in their_____ .

19. The number of multiple births has _____ (increased/decreased/remained unchanged) in many nations because of the increased use of _____ . Generally, the more embryos that develop together, the _____ , less _____ , and more _____ each one is.

20. (Changing Policy) Worldwide, slightly more _____ (females/males) than _____ (females/males) are born each year. However, because _____ (females/males) have a slightly higher rate of childhood death, a balance occurs when men and women reach _____ age.

21. (Changing Policy) After about age _____ , the sex ratio now favors women. This is due to the fact that in the past many women died in _____ , whereas today more men than women die from _____ _____ .

22. (Changing Policy) Today, choosing the sex of children _____ (is/is not) feasible and _____ (is/is not) widespread.

Genotype to Phenotype (pp. 77–86)

23. Most human characteristics are affected by many genes, and so are _____ ; and by many factors, and so are _____ .

24. The sum total of all the genes a person inherits is called the _____ . The sum total of all the genes that are actually expressed is called the _____ .

25. A person who has a gene in his or her genotype that is not expressed in the phenotype is said to be a _____ of that gene.

26. For any given trait, the phenotype arises from the interaction of the proteins synthesized from the specific _____ that make up the

genotype, and from the interaction between the genotype and the _____ .

27. A phenotype that reflects the sum of the contributions of all the genes involved in its determination illustrates the _____ pattern of genetic interaction. Examples include genes that affect _____ and _____ _____ .

28. Less often, genes interact in a _____ fashion. In one example of this pattern, some genes are more influential than others; this is called the _____-pattern. In this pattern, the more influential gene is called _____ , and the weaker gene is called _____ . In one variation of this pattern, the phenotype is influenced primarily, but not exclusively, by the dominant gene; this is the _____ _____ pattern. Hundreds of _____ characteristics follow this basic pattern.

29. Some recessive genes are located only on the *X* chromosome and so are called _____-_____ . Examples of such genes are the ones that determine _____ _____ . Because they have only one *X* chromosome, _____ (females/males) are more likely to have these characteristics in their phenotype.

30. Complicating inheritance further is the fact that dominant genes sometimes do not completely _____ the phenotype. This may be caused by _____ , _____ , or other factors. Furthermore, chromosome pairs sometimes do not split precisely, resulting in a mixture of cells called a _____ .

31. Whether a gene is inherited from the mother or the father _____ (does/does not) influence its behavior. This tendency of genes is called _____ _____ , or tagging.

32. The complexity of genetic interaction is particularly apparent in _____ , which is the study of the genetic origins of _____ characteristics. These include _____ traits such as _____ ; psychological disorders such as _____ _____ ; and _____ traits such as _____ .

33. Most behavioral traits are affected by the _____ of large numbers of _____ with _____ factors. Traits that are plastic early in life _____ (always/do not always) remain plastic thereafter.

34. To identify genetic influences on development, researchers must distinguish genetic effects from _____ effects. To this end, researchers study _____ and _____ children.

35. If _____ (monozygotic/dizygotic) twins are found to be much more similar on a particular trait than _____ (monozygotic/dizygotic) twins are, it is likely that genes play a significant role in the appearance of that trait.

36. Traits that show a strong correlation between adopted children and their _____ (adoptive/biological) parents suggest a genetic basis for those characteristics.

37. The best way to try to separate the effects of genes and environments is to study _____ twins who have been raised in _____ (the same/different) environments.

38. Environment, as broadly defined in the text, affects _____ (most/every/ few) human characteristic(s).

39. The study of the chemical codes that make up a particular molecule of DNA is called _____ _____ .

40. Researchers can now directly compare a pattern of genes shared by two individuals with a promising new statistical technique called _____ _____ _____ .

Explain how social scientists define environment.

Briefly explain how shyness (or inhibition), which is influenced by genes, is also affected by the social environment.

41. Other psychological traits that have strong genetic influences but may be affected by environment include _____ ,

_____ , _____

_____ , _____ , and

_____ .

42. If one monozygotic twin develops schizophrenia, about _____ of the time the other twin does, too. Researchers have pinpointed a gene on chromosome _____ , which predisposes schizophrenia.

43. Environmental influences _____ (do/do not) play an important role in the appearance of schizophrenia. One predisposing factor is birth during _____

_____ , probably because a certain _____ is more prevalent at this time of year.

44. Another disease that develops from the complex interaction of genes and environmental conditions is _____ _____ .

45. (A Life-Span View) Alcoholism _____ (is/is not) partly genetic; furthermore, its expression _____ (is/is not) affected by the environment. Certain temperamental traits correlate with abusive drinking, including _____ . A person is most likely to

become an active alcoholic between ages _____ and _____ .

(A Life-Span View) Briefly explain how genes for alcoholism might have evolved in certain groups.

Inherited Abnormalities (pp. 86–93)

Researchers study genetic and chromosomal abnormalities for three major reasons. They are:

46. (Research Report) When conception occurs in a laboratory dish, called _____ , cells can be analyzed for genetic defects before they are inserted into the uterus. This procedure is called _____ - _____

_____ . One test for neural-tube defects and Down syndrome analyzes the level of _____ in the mother's blood. An ultrasound, or _____ , uses high-frequency sound waves to produce an image of the fetus. Physicians use a device called a _____ to directly observe the fetus and the inside of the placenta.

47. (Research Report) The "mainstay" of prenatal diagnosis is _____ , in which a small amount of fluid surrounding the fetus, inside the placenta, is analyzed for chromosomal or genetic abnormalities. A test that provides the same information but can be performed much earlier during the pregnancy is called

_____ _____

_____ .

48. Chromosomal abnormalities occur during the formation of the _____ , producing a sperm or ovum that does not have the normal complement of chromosomes.

49. An estimated _____ of all zygotes have too few or too many chromosomes. Most of these _____ (do/do not) begin to develop, usually because a _____ occurs. Nevertheless, about 1 in every _____ newborns has one chromosome too few or one too many, leading to a cluster of characteristics called a _____ .

50. The most common extra-chromosome syndrome is _____ , which is also called _____ .

List several of the physical and psychological characteristics associated with Down syndrome.

51. About 1 in every 500 infants has either a missing _____ chromosome or two or more such chromosomes. One such syndrome is _____ _____ , in which a boy inherits the _____ chromosome pattern.

52. In some individuals, part of the X chromosome is attached by such a thin string of molecules that it seems about to break off; this abnormality is called _____-_____ syndrome.

53. The variable that most often correlates with chromosomal abnormalities is _____ _____ .

54. Chromosomal abnormalities such as Down syndrome _____ (rarely/almost always) follow an age-related pattern.

55. (In Person) Through _____ _____ _____ , couples today can learn more about their genes and about their chances of conceiving a child with chromosomal or other genetic abnormalities.

56. (In Person) List four situations in which genetic counseling is strongly recommended.

   a. _____

   b. _____

   c. _____

   d. _____

57. It is much _____ (more/less) likely that a person is a carrier of one or more harmful genes than that he or she has abnormal chromosomes.

58. Most of the known genetic disorders are _____ (dominant/recessive). Genetic disorders usually _____ (are/are not) seriously disabling.

59. Two exceptions are the central nervous system disease called _____ _____ and the disorder that causes its victims to exhibit uncontrollable tics and explosive outbursts, called _____ .

60. Genetic disorders that are _____ and _____ claim more victims than dominant ones. Three common recessive disorders are _____ _____ , _____ , and _____-_____ .

Progress Test 1

Circle your answers to the following questions and check them against the answers on page 50. If your answer is incorrect, read the explanation for why it is incorrect and then consult the appropriate pages of the text (in parentheses following the correct answer).

Multiple-Choice Questions

1. When a sperm and an ovum merge, a one-celled
   _____ is formed.
   a. zygote   c. gamete
   b. reproductive cell   d. monozygote

2. Genes are discrete segments that provide the biochemical instructions that each cell needs to
   become:
   a. a zygote.
   b. a chromosome.
   c. a specific part of a functioning human body.
   d. deoxyribonucleic acid.

3. In the male, the twenty-third pair of chromosomes is designated _____ ; in the
   female, this pair is designated _____ .
   a. XX; XY   c. XO; XXY
   b. XY; XX   d. XXY; XO

4. Since the twenty-third pair of chromosomes in
   females is *XX*, each ovum carries an:
   a. XX zygote.   c. XY zygote.
   b. X zygote.   d. X chromosome.

5. When a zygote splits, the two identical, independent clusters that develop become:
   a. dizygotic twins.   c. fraternal twins.
   b. monozygotic twins.   d. trizygotic twins.

6. In scientific research, the *best* way to separate the
   effects of genes and the environment is to study:
   a. dizygotic twins.
   b. adopted children and their biological parents.
   c. adopted children and their adoptive parents.
   d. monozygotic twins raised in different envi-
      ronments.

7. Most of the known genetic disorders are:
   a. dominant.
   b. recessive.
   c. seriously disabling.
   d. sex-linked.

8. When we say that a characteristic is multifactorial, we mean that:
   a. many genes are involved.
   b. many environmental factors are involved.
   c. many genetic and environmental factors are
      involved.
   d. the characteristic is polygenic.

9. Genes are segments of molecules of:
   a. genotype.
   b. deoxyribonucleic acid (DNA).
   c. karyotype.
   d. phenotype.

10. The potential for genetic diversity in humans is
    so great because:
    a. there are approximately 8 million possible
       combinations of chromosomes.
    b. when the sperm and ovum unite, genetic com-
       binations not present in either parent can be
       formed.
    c. just before a chromosome pair divides during
       the formation of gametes, genes cross over,
       producing recombinations.
    d. of all the above reasons.

11. A chromosomal abnormality that affects males
    only involves a(n):
    a. XO chromosomal pattern.
    b. XXX chromosomal pattern.
    c. YY chromosomal pattern.
    d. XXY chromosomal pattern.

12. Polygenic complexity is most apparent in
    _____ characteristics.
    a. physical   c. recessive gene
    b. psychological   d. dominant gene

13. Babies born with trisomy-21 (Down syndrome)
    are often:
    a. born to older parents.
    b. unusually aggressive.
    c. abnormally tall by adolescence.
    d. blind.

14. To say that a trait is polygenic means that:
    a. many genes make it more likely that the indi-
       vidual will inherit the trait.
    b. several genes must be present in order for the
       individual to inherit the trait.
    c. the trait is multifactorial.
    d. most people carry genes for the trait.

15. Some genetic diseases are recessive, so the child
    cannot inherit the condition unless both parents:
    a. have Kleinfelter syndrome.
    b. carry the same recessive gene.
    c. have XO chromosomes.
    d. have the disease.

Matching Items

Match each term with its corresponding description or definition.

Terms

_____   1. gametes
_____   2. chromosome
_____   3. genotype
_____   4. phenotype
_____   5. monozygotic
_____   6. dizygotic
_____   7. additive
_____   8. fragile-*X* syndrome
_____   9. carrier
_____   10. zygote
_____   11. alleles

Descriptions or Definitions

a. a person's entire genetic inheritance
b. identical twins
c. sperm and ovum
d. the first cell of the developing person
e. a person who has a recessive gene in his or he genotype that is not expressed in the phenotype
f. fraternal twins
g. a pattern in which each gene in question make an active contribution to the final outcome
h. a DNA molecule
i. the behavioral or physical expression of geneti potential
j. a chromosomal abnormality
k. alternate versions of a gene

Progress Test 2

Progress Test 2 should be completed during a final chapter review. Answer the following questions after you thoroughly understand the correct answers for the Chapter Review and Progress Test 1.

1. Which of the following provides the best broad description of the relationship between heredity and environment in determining height?
   a. Heredity is the primary influence, with environment affecting development only in severe situations.
   b. Heredity and environment contribute equally to development.
   c. Environment is the major influence on physical characteristics.
   d. Heredity directs the individual's potential and environment determines whether and to what degree the individual reaches that potential.

2. Research studies of monozygotic twins who were raised apart suggest that:
   a. virtually every human trait is affected by both genes and environment.
   b. only a few psychological traits, such as emotional reactivity, are affected by genes.
   c. most traits are determined by environmental influences.
   d. most traits are determined by genes.

3. Males with fragile-*X* syndrome are:
   a. feminine in appearance.
   b. less severely affected than females.
   c. frequently retarded intellectually.
   d. likely to have fatty deposits around th breasts.

4. Disorders that are _____ are mo likely to pass undetected from generation to gen eration.
   a. dominant
   b. dominant and polygenic
   c. recessive
   d. recessive and multifactorial

5. The effect of a gene on a particular physical cha acteristic depends on whether the gene come from the mother or the father. This is called:
   a. the dominant-recessive pattern.
   b. genetic imprinting.
   c. the additive pattern.
   d. molecular genetics.

6. Dizygotic twins result when:
   a. a single egg is fertilized by a sperm and the splits.
   b. a single egg is fertilized by two differe sperm.
   c. two eggs are fertilized by two different sperr
   d. either a single egg is fertilized by one spe or two eggs are fertilized by two differe sperm.

7. Molecules of DNA that in humans are organize into 23 complementary pairs are called:
   a. zygotes.   c. chromosomes.
   b. genes.   d. ova.

8. Shortly after the zygote is formed, it begins the processes of duplication and division. Each resulting new cell has:
   a. the same number of chromosomes as was contained in the zygote.
   b. half the number of chromosomes as was contained in the zygote.
   c. twice, then four times, then eight times the number of chromosomes as was contained in the zygote.
   d. all the chromosomes except those that determine sex.

9. If an ovum is fertilized by a sperm bearing a Y chromosome:
   a. a female will develop.
   b. cell division will result.
   c. a male will develop.
   d. spontaneous abortion will occur.

10. When the male cells in the testes and the female cells in the ovaries divide to produce gametes, the process differs from that in the production of all other cells. As a result of the different process, the gametes have:
   a. one rather than both members of each chromosome pair.
   b. 23 chromosome pairs.
   c. X but not Y chromosomes.
   d. chromosomes from both parents.

11. Most human traits are:
   a. polygenic.
   b. multifactorial.
   c. determined by dominant-recessive patterns.
   d. both a. and b.

12. Genotype is to phenotype as _____ is to _____ .
   a. genetic potential; physical expression
   b. physical expression; genetic potential
   c. sperm; ovum
   d. gamete; zygote

13. The genes that influence height and skin color interact according to the _____ pattern.
   a. dominant-recessive   c. additive
   b. X-linked   d. nonadditive

14. X-linked recessive genes explain why some traits seem to be passed from:
   a. father to son.
   b. father to daughter.
   c. mother to daughter.
   d. mother to son.

15. (Research Report) A 35-year-old woman who is pregnant is most likely to undergo which type of test for the detection of prenatal chromosomal or genetic abnormalities?
   a. pre-implantation testing
   b. ultrasound
   c. amniocentesis
   d. alphafetoprotein assay

True or False Items

Write T (*true*) or F (*false*) on the line in front of each statement.

_____ 1. Most human characteristics are multifactorial, caused by the interaction of genetic and environmental factors.

_____ 2. Less than 10 percent of all zygotes have harmful genes or an abnormal chromosomal makeup.

_____ 3. (A Life-Span View) Research suggests that susceptibility to alcoholism is at least partly the result of genetic inheritance.

_____ 4. The human reproductive cells (ova and sperm) are called gametes.

_____ 5. Only a very few human traits are polygenic.

_____ 6. The zygote contains all the biologically inherited information—the genes and chromosomes—that a person will have during his or her life.

_____ 7. A couple should probably seek genetic counseling if several earlier pregnancies ended in spontaneous abortion.

_____ 8. Many genetic conditions are recessive; thus, a child will have the condition even if only the mother carries the gene.

_____ 9. Two people who have the same phenotype may have a different genotype for a trait such as eye color.

_____ 10. When cells divide to produce reproductive cells (gametes), each sperm or ovum receives only 23 chromosomes, half as many as the original cell.

_____ 11. Most genes have only one function.

Thinking Critically About Chapter 3

Answer these questions the day before an exam as a final check on your understanding of the chapter's terms and concepts.

1. The international effort to map the complete human genetic code is complicated by the fact that:
   a. the total number of human genes is far greater than the 100,000 previously estimated.
   b. some genes appear in several different versions.
   c. genes are made up of thousands of DNA particles called alleles.
   d. All of the above have complicated the effort to map the genetic code.

2. Before their first child was born, Jack and Diane decided that they should be karyotyped, which means that:
   a. their chromosomes were photographed.
   b. a genetic counselor filled out a complete history of genetic diseases in their families.
   c. they each took a fertility test.
   d. they selected the sex of their child.

3. Which of the following is an inherited abnormality that quite possibly could develop into a recognizable syndrome?
   a. Just before dividing to form a sperm or ovum, corresponding gene segments of a chromosome pair break off and are exchanged.
   b. Just before conception, a chromosome pair splits imprecisely, resulting in a mosaic of cells.
   c. A person inherits an X chromosome in which part of the chromosome is attached to the rest of it by a very slim string of molecules.
   d. A person inherits a recessive gene on his Y chromosome.

4. Some men are color-blind because they inherit a particular recessive gene from their mother. That recessive gene is carried on the:
   a. X chromosome.
   b. XX chromosome pair.
   c. Y chromosome.
   d. X or Y chromosome.

5. If your mother is much taller than your father, it is most likely that your height will be:
   a. about the same as your mother's, because the X chromosome determines height.
   b. about the same as your father's, because the Y chromosome determines height.
   c. somewhere between your mother's and father's heights because of genetic imprinting.
   d. greater than both your mother's and father's because of your grandfather's dominant gene.

6. If a dizygotic twin develops schizophrenia, the likelihood of the other twin experiencing serious mental illness is much lower than is the case with monozygotic twins. This suggests that:
   a. schizophrenia is caused by genes.
   b. schizophrenia is influenced by genes.
   c. environment is unimportant in the development of schizophrenia.
   d. monozygotic twins are especially vulnerable to schizophrenia.

7. A person's skin turns yellow-orange as a result of a carrot-juice diet regimen. This is an example of
   a. an environmental influence.
   b. an alteration in genotype.
   c. polygenic inheritance.
   d. incomplete dominance.

8. The personality trait of inhibition (shyness) seems to be partly genetic. A child who inherits the genes for shyness will be shy:
   a. under most circumstances.
   b. only if shyness is the dominant gene.
   c. if the environment does not encourage greater sociability.
   d. if he or she is raised by biological rather than adoptive parents.

9. If a man carries the recessive gene for cystic fibrosis and his wife does not, the chances of their having a child with cystic fibrosis is:
   a. one in four.
   b. fifty-fifty.
   c. zero.
   d. dependent upon the wife's ethnic background.

10. One of the best ways to distinguish the relative influence of genetic and environmental factors on behavior is to compare children who have:
    a. the same genes and environments.
    b. different genes and environments.
    c. similar genes and environments.
    d. the same genes but different environments.

11. In the case of identical twins reared apart, research has confirmed that:
    a. most psychological characteristics and personal traits are genetically influenced.
    b. most psychological characteristics and personal traits are influenced by the environment.
    c. some traits are genetically influenced while others are due to environmental effects.
    d. both a. and b. are true.

12. (A Life-Span View) Laurie and Brad, who both have a history of alcoholism in their families, are concerned that the child they hope to have will inherit a genetic predisposition to alcoholism. Based on information presented in the text, what advice should you offer them?
    a. "Stop worrying, alcoholism is only weakly genetic."
    b. "It is almost certain that your child will become alcoholic."
    c. "Social influences, such as the family and peer environment, play a critical role in determining whether alcoholism is expressed."
    d. "Wait to have children until you are both middle aged, in order to see if the two of you become alcoholic."

13. Sixteen-year-old Joey experiences some mental slowness and hearing and heart problems, yet he is able to care for himself and is unusually sweet-tempered. Joey probably:
    a. is mentally retarded.
    b. has Alzheimer's disease.
    c. has Kleinfelter syndrome.
    d. has Down syndrome.

14. Genetically, Claude's potential height is 6'0. Because he did not receive a balanced diet, however, he grew to only 5'9". Claude's actual height is an example of a:
    a. recessive gene.
    b. dominant gene.
    c. genotype.
    d. phenotype.

15. Winona inherited a gene from her mother that, regardless of her father's contribution to her genotype, will be expressed in her phenotype. Evidently, the gene Winona received from her mother is a(n) _____ gene.
    a. polygenic
    b. recessive
    c. dominant
    d. X-linked

Key Terms

Writing Definitions

Using your own words, write on a separate piece of paper a brief definition or explanation of each of the following terms.

1. environment
2. heredity
3. gamete
4. zygote
5. genes
6. chromosome
7. genetic code
8. Human Genome Project
9. twenty-third pair
10. monozygotic twins
11. dizygotic twins
12. polygenic traits
13. multifactorial traits
14. genotype
15. phenotype
16. carrier
17. additive gene
18. dominant gene
19. recessive gene
20. X-linked gene
21. genetic imprinting
22. behavioral genetics
23. molecular genetics
24. spontaneous abortion
25. syndrome
26. Trisomy-21 (Down syndrome)
27. fragile-X syndrome
28. genetic counseling

Cross Check

After you have written the definitions of the key terms in this chapter, you should complete the crossword puzzle to ensure that you can reverse the process—recognize the term, given the definition.

ACROSS

2. Cluster of distinct characteristics that tend to occur together in a given disorder.
7. A person who has a gene in his or her genotype that is not evident in his or her phenotype.
8. The sum total of all the genes a person inherits.
10. The single cell formed from the fusing of an ovum and a sperm.
13. The stronger gene in an interacting pair of genes.
14. A tool of molecular genetics that pinpoints the chemical codes that make up a particular DNA molecule (abbrev.).
15. All of the genetic traits that are expressed in a person.
17. Genes that are on the X chromosome.
18. The sequence of chemical bases held within DNA molecules that directs development.
19. One of 46 in each normal human cell.
20. A genetic disease that nearly always develops in people with a particular allele of a particular gene.
21. The genes that affect height, hair curliness, and skin color are of this type.

DOWN

1. A genetic disorder in which part of the X chromosome is attached to the rest of it by a very slim string of molecules.
3. Fraternal twins.
4. All the nongenetic factors that can affect development.
5. The growth process in which cells begin to specialize, taking different forms and dividing at different rates.
6. The basic unit of genetic instruction.
7. The genetic process that during the formation of gametes adds greatly to genetic diversity.
9. A spontaneous abortion.
11. The international project that aims to map the complete human genetic code.
12. Type of trait produced by the interaction of many genes (rather than by a single gene).
13. The most common extra-chromosome syndrome (also called trisomy-21).
16. The weaker gene in an interacting pair of genes.

ANSWERS

CHAPTER REVIEW

1. gametes; sperm; ovum
2. zygote
3. duplicated; differentiate
4. every
5. genes; chromosome; DNA
6. adenine; guanine; cytosine; thymine; geneti code; sequence
7. Human Genome Project; alleles; several different
8. proteins; enzymes; grow, to repair damage, t take in nourishment, to multiply, to atrophy, an so forth
9. 46; 23
10. one; 23
11. twenty-third; *X*; *XX*; *X*; *Y*; *XY*
12. sperm
13. continuity; diversity
14. chance

5. crossing-over; 64 trillion

6. 270; monozygotic; are

7. dizygotic (fraternal); 50

8. 60; late 30s; early 20s

9. increased; fertility drugs; smaller; mature; vulnerable

0. males; females; males; reproductive

1. 45; childbirth; heart attacks

2. is; is not

3. polygenic; multifactorial

4. genotype; phenotype

5. carrier

6. genes; environment

7. additive; height; skin color

8. nonadditive; dominant-recessive; dominant; recessive; incomplete dominance; physical

9. X-linked; color-blindness, many allergies, several diseases, and some learning disabilities; males

0. penetrate; temperature; stress; mosaic

1. does; genetic imprinting

2. behavioral genetics; psychological; personality; sociability, assertiveness, moodiness, and fearfulness; schizophrenia, depression, and attention-deficit hyperactive disorder; cognitive; memory for numbers, spatial perception, and fluency of expression

3. interaction; genes; environmental; do not always

4. environmental; twins; adopted

5. monozygotic; dizygotic

6. biological

7. identical (or monozygotic); different

8. every

9. molecular genetics

0. quantitative trait loci

ocial scientists define *environment* broadly to refer to ne multitude of variables that can interact with the erson's genetic inheritance at every point of life.

genetically shy child whose parents are outgoing, or example, would have many more contacts with ther people and would observe his or her parents ocializing more freely than if this same child's parnts were also shy. In growing up, the child might arn to relax in social settings and would become less bservably shy than he or she would have been with nore introverted parents, despite the genetic predisosition toward shyness. Culture plays a role in the xpression of shyness.

1. intelligence; emotionality; activity level; aggression; religiosity

42. two-thirds; 6

43. do; late winter; virus

44. Alzheimer's disease

45. is; is; a quick temper, a willingness to take risks, and a high level of anxiety; 15; 25

Since the distillation process involved in producing alcohol killed the destructive bacteria that thrived in drinking water, being able to drink alcohol in quantity was adaptive for our ancestors in most of Europe. Because east Asians boiled their water and drank it as tea, however, about half lack the gene for an enzyme necessary to fully metabolize alcohol.

By studying genetic disruptions of normal development, researchers (a) gain a fuller appreciation of the complexities of genetic interaction, (b) reduce misinformation and prejudice directed toward those afflicted by such disorders, and (c) help individuals understand the likelihood of occurrence and to become better prepared to limit their harmful effects.

46. in vitro; pre-implantation testing; alphafetoprotein; sonogram; fetoscope

47. amniocentesis; chorionic villi sampling

48. gametes

49. half; do not; spontaneous abortion; 200; syndrome

50. Down syndrome; trisomy-21

Most people with Down syndrome have certain facial characteristics—a thick tongue, round face, slanted eyes—as well as distinctive hands, feet, and fingerprints. Many also have hearing problems, heart abnormalities, muscle weakness, and short stature. Almost all experience some mental slowness.

51. sex; Klinefelter syndrome; XXY

52. fragile-X

53. maternal age

54. almost always

55. prenatal genetic counseling

56. Genetic counseling is recommended for (a) those who have a parent, sibling, or child with a serious genetic condition; (b) those who have a history of spontaneous abortions, stillbirths, or infertility; (c) couples who are from the same ethnic group or subgroup; and (d) women over age 34.

57. more

58. dominant; are not

59. Huntington's chorea; Tourette syndrome

60. recessive; multifactorial; cystic fibrosis, thalassemia, sickle-cell anemia

PROGRESS TEST 1

Multiple-Choice Questions

1. **a.** is the answer. (p. 69)

    b. & c. The reproductive cells (sperm and ova), which are also called gametes, are individual entities.

    d. *Monozygote* refers to one member of a pair of identical twins.

2. **c.** is the answer. (p. 70)

    a. The zygote is the first cell of the developing person.

    b. Chromosomes are molecules of DNA that *carry* genes.

    d. DNA molecules contain genetic information.

3. **b.** is the answer. (p. 72)

4. **d.** is the answer. When the gametes are formed, one member of each chromosome pair splits off; because in females both are *X* chromosomes, each ovum must carry an *X* chromosome. (p. 72)

    a., b., & c. The zygote refers to the merged sperm and ovum that is the first new cell of the developing individual.

5. **b.** is the answer. *Mono* means "one." Thus, monozygotic twins develop from one zygote. (p. 75)

    a. & c. Dizygotic, or fraternal, twins develop from two (*di*) zygotes.

    d. A trizygotic birth would result in triplets (*tri*), rather than twins.

6. **d.** is the answer. In this situation, one factor (genetic similarity) is held constant while the other factor (environment) is varied. Therefore, any similarity in traits is strong evidence of genetic inheritance. (p. 81)

7. **a.** is the answer. (p. 90)

    c. & d. Most dominant disorders are neither seriously disabling, nor sex-linked.

8. **c.** is the answer. (p. 77)

    a., b., & d. *Polygenic* means "many genes"; *multifactorial* means "many factors," which are not limited to either genetic or environmental factors.

9. **b.** is the answer. (p. 70)

    a. Genotype is a person's genetic potential.

    c. A karyotype is a picture of a person's chromosomes.

    d. Phenotype is the actual expression of a genotype.

10. **d.** is the answer. (p. 73)

11. **d.** is the answer. (p. 89)

    a. & b. These chromosomal abnormalities affec[t] females.

    c. There is no such abnormality.

12. **b.** is the answer. (p. 79)

    c. & d. The text does not equate polygenic com[plexity] plexity with either recessive or dominant genes.

13. **a.** is the answer. (p. 89)

14. **b.** is the answer. (p. 77)

15. **b.** is the answer. (p. 92)

    a. & c. These abnormalities involve the sex chr[o]mosomes, not genes.

    d. In order for an offspring to inherit a recessiv[e] condition, the parents need only be carriers of th[e] recessive gene in their genotypes; they need n[ot] actually have the disease.

Matching Items

1. c (p. 69)	**5.** b (p. 75)	**9.** e (p. 77)
2. h (p. 70)	**6.** f (p. 76)	**10.** d (p. 69)
3. a (p. 77)	**7.** g (p. 77)	**11.** k (p. 71)
4. i (p. 77)	**8.** j (p. 89)	

PROGRESS TEST 2

Multiple-Choice Questions

1. **d.** is the answer. (p. 82)

2. **a.** is the answer. (p. 81)

3. **c.** is the answer. (p. 89)

    a. Physical appearance is usually normal in th[is] syndrome.

    b. Males are more frequently and more severe[ly] affected.

    d. This is true of the *XXY* chromosomal abno[r]mality, but not the fragile-*X* syndrome.

4. **d.** is the answer. (p. 92)

5. **b.** is the answer. (p. 79)

    a. & c. These patterns are based on the interacti[on] of both parents' genes.

    d. Molecular genetics is the study of the chemic[al] codes that make up a particular molecule [of] DNA.

6. **c.** is the answer. (p. 76)

    a. This would result in monozygotic twins.

    b. Only one sperm can fertilize an ovum.

d. A single egg fertilized by one sperm would produce a single offspring or monozygotic twins.

7. c. is the answer. (p. 70)

a. Zygotes are fertilized ova.

b. Genes are the smaller units of heredity that are organized into sequences on chromosomes.

d. Ova are female reproductive cells.

8. a. is the answer. (p. 70)

9. c. is the answer. The ovum will contain an *X* chromosome; with the sperm's *Y* chromosome, it will produce the male *XY* pattern. (p. 72)

a. Only if the ovum is fertilized by an *X* chromosome from the sperm will a female develop.

b. Cell division will occur regardless of whether the sperm contributes an *X* or a *Y* chromosome.

d. Spontaneous abortions are likely to occur when there are chromosomal or genetic abnormalities; the situation described is perfectly normal.

0. a. is the answer. (p. 72)

b. & d. These are true of all body cells *except* the gametes.

c. Gametes have either *X* or *Y* chromosomes.

1. d. is the answer. (p. 77)

2. a. is the answer. Genotype refers to the sum total of all the genes a person inherits; phenotype refers to the actual expression of the individual's characteristics. (p. 77)

3. c. is the answer. (p. 77)

4. d. is the answer. *X*-linked genes are located only on the *X* chromosome. Because males inherit only one *X* chromosome, they are more likely than females to have these characteristics in their phenotype. (p. 78)

5. c. is the answer. (p. 86)

a. Pre-implantation testing is conducted on zygotes grown *in vitro*.

b. Ultrasound is used to detect visible signs of abnormality.

d. Alphafetoprotein assay is used to detect the presences of AFP, an indicator of neural-tube defects.

rue or False Items

1. T (p. 77)

2. F   An estimated half of all zygotes have an odd number of chromosomes. (p. 87)

3. T (p. 84)

4. T (p. 69)

5. F   Most traits are polygenic. (p. 77)

6. T (p. 70)

7. T (p. 90)

8. F   A trait from a recessive gene will be part of the phenotype only when the person has two recessive genes for that trait. (p. 92)

9. T (pp. 77)

10. T (p. 72)

11. F   Most genes have several functions. (p. 71)

THINKING CRITICALLY ABOUT CHAPTER 3

1. b. is the answer. (p. 71)

a. In fact, the total number of human genes is probably *less* than 100,000.

c. Alleles are alternate versions of a specific gene.

2. a. is the answer. (p. 71)

3. c. is the answer. This describes the fragile-X syndrome. (p. 89)

a. This phenomenon, which is called *crossing over*, merely contributes to genetic diversity.

b. This is merely an example of a particular non-additive gene interaction pattern.

4. a. is the answer. (pp. 78, 79)

b. The male genotype is *XY*, not *XX*.

c. & d. The mother contributes only an *X* chromosome.

5. c. is the answer. (pp. 77–78)

a., c., & d. It is unlikely that these factors account for height differences from one generation to the next.

6. b. is the answer. Since monozygotic twins are genetically identical, while dizygotic twins share only 50 percent of their genes, greater similarity of traits between monozygotic twins suggests that genes are an important influence. (p. 83)

a. & c. Even though schizophrenia has a strong genetic component, it is not the case that if one twin has schizophrenia the other also automatically does. Therefore, the environment, too, is an important influence.

d. This does not necessarily follow.

7. a. is the answer. (p. 82)

b. Genotype is a person's genetic potential, established at conception.

c. Polygenic inheritance refers to the influence of many genes on a particular trait.

d. Incomplete dominance refers to the phenotype being influenced primarily, but not exclusively, by the dominant gene.

8. **c.** is the answer. (pp. 82–83)

   a. & b. Research on adopted children shows that shyness is affected by both genetic inheritance and the social environment. Therefore, if a child's environment promotes socializing outside the immediate family, a genetically shy child might grow up much less timid socially than he or she would have been with less outgoing parents.

   d. Either biological or adoptive parents are capable of nurturing, or not nurturing, shyness in their children.

9. **c.** is the answer. Cystic fibrosis is a recessive gene disorder; therefore, in order for a child to inherit this disease, he or she must receive the recessive gene from both parents. (pp. 78, 92)

10. **d.** is the answer. To separate the influences of genes and environment, one of the two must be held constant. (pp. 84–85)

    a., b., & c. These situations would not allow a researcher to separate the contributions of heredity and environment.

11. **d.** is the answer. (p. 81)

12. **c.** is the answer. (pp. 84–85)

    a. Some people's inherited biochemistry makes them highly susceptible to alcoholism.

    b. Despite a strong genetic influence, the environment plays a critical role in the expression of alcoholism.

    d. Not only is this advice unreasonable, but it might increase the likelihood of chromosomal abnormalities in the parents' sperm and ova.

13. **d.** is the answer. (p. 88)

14. **d.** is the answer. (p. 77)

    a. & b. Genes are discrete segments of a chromosome.

    c. Genotype refers to genetic potential.

15. **c.** is the answer. (pp. 77–78)

    a. There is no such thing as a "polygenic gene." *Polygenic* means "many genes."

    b. A recessive gene paired with a dominant gene will not be expressed in the phenotype.

    d. X-linked genes may be dominant or recessive.

KEY TERMS

1. When social scientists discuss the effects of the **environment** on genes, they are referring to everything—from the impact of the immediat cell environment on the genes to the multitude c elements in the outside world, such as nutrition climate, and family interactions—that can interac with the person's genetic inheritance at ever point of life. (p. 69)

2. **Heredity** refers to the specific genetic materia that an organism inherits from its parents. (p. 69)

3. **Gametes** are the human reproductive cells. (p. 69

4. The **zygote** (a term derived from the Greek wor for "joint") is the fertilized egg, that is, the on celled organism formed during conception by th union of sperm and ovum. (p. 69)

5. **Genes** are discrete segments of a chromosom which is a DNA molecule, that are the basic uni of heredity. (p. 70)

6. **Chromosomes** are molecules of DNA that cor tain the genes organized in precise sequences. (70)

7. The precise nature of a gene's instructions, calle the **genetic code**, is determined by the overa sequence of the four chemical bases along a seg ment of DNA. (p. 71)

8. The **Human Genome Project** is a worldwic effort to map the complete sequence of all of th base pairs that make up the genes in the huma genotype. (p. 71)

9. The **twenty-third pair** of chromosomes dete mines the individual's sex. (p. 72)

10. **Monozygotic**, or identical, **twins** develop from single fertilized ovum that splits in two, produ ing two genetically identical zygotes. (p. 75)

    Memory aid: Mono means "one"; **monozygot twins** develop from one fertilized ovum.

11. **Dizygotic**, or fraternal, **twins** develop from tw separate ova fertilized by different sperm roughly the same time, and therefore are no mo: genetically similar than ordinary siblings. (p. 76

    Memory aid: A fraternity is a group of two (*di*) more nonidentical individuals.

12. Most human traits, especially psychological trait are **polygenic traits**; that is, they are affected l many genes. (p. 77)

13. Most human traits are also **multifactorial traits** that is, influenced by many factors, includin genetic and environmental factors. (p. 77)

    Memory aid: The roots of the words *polygenic* ar *multifactorial* give their meaning: *poly* mear "many" and *genic* means "of the genes"; *mu* means "several" and *factorial* obviously refers factors.

14. The total of all the genes a person inherits—his or her genetic potential—is called the **genotype**. (p. 77)

15. The actual physical or behavioral expression of a genotype, the result of the interaction of the genes with each other and with the environment, is called the **phenotype**. (p. 77)

16. A person who has a recessive gene that is not expressed in his or her genotype is called a **carrier** of that gene. (p. 77)

17. When a trait is determined by **additive genes**, the phenotype reflects the sum of the contributions of all the genes involved. The genes affecting height, for example, interact in this fashion. (p. 77)

18. A **dominant gene** is the stronger, controlling member, of an interacting pair of genes. (p. 78)

19. A **recessive gene** is the weaker member of an interacting pair of genes. (p. 78)

20. **X-linked genes** are genes that are located only on the X chromosome. Since males have only one X chromosome, they are more likely to have the characteristics determined by these genes in their phenotype than are females. (p. 78)

21. **Genetic imprinting** is the tendency of certain genes to behave differently depending on whether they are inherited from the mother or from the father. (p. 79)

22. **Behavioral genetics** is the study of the effects of genes on personality, psychological disorders, intellectual abilities, and other psychological characteristics. (p. 79)

23. **Molecular genetics** is the study of the chemical codes that make up a particular molecule of DNA. (p. 81)

24. Also known as a *miscarriage*, a **spontaneous abortion** is the natural termination of a pregnancy before the fetus is fully developed. (p. 88)

25. A **syndrome** is a cluster of distinct characteristics that tend to occur together in a given disorder. (p. 88)

26. **Trisomy-21 (Down syndrome)** is a chromosomal disorder in which there is an extra chromosome at site 21. Most people with Down syndrome have distinctive physical and psychological characteristics, including rounded face, short stature, and mental slowness. (p. 88)

27. The **fragile-X syndrome** is a single-gene disorder in which part of the X chromosome is attached by such a thin string of molecules that it seems about to break off. Although the characteristics associated with this syndrome are quite varied, some mental deficiency is relatively common. (p. 89)

28. **Genetic counseling** involves a variety of tests through which couples can learn more about their genes, and can thus make informed decisions about their childbearing and child-rearing future. (p. 92)

Cross-Check

ACROSS
- 2. syndrome
- 7. carrier
- 8. genotype
- 10. zygote
- 13. dominant
- 14. QTL
- 15. phenotype
- 17. X-linked
- 18. genetic code
- 19. chromosome
- 20. Alzheimer's
- 21. additive

DOWN
- 1. fragile-X
- 3. dizygotic
- 4. environment
- 5. differentiation
- 6. gene
- 7. crossing-over
- 9. miscarriage
- 11. Human Genome
- 12. polygenic
- 13. Down syndrome
- 16. recessive

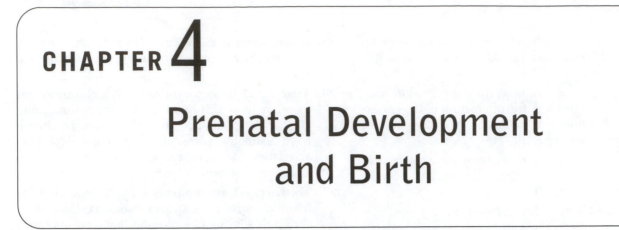

CHAPTER 4

Prenatal Development and Birth

Chapter Overview

Prenatal development is complex and startlingly rapid—more rapid than any other period of the life span. During the prenatal period, the individual develops from a one-celled zygote to a complex human baby. This development is outlined in Chapter 4, along with some of the problems that can occur—among them prenatal exposure to disease, drugs, and other hazards—and the factors that moderate the risks of teratogenic exposure.

For the developing person, birth marks the most radical transition of the entire life span. No longer sheltered from the outside world, the fetus becomes a separate human being who begins life almost completely dependent upon its caregivers. Chapter 4 also examines the process of birth and its possible variations and problems.

The chapter concludes with a discussion of the significance of the parent–newborn bond, including factors that affect its development.

NOTE: Answer guidelines for all Chapter 4 questions begin on page 66.

Guided Study

The text chapter should be studied one section at a time. Before you read, preview each section by skimming it, noting headings and boldface items. Then read the appropriate section objectives from the following outline. Keep these objectives in mind and, as you read the chapter section, search for the information that will enable you to meet each objective. Once you have finished a section, write out answers for its objectives.

From Zygote to Newborn (pp. 97–104)

1. Describe the significant developments of the germinal period.

2. Describe the significant developments of the period of the embryo.

3. Describe the significant developments of the period of the fetus, noting the importance of the age of viability.

(In Person) Describe the fetus's various responses to its immediate environment (the womb).

Low Birthweight (pp. 112–117)

8. Distinguish among low-birthweight (LBW), preterm, and small-for-gestational-age (SGA) infants, and identify the causes of low birthweight, focusing on the relationship of poverty to low birthweight.

sk Reduction (pp. 104–112)

Define teratology, and discuss several factors that determine whether a specific teratogen will be harmful.

The Normal Birth (pp. 117–121)

9. Describe the normal process of birth, specifying the events of each stage.

Identify at least five teratogens, and describe their effects on the developing embryo or fetus, focusing on the effects of psychoactive drugs.

10. Describe the test used to assess the neonate's condition at birth.

(Changing Policy) Discuss several protective steps that may be taken to prevent drug damage.

11. Discuss the importance of medical attention and the question of medical intervention.

Birth Complications (pp. 122–123)

12. Explain the causes of cerebral palsy, and discuss the special needs of high-risk infants.

The Beginning of Bonding (pp. 123–126)

13. (text and Research Report) Explain the concept of parent–newborn bonding and the current view of most developmentalists regarding bonding in humans.

Chapter Review

When you have finished reading the chapter, work through the material that follows to review it. Complete the sentences and answer the questions. As you proceed, evaluate your performance for each section by consulting the answers on page 66. Do not continue with the next section until you understand each answer. If you need to, review or reread the appropriate section in the textbook before continuing.

From Zygote to Newborn (pp. 97–104)

1. Prenatal development is divided into _____ main periods. The first two weeks of development are called the _____ period; from the _____ week through the _____ week is known as the period of the _____ ; and from this point until birth is the period of the _____ . Some developmentalists

prefer to divide pregnancy into 3-month period called _____ .

2. At least through the _____ (how many?) doubling of cells following conception, each of the zygote's cells is identical. Soon after clusters of cells begin to take on distinct traits. The first clear sign of this process, called _____ , occurs about _____ week(s) after conception, when the multiplying cells separate into outer cells that will become the _____ and inner cells that will become the

_____ .

3. The next significant event is the burrowing of t outer cells of the organism into the lining of the uterus, a process called _____ . T process _____ (is/is not) automat

4. At the beginning of the period of the embryo, a fold in the outer cells of the developing individ ual forms a structure that will become the _____ _____ , whic will develop into the _____

_____ _____ .

Briefly describe the major features of developm during the second month.

5. Eight weeks after conception, the embryo weig about _____ and is about _____ in length. The organism n becomes known as the _____ .

6. The first stage of development of the sex organ the appearance in the _____ week of the _____ _____ , a cluster of cells that can develop into male or female sex organs.

7. If the fetus has a(n) _____ (X/Y) chromosome, a gene on this chromosome send

biochemical signal that triggers the development of the _____ (male/female) sex organs. Without that gene, no signal is sent, and the fetus begins to develop _____ (male/female) sex organs. Not until the _____ week are the external male or female genital organs fully formed.

By the end of the _____ month, the fetus is fully formed, weighs approximately _____ , and is about _____ long. These figures _____ (vary/do not vary) from fetus to fetus.

The placenta connects the mother's _____ _____ with that of her growing embryo.

During the fourth, fifth, and six months the brain increases in size by a factor of _____ . This neurological maturation is essential to the regulation of such basic body functions as _____ and _____ .

The age at which a fetus has at least some chance of surviving outside the uterus is called the _____ _____ _____ , which occurs _____ weeks after conception.

At about _____ weeks after conception, brain-wave patterns begin to resemble the _____–_____ cycles of a newborn.

A 28-week-old fetus typically weighs about _____ and has more than a _____ percent chance of survival.

The normal due date is calculated at _____ days after conception.

Two crucial aspects of development in the last months of prenatal life are maturation of the _____ and _____ systems.

16. The average newborn weighs _____ .

17. An important part of the fetus's weight gain is the formation of body _____ , which will provide a layer of insulation to keep the newborn warm.

18. This weight gain also provides the fetus with _____ for use until the mother's breast milk is fully established.

Risk Reduction (pp. 104–112)

19. The scientific study of factors that contribute to birth defects is called _____ . Harmful agents that can cause birth defects, called _____ , include _____ _____ .

20. Substances that impair the child's action and intellect by harming the brain are called _____ _____ .

21. Teratology is a science of _____ _____ , which attempts to evaluate the factors that can make prenatal harm more or less likely to occur.

22. Three crucial factors that determine whether a specific teratogen will cause harm, and of what nature, are the _____ of exposure, the _____ of exposure, and the developing organism's _____ _____ to damage from the substance.

23. The time when a particular part of the body is most susceptible to teratogenic damage is called its _____ _____ . For physical structure and form, this is the entire period of the _____ . However, for _____ teratogens, which damage the _____ and _____ _____ , the entire prenatal period is critical.

24. Two especially critical periods are at the beginning of pregnancy, when _____ can impede _____ , and during the final weeks, when the fetus is particularly vulnerable to damage that can cause

    _____ _____ .

25. Some teratogens have a _____ effect—that is, the substances are harmless until exposure reaches a certain frequency or amount. However, the _____ of some teratogens when taken together may make them more harmful at lower dosage levels than when taken separately.

26. Genetic susceptibilities to the prenatal effects of alcohol and to certain birth disorders, such as cleft palate, may involve defective

    _____ .

27. When the mother-to-be's diet is deficient in

    _____ _____ ,

    neural-tube defects such as

    _____ _____

    or _____ may result.

28. Genetic vulnerability is also related to the sex of the developing organism. Generally, _____ (male/female) embryos and fetuses are more vulnerable to teratogens. This sex not only has a higher rate of teratogenic birth defects and later behavioral problems, but also a higher rate of

    _____ _____

    and later _____

    _____ .

29. When contracted during the critical period, German measles, also called _____ , is known to cause structural damage to the heart, eyes, ears, and brain.

30. The most devastating viral teratogen is

    _____ _____

    _____ , which gradually over-

whelms the body's natural immune responses and leads to a host of diseases that together constitute _____

_____ _____ . About one in every four infants born to women with the virus acquire it from the mother during

_____ or _____ . This disease's long incubation period—up to _____ years or more—complicates its prevention.

31. The best way to prevent pediatric AIDS is to prevent _____ _____ . The second best way is to _____

    _____

    A third preventive measure is to administer the drug _____ to HIV-infected women during pregnancy and at birth.

32. Some widely used medicinal drugs, including

    _____ ,

    are teratogenic in some cases.

33. Psychoactive drugs such as _____

    _____

    _____

    slow fetal _____ and can trigger premature _____ . The potential long-term teratogenic effects of such drugs include _____

    _____ .

34. (text and Table 4.3) Prenatal exposure to alcohol may lead to _____ _____

    _____ , which includes such symptoms as abnormal facial characteristics, slowed physical growth, behavior problems, and mental retardation. Likely victims of this syndrome are those whose mothers ingest more than

    _____ drinks daily during pregnancy. Even more moderate alcohol consumption can be teratogenic, causing _____ .

    _____ _____ .

(Table 4.3) List some of the effects of fetal exposure to tobacco.

. (Table 4.3) Infants born to heavy users of marijuana often show impairment to their

_____ _____

system.

(Table 4.3) List some of the effects of fetal exposure to cocaine.

. The specific effects of illicit drugs

_____ (are/are not) difficult to document because users often use multiple drugs and have other problems, including

_____ .

(Changing Policy) List five protective steps pregnant women should take to prevent drug damage to their offspring.

(Changing Policy) Babies born to women who recently emigrated to the United States often weigh _____ (more/less) than

babies of native-born women of the same ethnicity. One likely reason is that these women are more often _____-_____ .

38. (Changing Policy) Teratogenic effects of psychoactive drugs _____ (do/do not) accumulate throughout pregnancy.

Low Birthweight (pp. 112–117)

39. Newborns who weigh less than

_____ are classified as

_____ _____ babies.

Below 3 pounds, they are called _____

_____ _____ babies; at

less than 2 pounds they are _____

_____ _____

babies. Worldwide, rates of this condition

_____ (vary/do not vary) from

nation to nation.

40. Many factors can cause low birthweight, including _____ and

_____ .

41. Babies who are born 3 or more weeks early are called _____ .

State several factors that increase the likelihood of early birth.

42. Infants who weigh substantially less than they should, given how much time has passed since conception, are called _____

_____ _____

_____ .

43. About 25 percent of all low-birthweight (LBW) births in the United States are linked to maternal use of _____ , which is responsible for about _____ percent of LBW in many European nations.

44. Virtually all the risk factors for low birthweight are related to _____ . Mothers of low-birthweight babies are more likely to be

_____ , _____ , _____ , and _____ .

45. (A Life-Span View) Overall, rates of very-low-birthweight and extremely-low-birthweight babies in the United States are _____ (rising/falling/holding steady). Perhaps because LBW babies are more demanding and less responsive, the rates of child _____ and _____ are elevated for these children, especially if they are also

_____ .

46. Low-birthweight infants are often raised in low-income homes, which increases family _____ and reduces the chance of the initial handicap being overcome. The best preventive medicine for LBW includes ongoing

_____ , _____ , and _____ _____ .

The Normal Birth (pp. 117–121)

47. At about the 266th day, the fetal brain signals the release of certain _____ into the mother's bloodstream, which trigger her

_____ _____

to contract and relax. The normal birth process begins when these contractions become regular. The average length of labor is _____ for first births and _____ for subsequent births.

48. The newborn is usually rated on the

_____ _____ , which assigns a score of 0, 1, or 2 to each of the following five characteristics: _____ _____ . A score below _____ indicates that the newborn is in critical condition and requires immediate attention; if the score is

_____ or better, all is well. This ra[ting] is made twice, at _____ minute(s) after birth and again at _____ minutes.

49. The mother's birth experience is influenced by several factors, including _____ _____ .

50. When a normal vaginal delivery is likely to be hazardous, a doctor may recommend a surgical procedure called a _____ _____ . Another common procedure, which involves a minor incision of the tissue at the opening of the vagina, is the _____ .

51. In many nations, increasing numbers of trained _____ preside over uncomplicated births. Even in hospital births, an increasing number of deliveries occur in the

_____ _____ .

An even more family-oriented environment is t[he]

_____ _____ .

Birth Complications (pp. 122–123)

52. The disorder _____ _____ , which affects motor cente[rs] in the brain, often results from _____ vulnerability, worsened by exposure to _____ and episodes o[f] _____ , a temporary lack of _____ during birth.

53. Because they are often confined to an isolette o[r] hooked up to medical machinery, low-birthweight infants may be deprived of normal kind[s] of _____ , such as _____ .

54. Providing extra soothing stimulation to vulnera-ble infants in the hospital _____ (does/does not) aid weight gain and _____ (does/does not) increase overall alertness.

55. Among the minor developmental problems tha[t] accompany preterm birth are being late to

_____

High-risk infants are often more
_____ , less _____ ,
and slower to _____ .

The deficits related to low birthweight usually
_____ (can/cannot) be
overcome.

e Beginning of Bonding (pp. 123–126)

The term used to describe the close relationship
that begins within the first hours after birth is
the _____–_____

_____ .

(Research Report) The best evidence for such a
relationship comes from studies of various

species of _____ .

(Research Report) Three factors that contribute to
animal bonding are:

a. _____

b. _____

c. _____

Research suggests that such a period
_____ (does/does not) exist in
humans, leading some social scientists to conclude that bonding is a _____

_____ .

Some new mothers experience a profound feeling
of sadness called _____

_____ .

ogress Test 1

Jltiple-Choice Questions

cle your answers to the following questions and
ck them with the answers on page 67. If your
wer is incorrect, read the explanation for why it is
orrect and then consult the appropriate pages of
text (in parentheses following the correct answer).

The third through the eighth week after conception is called the:
a. period of the embryo.
b. period of the ovum.
c. period of the fetus.
d. germinal period.

2. The neural tube develops into the:
   a. respiratory system.
   b. umbilical cord.
   c. brain and spinal column.
   d. circulatory system.

3. To say that a teratogen has a "threshold effect"
   means that it is:
   a. virtually harmless until exposure reaches a
      certain level.
   b. harmful only to low-birthweight infants.
   c. harmful to certain developing organs during
      periods when these organs are developing
      most rapidly.
   d. harmful only if the pregnant woman's weight
      does not increase by a certain minimum
      amount during her pregnancy.

4. By the eighth week after conception, the embryo
   has almost all the basic organs except the:
   a. skeleton.   c. sex organs.
   b. elbows and knees. d. fingers and toes.

5. The most critical factor in attaining the age of viability is development of the:
   a. placenta.   c. brain.
   b. eyes.   d. skeleton.

6. An important nutrient that many women do not
   get in adequate amounts from the typical diet is:
   a. vitamin A.   c. guanine.
   b. zinc.   d. folic acid.

7. An embryo begins to develop male sex organs if
   _____ , and female sex organs if

   _____ .
   a. genes on the Y chromosome send a biochemi-
      cal signal; no signal is sent from an X chromo-
      some
   b. genes on the Y chromosome send a biochemi-
      cal signal; genes on the X chromosome send a
      signal
   c. genes on the X chromosome send a biochemi-
      cal signal; no signal is sent from an X chromo-
      some
   d. genes on the X chromosome send a biochemi-
      cal signal; genes on the Y chromosome send a
      signal

8. A teratogen:
   a. cannot cross the placenta during the period of
      the embryo.
   b. is usually inherited from the mother.
   c. can be counteracted by good nutrition most of
      the time.
   d. may be a virus, a drug, a chemical, radiation,
      or environmental pollutants.

9. Among the characteristics of babies born with fetal alcohol syndrome are:
   a. slowed physical growth and behavior problems.
   b. addiction to alcohol and methadone.
   c. deformed arms and legs.
   d. blindness.

10. The birth process begins:
   a. when the fetus moves into the right position.
   b. when the uterus begins to contract at regular intervals to push the fetus out.
   c. about 8 hours (in the case of firstborns) after the uterus begins to contract at regular intervals.
   d. when the baby's head appears at the opening of the vagina.

11. The Apgar scale is administered:
   a. only if the newborn is in obvious distress.
   b. once, just after birth.
   c. twice, 1 minute and 5 minutes after birth.
   d. repeatedly during the newborn's first hours.

12. Most newborns weigh about:
   a. 5 pounds.   c. 7 1/2 pounds.
   b. 6 pounds.   d. 8 1/2 pounds.

13. Low-birthweight babies born near the due d but weighing substantially less than they shou
   a. are classified as preterm.
   b. are called small for gestational age.
   c. usually have no sex organs.
   d. show many signs of immaturity.

14. Approximately 1 out of every 4 low-birthwei births in the United States is caused by mater use of:
   a. alcohol.
   b. tobacco.
   c. crack cocaine.
   d. household chemicals.

15. (Research Report) The idea of a parent–newb bond in humans arose from:
   a. observations in the delivery room.
   b. data on adopted infants.
   c. animal studies.
   d. studies of disturbed mother-newborn pairs

Matching Items

Match each definition or description with its corresponding term.

Terms

_____ 1. period of the embryo
_____ 2. period of the fetus
_____ 3. placenta
_____ 4. preterm
_____ 5. teratology
_____ 6. rubella
_____ 7. HIV
_____ 8. critical period
_____ 9. neural tube
_____ 10. fetal alcohol syndrome
_____ 11. germinal period

Definitions or Descriptions

a. term for the period during which a develop baby's body parts are most susceptible to dam
b. the scientific study of birth defects
c. the age when viability is attained
d. the precursor of the central nervous system
e. also called German measles
f. characterized by abnormal facial characteris slowed growth, behavior problems, and me retardation
g. a virus that gradually overwhelms the bo immune responses
h. the life-giving organ that nourishes the emb and fetus
i. when implantation occurs
j. the prenatal period when all major body st tures begin to form
k. a baby born 3 or more weeks early

Progress Test 2

Progress Test 2 should be completed during a final chapter review. Answer the following questions after you thoroughly understand the correct answers for the Chapter Review and Progress Test 1.

Multiple-Choice Questions

1. During which period does cocaine use affect the fetus and/or newborn?
   a. throughout pregnancy
   b. before birth
   c. after birth
   d. during all of the above periods

2. In order, the correct sequence of prenatal stages of development is:
   a. embryo; germinal; fetus
   b. germinal; fetus; embryo
   c. germinal; embryo; fetus
   d. ovum; fetus; embryo

3. Monika is preparing for the birth of her first child. If all proceeds normally, she can expect that her labor will last about:
   a. 3 hours.   c. 9 hours.
   b. 6 hours.   d. 12 hours.

4. Tetracycline, retinoic acid, and most hormones:
   a. can be harmful to the human fetus.
   b. have been proven safe for pregnant women after the period of the embryo.
   c. will prevent spontaneous abortions.
   d. are safe when used before the period of the fetus.

5. One of the first teratogens to be recognized, possibly causing deafness, blindness, and brain damage if the fetus is exposed early during the pregnancy, is:
   a. rubella (German measles).
   b. anoxia.
   c. acquired immune deficiency syndrome (AIDS).
   d. neural-tube defect.

6. (Changing Policy) The most realistic way for pregnant women to reduce the risk of birth defects in their unborn children is to avoid unnecessary drugs and:
   a. have a diagnostic x-ray or sonogram.
   b. improve their genetic predispositions.
   c. seek early and regular prenatal care.
   d. avoid exposure to any suspected pollutant.

7. Among the characteristics rated on the Apgar scale are:
   a. shape of the newborn's head and nose.
   b. presence of body hair.
   c. interactive behaviors.
   d. muscle tone and color.

8. A newborn is classified as low birthweight if he or she weighs less than:
   a. 7 pounds.
   b. 6 pounds.
   c. 5 1/2 pounds.
   d. 4 pounds.

9. The most critical problem for preterm babies is:
   a. the immaturity of the sex organs—for example, undescended testicles.
   b. spitting up or hiccupping.
   c. infection from intravenous feeding.
   d. breathing difficulties.

10. (In Person) The most remarkable examples of learning by the developing fetus involve the sense of:
    a. touch.
    b. vision.
    c. hearing.
    d. smell.

11. Many low-birthweight infants experience brain damage as the result of:
    a. anoxia.
    b. cerebral hemorrhaging.
    c. excessive analgesia.
    d. genetic defects.

12. Which Apgar score indicates that a newborn is in normal health?
    a. 4   c. 6
    b. 5   d. 7

13. Infants born with HIV always develop pediatric AIDS because drugs that reverse the course of HIV have not been tested on children and because:
    a. their mothers had to undergo a cesarean delivery.
    b. the virus overwhelms a very young body faster than a fully grown one.
    c. AZT does not pass through the placenta and so cannot immunize the fetus.
    d. prenatal care is not available for low-income women in developed countries.

14. Many of the factors that contribute to low birth-weight are related to poverty; for example, women of lower socioeconomic status tend to:
   a. be less well nourished.
   b. have less education.
   c. be subjected to stressful living conditions.
   d. be all of the above.

15. The critical period for preventing physical defects appears to be the:
   a. period of the zygote.
   b. period of the embryo.
   c. period of the fetus.
   d. entire pregnancy.

True or False Items

Write T (*true*) or F (*false*) on the line in front of each statement.

_____ 1. (In Person) Newborns can recognize some of what they heard while in the womb.

_____ 2. Eight weeks after conception, the embryo has formed almost all the basic organs.

_____ 3. Infants who are HIV-positive do not always develop pediatric AIDS.

_____ 4. In general, behavioral teratogens have the greatest effect during the period of the embryo.

_____ 5. The effects of cigarette smoking during pregnancy remain highly controversial.

_____ 6. The Apgar scale is used to measure vital signs such as heart rate, breathing, and reflexes.

_____ 7. Newborns usually cry on their own, moments after birth.

_____ 8. (Research Report) Research shows that immediate mother-newborn contact at birth is necessary for the normal emotional development of the child.

_____ 9. Low birthweight is often correlated with poverty and malnutrition.

_____ 10. Cesarean sections are rarely performed in the United States today because of the resulting danger to the fetus.

Thinking Critically About Chapter 4

Answer these questions the day before an exam as a final check on your understanding of the chapter's terms and concepts.

1. Babies born to mothers who are powerful addicted to a psychoactive drug are *most* likely suffer from:
   a. structural problems.
   b. behavioral problems.
   c. both a. and b.
   d. neither a. nor b.

2. I am about 1 inch long and 1 gram in weight have all of the basic organs (except sex orga and features of a human being. What am I?
   a. a zygote   c. a fetus
   b. an embryo   d. an indifferent gon

3. Karen and Brad report to their neighbors that weeks after conception, a sonogram of their chi to-be revealed female sex organs. The neighbo are skeptical of their statement because:
   a. sonograms are never administered before ninth week.
   b. sonograms only reveal the presence absence of male sex organs.
   c. the fetus does not begin to develop female organs until about the ninth week.
   d. it is impossible to determine that a woman pregnant until six weeks after conception.

4. Five-year-old Benjamin can't sit quietly and co centrate on a task for more than a minute. Simmons, who is a teratologist, suspects t Benjamin may have been exposed _____ during prenatal development
   a. human immunodeficiency virus
   b. a behavioral teratogen
   c. rubella
   d. lead

5. Sylvia and Stan, who are of British descent, hoping to have a child. Doctor Caruthers asks a complete nutritional history and is particula concerned when she discovers that Sylvia m have a deficiency of folic acid in her diet. Doc Caruthers is probably worried about the risk _____ in the couple's offspring.
   a. FAS   c. neural-tube defec
   b. brain damage   d. FAE

6. Three-year-old Kenny was born underwei and premature. Today, he is small for his age. doctor suspects that:
   a. Kenny is a victim of fetal alcohol syndrome
   b. Kenny suffers from fetal alcohol effects.
   c. Kenny's mother smoked heavily during pregnancy.
   d. Kenny's mother used cocaine during her pr nancy.

Which of these fetuses is most likely to experience serious prenatal damage?

a. a male whose 15-year-old mother has an unusually stressful home life

b. a female whose mother did not begin to receive prenatal care until the second month of her pregnancy

c. a female whose 30-year-old mother is on welfare

d. a male whose mother was somewhat undernourished early in the pregnancy

Fetal alcohol syndrome is common in newborns whose mothers were heavy drinkers during pregnancy, whereas newborns whose mothers were moderate drinkers may suffer fetal alcohol effects. This finding shows that to assess and understand risk we must know:

a. the kind of alcoholic beverage (for example, beer, wine, or whiskey).

b. the level of exposure to the teratogen.

c. whether the substance really is teratogenic.

d. the timing of exposure to the teratogen.

Your sister and brother-in-law, who are about to adopt a 1-year-old, are worried that the child will never bond with them. What advice should you offer?

a. Tell them that, unfortunately, this is true; they would be better off waiting for a younger child who has not yet bonded.

b. Tell them that, although the first year is a biologically determined critical period for attachment, there is a fifty-fifty chance that the child will bond with them.

c. Tell them that bonding is a long-term process between parent and child that is determined by the nature of interaction throughout infancy, childhood, and beyond.

d. Tell them that if the child is female, there is a good chance that she will bond with them, even at this late stage.

Which of the following newborns would be most likely to have problems in body structure and functioning?

a. Anton, whose Apgar score is 6

b. Debora, whose Apgar score is 7

c. Sheila, whose Apgar score is 3

d. Simon, whose Apgar score is 5

At birth, Clarence was classified as small for gestational age. It is likely that Clarence:

a. was born in a rural hospital.

b. suffered several months of prenatal malnutrition.

c. was born in a large city hospital.

d. comes from a family with a history of such births.

12. Of the following, who is *most* likely to give birth to a low-birthweight child?

a. 21-year-old Janice, who was herself a low-birthweight baby.

b. 25-year-old May Ling, who gained 25 pounds during her pregnancy.

c. 16-year-old Donna, who diets frequently despite being underweight, and is under a lot of stress.

d. 30-year-old Maria, who has already given birth to 4 children.

13. An infant born 266 days after conception, weighing 4 pounds, would be designated a _____ infant.

a. preterm

b. low-birthweight

c. small-for-gestational-age

d. b. & c.

14. An infant who was born at 35 weeks, weighing 6 pounds, would be called a _____ infant.

a. preterm

b. low-birthweight

c. small-for-gestational-age

d. premature

15. The five characteristics evaluated by the Apgar scale are:

a. heart rate, length, weight, muscle tone, and color.

b. orientation, muscle tone, reflexes, interaction, and responses to stress.

c. reflexes, breathing, muscle tone, heart rate, and color.

d. pupillary response, heart rate, reflex irritability, alertness, and breathing.

Key Terms

Using your own words, write a brief definition or explanation of each of the following terms on a separate piece of paper.

1. germinal period

2. period of the embryo

3. period of the fetus

 4. implantation

 5. neural tube

 6. placenta

 7. age of viability

 8. teratology

 9. teratogens

10. behavioral teratogens

11. risk analysis

12. critical period

13. threshold effect

14. interaction effect

15. rubella

16. human immunodeficiency virus (HIV)

17. acquired immune deficiency syndrome (AIDS)

18. fetal alcohol syndrome (FAS)

19. low-birthweight (LBW) infant

20. preterm

21. small for gestational age (SGA)

22. Apgar scale

23. Cesarean section

24. cerebral palsy

25. anoxia

26. parent-newborn bond

27. postpartum depression

ANSWERS

CHAPTER REVIEW

 1. three; germinal; third; eighth; embryo; fetus; trimesters

 2. third; differentiation; one; placenta; embryo

 3. implantation; is not

 4. neural tube; central nervous system

First, the upper arms, then the forearms, palms, and webbed fingers appear. Legs, feet, and webbed toes follow. At eight weeks, the embryo's head is more rounded, and the facial features are fully formed. The fingers and toes are distinct and separate. The "tail" is no longer visible.

 5. 1/30 of an ounce (1 gram); 1 inch (2.5 centimeters); fetus

 6. sixth; indifferent gonad

 7. Y; male; female; twelfth

 8. third; 3 ounces (87 grams); 3 inches (7.5 centimeters); vary

 9. circulatory system

10. six; breathing; sucking

11. age of viability; 22

12. 28; sleep–wake

13. 3 pounds (1,300 grams); 90

14. 266

15. respiratory; cardiovascular

16. 7 1/2 pounds (3,400 grams)

17. fat

18. calories

19. teratology; teratogens; viruses, drugs, chemicals, pollutants, stressors, and malnutrition

20. behavioral teratogens

21. risk analysis

22. timing; amount; genetic vulnerability

23. critical period; embryo; behavioral; brain; nervous system

24. stress; implantation; learning disabilities

25. threshold; interaction

26. enzymes

27. folic acid; spina bifida; anencephaly

28. male; spontaneous abortions; learning disabilities

29. rubella

30. human immunodeficiency virus (HIV); acquired immune deficiency syndrome (AIDS); pregnancy; birth; 10

31. adult AIDS; prevent pregnancy in HIV-positive women; AZT

32. tetracycline, anticoagulants, phenobarbital, bromides, retinoic acid, most hormones, aspirin, antacids, diet pills

33. beer, wine, liquor, cigarettes, smokeless tobacco, heroin, methadone, LSD, marijuana, cocaine, inhalants, and antidepressant pills; growth; labor

learning difficulties, impaired self-control, poor concentration, overall irritability

fetal alcohol syndrome; three; fetal alcohol effects

⌐oking increases the risk of abnormalities and ⌐uces birthweight and size. Babies born to regular ⌐okers tend to have respiratory problems and, in ⌐lthood, increased risk of becoming smokers them-⌐ves.

central nervous

⌐caine use causes overall growth retardation, ⌐reases the risk of problems with the placenta, and ⌐en leads to learning problems in the first months of ⌐.

are; malnutrition, stress, sickness, poor family support and health care

⌐ five protective steps are:

a. Abstain from drugs altogether, even before pregnancy.

b. Abstain from drugs after the first month.

c. Use drugs in moderation throughout pregnancy (if abstinence is impossible).

d. Seek social support.

e. Keep up with postnatal care.

more; drug-free

do

2,500 grams (5 $\frac{1}{2}$ pounds); low birthweight; very low birthweight; extremely low birthweight; vary

malnutrition; poverty

preterm

⌐ possible causes of early birth include infections, ⌐gs, extreme stress, exhaustion, a placenta that ⌐omes detached from the uterine wall, and a uterus ⌐t cannot accommodate further growth.

small for gestational age

tobacco; 50

poverty; ill, malnourished, teenaged, stressed

rising: abuse; neglect; disabled

stress; education, nutrition, family support

hormones; uterine muscles; 6 hours; 3 hours

Apgar scale; heart rate, breathing, muscle tone, color, and reflexes; 4; 7; 1; 5

the mother's preparation for birth, the physical and emotional support provided by birth atten-dants, the position and size of the fetus, the cul-tural context, the nature and degree of medical intervention

50. cesarean section; episiotomy

51. midwives; labor room; birthing center

52. cerebral palsy; genetic; teratogens; anoxia; oxygen

53. stimulation; rocking (or regular handling)

54. does; does

55. smile, hold a bottle, and to communicate; dis-tractible; obedient; talk

56. can

57. parent–newborn bond

58. mammals

59. a. birth hormones that trigger maternal feelings

   b. the mother's identification of her infant by its smell

   c. the timing of the first contact between mother and newborn

60. does not; social construction

61. postpartum depression

PROGRESS TEST 1

Multiple-Choice Questions

1. **a.** is the answer. (p. 97)

   b. This term, which refers to the germinal period, is not used in the text.

   c. The period of the fetus is from the ninth week until birth.

   d. The germinal period covers the first two weeks.

2. **c.** is the answer. (p. 98)

3. **a.** is the answer. (p. 106)

   b., c., & d. Although low birthweight (b), critical periods of organ development (c), and maternal malnutrition (d) are all hazardous to the develop-ing person during prenatal development, none is an example of a threshold effect.

4. **c.** is the answer. The sex organs do not begin to take shape until the period of the fetus. (p. 100)

5. **c.** is the answer. (p. 101)

6. **d.** is the answer. (p. 107)

7. **a.** is the answer. (p. 100)

8. **d.** is the answer. (p. 105)

a. In general, teratogens can cross the placenta at any time.

b. Teratogens are agents in the environment, not heritable genes (although *susceptibility* to individual teratogens has a genetic component).

c. Although nutrition is an important factor in healthy prenatal development, the text does not suggest that nutrition alone can usually counteract the harmful effects of teratogens.

9. **a.** is the answer. (p. 112)

10. **b.** is the answer. (p. 117)

11. **c.** is the answer. (p. 118)

12. **c.** is the answer. (p. 104)

13. **b.** is the answer. (p. 114)

14. **b.** is the answer. (p. 114)

15. **c.** is the answer. (p. 125)

Matching Items

1. j (p. 97)
2. c (p. 97)
3. h (p. 101)
4. k (p. 113)
5. b (p. 105)
6. e (p. 107)
7. g (p. 110)
8. a (p. 105)
9. d (p. 98)
10. f (p. 112)
11. i (p. 97)

PROGRESS TEST 2

Multiple-Choice Questions

1. **d.** is the answer. (pp. 111, 112)

2. **c.** is the answer. (p. 97)

3. **b.** is the answer. (p. 117)

   a. The average length of labor for subsequent births is 3 hours.

4. **a.** is the answer. (pp. 110–111)

5. **a.** is the answer. (p. 107)

6. **c.** is the answer. (p. 108)

7. **d.** is the answer. (p. 118)

8. **c.** is the answer. (p. 112)

9. **d.** is the answer. (p. 103)

10. **c.** is the answer. (p. 102)

11. **c.** is the answer. (p. 122)

12. **d.** is the answer. (p. 118)

13. **b.** is the answer. (p. 110)

14. **d.** is the answer. (p. 116)

15. **b.** is the answer. (p. 103)

True or False Items

1. T (p. 102)

2. T (pp. 99–100)

3. F   Sadly, within months or years, infants w are HIV-positive always develop AIDS. (p. 110

4. F   Behavioral teratogens can affect the fetus any time during the prenatal period. (p. 105)

5. F   There is no controversy about the damag effects of smoking during pregnancy. (111–112)

6. T (p. 118)

7. T (p. 117)

8. F   Though highly desirable, mother–newb contact at birth is not necessary for the chi normal development or for a good parent–ch relationship. Many opportunities for bond occur throughout childhood. (p. 125)

9. T (p. 112)

10. F   Nearly one in four births in the United St are now cesarean. (p. 119)

THINKING CRITICALLY ABOUT CHAPTER

1. **c.** is the answer. (p. 112)

2. **b.** is the answer. (pp. 99–100)

   a. The zygote is the fertilized ovum.

   c. The developing organism is designated a f starting at the ninth week.

   d. The indifferent gonad is the mass of cells will eventually develop into female or male organs.

3. **c.** is the answer. (p. 100)

4. **b.** is the answer. (p. 105)

   a. This is the virus that causes AIDS.

   c. Rubella may cause blindness, deafness, brain damage.

   d. The text does not discuss the effects of ex sure to lead.

5. **c.** is the answer. (p. 107)

   a. FAS is caused in infants by the mother-to drinking three or more drinks daily during p nancy.

   b. Brain damage is caused by the use of so drugs during pregnancy.

d. FAE is caused in infants by the mother-to-be drinking 1 ounce of alcohol per day.

c. is the answer. (p. 111)

a. is the answer. (p. 116)

b. is the answer. (p. 106)

c. is the answer. (p. 124)

a. & b. Bonding in humans is not a biologically determined event limited to a critical period, as it is in many other animal species.

d. There is no evidence of any gender differences in the formation of the parent-newborn bond.

c. is the answer. If a neonate's Apgar score is below 4, the infant is in critical condition and needs immediate medical attention. (p. 118)

b. is the answer. (p. 114)

a., c., & d. Prenatal malnutrition is the most common cause of a small-for-dates neonate.

c. is the answer. Donna has three risk factors that are related to having an LBW baby, including being a teenager; underweight, and stressed. (p. 116)

a., & d. Neither of these has been linked to increased risk of having LBW babies.

b. In fact, based only on her age and normal weight gain, May Ling's baby would *not* be expected to be LBW.

d. is the answer. (pp. 114, 117)

a. & c. At 266 days, this infant is full term.

a. is the answer. (p. 113)

b. Low birthweight is defined as weighing less than 5 1/2 pounds.

c. Although an infant can be both preterm and small for gestational age, this baby's weight is within the normal range of healthy babies.

d. This term is no longer used to describe early births.

c. is the answer. (p. 118)

KEY TERMS

The first two weeks of development, characterized by rapid cell division and the beginning of cell differentiation, are called the **germinal period**. (p. 97)

Memory aid: A *germ cell* is one from which a new organism can develop. The *germinal period* is the

first stage in the development of the new organism.

2. The **period of the embryo** is the third through the eighth week of prenatal development, when the rudimentary forms of all anatomical structures develop. (p. 97)

3. From the ninth week until birth is the **period of the fetus**, when the organs grow in size and complexity. (p. 97)

4. **Implantation** is the process by which the outer cells of the organism burrow into the uterine lining and rupture its blood vessels to obtain nourishment and trigger the bodily changes that signify the beginning of pregnancy. (p. 98)

5. The **neural tube** forms from a fold of outer embryonic cells during the period of the embryo; it is the precursor of the central nervous system. (p. 98)

Memory aid: Neural means "of the nervous system." The **neural tube** is the precursor of the central nervous system.

6. The **placenta** is the organ that connects the mother's circulatory system with that of her growing embryo, providing nourishment to the developing organism and removing wastes (p. 101).

7. About 22 weeks after conception, the fetus attains the **age of viability**, at which point it has at least some slight chance of survival outside the uterus if specialized medical care is available. (p. 101)

8. **Teratology** is the scientific study of the factors that can contribute to birth defects. (p. 105)

9. **Teratogens** are external agents and conditions, such as viruses, bacteria, drugs, chemicals, stressors, and malnutrition, that can cause damage to the developing organism. (p. 105)

10. **Behavioral teratogens** tend to damage the brain and nervous system, impairing the future child's intellectual and emotional functioning. (p. 105)

11. The science of teratology is a science of **risk analysis**, meaning that it attempts to evaluate what factors make prenatal harm more or less likely to occur. (p. 105)

12. The first eight weeks, as well as the last months, of pregnancy are often called a **critical period**, because teratogenic exposure during these time periods can produce malformations of basic body organs and structure. (p. 105)

13. A **threshold effect** is the harmful effect of a sub-

stance that occurs when exposure to it reaches a certain level. (p. 106)

14. An **interaction effect** occurs when one teratogen intensifies the harmful effects of another. (p. 106)

15. **Rubella** (German measles) is a viral disease that, if contracted by the expectant mother early in pregnancy, is likely to cause birth handicaps, including blindness, deafness, heart abnormalities, and brain damage. (p. 107)

16. **Human immunodeficiency virus (HIV)** is the most devastating viral teratogen. HIV gradually overwhelms the body's immune system, making the individual vulnerable to the host of diseases and infections that constitute AIDS. (p. 110)

17. The **acquired immune deficiency syndrome (AIDS)** is the conglomerate of diseases and infections caused by the HIV virus. (p. 110)

18. Prenatal alcohol exposure may cause **fetal alcohol syndrome (FAS)**, which includes abnormal facial characteristics, slowed physical growth, behavior problems, and mental retardation. Likely victims are those who are genetically vulnerable and whose mothers drink three or more drinks daily during pregnancy. (p. 112)

19. Newborns who weigh less than 2,500 grams (5 1/2 pounds) are called **low-birthweight (LBW) infants**. Such infants are at risk for many immediate and long-term problems. (p. 112)

20. Infants who are born three or more weeks before the due date are called **preterm**. (p. 113)

21. Infants who weigh substantially less than the should, given how much time has passed since conception, are called **small for gestational a (SGA)**, or small-for-dates. (p. 114)

22. Newborns are rated at one and then at five minutes after birth according to the **Apgar scale**. The scale assigns a score of 0, 1, or 2 to each of five characteristics: heart rate, breathing, muscle tone color, and reflexes. A score of 7 or better indicates that all is well. (p. 118)

23. In a **cesarean section**, the fetus is removed from the mother surgically. (p. 119)

24. **Cerebral palsy** is a muscular control disorder caused by damage to the brain's motor center during or before birth. (p. 122)

25. **Anoxia** is a temporary lack of fetal oxygen during the birth process that, if prolonged, can cause brain damage or even death. (p. 122)

26. The term **parent–newborn bond** describes the strong feelings of attachment between parent and child in the early moments of their relationship together. (p. 123)

27. **Postpartum depression** is a profound feeling sadness and inadequacy sometimes experienced by new mothers. (p. 124)

5

The First Two Years:
Biosocial Development

Chapter Overview

Chapter 5 is the first of a three-chapter unit that describes the developing person from birth to age 2 in terms of biosocial, cognitive, and psychosocial development. Physical development is the first to be examined.

The chapter begins with observations on the overall growth and health of infants, including their size and shape and the importance of immunizations during the first two years. Following is a discussion of brain growth and development and the importance of experience in brain development. The chapter then turns to a discussion of motor abilities and the ages at which the average infant acquires them. Vision and hearing are discussed next, along with research on infant perception. The final section discusses the importance of nutrition during the first two years and the consequences of severe malnutrition and undernutrition.

NOTE: Answer guidelines for all Chapter 5 questions begin on page 83.

Guided Study

The text chapter should be studied one section at a time. Before you read, preview each section by skimming it, noting headings and boldface items. Then read the appropriate section objectives from the following outline. Keep these objectives in mind and, as you read the chapter section, search for the information that will enable you to meet each objective. Once you have finished a section, write out answers for its objectives.

Physical Growth and Health (pp. 131–133, 134–135)

1. Describe the size and proportions of an infant's body, including how they change during the first two years and how they compare with those of an adult.

2. (A Life-Span View) Discuss the role of immunization in the relatively recent improvement in the survival of young children.

3. Identify risk factors and possible explanations for sudden infant death syndrome.

Brain Growth and Development (pp. 133, 136–138)

4. Describe the ways in which the brain changes or matures during infancy.

5. Discuss the role of experience in brain development.

Motor Skills (pp. 138–145)

6. Describe the basic reflexes of the newborn, and distinguish between gross motor skills and fine motor skills.

7. Describe the basic pattern of motor-skill development, and discuss variations in the timing of motor-skill acquisition.

Sensory and Perceptual Capacities (pp. 145–151)

8. Distinguish between sensation and perception and describe the extent and development of infant's perceptual abilities in terms of the sense of vision.

9. Describe how and why habituation is used in research on infant perception, focusing on the sense of hearing.

10. (text and Research Report) Identify the cause of most mild hearing losses in infants, and discuss chronic otitis media, focusing on its potential developmental consequences and treatment.

11. Describe the extent and development of infant's perceptual abilities in terms of the sense of taste, smell, and touch.

Nutrition (pp. 151–155)

12. Describe the nutritional needs of infants.

(text and Changing Policy) Discuss the causes and effects of malnutrition and undernutrition in the first years, and explain ways of preventing undernutrition.

hapter Review

nen you have finished reading the chapter, work ·ough the material that follows to review it. ·mplete the sentences and answer the questions. As ·u proceed, evaluate your performance for each sec- ·n by consulting the answers on page 83. Do not ·tinue with the next section until you understand ·h answer. If you need to, review or reread the ·propriate section in the textbook before continuing.

·ysical Growth and Health (pp. 131–133, 134–135)

With the exception of _____ development, infancy is the period of the fastest and most notable increases in _____ and changes in _____ .

The average North American newborn measures _____ and weighs a little more than _____ .

In the first days of life, most newborns _____ (gain/lose) between 5 and 10 percent of their body weight.

By age 1, the typical baby weighs about _____ and measures almost _____ . The typical 2-year-old is almost _____ (what proportion?) of his or her adult weight and _____ (what proportion?) of his or her adult height.

Newborns often seem top-heavy because their heads are equivalent to about _____ (what proportion?) of their total length, com- pared to about _____ at 1 year and _____ in adulthood.

6. Newborns' legs represent about _____ (what proportion?) of their total length, whereas an adult's legs represent about _____ of it.

7. One common cause of infant death that is not related to any obvious problem is

_____ _____

_____ _____ , also

called _____ _____ in

Great Britain or _____

_____ in the United States.

8. The cause of SIDS is an unsteady

_____ _____ , usually

between _____ and _____ months.

9. There is less of a risk for SIDS when healthy infants sleep on their _____ .

Identify several other preventive measures for reduc- ing an infant's risk of SIDS.

10. (A Life-Span View) The chance of infants dying from infectious disease within the first year in North America and most developed nations is less than 1 in _____ . The single most important cause of the improvement in child survival is _____ .

11. Among the childhood diseases that have either been completely eradicated, or nearly so, are

_____ , _____ , and

_____ .

Brain Growth and Development (pp. 133, 136–138)

12. At birth, the brain has attained about _____ percent of its adult weight; by age 2 the brain is about _____ percent of its adult weight. In comparison, body weight at age 2 is about _____ per- cent of what it will be in adulthood.

13. The brain's communication system consists primarily of nerve cells called _____ connected by intricate networks of nerve fibers, called _____ and _____ . Each neuron has many _____ , but only a single _____ .

14. Neurons communicate with one another at intersections called _____ . After travelling down the length of the _____ , electrical impulses trigger chemicals called _____ that diffuse across the _____ _____ to the _____ of a "receiving" neuron. Most of the nerve cells _____ (are/are not) present at birth, whereas the fiber networks _____ (are/are not) rudimentary.

15. During the first months of life, brain development is most noticeable in its outer layer, which is called the _____ . This area of the brain controls _____ and _____ .

16. From birth until age 2, the density of dendrites in the cortex _____ (increases/decreases) by a factor of _____ . The phenomenal increase in neural connections over the first two years has been called _____ _____ .

17. The fibers that transmit impulses also become coated with the insulating substance called _____ that speeds neural transmission and enables _____ brain activity. This coating process proceeds most rapidly from birth to age _____ and continues through _____ .

18. The _____ area of the cortex, which assists in _____ and _____ , becomes more mature during infancy, giving infants greater regulation of their _____-_____ patterns and increasing control over their early _____ . With continued development in this area, _____ skills

requiring deliberation begin to emerge, along with a basic capacity for _____ self-control.

19. Brain development _____ (is/is n influenced by the infant's experiences.

20. Kittens that are _____ for the firs several weeks of life never acquire normal visi This visual deficit occurs because the _____ _____ of the brain fail to develop normally. Kittens who are temporarily blinded in one eye never acquire _____ _____ , whic the ability to focus two eyes together on an obj

21. Research studies involving sensory restriction enriched stimulation demonstrate that the brai retains some _____ as long as sti ulating _____ continue.

Motor Skills (pp. 138–145)

22. The maturation of movement skills is called _____ _____ .

23. An involuntary physical response to a stimulu called a _____ .

24. The involuntary response of breathing, which causes the newborn to take the first breath eve before the umbilical cord is cut, is called the _____ _____ . Beca breathing is irregular during the first few days other reflexive behaviors, such as _____ , _____ , and _____ , are common.

25. Shivering, crying, and tucking the legs close to the body are examples of reflexes that help to maintain _____ _____ .

26. A third set of reflexes fosters _____ One of these is the tendency of the newborn to suck anything that touches the lips; this is the _____ reflex. Another is the tend cy of newborns to turn their heads and start to suck when something brushes against their cheek; this is the _____ reflex.

27. Large movements such as running and climbi are called _____ _____ skills.

. Most infants are able to crawl on all fours (sometimes called creeping) between _____ and _____ months of age.

st the major landmarks in children's mastery of alking.

. Babies who have just begun to walk are given the name _____ for the characteristic way they move their bodies from side to side.

. Abilities that require more precise, small movements, such as picking up a coin, are called _____ _____ skills. By _____ of age, most babies can reach for, grab, and hold onto almost any object of the right size.

. Although the _____ in which motor skills are mastered is the same in all healthy infants, the _____ of acquisition of skills varies greatly.

. The average ages at which most infants master major motor skills are known as _____ . These averages are based on a large sample of infants drawn from _____ (a single/many) ethnic group(s).

. Motor skill norms vary from one _____ group to another.

st several factors that account for the variation in e acquisition of motor skills.

. Motor skill acquisition in identical twins _____ (is/is not) more similar than

in fraternal twins, suggesting that genes _____ (do/do not) play an important role.

35. Most developmentalists would say that the age at which a particular baby first displays a particular skill depends on the interaction between _____ and _____ factors.

Sensory and Perceptual Capacities (pp. 145–151)

36. The process by which the visual, auditory, and other sensory systems detect stimuli is called _____ ; _____ occurs when the brain tries to make sense out of a stimulus so that the individual becomes aware of it. At birth, both of these processes _____ (are/are not) apparent.

Briefly describe the sensory abilities of the newborn.

37. Newborns' visual focusing is best for objects between _____ and _____ inches away, giving them distance vision of about 20/_____ . Distance vision improves rapidly, reaching 20/20 by _____ of age.

38. Increasing maturation of the visual cortex accounts for improvements in other visual abilities, such as the infant's ability to _____ an object and _____ to its critical areas. The ability to use both eyes together to focus on one object, which is called _____ _____ , develops at about _____ of age. As a result of these changes, _____ and _____ perception improve

dramatically, as evidenced by infants' ability to _____ moving objects.

39. Color vision _____ (is/is not) present at birth.

40. Generally speaking, newborns' hearing is _____ (more/less) sensitive than their vision. By _____ of age, infants can perceive differences between very similar speech sounds.

41. An infant presented with an unfamiliar stimulus will respond with intensified sucking on a pacifier or concentrated gazing. When the stimulus becomes so familiar that these responses no longer occur, _____ is said to have occurred. If the infant reacts to a new stimulus, researchers conclude that the infant _____ (can/cannot) perceive a difference between the stimuli.

42. Young infants _____ (can/cannot) distinguish between speech sounds that are not used in their native language.

43. About 1 in every _____ infants is profoundly deaf.

44. A common cause of temporary hearing loss during infancy is a middle ear infection, or _____ _____ . When this condition becomes chronic, the _____ ear fills with fluid. This condition may last for weeks or months, causing impairment in one or both ears.

45. (Research Report) Chronic otitis media may cause developmental lags in the ability to _____ , make _____ , and solve _____ problems, and deflect _____ . Treatments include the use of _____ drugs and placement of a _____ to drain fluid from the inner ear.

46. At birth, infants can distinguish most of the basic tastes except _____ tastes. Compared to their sense of taste, infants' sense of smell is _____ (more/less) acute. By

_____ of age, taste and smell become quite sensitive.

47. The sense of touch _____ (is/is not) very acute during the first year. By 6 months, infants can distinguish objects on the basis of their _____ , _____ , _____ , and _____ .

Nutrition (pp. 151–155)

48. More important than an infant's feeding schedule in fostering development is the overall _____ and _____ of the infant's nutritional intake.

State several advantages of breast milk over cow milk for the developing infant.

49. The most serious nutritional problem of infancy is _____-_____ _____ .

50. Severe protein-calorie deficiency in early infancy causes a disease called _____ . In toddlers, protein-calorie deficiency is more likely to cause a disease called _____ , which involves swelling or bloating of the face, legs, and abdomen.

51. The primary cause of malnutrition in developing countries is _____ _____ .

(Changing Policy) Identify several possible causes of infant undernutrition.

. Children who were undernourished as infants show impaired learning, especially in their ability to _____ and in their _____ skills.

rogress Test 1

ultiple-Choice Questions

rcle your answers to the following questions and eck them with the answers on page 83. If your swer is incorrect, read the explanation for why it is correct and then consult the appropriate pages of e text (in parentheses following the correct answer).

. The average North American newborn:
   a. weighs approximately 6 pounds.
   b. weighs approximately 7 pounds.
   c. is "overweight" because of the diet of the mother.
   d. weighs 10 percent less than what is desirable.

. Compared to the first year, growth during the second year:
   a. proceeds at a slower rate.
   b. continues at about the same rate.
   c. includes more insulating fat.
   d. includes more bone and muscle.

. The major motor skill most likely to be mastered by an infant before the age of 6 months is:
   a. rolling over.
   b. sitting without support.
   c. turning the head in search of a nipple.
   d. grabbing an object with thumb and forefinger.

. Norms suggest that the earliest walkers in the world are infants from:
   a. Western Europe.   c. Uganda.
   b. the United States.   d. Denver.

. The interaction between inherited and environmental factors is responsible for:
   a. variation in the age at which infants master specific motor skills.
   b. physical growth, but not the development of motor skills.
   c. the fact that babies in the United States walk earlier than do Ugandan babies.
   d. the fact that infants master motor skills more slowly today than they did fifty years ago.

6. The development of binocular vision at about 14 months results in:
   a. a dramatic improvement in depth and motion perception.
   b. the rapid development of distance vision.
   c. the refinement of the ability to discriminate colors.
   d. both a. and b.

7. Proportionally, the head of the infant is about _____ of total body length; the head of an adult is about _____ of total body length.
   a. one-fourth; one-third
   b. one-eighth; one-fourth
   c. one-fourth; one-eighth
   d. one-third; one-fourth

8. Research has shown that young animals prevented from using their senses in a normal way experience:
   a. no significant impairment.
   b. harmful overstimulation.
   c. deficits in behavior only.
   d. permanent impairment.

9. Compared with formula-fed infants, breast-fed infants tend to have:
   a. greater weight gain.
   b. fewer allergies and digestive upsets.
   c. less frequent feedings during the first few months.
   d. more social approval.

10. Marasmus and kwashiorkor are caused by:
   a. bloating.
   b. protein-calorie deficiency.
   c. living in a developing country.
   d. poor family food habits.

11. The infant's first motor skills are:
   a. fine motor skills.   c. reflexes.
   b. gross motor skills.   d. unpredictable.

12. Babies are referred to as toddlers when:
   a. their newborn reflexes have disappeared.
   b. they can walk well unassisted.
   c. they begin to creep or crawl.
   d. they speak their first word.

13. Which of the following is true of motor-skill development in healthy infants?
    a. It follows the same basic sequence the world over.
    b. It occurs at different rates from individual to individual.
    c. It follows norms that vary from one ethnic group to another.
    d. All of the above are true.

14. Most of the nerve cells a human brain will ever possess are present:
    a. at conception.
    b. about 1 month following conception.
    c. at birth.
    d. at age 5 or 6.

15. (Research Report) Toddlers with a history of f[r]equent ear infections are much more likely to:
    a. lag behind in language development.
    b. play by themselves.
    c. be uninterested in watching other childr[en] play.
    d. do all of the above.

Matching Items

Match each definition or description with its corresponding term.

Terms

_____ 1. neurons
_____ 2. dendrites
_____ 3. myelination
_____ 4. kwashiorkor
_____ 5. marasmus
_____ 6. habituation
_____ 7. gross motor skill
_____ 8. fine motor skill
_____ 9. reflex
_____ 10. sucking reflex
_____ 11. protein-calorie malnutrition
_____ 12. transient exuberance
_____ 13. developmental biodynamics
_____ 14. otitis media
_____ 15. neurotransmitter

Definitions or Descriptions

a. ear infection
b. protein deficiency during the first year in wh[ich] growth stops and body tissues waste away
c. picking up an object
d. the most common serious nutrition problem [in] infancy
e. protein deficiency during toddlerhood
f. newborns suck anything that touches their lips
g. communication networks among nerve cells
h. declining physiological response to a famil[iar] stimulus
i. running or climbing
j. the process in which axons are coated with [an] insulating sheath
k. an involuntary response
l. the phenomenal increase in neural connectio[ns] over the first 2 years
m. nerve cells
n. maturation of the developing person's ability [to] move through, and with, the environment
o. a brain chemical that carries information acr[oss] the synaptic gap between two neurons

Progress Test 2

Progress Test 2 should be completed during a final chapter review. Answer the following questions after you thoroughly understand the correct answers for the Chapter Review and Progress Test 1.

Multiple-Choice Questions

1. Dendrite is to axon as neural _____ is to neural _____ .
   a. input; output
   b. output; input
   c. myelin; synapse
   d. synapse; myelin

2. A reflex is best defined as a(n):
   a. fine motor skill.
   b. motor ability mastered at a specific age.
   c. involuntary physical response to a given stimulus.
   d. gross motor skill.

3. Habituation describes the:
   a. increased physiological arousal of the newborn to unfamiliar or interesting stimuli.
   b. decreased physiological arousal of the newborn to stimuli that are familiar or no longer interesting.
   c. preterm infant's immature brain-wave patterns.
   d. universal sequence of motor-skill development in children.

4. Most babies can reach for, grasp, and hold onto an object by about the _____ month.
   a. second
   b. sixth
   c. ninth
   d. fourteenth

5. Activity level, rate of physical maturation, and how fat the infant is affect the age at which an infant walks and acquires other motor skills. They are examples of:
   a. norms.
   b. environmental factors.
   c. inherited factors.
   d. the interaction of environment and heredity.

6. During the first weeks of life, babies seem to focus reasonably well on:
   a. little in their environment.
   b. objects at a distance of 4 to 30 inches.
   c. objects at a distance of 1 to 3 inches.
   d. objects several feet away.

7. Which of the following provides evidence that some aspects of early speech perception are innate?

   a. Young infants are able to distinguish their mother's voice from others.
   b. Girls master the rules of grammar more readily than do boys.
   c. Young infants can distinguish between speech sounds that are not used in their native language.
   d. Newborns habituate rapidly to soothing sounds.

8. An advantage of breast milk over formula is that it:
   a. is always sterile and at body temperature.
   b. contains traces of medications ingested by the mother.
   c. can be given without involving the father.
   d. contains more protein and vitamin D than does formula.

9. The primary cause of malnutrition in developing countries is:
   a. formula feeding.
   b. inadequate food supply.
   c. disease.
   d. early cessation of breast-feeding.

10. The cause of sudden infant death syndrome (SIDS) is:
    a. an inborn heart defect.
    b. a neurological disorder.
    c. inadequate infant care.
    d. an unsteady breathing reflex.

11. Climbing is to using a crayon as _____ is to _____ .
    a. fine motor skill; gross motor skill
    b. gross motor skill; fine motor skill
    c. reflex; fine motor skill
    d. reflex; gross motor skill

12. Some infant reflexes are critical for survival. Hiccups and sneezes help the infant maintain the _____ and leg tucking maintains _____ .
    a. feeding; oxygen supply
    b. feeding; a constant body temperature
    c. oxygen supply; feeding
    d. oxygen supply; a constant body temperature

13. (A Life-Span View) The single most important cause of the dramatic improvement in child survival is:
    a. better nutrition.
    b. improved public health measure.
    c. immunization.
    d. new technologies for high-risk infants.

14. (Research Report) A common cause of undernutrition in young children is:
    a. ignorance of the infant's nutritional needs.
    b. the absence of socioeconomic policies that reflect the importance of infant nutrition.
    c. problems in the family.
    d. all of the above.

15. Neurotransmitters are chemical messengers that diffuse across the:
    a. axon.
    b. myelin sheath.
    c. dendrite.
    d. synaptic gap.

True or False Items

Write T (*true*) or F (*false*) on the line in front of each statement.

_____ 1. By age 2, boys are slightly taller than girls, but girls are slightly heavier.

_____ 2. Putting babies to sleep on their stomachs increases the risk of SIDS.

_____ 3. Reflexive hiccups, sneezes, and thrashing are signs that the infant's reflexes are not functioning properly.

_____ 4. Infants of all ethnic backgrounds develop the same motor skills at approximately the same age.

_____ 5. The typical 2-year-old is almost one-fifth its adult weight and one-half its adult height.

_____ 6. Vision is better developed than hearing in most newborns.

_____ 7. Myelination and other processes of brain maturation are completed within the first few years of childhood.

_____ 8. Certain basic sensory experiences seem necessary to ensure full brain development in the human infant.

_____ 9. Severe malnutrition is not widespread among young children in the United States.

_____ 10. Ear infections are common during infancy and rarely a cause for concern.

Thinking Critically About Chapter 5

Answer these questions the day before an exam as a final check on your understanding of the chapter's terms and concepts.

1. Newborns cry, shiver, and tuck their legs close to their bodies. This set of reflexes helps them:
   a. ensure proper muscle tone.
   b. learn how to signal distress.
   c. maintain constant body temperature.
   d. communicate serious hunger pangs.

2. If a baby sucks harder on a nipple, evidences change in heart rate, or stares longer at one imag than at another when presented with a change stimulus, the indication is that the baby:
   a. is annoyed by the change.
   b. is both hungry and angry.
   c. has become habituated to the new stimulus.
   d. perceives some differences between stimuli.

3. A classic experiment on hearing in infants (Eim et al., 1971) showed that even 1-month-olds ca detect:
   a. the father's voice more quickly than the mot er's.
   b. sounds they won't be able to hear at age 2.
   c. differences between very similar sounds.
   d. the correct location of auditory stimuli abo 80 percent of the time.

4. The Farbers, who are first-time parents, are wo dering whether they should be concerne because their 12-month-old daughter, wh weighs 22 pounds and measures 30 inches, is n growing quite as fast as she did during her fir year. You should tell them that:
   a. any slowdown in growth during the secor year is a cause for immediate concern.
   b. their daughter's weight and height are we below average for her age.
   c. growth patterns for a first child are ofte erratic.
   d. physical growth is somewhat slower in tl second year.

5. The brain development that permits seeing ar hearing in human infants appears to be:
   a. totally dependent upon genetic programmir present at birth.
   b. totally dependent upon visual and audito experiences in the first few months.
   c. "fine-tuned" by visual and auditory expe ences in the first few months.
   d. independent of both genetic and environme tal influences.

6. Intellectual functioning is enhanced as childr develop increasing neurological control over th motor functions and sensory abilities. This co trol is made possible by:
   a. dendrites.   c. axons.
   b. neurotransmitters.   d. myelin.

7. Michael has 20/400 vision and is able to discriminate subtle sound differences. Michael most likely:
  a. is a preterm infant.
  b. has brain damage in the visual processing areas of the cortex.
  c. is a newborn.
  d. is slow-to-mature.

8. A baby turns her head and starts to suck when her receiving blanket is brushed against her cheek. The baby is displaying the:
  a. sucking reflex.   c. thrashing reflex.
  b. rooting reflex.   d. tucking reflex.

9. (Research Report) Toddlers whose parents give them a bottle of milk before every nap and with every meal:
  a. may be at increased risk of undernutrition, because the milk reduces the child's appetite for other foods.
  b. are ensured of receiving a sufficient amount of iron in their diets.
  c. are more likely to develop lactose intolerance.
  d. are likely to be overweight throughout life.

10. Sensation is to perception as _____ is to _____ .
  a. hearing; seeing
  b. detecting a stimulus; making sense of a stimulus
  c. making sense of a stimulus; detecting a stimulus
  d. tasting; smelling

11. Sharetta's pediatrician informs her parents that Sharetta's 1-year-old brain is exhibiting transient exuberance. In response to this news, Sharetta's parents:
  a. smile, because they know their daughter's brain is developing new neural connections.
  b. worry, because this may indicate increased vulnerability to a later learning disability.
  c. know that this process, in which axons become coated with insulation, is normal.
  d. are alarmed, since this news indicates that the frontal area of Sharetta's cortex is immature.

12. Kittens who are blindfolded for the first several weeks of life:
  a. do not develop the visual pathways in their brains to allow normal vision.
  b. recover fully if visual stimulation is normal thereafter.
  c. develop only binocular vision.
  d. can see clearly, but lack sensitivity to color.

13. Your sister is worried that her 2-year-old son's first middle ear infection, which is being treated with antibiotics, is a sign of chronic otitis media. To help her reason about her son's condition, you wisely point out that:
  a. middle ear infections are common in infancy.
  b. most middle ear infections can be successfully treated with antibiotics and involve no permanent hearing damage.
  c. chronic otitis media is an inner ear disorder.
  d. all of the above are true.

14. Three-week-old Nathan should have the *least* difficulty focusing on the sight of:
  a. stuffed animals on a bookshelf across the room from his crib.
  b. his mother's face as she holds him in her arms.
  c. the checkerboard pattern in the wallpaper covering the ceiling of his room.
  d. the family dog as it dashes into the nursery.

15. (text and Changing Policy) Geneva has been undernourished throughout childhood. It is likely that she will be:
  a. smaller and shorter than her genetic potential would dictate.
  b. slow in intellectual development.
  c. less resistant to disease.
  d. all of the above.

Key Terms

Writing Definitions

Using your own words, write a brief definition or explanation of each of the following terms on a separate piece of paper.

1. neuron
2. axon
3. dendrites
4. synapses
5. neurotransmitter
6. cortex
7. transient exuberance
8. myelination
9. binocular vision
10. developmental biodynamics
11. reflexes
12. breathing reflex

13. sucking reflex
14. rooting reflex
15. gross motor skills
16. toddler
17. fine motor skills
18. norm
19. sensation

20. perception
21. habituation
22. otitis media
23. protein-calorie malnutrition
24. marasmus
25. kwashiorkor

Cross Check
After you have written the definitions of the key terms in this chapter, you should complete the crossword puzzle to ensure that you can reverse the process—recognize the term, given the definition.

ACROSS

1. The main component of the nervous system.
5. Process that simulates the body's own defensive system to defend against an infectious disease.
8. Nerve fiber extension that transmits an electrical impulse from one neuron to the dendrites of another neuron.
10. Average age for the acquisition of a particular behavior, developed for a specified group population.
11. Decline in physiological responsiveness to a familiar stimulus.
12. Reflex that causes babies to turn their heads and start sucking when something brushes their cheek.
13. Thin outer layer of the brain.
15. Form of malnutrition that results when a person does not consume enough nourishment to thrive.
16. Disease caused by protein-calorie deficiency during toddlerhood.
17. Physical abilities that require precise, small movements.
18. Nerve fiber extensions that receive impulses from the axon of another neuron.

DOWN

1. Chemical that transmits information across the synaptic gap.
2. Middle ear infection.

3. Vision involving the use of both eyes together.
4. Physical abilities that demand large body movements.
6. Process by which axons become coated with the fatty sheath that speeds neural communication.
7. Name given to infants once they are able to walk well without assistance.
9. Process by which the brain tries to make sense of a stimulus.
14. Disease caused by severe protein-calorie deficiency during the first year of life.

ANSWERS
CHAPTER REVIEW

1. prenatal; size; proportion
2. 20 inches (51 centimeters); 7 pounds (3.2 kilograms)
3. lose
4. 22 pounds (10 kilograms); 30 inches (75 centimeters); one-fifth; half
5. one-fourth; one-fifth; one-eighth
6. one-fourth; one-half
7. sudden infant death syndrome; cot death; crib death
8. breathing reflex; 2; 4
9. backs

Other preventive measures include removing soft bedding, eliminating second-hand smoke, and prolonging breast-feeding.

10. 500; immunization
11. smallpox; polio; measles
12. 25; 75; 20
13. neurons; dendrites; axons; dendrites; axon
14. synapses; axon; neurotransmitters; synaptic gap; dendrites; are; are
15. cortex; perception; thinking
16. increases; five; transient exuberance
17. myelin; complex; 4; adolescence
18. frontal; self-control; self-regulation; sleep–wake; reflexes; cognitive; emotional
19. is
20. blindfolded; neural pathways; binocular vision
21. plasticity; experiences
22. developmental biodynamics
23. reflex
24. breathing reflex; hiccups, sneezes, thrashing
25. body temperature
26. feeding; sucking; rooting
27. gross motor
28. 8; 10

On average, a child can walk while holding a hand at 9 months, can stand alone momentarily at 10 months, and can walk well unassisted at 12 months.

29. toddler
30. fine motor; 6 months
31. sequence; age
32. norms; many

33. ethnic

Of primary importance in variations in the acquisition of motor skills are inherited factors, such as activity level, rate of physical maturation, and how fat the infant is. Particular patterns of infant care may also be influential.

34. is; do
35. inherited; environmental
36. sensation; perception; are

Although their sensory abilities are selective, newborns see, hear, smell, taste, and respond to pressure, motion, temperature, and pain.

37. 4; 30; 400; 1 year
38. scan; attend; binocular vision; 14 weeks; depth; motion; track
39. is not
40. more; 1 month
41. habituation; can
42. can
43. 1,000
44. otitis media; inner
45. learn; friends; social; aggression; antibiotic; tube
46. salty; more; 1 year
47. is; temperature; size; hardness; texture
48. quality; quantity

Breast milk is always sterile and at body temperature; it contains more iron, vitamin C, and vitamin A; it contains antibodies that provide the infant some protection against disease; it is more digestible than any formula; and it decreases the frequency of almost every common infant ailment.

49. protein-calorie malnutrition
50. marasmus; kwashiorkor
51. early cessation of breast-feeding

Undernutrition is caused by the interaction of many factors, with insufficient food as the immediate cause, and problems in the family and/or society as underlying causes. For example, depressed mothers tend to feed their infants erratically, and some may be ignorant of the infant's nutritional needs.

52. concentrate; language

PROGRESS TEST 1

Multiple-Choice Questions

1. **b.** is the answer. (p. 131)
2. **a.** is the answer. (p. 132)
3. **a.** is the answer. (p. 143)

    b. The age norm for this skill is 7.8 months.

c. This is a reflex, rather than an acquired motor skill.

d. This skill is acquired between 9 and 14 months.

4. **c.** is the answer. (p. 143)

5. **a.** is the answer. (p. 145)

b. Inherited and environmental factors are important for both physical growth *and* the development of motor skills.

c. On average, Ugandan babies walk earlier than do babies in the United States.

d. In fact, just the opposite is true.

6. **a.** is the answer. (p. 147)

7. **c.** is the answer. (p. 132)

8. **d.** is the answer. (p. 138)

a. & c. Research has shown that deprivation of normal sensory experiences prevents the development of normal neural pathways that transmit sensory information.

b. On the contrary, these studies demonstrate harmful sensory *restriction.*

9. **b.** is the answer. This is because breast milk is more digestible than cow's milk or formula. (p. 152)

a., c., & d. Breast- and bottle-fed babies do not differ in these attributes.

10. **b.** is the answer. (p. 153)

11. **c.** is the answer. (p. 139)

a. & b. These motor skills do not emerge until somewhat later; reflexes are present at birth.

d. On the contrary, reflexes are quite predictable.

12. **b.** is the answer. (p. 141)

13. **d.** is the answer. (p. 143)

14. **c.** is the answer. (p. 133)

15. **b.** is the answer. (p. 149)

Matching Items

1. m (p. 133) **6.** h (p. 148) **11.** d (p. 153)
2. g (p. 133) **7.** i (p. 140) **12.** l (p. 136)
3. j (p. 136) **8.** c (p. 141) **13.** n (p. 139)
4. e (p. 153) **9.** k (p. 139) **14.** a (p. 148)
5. b (p. 153) **10.** f (p. 140) **15.** o (p. 136)

PROGRESS TEST 2

Multiple-Choice Questions

1. **a.** is the answer. (p. 133)

2. **c.** is the answer. (p. 139)

a., b., & d. Each of these refers to voluntary responses that are acquired only after a certain amount of practice; reflexes are involuntary responses that are present at birth and require no practice.

3. **b.** is the answer. (p. 148)

4. **b.** is the answer. (p. 141)

5. **c.** is the answer. (p. 143)

a. Norms are average ages at which certain motor skills are acquired.

6. **b.** is the answer. (p. 146)

a. Although focusing ability seems to be limited to a certain range, babies do focus on many objects in this range.

c. This is not within the range at which babies *can* focus.

d. Babies have very poor distance vision.

7. **c.** is the answer. (p. 148)

a. & c. These are examples of learned rather than innate behaviors.

b. This text chapter does not discuss the development of grammar.

8. **a.** is the answer. (pp. 151–152)

b. If anything, this is a potential *disadvantage* of breast milk over formula.

c. So can formula.

d. Breast milk contains more iron, vitamin C, and vitamin A than cow's milk; it does not contain more protein and vitamin D, however.

9. **d.** is the answer. (p. 154)

10. **d.** is the answer. (p. 132)

11. **b.** is the answer. (pp. 140, 141)

c. & d. Reflexes are involuntary responses; climbing and using a crayon are both voluntary responses.

12. **d.** is the answer. (pp. 139–140)

13. **c.** is the answer. (p. 134)

14. **d.** is the answer. (p. 155)

15. **d.** is the answer. (p. 136)

True or False Items

1. F Boys are both slightly heavier and taller than girls at 2 years. (p. 132)

2. T (pp. 132–133)

3. F Hiccups, sneezes, and thrashing are common during the first few days, and they are entirely normal reflexes. (p. 139)

4. F   Although all healthy infants develop the same motor skills in the same sequence, the age at which these skills are acquired can vary greatly from infant to infant. (p. 143)

5. T (p. 132)

6. F   Vision is relatively poorly developed at birth, whereas hearing is well developed. (pp. 146, 147)

7. F   Myelination is not complete until adolescence. (p. 136)

8. T (p. 137)

9. T (p. 154)

0. F   Although ear infections are common, they need prompt attention, since they can lead to hearing problems and social and cognitive difficulties. (pp. 148–149)

THINKING CRITICALLY ABOUT CHAPTER 5

1. **c.** is the answer. (p. 139)

2. **d.** is the answer. (p. 148)

   a. & b. These changes in behavior indicate that the newborn has perceived an unfamiliar stimulus, not that he or she is hungry, annoyed, or angry.

   c. Habituation refers to a *decrease* in physiological responsiveness to a familiar stimulus.

3. **c.** is the answer. (p. 148)

   a. & b. There is no evidence that infants can detect one parent's voice more easily than the other's, or that sounds perceived at 1 month can not be discriminated later.

   d. This experiment was not concerned with sound localization.

4. **d.** is the answer. (p. 132)

   a. & b. Although slowdowns in growth during infancy are often a cause for concern, their daughter's weight and height are typical of 1-year-old babies.

   c. Growth patterns are no more erratic for first children than for later children.

5. **c.** is the answer. The evidence for this comes from studies in which animals were prevented from using their senses in infancy; such animals became permanently handicapped. (p. 138)

   a. If this were true, research would show that restriction had no effect on sensory abilities.

   b. If this were true, sensory restriction would cause much more serious impairment than it does.

   d. Sensory restriction research demonstrates that both genetic and environmental factors are important in the development of sensory abilities.

6. **d.** is the answer. (pp. 136)

   a. Dendrites are the "receiving" end of neurons.

   b. Neurotransmitters are chemicals that carry neural information across the synaptic gap.

   c. Axons are the single nerve fibers that extend from neurons and transmit impulses from that neuron to the dendrites of other neurons.

7. **c.** is the answer. (p. 146)

8. **b.** is the answer. (p. 140)

   a. This is the reflexive sucking of newborns in response to anything that touches their *lips*.

   c. This is the response that infants make when their feet are stroked.

   d. In this response to startling noises, newborns fling their arms outward and then bring them together on their chests as if to hold on to something.

9. **a.** is the answer. (p. 155)

10. **b.** is the answer. (p. 145)

   a. & d. Sensation and perception operate in all of these sensory modalities.

11. **a.** is the answer. Transient exuberance results in a proliferation of neural connections during infancy, some of which will disappear because they are not used; that is, they are not needed to process information. (p. 136)

   b. & d. Transient exuberance is a normal developmental process that occurs in all healthy infants.

   c. This describes myelination.

12. **a.** is the answer. (p. 138)

13. **d.** is the answer. (p. 149)

14. **b.** is the answer. This is true because, at birth, focusing is best for objects between 4 and 30 inches away. (p. 146)

   a., c., & d. Newborns have very poor distance vision; each of these situations involves a distance greater than the optimal focus range.

15. **d.** is the answer. (pp. 154–155)

KEY TERMS

Writing Definitions

1. A **neuron**, or nerve cell, is the main component of the central nervous system. (p. 133)

2. An **axon** is the nerve fiber extension that sends impulses from one neuron to the dendrites of other neurons. (p. 133)

3. **Dendrites** are nerve fiber extensions that receive the impulses transmitted from other neurons via their axons. (p. 133)

4. A **synapse** is the point at which the axon of a sending neuron meets the dendrites of a receiving neuron. (p. 133)

5. A **neurotransmitter** is a chemical that transmits information across the synaptic gap between the axon of one neuron and the dendrite of another. (p. 136)

6. The **cortex** is the thin outer layer of the brain that is involved in the voluntary, cognitive aspects of the mind. (p. 136)

   Memory aid: **Cortex** in Latin means "bark." As bark covers a tree, the cortex is the "bark of the brain."

7. **Transient exuberance** is the dramatic increase in neural connections that occurs in an infant's brain over the first 2 years of life. (p. 136)

8. **Myelination** is the process in which axons are coated with myelin, a fatty substance that speeds neural communication. (p. 136)

9. **Binocular vision** is the ability to use both eyes together to focus on a single object. (p. 138)

   Memory aid: Bi- indicates "two"; *ocular* means something pertaining to the eye. **Binocular vision** is vision for "two eyes."

10. **Developmental biodynamics** is the maturation of movement skills. (p. 139)

11. **Reflexes** are involuntary physical responses to specific stimuli. (p. 139)

12. The **breathing reflex** is an involuntary physical response that ensures that the infant has an adequate supply of oxygen and discharges carbon dioxide. (p. 139)

13. The **sucking reflex** is the involuntary tendency of newborns to suck anything that touches their lips. This reflex fosters feeding. (p. 140)

14. The **rooting reflex**, which helps babies find a nipple, causes them to turn their heads and start to suck when something brushes against their cheek. (p. 140)

15. **Gross motor skills** are physical abilities that demand large body movements, such as climbing, jumping, or running. (p. 140)

16. When babies can walk well without assistance (usually at about 12 months), they are given the name **toddler** because of the characteristic way they move their bodies from side to side. (p. 141)

17. **Fine motor skills** are physical abilities th. require precise, small movements, such as pic ing up a coin. (p. 141)

18. A **norm** is an average age for the acquisition of particular behavior, developed for a specif group population. (p. 143)

19. **Sensation** is the process by which a sensory sy tem detects a particular stimulus. (p. 145)

20. **Perception** is the process by which the brain tri to make sense of a stimulus such that the indivi ual becomes aware of it. (p. 145)

21. **Habituation** refers to the decline in physiologic responsiveness that occurs when a stimul becomes familiar. Habituation to stimuli is use by researchers to assess infants' ability to pe ceive by testing their ability to discrimina between very similar stimuli. (p. 148)

22. **Otitis media** is a middle ear infection that ca impair hearing temporarily, which can slow la guage development and interfere with soci development if allowed to continue too lon (p. 148)

23. **Protein-calorie malnutrition** results when a pe son does not consume enough nourishment thrive. (p. 153)

24. **Marasmus** is a disease caused by severe protei calorie deficiency during the first year of li Growth stops, body tissues waste away, and t infant dies. (p. 153)

25. **Kwashiorkor** is a disease caused by protein-ca rie deficiency during toddlerhood. The chilc face, legs, and abdomen swell with water, som times making the child appear well fed. Oth body parts are degraded, including the ha which becomes thin, brittle, and colorless. (p. 15

Cross-Check

ACROSS	DOWN
1. neuron	1. neurotransmitter
5. immunization	2. otitis media
8. axon	3. binocular
10. norm	4. gross motor
11. habituation	6. myelination
12. rooting	7. toddler
13 cortex	9. perception
15. protein-calorie	14. marasmus
16. kwashiorkor	
17. fine motor	
18. dendrites	

CHAPTER 6

The First Two Years: Cognitive Development

Chapter Overview

Chapter 6 explores the ways in which the infant comes to learn about, think about, and adapt to his or her surroundings. It focuses on the various ways in which infant intelligence is revealed: through perception, cognition, memory, sensorimotor intelligence, and language development. The chapter begins with a description of infant perception and Eleanor and James Gibson's influential theory. Central to this theory is the idea that infants gain cognitive understanding of their world through the affordances of objects, that is, the activities they can do with them.

The second section discusses the key cognitive elements needed by the infant to structure the environment discovered through its newfound perceptual abilities. Using the habituation procedure, researchers have found that the speed with which infants recognize familiarity and seek something novel is related to later cognitive skill. It points out the importance of memory to cognitive development.

The third section describes Jean Piaget's theory of sensorimotor intelligence, which maintains that infants think exclusively with their senses and motor skills. Piaget's six stages of sensorimotor intelligence are examined.

Finally, the chapter turns to the most remarkable cognitive achievement of the first two years, the acquisition of language. Beginning with a description of the infant's first attempts at language, the chapter follows the sequence of events that leads to the child's ability to utter two-word sentences. The chapter concludes with an examination of language learning as teamwork involving babies and adults, who, in a sense, teach each other the unique human process of verbal communication.

NOTE: Answer guidelines for all Chapter 6 questions begin on page 97.

Guided Study

The text chapter should be studied one section at a time. Before you read, preview each section by skimming it, noting headings and boldface items. Then read the appropriate section objectives from the following outline. Keep these objectives in mind and, as you read the chapter section, search for the information that will enable you to meet each objective. Once you have finished a section, write out answers for its objectives.

Perception and Cognition (pp. 159–164)

1. Explain the Gibsons' contextual view of perception, and discuss the idea of affordances, giving examples of the affordances perceived by infants.

2. Explain how the infant's focus on movement and change enhances sensory and perceptual skills and thus overall cognitive growth.

3. (text and Research Report) Explain what object permanence is, how it is tested in infancy, and what these tests reveal.

8. Identify and describe stages 5 and 6 of Piaget theory of sensorimotor intelligence.

Key Elements of Cognitive Growth (pp. 164–170)

4. Explain what research has revealed about the infant's ability to categorize.

Language Development (pp. 174–183)

9. Describe language development during infancy and identify its major hallmarks.

5. (text and A Life-Span View) Discuss research findings on infant long-term memory and infants' understanding of causal relationships.

10. Contrast the theories of Skinner and Chomsky regarding early language development, and explain current views on language learning.

Piaget's Sensorimotor Intelligence (pp. 170–174)

6. Identify and describe the first two of Piaget's stages of sensorimotor intelligence.

11. (text and Changing Policy) Explain the importance of baby talk, and identify its main features.

7. Identify and describe stages 3 and 4 of Piaget's theory of sensorimotor intelligence.

Chapter Review

When you have finished reading the chapter, work through the material that follows to review it. Complete the sentences and answer the questions. As you proceed, evaluate your performance for each section by consulting the answers on page 97. Do not continue with the next section until you understand each answer. If you need to, review or reread the appropriate section in the textbook before continuing.

Perception and Cognition (pp. 159–164)

1. The first major theorist to realize that infants are active learners was _____ .

2. Much of the current research in perception and cognition has been inspired by the work of the Gibsons, who stress that perception is a(n) _____ (active/passive/automatic) cognitive phenomenon.

3. According to the Gibsons, any object in the environment offers diverse opportunities for interaction; this property of an object is called an _____ .

4. Which of these an individual perceives in an object depends on the individual's _____ _____ and _____ _____ , on his or her _____ _____ , and on his or her _____ _____ of what the object might be used for.

5. Infants perceive the affordance of _____ long before their manual dexterity has matured. The time it takes infants to grab objects successfully demonstrates that deliberate and thoughtful perception _____ (precedes/does not precede) the action.

List other affordances perceived by infants from a very early age.

6. A firm surface that appears to drop off is called a _____ _____ .

Although perception of this drop off was once linked to _____ maturity, later research found that infants as young as _____ are able to perceive the drop off, as evidenced by changes in their _____ _____ and their wide open eyes.

7. Perception that is primed to focus on movement and change is called _____ _____ .

Give several examples of how infants use movement cues in perceiving objects.

8. A major cognitive accomplishment of infancy is the ability to understand that objects exist independently of _____ . This awareness is called _____ _____ .

9. To test for this awareness, Piaget devised a procedure to observe whether an infant will _____ for a hidden object. Using this test, Piaget concluded that this awareness does not develop until about _____ of age.

10. (Research Report) Using the habituation procedure, Renée Baillargeon has demonstrated that infants as young as _____ months have an awareness of object permanence that is concealed by the traditional Piagetian hidden-object tests.

Key Elements of Cognitive Growth (pp. 164–170)

11. From a very early age, infants coordinate and organize their perceptions into _____ . Researchers use the phenomenon of infant _____ to study these abilities.

12. Infants younger than 6 months can categorize objects according to their _____, _____, _____, _____, _____, and _____. By the end of the first year, they can categorize _____, _____, and _____, for example.

13. According to _____, no one can remember anything that happened before the age of _____. This hypothesized inability is called _____ _____. Piaget _____ (agreed/disagreed) with this hypothesis.

14. Researchers have generally considered infants' long-term memory to be quite _____ (good/poor).

15. More recent studies demonstrate that babies have great difficulty storing new memories in their first _____ (how long?), but they can show that they remember when three conditions are met:

    (a) _____

    (b) _____

    (c) _____

16. When these conditions are met, infants as young as _____ months "remembered" events from one week earlier or two weeks earlier, if they experienced a _____ prior to retesting.

17. The ability to remember and imitate behaviors that have been observed but never actually performed is called _____ _____. This ability becomes apparent toward the _____.

18. (A Life-Span View) Improvement in infant memory ability seems tied to _____ maturation and _____ development. Notable increases in memory capacity and duration occur at about _____ months, again at about _____ months, and again at age _____. Research also demonstrates the importance of the _____ aspects of memory.

19. Another important cognitive accomplishment of infancy is the ability to recognize and associate _____-_____-_____ relations. Research using the _____ _____ procedure reveals that infants as young as _____ months have a rudimentary understanding of such relations.

Piaget's Sensorimotor Intelligence (pp. 170–174)

20. A central concept in Piaget's theory of cognitive development is the notion of _____ intelligence.

21. When infants begin to explore the environment through sensory and motor skills, they are displaying what Piaget called _____ intelligence. In number, Piaget described _____ stages of development of this type of intelligence.

22. Sensorimotor intelligence begins with newborns' reflexes, such as _____, _____, _____, and _____. It lasts from birth to _____ of age.

23. Stage 2 begins when newborns show signs of _____ of their reflexes to the specifics of the environment. This is revealed in two ways: by _____ of new information into previously developed mental categories, or _____; and _____ of previous mental categories to incorporate new information.

Describe the development of the sucking reflex during stages one and two.

24. During stage three, which occurs between _____ and _____ months of age, infants repeat a specific action that has just elicited a pleasing response.

Describe a typical stage-three behavior.

5. In stage four, which lasts from _____ to _____ months of age, infants can better _____ events. At this stage, babies also engage in purposeful actions, or _____-_____ behavior.

6. During stage five, which lasts from _____ to _____ months, goal-directed activities become more expansive and creative.

Explain what Piaget meant when he described the stage-five infant as a "little scientist."

7. Stage six, which lasts from _____ to _____ months, is the stage of achieving new means by using _____ _____ .

8. One sign that children have reached stage six is their ability to enjoy a broader range of _____ activities.

Language Development (pp. 174–183)

9. Children the world over _____ (follow/do not follow) the same sequence of early language development. The timing of this sequence _____ (varies/does not vary).

10. Newborns show a preference for hearing _____ over other sounds.

11. By 4 months of age, most babies' verbal repertoire consists of _____ _____ .

32. At _____ months of age, babies begin to repeat certain syllables, a phenomenon referred to as _____ .

33. Deaf babies begin oral babbling _____ (earlier/later) than hearing babies do. Deaf babies may also babble _____ , with this behavior emerging (earlier than/at the same time as/later than) hearing infants begin oral babbling.

34. The average baby speaks a few words at about _____ of age. When vocabulary reaches approximately 50 words, it suddenly begins to build rapidly, at a rate of _____ or more words a month.

35. Toddlers who primarily learn naming words first are called _____ , whereas those who acquire mainly words that can be used in social interaction are called _____ . Language acquisition is also shaped by our _____ , as revealed by the fact that North American infants are more _____ than Japanese infants.

36. One characteristic of infant speech is _____ , or overgeneralization, in which the infant applies a known word to a variety of objects and contexts. Initially, however, infants tend toward _____ of word meanings. Infants also might learn one name for something and refuse to use alternative names; this is called the _____ _____ .

37. Another characteristic is the use of the _____ , in which a single word expresses a complete thought.

38. Children begin to produce their first two-word sentences at about _____ months.

39. Reinforcement and other conditioning processes account for language development, according to the learning theory of _____ .

40. The theorist who stressed the infant's innate language abilities is _____ , who maintained that all children are born with a LAD, or

_____ _____

_____ .

Summarize the conclusions of recent research regarding the theories of Skinner and Chomsky.

41. Adults talk to infants using a special form of language called _____

_____ .

(text and Changing Policy) Briefly describe the type of speech adults use with infants.

42. Four ways that adults support infants in their acquisition of language are: (a) _____

_____ ; (b) _____

_____ ; (c) _____

_____ ; and (d) _____

_____ .

Progress Test 1

Multiple-Choice Questions

Circle your answers to the following questions and check them with the answers on page 98. If your answer is incorrect, read the explanation for why it is incorrect and then consult the appropriate pages of the text (in parentheses following the correct answer).

1. In general terms, the Gibsons' concept of affordances emphasizes the idea that the individual perceives an object in terms of its:
   a. economic importance.
   b. physical qualities.
   c. function or use to the individual.
   d. role in the larger culture or environment.

2. According to Piaget, when a baby repeats an action that has just triggered a pleasing response from his or her caregiver, a stage _____ behavior has occurred.
   a. one   c. three
   b. two   d. six

3. Sensorimotor intelligence begins with a baby first:
   a. attempt to crawl.
   b. reflex actions.
   c. auditory perception.
   d. adaptation of a reflex.

4. Piaget and the Gibsons would most likely agree that:
   a. perception is largely automatic.
   b. language development is biologically predisposed in children.
   c. learning and perception are active cognitive processes.
   d. it is unwise to "push" children too hard academically.

5. By the end of the first year, infants usually learn how to:
   a. accomplish simple goals.
   b. manipulate various symbols.
   c. solve complex problems.
   d. pretend.

6. When an infant begins to understand that objects exist even when they are out of sight, she or he has begun to understand the concept of object:
   a. displacement.   c. permanence.
   b. importance.   d. location.

7. Today, most cognitive psychologists view language acquisition as:
   a. primarily the result of imitation of adult speech.
   b. a behavior that is determined primarily by biological maturation.
   c. a behavior determined entirely by learning.
   d. determined by both biological maturation and learning.

8. Despite cultural differences, children all over the world attain very similar language skills:
   a. according to ethnically specific timetables.
   b. in the same sequence according to a variable timetable.
   c. according to culturally specific timetables.
   d. according to timetables that vary from child to child.

9. The average baby speaks a few words at about:

  a. 6 months.   **c.** 12 months.

  b. 9 months.   **d.** 24 months.

0. A single word used by toddlers to express a complete thought is:

  a. a holophrase.   **c.** an overextension.

  b. baby talk.   **d.** an underextension.

1. Which of the following theorists would most likely agree that the interactive, social context of early language development is of paramount importance?

  a. B. F. Skinner

  b. Noam Chomsky

  c. Lev Vygotsky

  d. Eleanor Gibson

2. A distinctive form of language, with a particular pitch, structure, etc., that adults use in talking to infants is called:

  a. a holophrase.   **c.** baby talk.

  b. the LAD.   **d.** conversation.

13. At 8 months, infants can categorize objects on the basis of

  a. angularity.   **c.** density.

  b. shape.   **d.** all of the above.

14. By what age can most infants properly interpret the cause-and-effect relations of the launching event experiment?

  a. 5 months   **c.** 10 months

  b. 6 months   **d.** 12 months

15. A toddler who taps on the computer's keyboard after observing her mother sending e-mail is demonstrating:

  a. assimilation.   **c.** deferred imitation.

  b. accommodation.   **d.** dynamic perception.

Matching Items

Match each definition or description with its corresponding term.

Terms

      1. mental combinations

      2. affordances

      3. object permanence

      4. Noam Chomsky

      5. B. F. Skinner

      6. sensorimotor intelligence

      7. babbling

      8. holophrase

      9. overextension

      10. deferred imitation

      11. dynamic perception

Definitions or Descriptions

  a. overgeneralization of a word to inappropriate objects, etc.

  b. repetitive utterance of certain syllables

  c. perception that focuses on movement and change

  d. the ability to witness, remember, and later copy a behavior

  e. the realization that something that is out of sight continues to exist

  f. trying out actions mentally

  g. opportunities for interaction that an object offers

  h. theorist who believed that verbal behavior is conditioned

  i. a single word used to express a complete thought

  j. theorist who believed that language ability is innate

  k. thinking through the senses and motor skills

Progress Test 2

Progress Test 2 should be completed during a final chapter review. Answer the following questions after you thoroughly understand the correct answers for the Chapter Review and Progress Test 1.

Multiple-Choice Questions

1. Stage five (12 to 18 months) of sensorimotor intelligence is best described as:
   a. first acquired adaptations.
   b. the period of the "little scientist."
   c. procedures for making interesting sights last.
   d. new means through symbolization.

2. Which of the following is not evidence of dynamic perception during infancy?
   a. Babies prefer to look at things in motion.
   b. Babies form simple expectations of the path that a moving object will follow.
   c. Babies use movement cues to discern the boundaries of objects.
   d. Babies quickly grasp that even though objects look different when seen from different viewpoints, they are the same objects.

3. (text and Research Report) Research suggests that the concept of object permanence:
   a. fades after a few months.
   b. is a skill some children never acquire.
   c. may occur earlier and more gradually than Piaget recognized.
   d. involves pretending as well as mental combinations.

4. According to the Gibsons, graspability is:
   a. an opportunity perceived by a baby.
   b. a quality that resides in toys and other objects.
   c. an ability that emerges at about 6 months.
   d. evidence of manual dexterity in the infant.

5. Toddlers whose first words are mainly those that can be used in social interaction are referred to as:
   a. referential.
   b. overextenders.
   c. expressive.
   d. underextenders.

6. According to Piaget, assimilation and accommodation are two ways in which:
   a. infants adapt their reflexes to the specifics of the environment.
   b. goal-directed behavior occurs.
   c. infants form mental combinations.
   d. language begins to emerge.

7. For Noam Chomsky, the "language acquisition device" refers to:
   a. the human predisposition to acquire language.
   b. the portion of the human brain that processes speech.
   c. the vocabulary of the language the child is exposed to.
   d. all of the above.

8. The first stage of sensorimotor intelligence lasts until:
   a. infants can anticipate events that will fulfill their needs.
   b. infants begin to adapt their reflexes to the environment.
   c. infants interact with objects to produce exciting experiences.
   d. infants are capable of thinking about past and future events.

9. Whether or not an infant perceives certain characteristics of objects, such as "suckability" or "graspability," seems to depend on:
   a. his or her prior experiences.
   b. his or her needs.
   c. his or her sensory awareness.
   d. all of the above.

10. Piaget was incorrect in his belief that infants do not have:
    a. object permanence.
    b. intelligence.
    c. goal-directed behavior.
    d. all of the above.

11. The purposeful actions that begin to develop in sensorimotor stage four are called:
    a. reflexes.
    b. affordances.
    c. goal-directed behaviors.
    d. mental combinations.

12. What is the correct sequence of stages of language development?
    a. crying, babbling, cooing, first word
    b. crying, cooing, babbling, first word
    c. crying, babbling, first word, cooing
    d. crying, cooing, first word, babbling

13. Compared with hearing babies, deaf babies:
    a. are less likely to babble.
    b. are more likely to babble.
    c. begin to babble vocally at about the same age.
    d. begin to babble manually at about the same age as hearing babies begin to babble vocally.

14. According to Skinner, children acquire language:
  a. as a result of an inborn ability to use the basic structure of language.
  b. through reinforcement and other aspects of conditioning.
  c. mostly because of biological maturation.
  d. in a fixed sequence of predictable stages.

15. (A Life-Span View) Which of the following is most closely tied to language development?
  a. the development of affordances
  b. object permanence
  c. improvement in memory ability
  d. dynamic perception

Matching Items

Match each definition or description with its corresponding term.

Terms

_____ **1.** goal-directed behavior
_____ **2.** visual cliff
_____ **3.** infantile amnesia
_____ **4.** baby talk
_____ **5.** assimilation
_____ **6.** little scientist
_____ **7.** launching event
_____ **8.** underextension
_____ **9.** accommodation
_____ **10.** LAD

Definitions or Descriptions

a. a device for studying depth perception
b. incorporating new information into an existing schema
c. research procedure for investigating cause-and-effect relations
d. the inability to access memories from the first years of life
e. a word used more narrowly than its true meaning allows
f. a hypothetical device that facilitates language development
g. also called "Motherese"
h. Piaget's term for the stage-five toddler
i. purposeful actions
j. modifying an existing schema to reflect new information

Thinking Critically About Chapter 6

Answer these questions the day before an exam as a final check on your understanding of the chapter's terms and concepts.

1. A 9-month-old repeatedly reaches for his sister's doll, even though he has been told "no" many times. This is an example of:
  a. pretend play.
  b. an overextension.
  c. delayed imitation.
  d. goal-directed behavior.

2. Concluding her presentation on theories of language development, Rosa states that:
  a. Chomsky's view that infants are genetically primed to pick up language is correct.
  b. Skinner's view that caregivers help condition infants' language learning is correct.
  c. Both Skinner's and Chomsky's theories have been discarded.

  d. Although both Skinner's and Chomsky's theories have some validity, neither recognizes the importance of the social context in language development.

3. (A Life-Span View) In one study, 6-month-old infants were trained to reach for a dangling Big Bird toy. When the responses of these children, 2 years later, were compared to those of a control group that had not received the training, the researchers discovered that:
  a. those that had been trained at 6 months were more likely to reach for and grab the toy.
  b. children in both groups had equal success in reaching for and grabbing the toy.
  c. children in the control group were more interested in the previously unseen toy and reached more for it.
  d. both groups of children quickly became bored with the toy and did not reach for it.

4. According to Skinner's theory, an infant who learns to delight his father by saying "da-da" is probably benefiting from:
   a. social reinforcers, such as smiles and hugs.
   b. modeling.
   c. learning by imitation.
   d. an innate ability to use language.

5. The child's tendency to call every animal "doggie" is an example of:
   a. using a holophrase.   c. motherese.
   b. babbling.   d. overextension.

6. About six months after speaking his or her first words, the typical child will:
   a. have a vocabulary of between 250 and 350 words.
   b. begin to speak in holophrases.
   c. put words together to form rudimentary sentences.
   d. do all of the above.

7. A 20-month-old girl who is able to try out various actions mentally without having to actually perform them is learning to solve simple problems by using:
   a. dynamic perception.
   b. object permanence.
   c. affordances.
   d. mental combinations.

8. A baby who repeats an action he or she has seen trigger a reaction in someone else is demonstrating an ability that typically occurs in which stage of sensorimotor development?
   a. one   c. three
   b. two   d. four

9. Sixteen-month-old Courtney reserves the word "cat" for her pet feline. Her failure to refer to other felines as cats is an example of:
   a. a holophrase.
   b. an overextension.
   c. babbling.
   d. an underextension.

10. A baby who realizes that a rubber duck that has fallen out of the tub must be somewhere on the floor has achieved:
    a. object permanence.
    b. deferred imitation.
    c. mental combinations.
    d. goal-directed behavior.

11. As soon as her babysitter arrives, 21-month-old Christine holds on to her mother's legs and, in a questioning manner, says "bye-bye." Because Christine clearly is "asking" her mother not to leave, her utterance can be classified as:
    a. babbling.
    b. an overextension.
    c. a holophrase.
    d. subject-predicate order.

12. The 6-month-old infant's continual repetition of sound combinations such as "ba-ba-ba" is called:
    a. cooing.   c. a holophrase.
    b. babbling.   d. an overextension.

13. Which of the following is an example of a linguistic overextension that a 2-year-old might make?
    a. saying "bye-bye" to indicate that he or she wants to go out
    b. pointing to a cat and saying "doggie"
    c. repeating certain syllables, such as "ma-ma"
    d. reversing word order, such as "want it paper"

14. Many researchers believe that the infant's ability to detect the similarities and differences between shapes and colors marks the beginning of:
    a. mental combinations.
    b. the stage of the little scientist.
    c. category or concept formation.
    d. full object permanence.

15. Like most Japanese toddlers, Noriko has acquired a greater number of _____ words than her North American counterparts, who tend to be more _____ .
    a. referential; expressive
    b. expressive; referential
    c. labeling; expressive
    d. social; referential

Key Terms

Using your own words, write a brief definition or explanation of each of the following terms on a separate piece of paper.

1. affordance
2. graspability
3. visual cliff
4. dynamic perception
5. object permanence
6. infantile amnesia

7. reminder session

8. deferred imitation

9. launching event

0. sensorimotor intelligence

1. goal-directed behavior

2. little scientist

3. mental combinations

4. babbling

5. underextension

6. overextension

7. holophrase

8. language acquisition device (LAD)

9. baby talk

ANSWERS

CHAPTER REVIEW

1. Piaget

2. active

3. affordance

4. past experiences; developmental level; present needs; sensory awareness

5. graspability; precedes

From a very early age, infants understand which objects afford digestibility and suckability, which afford noisemaking, which afford movability, and so forth.

6. visual cliff; visual; 3 months; heart rate

7. dynamic perception

Infants use movement cues to discern not only the boundaries of objects but also their rigidity, wholeness, shape, and size. They even form expectations of the path that a moving object will follow.

8. one's perception of them even when they are moved out of sight; object permanence

9. search; 8 months

0. 4 $^1/_2$

1. categories; habituation

2. angularity; shape; color; density; relative size; number (up to 3 objects); faces; animals; birds

3. Freud; 2 years; infantile amnesia; agreed

4. poor

5. 6 months; (a) real-life situations are used; (b) motivation is high; (c) special measures aid memory retrieval

16. 3 months; reminder session

17. deferred imitation; end of the first year

18. brain; language; 8; 18; 5; social

19. cause-and-effect; launching event; 6

20. active

21. sensorimotor; 6

22. sucking; grasping; looking; listening; 1 month

23. adaptation; assimilation; schemas; accommodation

Stage-one infants suck everything that touches their lips. At about 1 month, they start to adapt their sucking to specific objects. By 3 months, they have organized the world into objects to be sucked for nourishment, objects to be sucked for pleasure, and objects not to be sucked at all.

24. 4; 8

A stage-three infant may squeeze a duck, hear a quack, and squeeze the duck again.

25. 8; 12; anticipate; goal-directed

26. 12; 18

Having discovered some action or set of actions that is possible with a given object, stage-five "little scientists" seem to ask, "What else can I do with this?"

27. 18; 24; mental combinations

28. pretend

29. follow; varies

30. speech

31. squeals, growls, grunts, croons, and yells, as well as some speechlike sounds

32. 6 or 7; babbling;

33. later; manually; at the same time as

34. 1 year; 100

35. referential; expressive; culture; referential

36. overextension; underextension; mutual exclusivity bias

37. holophrase

38. 21

39. B. F. Skinner

40. Noam Chomsky; language acquisition device

Recent research has suggested that both Skinner's and Chomsky's theories have some validity but that both miss the mark. Developmentalists today believe that language acquisition is an interactional process between the infant's genetic predisposition and the communication that occurs in the caregiver-child relationship.

41. baby talk

Baby talk is higher in pitch; has a characteristically low-to-high intonation pattern; uses simpler and more concrete vocabulary and shorter sentence length; and employs more questions, commands, and repetitions, and fewer past tenses, pronouns, and complex sentences.

42. (a) holding prelinguistic "conversations" with the infant; (b) engaging in baby talk; (c) persistently naming objects and events that capture the child's attention; and (d) expanding the child's sounds and words into meaningful communications

PROGRESS TEST 1

Multiple-Choice Questions

1. **c.** is the answer. (p. 160)

2. **c.** is the answer. (p. 172)

3. **b.** is the answer. This was Piaget's most basic contribution to the study of infant cognition—that intelligence is revealed in behavior at every age. (p. 171)

4. **c.** is the answer. (pp. 160, 171)

   b. This is Chomsky's position.

   d. This issue was not discussed in the text.

5. **a.** is the answer. (p. 173)

   b. & c. These abilities are not acquired until children are much older.

   d. Pretending is associated with stage six (18 to 24 months).

6. **c.** is the answer. (pp. 163–164)

7. **d.** is the answer. (pp. 180–181)

8. **b.** is the answer. (p. 175)

   a., c., & d. Children the world over, and in every Piagetian stage, follow the same sequence, but the timing of their accomplishments may vary considerably.

9. **c.** is the answer. (p. 176)

10. **a.** is the answer. (p. 178)

    b. Baby talk is the speech adults use with infants.

    c. An overextension is a grammatical error in which a word is generalized to an inappropriate context.

    e. An underextension is the use of a word to refer to a narrower category of objects or events than the term signifies.

11. **c.** is the answer. Vygotsky's concept of an "apprenticeship in thinking" is very much in keeping with the interactive, social nature of language development. (p. 182)

    a. & b. Skinner and Chomsky both overlooked the social context of language development in their theories.

    d. Gibson's research was not directly concerned with language development.

12. **c.** is the answer. (p. 180)

    a. A holophrase is a single word uttered by a toddler to express a complete thought.

    b. According to Noam Chomsky, the LAD, or language acquisition device, is an innate ability in humans to acquire language.

    d. These characteristic differences in pitch and structure are precisely what distinguish baby talk from regular conversation.

13. **d.** is the answer. (p. 166)

14. **c.** is the answer. (p. 170)

15. **c.** is the answer (p. 168)

    a. & b. In Piaget's theory, these refer to processes by which mental concepts incorporate new experiences (assimilation) or are modified in response to new experiences (accommodation).

    d. Dynamic perception is perception that primed to focus on movement and change.

Matching Items

1. f (p. 174)	**5.** h (p. 178)	**9.** a (p. 177)
2. g (p. 160)	**6.** k (p. 171)	**10.** d (p. 168)
3. e (p. 164)	**7.** b (p. 176)	**11.** c (p. 163)
4. j (p. 179)	**8.** i (p. 178)	

PROGRESS TEST 2

Multiple-Choice Questions

1. **b.** is the answer. (p. 174)

   a. & c. These are stages two and three.

   d. This is not one of Piaget's stages of sensorimotor intelligence.

2. **d.** is the answer. This is an example of perceptual constancy. (p. 163)

3. **c.** is the answer. (pp. 164, 165)

4. **a.** is the answer. (p. 161)

   b. Affordances are perceptual phenomena.

   c. & d. Infants perceive graspability at an earlier age and long before their manual dexterity enables them to actually grasp successfully.

5. c. is the answer. (pp. 177)

a. Referential children primarily learn naming words.

b. & d. All children demonstrate overextension and underextension during the course of their language development.

6. a. is the answer. (p. 172)

b. Assimilation and accommodation are cognitive processes, not behaviors.

c. Mental combinations are sequences of actions that are carried out mentally.

d. Assimilation and accommodation do not directly pertain to language use.

7. a. is the answer. Chomsky believed that this device is innate. (p. 179)

8. b. is the answer. (pp. 171–172)

a. & c. Both of these occur later than stage one.

d. This is a hallmark of stage six.

9. d. is the answer. (p. 160)

10. a. is the answer. (p. 164)

11. c. is the answer. (p. 173)

a. Reflexes are involuntary (and therefore unintentional) responses.

b. Affordances are perceived opportunities for interaction with objects.

d. Mental combinations are actions that are carried out mentally, rather than behaviorally. Moreover, mental combinations do not develop until a later age, during sensorimotor stage six.

12. b. is the answer. (pp. 175–177)

13. d. is the answer. (p. 176)

a. & b. Hearing and deaf babies do not differ in the overall likelihood that they will babble.

c. Deaf babies begin to babble vocally several months later than hearing babies do.

14. b. is the answer. (p. 178)

a., c., & d. These views on language acquisition describe the theory offered by Noam Chomsky.

15. c. is the answer. (p. 169)

Matching Items

1. i (p. 173)   5. b (p. 172)   9. j (p. 172)
2. a (p. 161)   6. h (p. 174)   10. f (p. 179)
3. d (p. 167)   7. c (p. 170)
4. g (p. 180)   8. e (p. 177)

THINKING CRITICALLY ABOUT CHAPTER 6

1. d. is the answer. The baby is clearly behaving purposefully, the hallmark of goal-directed behavior. (p. 173)

a. There is nothing imaginary in the child's behavior.

b. An overextension occurs when the infant overgeneralizes the use of a word to an inappropriate object or context.

c. Delayed imitation is the ability to imitate actions seen in the past.

2. d. is the answer. (p. 180)

3. a. is the answer. (p. 169)

4. a. is the answer. The father's expression of delight is clearly a reinforcer in that it has increased the likelihood of the infant's vocalization. (p. 178)

b. & c. Modeling, or learning by imitation, would be implicated if the father attempted to increase the infant's vocalizations by repeatedly saying "da-da" himself, in the infant's presence.

d. This is Chomsky's viewpoint; Skinner maintained that language is acquired through learning.

5. d. is the answer. The child is clearly overgeneralizing the word "dog" by applying it to other animals. (p. 177)

a. The holophrase is a single word that is used to express a complete thought.

b. Babbling is the repetitious uttering of certain syllables, such as "ma-ma," or "da-da."

c. Motherese, or baby talk, is the characteristic manner in which adults change the structure and pitch of their speech when conversing with infants.

6. c. is the answer. (p. 178)

a. At 18 months of age, most children have much smaller vocabularies.

b. Speaking in holophrases is typical of younger infants.

7. d. is the answer. (p. 174)

a. Dynamic perception is perception primed to focus on movement and change.

b. Object permanence is the awareness that objects do not cease to exist when they are out of sight.

c. Affordances are the opportunities for perception and interaction that an object or place offers to any individual.

8. c. is the answer. (p. 173)

9. **d.** is the answer. (p. 177)

10. **a.** is the answer. Before object permanence is attained, an object that disappears from sight ceases to exist for the infant. (pp. 163–164)

    b. Deferred imitation is the ability to witness, remember, and later copy a particular behavior.

    c. Mental combinations are actions that are carried out mentally.

    d. Goal-directed behavior refers to purposeful actions initiated by infants in anticipation of events that will fulfill their needs and wishes.

11. **c.** is the answer. (p. 178)

    a. Because Christine is expressing a complete thought, her speech is much more than babbling.

    b. An overextension is the application of a word the child knows to an inappropriate context, such as "doggie" to all animals the child sees.

    d. The ability to understand subject-predicate order emerges later, when children begin forming 2-word sentences.

12. **b.** is the answer. (p. 176)

    a. Cooing is the pleasant-sounding utterances of the infant at about 2 months.

    c. The holophrase occurs later and refers to the toddler's use of a single word to express a complete thought.

    d. An overextension, or overgeneralization, is the application of a word to an inappropriate context, such as "doed" for the past tense of "do."

13. **b.** is the answer. In this example, the 2-year-old has overgeneralized the concept "doggie" to all four-legged animals. (p. 177)

14. **c.** is the answer. (pp. 164, 166)

    a. Mental combinations—sequences of actions that are carried out mentally—are a hallmark of Piaget's stage 4 infant.

    b. The stage of the little scientist is Piaget's way of describing the infant as he or she begins to experiment and be creative.

    d. Object permanence, or the awareness that objects do not cease to exist simply because they are not in view, is not based on perceiving similarities among objects.

15. **b.** is the answer. (p. 177)

    c. & d. Referential language focuses on labeling; expressive language focuses on social interaction.

KEY TERMS

1. **Affordances** are perceived opportunities fo interacting with objects or places in the environ ment. Infants perceive sucking, grasping, noise making, and many other affordances of objects a an early age. (p. 160)

2. **Graspability** is the perception of whether or nc an object is of the proper size, shape, texture, an distance to afford grasping or grabbing. (p. 161)

3. A **visual cliff** is an apparent (but not actual) dro between one surface and another. (p. 161)

4. **Dynamic perception** is perception that is prime to focus on movement and change. (p. 163)

5. **Object permanence** is the understanding tha objects continue to exist even when they canno be seen, touched, or heard. (p. 164)

6. **Infantile amnesia** is the inability, according t Freud, to remember events before age 2. (p. 167)

7. A **reminder session** involves the experiencing some aspect of an event that triggers the enti memory of the event. (p. 167)

8. **Deferred imitation** is the ability to witnes remember, and later copy a particular behavio (p. 168)

9. The **launching event** is a commonly used habit ation technique for studying infants' awarene of cause-and-effect relationships. (p. 170)

10. Piaget's stages of **sensorimotor intelligen** (from birth to about 2 years old) are based on h theory that infants think exclusively with the senses and motor skills. (p. 171)

11. **Goal-directed behavior** refers to purposeful a tions initiated by infants in anticipation of even that will fulfill their needs and wishes. (p. 173)

12. **"Little scientist"** is Piaget's term for the stag five toddler who learns about the properties objects in his or her world through active exper mentation. (p. 174)

13. In Piaget's theory, **mental combinations** a sequences of actions that are carried out mental Mental combinations enable stage-six toddlers begin to anticipate and solve problems witho resorting to trial-and-error experiments. (p. 174)

14. **Babbling**, which begins at 6 or 7 months, is cha acterized by the extended repetition of certa syllables (such as "ma-ma"). (p. 176)

15. An **underextension** of word meaning occurs when a baby applies a word more narrowly than its full meaning allows. (p. 177)

16. **Overextension** is a characteristic of infant speech in which the infant overgeneralizes a known word by applying it to a large variety of objects or contexts. (p. 177)

    Memory aid: In this behavior, the infant *extends* a word or grammatical rule beyond, or *over* and above, its normal boundaries.

17. Another characteristic of infant speech is the use of the **holophrase**, in which a single word is used to convey a complete thought. (p. 178)

18. According to Chomsky, children possess an innate **language acquisition device (LAD)** that enables them to acquire language, including the basic aspects of grammar. (p. 179)

19. **Baby talk** is a form of speech used by adults when talking to infants. Its hallmark is exaggerated expressiveness; it employs more questions, commands, and repetitions and fewer past tenses, pronouns, and complex sentences; it uses simpler vocabulary and grammar; it has a higher pitch and more low-to-high fluctuations. (p. 180)

7

The First Two Years: Psychosocial Development

Chapter Overview

Chapter 7 describes the emotional and social life of the developing person during the first two years. It begins with a description of the infant's emerging emotions and how they reflect increasing cognitive abilities. Newborns are innately predisposed to sociability, and capable of expressing distress, sadness, pleasure, and many other emotions, as well as responding to the emotions of other people. This section also explores the social context in which emotions develop. By referencing their caregivers' signals, infants learn when and how to express their emotions. As self-awareness develops, many new emotions emerge, including embarrassment, shame, guilt, and pride.

The second section presents the theories of Freud and Erikson that help us understand how the infant's emotional and behavioral responses begin to take on the various patterns that form personality. Important research on the nature and origins of temperament, which informs virtually every characteristic of the individual's developing personality, is also considered.

In the final section, emotions and relationships are examined from a different perspective—that of parent–infant interaction. Videotaped studies of parents and infants, combined with laboratory studies of attachment, have greatly expanded our understanding of psychosocial development.

NOTE: Answer guidelines for all Chapter 7 questions begin on page 113.

Guided Study

The text chapter should be studied one section at a time. Before you read, preview each section by skimming it, noting headings and boldface items. Then read the appropriate section objectives from the following outline. Keep these objectives in mind and, as you read the chapter section, search for the information that will enable you to meet each objective. Once you have finished a section, write out answers for its objectives.

Early Emotions (pp. 187–192)

1. Describe the basic emotions expressed by infants during the first days and months.

2. Describe the main developments in the emotional life of the child between 6 months and 2 years.

3. Discuss the concept of social referencing, noting the difference in how the infant interacts with mother and father.

Discuss the links between the infant's emerging self-awareness and its continuing emotional development.

9. Discuss the origins and development of temperament as an interaction of nature and nurture.

10. (Research Report) Identify the nine characteristics of temperament, and explain the significance of research on temperament for parents and caregivers.

e Origins of Personality (pp. 193–201)

Describe the evolution of learning theory with regard to personality development.

Describe Freud's psychosexual stages of infant development.

Interaction Again (pp. 202–213)

11. Describe the synchrony of parent–infant interaction during the first year, and discuss its significance for the developing person.

Describe Erikson's psychosocial stages of infant development.

12. Define attachment, explain how it is measured and how it is influenced by context, and discuss the long-term consequences of secure and insecure attachment.

(Changing Policy) Discuss concerns regarding day care, and identify the factors that define high-quality day care.

13. (Research Report) Describe four categories of adult attachments and how each affects the child's attachment to the parent.

Chapter Review

When you have finished reading the chapter, work through the material that follows to review it. Complete the sentences and answer the questions. As you proceed, evaluate your performance for each section by consulting the answers on page 114. Do not continue with the next section until you understand each answer. If you need to, review or reread the appropriate section in the textbook before continuing.

1. Developmentalists believe that infants _____ (are/are not) innately predisposed to sociability.

Early Emotions (pp. 187–192)

2. The first emotion that can be reliably discerned in infants is _____ . Other early infant emotions include _____ , _____ , and _____ .

3. The infant's smile in response to a human face or voice, which is called a _____ , begins to appear at about _____ of age. Full smiles are easy to elicit at _____ months.

4. Infant emotions become more differentiated and distinct sometime between _____ and _____ months of age. Infants begin to express anger by about _____ months. At this age, individual differences in the _____ and _____ with which emotions occur are also apparent.

5. Three universals that make the emotions of the older baby more selective and diverse are _____ maturation, growing _____ skills, and more varied _____ .

6. Stranger _____ is first noticeable about _____ of age.

7. An infant's fear of being left by the mother or other caregiver, called _____ _____ , emerges at about _____ months, peaks at about _____ months, and then graduall subsides. Whether separation distresses an infa depends on such factors as _____ .

8. As early as _____ months of age, infants associate _____ meanings with specific _____ expressions a with different tones of voice. For example, infa look to trusted adults for emotional cues in unc tain situations; this is called _____ _____ . This becomes increasingl important as the infant becomes more _____ .

9. Infants use their fathers for social reference _____ (less than/about the same as/more than) their mothers. Fathers tend to be more _____ , and mothers are mo _____ .

Briefly contrast how mothers and fathers tend to p with their infants.

10. The emerging sense of "me and mine" is part c what psychologists call _____ . This makes possible many new self-conscious emotions, including _____ , _____ , _____ , and _____ . This awareness emerges between _____ and _____ months.

riefly describe the nature and findings of the classic
uge-and-mirror experiment on self-awareness in
fants.

. Developing self-awareness also enhances the toddler's _____ reactions and emotion-
al responses such as _____ .
Furthermore, it allows the child to react to his or
her misdeeds with _____ at going
against another's wishes.

ue Origins of Personality (pp. 193–201)

. Personality is defined as _____

_____ .

. An early prevailing view among psychologists
was that the individual's personality was permanently molded by the actions of his or her
_____ . Two versions of this theory
were the _____ and
_____ theories.

. According to early learning theory, personality is
molded through the processes of
_____ and _____
of the child's various behaviors. A strong proponent of this position was _____ .

. Later theorists incorporated the role of
_____ learning, that is, infants' tendency to _____ the personality
traits of their parents. This form of learning is
strengthened by _____

_____ .

riefly explain how the kinds of signals caregivers
nd to toddlers influence their overall emotionality.

16. According to Freud, the experiences of the first
_____ years of life and the child's
relationship with his or her
_____ were decisive in personality
formation.

17. In Freud's theory, development begins with the
_____ stage, so named because the
_____ is the infant's prime source of
gratification and pleasure.

18. According to Freud, in the second year the prime
focus of gratification comes from stimulation and
control of the bowels. Freud referred to this period as the _____ stage. This stage
represents a shift in the way the infant interacts
with others, from the more _____ ,
_____ mode of orality to the more
_____ , _____ mode of
anality.

Describe Freud's ideas on the importance of early oral
experiences to later personality development.

19. Research has shown that the parents' overall pattern of _____
is more important to the child's emotional development than the particulars of feeding and wean-
ing or toilet training.

20. The theorist who believed that development
occurs through a series of psychosocial crises is
_____ . According to his theory, the
crisis of infancy is one of

_____ ,

whereas the crisis of toddlerhood is one of

_____ .

He maintained that experiences later in life

_____ (can alter/have little impact on) the effects of early experiences on personality development.

21. The traditional views of personality emphasize the importance of early _____ , particularly that provided by a child's

_____ .

22. (Changing Policy) According to Jay Belsky, extended infant day care _____ (is/is not) likely to result in negative developmental outcomes. Belsky admits, however—and other research has convincingly demonstrated—that when preschoolers experience early and extended amounts of high-quality day care, they show more _____ (positive/negative) outcomes than children without such experience.

23. (Changing Policy) Researchers have identified four factors that seem essential to high-quality day care:

    a. _____

    b. _____

    c. _____

    d. _____

24. (Changing Policy) A large-scale study of day care in the United States found that infants were likely to become insecurely attached only under three circumstances:

    a. _____

    b. _____

    c. _____

25. A person's inherent, relatively consistent, basic dispositions define his or her _____ . This overall makeup, which _____ (is/is not) evident at birth, begins in the _____ codes that guide the development of the brain and is affected by many prenatal experiences, including _____ _____ . However, as the person develops, the _____ _____ and the individual's _____ increasingly influence the

nature and expression of this trait. Thus, this makeup is _____ .

26. (Research Report) List the nine temperamental characteristics measured in the NYLS study:

    _____

    _____

27. (Research Report) Most young infants can be described as one of three types: _____ _____ _____ _____ _____ or _____ .

28. (Research Report) The "big five" dimensions of personality are _____ , _____ , _____ , _____ , and _____ .

29. (Research Report) Temperament is linked to _____ . This means that parents _____ (can/cannot) be blamed, or credited, for all their infants' actions.

(Research Report) Describe two ways in which the environment can influence a child's temperamental characteristics.

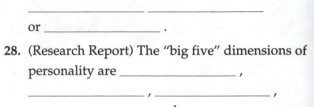

Interaction Again (pp. 202–213)

30. Although infants are social from birth, they are not necessarily socially _____ .

31. Infants under 3 months of age often become ups for reasons that have little to do with the _____ they receive. At this age, _____ (boys/girls) tend to be fussier than _____ (boys/girls).

32. Babies begin to respond especially to their prima ry caregivers by _____ months of age. At this time, caregivers begin to initiate focused episodes of _____-_____-_____ play.

3. The coordinated interaction of response between infant and caregiver is called _____ . Partly through this interaction, infants learn to _____ and _____ emotions.

escribe the social play behaviors of adults with fants.

.. Episodes of face-to-face play _____ (are/are not) a universal feature of early interaction with infants.

. Cultural variations in the _____ and _____ of social play, as well as the _____ of the adults who initiate face-to-face episodes, are common.

. (In Person) The signs of dyssynchrony include _____ _____ . The ease of synchrony is affected not only by the caregiver's personality but also by the infant's _____ and _____ .

. The emotional bond that develops between parents and infants is called _____ .

. Approaching, following, and climbing onto the caregiver's lap are signs of _____-_____ behaviors, while clinging and resisting being put down are signs of _____-_____ behaviors.

. An infant who derives comfort and confidence from the secure base provided by the caregiver is displaying _____ _____ . By contrast, _____ _____ is characterized by an infant's fear, anger, or seeming indifference to the caregiver.

40. The procedure developed by Ainsworth to measure attachment is called the _____ _____ . Approximately _____ (what proportion?) of all normal infants tested with this procedure demonstrate secure attachment.

(text and Table 7.1) Briefly describe three types of insecure attachment.

41. Among the features of caregiving that affect the quality of attachment are the following:

a. _____

b. _____

c. _____

42. Attachment may also be affected by the broader family context, including the quality of the _____'s involvement in child care, the _____ _____ and the _____ _____ _____ . It is also affected by _____ and by the infant's _____ .

43. Most infants _____ (do/ do not) show signs of attachment to other caregivers, such as fathers, siblings, and day-care workers.

44. By itself, a secure or insecure attachment in infancy _____ (determines/ does not determine) a child's later social relationships.

45. When a child's attachment is insecure, the parents _____ (are/are not) always to blame. Recent research studies have found that the child's temperament has a _____ (smaller/greater) impact on attachment than the parent's caregiving pattern.

46. (Research Report) Mary Main has found that adults can be classified into one of four categories of attachment: _____ adults, who value attachment relationships but can discuss them objectively; _____ adults, who devalue attachment; _____ adults, who dwell on past relationships; and _____ adults, who have not yet reconciled their past experiences with the present.

47. (Research Report) Autonomous mothers tend to have infants who are _____ attached, dismissing mothers tend to have _____ babies, and preoccupied mothers tend to have _____ infants. A recent study found that mothers who describe their own past attachment as _____ tend to express more joy in their infants, while mothers who are _____ of their past relationship tend to show anger toward their infants.

(Research Report) State several possible reasons for the link between adult and infant attachment.

Progress Test 1

Multiple-Choice Questions

Circle your answers to the following questions and check them with the answers on page 114. If your answer is incorrect, read the explanation for why it is incorrect and then consult the appropriate pages of the text (in parentheses following the correct answer).

1. One of the first emotions that can be discerned in infancy is:
   a. shame.   c. guilt.
   b. distress.   d. pride.

2. The social smile begins to appear:
   a. at about 6 weeks.
   b. at about 8 months.
   c. after stranger wariness has been overcome.
   d. after the infant has achieved a sense of self.

3. An infant's fear of being left by the mother other caregiver, called _____ , pea at about _____ .
   a. separation anxiety; 14 months
   b. stranger wariness; 8 months
   c. separation anxiety; 8 months
   d. stranger wariness; 14 months

4. Social referencing refers to:
   a. parenting skills that change over time.
   b. changes in community values regarding, f example, the acceptability of using physic punishment with small children.
   c. the support network for new parents provi ed by extended family members.
   d. the infant response of looking to trust adults for emotional cues in uncertain situ tions.

5. (Research Report) The "big five" personali dimensions are:
   a. emotional stability, openness, introversic sociability, locus of control
   b. neuroticism, extroversion, openness, emotio al stability, sensitivity
   c. agreeableness, conscientiousness, neuroticis openness, extroversion
   d. neuroticism, gregariousness, extroversion, i pulsiveness, sensitivity

6. Psychologists who favored the _____ p spective believed that the personality of the ch was virtually "created" through reinforceme and punishment.
   a. psychoanalytic   c. psychosocial
   b. learning   d. epigenetic

7. Freud's oral stage corresponds to Erikson's cri of:
   a. orality versus anality.
   b. trust versus mistrust.
   c. autonomy versus shame and doubt.
   d. secure versus insecure attachment.

8. Erikson felt that the development of a sense trust in early infancy depends on the quality the:
   a. infant's food.
   b. child's genetic inheritance.
   c. maternal relationship.
   d. introduction of toilet training.

Research studies demonstrate that the _____ is more influential than the _____ in determining the parent-child connection.

a. parent's caregiving pattern; child's temperament
b. child's temperament; parent's caregiving pattern
c. child's gender; child's age
d. parent's age; child's temperament

(Research Report) "Easy," "slow to warm up," and "difficult" are descriptions of different:

a. forms of attachment.
b. types of temperament.
c. types of parenting.
d. toddler responses to the Strange Situation.

The more physical play of fathers probably helps the children master motor skills and may contribute to the:

a. infant's self-awareness.
b. growth of the infant's social skills and emotional expression.
c. tendency of the infant to become securely attached.
d. infant's fear of strangers and separation anxiety.

Synchrony is a term that describes:

a. the carefully coordinated interaction between parent and infant.
b. a mismatch of the temperaments of parent and infant.
c. a research technique involving videotapes.
d. the concurrent evolution of different species.

The emotional tie that develops between an infant and his or her primary caregiver is called:

a. self-awareness.   c. affiliation.
b. synchrony.   d. attachment.

An important effect of secure attachment is the promotion of:

a. self-awareness.
b. curiosity and self-directed behavior.
c. dependency.
d. all of the above.

The sight of almost any human face is most likely to produce a smile in a _____-month-old.

a. 3   c. 9
b. 6   d. 12

True or False Items

Write T (*true*) or F (*false*) on the line in front of each statement.

_____ 1. Most developmentalists think that infants must learn to be sociable.
_____ 2. The major difference between a 6-month-old and a 12-month-old is that emotions become less intense.
_____ 3. A baby at 11 months is likely to display both stranger wariness and separation anxiety.
_____ 4. Emotional development is affected by cognitive development.
_____ 5. A securely attached toddler is most likely to stay close to his or her mother even in a familiar environment.
_____ 6. (Changing Policy) Current research shows that the majority of infants in day care are slow to develop cognitive and social skills.
_____ 7. Infants use their fathers for social referencing as much as they use their mothers.
_____ 8. Temperament is genetically determined and is unaffected by environmental factors.
_____ 9. Self-awareness enables toddlers to be self-critical and to feel guilt.
_____ 10. (Research Report) Adult attachment classifications parallel those of infancy.

Progress Test 2

Progress Test 2 should be completed during a final chapter review. Answer the following questions after you thoroughly understand the correct answers for the Chapter Review and Progress Test 1.

Multiple-Choice Questions

1. Infants give their first real smiles, called _____ , when they are about _____ of age.
   a. play smiles; 3 months
   b. play smiles; 6 weeks
   c. social smiles; 3 months
   d. social smiles; 6 weeks

2. Freud's anal stage corresponds to Erikson's crisis of:
   a. autonomy versus shame and doubt.
   b. trust versus mistrust.
   c. orality versus anality.
   d. identity versus role confusion.

3. Not until the sense of self begins to emerge do babies realize that they are seeing their own faces in the mirror. This realization usually occurs:
   a. shortly before 3 months.
   b. at about 6 months.
   c. between 15 and 24 months.
   d. after 24 months.

4. (Changing Policy) Infants placed in day care are most likely to become insecurely attached if they are in day care more than 20 hours a week, if the day care quality is poor, and if:
   a. their mothers are insensitive.
   b. they come from broken homes.
   c. they have a difficult temperament.
   d. their own parents were insecurely attached.

5. Emotions such as shame, guilt, embarrassment, and pride emerge at the same time that:
   a. the social smile appears.
   b. aspects of the infant's temperament can first be discerned.
   c. self-awareness begins to emerge.
   d. parents initiate toilet training.

6. (Research Report) The NYLS temperamental characteristics are not identical to the Big Five, but there are similarities, indicating that:
   a. temperament is probably innate.
   b. the interaction of parent and child determines later personality.
   c. parents pass their temperaments on to their children through modeling.
   d. self-awareness contributes to the development of temperament.

7. In the second six months, stranger wariness is a:
   a. result of insecure attachment.
   b. result of social isolation.
   c. normal emotional response.
   d. setback in emotional development.

8. (Research Report) The caregiving environment can affect a child's temperament through:
   a. the child's temperamental pattern and the demands of the home environment.
   b. parental expectations.
   c. both a. and b.
   d. neither a. nor b.

9. Compared to children who are insecurely attached, those who are securely attached are:
   a. more independent.
   b. more curious.
   c. more sociable.
   d. characterized by all of the above.

10. The later consequences of secure attachment a insecure attachment for children are:
    a. balanced by the child's current rearing cumstances.
    b. irreversible, regardless of the child's curr rearing circumstances.
    c. more significant in girls than in boys.
    d. more significant in boys than in girls.

11. Beginning at _____ of age, infa begin to associate emotional meaning with diff ent facial expressions of emotion.
    a. 3 months   c. 5 months
    b. 4 months   d. 6 months

12. Compared with mothers, fathers are more lik to:
    a. engage in noisier, more boisterous play.
    b. encourage intellectual development in th children.
    c. encourage social development in their c dren.
    d. read to their toddlers.

13. Unlike Freud, Erikson believed that:
    a. problems arising in early infancy can las lifetime.
    b. experiences later in life can alter the effect early experiences.
    c. the first two years of life are fraught w potential conflict.
    d. all of the above are true.

14. Which of the following most accurately summ rizes the relationship between early attachm and later social relationships?
    a. Attachment in infancy determines whethe child will grow to be sociable.
    b. Attachment relationships are sometin though rarely, altered as children grow old
    c. There is, at best, only a weak correlat between early attachment and later social r tionships.
    d. Early attachment biases, but does inevitably determine, later social relati ships.

15. (Research Report) In her research, Mary Main discovered that:
    a. adult attachment classifications parallel th of infancy.
    b. autonomous mothers tend to have insecu attached babies.
    c. preoccupied mothers tend to have avoid babies.
    d. all of the above are true.

Matching Items

Match each theorist, term, or concept with its corresponding description or definition.

Theorists, Terms, or Concepts

_____ 1. temperament
_____ 2. Erikson
_____ 3. the Strange Situation
_____ 4. synchrony
_____ 5. trust versus mistrust
_____ 6. Freud
_____ 7. social referencing
_____ 8. autonomy versus shame and doubt
_____ 9. self-awareness
_____ 10. Ainsworth
_____ 11. proximity-seeking behaviors
_____ 12. contact-maintaining behaviors

Descriptions or Definitions

a. looking to caregivers for emotional cues
b. the crisis of infancy
c. the crisis of toddlerhood
d. approaching, following, and climbing
e. theorist who described psychosexual stages of development
f. researcher who devised a laboratory procedure for studying attachment
g. laboratory procedure for studying attachment
h. the relatively consistent, basic dispositions inherent in a person
i. clinging and resisting being put down
j. coordinated interaction between parent and infant
k. theorist who described psychosocial stages of development
l. a person's sense of being distinct from others

Thinking Critically About Chapter 7

Answer these questions the day before an exam as a final check on your understanding of the chapter's terms and concepts.

1. In laboratory tests of attachment, when the mother returns to the playroom after a short absence, a securely attached infant is most likely to:
   a. cry and protest the mother's return.
   b. climb into the mother's lap, then leave to resume play.
   c. climb into the mother's lap and stay there.
   d. continue playing without acknowledging the mother.

2. After a scary fall, 18-month-old Miguel looks to his mother to see if he should cry or laugh. Miguel's behavior is an example of:
   a. proximity-seeking behavior.
   b. contact-maintaining behavior.
   c. insecure attachment.
   d. the crisis of trust versus mistrust.

3. Which of the following is a clear sign of an infant's attachment to a particular person?
   a. The infant turns to that person when distressed.
   b. The infant protests when that person leaves a room.
   c. The infant may cry when strangers appear.
   d. They are all signs of infant attachment.

4. (Research Report) If you had to predict a newborn baby's personality "type" solely on the basis of probability, which classification would be the most likely?
   a. easy
   b. slow-to-warm-up
   c. difficult
   d. There is not enough information to make a prediction.

5. (Research Report) Kenny becomes very emotional when talking about his relationship with his parents; consequently, he is unable to discuss his early attachment experiences objectively. Kenny's attachment classification is probably:
   a. autonomous.   c. preoccupied.
   b. dismissing.   d. unresolved.

6. (Research Report) Which of the following mothers is most likely to have an avoidant son or daughter?
   a. Claudia, who is still coping with the loss of her parents
   b. Kaleen, who idealizes her parents, yet devalues the importance of her own relationships
   c. Pearl, who is able to discuss her own early attachment experiences quite objectively, despite their painful nature
   d. Carmen, who spends a lot of time thinking about her own relationship with her parents

7. (Changing Policy) One way in which infant psychosocial development has changed is that today:
   a. many infants have their first encounters with other infants at a younger age.
   b. parental influence is less important than it was in the past.
   c. social norms are nearly the same for the sexes.
   d. infants tend to have fewer social encounters than in the past.

8. Mashiyat, who advocates epigenetic systems theory in explaining the origins of personality, points to research evidence that:
   a. infants are born with definite and distinct temperaments that can change.
   b. early temperamental traits almost never change.
   c. an infant's temperament does not begin to clearly emerge until 2 years of age.
   d. temperament appears to be almost completely unaffected by the social context.

9. Kalil's mother left him alone in the room for a few minutes. When she returned, Kalil seemed indifferent to her presence. According to Mary Ainsworth's research with children in the Strange Situation, Kalil is probably:
   a. a normal, independent infant.
   b. an abused child.
   c. insecurely attached.
   d. securely attached.

10. (Research Report) Connie and Lev, who are first-time parents, are concerned because their 1-month-old baby is difficult to care for and hard to soothe. They are worried that they are doing something wrong. You inform them that their child is probably that way because:
    a. they are reinforcing the child's tantrum behaviors.
    b. they are not meeting some biological need of the child's.
    c. of his or her inherited temperament.
    d. at 1 month of age all children are difficult to care for and hard to soothe.

11. Two-year-old Anita and her mother visit a day-care center. Seeing an interesting toy, Anita runs a few steps toward it, then stops and looks back to see if her mother is coming. Anita's behavior illustrates:
    a. the crisis of autonomy versus shame and doubt.
    b. synchrony.
    c. dyssynchrony.
    d. social referencing.

12. Felix has a biting, sarcastic manner. Freud wou probably say that Felix is:
    a. anally expulsive.
    b. anally retentive.
    c. fixated in the oral stage.
    d. experiencing the crisis of trust versus mi trust.

13. A researcher at the child development cent places a dot on an infant's nose and watches see if the infant reacts to her image in a mirror touching her nose. Evidently, the researcher testing the child's:
    a. attachment.
    b. temperament.
    c. self-awareness.
    d. social referencing.

14. Four-month-old Carl and his 13-month-old sist Carla are left in the care of a babysitter. As the parents are leaving, it is to be expected that:
    a. Carl will become extremely upset, while Ca will calmly accept her parents' departure.
    b. Carla will become more upset over her p ents' departure than will Carl.
    c. Carl and Carla will both become quite ups as their parents leave.
    d. Neither Carl nor Carla will become very ups as their parents leave.

15. You have been asked to give a presentation "Mother–Infant Attachment" to a group of expe tant mothers. Basing your presentation on t research of Mary Ainsworth, you conclude yo talk by stating that mother–infant attachme depends mostly on:
    a. an infant's innate temperament.
    b. the amount of time mothers spend with the infants.
    c. sensitive and responsive caregiving in t early months.
    d. whether the mother herself was secure attached as an infant.

Key Terms

Using your own words, write a brief definition explanation of each of the following terms on a sep rate piece of paper.

1. social smile
2. stranger wariness
3. separation anxiety
4. social referencing

5. self-awareness

6. personality

7. oral stage

8. anal stage

9. trust versus mistrust

10. autonomy versus shame and doubt

11. temperament

12. goodness of fit

13. synchrony

14. attachment

15. proximity-seeking behaviors

16. contact-maintaining behaviors

17. secure attachment

18. insecure attachment

19. Strange Situation

NSWERS

HAPTER REVIEW

1. are

2. distress; sadness; interest; pleasure

3. social smile; 6 weeks; 5

4. 6; 9; 7; intensity; speed

5. physical; cognitive; experiences

6. wariness; 6 months

7. separation anxiety; 8 or 9; 14; the baby's prior experiences with separation and the manner in which the caregiver departs

8. 5; emotional; facial; social referencing; mobile

9. about the same as; encouraging; protective

thers' play is more noisy, emotional, boisterous, hysical, and idiosyncratic. Mothers are more likely caress, sing soothingly, and to combine play with retaking activities.

10. self-awareness; embarrassment; guilt; shame; pride; 9; 15

the classic self-awareness experiment, babies look a mirror after a dot of rouge is put on their nose. If e babies react to the mirror image by touching their ose, it is clear they know they are seeing their own ce. Most babies demonstrate this self-awareness tween 15 and 24 months of age.

11. self-critical; shame; guilt

12. the emotions, behaviors, and attitudes that make an individual unique

13. parents; learning; psychoanalytic

14. reinforcement; punishment; John Watson

15. social; imitate; social referencing

If toddlers receive more signals of interest and encouragement than of fear and prohibition as they explore, they are likely to be friendlier and less aggressive. If an infant or toddler sees few signals of any kind, the child becomes relatively passive and emotionless.

16. 4; mother

17. oral; mouth

18. anal; passive; dependent; active; controlling

Freud believed that the oral and anal stages are fraught with potential conflict that can have long-term consequences for the infant. If nursing is a hurried or tense event, for example, the child may become fixated at the oral stage, excessively eating, drinking, smoking, or talking in quest of oral satisfaction.

19. warmth and sensitivity or coldness and domination

20. Erikson; trust versus mistrust; autonomy versus shame and doubt; can alter

21. nurture; mother

22. is; positive

23. (a) adequate attention to each child; (b) encouragement of sensorimotor exploration and language development; (c) attention to health and safety; (d) well-trained and professional caregivers.

24. (a) if their mothers were insensitive; (b) if the day-care quality was poor, (c) if they were in day care more than 20 hours per week

25. temperament; is; genetic; the nutrition and health of the mother; social context; experiences; epigenetic

26. activity level; rhythmicity; approach-withdrawal; adaptability; intensity of reaction; threshold of responsiveness; quality of mood; distractibility; attention span

27. easy; slow to warm up; difficult

28. extroversion; agreeableness; conscientiousness; neuroticism; openness

29. biological and neurological patterns that appear in the first month of life; cannot

One way is through the "goodness of fit" between the child's temperamental patterns and the demands of the home environment. Parents' expectations also can influence temperament.

30. competent

31. care; boys; girls

32. 2 to 3; face-to-face

33. synchrony; express; read

Adults tend to open their eyes and mouths wide in exaggerated expressions, make rapid clucking noises or repeated one-syllable sounds, raise and lower the pitch of their voice, change the pace of their movements, and imitate the infant's actions, for example.

34. are

35. frequency; duration; goals

36. the baby's averted eyes, stiffening or abrupt shifting of the body, and/or an unhappy noise; personality; predispositions

37. attachment

38. proximity-seeking; contact-maintaining

39. secure attachment; insecure attachment

40. Strange Situation; two-thirds

Some infants are avoidant: They engage in little interaction with their mother before and after her departure. Others are anxious and resistant: They cling nervously to their mother, are unwilling to explore, cry loudly when she leaves, and refuse to be comforted when she returns. Others are disorganized and/or disoriented: They show an inconsistent mixture of behavior toward the mother.

41. a.   general sensitivity to the infant's needs

    b.   responsiveness to the infant's specific signals

    c.   talking and playing with the infant in ways that actively encourage growth and development

42. father; marital relationship; overall social context; changes in family circumstances; temperament

43. do

44. does not determine

45. are not; greater

46. autonomous; dismissing; preoccupied; unresolved

47. securely; avoidant; resistant; autonomous; dismissing

(a) Parents who value attachment may be more sensitive to their offspring and inspire secure attachment as a result; (b) inherited temperament may predispose a certain attachment pattern across most relationships; (c) the nature of parents' attachment with their children may influence their memories of, and

attitudes about, other attachments; (d) some cultur[al] contexts may encourage attachments while others [do] not; (e) life experiences after infancy may have [an] impact.

PROGRESS TEST 1

Multiple-Choice Questions

1. **b.** is the answer. (p. 187)

    a., c., & d. These emotions emerge later in infan[cy], at about the same time as self-awaren[ess] emerges.

2. **a.** is the answer. (p. 188)

3. **a.** is the answer. (p. 188)

    b. & d. This fear, which is also called fear [of] strangers, peaks by 10 to 14 months.

4. **d.** is the answer. (p. 189)

5. **c.** is the answer. (pp. 200–201)

6. **b.** is the answer. (p. 193)

    a. Reinforcement and punishment have no pla[ce] in the psychoanalytic perspective.

    c. This is Erikson's theory, which sees develop[ment] as occurring through a series of basic crise[s].

    d. This perspective analyzes how genes and env[i]ronment contribute to development.

7. **b.** is the answer. (pp. 194, 195)

    a. Orality and anality refer to personality tra[its] that result from fixation in the oral and an[al] stages, respectively.

    c. According to Erikson, this is the crisis of to[d]dlerhood, which corresponds to Freud's an[al] stage.

    d. This is not a developmental crisis in Erikso[n's] theory.

8. **c.** is the answer. (p. 195)

9. **b.** is the answer. (p. 211)

    c. & d. Neither gender nor age (of child or paren[t]) was discussed as a factor in attachment.

10. **b.** is the answer. (p. 200)

    a. "Secure" and "insecure" are different forms [of] attachment.

    c. The chapter does not describe different types [of] parenting.

    d. The Strange Situation is a test of attachme[nt] rather than of temperament.

11. **b.** is the answer. (p. 190)

12. **a.** is the answer. (p. 203)

d. is the answer. (p. 206)

a. Self-awareness refers to the infant's developing sense of "me and mine."

b. Synchrony describes the coordinated interaction between infant and caregiver.

c. Affiliation describes the tendency of people at any age to seek the companionship of others.

b. is the answer. (p. 210)

a. The text does not link self-awareness to secure attachment.

c. On the contrary, secure attachment promotes *independence* in infants and children.

a. is the answer. (p. 188)

b., c., & d. As infants become older, they smile more selectively.

ue or False Items

F   Most developmentalists believe that infants are born with a tendency toward sociability as a means of survival. (p. 187)

F   Emotions become more intense and are manifested more quickly and more persistently. (p. 188)

T (p. 188)

T (p. 188)

F   A securely attached toddler is most likely to explore the environment, the mother's presence being enough to give him or her the courage to do so. (p. 207)

F   Jay Belsky and other researchers believe that high-quality day care is not likely to harm the child. In fact, it is thought to be beneficial to the development of cognitive and social skills. (p. 196)

T (p. 190)

F   Temperament is a product of both nature and nurture. (p. 199)

T (p. 192)

T (pp. 212–213)

OGRESS TEST 2

ltiple-Choice Questions

d. is the answer. (p. 188)

a. is the answer. (pp. 194, 195)

c. is the answer. (p. 192)

a. is the answer. (pp. 196–197)

c. is the answer. (pp. 191–192)

a. & b. The social smile, as well as temperamental characteristics, emerge well before the first signs of self-awareness.

d. Contemporary developmentalists link these emotions to self-consciousness, rather than any specific environmental event such as toilet training.

6. **a.** is the answer. (p. 201)

   b. & c. Although environment, especially parents, affects temperamental tendencies, the similarities point to a genetic component.

   d. Self-awareness is not a temperamental characteristic.

7. **c.** is the answer. (p. 188)

8. **c.** is the answer. (p. 201)

9. **d.** is the answer. (pp. 209–210)

10. **a.** is the answer. (p. 210)

    c. & d. The text does not suggest that the consequences of secure and insecure attachment differ in boys and girls.

11. **c.** is the answer. (p. 189)

12. **a.** is the answer. (p. 190)

13. **b.** is the answer. (p. 195)

    a. & c. Freud would have agreed with both of these statements.

14. **d.** is the answer. (p. 210)

15. **a.** is the answer. (p. 212)

    b. Autonomous mothers tend to have securely attached infants.

    c. Preoccupied mothers tend to have resistant infants.

Matching Items

1. h (p. 198)	5. b (p. 195)	9. l (p. 191)
2. k (p. 195)	6. e (p. 194)	10. f (p. 207)
3. g (p. 207)	7. a (p. 189)	11. d (p. 206)
4. j (p. 203)	8. c (p 195)	12. i (p. 206)

THINKING CRITICALLY ABOUT CHAPTER 7

1. **b.** is the answer. (pp. 207–208)

   a., c., & d. These responses are more typical of insecurely attached infants.

2. **b.** is the answer. (p. 206)

3. **d.** is the answer. (pp. 206–207)

4. **a.** is the answer. About 40 percent of young infants can be described as "easy." (p. 200)

   b. About 15 percent of infants are described as "slow to warm up."

   c. About 10 percent of infants are described as "difficult."

5. c. is the answer. (p. 212)

a. Autonomous adults are able to talk objectively about their own early attachments.

b. Dismissing adults devalue the importance of attachment relationships.

d. Unresolved adults have not yet reconciled their own early attachments.

6. b. is the answer. (p. 212)

a. Claudia would be classified as "unresolved."

c. Autonomous adults, such as Pearl, tend to have securely attached infants.

d. Preoccupied adults, such as Carmen, tend to have resistant offspring.

7. a. is the answer. (p. 196)

8. a. is the answer. (pp. 199)

b. Although temperament is genetic in origin, early temperamental traits *can* change.

c. Temperament is apparent shortly after birth.

d. As the person develops, the social context exerts a strong effect on temperament.

9. c. is the answer. (pp. 207–208)

a. & d. When their mothers return following an absence, securely attached infants usually re-establish social contact (with a smile or by climbing into their laps) and then resume playing.

b. There is no evidence in this example that Kalil is an abused child.

10. c. is the answer. (p. 200)

a. & b. There is no evidence in the question that the parents are reinforcing tantrum behavior or failing to meet some biological need of the child's.

d. On the contrary, about 40 percent of infants are "easy" in temperamental style.

11. d. is the answer. (p. 189)

a. According to Erikson, this is the crisis of toddlerhood.

b. This describes a moment of coordinated and mutually responsive interaction between a parent and an infant.

c. Dyssynchrony occurs when the coordinated pace and timing of a synchronous interaction are temporarily lost.

12. c. is the answer. (p. 195)

a. & b. In Freud's theory, a person who is fixated in the anal stage exhibits messiness and disorganization or compulsive neatness.

d. Erikson, rather than Freud, proposed crises of development.

13. c. is the answer. (pp. 191–192)

14. b. is the answer. The fear of being left by a caregiver (separation anxiety) emerges at about 8 or months, and peaks at about 14 months. For t reason, 4-month-old Carl can be expected to come less upset than his older sister. (p. 188)

15. c. is the answer. (pp. 208–209)

KEY TERMS

1. The **social smile**—a smile of pleasure in respo to a human face or voice—appears at abou weeks. (p. 188)

2. A common early fear, **stranger wariness** (a called fear of strangers) is first noticeable at ab 6 months. (p. 188)

3. **Separation anxiety**, which is the infant fear being left by the mother or other caregi emerges at about 8 or 9 months, peaks at abou months, and then gradually subsides. (p. 188)

4. When infants engage in **social referencing**, t are looking to trusted adults for emotional c on how to interpret uncertain situations. (p. 18

5. **Self-awareness** refers to a person's sense of h self or herself as being distinct from other pec that makes possible many new self-consci emotions, including shame, guilt, embarrassme and pride. (p. 191)

6. **Personality** refers to the emotions, behaviors, attitudes that make an individual unique. (p. 1

7. In Freud's first stage of psychosexual devel ment, the **oral stage**, the mouth is the most portant source of gratification for the inf (p. 194)

8. According to Freud, during the second y infants are in the **anal stage** of psychose development and derive sensual pleasure fr the stimulation of the bowels and psycholog pleasure from their control. (p. 194)

9. In Erikson's theory, the crisis of infancy is on **trust versus mistrust**, in which the infant lea whether the world is a secure place in wh basic needs will be met. (p. 195)

10. In Erikson's theory, the crisis of toddlerhoo one of **autonomy versus shame and doubt** which toddlers strive to rule their own acti and bodies. (p. 195)

11. **Temperament** refers to the set of innate tend cies, or dispositions, that underlie and affect e person's interactions with people, situations, events. (p. 198)

2. Goodness of fit is the match between the child's temperamental pattern and the demands of the environment. (p. 201)

3. Synchrony refers to the coordinated interaction between caregiver and infant that helps infants learn to express and read emotions. (p. 203)

4. Attachment is the enduring emotional tie that a person or animal forms with another. (p. 206)

5. Following, approaching, and other **proximity-seeking behaviors** are intended to place an individual close to another person to whom he or she is attached. (p. 206)

6. Clinging, resisting being put down, and other **contact-maintaining behaviors** are intended to keep a person near another person to whom he or she is attached. (p. 206)

17. A **secure attachment** is one in which the infant derives comfort and confidence from the "secure base" provided by a caregiver. (p. 207)

18. Insecure attachment is characterized by the infant's fear, anger, or seeming indifference toward the caregiver. (p. 207)

19. The **Strange Situation** is a laboratory procedure developed by Ainsworth for assessing attachment. Infants are observed in a playroom, in several successive episodes, while the caregiver (usually the mother) and a stranger move in and out of the room. (p. 207)

CHAPTER 8

The Play Years: Biosocial Development

Chapter Overview

Chapter 8 introduces the developing person between the ages of 2 and 6. This period is called the play years, emphasizing the central importance of play to the biosocial, cognitive, and psychosocial development of preschoolers.

The chapter begins by outlining the changes in size and shape that occur from ages 2 through 6. This is followed by a look at brain growth and development and its role in the development of physical and cognitive abilities. The Changing Policy box addresses the important issues of injury control and accidents, the major cause of childhood death in all but the most disease-ridden or war-torn countries. A description of the acquisition of gross and fine motor skills follows, noting that mastery of such skills develops steadily during the play years along with intellectual growth. The chapter concludes with an in-depth exploration of child maltreatment, including its prevalence, contributing factors, consequences for future development, treatment, and prevention.

NOTE: Answer guidelines for all Chapter 8 questions begin on page 128.

Guided Study

The text chapter should be studied one section at a time. Before you read, preview each section by skimming it, noting headings and boldface items. Then read the appropriate section objectives from the following outline. Keep these objectives in mind and, as you read the chapter section, search for the information that will enable you to meet each objective. Once you have finished a section, write out answers for its objectives.

Size and Shape (pp. 219–220)

1. Describe normal physical growth during the play years, and account for variations in height and weight.

2. (Research Report) Describe changes in eating habits during the preschool years.

Brain Growth and Development (pp. 221–227)

3. Discuss brain growth and development and effect on development during the play years.

4. Identify several factors that contribute to variation in the risk of accidental injury among children.

5. (Changing Policy) Explain what is meant by "injury control," and describe some measures that have significantly reduced accidental death rates for children.

6. Explain how the maturation of the visual pathways and cerebral hemispheres allows for formal education to begin at about age 6.

Mastering Motor Skills (pp. 227–230)

7. Distinguish between gross and fine motor skills, and discuss the development of each during the play years.

8. (In Person) Discuss the significance of drawing during the play years.

Child Maltreatment (pp. 230–242)

9. Identify the various categories of child maltreatment, and discuss several factors that contribute to its occurrence.

10. (text and A Life-Span View) Discuss the consequences of child maltreatment and the inevitability of intergenerational transmission of maltreatment.

11. Describe current efforts to treat child maltreatment, focusing on the concept of differential response.

12. Discuss foster care, kinship care, and adoption as intervention options in cases of child maltreatment.

13. Compare and contrast three approaches to the prevention of child maltreatment.

Chapter Review

When you have finished reading the chapter, work through the material that follows to review it. Complete the sentences and answer the questions. As you proceed, evaluate your performance for each section by consulting the answers on page 128. Do not continue with the next section until you understand each answer. If you need to, review or reread the appropriate section in the textbook before continuing.

Size and Shape (pp. 219–220)

1. During the preschool years, from age _____ to _____ , children add almost _____ in height and gain about _____ in weight per year. By age 6, the average child in a developed nation weighs about _____ and measures _____ in height.

2. The range of normal physical development is quite _____ (narrow/broad).

3. Of the many factors that influence height and weight, the most influential are the child's

_____ _____ ,
_____ _____ ,
and _____ .

4. The dramatic differences between physical development in developed and underdeveloped nations are largely due to differences in the average child's _____ .

5. In multiethnic countries, children of _____ descent tend to be tallest, followed by _____ , then _____ , and then _____ . The impact of _____ patterns on physical develop-

ment can be seen in families in South Asia and the Indian subcontinent, where _____ (which gender?) are more highly valued and consequently better fed than the other sex when food is scarce.

6. (Research Report) During the preschool years, annual height and weight gain is much _____ (greater/less) than during infancy. This means that children need _____ (fewer/more) calories per pound during this period.

7. (Research Report) The most prevalent nutritional problem in developed countries during the preschool years is _____ _____ _____ , the chief symptom of which is _____ _____ . This problem stems from a diet deficient in _____ _____ This problem is _____ (more/ less) common among low-income families than among others.

8. (Research Report) An additional problem for American children is that they, like most American adults, consume too much _____ and too much _____ .

Brain Growth and Development (pp. 221–227)

9. By age 5, the brain has attained about _____ percent of its adult weight; by age 7 it is _____ . In contrast, total body weight of the average 7-year-old is about _____ percent of that of the average adult.

10. Part of the brain's increase in size during childhood is due to the continued proliferation of _____ pathways and the ongoing process of _____ . In addition, there is notable expansion of brain areas dedicated to _____ and _____ , the _____ , and _____

processes. This helps children to develop
_____ reactions to stimuli and to be
able to control their reactions.

The band of nerve fibers that connects the right
and left sides of the brain, called the
_____ _____ ,
becomes thicker due to _____
growth and _____ . This helps children better coordinate functions that involve
_____ .

In all but the most disease-ridden or war-torn
countries of the world, the leading cause of childhood death is _____ .

The accident risk for particular children depends
on several factors, including their
_____ , _____
_____ , and _____ .

Injuries and accidental deaths are
_____ (more/less) frequent among
boys than girls.

The clearest risk factor in accident rates is
_____ _____ , with
_____ (high/low)-status children
being three times more likely than other children
to die an accidental death.. The impact of this factor is greatest during _____
_____ , when
_____ immaturity makes children
least able to understand danger.

(Changing Policy) Instead of "accident prevention," many experts speak of _____
_____ , an approach based on the
belief that most accidents _____
(are/are not) preventable.

(Changing Policy) Safety laws that include penalties for noncompliance seem to be even
_____ (less/more) effective than
educational measures in reducing injury rates.

(Changing Policy) The accidental death rate for
American children between the ages of 1 and 5
has _____ (increased/ decreased)
between 1980 and 1996.

19. Throughout the preschool years, the visual path-
    ways of the brain that are associated with control
    of _____ _____ and
    _____ undergo considerable
    growth. This, along with improved
    _____ between the left and right
    sides of the brain, enhances children's
    _____–_____
    coordination.

20. Brain growth during childhood
    _____ (is/is not) necessarily linear,
    sometimes occurring in _____
    and _____ .

21. Development of the corpus callosum and the
    frontal lobes of the brain as well as other qualita-
    tive changes in the brain at around age 5 facili-
    tates formal schooling, because children are now
    able to begin forming links between
    _____ and _____
    _____ .

Mastering Motor Skills (pp. 227–230)

22. Large body movements such as running, climb-
    ing, jumping, and throwing are called
    _____ _____ skills.
    These skills, which improve dramatically during
    the preschool years, require guided
    _____ , as well as a certain level of
    _____ _____ . Most
    children learn these skills _____ (by
    themselves/from parents).

23. Skills that involve small body movements, such
    as pouring liquids and cutting food, are called
    _____ _____ skills.
    Preschoolers have greater difficulty with these
    skills primarily because they have not developed
    the _____ control, patience, or
    _____ needed—in part because the
    _____ of the central nervous system
    is not complete.

24. (In person) Many developmentalists believe that
    _____ is a form of play that
    enhances the child's sense of accomplishment.

This form of play also provides a testing ground for another important skill, _____ . Mastery of this skill is related to overall _____ growth.

Child Maltreatment (pp. 230–242)

25. Until a few decades ago, the concept of child maltreatment was mostly limited to obvious _____ assault, which was thought to be the outburst of a mentally disturbed person. Today, it is known that most perpetrators of maltreatment _____ (are/are not) mentally ill.

26. Intentional harm to, or avoidable endangerment of, someone under age 18 defines child _____ . Actions that are deliberately harmful to a child's well-being are classified as _____ . A failure to act appropriately to meet a child's basic needs is classified as _____ .

27. Ideas about what constitutes child maltreatment vary with _____ and _____ norms.

28. Before a particular practice can be considered abusive, _____ and _____ must be taken into account.

29. Two aspects of the overall context that seem universally conducive to maltreatment are _____ and _____ . _____

Describe some of the deficits of children who have been maltreated.

30. (A Life-Span View) The phenomenon of maltreated children growing up to become abusive or neglectful parents themselves is called _____ _____ . A wide-ly held misconception is that this phenomenon _____ (is/is not) avoidable.

31. (A Life-Span View) Approximately _____ percent of abused children actually become abusive parents.

32. New laws requiring teachers, social workers, a other professionals to report possible maltreatment _____ (have/have not) resued in increased reporting. Out of their concern that reporting does not create enough protectic for a maltreated child, some experts advocate a policy of _____ _____ . This policy separates high risk cases that may require complete investigation and _____ of the child from low-risk cases that may require some sort of _____ measure.

33. Some children are officially removed from thei parents and placed in a _____ _____ arrangement with another adult or family who is paid to nurture them.

34. The process of finding a long-term solution to care of a child who has been abused is called _____ _____ .

35. The average length of stay in foster care in the United States has _____ (increased/decreased), and the number of chil dren needing foster placement has _____ (increased/decreased).

36. In another type of foster care, called _____ _____ , a rela tive of the maltreated child becomes the approved caregiver. A final option is _____ , which is ideal when fami lies are _____ and children are _____ .

37. Public policy measures and other efforts desig to prevent maltreatment from ever occurring a called _____ _____ An approach that focuses on spotting and trea ing the first symptoms of maltreatment is calle _____ _____ . A sp cific example of this approach occurs in countr

such as England and New Zealand, where

_____ _____ of families with young infants is routinely practiced. Last ditch measures such as removing a child from an abusive home, jailing the perpetrator, and so forth constitute _____

_____ .

rogress Test 1

ultiple-Choice Questions

ircle your answers to the following questions and eck them with the answers on page 128. If your swer is incorrect, read the explanation for why it is correct and then consult the appropriate pages of e text (in parentheses following the correct answer).

. (Research Report) During the preschool years, the most common nutritional problem in developed countries is:
   a. serious malnutrition.
   b. excessive intake of sweets.
   c. iron deficiency anemia.
   d. excessive caloric intake.

. The brain center for speech is usually located in the:
   a. right brain.
   b. left brain.
   c. corpus callosum.
   d. space just below the right ear.

. Which of the following is an example of tertiary prevention of child maltreatment?
   a. removing a child from an abusive home
   b. home visitation of families with infants by health professionals
   c. new laws establishing stiff penalties for child maltreatment
   d. public-policy measures aimed at creating stable neighborhoods

. (Changing Policy) Which of the following is *not* true regarding injury control?
   a. Broad-based television announcements do not have a direct impact on children's risk taking.
   b. Unless parents become involved, classroom safety education has little effect on children's actual behavior.
   c. Safety laws that include penalties are more effective than educational measures.
   d. Accidental deaths of 1- to 5-year-olds have held steady in the United States over the past two decades.

5. (Research Report) Like most Americans, children tend to have too much _____ in their diet.
   a. iron   c. sugar
   b. fat   d. b. and c.

6. Skills that involve large body movements, such as running and jumping, are called:
   a. activity-level skills.
   b. fine motor skills.
   c. gross motor skills.
   d. left-brain skills.

7. The brain's ongoing myelination during childhood helps children:
   a. control their actions more precisely.
   b. react more quickly to stimuli.
   c. focus more easily on printed letters.
   d. do all of the above.

8. The leading cause of death in childhood is:
   a. accidents.
   b. untreated diabetes.
   c. malnutrition.
   d. iron deficiency anemia.

9. At age 6, the proportions of a child's body:
   a. still retain the "top-heavy" look of infancy.
   b. are more adultlike in girls than in boys.
   c. are not very different from those of an adult.
   d. are influenced more by heredity than by health care or nutrition.

10. Which of the following factors is *most* responsible for differences in height and weight between children in developed and developing countries?
    a. the child's genetic background
    b. health care
    c. nutrition
    d. age of weaning

11. In which of the following age periods is serious malnutrition *least* likely to occur?
    a. infancy
    b. early childhood
    c. adolescence
    d. Serious malnutrition is equally likely in each of these age groups.

12. The relationship between accident rate and SES can be described as:
    a. a positive correlation.
    b. a negative correlation.
    c. curvilinear.
    d. no correlation.

13. Which of the following is true of the corpus callo-
    sum?
    a. It enables short-term memory.
    b. It connects the two halves of the brain.
    c. It must be fully myelinated before gross motor
       skills can be acquired.
    d. All of the above are correct.

14. Eye–hand coordination improves during the play
    years, in part because:
    a. the brain areas associated with this ability
       become more fully myelinated.
    b. the corpus callosum begins to function.
    c. fine motor skills have matured by age 2.
    d. gross motor skills have matured by age 2.

15. Adoption is most likely to be successful as an
    intervention for maltreatment when:
    a. children are young and biological families are
       inadequate.
    b. efforts at tertiary prevention have already
       failed.
    c. children have endured years of maltreatment
       in their biological family.
    d. foster care and kinship care have failed.

True or False Items

Write T (*true*) or F (*false*) on the line in front of each
statement.

_____ 1. Growth between ages 2 and 6 is more
            rapid than at any other period in the life
            span.

_____ 2. During childhood, the legs develop
            faster than any other part of the body.

_____ 3. For most people, the brain center for
            speech is located in the left hemisphere .

_____ 4. The health care, genetic background,
            and nutrition of the preschool child are
            major influences on growth.

_____ 5. Brain growth during childhood pro-
            ceeds in spurts and plateaus.

_____ 6. Fine motor skills are usually easier for
            preschoolers to master than are gross
            motor skills.

_____ 7. (Changing Policy) Most serious child-
            hood injuries truly are "accidents."

_____ 8. Children often fare as well in kinship
            care as they do in conventional foster
            care.

_____ 9. Concern for and protection of the well-
            being of children varies markedly from
            culture to culture.

_____ 10. Most child maltreatment does not
             involve serious physical abuse.

Progress Test 2

Progress Test 2 should be completed during a fir
chapter review. Answer the following questions aft
you thoroughly understand the correct answers f
the Chapter Review and Progress Test 1.

Multiple-Choice Questions

1. Each year from ages 2 to 6, the average chi
   gains and grows, respectively:
   a. 2 pounds and 1 inch.
   b. 3 pounds and 2 inches.
   c. 4 1/2 pounds and 3 inches.
   d. 6 pounds and 6 inches.

2. The center for perceiving various types of visu
   configurations is usually located in the brain's:
   a. right hemisphere.
   b. left hemisphere.
   c. right or left hemisphere.
   d. corpus callosum.

3. Which of the following best describes bra
   growth during childhood?
   a. It proceeds at a slow, steady, linear rate.
   b. The left hemisphere develops more rapid
      than the right.
   c. The right hemisphere develops more rapid
      than the left.
   d. It involves a nonlinear series of spurts a
      plateaus.

4. (In Person) The text notes that art provides
   important opportunity for the child to devel
   the skill of:
   a. realistic representation of objects.
   b. reading.
   c. perspective.
   d. self-correction.

5. Which of the following is an example of se
   ondary prevention of child maltreatment?
   a. removing a child from an abusive home
   b. jailing a maltreating parent
   c. home visitation of families with infants
      health professionals
   d. public-policy measures aimed at creating s
      ble neighborhoods

6. When parents or caregivers do not provide a
   quate food, shelter, attention, or supervision, it
   referred to as:
   a. abuse.   c. endangering.
   b. neglect.   d. maltreatment.

7. Which of the following is true of a developed nation in which many ethnic groups live together?
   a. Ethnic variations in height and weight disappear.
   b. Ethnic variations in stature persist, but are substantially smaller.
   c. Children of African descent tend to be tallest, followed by Europeans, Asians, and Latinos.
   d. Cultural patterns exert a stronger-than-normal impact on growth patterns.

8. Which of the following is *not* true regarding foster care?
   a. Foster children often have behavioral problems.
   b. The number of foster children in the United States is increasing.
   c. Most foster children become maltreating caregivers.
   d. The average stay in foster care has decreased.

9. Which of the following is an example of a fine motor skill?
   a. kicking a ball
   b. running
   c. drawing with a pencil
   d. jumping

10. Children who have been maltreated often:
   a. regard other children and adults as hostile and exploitative.
   b. are less friendly and more aggresssive.
   c. are more isolated than other children.
   d. are all of the above.

11. (Changing Policy) As a means of preventing childhood injuries, safety laws that include penalties:
   a. are less effective than educational programs in schools.
   b. are more effective in low-SES districts than in high-SES districts.
   c. are more effective in high-SES districts than in low-SES districts.
   d. are more effective than educational measures.

12. Most gross motor skills can be learned by healthy children by about age:
   a. 2.   c. 5.
   b. 3.   d. 7.

13. Two of the most important factors that affect height during the play years are:
   a. socioeconomic status and health care.
   b. gender and health care.
   c. heredity and nutrition.
   d. heredity and activity level.

14. (Changing Policy) Over the past two decades, the accidental death rate for American children between the ages of 1 and 5 has:
   a. decreased, largely as a result of new city, state, and federal safety laws.
   b. decreased, largely because parents are more knowledgeable about safety practices.
   c. increased.
   d. remained unchanged.

15. During the play years, because growth is slow, children's appetites seem _____ they were in the first two years of life.
   a. larger than
   b. smaller than
   c. about the same as
   d. erratic, sometimes smaller and sometimes larger than

Matching Items

Match each term or concept with its corresponding description or definition.

Terms or Concepts

_____ 1. corpus callosum
_____ 2. gross motor skills
_____ 3. fine motor skills
_____ 4. kinship care
_____ 5. foster care
_____ 6. injury control
_____ 7. right hemisphere
_____ 8. left hemisphere
_____ 9. abuse
_____ 10. neglect
_____ 11. primary prevention
_____ 12. secondary prevention
_____ 13. tertiary prevention

Descriptions or Definitions

a. brain area that is primarily responsible for pr cessing language
b. brain area that is primarily responsible for reco nizing visual shapes
c. legal placement of a child in the care of someo other than his or her biological parents
d. a form of care in which a relative of a maltreat child takes over from the biological parents
e. procedures to prevent child maltreatment fro ever occurring
f. running and jumping
g. actions that are deliberately harmful to a chil well-being
h. procedures for spotting and treating the ea warning signs of child maltreatment
i. painting a picture or tying shoelaces
j. failure to appropriately meet a child's basic nee
k. an approach emphasizing "accident" preventio
l. procedures to halt maltreatment that has alrea occurred
m. band of nerve fibers connecting the right and l hemispheres of the brain

Thinking Critically About Chapter 8

Answer these questions the day before an exam as a final check on your understanding of the chapter's terms and concepts.

1. An editorial in the local paper claims that there is no reason children younger than 6 cannot be taught basic literacy skills. You write to the editor, noting that:
   a. she has an accurate grasp of developmental processes.
   b. before age 6, brain myelination and development are too immature to enable children to form links between spoken and written language.
   c. although the right hemisphere is relatively mature at age 6, the left is not.
   d. although this may be true for girls, boys (who are slower to mature neurologically) would struggle.

2. (Research Report) Four-year-old Deon is tired all the time. On questioning Deon's mother, the pediatrician learns that Deon's diet is deficient in quality meats, whole grains, eggs, and dark green vegetables. The doctor believes that Deon may suffering from:
   a. malnutrition.
   b. protein anemia.
   c. iron deficiency anemia.
   d. an inherited fatigue disorder.

3. Following an automobile accident, Amira dev oped severe problems with her speech. Her do tor believes that the accident injured t _____ of her brain.
   a. left side
   b. right side
   c. communication pathways
   d. corpus callosum

4. Two-year-old Ali is quite clumsy, falls down f quently, and often bumps into stationary objec Ali most likely:
   a. has a neuromuscular disorder.
   b. has an underdeveloped right hemisphere the brain.
   c. is suffering from iron deficiency anemia.
   d. is a normal 2-year-old whose gross mo skills will improve dramatically during preschool years.

Climbing a fence is an example of a:

a. fine motor skill.
b. gross motor skill.
c. circular reaction.
d. launching event.

(Changing Policy) To prevent accidental death in childhood, some experts urge forethought and planning for safety and measures to limit the damage of such accidents as do occur. This approach is called:

a. protective analysis.
b. safety education.
c. injury control.
d. childproofing.

Recent research reveals that some children are poor readers because they have trouble connecting visual symbols, phonetic sounds, and verbal meanings. This occurs because:

a. their sugary diets make concentration more difficult.
b. the brain areas involved in reading have not become localized in the left hemisphere.
c. they use one side of the brain considerably more than the other.
d. their underdeveloped corpus callosums limit communication between the two brain hemispheres.

Which of the following activities would probably be the most difficult for a 5-year-old child?

a. climbing a ladder
b. catching a ball
c. throwing a ball
d. pouring juice from a pitcher without spilling it

Of the following children, the child with the greatest risk of accidental injury is:

a. 6-year-old Brandon, whose family lives below the poverty line.
b. 6-year-old Stacey, whose family lives below the poverty line.
c. 3-year-old Daniel, who comes from an affluent family.
d. 3-year-old Bonita, who comes from an affluent family.

Most child maltreatment:

a. does not involve serious physical abuse.
b. involves a rare outburst from the perpetrator.
c. involves a mentally ill perpetrator.
d. can be predicted from the victim's personality characteristics.

11. A mayoral candidate is calling for sweeping policy changes to help ensure the well-being of children by promoting home ownership, high-quality community centers, and more stable neighborhoods. If these measures are effective in reducing child maltreatment, they would be classified as:

a. primary prevention.
b. secondary prevention.
c. tertiary prevention.
d. differential response.

12. A factor that would figure very little into the development of fine motor skills, such as drawing and writing, is:

a. strength.
b. muscular control.
c. judgment.
d. short, fat fingers.

13. (A Life-Span View) Parents who were abused as children:

a. almost always abuse their children.
b. are more likely to neglect, but not necessarily abuse, their children.
c. are no more likely than anyone else to mistreat their children .
d. do none of the above.

14. Which aspect of brain development during the play years contributes *most* to enhancing communication among the brain's various specialized areas?

a. increasing brain weight
b. proliferation of dendrite networks
c. myelination
d. increasing specialization of brain areas

15. (Research Report) Three-year-old Kyle's parents are concerned because Kyle, who generally seems healthy, doesn't seem to have the hefty appetite or rate of growth he had as an infant. Should they be worried?

a. Yes, because both appetite and growth rate normally increase throughout the preschool years.
b. Yes, because appetite (but not necessarily growth rate) normally increases during the preschool years.
c. No, because growth rate (and hence caloric need) is less during the preschool years than during infancy.
d. There is not enough information to determine whether Kyle is developing normally.

Key Terms

Using your own words, write a brief definition or explanation of each of the following terms on a separate piece of paper.

1. myelination
2. corpus callosum
3. injury control
4. child maltreatment
5. abuse
6. neglect
7. intergenerational transmission
8. differential response
9. foster care
10. permanency planning
11. kinship care
12. primary prevention
13. secondary prevention
14. tertiary prevention

ANSWERS

CHAPTER REVIEW

1. 2; 6; 3 inches (7 centimeters); 4 1/2 pounds (2 kilograms); 46 pounds (21 kilograms); 46 inches (117 centimeters)
2. broad
3. genetic background; health care; nutrition
4. nutrition
5. African; Europeans; Asians; Latinos; cultural; boys
6. less; fewer
7. iron deficiency anemia; chronic fatigue; quality meats, whole grains, eggs, and dark green vegetables; more
8. sugar; fat
9. 90; full-grown; 33
10. communication; myelination; control; coordination; emotions; thinking; quicker
11. corpus callosum; dendrite; myelination; both sides of the brain and body
12. accidents
13. sex; socioeconomic status; neighborhood
14. more
15. socioeconomic status (SES); low; infancy and the play years; brain

16. injury control; are
17. more
18. decreased
19. eye movements; focusing; communicati eye–hand
20. is not; spurts; plateaus
21. spoken; written language
22. gross motor; practice; brain maturation; by the selves
23. fine motor; muscular; judgment; myelination
24. drawing; self-correction; intellectual
25. physical; are not
26. maltreatment; abuse; neglect
27. historical; cultural
28. customs; community standards
29. poverty; social isolation

Compared to well-cared-for children, chronica abused and neglected children are slower to ta underweight, less able to concentrate, and behind school. They also tend to regard others as hostile a exploitative, and so are less friendly, more aggressi and more isolated than other children. As adolesce and adults, they often engage in self-destruct and/or other destructive behaviors.

30. intergenerational transmission; is not
31. 30–40
32. have; differential response; removal; supportiv
33. foster care
34. permanency planning
35. decreased; increased
36. kinship care; adoption; inadequate; young
37. primary prevention; secondary prevention; ho visitation; tertiary prevention

PROGRESS TEST 1

Multiple-Choice Questions

1. **c.** is the answer. (p. 220)

   a. Serious malnutrition is much more likely occur in infancy or in adolescence than in ea childhood.

   b. Although an important health problem, eat too much candy or other sweets is not as seri as iron deficiency anemia.

   d. Since growth is slower during the presch years, children need fewer calories per pou during this period.

b. is the answer. (p. 227)

a. & d. The right brain is the location of areas associated with recognition of visual configurations.

c. The corpus callosum helps integrate the functioning of the two halves of the brain; it does not contain areas specialized for particular skills.

a. is the answer. (p. 241)

b. This is an example of secondary prevention.

c. & d. These are examples of primary prevention.

d. is the answer. Accident rates have *decreased* during this time period. (p. 225)

d. is the answer. (p. 220)

c. is the answer. (p. 227)

d. is the answer. (pp. 222, 226)

a. is the answer. (p. 223)

c. is the answer. (p. 219)

b. The proportions are more adultlike in both girls and boys.

d. Nutrition is a bigger factor in growth at this age than either heredity or health care.

c. is the answer. (p. 220)

b. is the answer. (p. 220)

b. is the answer. Children with *lower* SES have *higher* accident rates. (p. 226)

b. is the answer. (p. 223)

a. The corpus callosum is not directly involved in memory.

c. Myelination of the central nervous system is important to the mastery of *fine* motor skills.

a. is the answer. (p. 226)

b. The corpus callosum begins to function long before the play years.

c. & d. Neither fine nor gross motor skills have fully matured by age 2.

a. is the answer. (p. 239)

b. Removing a child from an abusive home is itself a form of tertiary prevention.

c. Such children tend to fare better in group homes.

d. Although adoption is the final option, children who have been unable to thrive in foster care or kinship care will probably not thrive in an adoptive home either.

ue or False Items

F   Growth actually slows down during the play years. (p. 219)

2. F   During childhood, the brain develops faster than any other part of the body. (p. 222)

3. T (p. 227)

4. T (p. 219)

5. T (p. 227)

6. F Fine motor skills are more difficult for preschoolers to master than are gross motor skills. (p. 228)

7. F   Most serious accidents involve someone's lack of forethought. (p. 224)

8. T (p. 239)

9. T (pp. 232–233)

10. T (p. 231)

PROGRESS TEST 2

Multiple-Choice Questions

1. **c.** is the answer. (p. 219)

2. **a.** is the answer. (p. 227)

   b. & c. The left hemisphere of the brain contains areas associated with language development.

   d. The corpus callosum does not contain areas for specific behaviors.

3. **d.** is the answer. (p. 227)

   b. & c. The left and right hemispheres develop at similar rates.

4. **d.** is the answer. (p. 229)

5. **c.** is the answer. (p. 240)

   a. & b. These are examples of tertiary prevention.

   d. This is an example of primary prevention.

6. **b.** is the answer. (p. 231)

   a. Abuse is deliberate, harsh injury to the body.

   c. Endangerment was not discussed.

   d. Maltreatment is too broad a term.

7. **c.** is the answer. (p. 221)

8. **c.** is the answer. Foster children often become good, nonmaltreating caregivers. (p. 238)

9. **c.** is the answer. (pp. 228, 230)

   a., b., & d. These are gross motor skills.

10. **d.** is the answer. (p. 244)

11. **d.** is the answer. (p. 225)

    b. & c. The effectiveness of safety laws does not vary with SES.

12. **c.** is the answer. (p. 228)

13. **c.** is the answer. (p. 219)

14. a. is the answer. (p. 225)

b. Although safety education is important, the decrease in accident rate is largely the result of new safety laws.

15. b. is the answer. (p. 220)

Matching Items

1. m (p. 223)	**6.** k (p. 226)	**11.** e (p. 240)
2. f (p. 227)	**7.** b (p. 223)	**12.** h (p. 240)
3. i (p. 228)	**8.** a (p. 223)	**13.** l (p. 241)
4. d (p. 238)	**9.** g (p. 231)	
5. c (p. 234)	**10.** j (p. 231)	

THINKING CRITICALLY ABOUT CHAPTER 8

1. b. is the answer. (p. 227)

2. c. is the answer. Chronic fatigue is the major symptom of iron deficiency anemia, which is caused by a diet deficient in quality meats, whole grains, eggs, and dark green vegetables and is the most prevalent nutritional deficiency in developed countries. (p. 220)

3. a. is the answer. In most people, the left hemisphere of the brain contains centers for language, including speech. (p. 227)

4. d. is the answer. (pp. 227–228)

5. b. is the answer. (p. 227)

a. Fine motor skills involve small body movements, such as the hand movements used in painting.

c. & d. These events were not discussed in this chapter.

6. c. is the answer. (p. 224)

7. c. is the answer. Analysis of the brain's electrical activity reveals that areas in both halves of the brain are involved in reading. (p. 227)

8. d. is the answer. (pp. 228–229)

a., b., & c. Preschoolers find these gross motor skills easier to perform than fine motor skills such as that described in d.

9. a. The strongest risk factor in accidental injuries is low SES. (p. 226)

b. & d. Boys, as a group, suffer more injuries than girls do.

10. a. is the answer. (p. 231)

11. a. is the answer. (p. 240)

b. Had the candidate called for measures to spot the early warning signs of maltreatment, this answer would be true.

c. Had the candidate called for jailing those who maltreat children or providing greater counseling and health care for victims, this answer would be true.

d. Differential response is not an approach to prevention of maltreatment; rather, it refers to separate reporting procedures for high- and low-risk families.

12. a. is the answer. Strength is a more important factor in the development of gross motor skills. (p. 230)

13. d. is the answer. Approximately 30 percent of adults who were abused as children themselves become abusive parents. (p. 235)

14. b. is the answer. (p. 222)

15. c. is the answer. (p. 220)

KEY TERMS

1. Myelination is the insulating process that speeds up the transmission of neural impulses. (p. 222)

2. The corpus callosum is a band of nerve fibers that connects the right and left hemispheres of the brain. (p. 223)

3. Injury control is the practice of limiting the extent of injuries by planning ahead, controlling the circumstances, preventing certain dangerous activities, and adding safety features to others. (p. 226)

4. Child maltreatment is intentional harm to, or avoidable endangerment of, anyone under age 18. (p. 231)

5. Abuse refers to deliberate actions that are harmful to a child's well-being. (p. 231)

6. Neglect refers to failure to appropriately meet a child's basic needs. (p. 231)

7. Intergenerational transmission is the assumption that mistreated children grow up to become abusive or neglectful parents themselves. (p. 231)

8. Differential response refers to separating child maltreatment reports into two categories: high-risk cases that require immediate investigation and possible removal of the child, and low-risk cases that require supportive measures to encourage better parental care. (p. 236)

9. Foster care is a legally sanctioned, publicly supported arrangement in which children are removed from their biological parents and temporarily given to another adult to nurture. (p. 238)

0. **Permanency planning** is the process of finding a long-term solution to the care of a child who has been abused. (p. 238)

1. **Kinship care** is a form of foster care in which a relative of a maltreated child becomes the child's legal caregiver. (p. 238)

2. **Primary prevention** refers to public policy measures designed to prevent child maltreatment (or other harm) from ever occurring. (p. 240)

3. **Secondary prevention** involves home visitation and other efforts to spot and treat the early warn- ing signs of maltreatment before problems become severe. (p. 240)

14. **Tertiary prevention** involves efforts to stop child maltreatment after it occurs and to treat the victim. Removing a child from an abusive home, jailing the perpetrator, and providing health care to the victim are examples of tertiary prevention. (p. 241)

CHAPTER 9

The Play Years: Cognitive Development

Chapter Overview

In countless everyday instances, as well as in the findings of numerous research studies, young children reveal themselves to be remarkably thoughtful, insightful, and perceptive thinkers whose grasp of the causes of everyday events, memory of the past, and mastery of language is sometimes astonishing. Chapter 9 begins by comparing Piaget's and Vygotsky's views of cognitive development at this age. According to Piaget, young children's thought is prelogical: between the ages of 2 and 6, they are unable to perform many logical operations and are limited by irreversible, centered, and static thinking. Lev Vygotsky, a contemporary of Piaget's, saw learning as a social activity more than as a matter of individual discovery. Vygotsky focused on the child's "zone of proximal development" and the relationship between language and thought.

The chapter next focuses on what preschoolers can do, including their competence in storing and retrieving memories, and theorizing about the world. This leads into a description of language development during the play years. Although young children demonstrate rapid improvement in vocabulary and grammar, they have difficulty with abstractions, metaphorical speech, and certain rules of grammar. The chapter concludes with a discussion of preschool education, including a description of "quality" preschool programs and an evaluation of their lifelong impact on children.

NOTE: Answer guidelines for all Chapter 9 questions begin on page 142.

Guided Study

The text chapter should be studied one section at a time. Before you read, preview each section by skimming it, noting headings and boldface items. Then read the appropriate section objectives from the following outline. Keep these objectives in mind and, as you read the chapter section, search for the information that will enable you to meet each objective. Once you have finished a section, write out answers for its objectives.

In Theory: How Young Children Think (pp. 245–253)

1. Describe and discuss the major characteristics of preoperational thought, according to Piaget.

2. Discuss Vygotsky's views on cognitive development, focusing on the concept of guided participation.

Explain the significance of the zone of proximal development and scaffolding in promoting cognitive growth.

Describe Vygotsky's view of the role of language in cognitive growth.

(Research Report) Compare and contrast the theories of Piaget and Vygotsky and explain why findings have led to qualification or revision of their description of cognition during the play years.

Fact: What Children Think (pp. 253–259)

Discuss young children's memory abilities and limitations, noting the role of meaning in their ability to recall events.

(Changing Policy) Discuss the reliability of children's eyewitness testimony.

8. Explain the typical young child's theory of mind, noting how it is affected by cultural context, and relate it to the child's developing ability to understand pretense.

Language (pp. 259–264)

9. (text and A Life-Span View) Describe the development of vocabulary in children, and explain the role of fast mapping in this process.

10. Describe the development of grammar during the play years and discuss limitations in the young child's language abilities.

Preschool Education (pp. 264–268)

11. Identify the characteristics of a high-quality preschool program, and discuss the long-term benefits of preschool education for the child and his or her family.

Chapter Review

When you have finished reading the chapter, work through the material that follows to review it. Complete the sentences and answer the questions. As you proceed, evaluate your performance for each section by consulting the answers on page 142. Do not continue with the next section until you understand each answer. If you need to, review or reread the appropriate section in the textbook before continuing.

In Theory: How Young Children Think (pp. 245–253)

1. For many years, researchers maintained that young children's thinking abilities were sorely limited by their _____ .

2. According to Piaget, the most striking difference between cognition during infancy and the preschool years is _____ _____ . He referred to cognitive development between the ages of 2 and 6 as _____ thought.

3. Young children's tendency to think about one aspect of a situation at a time is called _____ . One particular form of this characteristic is children's tendency to contemplate the world exclusively from their personal perspective, which is referred to as _____ . They also tend to focus on _____ to the exclusion of other attributes of objects and people.

4. Preschoolers' understanding of the world tends to be _____ (static/dynamic), which means that they tend to think of their world as _____ . A closely related characteristic is _____ —the inability to recognize that reversing a process will restore the original conditions from which the process began.

5. The idea that amount is unaffected by changes in shape or configuration is called _____ . In the case of _____ _____ , preschoolers who are shown pairs of checkers in two even rows and who then observe one row being spaced out will say that the spaced-out row has more checkers.

6. The idea that children are "apprentices in thinking" emphasizes that children's intellectual growth is stimulated by their _____ in _____ experiences of their environment. The critical element in this process is that the mentor and the child _____ to accomplish a task.

7. Much of the research from the sociocultural perspective on the young child's emerging cognition is inspired by the Russian psychologist _____ .

8. Unlike Piaget, this psychologist believed that cognitive growth is a _____ _____ more than a matter of individual discovery.

9. Vygotsky suggested that for each developing individual there is a _____ _____ _____ , a range of skills that the person can exercise with assistance but is not yet able to perform independently.

10. How and when new skills are developed depends, in part, on the willingness of tutors to _____ the child's participation in learning encounters.

11. Vygotsky believed that language is essential to the advancement of thinking in two crucial ways. The first is through the internal dialogue in which a person talks to himself or herself, called _____ _____ . In preschoolers, this dialogue is likely to be _____ (expressed silently/uttered aloud).

12. According to Vygotsky, another way language advances thinking is as the _____ of social interaction.

13. (Research Report) Piaget believed that it is _____ (possible/impossible) for preoperational children to grasp logical reasoning processes. It is now clear that with special training, preschoolers can succeed at some tests of _____ .

. (Research Report) Vygotsky would have placed the blame for preschoolers' difficulty mastering conservation squarely in the child's _____ context. According to his view, the presence of a _____ adult, who uses an _____ game to measure this ability, can elicit such thinking years before age 6. However, a responsive adult _____ (is/is not) always available, and children _____ (are/are not) always interested in learning what adults want to teach.

Fact: What Children Think (pp. 253–259)

. Preschoolers are notorious for having a poor _____ . This shortcoming is due to the fact that they have not yet acquired skills for deliberate _____ and efficient _____ of information.

. One way in which preschoolers are quite capable of storing in mind a representation of past events is by retaining _____ of familiar, recurrent past experiences. These devices reflect an awareness of the correct _____ and causal _____ of remembered events.

. A study compared preschoolers' memory of Disney World in response to a series of focused questions. The results showed that age _____ (did/did not) significantly affect the amount of information the children remembered when they were asked specific questions.

. The "Disney World" study strongly suggests that even very young preschoolers can recall a great deal of information when they are given appropriate cues, such as _____ and when the material is _____ to them.

. (Changing Policy) Until quite recently, young children in most countries _____ (were/were not) prohibited from providing courtroom testimony.

. (Changing Policy) Research has found that, par-ticularly for young children, the _____ context in which children considered to be eyewitnesses are questioned is an important factor in the accuracy of their memory. Specifically, the _____ of the child to the questioner, the _____ of the questioner, and the _____ of the interview have a substantial influence on the child's testimony.

21. (Changing Policy) Research demonstrates that the great majority of children when questioned as eyewitnesses _____ (resist/fail to resist) suggestive questioning.

22. As a result of their experiences with others, young children acquire a _____ _____ _____ that reflects their developing concepts about human mental processes.

Describe the young child's theory of mind by age 3 or 4.

23. Most 3-year-olds _____ (have/do not have) difficulty realizing that a belief can be false.

24. Research studies reveal that theory-of-mind development depends as much on general _____ ability as it does on _____ _____ . A third helpful factor is having at least one _____ . Finally, _____ may be a factor.

Language (pp. 259–264)

25. During the preschool years, a dramatic increase in language occurs, with _____ increasing exponentially.

26. Through the process called _____ _____ preschoolers often learn words after only one or two hearings.

27. Abstract nouns, metaphors, and analogies are _____ (more/no more) difficult for preschoolers to understand.

28. Because preschool children tend to think in absolute terms, they have difficulty with words that express _____ , as well as words expressing relativities of _____ and _____ .

29. The structures, techniques, and rules that a language uses to communicate meaning define its _____ . By age _____ , children typically demonstrate extensive understanding of this aspect of language.

30. Children's understanding of grammar is also facilitated by _____ and by _____ .

31. Most North American children have trouble with the _____ voice. Rather than brain maturation, as researchers once believed, it is _____ that is responsible for this limitation.

32. Preschoolers' tendency to apply rules of grammar when they should not is called _____ .

Give several examples of this tendency.

33. During the preschool years, children are able to comprehend _____ (more/less) complex grammar and vocabulary than they can produce.

Preschool Education (pp. 264–268)

List several characteristics of a high-quality preschool program.

34. Japanese culture places great emphasis on _____ _____ and _____ . Reflecting this emphasis, Japanese preschools provide training in the behavior and attitudes appropriate for _____ _____ . In contrast, preschools in the United States are often designed to foster _____ and _____ .

35. In 1965, _____ _____ _____ was inaugurated to give low-income children some form of compensatory education during the preschool years. Longitudinal research found that, as they made their way through elementary school, graduates of this program scored _____ (higher/no higher) on achievement tests and had more positive school report cards than their non–Headstart counterparts.

Progress Test 1

Multiple-Choice Questions

Circle your answers to the following questions and check them with the answers on page 142. If your answer is incorrect, read the explanation for why it is incorrect and then consult the appropriate pages of the text (in parentheses following the correct answer).

1. Piaget believed that children are in the preoperational stage from ages:
   a. 6 months to 1 year.   c. 2 to 6 years.
   b. 1 to 3 years.   d. 5 to 11 years.

2. Compared with children in other developed countries, _____ children in the United States attend preschool.

   a. fewer
   b. about the same number of
   c. a slightly higher percentage of
   d. a significantly higher percentage of

3. (Changing Policy) When questioned as eyewitnesses to an event, most young children:

   a. are unable to resist suggestive questioning.
   b. are able to resist suggestive questioning.
   c. provide very inaccurate answers.
   d. have reliable short-term memories, but very unreliable long-term memories.

4. The typical script of a 4-year-old:

   a. has a beginning and an end.
   b. fails to recognize the causal flow of events.
   c. pertains only to the most familiar routines.
   d. is very difficult to follow for most adults.

5. Preschoolers' poor performance on memory tests is primarily due to:

   a. their tendency to rely too extensively on scripts.
   b. their lack of efficient storage and retrieval skills.
   c. the incomplete myelination of cortical neurons.
   d. their short attention span.

6. The vocabulary of preschool children consists primarily of:

   a. metaphors.
   b. self-created words.
   c. abstract nouns.
   d. verbs and concrete nouns.

7. Preschoolers sometimes apply the rules of grammar even when they shouldn't. This tendency is called:

   a. overregularization.   c. practical usage.
   b. literal language.   d. single-mindedness.

8. The Russian psychologist Vygotsky emphasized that:

   a. language helps children form ideas.
   b. children form concepts first, then find words to express them.
   c. language and other cognitive developments are unrelated at this stage.
   d. preschoolers learn language only for egocentric purposes.

9. Private speech can be described as:

   a. a way of formulating ideas to oneself.
   b. fantasy.
   c. an early learning difficulty.
   d. the beginnings of deception.

10. The child who has not yet grasped the principle of conservation is likely to:

    a. insist that a tall, narrow glass contains more liquid than a short, wide glass, even though both glasses actually contain the same amount.
    b. be incapable of egocentric thought.
    c. be unable to reverse an event.
    d. do all of the above.

11. In later life, Head Start graduates showed:

    a. better report cards, but more behavioral problems.
    b. significantly higher IQ scores.
    c. higher scores on achievement tests.
    d. alienation from their original neighborhoods and families.

12. The best preschool programs are generally those that provide the greatest amount of:

    a. behavioral control.
    b. adult-child conversation.
    c. instruction in conservation and other logical principles.
    d. demonstration of toys by professionals.

13. Compared with their rate of speech development, children's understanding of language develops:

    a. more slowly.
    b. at about the same pace.
    c. more rapidly.
    d. more rapidly in some cultures than in others.

14. (Research Report) Relatively recent experiments have demonstrated that preschoolers *can* succeed at tests of conservation when:

    a. they are allowed to work cooperatively with other children.
    b. the test is presented as a competition.
    c. the children are informed that they are being observed by their parents.
    d. the test is presented in a simple, gamelike way.

15. Through the process called fast mapping, children:
    a. immediately assimilate new words by connecting them through their assumed meaning to categories of words they have already mastered.
    b. acquire the concept of conservation at an earlier age than Piaget believed.
    c. are able to move beyond egocentric thinking.
    d. become skilled in the practical use of language.

True or False Items

Write T (true) or F (false) on the line in front of each statement.

_____ 1. (Research Report) Piaget's description of cognitive development in early childhood has been universally rejected by contemporary developmentalists.

_____ 2. In conservation problems, many preschoolers are unable to understand the transformation because they focus exclusively on appearances.

_____ 3. Preschoolers who use private speech have slower cognitive growth than those who do not.

_____ 4. (Research Report) Whether or not a preschooler demonstrates conservation in an experiment depends in part on the conditions of the experiment.

_____ 5. Preoperational children tend to focus on one aspect of a situation to the exclusion of all others.

_____ 6. Piaget believed that preschoolers' acquisition of language makes possible their cognitive development.

_____ 7. With the beginning of preoperational thought, most preschoolers can understand abstract words.

_____ 8. A preschooler who says "You comed up and hurted me" is demonstrating a lack of understanding of English grammar.

_____ 9. Successful preschool programs generally have a low teacher-to-child ratio.

_____ 10. Vygotsky believed that cognitive growth is largely a social activity.

Progress Test 2

Progress Test 2 should be completed during a final chapter review. Answer the following questions after you thoroughly understand the correct answers for the Chapter Review and Progress Test 1.

Multiple-Choice Questions

1. (Changing Policy) When children are required t give eyewitness testimony:
    a. they should be interviewed by a neutral pro fessional.
    b. they should be interviewed by a famil member.
    c. the atmosphere of the interview should b fairly intense, to impress upon them th importance of their answers.
    d. both b. and c. should be done.

2. In one study, 3- and 4-year-old children wer interviewed after visiting Disney World. Th results demonstrated that:
    a. age did not significantly affect the amount information children remembered.
    b. the children provided much more informatic in response to open-ended questions tha they did to directive questions.
    c. older children recalled less information spo taneously than did younger children.
    d. all of the above were true.

3. A preschooler who focuses his or her attention c only one feature of a situation is demonstrating characteristic of preoperational thought called:
    a. centration.   c. reversibility.
    b. overregularization.   d. egocentrism.

4. One characteristic of preoperational thought is:
    a. the ability to categorize objects.
    b. the ability to count in multiples of 5.
    c. the inability to perform logical operations.
    d. difficulty adjusting to changes in routine.

5. The zone of proximal development represen the:
    a. skills or knowledge that are within the pote tial of the learner but are not yet mastered.
    b. influence of a child's peers on cognitive deve opment.
    c. explosive period of language developme during the play years.
    d. normal variations in children's language pr ficiency.

6. According to Vygotsky, language advances thin ing through private speech, and by:
    a. helping children to privately review wh they know.
    b. helping children explain events to themselve
    c. serving as a mediator of the social interacti that is a vital part of learning.
    d. facilitating the process of fast mapping.

. Irreversibility refers to the:
   a. inability to understand that other people view the world from a different perspective than one's own.
   b. inability to think about more than one idea at a time.
   c. failure to understand that changing the arrangement of a group of objects doesn't change their number.
   d. failure to understand that undoing a process will restore the original conditions.

. According to Piaget:
   a. it is impossible for preoperational children to grasp the concept of conservation, no matter how carefully it is explained.
   b. preschoolers fail to solve conservation problems because they center their attention on the transformation that has occurred and ignore the changed appearances of the objects.
   c. with special training, even preoperational children are able to grasp some aspects of conservation.
   d. preschoolers fail to solve conservation problems because they have no theory of mind.

. Scaffolding of a child's cognitive skills can be provided by:
   a. a mentor.
   b. the objects or experiences of a culture.
   c. the child's past learning.
   d. all of the above.

. Which theorist would be most likely to agree with the statement, "Learning is a social activity more than it is a matter of individual discovery"?
   a. Piaget   c. both a. and b.
   b. Vygotsky   d. neither a. nor b.

Children first demonstrate some understanding of grammar:
   a. as soon as the first words are produced.

   b. once they begin to use language for practical purposes.
   c. through the process called fast mapping.
   d. in their earliest two-word sentences.

12. Preschoolers sometimes seem forgetful because they:
   a. are unable to benefit from using mental scripts.
   b. often do not attend to event features that are pertinent to older people.
   c. are egocentric in their thinking.
   d. have all of the above limitations.

13. Most 5-year-olds have difficulty understanding analogies because:
   a. they have not yet begun to develop grammar.
   b. the literal nature of the fast-mapping process allows only one meaning per word.
   c. of their limited vocabulary.
   d. of their tendency to overregularize.

14. Overregularization indicates that a child:
   a. is clearly applying rules of grammar.
   b. persists in egocentric thinking.
   c. has not yet mastered the principle of conservation.
   d. does not yet have a theory of mind.

15. Regarding the value of preschool education, most developmentalists believe that:
   a. most disadvantaged children will not benefit from an early preschool education.
   b. most disadvantaged children will benefit from an early preschool education.
   c. the early benefits of preschool education are likely to disappear by grade 3.
   d. the relatively small benefits of antipoverty measures such as Head Start do not justify their huge costs.

Matching Items

Match each term or concept with its corresponding description or definition.

Terms or Concepts

_____ 1. script
_____ 2. scaffold
_____ 3. theory of mind
_____ 4. zone of proximal development
_____ 5. overregularization
_____ 6. fast mapping
_____ 7. irreversibility
_____ 8. centration
_____ 9. conservation
_____ 10. private speech
_____ 11. guided participation

Descriptions or Definitions

a. the idea that amount is unaffected by changes shape or placement
b. memory-facilitating outline of past experiences
c. the cognitive distance between a child's actu and potential levels of development
d. the tendency to think about one aspect of a situ tion at a time
e. the process whereby the child learns throu social interaction with a "tutor"
f. our understanding of mental processes in ou selves and others
g. the process by which words are learned after or one hearing
h. an inappropriate application of rules of gramm
i. the internal use of language to form ideas
j. the inability to understand that original con tions are restored by the undoing of some proce
k. to structure a child's participation in learni encounters

Thinking Critically About Chapter 9

Answer these questions the day before an exam as a final check on your understanding of the chapter's terms and concepts.

1. An experimenter first shows a child two rows of checkers that each have the same number of checkers. Then, with the child watching, the experimenter elongates one row and asks the child if each of the two rows still has an equal number of checkers. This experiment tests the child's understanding of:
   a. reversibility.
   b. conservation of matter.
   c. conservation of number.
   d. centration.

2. A preschooler believes that a "party" is the one and only attribute of a birthday. She says that Daddy doesn't have a birthday because he never has a party. This thinking demonstrates the tendency Piaget called:
   a. egocentrism.
   b. centration.
   c. conservation of events.
   d. mental representation.

3. A child who understands that 6 + 3 = 9 mea that 9 – 6 = 3 has had to master the concept of:
   a. reversibility.   c. conservation.
   b. number.   d. egocentrism.

4. A 4-year-old tells the teacher that a clown shou not be allowed to visit the class because "Pat 'fraid of clowns." The 4-year-old thus shows t he can anticipate how another will feel. This evidence of the beginnings of:
   a. egocentrism.
   b. deception.
   c. a theory of mind.
   d. conservation.

5. A Chinese visitor to an American presch would probably be struck by its emphasis on f tering _____ in children.
   a. conformity
   b. concern for others
   c. cooperation
   d. self-reliance

A nursery school teacher is given the job of selecting holiday entertainment for a group of preschool children. If the teacher agrees with the ideas of Vygotsky, she is most likely to select:

a. a simple TV show that every child can understand.

b. a hands-on experience that requires little adult supervision.

c. brief, action-oriented play activities that the children and teachers will perform together.

d. holiday puzzles for children to work on individually.

When asked to describe her dinner last night, 3-year-old Hilary says, "We sat at the table, mommy served meat and potatoes, we ate, we left the table." Hilary evidently:

a. is very egocentric in her thinking.

b. is retrieving from a "dinner script."

c. failed to retrieve the memory that they ate out last night.

d. has acquired a sophisticated theory of mind.

That a child produces sentences that follow such rules of word order as "the initiator of an action precedes the verb, the receiver of an action follows it" demonstrates a knowledge of:

a. grammar.   **c.** pragmatics.

b. semantics.   **d.** phrase structure.

The 2-year-old child who says, "We goed to the store," is making a grammatical:

a. centration.   **c.** extension.

b. overregularization. **d.** script.

An experimenter who makes two balls of clay of equal amount, then rolls one into a long, skinny rope and asks the child if the amounts are still the same, is testing the child's understanding of:

a. conservation.   **c.** perspective-taking.

b. reversibility.   **d.** centration.

Dr. Jones, who believes that children's language growth greatly contributes to their cognitive growth, evidently is a proponent of the ideas of:

a. Piaget.   **c.** Flavell.

b. Chomsky.   **d.** Vygotsky.

Jack constantly "talks down" to his 3-year-old son's speech level. Jack's speech is:

a. appropriate, because 3-year-olds have barely begun to comprehend grammatical rules.

b. commendable, given the importance of scaffolding in promoting cognitive growth.

c. unnecessary, because preschoolers are able to comprehend more complex grammar and vocabulary than they can produce.

d. clearly within his son's zone of proximal development.

13. In describing the limited logical reasoning of preschoolers, a developmentalist is *least* likely to emphasize:

a. irreversibility.   **c.** its action-bound nature.

b. centration.   **d.** its static nature.

14. A preschooler fails to put together a difficult puzzle on her own, so her mother encourages her to try again, this time guiding her by asking questions such as, "For this space do we need a big piece or a little piece?" With Mom's help, the child successfully completes the puzzle. Lev Vygotsky would attribute the child's success to:

a. additional practice with the puzzle pieces.

b. imitation of her mother's behavior.

c. the social interaction with her mother that restructured the task to make its solution more attainable.

d. modeling and reinforcement.

15. Mark is answering an essay question that asks him to "discuss the positions of major developmental theorists regarding the relationship between language and cognitive development." To help organize his answer, Mark jots down a reminder that _____ contended that language is essential to the advancement of thinking, as private speech, and as a _____ of social interactions.

a. Piaget; mediator   **c.** Piaget; theory

b. Vygotsky; mediator **d.** Vygotsky; theory

Key Terms

Using your own words, write a brief definition or explanation of each of the following terms on a separate piece of paper.

1. symbolic thought

2. preoperational thought

3. centration

4. egocentrism

5. conservation

6. guided participation

7. zone of proximal development

8. scaffold

9. private speech

10. social mediation

11. scripts

12. theory of mind

13. fast mapping

14. overregularization

ANSWERS

CHAPTER REVIEW

1. self-absorption

2. symbolic thinking; preoperational

3. centration; egocentrism; appearances

4. static; unchanging; irreversibility

5. conservation; conservation of number

6. guided participation; social; interact

7. Lev Vygotsky

8. social activity

9. zone of proximal development

10. scaffold

11. private speech; uttered aloud

12. mediator

13. impossible; conservation

14. social; responsive; interactive; is not; are not

15. memory; storage; retrieval

16. scripts; sequence; flow

17. did not

18. photographs of their experiences; meaningful

19. were

20. social; relationship; age; atmosphere

21. resist

22. theory of mind

By age 3 or 4, young children distinguish between mental phenomena and the physical events to which they refer; they appreciate how mental states arise from experiences in the world; they understand that mental phenomena are subjective; they recognize that people have differing opinions and preferences; they realize that beliefs and desires can form the basis for human action; and they realize that emotion arises not only from physical events but also from goals and expectations.

23. have

24. language; brain maturation; brother or sist●
culture

25. vocabulary

26. fast mapping

27. more

28. comparisons; time; place

29. grammar; 3

30. hearing conversations at home that model go●
grammar; receiving helpful feedback about th●
language use

31. passive; context

32. overregularization

Many preschoolers overapply the rule of adding "●
to form the plural, as well as the rule of adding "e●
to form the past tense. Thus, preschoolers are likely
say "foots" and "snows," and that someone "broke
a toy.

33. more

High-quality preschools are characterized by (a)●
low teacher-child ratio, (b) a staff with training a●
credentials in early-childhood education, (c) a cu●
riculum geared toward cognitive development, a●
(d) an organization of space that facilitates creati●
and constructive play.

34. social consensus; conformity; group activity; se●
confidence; self-reliance

35. Project Head Start; higher

PROGRESS TEST 1

Multiple-Choice Questions

1. c. is the answer. (p. 247)

2. a. is the answer. Unlike the U.S. government, ●
governments of many other developed countr●
sponsor preschool education. (p. 264)

3. b. is the answer. (p. 254)

   c. & d. Research demonstrates that even you●
   children often have very accurate long-te●
   recall.

4. a. is the answer. (p. 256)

   b. & d. Because preschoolers' scripts do recogn●
   the causal flow of events, they are not hard to f●
   low.

   c. Preschoolers use scripts not only when recou●
   ing familiar routines but also in pretend play.

5. b. is the answer. (p. 254)

   a. Scripts tend to improve preschoolers' memory

c. & d. Although true, neither of these is the *primary* reason for preschoolers' poor memory.

6. **d.** is the answer. (p. 262)

a. & c. Preschoolers generally have great difficulty understanding, and therefore using, metaphors and abstract nouns.

b. Other than the grammatical errors of overregularization, the text does not indicate that preschoolers use a significant number of self-created words.

7. **a.** is the answer. (p. 263)

b. & d. These terms are not identified in the text and do not apply to the use of grammar.

c. Practical usage, which also is not discussed in the text, refers to communication between one person and another in terms of the overall context in which language is used.

8. **a.** is the answer. (p. 252)

b. This expresses the views of Piaget.

c. Because he believed that language facilitates thinking, Vygotsky obviously felt that language and other cognitive developments are intimately related.

d. Vygotsky did not hold this view.

9. **a.** is the answer. (p. 252)

10. **a.** is the answer. (pp. 247–248)

b., c., & d. Failure to conserve is the result of thinking that is centered on appearances. Egocentrism and irreversibility are also examples of centered thinking.

11. **c.** is the answer. (p. 267)

b. This is not discussed in the text. However, although there was a slight early IQ advantage in Head Start graduates, the difference disappeared by grade 3.

a. & d. There was no indication of greater behavioral problems or alienation in Head Start graduates.

12. **b.** is the answer. (p. 264)

13. **c.** is the answer. (p. 264)

14. **d.** is the answer. (p. 250)

15. **a.** is the answer. (pp. 259–260)

True or False Items

1. **F**   More recent research has found that children may understand conservation earlier than Piaget thought, given a more gamelike presentation. His theory has not been rejected overall, however. (p. 250)

2. **T** (pp. 247–248)

3. **F**   In fact, just the opposite is true. Children who have learning difficulties tend to be slower to develop private speech. (p. 252)

4. **T** (p. 250)

5. **T** (p. 246)

6. **F**   Piaget believed that language ability builds on the sensorimotor and conceptual accomplishments of infancy and toddlerhood. (p. 246)

7. **F**   Preschoolers have difficulty understanding abstract words; their vocabulary consists mainly of concrete nouns and verbs. (p. 262)

8. **F**   In adding "ed" to form a past tense, the child has indicated an understanding of the grammatical rule for making past tenses in English, even though the construction in these two cases is incorrect. (pp. 263–264)

9. **T** (p. 264)

10. **T** (p. 249)

PROGRESS TEST 2

Multiple-Choice Questions

1. **a.** is the answer. (p. 255)

2. **a.** is the answer. (p. 256)

b. The children provided more information in response to *directive* questions.

c. Older children recalled *more* information spontaneously than did younger children.

3. **a.** is the answer. (p. 246)

b. Overregularization is the child's tendency to apply grammatical rules even when he or she shouldn't.

c. Reversibility is the concept that reversing an operation, such as addition, will restore the original conditions.

d. This term is used to refer to the young child's belief that people think as he or she does.

4. **c.** is the answer. This is why the stage is called *pre*operational. (p. 246)

5. **a.** is the answer. (p. 252)

6. **c.** is the answer. (pp. 252–253)

a. & b. These are both advantages of private speech.

d. Fast mapping is the process by which new words are acquired, often after only one hearing.

7. **d.** is the answer. (p. 247)

a. This describes egocentrism.

b. This is the opposite of centration.

c. This defines conservation of number.

8. **a.** is the answer. (pp. 247–248)

b. According to Piaget, preschoolers fail to solve conservation problems because they focus on the *appearance* of objects and ignore the transformation that has occurred.

d. Piaget did not relate conservation to a theory of mind.

9. **d.** is the answer. (p. 252)

10. **b.** is the answer. (p. 249)

a. Piaget believed that learning is a matter of individual discovery.

11. **d.** is the answer. Preschoolers almost always put subject before verb in their two-word sentences. (p. 262)

12. **b.** is the answer. (p. 256)

a. Preschoolers *do* tend to use mental scripts.

c. Although this type of thinking is somewhat characteristic of preschoolers, it has no impact on memory per se.

13. **b.** is the answer. (p. 262)

a. By the time children are 3 years old, their grammar is quite impressive.

c. On the contrary, vocabulary develops so rapidly that, by age 5, children seem to be able to understand and use almost any term they hear.

d. This tendency to make language more logical by overapplying certain grammatical rules has nothing to do with understanding the *meaning* of analogies.

14. **a.** is the answer. (pp. 263–264)

b. c, & d. Overregularization is a *linguistic* phenomenon rather than a characteristic type of thinking (b. and d.), or a logical principle (c.).

15. **b.** is the answer. (p. 267)

Matching Items

1. b (p. 256)
2. k (p. 252)
3. f (p. 257)
4. c (p. 252)
5. h (p. 263)
6. g (p. 260)
7. j (p. 247)
8. d (p. 246)
9. a (p. 247)
10. i (p. 252)
11. e (p. 249)

THINKING CRITICALLY ABOUT CHAPTER 9

1. **c.** is the answer. (p. 248)

a. A test of reversibility would ask a child to perform an operation, such as adding 4 to 3, and then reverse the process (subtract 3 from 7) to determine whether the child understood that the original condition (the number 4) was restored.

b. A test of conservation of matter would transform the appearance of an object, such as a ball of clay, to determine whether the child understoo that the object remained the same.

d. A test of centration would involve the child ability to see various aspects of a situation.

2. **b.** is the answer. (p. 246)

a. Egocentrism is thinking that is self-centered.

c. This is not a concept in Piaget's theory.

d. Mental representation is an example of sym bolic thought.

3. **a.** is the answer. (p. 247)

4. **c.** is the answer. (p. 257)

a. Egocentrism is self-centered thinking.

b. Although deception provides evidence of theory of mind, the child in this example is n deceiving anyone.

d. Conservation is the understanding that th amount of a substance is unchanged by change in its shape or placement.

5. **d.** is the answer. (p. 265)

a., b., & c. Chinese preschools place *more* empha sis on these attitudes and behaviors than American preschools.

6. **c.** is the answer. In Vygotsky's view, learning is social activity more than a matter of individu discovery. Thus, social interaction that provide motivation and focuses attention facilitates lear ing. (p. 249)

a., b., & d. These situations either provide r opportunity for social interaction (b. & d.) or not challenge the children (a.).

7. **b.** is the answer. (p. 283)

a. Egocentrism is thinking that is self-focused.

c. Preschoolers do have poor retrieval strategie but the question doesn't indicate that she co fused the events of the preceding evening.

d. This refers to preschoolers' emerging soci understanding of others' perspectives.

8. **a.** is the answer. (p. 262)

b. & d. The text does not discuss these aspects language.

c. Pragmatics, which is not mentioned in the te refers to the practical use of language in varyir social contexts.

9. **b.** is the answer. (p. 263)

10. **a.** is the answer. (pp. 247–248)

11. **d.** is the answer. (p. 252)

a. Piaget believed that cognitive growth preced language development.

b. & c. Chomsky focused on the *acquisition* of language, and Flavell emphasizes cognition.

. **c.** is the answer. (p. 264)

. **c.** is the answer. This is typical of cognition during the first two years, when infants think exclusively with their senses and motor skills. (p. 247)

. **c.** is the answer. (p. 249)

. **b.** is the answer. (p. 252)

EY TERMS

. **Symbolic thought** is thinking that involves the use of words, gestures, pictures, or actions to represent other objects, behaviors, or experiences. (p. 246)

. According to Piaget, thinking between ages 2 and 6 is characterized by **preoperational thought**, meaning that children cannot yet perform logical operations; that is, they cannot use logical principles. (p. 246)

Memory aid: Operations are mental transformations involving the manipulation of ideas and symbols. *Pre*operational children, who lack the ability to perform transformations, are "before" this developmental milestone.

. **Centration** is the tendency of young children to focus only on a single aspect of a situation or object. (p. 246)

. **Egocentrism** refers to the tendency of young children to view the world exclusively from their own perspective. (p. 247)

. **Conservation** is the understanding that the amount or quantity of a substance or object is unaffected by changes in its shape or configuration. (p. 247)

According to Vygotsky, intellectual growth in young children is stimulated and directed by their **guided participation** in learning experiences. As guides, parents, teachers, and older children offer assistance with challenging tasks, model problem-solving approaches, provide explicit instructions as needed, and support the child's interest and motivation. (p. 249)

7. According to Vygotsky, for each individual there is a **zone of proximal development**, which represents the skills that are within the potential of the learner but cannot be performed independently. (p. 252)

8. Tutors who **scaffold** structure children's learning experiences in order to foster their emerging capabilities. (p. 252)

9. **Private speech** is the internal dialogue in which a person talks to himself or herself. Private speech, which often is uttered aloud, helps preschoolers to think, review what they know, and decide what to do. (p. 252)

10. In Vygotsky's theory, **social mediation** refers to the use of speech as a tool to bridge the gap in understanding or knowledge between a child and a tutor. (p. 252)

11. **Scripts** are mental outlines of familiar, recurrent past experiences used to facilitate the storage and retrieval of memories. (p. 256)

12. A **theory of mind** is an understanding of mental processes, that is, of one's own or another's emotions, perceptions, intentions, and thoughts. (p. 257)

13. **Fast mapping** is the process by which children rapidly learn new words by quickly connecting them to words and categories that are already understood. (p. 260)

14. **Overregularization** occurs when children apply rules of grammar when they should not. It is seen in English, for example, when children add "s" to form the plural even in irregular cases that form the plural in a different way. (p. 263)

CHAPTER 10

The Play Years: Psychosocial Development

Chapter Overview

Chapter 10 explores the ways in which young children begin to relate to others in an ever-widening social environment. The chapter begins where social understanding begins, with the emergence of the sense of self. With their increasing social awareness, children become more concerned with how others evaluate them and better able to regulate their emotions.

The next section explores the origins of helpful, prosocial behaviors in young children, as well as antisocial behaviors such as the different forms of aggressive behavior. The child's social skills reflect many influences, including learning from playmates through various types of play as well as from television and parenting patterns

The chapter concludes with a description of children's emerging awareness of male-female differences and gender identity. Five major theories of gender-role development are considered.

NOTE: Answer guidelines for all Chapter 10 questions begin on page 157.

Guided Study

The text chapter should be studied one section at a time. Before you read, preview each section by skimming it, noting headings and boldface items. Then read the appropriate section objectives from the following outline. Keep these objectives in mind and, as you read the chapter section, search for the information that will enable you to meet each objective. Once you have finished a section, write out answers for its objectives.

The Self and the Social World (pp. 271–277)

1. Discuss the relationship between the child developing sense of self and social awareness.

2. (Changing Policy) Discuss the impact of being only child on cognitive and social development.

3. Discuss emotional development during ea childhood, focusing on emotional regulation, a how it relates to attachment.

Antisocial and Prosocial Behavior (pp. 277–287)

4. Differentiate four types of aggression during play years and explain why certain types more troubling to developmentalists.

. Discuss the nature and significance of rough-and-tumble and sociodramatic play during the play years.

. (A Life-Span View) Discuss how watching television contributes to the development of aggression and other antisocial behaviors.

. Compare and contrast three classic patterns of parenting and their effect on children.

. (text and Research Report) Discuss the pros and cons of punishment, and describe the most effective method for disciplining a child.

y or Girl: So What? (pp. 287–295)

Describe the developmental progression of gender awareness in young children.

10. Summarize five theories of gender-role development during the play years, noting important contributions of each.

Chapter Review

When you have finished reading the chapter, work through the material that follows to review it. Complete the sentences and answer the questions. As you proceed, evaluate your performance for each section by consulting the answers on page 157. Do not continue with the next section until you understand each answer. If you need to, review or reread the appropriate section in the textbook before continuing.

The Self and the Social World (pp. 271–277)

1. Between 3 and 6 years of age, according to Erikson, children are in the stage of

   _____ _____

   _____ .

2. The play years are filled with examples of the child's emerging _____ .

3. The growth of preschoolers' self-awareness is especially apparent in their _____ with others.

4. As their theory of mind expands, preschoolers become less _____ and more

   _____ .

5. Psychologists emphasize the importance of children's developing a positive _____ . Preschoolers typically form impressions of themselves that are quite _____ . One manifestation of this tendency is that preschoolers regularly _____ (overestimate/underestimate) their own abilities. Most preschoolers think of themselves as competent _____ (in all/only in certain) areas.

6. As they grow, preschoolers become
_____ (more/less) concerned with
how others evaluate their behavior.

7. (Changing Policy) Worldwide, the number of
only children is _____ (increas-
ing/decreasing). The largest average family size
occurs _____ (in which country?).
In most ways, only children fare _____
(as well as or better/ worse) than children with
siblings. Only children are particularly likely to
benefit _____ , becoming more
_____ and more _____ .
A potential problem for only children is in their
development of _____ skills.

8. The most significant emotional development during early childhood is _____
_____ , which is the growing ability
to direct or modify one's feelings in response to
expectations from _____ . This abili-
ty develops partly as the result of
_____ maturation and partly as a
result of _____ .

9. The development of fears during the play years is
_____ (common/rare). Some
preschoolers develop strong irrational fears
called _____ ; this is particularly
likely if the child's _____ share
these fears. During these years, the child's
enhanced _____ contributes to an
increase in _____ .

10. How children regulate their emotions reflects the
results of past _____ . For example,
children who respond unsympathetically to
another child's distress may have
_____ _____ .

11. Another example of emotional regulation is
appropriate expression of _____ .
According to _____ , the ability to
direct emotions is crucial to the development of
_____ _____ .

Antisocial and Prosocial Behavior (pp. 277–287)

12. Sharing, cooperating, and sympathizing are
examples of _____ .
_____
These attitudes correlate with _____
_____ . As the
capacity for self-control increases between 2 and
5 years, there is a decrease in _____
_____
_____
Conversely, actions that are destructive or deliberately hurtful are called _____
_____ . Such actions are often predicted by a lack of _____
_____ .

13. The roots of aggression are a negative
_____ and inadequate _____
_____ during the early preschool
years.

14. Developmentalists distinguish three types of
physical aggression: _____ , used to
obtain or retain a toy or other object;
_____ , used in angry retaliation
against an intentional or accidental act committe
by a peer; and _____ , used in an
unprovoked attack on a peer.

15. The form of aggression that is most likely to
increase from age 2 to 6 is _____
_____ . Of greater concern are
_____ _____ , because it ca
indicate a lack of _____
_____ , and _____
_____ , which is most worrisome ove
all.

16. Social aggression that involves insults or social
rejection is called _____
_____ .
Victims of this type of aggression are more com
monly preschoolers who are
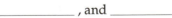

7. The type of physical play that mimics aggression is called _____-_____ _____ play. A distinctive feature of this form of play, which _____ (occurs only in some cultures/is universal), is the positive facial expression that characterizes the _____ _____ . Age differences are evident, because this type of play relies on the child's _____ _____ . Gender differences _____ (are/are not) evident in rough-and-tumble play.

8. In _____ play, children act out various roles and themes in stories of their own creation. The increase in this form of play is related to the development of the child's _____ _____ _____ and emotional regulation, as well as the development of _____ . _____ (Girls/Boys) tend to engage in this type of play more often than do _____ (girls/boys).

9. (A Life-Span View) A typical preschool child In the United States watches more than _____ hours of television per day. This amount _____ (is/is not) greater than any other age group.

A Life-Span View) State several negative effects of ·levision from a developmental perspective.

). (A Life-Span View) Another criticism of television is that it encourages _____ _____ in young children, in part by _____ them to violence in real life. Children who watch large amounts of video violence are more likely than others to be _____ _____ .

21. A significant influence on early psychosocial growth is the style of _____ that characterizes a child's family life.

22. The seminal research on parenting styles, which was conducted by _____ , found that parents varied in their _____ toward offspring, in their strategies for _____ , in how well they _____ , and in their expectations for _____ .

23. Parents who adopt the _____ style demand unquestioning obedience from their children. In this style of parenting, nurturance tends to be _____ (low/ high), maturity demands are _____ (low/high), and parent–child communication tends to be _____ (low/high).

24. Parents who adopt the _____ style make few demands on their children and are lax in discipline. Such parents _____ (are/are not very) nurturant, communicate _____ (well/poorly), and make _____ (few/extensive) maturity demands.

25. Parents who adopt the _____ style democratically set limits and enforce rules. Such parents make _____ (high/low) maturity demands, communicate _____ (well/poorly), and _____ (are/are not) nurturant.

26. Follow-up studies indicate that children raised by _____ parents are likely to be obedient but unhappy; those raised by _____ parents are likely to lack self-control; and those raised by _____ parents are more likely to be successful, happy with themselves, and generous with others. These advantages _____ (grow stronger/weaken) over time.

27. An important factor in the effectiveness of parenting style is the child's _____ .

28. To be effective, punishment should be more _____ than _____ .

29. (Research Report) A 1994 study investigated the relationship between spanking and aggressive behavior in the child. Observers scored kindergartners for instances of aggressive behavior. Compared with children who were not spanked, those children who were spanked were more likely to engage in _____ aggression.

30. Japanese mothers tend to use _____ as disciplinary techniques more often than do North American mothers, who are more likely to encourage _____ expressions of all sorts in their children. Throughout the world, most parents _____ (believe/do not believe) that spanking is acceptable at times. Although spanking _____ (is/is not) effective, it may teach children to be more _____ .

Boy or Girl: So What? (pp. 287–295)

31. Social scientists distinguish between biological, or _____ differences between males and females, and cultural, or _____ differences in the _____ and behaviors of the two sexes.

32. True sex differences are _____ (more/less) apparent in childhood than in adulthood; _____ differentiation seems more significant to children than to adults.

33. By age _____ , children can consistently apply gender labels and have a rudimentary understanding of the permanence of their own gender. By age _____ , most children express stereotypic ideas of each sex. Such stereotyping _____ (does/does not) occur in children whose parents provide nontraditional gender role models. Awareness that sex is a fixed biological characteristic does not become solid until about age _____ .

34. Freud called the period from age 3 to 7 the _____ _____ . According to his view, boys in this stage develop sexual feelings about their _____

and become jealous of their _____ . Freud called this phenomenon the _____ _____ .

35. In Freud's theory, preschool boys resolve their guilty feelings defensively through _____ with their father. Boys also develop, again in self-defense, a powerful conscience called the _____ .

36. According to Freud, during the phallic stage little girls may experience the _____ _____ , in which they want to get rid of their mother and become intimate with their father. Alternatively, they may become jealous of boys because they have a penis; this emotion Freud called _____ _____ .

37. According to learning theory, preschool children develop gender-role ideas by being _____ for behaviors deemed appropriate for their sex and _____ for behaviors deemed inappropriate.

38. Social learning theorists maintain that children learn gender-appropriate behavior by _____ .

39. Cognitive theorists focus on children's _____ of male-female differences. When their experience is ambiguous, preschoolers search for the simple _____ they have formed regarding gender roles.

40. According to the _____ theory, gender education varies by region, socioeconomic status, and historical period. Gender distinctions are emphasized in many _____ cultures. This theory points out that children can maintain a balance of male and female characteristics, or _____ , only if their culture promotes that idea.

41. According to _____ _____ theory, gender attitudes and roles are the result of interaction between _____ and _____ .

2. One idea that has recently found greater acceptance is the idea that some gender differences are _____ rather than _____ based.

3. In some respects, the two sexes are different because there are subtle differences in _____ development.

escribe several of these differences.

. These differences probably _____ (are/are not) the result of any single gene. More likely, they result from the differing

_____ _____

that influence brain development.

rogress Test 1

ultiple-Choice Questions

rcle your answers to the following questions and eck them with the answers on page 157. If your swer is incorrect, read the explanation for why it is correct and then consult the appropriate pages of e text (in parentheses following the correct answer).

. Preschool children have a clear (but not necessarily accurate) concept of self. Typically, the preschooler believes that she or he:
   a. owns all objects in sight.
   b. is great at almost everything.
   c. is much less competent than peers and older children.
   d. is more powerful than her or his parents.

. According to Freud, the third stage of psychosexual development, during which the penis is the focus of psychological concern and pleasure, is the:
   a. oral stage.   c. phallic stage.
   b. anal stage.   d. latency period.

3. Because it helps children rehearse social roles, work out fears and fantasies, and learn cooperation, an important form of social play is:
   a. sociodramatic play.
   b. mastery play.
   c. rough-and-tumble play.
   d. sensorimotor play.

4. The three *basic* patterns of parenting described by Diana Baumrind are:
   a. hostile, loving, and harsh.
   b. authoritarian, permissive, and authoritative.
   c. positive, negative, and punishing.
   d. indulgent, neglecting, and traditional.

5. Authoritative parents are receptive and loving, but they also normally:
   a. set limits and enforce rules.
   b. have difficulty communicating.
   c. withhold praise and affection.
   d. encourage aggressive behavior.

6. Children who watch a lot of violent television:
   a. are more likely to be aggressive.
   b. become desensitized to violence.
   c. are less likely to attempt to mediate a quarrel between other children.
   d. have all of the above characteristics.

7. Between 2 and 6 years of age, the form of aggression that is most likely to increase is:
   a. reactive
   b. instrumental
   c. relational
   d. bullying

8. During the play years, a child's self-concept is defined largely by his or her:
   a. expanding range of skills and competencies.
   b. physical appearance.
   c. gender.
   d. relationship with family members.

9. Learning theorists emphasize the importance of _____ in the development of the preschool child.
   a. identification   c. initiative
   b. praise and blame   d. a theory of mind

10. Children apply gender labels and have definite ideas about how boys and girls behave as early as age:
   a. 3.   c. 5.
   b. 4.   d. 7.

11. Psychologist Daniel Goleman believes that emotional regulation is especially crucial to the preschooler's developing:
    a. sense of self.
    b. social awareness.
    c. emotional intelligence.
    d. sense of gender.

12. Six-year-old Leonardo has superior verbal ability rivaling that of most girls his age. Dr. Laurent believes this is due to the fact that although his sex is predisposed to slower language development, Leonardo's upbringing in a linguistically rich home enhanced his biological capabilities. Dr. Laurent is evidently a proponent of:
    a. cognitive theory.
    b. gender-schema theory.
    c. sociocultural theory.
    d. epigenetic systems theory.

13. (Changing Policy) Compared with children with siblings, only children are likely to:
    a. be less verbal.
    b. fare as well or better in most ways.
    c. have greater competence in social skills.
    d. be less creative.

14. Compared to Japanese mothers, North American mothers are more likely to:
    a. use reasoning to control their preschoolers' social behavior.
    b. use expressions of disappointment to control their preschoolers' social behavior.
    c. encourage emotional expressions of all sorts in their preschoolers.
    d. do all of the above.

15. When her friend hurts her feelings, Maya shouts that she is a "mean old stinker!" Maya's behavior is an example of:
    a. instrumental aggression.
    b. reactive aggression.
    c. bullying aggression.
    d. relational aggression.

True or False Items

Write *T (true)* or *F (false)* on the line in front of each statement.

_____ 1. According to Baumrind, only authoritarian parents make maturity demands on their children.

_____ 2. Children of authoritative parents tend to be successful, happy with themselves, and generous with others.

_____ 3. True sex differences are more apparent in childhood than in adulthood.

_____ 4. (Research Report) Spanking is associated with higher rates of aggression toward peers.

_____ 5. Many gender differences are genetically based.

_____ 6. Children from feminist or nontraditional homes seldom have stereotypic ideas about feminine and masculine roles.

_____ 7. Developmentalists do not agree about how children acquire gender roles.

_____ 8. By age 4, most children have definite ideas about what constitutes typical masculine and feminine behavior.

_____ 9. Identification was defined by Freud as a defense mechanism in which people identify with others who may be stronger and more powerful than they.

_____ 10. Sociodramatic play allows children free expression of their emotions.

Progress Test 2

Progress Test 2 should be completed during a final chapter review. Answer the following questions after you thoroughly understand the correct answers for the Chapter Review and Progress Test 1.

Multiple-Choice Questions

1. Children of permissive parents are *most* likely to lack:
   a. social skills.   c. initiative and guilt.
   b. self-control.   d. care and concern.

2. Children learn how to manage conflict through the use of humor most readily from their interaction with:
   a. their mothers.   c. friends.
   b. their fathers.   d. others of the same sex.

3. The initial advantages of parenting style:
   a. do not persist past middle childhood.
   b. remain apparent through adolescence.
   c. are likely to be even stronger over time.
   d. have an unpredictable impact later in children's lives.

4. When they are given a choice of playmates, 2-5-year-old children:
   a. play with children of their own sex.
   b. play equally with girls and boys.
   c. segregate by gender in cultures characterized by traditional gender roles.
   d. prefer to play alone.

5. Which of the following best summarizes the current view of developmentalists regarding gender differences?

  a. Some gender differences are biological in origin.
  b. Most gender differences are biological in origin.
  c. Nearly all gender differences are cultural in origin.
  d. There is no consensus among developmentalists regarding the origin of gender differences.

6. According to Freud, a young boy's jealousy of his father's relationship with his mother, and the guilt feelings that result, are part of the:

  a. Electra complex.
  b. Oedipus complex.
  c. phallic complex.
  d. penis envy complex.

7. The style of parenting in which the parents make few demands on children, the discipline is lax, and the parents are nurturant and accepting is:

  a. authoritarian.
  b. authoritative.
  c. permissive.
  d. traditional.

8. Cooperating with a playmate is to _____ as insulting a playmate is to _____ .

  a. antisocial behavior; prosocial behavior
  b. prosocial behavior; antisocial behavior
  c. emotional regulation; antisocial behavior
  d. prosocial behavior; emotional regulation

9. Which of the following children would probably be said to have a phobia?

  a. Nicky, who has an exaggerated and irrational fear of furry animals
  b. Nairobi, who is frightened by loud thunder
  c. Noriko, who doesn't like getting shots
  d. All of the above have phobias.

10. Which of the following theories advocates the development of gender identification as a means of avoiding guilt over feelings for the opposite-sex parent?

  a. learning   c. psychoanalytic
  b. sociocultural   d. social learning

11. (Changing Policy) Compared to children with siblings, only children are more likely to be:

  a. overly dependent upon their parents.
  b. very spoiled.
  c. both a. and b.
  d. neither a. nor b.

12. The preschooler's readiness to learn new tasks and play activities reflects his or her:

  a. emerging competency and self-awareness.
  b. theory of mind.
  c. relationship with parents.
  d. growing identification with others.

13. Emotional regulation is in part related to maturation of a specific part of the brain in the:

  a. frontal cortex.
  b. parietal cortex.
  c. temporal lobe.
  d. occipital lobe.

14. In which style of parenting is the parents' word law and misbehavior strictly punished?

  a. permissive
  b. authoritative
  c. authoritarian
  d. traditional

15. Erikson noted that preschoolers eagerly begin many new activities but are vulnerable to criticism and feelings of failure; they experience the crisis of:

  a. identity versus role confusion.
  b. initiative versus guilt.
  c. basic trust versus mistrust.
  d. efficacy versus helplessness.

Matching Items

Match each term or concept with its corresponding description or definition.

Terms or Concepts

_____ 1. rough-and-tumble play
_____ 2. androgyny
_____ 3. sociodramatic play
_____ 4. prosocial behavior
_____ 5. antisocial behavior
_____ 6. Electra complex
_____ 7. Oedipus complex
_____ 8. authoritative
_____ 9. authoritarian
_____ 10. identification
_____ 11. instrumental aggression

Descriptions or Definitions

a. aggressive behavior whose purpose is to obtain an object desired by another
b. Freudian theory that every daughter secretly wishes to replace her mother
c. parenting style associated with high maturity demands and low parent-child communication
d. an action performed for the benefit of another person without the expectation of reward
e. Freudian theory that every son secretly wishes to replace his father
f. parenting style associated with high maturity demands and high parent-child communication
g. two children wrestle without serious hostility
h. an action that is intended to harm someone else
i. two children act out roles in a story of their own creation
j. a defense mechanism through which children cope with their feelings of guilt during the phallic stage
k. a balance of traditional male and female characteristics in an individual

Thinking Critically About Chapter 10

Answer these questions the day before an exam as a final check on your understanding of the chapter's terms and concepts.

1. Bonita eventually copes with the fear and anger she feels over her hatred of her mother and love of her father by:
   a. identifying with her mother.
   b. copying her brother's behavior.
   c. adopting her father's moral code.
   d. competing with her brother for her father's attention.

2. A little girl who says she wants her mother to go on vacation so that she can marry her father is voicing a fantasy consistent with the _____ described by Freud.
   a. Oedipus complex
   b. Electra complex
   c. theory of mind
   d. crisis of initiative versus guilt

3. According to Erikson, before the preschool years children are incapable of feeling guilt because:
   a. guilt depends on a sense of self, which is not sufficiently established in preschoolers.

b. they do not yet understand that they are male or female for life.
c. this emotion is unlikely to have been reinforced at such an early age.
d. guilt is associated with the resolution of the Oedipus complex, which occurs later in life.

4. Parents who are strict and aloof are *most* likely to make their children:
   a. cooperative and trusting.
   b. obedient but unhappy.
   c. violent.
   d. withdrawn and anxious.

5. When 4-year-old Seema grabs for Vincenzo's Beanie Baby, Vincenzo slaps her hand away, displaying an example of:
   a. bullying aggression.
   b. reactive aggression.
   c. instrumental aggression.
   d. relational aggression.

6. The belief that almost all sexual patterns are learned rather than inborn would find its strongest adherents among _____ theorists.
   a. cognitive　　　　c. psychoanalytic
   b. learning　　　　d. epigenetic systems

7. In explaining the origins of gender distinctions, Dr. Christie notes that every society teaches its children its values and attitudes regarding preferred behavior for men and women. Dr. Christie is evidently a proponent of:
   a. gender-schema theory.
   b. sociocultural theory.
   c. epigenetic systems theory.
   d. psychoanalytic theory.

8. Five-year-old Rodney has a better-developed sense of self and is more confident than Darnell. According to the text, it is likely that Rodney will also be more skilled at:
   a. tasks involving verbal reasoning.
   b. social interaction.
   c. deception.
   d. all of the above.

9. (Changing Policy) Your sister and brother-in-law are thinking of having a second child because they are worried that only children miss out on the benefits of social play. You tell them that:
   a. parents can compensate by making sure the child has regular contact with other children.
   b. only children are likely to possess *superior* social skills because of the greater attention they receive from their parents.
   c. the style of parenting, rather than the presence of siblings, is the most important factor in social and intellectual development.
   d. unfortunately, this is true and nothing can replace the opportunities for acquiring social skills that siblings provide.

10. Concerning children's concept of gender, which of the following statements is true?
    a. Before the age of 3 or so, children think that boys and girls can change gender as they get older.
    b. Children as young as 1 year have a clear understanding of the physical differences between girls and boys and can consistently apply gender labels.
    c. Not until age 5 or 6 do children show a clear preference for gender-typed toys.
    d. All of the above are true.

11. Which of the following is *not* one of the features of parenting used by Baumrind to differentiate authoritarian, permissive, and authoritative parents?
    a. maturity demands for the child's conduct
    b. efforts to control the child's actions
    c. nurturance
    d. adherence to stereotypic gender roles

12. Seeking to discipline her 3-year-old son for snatching a playmate's toy, Cassandra gently says, "How would you feel if Juwan grabbed your car?" Developmentalists would probably say that Cassandra's approach:
    a. is too permissive, and would therefore be ineffective in the long run.
    b. would probably be more effective with a girl.
    c. will be effective in increasing prosocial behavior because it promotes empathy.
    d. will backfire and threaten her son's self-confidence.

13. Which of the following is *not* a gender difference cited in the text?
    a. Right hemisphere activity is more pronounced in females.
    b. The corpus callosum is thicker in females.
    c. Brain maturation is faster in females.
    d. Right hemisphere dendrite formation is more pronounced in males.

14. (Research Report) Which of the following is true regarding the effects of spanking?
    a. Spanking seems to reduce reactive aggression.
    b. When administered appropriately, spanking promotes psychosocial development.
    c. Spanking is associated with increased aggression toward peers.
    d. None of the above is true.

15. Aldo and Jack are wrestling and hitting each other. Although this rough-and-tumble play mimics negative, aggressive behavior, it serves a useful purpose, which is to:
    a. rehearse social roles.
    b. develop interactive skills.
    c. improve fine motor skills.
    d. do both b. and c.

Key Terms

Writing Definitions

Using your own words, write a brief definition or explanation of each of the following terms on a separate piece of paper.

1. initiative versus guilt
2. emotional regulation
3. phobia
4. prosocial behavior
5. antisocial behavior
6. instrumental aggression
7. reactive aggression

8. relational aggression
9. bullying aggression
10. rough-and-tumble play
11. sociodramatic play
12. authoritarian parenting
13. permissive parenting
14. authoritative parenting
15. sex differences

16. gender differences
17. phallic stage
18. Oedipus complex
19. identification
20. superego
21. Electra complex
22. androgyny

Cross Check

After you have written the definitions of the key terms in this chapter, you should complete the crossword puzzle to ensure that you can reverse the process—recognize the term, given the definition.

ACROSS

1. Physical play that often mimics aggression but involves no intent to harm.
3. A behavior, such as cooperating or sharing, performed to benefit another person without the expectation of a reward.
8. In psychoanalytic theory, the self-critical and judgmental part of personality that internalizes the moral standards set by parents and society.
9. An exaggerated and irrational fear of an object or experience.
13. Behavior that takes the form of insults or social rejection is called _____ aggression.
15. Act intended to obtain or retain an object desired by another is called _____ aggression.
16. Style of parenting in which parents make few demands on their children yet are nurturant and accepting and communicate well with their children.

DOWN

2. Cultural differences in the roles and behaviors of males and females.
4. Defense mechanism through which a person takes on the role and attitudes of a person more powerful than himself or herself.
5. Ability to manage and modify one's feelings, particularly feelings of fear, frustration, and anger.
6. In Freud's phallic stage of psychosexual development, a boy's sexual attraction toward the mother and resentment of the father.

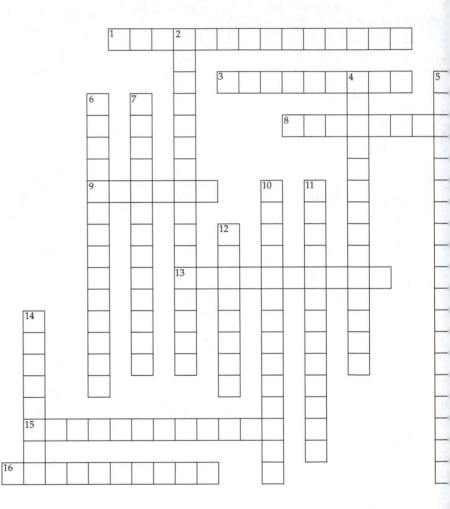

7. Style of child-rearing in which the parents show little affection or nurturance for their children, maturity demands are high, and parent–child communication is low.
10. In Freud's phallic stage of psychosexual development, a girl's sexual attraction toward the father and resentment of the mother.
11. Style of parenting in which the parents set limits and enforce rules but do so more democratically than do authoritarian parents.
12. Form of aggression involving an unprovoked attack on another child.
14. Aggressive behavior that is an angry retaliation for some intentional or incidental act by another person.

ANSWERS

CHAPTER REVIEW

. initiative versus guilt

. self-definition

. negotiations

. stubborn (or demanding); compromising

. self concept; optimistic; overestimate; in all

. more

. increasing; Africa; as well as or better; intellectually; verbal; creative; social

. emotional regulation; society; neurological; learning

. common; phobias; parents; imagination; nightmares

. caregiving; insecure attachments

. friendliness; Daniel Goleman; emotional intelligence

. prosocial behavior; the making of new friends; violent temper tantrums, uncontrollable crying, and terrifying phobias; antisocial behavior; emotional regulation

. self-concept; emotional regulation

. instrumental; reactive; bullying

. instrumental aggression; reactive aggression; emotional regulation; bullying aggression

. relational aggression; less prosocial and less likely to have friends

. rough-and-tumble; is universal; play face; social experience; are

. sociodramatic; theory of mind; self-understanding; Girls; boys

. 3; is

television takes away from active, interactive, and imaginative play; exposes children to faulty nutrition-messages and sexist, racist, and ageist stereotypes; undermines sympathy for emotional pain; and undercuts values that lead to prosocial activity.

. physical aggression; desensitizing; bullies, to retaliate physically, to be passive victims, and to be onlookers rather than mediators when other children fight

. parenting

. Baumrind; nurturance; discipline; communicate; maturity

. authoritarian; low; high; low

. permissive; are; well; few

. authoritative; high; well; are

26. authoritarian; permissive; authoritative; grow stronger

27. temperament

28. proactive; punitive

29. reactive

30. reasoning; emotional; believe; is; aggressive

31. sex; gender; roles

32. less; gender

33. 2; 6; does; 8

34. phallic stage; mother; father; Oedipus complex

35. identification; superego

36. Electra complex; penis envy

37. reinforced; punished

38. observing and interacting with other people

39. understanding; script

40. sociocultural; traditional; androgyny

41. epigenetic systems; genes; early experience

42. biologically; culturally

43. brain

In females, the corpus callosum is thicker, and overall brain maturation occurs more quickly. In males, right-hemisphere activity and dendrite formation tend to be more pronounced.

44. are not; sex hormones

PROGRESS TEST 1

Multiple-Choice Questions

1. **b.** is the answer. (pp. 272–273)

2. **c.** is the answer. (p. 289)

   a. & b. In Freud's theory, the oral and anal stages are associated with infant and early childhood development, respectively.

   d. In Freud's theory, the latency period is associated with development during the school years.

3. **a.** is the answer. (p. 280)

   b. & d. These two types of play are not discussed in this chapter. Mastery play is play that helps children develop new physical and intellectual skills. Sensorimotor play captures the pleasures of using the senses and motor skills.

   c. Rough-and-tumble play is physical play that mimics aggression.

4. **b.** is the answer. (p. 283)

   d. Traditional is a variation of the basic styles uncovered by later research. Indulgent and neglecting are not discussed in the text.

5. **a.** is the answer. (p. 283)

   b. & c. Authoritative parents communicate very well and are quite affectionate.

   d. This is not typical of authoritative parents.

6. **d.** is the answer. (p. 281)

7. **b.** is the answer. (p. 278)

8. **a.** is the answer. (p. 272)

9. **b.** is the answer. (p. 290)

   a. This is the focus of Freud's phallic stage.

   c. This is the focus of Erikson's psychosocial theory.

   d. This is the focus of cognitive theorists.

10. **a.** is the answer. (p. 288)

11. **c.** is the answer. (p. 277)

12. **d.** is the answer. In accounting for Leonardo's verbal ability, Dr. Laurent alludes to both genetic and environmental factors, a dead-giveaway for epigenetic systems theory. (p. 294)

    a., b., & c. These theories do not address biological or genetic influences on development.

13. **b.** is the answer. (p. 274)

    a. & d. Only children often benefit intellectually, becoming more verbal and more creative.

    c. Because only children may miss out on the benefits of social play, they may be weaker in their social skills.

14. **c.** is the answer. (p. 286)

    a., & b. These strategies are more typical of Japanese mothers.

15. **d.** is the answer. (p. 278)

True or False Items

1. F   All parents make some maturity demands on their children; maturity demands are high in both the authoritarian and authoritative parenting styles. (p. 283)

2. T (p. 285)

3. F   Just the opposite is true. (p. 287)

4. T (p. 285)

5. T (p. 294)

6. F   Children raised in feminist or nontraditional homes often surprise their parents by expressing stereotypic ideas about feminine and masculine roles. (p. 288)

7. T (pp. 289–295)

8. T (p. 288)

9. T (p. 290)

10. F   The reverse is true; it provides a way for children to learn emotional regulation. (p. 280)

PROGRESS TEST 2

Multiple-Choice Questions

1. **b.** is the answer. (p. 285)

2. **c.** is the answer. (p. 279)

   a. & b. Parents, especially mothers, are more understanding and self-sacrificing than playmates and so less able to teach this lesson.

   d. The text does not indicate that same-sex friends are more important in learning these than friends of the other sex.

3. **c.** is the answer. (pp. 285–286)

4. **a.** is the answer. (p. 288)

   c. & d. The preference for same-sex playmates universal.

5. **a.** is the answer. Recent research has found that the sexes are different in part because of subtle differences in brain development. (p. 294)

6. **b.** is the answer. (p. 289)

   a. & d. These are Freud's versions of phallic-stage development in little girls.

   c. There is no such thing as the "phallic complex."

7. **c.** is the answer. (p. 283)

   a. & b. Both authoritarian and authoritative parents make high demands on their children.

   d. This is not one of the three parenting styles. Traditional parents could be any one of the types.

8. **b.** is the answer. (p. 277)

9. **a.** is the answer. Exaggeration and irrationality are two hallmarks of phobias. (p. 276)

   b. & c. Neither of these fears seems exaggerated or irrational.

10. **c.** is the answer. (p. 290)

    a. & d. Learning and social learning theories emphasize that children learn about gender rewards and punishments and by observing others.

    b. Sociocultural theory focuses on the impact the environment on gender identification.

11. **d.** is the answer. (p. 274)

12. **a.** is the answer. (p. 273)

    b. This viewpoint is associated only with cognitive theory.

c. Although parent-child relationships are important to social development, they do not determine readiness.

d. Identification is a Freudian defense mechanism.

3. **a.** is the answer. (p. 275)

4. **c.** is the answer. (p. 283)

5. **b.** is the answer. (pp. 271–272)

a. & c. According to Erikson, these are the crises of adolescence and infancy, respectively.

d. This is not a crisis described by Erikson.

Matching Items

1. g (p. 279)	5. h (p. 277)	9. c (p. 283)
2. k (p. 293)	6. b (p. 290)	10. j (p. 290)
3. i (p. 280)	7. e (p. 289)	11. a (p. 278)
4. d (p. 277)	8. f (p. 283)	

THINKING CRITICALLY ABOUT CHAPTER 10

1. **a.** is the answer. (p. 290)

2. **b.** is the answer. (p. 290)

a. According to Freud, the Oedipus complex refers to the male's sexual feelings toward his mother and resentment toward his father.

c. & d. These are concepts introduced by cognitive theorists and Erik Erikson, respectively.

3. **a.** is the answer. (p. 272)

b. Erikson did not equate gender constancy with the emergence of guilt.

c. & d. These reflect the viewpoints of learning theory and Freud, respectively.

4. **b.** is the answer. (p. 284)

5. **c.** is the answer. The purpose of Vincenzo's action is clearly to retain the Beanie Baby, rather than to retaliate (b), or bully Seema (a). (p. 278)

d. Relational aggression takes the form of a verbal insult.

6. **b.** is the answer. (p. 290)

7. **b.** is the answer. (p. 293)

8. **b.** is the answer. (pp. 272–273)

a. & c. The chapter does not link self-understanding with verbal reasoning or deception.

9. **a.** is the answer. (p. 274)

10. **a.** is the answer. (p. 288)

b. Not until about age 3 can children consistently apply gender labels.

c. By age 2, children prefer gender-typed toys.

11. **d.** is the answer. (p. 283)

12. **c.** is the answer. (p. 277)

13. **a.** is the answer. Right hemisphere activity is more pronounced in males. (p. 294)

14. **c.** is the answer. (pp. 284–285)

15. **b.** is the answer. (p. 279)

KEY TERMS

1. According to Erikson, the crisis of the preschool years is **initiative versus guilt**. In this crisis, young children eagerly take on new tasks and play activities and feel guilty when their efforts result in failure or criticism. (p. 272)

2. **Emotional regulation** is the ability to manage and modify one's feelings, particularly feelings of fear, frustration, and anger. (p. 275)

3. A **phobia** is an exaggerated and irrational fear of an object or experience. (p. 276)

4. **Prosocial behavior** is an action, such as cooperating or sharing, that is performed to benefit another person without the expectation of reward. (p. 277)

5. **Antisocial behavior** is an action, such as hitting or insulting, that is intended to hurt another person. (p. 277)

6. **Instrumental aggression** is an action whose purpose is to obtain or retain an object desired by another. (p. 278)

7. **Reactive aggression** is aggressive behavior that is an angry retaliation for some intentional or incidental act by another person. (p. 278)

Memory aid: Instrumental aggression is behavior that is *instrumental* in allowing a child to retain a favorite toy. **Reactive aggression** is a *reaction* to another child's behavior.

8. Aggressive behavior that takes the form of verbal insults or social rejection is called **relational aggression**. (p. 278)

9. An unprovoked attack on another child is an example of **bullying aggression**. (p. 278)

10. **Rough-and-tumble play** is physical play that often mimics aggression but involves no intent to harm. (p. 279)

11. In **sociodramatic play**, children act out roles and themes in stories of their own creation, allowing them to examine personal concerns in a non-threatening manner. (p. 280)

12. **Authoritarian parenting** is a style of child rearing in which the parents show little affection or nurturance for their children; maturity demands are

high and parent–child communication is low. (p. 283)

Memory aid: Someone who is an **authoritarian** demands unquestioning obedience and acts in a dictatorial way.

13. **Permissive parenting** is a style of parenting in which the parents make few demands on their children, yet are nurturant and accepting, and communicate well with their children. (p. 283)

14. **Authoritative parenting** is a style of parenting in which the parents set limits and enforce rules but do so more democratically than do authoritarian parents. (p. 283)

Memory aid: **Authoritative parents** act as *authorities* do on a subject—by discussing and explaining why certain family rules are in place.

15. **Sex differences** are biological differences between females and males. (p. 287)

16. **Gender differences** are cultural differences in the roles and behavior of males and females. (p. 287)

17. In psychoanalytic theory, the **phallic stage** is the third stage of psychosexual development, in which the penis becomes the focus of psychological concerns and physiological pleasure. (p. 289)

18. According to Freud, boys in the phallic stage of psychosexual development develop a collection of feelings, known as the **Oedipus complex**, that center on sexual attraction to the mother and resentment of the father. (p. 289)

19. In Freud's theory, **identification** is the defense mechanism through which a person takes on the role and attitudes of a person more powerful than himself or herself. (p. 290)

20. In psychoanalytic theory, the **superego** is the self-critical and judgmental part of personality that internalizes the moral standards set by parents and society. (p. 290)

21. According to Freud, girls in the phallic stage may develop a collection of feelings, known as the **Electra complex**, that center on sexual attraction to the father and resentment of the mother. (p. 290)

22. **Androgyny** is a balance of traditionally female and male gender characteristics in a person. (p. 293)

Cross-Check

ACROSS

1. rough-and-tumble
3. prosocial
8. superego
9. phobia
13. relational
15. instrumental
16. permissive

DOWN

2. gender difference
4. identification
5. emotional regulation
6. Oedipus complex
7. authoritarian
10. Electra complex
11. authoritative
12. bullying
14. reactive

CHAPTER 11

The School Years: Biosocial Development

Chapter Overview

This chapter introduces middle childhood, the years from 7 to 11. Changes in physical size and shape are described, and the problem of obesity is addressed. The discussion then turns to the continuing development of motor and intellectual skills during the school years, culminating in an evaluation of intelligence testing. A final section examines the experiences of children with special needs, such as autistic children, children with learning disabilities, and those diagnosed as having attention-deficit hyperactivity disorder. The causes of and treatments for these problems are discussed, with emphasis placed on insights arising from the new developmental psychopathology perspective. This perspective makes it clear that the manifestations of any special childhood problem will change as the child grows older and that treatment must often focus on all three domains of development.

NOTE: Answer guidelines for all Chapter 11 questions begin on page 172.

Guided Study

The text chapter should be studied one section at a time. Before you read, preview each section by skimming it, noting headings and boldface items. Then read the appropriate section objectives from the following outline. Keep these objectives in mind and, as you read the chapter section, search for the information that will enable you to meet each objective. Once you have finished a section, write out answers for its objectives.

Size and Shape (pp. 301–306)

1. Describe normal physical growth and development during middle childhood, and account for the usual variations among children.

2. Discuss the problems—both physical and psychological—of obese children in middle childhood.

3. (Research Report) Identify the major causes of obesity, and outline the best approaches to treating obesity.

4. Explain why differences in physique and health among children are important.

8. (A Life-Span View) Describe Sternberg's and Gardner's theories of multiple intelligences, and explain the significance of these theories.

5. (Changing Policy) Discuss the causes, treatments, and impact of asthma on development during the school years.

Children with Special Needs (pp. 313–323)

9. Explain the new developmental psychopathology perspective, and discuss its value in treating children with special needs.

Skill Development (pp. 306–313)

6. Describe motor-skill development during the school years, focusing on variations due to gender, culture, and genetics.

10. Identify the symptoms of autism, and describe its most effective treatment.

7. Explain how achievement and aptitude tests are used in evaluating individual differences in cognitive growth, and discuss why use of such tests is controversial.

11. Discuss the characteristics of learning disabilities

2. Describe the symptoms and possible causes of ADHD (attention-deficit hyperactivity disorder) and ADHDA (attention-deficit hyperactivity disorder with aggression).

3. Discuss the types of treatment available for children with ADHD.

4. (In Person) Describe techniques that have been tried in efforts to educate children with special needs.

hapter Review

When you have finished reading the chapter, work through the material that follows to review it. Complete the sentences and answer the questions. As you proceed, evaluate your performance for each section by consulting the answers on page 172. Do not continue with the next section until you understand each answer. If you need to, review or reread the appropriate section in the textbook before continuing.

. Compared with biosocial development during other periods of the life span, biosocial development during middle childhood is _____ (relatively smooth/often fraught with problems). For example, disease and

death during these years are _____ (more common/rarer) than during any other period. For another, sex differences in physical development and ability are _____ (very great/minimal).

Size and Shape (pp. 301–306)

2. Children grow _____ (faster/more slowly) during middle childhood than they did earlier or than they will in adolescence. The typical child gains about _____ pounds and _____ inches per year.

Describe several other features of physical development during the school years.

3. In some undeveloped countries, most of the variation in children's height and weight is caused by differences in _____ . In developed countries, most children grow as tall as their _____ allow.

4. The precise point at which a child is considered obese depends on _____ _____ , on the proportion of _____ to _____ , and on _____ _____ .

5. One measure of obesity is the _____ _____ _____ , which is the child's weight in _____ divided by the square of the _____ in meters. At age 6, obesity begins at a value of _____ on this index. At age 10, obesity begins at a value of _____ .

6. Experts estimate that between _____ and _____ percent of American children are obese.

7. Two physical problems associated with childhood obesity are _____ and _____ problems.

(Research Report) Identify several inherited characteristics that might contribute to obesity.

8. (Research Report) Inactive people burn _____ (more/fewer) calories and are _____ (no more/more) likely to be obese than active people.

9. (Research Report) Excessive television-watching by children _____ (is/is not) directly correlated with obesity. When children watch TV, their metabolism _____ (slows down/speeds up).

(Research Report) Identify three factors that make television-watching fattening.

10. (Research Report) American children whose parents were immigrants from developing countries are _____ (more/less) likely to be overweight. This demonstrates the importance of another factor in obesity: _____ _____ .

11. (Research Report) The onset of childhood obesity _____ (is/is not) commonly associated with a traumatic experience.

12. (Research Report) Fasting and/or repeated dieting _____ (lowers/raises) the rate of metabolism. For this reason, after a certain amount of weight loss, additional pounds become _____ (more/less) difficult to lose.

13. (Research Report) Strenuous dieting during childhood _____ (is/is not) potentially dangerous.

14. The best way to get children to lose weight is to increase their _____ _____ . Developmentalists agree that treating obesity early in life _____ (is/is not) very important in ensuring the child's overall health later in life.

15. (Changing Policy) A chronic inflammatory disorder of the airways is called _____. This health problem is becoming increasingly prevalent in _____ nations. It usually disappears by _____ _____ . Crucial in the epidemiology of this disorder are _____ factors.

16. (Changing Policy) Among the aspects of modern life that contribute to asthma are _____ _____ _____ .

(Changing Policy) List three environmental factors that are implicated in asthma.

Skill Development (pp. 306–313)

17. Children become more skilled at controlling their bodies during the school years, in part because they _____

18. The length of time it takes a person to respond to a particular stimulus is called _____ _____ . A key factor in this motor skill is _____ _____

19. Other important abilities that continue to develop during the school years are _____ _____ _____ , balance and judgment of _____ .

20. Because during the school years boys have greater _____-_____ strength than girls, they tend to have an advantage in sports such as _____ ,

whereas girls have an advantage in sports such as

_____ .

21. For most physical activities during middle childhood, biological sex differences are _____ , with expertise depending on three elements: _____ , _____ , and _____ . The development of specific motor skills also depends on _____ _____ and _____ .

22. Many of the sports that adults value _____ (are/are not) well suited for children.

23. Due to _____ differences, some children are simply more gifted in developing specific motor skills.

24. Motor habits that rely on coordinating both sides of the body improve because the _____ _____ between the brain's hemispheres continues to mature. Animal research also demonstrates that brain development is stimulated through _____ . In addition, _____ play may help boys overcome their tendencies toward _____ because it helps with regulation in the _____ _____ of the brain.

25. Tests that are designed to measure what a child has learned are called _____ tests. Tests that are designed to measure learning potential are called _____ tests.

26. The most commonly used aptitude tests are _____ _____ . In the original version of the most commonly used test of this type, a person's score was calculated as a _____ (the child's _____ divided by the child's _____ _____ and multiplied by 100 to determine his or her _____).

27. Two highly regarded IQ tests are the _____ - _____ and the _____ .

28. (Figure 11.4) On current tests, 70 percent of all children score somewhere between _____ and _____ . Children who score above _____ are considered gifted, whereas those who score in the _____ - _____ range are considered to be slow learners.

29. Testing is controversial in part because a child's test performance can be affected by nonacademic factors, such as _____ .

30. IQ scores may seriously underestimate the intellectual potential of a _____ child or overestimate that of a child from an _____ background.

31. (A Life-Span View) Robert Sternberg believes that there are three distinct types of intelligence: _____ , _____ , and _____ . Similarly, Howard Gardner describes _____ (how many?) distinct intelligences.

Children with Special Needs (pp. 313–323)

32. Among the psychological disorders that impair the development of children with special needs are _____ _____ .

33. The field of study that is concerned with childhood psychological disorders is _____ _____ .

34. This perspective has made diagnosticians much more aware of the _____ _____ of childhood problems. This awareness is reflected in the official diagnostic guide of the American Psychiatric Association, which is the _____ _____ .

35. One of the most severe disturbances of early childhood is _____ , a term that Leo Kanner first used to describe children who are _____ .

36. Children who have autistic symptoms that are less severe than those in the classic syndrome are sometimes diagnosed with _____ _____ .

37. Autism is more common in _____ (boys/girls).

38. In early childhood autism, severe deficiencies appear in three areas: _____ _____ , _____ _____ , and _____ _____ . The first two deficiencies are usually apparent during _____ .

39. Some autistic children engage in a type of speech called _____ , in which they repeat, word for word, things they have heard.

40. The unusual play patterns of autistic children are characterized by repetitive _____ and an absence of spontaneous _____ play.

41. The most devastating problem of autistic children often proves to be the lack of _____ _____ . Autistic children appear to lack a _____ _____ _____ .

42. Unaffected by others' opinions, autistic children also lack _____ _____ .

43. Some children have difficulty in school due to an overall slowness in development; that is, they suffer _____ _____ . If that difficulty _____ (is/is not) attributable to an overall intellectual slowness, a physical handicap, a severely stressful situation, or a lack of basic education, the child is said to have a _____ _____ .

44. A disability in reading is called _____ ; in math, it is called _____ . Other specific academic subjects that may show a learning disability are _____ and _____ .

45. A disability that manifests itself in a difficulty in concentrating for more than a few moments and a need to be active, often accompanied by excitability and impulsivity, is called _____ - _____ _____ _____ . The crucial problem in these conditions seems to be a neurological difficulty in paying _____ .

46. Researchers have identified several factors that may contribute to ADHD. These include _____ _____ , prenatal damage from _____ , and postnatal damage, such as from _____ _____ _____ .

47. Children with attention-deficit disorder without hyperactivity appear to be prone to _____ and _____ .

48. Many children with ADHD are prone to _____ , a fact that has led some researchers to propose a subtype of the disorder called _____ . Such children also are at risk for developing _____ and _____ disorders.

49. Developmental and contextual variations in ADHD help explain _____ differences in the frequency of this disorder. For example, children in _____ _____ are less likely to be diagnosed as having ADHD than U.S. children, but they are more likely to be diagnosed with _____ _____ .

50. Children with ADHD _____ (do/do not) tend to have continuing problems as adults.

51. In childhood, the most effective forms of treatment for ADHD are _____ , _____ therapy, and changes in the _____ .

52. Certain drugs that stimulate adults, such as _____ and _____ , have a reverse effect on many hyperactive children.

53. Teacher behavior that is too _____ or too _____ tends to exacerbate ADHD.

54. (In-Person) The training approach in which learning-disabled children are not separated into special classes is called _____ . More recently, some schools have developed a

_____ _____ , in which such children spend part of each day with a teaching specialist. In the most recent approach, called _____ , learning-disabled children receive targeted help within the setting of a regular classroom.

Progress Test 1

Multiple-Choice Questions

Circle your answers to the following questions and check them with the answers on page 173. If your answer is incorrect, read the explanation for why it is incorrect and then consult the appropriate pages of the text (in parentheses following the correct answer).

1. As children move into middle childhood:
   a. the rate of accidental death increases.
   b. sexual urges intensify.
   c. the rate of weight gain increases.
   d. biological growth slows and steadies.

2. During middle childhood:
   a. girls are usually stronger than boys.
   b. boys have greater physical flexibility than girls.
   c. boys have greater upper-arm strength than girls.
   d. the development of motor skills slows drastically.

3. (Research Report) To help obese children, nutritionists usually recommend:
   a. strenuous dieting to counteract early overfeeding.
   b. the use of amphetamines and other drugs.
   c. more exercise, stabilization of weight, and time to "grow out" of the fat.
   d. no specific actions.

4. A factor that is *not* primary in the development of motor skills during middle childhood is:
   a. practice.   c. brain maturation.
   b. gender.   d. age.

5. Dyslexia is a learning disability that affects the ability to:
   a. do math.   c. write.
   b. read.   d. speak.

6. (Research Report) In relation to weight in later life, childhood obesity is:
   a. not an accurate predictor of adolescent or adult weight.
   b. predictive of adolescent but not adult weight.
   c. predictive of adult but not adolescent weight.
   d. predictive of both adolescent and adult weight.

7. The developmental psychopathology perspective is characterized by its:
   a. contextual approach.
   b. emphasis on individual therapy.
   c. emphasis on the cognitive domain of development.
   d. concern with all of the above.

8. The time—usually measured in fractions of a second—it takes for a person to respond to a particular stimulus is called:
   a. the interstimulus interval.
   b. reaction time.
   c. the stimulus-response interval.
   d. response latency.

9. Researchers have suggested that excessive television-watching is a possible cause of childhood obesity because:
   a. TV bombards children with persuasive junk food commercials.
   b. children often snack while watching TV.
   c. body metabolism slows while watching TV.
   d. of all the above reasons.

10. The underlying problem in attention-deficit hyperactivity disorder appears to be:
    a. low overall intelligence.
    b. a neurological difficulty in paying attention.
    c. a learning disability in a specific academic skill.
    d. the existence of a conduct disorder.

11. Teacher behavior that seems to aggravate or increase problems in children with attention-deficit hyperactivity disorder tends to be:
    a. too rigid.
    b. too permissive.
    c. too rigid or permissive.
    d. none of the above.

12. In developed countries, most of the variation in children's size and shape can be attributed to:
    a. the amount of daily exercise.
    b. nutrition.
    c. genes.
    d. the interaction of the above factors.

13. Autistic children generally have severe deficiencies in all but which of the following?
    a. social skills
    b. imaginative play
    c. echolalia
    d. communication ability

14. (Changing Policy) Although asthma has genetic origins, several environmental factors contribute to its onset, including:
    a. urbanization.
    b. airtight windows.
    c. dogs and cats living inside the house.
    d. all of the above.

15. Psychoactive drugs are most effective in treating attention-deficit hyperactivity disorder when they are administered:
    a. before the diagnosis becomes certain.
    b. for several years after the basic problem has abated.
    c. as part of the labeling process.
    d. with psychological support or therapy.

16. Tests that measure a child's potential to learn a new subject are called _____ tests.
    a. aptitude
    b. achievement
    c. vocational
    d. intelligence

17. In the earliest aptitude tests, a child's score was calculated by dividing the child's _____ age by his or her _____ age to find the _____ quotient.
    a. mental; chronological; intelligence
    b. chronological; mental; intelligence
    c. intelligence; chronological; mental
    d. intelligence; mental; chronological

True or False Items

Write T *(true) or* F *(false)* on the line in front of each statement.

_____ 1. Physical variations in North American children are usually caused by diet rather than heredity.

_____ 2. Childhood obesity usually does not correlate with adult obesity.

_____ 3. Research shows a direct correlation between television-watching and obesity.

_____ 4. The quick reaction time that is crucial in some sports can be readily achieved with practice.

_____ 5. (In Person) Despite the efforts of teachers and parents, most children with learning disabilities can expect their disabilities to persist and even worsen as they enter adulthood.

_____ 6. (Research Report) The best way for children to lose weight is through strenuous dieting.

_____ 7. Autistic children have their own unique theory of mind.

_____ 8. Stressful living conditions is an important consideration in diagnosing a learning disability.

_____ 9. ADHD is diagnosed more often in Great Britain than in the United States.

_____ 10. The drugs sometimes given to children to reduce hyperactive behaviors have reverse effect on adults.

Progress Test 2

Progress Test 2 should be completed during a final chapter review. Answer the following questions after you thoroughly understand the correct answers for the Chapter Review and Progress Test 1.

Multiple-Choice Questions

1. During the years from 7 to 11, the average child:
   a. becomes slimmer.
   b. gains about 12 pounds a year.
   c. has decreased lung capacity.
   d. is more likely to become obese than at any other period in the life span.

2. (Research Report) Among the factors that are known to contribute to obesity are activity level, quantity and types of food eaten, and:
   a. a traumatic event.
   b. television-watching.
   c. attitudes toward food.
   d. all of the above.

3. A specific learning disability that becomes apparent when a child experiences unusual difficulty in learning to read is:
   a. dyslexia.   c. ADHD.
   b. dyscalcula.   d. ADHDA.

4. Problems in learning to write, read, and do math are collectively referred to as:
   a. learning disabilities.
   b. attention-deficit hyperactivity disorder.
   c. hyperactivity.
   d. dyscalcula.

5. A measure of obesity in which weight in kilograms is divided by the square of height in meters is the:
   a. basal metabolic rate (BMR)
   b. body mass index (BMI)
   c. body fat index (BFI)
   d. basal fat ratio (BFR)

6. Aptitude and achievement testing are controversial because:
   a. most tests are unreliable with respect to the individual scores they yield.
   b. test performance can be affected by many factors other than the child's intellectual potential or academic achievement.
   c. they often fail to identify serious learning problems.
   d. of all of the above reasons.

7. The most effective form of help for children with ADHD is:
   a. medication.
   b. psychological therapy.
   c. environmental change.
   d. a combination of some or all of the above.

8. A key factor in reaction time is:
   a. whether the child is male or female.
   b. brain maturation.
   c. whether the stimulus to be reacted to is an auditory or visual one.
   d. all of the above.

9. The first noticeable symptom of autism is usually:
   a. the lack of spoken language.
   b. abnormal social responsiveness.
   c. both a. and b.
   d. unpredictable.

10. Which of the following is true of children with a diagnosed learning disability?
    a. They are, in most cases, average in intelligence.
    b. They often have a specific physical handicap, such as hearing loss.
    c. They often lack basic educational experiences.
    d. All of the above are true.

11. During the school years:
    a. boys are, on average, at least a year ahead of girls in the development of physical abilities.
    b. girls are, on average, at least a year ahead of boys in the development of physical abilities.
    c. boys and girls are about equal in physical abilities.
    d. motor-skill development proceeds at a slower pace, since children grow more rapidly at this age than at any other time.

12. Whether a particular child is considered obese depends on:
    a. the child's body type.
    b. the proportion of fat to muscle.
    c. cultural standards.
    d. all of the above.

13. (In Person) Which approach to education may best meet the needs of learning-disabled children in terms of both skill remediation and social interaction with other children?
    a. mainstreaming
    b. special education
    c. inclusion
    d. resource rooms

14. Asperger syndrome is a disorder in which:
    a. body weight fluctuates dramatically over short periods of time.
    b. verbal skills seem normal, but social perceptions and skills are abnormal.
    c. an autistic child is extremely aggressive.
    d. a child of normal intelligence has difficulty In mastering a specific cognitive skill.

15. Which of the following is *not* a contributing factor in most cases of ADHD?
    a. genetic inheritance
    b. dietary sugar and caffeine
    c. prenatal damage
    d. postnatal damage

16. Tests that measure what a child has already learned are called _____ tests.
    a. aptitude
    b. vocational
    c. achievement
    d. intelligence

17. (A Life-Span View) Which of the following is not a type of intelligence identified in Robert Sternberg's theory?
    a. academic   c. achievement
    b. practical   d. creative

Matching Items

Match each term or concept with its corresponding description or definition.

Terms or Concepts

_____ **1.** dyslexia
_____ **2.** dyscalcula
_____ **3.** mental retardation
_____ **4.** attention-deficit hyperactivity disorder
_____ **5.** asthma
_____ **6.** echolalia
_____ **7.** autism
_____ **8.** developmental psychopathology
_____ **9.** DSM-IV
_____ **10.** learning disability
_____ **11.** mainstreaming

Descriptions or Definitions

a. an unexpected difficulty with one or more acade mic skills
b. speech that repeats, word for word, what has ju been heard
c. the diagnostic guide of the American Psychiat Association
d. a pervasive delay in cognitive development
e. system in which learning-disabled children a taught in general education classrooms
f. disorder characterized by the absence of a theo of mind
g. difficulty in reading
h. chronic inflammation of the airways
i. behavior problem involving difficulty in conce trating, as well as excitability and impulsivity
j. difficulty in math
k. applies insights from studies of normal develo ment to the study of childhood disorders

Thinking Critically About Chapter 11

Answer these questions the day before an exam as a final check on your understanding of the chapter's terms and concepts.

1. According to developmentalists, the best game for a typical group of 8-year-olds would be:
  a. football or baseball.
  b. basketball.
  c. one in which reaction time is not crucial.
  d. a game involving one-on-one competition.

2. Dr. Rutter, who believes that knowledge about normal development can be applied to the study and treatment of psychological disorders evidently is working from which of the following perspectives?
  a. clinical psychology
  b. developmental psychopathology
  c. behaviorism
  d. psychoanalysis

3. Nine-year-old Jack has difficulty concentrating on his classwork for more than a few moments, repeatedly asks his teacher irrelevant questions, and is constantly disrupting the class with loud noises. If his difficulties persist, Jack is likely to be diagnosed as suffering from:

  a. dyslexia.
  b. dyscalcula.
  c. autism.
  d. attention-deficit hyperactivity disorder.

4. Angela was born in 1984. In 1992, she scored 1 on an intelligence test. Using the original form la, what was Angela's mental age when she to the test?
  a. 6
  b. 8
  c. 10
  d. 12

5. Ten-year-old Clarence is quick-tempered, eas frustrated, and is often disruptive in the cla room. Clarence may be suffering from:
  a. dyslexia.
  b. dyscalcula.
  c. attention-deficit disorder.
  d. attention-deficit hyperactivity disorder.

6. Because 11-year-old Wayne is obese, he runs greater risk of developing:
  a. orthopedic problems.
  b. respiratory problems.
  c. psychological problems.
  d. all of the above.

7. Of the following individuals, who is likely to have the fastest reaction time?

  a. a 7-year-old   **c.** an 11-year-old

  b. a 9-year-old   **d.** an adult

8. Harold weighs about 20 pounds more than his friend Jay. During school recess, Jay can usually be found playing soccer with his classmates, while Harold sits on the sidelines by himself. Harold's rejection is likely due to his:

  a. being physically different.

  b. being dyslexic.

  c. intimidation of his schoolmates.

  d. being hyperactive.

9. In determining whether an 8-year-old has a learning disability, a teacher looks primarily for:

  a. exceptional performance in a subject area.

  b. the exclusion of other explanations.

  c. a family history of the learning disability.

  d. both a. and b.

0. When she moved her practice to England, Dr. Williams was struck by the fact that British doctors seemingly applied the criteria she used to diagnose ADHD to diagnose:

  a. dyslexia.

  b. dyscalcula.

  c. conduct disorder.

  d. antisocial personality.

1. If you were to ask an autistic child with echolalia, "what's your name?" the child would probably respond by saying:

  a. nothing.

  b. "what's your name?"

  c. "your name what's?"

  d. something that was unintelligible.

2. Although 12-year-old Brenda is quite intelligent, she has low self-esteem and few friends, and is often teased. Knowing nothing else about Brenda, you conclude that she may be:

  a. unusually aggressive.   **c.** arrogant.

  b. obese.   **d.** socially inept.

3. Danny has been diagnosed as having attention-deficit hyperactivity disorder. Every day his parents make sure that he takes the proper dose of Ritalin. His parents should:

  a. continue this behavior until Danny is an adult.

  b. try different medications when Danny seems to be reverting to his normal overactive behavior.

  c. make sure that Danny also has psychotherapy.

  d. not worry about Danny's condition; he will outgrow it.

14. In concluding her presentation entitled "Facts and falsehoods regarding childhood obesity," Cheryl states that, contrary to popular belief, _____ is *not* a common cause of childhood obesity.

  a. television-watching

  b. a traumatic event

  c. overeating of high-fat foods

  d. a prenatal teratogen

15. Curtis is 21 years old, 2 meters tall, and weighs 80 kilograms. His BMI equals _____ , making him statistically _____ .

  a. 40; obese

  b. 40; overweight

  c. 20; normal body weight

  d. 20; obese

16. (A Life-Span View) Howard Gardner and Robert Sternberg would probably be most critical of traditional aptitude and achievement tests because they:

  a. inadvertently reflect certain nonacademic competencies.

  b. do not reflect knowledge of cultural ideas.

  c. measure only a limited set of abilities.

  d. underestimate the intellectual potential of disadvantaged children.

Key Terms

Using your own words, write a brief definition or explanation of each of the following terms on a separate piece of paper.

  1. body mass index (BMI)

  2. asthma

  3. reaction time

  4. achievement tests

  5. aptitude tests

  6. IQ tests

  7. child with special needs

  8. developmental psychopathology

  9. DSM-IV

  10. autism

  11. Asperger syndrome

  12. mental retardation

13. learning disability
14. dyslexia
15. dyscalcula
16. ADHD (attention-deficit hyperactivity disorder)
17. mainstreaming
18. resource room
19. inclusion

ANSWERS

CHAPTER REVIEW

1. relatively smooth; rarer; minimal
2. more slowly; 5; 2 1/2

During the school years, children generally become slimmer, muscles become stronger, and lung capacity increases.

3. nutrition; genes
4. body type; fat; muscle; cultural standards
5. body mass index (BMI); kilograms; height; 19; 24
6. 20; 30
7. orthopedic; respiratory

Body type, including the amount and distribution of fat, as well as height and bone structure; individual differences in metabolic rate; and activity level are all influenced by heredity and can contribute to obesity.

8. fewer; more
9. is; slows down

While watching television, children (a) are bombarded with commercials for junk food, (b) consume many snacks, and (c) burn fewer calories than they would if they were actively playing.

10. more; cultural attitudes toward food
11. is
12. lowers; more
13. is
14. physical activity; is
15. asthma; developed; late adolescence; environmental
16. carpeted floors, more bedding, dogs and cats living inside the house, airtight windows, less outdoor play, crowded living conditions

The rate of asthma has at least doubled since 1980 in virtually every developed nation. Asthma patients tend to be those least susceptible to other childhood illnesses. Asthma is at least 10 times more common in urban areas than in rural areas.

17. grow slowly

18. reaction time; brain maturation
19. hand-eye coordination; movement
20. upper-arm; baseball; gymnastics
21. minimal; motivation; guidance; practice; national policy; genetics
22. are not
23. hereditary
24. corpus callosum; play; rough-and-tumble; hyper activity and learning disabilities; frontal lobes
25. achievement; aptitude
26. intelligence tests; quotient; mental age; chrono logical age; IQ
27. Stanford-Binet; Wechsler
28. 85; 115; 130; 70–85
29. the capacity to pay attention and concentrate emotional stress, health, language difficultie and test-taking anxiety
30. disadvantaged; advantaged
31. academic; creative; practical; seven
32. aggression, anxiety, autism, conduct disorde depression, developmental delay, hyperactivit learning disabilities, mutism, and mental slow ness
33. developmental psychopathology
34. social context; *Diagnostic and Statistical Manual Mental Disorders* (DSM-IV)
35. autism; self-absorbed
36. Asperger syndrome
37. boys
38. communication ability; social skills; imaginativ play; infancy
39. echolalia
40. rituals; imaginative
41. social understanding; theory of mind
42. emotional regulation
43. mental retardation; is not; learning disability
44. dyslexia; dyscalcula; spelling; handwriting
45. attention-deficit hyperactivity disorder; attentio
46. genetic inheritance; teratogens; lead poisoning repeated blows to the head
47. anxiety; depression
48. aggression; attention-deficit hyperactivity diso der with aggression (ADHDA); oppositional; co duct
49. cultural; Britain; conduct disorder
50. do
51. medication; psychological; family and scho environment

52. amphetamines; methylphenidate (Ritalin)

53. rigid; permissive

54. mainstreaming; resource room; inclusion

PROGRESS TEST 1

Multiple-Choice Questions

1. **d.** is the answer. (p. 301)

2. **c.** is the answer. (p. 308)

   a. Especially in forearm strength, boys are usually stronger than girls during middle childhood.

   b. During middle childhood, girls usually have greater overall flexibility than boys.

   d. Motor-skill development improves greatly during middle childhood.

3. **c.** is the answer. (p. 305)

   a. Strenuous dieting can be physically harmful and often makes children irritable, listless, and even sick—adding to the psychological problems of the obese child.

   b. Although not specifically mentioned in the box, the use of amphetamines to control weight is not recommended at any age.

4. **b.** Boys and girls are just about equal in physical abilities during the school years. (pp. 307–308)

5. **b.** is the answer. (p. 317)

   a. This is dyscalcula.

   c. & d. The text does not give labels for learning disabilities in writing or speaking.

6. **d.** is the answer. (p. 305)

7. **a.** is the answer. (p. 314)

   b. & c. Because of its contextual approach, developmental psychopathology emphasizes *group* therapy and *all* domains of development.

8. **b.** is the answer. (p. 307)

9. **d.** is the answer. (p. 304)

10. **b.** is the answer. (pp. 319–320)

11. **c.** is the answer. (p. 321)

12. **c.** is the answer. (p. 302)

    a. The amount of daily exercise a child receives is an important factor in his or her tendency toward obesity; exercise, however, does not explain most of the variation in childhood physique.

    b. In some parts of the world malnutrition accounts for most of the variation in physique; this is not true of developed countries, where most children get enough food to grow as tall as their genes allow.

13. **c.** is the answer. Echolalia *is* a type of communication difficulty. (p. 316)

14. **d.** is the answer. (p. 306)

15. **d.** is the answer. (pp. 320–321)

16. **a.** is the answer. (p. 31-)

    b. Achievement tests measure what has already been learned.

    c. Vocational tests, which, as their name implies, measure what a person has learned about a particular trade, are achievement tests.

    d. Intelligence tests measure general aptitude, rather than aptitude for a specific subject.

17. **a.** is the answer. (pp. 310–311)

True or False Items

1. F   Physical variations in children from developed countries are caused primarily by heredity. (p. 302)

2. F. If obesity is established in middle childhood, it tends to continue into adulthood. (p. 305)

3. T (p. 304)

4. F   Reaction time depends on brain maturation and is not readily affected by practice. (pp. 307–308)

5. F   With the proper assistance, many learning-disabled children develop into adults who are virtually indistinguishable from other adults in their educational and occupational achievements. (pp. 322–323)

6. F   Strenuous dieting during childhood can be dangerous. The best way to get children to lose weight is by increasing their activity level. (p. 305)

7. F   Autistic children seem to lack a theory of mind. (p. 316)

8. F   Stressful living conditions must be excluded before diagnosing a learning disability. (p. 317)

9. F   ADHD is more often diagnosed in the United States than in Britain. (p. 320)

10. T (p. 320)

PROGRESS TEST 2

Multiple-Choice Questions

1. **a.** is the answer. (p. 301)

   b. & c. During this period children gain about 5 pounds per year and experience increased lung capacity.

d. Although childhood obesity is a common problem, the text does not indicate that a person is more likely to become obese at this age than at any other.

2. **d.** is the answer. (p. 304)

3. **a.** is the answer. (p. 317)

b. This learning disability involves math rather than reading.

c. & d. These disorders do not manifest themselves in a particular academic skill but instead appear in psychological processes that affect learning in general.

4. **a.** is the answer. (p. 317)

b. & c. ADHD is a general learning disability that usually does not manifest itself in specific subject areas. Hyperactivity is a facet of this disorder.

d. Dyscalcula is a learning disability in math only.

5. **b.** is the answer. (p. 302)

6. **b.** is the answer. (pp. 311–312)

7. **d.** is the answer. (p. 320)

8. **b.** is the answer. (pp. 307–308)

9. **c.** is the answer. (p. 315)

10. **a.** is the answer. (p. 317)

11. **c.** is the answer. (p. 308)

12. **d.** is the answer. (p. 302)

13. **c.** is the answer. (p. 322)

a. Many general education teachers are unable to cope with the special needs of some children.

b. & d. These approaches undermined the social integration of children with special needs.

14. **b.** is the answer. (p. 315)

15. **b.** is the answer. (p. 319)

16. **c.** is the answer. (p. 310)

17. **c.** is the answer. (p. 312)

Matching Items

1. g (p. 317)   5. h (p. 306)   9. c (p. 314)
2. j (p. 318)   6. b (p. 316)   10. a (p. 317)
3. d (p. 317)   7. f (p. 315)   11. e (p. 322)
4. i (p. 319)   8. k (p. 314)

THINKING CRITICALLY ABOUT CHAPTER 11

1. **c.** is the answer. (p. 308)

a. & b. Each of these games involves skills that are hardest for schoolchildren to master.

d. Because one-on-one sports are likely to accentuate individual differences in ability, they may be especially discouraging to some children.

2. **b.** is the answer. (p. 314)

3. **d.** is the answer. (p. 319)

a. & b. Jack's difficulty is in concentrating, not in reading (dyslexia) or math (dyscalcula).

c. Autism is characterized by a lack of communication skills.

4. **c.** is the answer. At the time she took the test, Angela's chronological age was 8. Knowing that her IQ was 125, we can solve the equation to yield a mental age value of 10. (pp. 310–311)

5. **d.** is the answer. (p. 319)

6. **d.** is the answer. (p. 303)

7. **d.** is the answer. (pp. 307–308)

8. **a.** is the answer. (p. 303)

b., c., & d. Obese children are no more likely to be dyslexic, physically intimidating, or hyperactive than other children.

9. **d.** is the answer. (p. 317)

10. **c.** is the answer. (p. 320)

11. **b.** is the answer. (p. 316)

12. **b.** is the answer. (p. 303)

13. **c.** is the answer. Medication alone cannot ameliorate all the problems of ADHD. (p. 321)

14. **d.** is the answer. There is no evidence that teratogens have anything to do with obesity. (pp. 304–305)

15. **c.** is the answer. BMI = *weight/height squared*. Therefore, BMI for Curtis = 80/4, or 20. For adults, overweight begins at 25 BMI, and obesity begins at about 28 BMI (p. 302)

16. **c.** is the answer. Both Sternberg and Gardner believe that there are multiple intelligences rather than the narrowly defined abilities measured by traditional aptitude and achievement tests. (pp. 312–313)

a., b., & d. Although these criticisms are certainly valid, they are not specifically associated with Sternberg or Gardner.

KEY TERMS

1. **Body mass index (BMI)** is a measure of obesity in which a person's weight in kilograms is divided by his or her height squared in meters (p. 302)

2. **Asthma** is a disorder in which the airways are chronically inflamed. (p. 306)

. **Reaction time** is the length of time it takes a person to respond to a particular stimulus. (p. 307)

. **Achievement tests** are tests that measure what a child has already learned in a particular academic subject or subjects. (p. 310)

. **Aptitude tests** are tests designed to measure potential, rather than actual, accomplishment. (p. 310)

. **IQ tests** are aptitude tests, which were originally designed to yield a measure of intelligence, calculated as mental age divided by chronological age, multiplied by 100. (p. 310)

. A **child with special needs** requires particular physical, intellectual, or social accommodations in order to learn. (p. 313)

. **Developmental psychopathology** is a new field that applies the insights from studies of normal development to the study and treatment of childhood disorders. (p. 314)

. **DSM-IV** is the fourth edition of the *Diagnostic and Statistical Manual of Mental Disorders*, developed by the American Psychiatric Association, the leading means of distinguishing various emotional and behavioral disorders. (p. 314)

. **Autism** is a severe disturbance of early childhood characterized by an inability or unwillingness to communicate with others, poor social skills, and diminished imagination. (p. 315)

. **Asperger syndrome** is a disorder in which a person has many symptoms of autism, despite having near normal communication skills. (p. 315)

12. **Mental retardation** is a pervasive delay in cognitive development. (p. 317)

13. A **learning disability** is a difficulty in a particular cognitive skill that is not attributable to overall intellectual slowness, a physical handicap, a severely stressful living condition, or a lack of basic education. (p. 317)

14. **Dyslexia** is a learning disability in reading. (p. 317)

15. **Dyscalcula** is a learning disability in math. (p. 318)

16. **ADHD (attention-deficit hyperactivity disorder)** is a behavior problem in which the individual has great difficulty concentrating, is often excessively excitable and impulsive, and is sometimes aggressive. (p. 319)

17. **Mainstreaming** is an educational approach in which children with special needs are included in regular classrooms. (p. 322)

18. A **resource room** is a classroom equipped with special material, in which children with special needs spend part of their day working with a trained specialist in order to learn basic skills. (p. 322)

19. **Inclusion** is an educational approach in which children with special needs receive individualized instruction within a regular classroom setting. (p. 322)

The School Years: Cognitive Development

Chapter Overview

Chapter 12 examines the development of cognitive abilities in children from age 7 to 11. The first section focuses on changes in the child's selective attention, processing speed and capacity, memory strategies, knowledge base, and problem-solving strategies. The second section discusses Piaget's view of the child's cognitive development, which involves a growing ability to use logic and reasoning. Because the school years are also a time of expanding moral reasoning, this section also examines Kohlberg's stage theory of moral development as well as current reevaluations of his theory.

The third section looks at learning and schooling during middle childhood. During this time, children develop a more analytic understanding of words and show a marked improvement in pragmatic skills, such as changing from one form of speech to another when the situation so demands. The linguistic and cognitive advantages of bilingualism are discussed, as are educational and environmental conditions that are conducive to fluency in a second language. The chapter concludes by examining cultural variations in schooling.

NOTE: Answer guidelines for all Chapter 12 questions begin on page 187.

Guided Study

The text chapter should be studied one section at a time. Before you read, preview each section by skimming it, noting headings and boldface items. Then read the appropriate section objectives from the following outline. Keep these objectives in mind and, as you read the chapter section, search for the information that will enable you to meet each objective. Once you have finished a section, write out answers for its objectives.

Remembering, Knowing, and Processing (pp. 327–33

1. Describe the components of the informatio processing system, noting how they interact.

2. Discuss advances in selective attention a metacognition during middle childhood.

3. (A Life-Span View) Explain how processi speed increases in middle childhood as the resu of advances in automatization and a larg knowledge base.

ages of Thinking (pp. 332–341)

. Identify and discuss the logical operations of concrete operational thought, and give examples of how these operations are demonstrated by schoolchildren.

. Outline Kohlberg's stage theory of moral development.

. Identify and evaluate several criticisms of Kohlberg's theory, and discuss sociocultural effects on moral development.

8. Describe the development of communication skills during the school years, noting changing abilities in vocabulary and code switching.

9. Identify several conditions that foster the learning of a second language, and describe the best approaches to bilingual education.

10. Discuss how cultural needs and standards direct cognitive growth and have led to changes in how schoolchildren in the United States spend their time.

arning, and Schooling (pp. 341–352)

. (text and Changing Policy) Discuss variations in the schooling of children, focusing on the interactive approach to education.

Chapter Review

When you have finished reading the chapter, work through the material that follows to review it. Complete the sentences and answer the questions. As you proceed, evaluate your performance for each section by consulting the answers on page 187. Do not continue with the next section until you understand each answer. If you need to, review or reread the appropriate section in the textbook before continuing.

Remembering, Knowing, and Processing (pp. 327–332)

1. During middle childhood, children not only know more but also are more resourceful in using their cognitive resources in _____ _____ . In the words of John Flavell, they have acquired a sense of "the _____ of thinking."

2. The idea that the advances in thinking that accompany middle childhood occur because of basic changes in how children _____ and _____ data is central to the _____-_____ theory.

3. Incoming stimulus information is held for a split second in the _____ _____ , after which most of it is lost.

4. Meaningful material is transferred into _____ _____ , which is sometimes called _____-_____ _____ . This part of memory handles mental activity that is _____ .

5. The part of memory that stores information for days, months, or years is _____-_____ _____ .

6. The part of the information-processing system that regulates the analysis and flow of information is the _____ _____ .

7. The ability to use _____ _____—to screen out distractors and concentrate on relevant information—improves steadily during the school years.

8. (A Life-Span View) Children in the school years are better learners and problem solvers than younger children are, because they have faster _____ _____ , and they have a larger _____ _____ .

9. (A Life-Span View) One reason for the cognitive advances of middle childhood is _____ maturation, especially the _____ of nerve pathways and the development of the _____ _____ .

10. (A Life-Span View) Processing capacity also becomes more efficient through _____ , as familiar mental activities become routine.

11. (A Life-Span View) Memory ability improves during middle childhood in part because of the child's expanded _____ _____ .

12. (A Life-Span View) Research suggests that high IQ children _____ (are/are not) always more cognitively competent than low-IQ children, and that a larger _____ may be sufficient to overcome slower thinking.

13. The ability to evaluate a cognitive task to determine what to do—and to monitor one's performance—is called _____ . When such efforts involve memory techniques, they are called _____ _____ .

List some indicators of this developmental change during the school years.

tages of Thinking (pp. 332–341)

4. The information-processing perspective sees cognitive development as occurring in

_____ _____ . In contrast, Jean Piaget sees cognitive development as occurring in _____ .

5. The rapid change in intellectual competence that many children experience during middle childhood is known as the _____-

_____-_____

_____ . As a result, older children are more logical thinkers who seek explanations that are _____ , _____ ,

and _____ .

6. According to Piaget, between ages 7 and 11 children are in the stage of _____

_____ _____ .

7. The logical principle that certain characteristics of an object remain the same even when other characteristics change is _____ . The idea that a transformation process can be reversed to restore the original condition is

_____ .

8. Many concrete operations underlie the basic ideas of elementary-school _____

and _____ ; they are also relevant to everyday _____

problem solving.

9. The theorist who has extensively studied moral development by presenting subjects with stories that pose ethical dilemmas is

_____ . According to his theory, the three levels of moral reasoning are

_____ , _____ , and

_____ .

0. (Table 12.2) In preconventional reasoning, emphasis is on getting _____ and avoiding _____ . "Might makes right" describes stage _____ (1/2), whereas "look out for number one" describes stage _____ (1/2).

1. (Table 12.2) In conventional reasoning, emphasis is on _____ _____ ,

such as being a dutiful citizen, in stage

_____ (3/4), or winning approval from others, in stage _____ (3/4).

22. (Table 12.2) In postconventional reasoning, emphasis is on _____ .

_____ , such as _____

_____ (stage 5) and _____

_____ _____ (stage 6).

23. Although moral values begin to develop by age _____ , childhood is the time when moral values are _____ .

24. One criticism of Kohlberg's theory was that his dilemmas were too _____ and

_____ . A second is that the later stages reflect values associated with

_____ , _____ cultures.

25. Carol Gilligan believes that females develop a

_____ _____

_____ , based on concern for the well-being of others, more than a

_____ _____

_____ based on depersonalized standards of right and wrong.

26. Most researchers believe that abstract reasoning about hypothetical moral dilemmas

_____ (is/is not) the only way to measure moral judgment.

27. Recent studies have found that cognitive development is _____ (less/more) erratic than Piaget's descriptions would suggest. Cognitive development seems to be more affected by _____ factors than Piaget's descriptions imply.

Learning and Schooling (pp. 341–352)

28. There _____ (is/is not) universal agreement on how best to educate schoolchildren.

29. Historically, _____ (boys/girls) and wealthier children have been most likely to be formally taught and to have the greatest educational demands placed upon them.

30. Teaching techniques vary from the
    _____ _____
    method to _____
    _____ , in which students are
    encouraged to interact and make use of all class-
    room resources.

31. (Changing Policy) Worldwide, teachers have
    become more _____ of children's
    efforts. Although the specific styles and methods
    of education will vary, depending on
    _____ _____ and
    _____ _____ ,
    any developmental approach attempts to engage
    every student in an _____ learning
    process. A new approach in math replaces rote
    learning with _____-
    _____ materials and active discus-
    sion, promoting a problem-solving approach to
    learning.

32. One of the most important skills for children to
    learn in school is _____ .

33. Schoolchildren's love of words is evident in their
    _____ , secret _____ ,
    and _____ that they create.

34. Children become more _____ and
    _____ in their processing of vocabu-
    lary and are better able to define words by ana-
    lyzing their _____ to other words.

35. Changing from one form of speech to another is
    called _____-_____ .
    The _____ _____ ,
    which children use in situations such as the class-
    room, is characterized by extensive
    _____ , complex _____ ,
    and lengthy _____ . With their
    friends, children tend to use the _____
    _____ , which
    has a more limited use of vocabulary and syntax
    and relies more on _____ and
    _____ to convey meaning.

36. Compared with the formal code, which is con-
    text-_____ (free/bound), the informal
    code is context-_____ (free/bound).

While adults often stress the importance of mastery of the formal code, the informal code is also
evidence of the child's _____ .

37. Cognitively and linguistically, it is a(n)
    _____ (advantage/disadvantage)
    for children to learn more than one language.

38. The approach to bilingual education in which the
    child's instruction occurs entirely in the second
    language is called _____ . In
    _____ _____ pro-
    grams, the child is taught first in his or her native
    language, until the second language is taught as a
    "foreign" language.

39. In ESL, or _____
    programs, children must master the basics of
    English before joining regular classes with other
    children. In contrast, _____
    _____ requires that
    teachers instruct children in both their native lan-
    guage as well as in English. An approach to
    teaching a second language that recognizes the
    importance of nonnative cultural strategies in
    learning is called _____-
    _____ _____ .

40. Immersion programs have been successful in
    _____ , with English-speaking chil-
    dren who were initially placed in French-only
    classrooms. In Guatemala, however,
    _____ _____ (which
    strategy?) seems to work best in teaching children
    a second language. Immersion tends to fail if the
    child feels _____ , _____
    or _____ _____ .

41. The crucial difference between success and fail-
    ure in second-language learning rests with
    _____
    _____ , who
    indicate to the children whether learning a sec-
    ond language is really valued.

42. Ideally, children learn a first and second spoken
    language best under age _____ .

43. The best teachers of a second language are
    _____ .

4. (Table 12.3) Compared to their counterparts in 1981, schoolchildren in the United States in 1997 spend more time _____ _____ , and less time _____ _____ . This shift is a result of the perception that the superior academic performance of children from _____ is due to this distribution of activities and time.

Progress Test 1

Multiple-Choice Questions

Circle your answers to the following questions and check them with the answers on page 187. If your answer is incorrect, read the explanation for why it is incorrect and then consult the appropriate pages of the text (in parentheses following the correct answer).

1. According to Piaget, the stage of cognitive development in which a person understands specific logical ideas and can apply them to concrete problems is called:
   a. preoperational thought.
   b. operational thought.
   c. concrete operational thought.
   d. formal operational thought.

2. The "5-to-7 shift" refers to the rapid change in _____ that children experience between ages 5 and 7.
   a. social competence
   b. moral reasoning
   c. friendship networks
   d. every domain of thinking

3. The idea that an object that has been transformed in some way can be restored to its original form by undoing the process is:
   a. identity.   c. total immersion.
   b. reversibility.   d. automatization.

4. Information-processing theorists contend that major advances in cognitive development occur during the school years because:
   a. the child's mind becomes more like a computer as he or she matures.
   b. children become better able to process and analyze information.

   c. most mental activities become automatic by the time a child is about 13 years old.
   d. the major improvements in reasoning that occur during the school years involve increased long-term memory capacity.

5. The ability to filter out distractions and concentrate on relevant details is called:
   a. metacognition.
   b. information processing.
   c. selective attention.
   d. decentering.

6. Concrete operational thought is Piaget's term for the school-age child's ability to:
   a. reason logically about things and events he or she perceives.
   b. think about thinking.
   c. understand that certain characteristics of an object remain the same when other characteristics are changed.
   d. understand that moral principles may supercede the standards of society.

7. The term for the ability to monitor one's cognitive performance—to think about thinking—is:
   a. pragmatics.
   b. information processing.
   c. selective attention.
   d. metacognition.

8. Long-term memory is _____ permanent and _____ limited than working memory.
   a. more; less
   b. less; more
   c. more; more
   d. less; less

9. In making moral choices, according to Gilligan, females are more likely than males to:
   a. score at a higher level in Kohlberg's system.
   b. emphasize the needs of others.
   c. judge right and wrong in absolute terms.
   d. formulate abstract principles.

10. During middle childhood, children become more analytical and logical in their understanding of words. This means that they:
    a. learn more words per year than they did during the play years.
    b. can first learn a second language.
    c. no longer engage in verbal play.
    d. become much more "teachable."

11. The formal code that children use in the classroom is characterized by:
    a. limited use of vocabulary and syntax.
    b. context-bound grammar.
    c. extensive use of gestures and intonation to convey meaning.
    d. extensive vocabulary, complex syntax, and lengthy sentences.

12. Which of the following is *not* an approach used in the United States to avoid the shock of complete immersion in the teaching of English?
    a. reverse immersion
    b. English as a second language
    c. bilingual education
    d. bilingual-bicultural education

13. Information-processing theorists see cognitive development as occurring in _____ , and Jean Piaget sees cognitive development as occurring in _____ .
    a. stages; small steps
    b. small steps; stages
    c. unpredictable ways; predictable ways
    d. predictable ways; unpredictable ways

14. Historically, boys and wealthier children were more likely to be formally taught and to have greater educational demands placed on them than girls or poor children. Today, this inequality:
    a. can be found only in developing countries.
    b. has largely disappeared.
    c. persists, even in developed countries.
    d. has been eliminated for girls but not for poor children.

15. Of the following, which was not identified as an important factor in the difference between success and failure in second-language learning?
    a. the age of the child
    b. the attitudes of the parents
    c. community values regarding second language learning
    d. the difficulty of the language

True or False Items

Write T (*true*) or F (*false*) on the line in front of each statement.

_____ 1. A major objection to Piaget's theory is that it describes the schoolchild as an active learner, a term appropriate only for preschoolers.

_____ 2. Learning a second language fosters children's overall linguistic and cognitive development.

_____ 3. (Table 12.3) American children spe[n] less time in school today than did the[ir] counterparts in the 1980s

_____ 4. (Changing Policy) Developmentali[sts] encourage an interactive teachi[ng] approach in the classroom

_____ 5. The process of telling a joke involv[es] pragmatic language skills usually n[ot] mastered before age 7.

_____ 6. Code switching, especially the occasio[n]al use of slang, is a behavior character[is]tic primarily of children in the low[er] social strata.

_____ 7. The best time to learn a second la[n]guage by listening and talking is duri[ng] middle childhood.

_____ 8. Most information that comes into t[he] sensory register is lost or discarded.

_____ 9. Information-processing theorists belie[ve] that advances in the thinking of scho[ol]age children occur primarily because [of] changes in long-term memory.

_____ 10. New standards of math education [in] many nations emphasize proble[m] solving skills rather than simple men[mo]rization of formulas.

Progress Test 2

Progress Test 2 should be completed during a fi[nal] chapter review. Answer the following questions af[ter] you thoroughly understand the correct answers [to] the Chapter Review and Progress Test 1.

Multiple-Choice Questions

1. According to Piaget, 8- and 9-year-olds can r[ea]son only about concrete things in their liv[es]. "Concrete" means:
   a. logical.
   b. abstract.
   c. tangible or specific.
   d. mathematical or classifiable.

2. Recent research regarding Piaget's theory h[as] found that:
   a. Cognitive development seems to be consid[er]ably less affected by sociocultural factors th[an] Piaget's descriptions imply.
   b. The movement to a new level of thinking [is] much more erratic than Piaget predicted
   c. There is no "5-to-7 shift."
   d. All of the above are true.

3. The increase in processing speed that occurs during middle childhood is partly the result of:
   a. ongoing myelination of axons.
   b. neurological development in the limbic system.
   c. the streamlining of the knowledge base.
   d. all of the above.

4. When psychologists look at the ability of children to receive, store, and organize information, they are examining cognitive development from a view based on:
   a. the observations of Piaget.
   b. information processing.
   c. learning theory.
   d. the idea that the key to thinking is the sensory register.

5 Kohlberg's stage theory of moral development is based on his research on a group of boys and on:
   a. psychoanalytic ideas.
   b. Piaget's theory of cognitive development.
   c. Carol Gilligan's research on moral dilemmas.
   d. questionnaires distributed to a nationwide sample of high school seniors.

6. The logical operations of concrete operational thought are particularly important to an understanding of the elementary-school subject(s) of:
   a. spelling.   c. math and science.
   b. reading.   d. social studies.

7. Although older school-age children are generally at the conventional level of moral reasoning, *when* they reach a particular level depends on:
   a. the specific context and the child's opportunity to discuss moral issues.
   b. the level of moral reasoning reached by their parents.
   c. how strongly their peers influence their thinking.
   d. whether they are male or female.

8. Which of the following Piagetian ideas is *not* widely accepted by developmentalists today?
   a. The thinking of school-age children is characterized by a more comprehensive logic than that of preschoolers.
   b. Children are active learners.
   c. How children think is as important as what they know.
   d. Once a certain type of reasoning ability emerges in children, it is evenly apparent in all domains of thinking.

9. Processing capacity refers to:
   a. the ability to selectively attend to more than one thought.
   b. the amount of information that a person is able to hold in working memory.
   c. the size of the child's knowledge base.
   d. all of the above.

10. The retention of new information is called:
    a. retrieval.   c. automatization.
    b. storage.   d. metacognition.

11. According to Kohlberg, a person who is a dutiful citizen and obeys the laws set down by society would be at which level of moral reasoning?
    a. preconventional stage one
    b. preconventional stage two
    c. conventional
    d. postconventional

12. Which aspect of the information-processing system assumes an executive role in regulating the analysis and transfer of information?
    a. sensory register   c. long-term memory
    b. working memory   d. control processes

13. An example of schoolchildren's growth in metacognition is their understanding that:
    a. transformed objects can be returned to their original state.
    b. rehearsal is a good strategy for memorizing, but outlining is better for understanding.
    c. objects may belong to more than one class.
    d. they can use different language styles in different situations.

14. A new approach to math education focuses on:
    a. rote memorization of formulas before problems are introduced.
    b. "hands-on" materials and active discussion of concepts.
    c. one-on-one tutorials.
    d. grouping children by ability.

15. Regarding bilingual education, many contemporary developmentalists believe that:
    a. the attempted learning of two languages is confusing to children and delays proficiency in either one or both languages.
    b. bilingual education is linguistically, culturally, and cognitively advantageous to children.
    c. second-language education is most effective when the child has not yet mastered the native language.
    d. bilingual education programs are too expensive to justify the few developmental advantages they confer.

Matching Items
Match each term or concept with its corresponding description or definition.

Terms or Concepts

_____ 1. automatization
_____ 2. reversibility
_____ 3. conventional
_____ 4. identity
_____ 5. information processing
_____ 6. selective attention
_____ 7. retrieval
_____ 8. storage
_____ 9. metacognition
_____ 10. immersion
_____ 11. postconventional
_____ 12. preconventional

Descriptions or Definitions

a. the ability to screen out distractions and conce trate on relevant information
b. the idea that a transformation process can undone to restore the original conditions
c. the idea that certain characteristics of an obj remain the same even when other characteristi change
d. developmental perspective that conceives of cc nitive development as the result of changes in t processing and analysis of information
e. moral reasoning in which the individual focus on his or her own welfare
f. moral reasoning in which the individual follov principles that supersede the standards of socie
g. an educational technique in which instructi occurs entirely in the second language
h. accessing previously learned information
i. holding information in memory
j. moral reasoning in which the individual consi ers social standards and laws to be primary
k. process by which familiar mental activiti become routine
l. the ability to evaluate a cognitive task and monitor one's performance on it

Thinking Critically About Chapter 12

Answer these questions the day before an exam as a final check on your understanding of the chapter's terms and concepts.

1. Of the following statements made by children, which best exemplifies the logical principle of identity?

    a. "You can't leave first base until the ball is hit!"
    b. "See how the jello springs back into shape after I poke my finger into it?"
    c. "I know it's still a banana, even though it's mashed down in my sandwich."
    d. "You're my friend, so I don't have to use polite speech like I do with adults."

2. Which of the following statements is the clearest indication that the child has grasped the principle of reversibility?

    a. "See, the lemonade is the same in both our glasses; even though your glass is taller than mine, it's narrower."

    b. "Even though your dog looks funny, I kno it's still a dog."
    c. "I have one sister and no brothers. My pa ents have two children."
    d. "I don't cheat because I don't want to be pu ished."

3. Compared to her 4-year-old sister, 9-year-o Andrea is more likely to seek explanations th are:

    a. intuitive.   c. subjective.
    b. generalizable.   d. all of the above.

4. (A Life-Span View) Dr. Larsen believes that t cognitive advances of middle childhood occ because of basic changes in children's thinki speed, knowledge base, and memory retriev skills. Dr. Larsen evidently is working from t _____ perspective.

    a. Piagetian
    b. Vygotskian
    c. information-processing
    d. psychoanalytic

5. Some researchers believe that cognitive processing speed and capacity increase during middle childhood because of:
   a. the myelination of nerve pathways.
   b. the maturation of the frontal cortex.
   c. better use of cognitive resources.
   d. all of the above.

6. A child's ability to tell a joke that will amuse his or her audience always depends on:
   a. the child's mastery of reciprocity and reversibility.
   b. code switching.
   c. the child's ability to consider another's perspective.
   d. an expansion of the child's processing capacity.

7. (A Life-Span View) For a 10-year-old, some mental activities have become so familiar or routine as to require little mental work. This development is called:
   a. selective attention.   c. metacognition.
   b. identity.   d. automatization.

8. Lana is 4 years old and her brother Roger is 7. The fact that Roger remembers what their mother just told them about playing in the street while Lana is more interested in the children playing across the street is due to improvements in Roger's:
   a. control processes.   c. selective attention.
   b. automatization.   d. long-term memory.

9. Which of the following statements is the best example of Kohlberg's concept of stage 1 preconventional moral reasoning?
   a. "Might makes right."
   b. "Law and order."
   c. "Nice boys do what is expected of them."
   d. "Look out for number one."

10. According to Carol Gilligan, a girl responding to the hypothetical question of whether an impoverished child should steal food to feed her starving dog is most likely to:
    a. respond according to a depersonalized standard of right and wrong.
    b. hesitate to take a definitive position based on the abstract moral premise of "right and wrong."
    c. immediately respond that the child was justified in stealing the food.
    d. respond unpredictably, based on her own personal experiences.

11. Compared to their counterparts 20 years ago, a typical American schoolchild in 1997 spent more time:
    a. attending school.   c. watching TV.
    b. playing.   d. at all the above.

12. As compared with her 5-year-old brother, 7-year-old Althea has learned to adjust her vocabulary to her audience. This is known as:
    a. selective attention.   c. code-switching.
    b. retrieval.   d. reversibility.

13. (Changing Policy) Compared with her mother, who attended elementary school in the 1950s, Bettina, who is now in the third grade, is likely to be in a class that places greater emphasis on:
    a. individualized learning.
    b. active learning.
    c. learning by discovery, discussion, and deduction.
    d. all of the above.

14. Critics of Kohlberg's theory of moral development argue that it:
    a. places too much emphasis on sociocultural factors.
    b. places too much emphasis on traditional, religious beliefs.
    c. is biased toward liberal, Western cultural beliefs.
    d. can't be tested.

15. (A Life-Span View) The study of fourth-graders' memory of a written passage about soccer revealed that:
    a. high-IQ children always did better than low-IQ children.
    b. expert soccer players outperformed novices, even when their IQ was lower.
    c. the size of a child's knowledge base was less important as a factor in their memory than their IQ.
    d. novice soccer players performed poorly, regardless of their IQ.

Key Terms

Writing Definitions

Using your own words, write a brief definition or explanation of each of the following terms on a separate piece of paper.

1. information-processing theory
2. sensory register
3. working memory

4. long-term memory
5. control processes
6. selective attention
7. automatization
8. metacognition
9. knowledge base
10. concrete operational thought
11. 5-to-7 shift
12. identity
13. reversibility
14. preconventional moral reasoning

15. conventional moral reasoning
16. postconventional moral reasoning
17. morality of care
18. morality of justice
19. code-switching
20. formal code
21. informal code
22. total immersion
23. English as a second language (ESL)
24. bilingual education
25. bilingual-bicultural education

Cross Check

After you have written the definitions of the key terms in this chapter, you should complete the crossword puzzle to ensure that you can reverse the process—recognize the term, given the definition.

ACROSS

2. Processes that regulate the analysis and flow of information in memory.
6. According to Gilligan, men develop a morality of _____ .
10. The part of memory that stores unlimited amounts of information for days, months, or years.
11. English as a second language.
12. Psychologist who developed an influential theory of cognitive development.
13. According to the theorist in 12 across, cognitive development occurs in _____ .
14. Speech code used by children in school and with adults.
16. Speech code used by children in casual situations.
17. One of Kohlberg's harshest critics.
18. According to Piaget, the type of cognitive operations that occur during middle childhood.
19. Moral reasoning in which the individual considers social standards and laws to be primary.

DOWN

1. The part of memory that handles current, conscious mental activity.
2. According to Gilligan, females develop a morality of

_____ .

3. The ability to evaluate a cognitive task in order to determine what to do.

4. Process by which familiar mental activities become routine.
5. Ongoing neural process that speeds up neural processing.
7. Changing from one form of speech to another.
8. An approach to teaching a second language in which the teacher instructs the children in school subjects using their native language as well as the second language.
9. The body of knowledge that has been learned about a particular area.
15. Neurological development in the _____ cortex during middle childhood helps speed neural processing.

ANSWERS

CHAPTER REVIEW

1. problem solving; game
2. process; analyze; information-processing
3. sensory register
4. working memory; short-term memory; conscious
5. long-term memory
6. control processes
7. selective attention
8. processing speed; processing capacity
9. neurological; myelination; frontal cortex
10. automatization
11. knowledge base
12. are not; knowledge base
13. metacognition; cognitive strategies

School-age children's better use of cognitive strategies derives from metacognitive growth. Furthermore, they know how to identify challenging tasks and devote greater effort to them; they also know how to evaluate their learning progress and how to distinguish fantasy from reality. In short, they approach cognitive tasks in a more strategic and analytic manner.

14. small steps; stages
15. 5-to-7 shift; rational; consistent; generalizable
16. concrete operational thought
17. identity; reversibility
18. math; science; social
19. Kohlberg; preconventional; conventional; post-conventional
20. rewards; punishments; 1; 2
21. social rules; 4; 3
22. moral principles; social contracts; universal ethical principles
23. 2; taught
24. narrow; restricted; liberal Western
25. morality of care; morality of justice
26. is not
27. more; sociocultural
28. is not
29. boys
30. strict lecture; open education
31. encouraging; teacher personality; cultural assumptions; interactive; hands-on
32. communication
33. poems; languages; jokes

34. logical; analytical; connections
35. code-switching; formal code; vocabulary; syntax; sentences; informal code; gestures; intonation
36. free; bound; ability
37. advantage
38. immersion; reverse immersion
39. English as a second language; bilingual education; bilingual-bicultural education
40. Canada; reverse immersion; shy; stupid; socially isolated
41. the attitudes of parents, teachers, and the community
42. 5
43. peers
44. in school, playing sports, studying, doing art, reading; being outdoors, playing, watching TV; Asia

PROGRESS TEST 1

Multiple-Choice Questions

1. **c.** is the answer. (p. 332)

   a. Preoperational thought is "pre-logical" thinking.

   b. There is no such stage in Piaget's theory.

   d. Formal operational thought extends logical reasoning to abstract problems.

2. **d.** is the answer. (p. 332)

3. **b.** is the answer. (p. 334)

   a. This is the concept that certain characteristics of an object remain the same even when other characteristics change.

   c. This is a form of bilingual education in which the child is taught totally in his or her nonnative language.

   d. This is the process by which familiar mental activities become routine and automatic.

4. **b.** is the answer. (p. 327)

   a. Information-processing theorists use the mind-computer metaphor at every age.

   c. Although increasing automatization is an important aspect of development, the information-processing perspective does not suggest that most mental activities become automatic by age 13.

   d. Most of the important changes in reasoning that occur during the school years are due to the improved processing capacity of the person's *working memory*.

5. **c.** is the answer. (p. 329)

a. This is the ability to evaluate a cognitive task and to monitor one's performance on it.

b. Information processing is a perspective on cognitive development that focuses on how the mind analyzes, stores, retrieves, and reasons about information.

d. Decentering, which refers to the school-age child's ability to consider more than one aspect of a problem simultaneously, is not discussed in this chapter.

6. **a.** is the answer. (p. 332)

b. This refers to metacognition.

c. This refers to Piaget's concept of identity.

d. This is characteristic of Kohlberg's postconventional moral reasoning.

7. **d.** is the answer. (p. 330)

a. Pragmatics refers to the practical use of language to communicate with others.

b. The information-processing perspective views the mind as being like a computer.

c. This is the ability to screen out distractions in order to focus on important information.

8. **a.** is the answer. (p. 328)

9. **b.** is the answer. (pp. 337–338)

10. **d.** is the answer. (p. 343)

a. In fact, vocabulary growth is less explosive than in earlier years.

b. Second language learning proceeds most smoothly when it begins at a younger age.

c. This is "prime time" for verbal play, as evidenced in the jokes and poems children create during the school years.

11. **d.** is the answer. (p. 345)

a., b., & c. These are characteristic of the informal code that children use with friends in other settings.

12. **a.** is the answer. (p. 348)

13. **b.** is the answer. (p. 332)

c. & d. Both theorists view cognitive development as being at least somewhat predictable.

14. **c.** is the answer. (p. 341)

15. **d.** is the answer. (pp. 348)

True or False Items

1. F Most educators agree that the school-age child, like the preschooler, is an active learner. (p. 332)

2. T (p. 346)

3. T (p. 351)

4. T (p. 343)

5. T (p. 342)

6. F Code switching (including occasional use slang) is a behavior demonstrated by all children (p. 345)

7. F The best time to learn a second language listening and talking is during *early* childhood. 346)

8. T (p. 328)

9. F They believe that the changes are due to bas changes in control processes. (p. 329)

10. T (pp. 351–352)

PROGRESS TEST 2

Multiple-Choice Questions

1. **c.** is the answer. (p. 332)

2. **b.** is the answer. (p. 339)

3. **a.** is the answer. (pp. 330–331)

b. Neurological development in the frontal corte facilitates processing speed during middle chil hood. The limbic system, which was not di cussed in this chapter, is concerned with em tions.

c. Processing speed is facilitated by *growth*, rath than streamlining, of the knowledge base.

4. **b.** is the answer. (p. 328)

5. **b.** is the answer. (p. 334)

6. **c.** is the answer. (pp. 332–334)

7. **a.** is the answer. (p. 337)

b., c., & d. Although these may be factors, the don't necessarily determine the child's level moral reasoning.

8. **d.** is the answer. (p. 339)

9. **b.** is the answer. (p. 330)

10. **b.** is the answer. (p. 328)

a. This the *accessing* of already learned inform tion.

c. Automatization is the process by which we learned activities become routine and automatic

d. This is the ability to evaluate a task and monitor one's performance on it.

11. **c.** is the answer. (p. 336)

12. **d.** is the answer. (pp. 328–329)

a. The sensory register stores incoming inform tion for a split second.

b. Working memory is the part of memory th handles current, conscious mental activity.

c. Long-term memory stores information for days, months, or years.

3. b. is the answer. (pp. 330–332)

4. b. is the answer. (p. 343)

5. b. is the answer. (p. 346)

Matching Items

1. k (p. 330)	**5.** d (p. 328)	**9.** l (p. 330)
2. b (p. 334)	**6.** a (p. 329)	**10.** g (p. 346)
3. j (p. 334)	**7.** h (p. 328)	**11.** f (p. 334)
4. c (p. 333)	**8.** i (p. 328)	**12.** e (p. 334)

THINKING CRITICALLY ABOUT CHAPTER 12

1. c. is the answer. (p. 333)

a., b., & d. Identity is the logical principle that certain characteristics of an object (such as the shape of a banana) remain the same even when other characteristics change.

2. a. is the answer. (p. 334)

b., c., & d. Reversibility is the logical principle that something that has been changed (such as the height of lemonade poured from one glass into another) can be returned to its original shape by reversing the process of change (pouring the liquid back into the other glass).

3. b. is the answer. (pp. 333–334)

4. c. is the answer. (pp. 330–331)

a. This perspective emphasizes the logical, active nature of thinking during middle childhood.

b. This perspective emphasizes the importance of social interaction in learning.

d. This perspective does not address the development of cognitive skills.

5. d. is the answer. (p. 330)

6. c. is the answer. Joke-telling is one of the clearest demonstrations of schoolchildren's improved pragmatic skills, including the ability to know what someone else will think is funny. (p. 342)

7. d. is the answer. (p. 330)

a. Selective attention is the ability to focus on important information and screen out distractions.

b. Identity is the logical principle that certain characteristics of an object remain the same even when other characteristics change.

c. Metacognition is the ability to evaluate a task and to monitor one's performance on it.

8. c. is the answer. (p. 329)

a. Control processes regulate the analysis and flow of information.

b. Automatization refers to the tendency of well-rehearsed mental activities to become routine and automatic.

d. Long-term memory is the part of memory that stores information for days, months, or years.

9. a. is the answer. (p. 336)

b. & c. These exemplify conventional moral reasoning.

b. This exemplifies stage 2 preconventional moral reasoning.

10. b. is the answer. Gilligan contends that females' morality of care makes them reluctant to judge right and wrong in absolute terms because they are socialized to be nurturant and caring. (p. 337)

11. a. is the answer. (p. 351)

12. c. is the answer. (p. 345)

13. d. is the answer. (pp. 342–343)

14. c. is the answer. (p. 337)

15. b. is the answer. (p. 331)

KEY TERMS

Writing Definitions

1. According to **information-processing theory**, human thinking is analogous to a computer in sorting, categorizing, storing, and retrieving stimuli. (p. 327)

2. **Sensory register** is the memory system that stores incoming stimuli for a fraction of a second, after which it is passed into working memory, or discarded as unimportant. (p. 328)

3. **Working memory** is the part of memory that handles current, conscious mental activity; also called short-term memory. (p. 328)

4. **Long-term memory** is the part of memory that stores unlimited amounts of information for days, months, or years. (p. 328)

5. **Control processes** (such as selective attention and retrieval strategies) regulate the analysis and flow of information in memory. (p. 328)

6. **Selective attention** is the ability to screen out distractions and concentrate on relevant information. (p. 329)

7. **Automatization** is the process by which familiar and well-rehearsed mental activities become routine and automatic. (p. 330)

8. **Metacognition** is the ability to evaluate a cognitive task to determine what to do and to monitor one's performance on that task. (p. 330)

9. The **knowledge base** is a body of knowledge in a particular area that has been learned and on which additional learning can be based. (p. 331)

10. During Piaget's stage of **concrete operational thought**, lasting from ages 7 to 11, children can think logically about concrete events and objects but are not able to reason abstractly. (p. 332)

11. The **5-to-7 shift** is the reorganization of all domains of the thinking process that occurs between ages 5 and 7, making children more systematic, objective, and educable thinkers. (p. 332)

12. In Piaget's theory, **identity** is the logical principle that certain characteristics of an object remain the same even when other characteristics change. (p. 333)

13. **Reversibility** is the logical principle that a transformation process can be reversed to restore the original conditions. (p. 334)

14. Kohlberg's first level of moral reasoning, **preconventional moral reasoning**, emphasizes obedience to authority in order to avoid punishment (stage 1) and being nice to other people so they will be nice to you (stage 2). (p. 334)

15. Kohlberg's second level of moral reasoning, **conventional moral reasoning**, emphasizes winning the approval of others (stage 3) and obeying the laws set down by those in power (stage 4). (p. 334)

16. Kohlberg's third level, **postconventional moral reasoning**, emphasizes the social and contractual nature of moral principles (stage 5) and the existence of universal ethical principles (stage 6). (p. 334)

17. Compared with boys and men, girls and women are more likely to develop a **morality of care** that is based on comparison, nurturance, and concern for the well-being of others. (p. 337)

18. Compared with girls and women, boys and men are more likely to develop a **morality of justice** based on depersonalized standards of right and wrong. (p. 337)

19. **Code-switching** is a pragmatic communication skill involving changing from one form of speech to another. (p. 345)

20. The **formal code** is a form of speech used by children in school and other formal situations, characterized by extensive vocabulary, complex syntax, lengthy sentences, and conformity to other social norms for correct language. (p. 345)

21. The **informal code** is a form of speech used by children in casual situations, characterized by limited vocabulary and syntax. (p. 345)

22. **Total immersion** is an approach to bilingual education in which the child's instruction occurs entirely in the new language. (p. 346)

23. **English as a second language (ESL)** is an approach to teaching English in which all instruction is in English, and the teacher does not speak the child's native language. (p. 347)

24. **Bilingual education** is an approach to teaching a second language in which the teacher instructs the children in school subjects using their native language as well as the second language. (p. 347)

25. **Bilingual-bicultural education** is an approach to teaching a second language that incorporates the child's native, cultural symbols in the learning process. (p. 347)

Cross Check

ACROSS	DOWN
2. control	1. working
6. justice	2. care
10. long-term	3. metacognition
11. ESL	4. automatization
12. Piaget	5. myelination
13. stages	7. code-switching
14. formal	8. bilingual
16. informal	9. knowledge base
17. Gilligan	15. frontal
18. concrete	
19. conventional	

CHAPTER 13

The School Years: Psychosocial Development

Chapter Overview

This chapter brings to a close the unit on the school years. We have seen that from ages 7 to 11, the child becomes stronger and more competent, mastering the biosocial and cognitive abilities that are important in his or her culture. Psychosocial accomplishments are equally impressive.

The first section of the chapter begins by exploring the growing social competence of children, as described by Freud, Erikson, learning, cognitive, sociocultural, and epigenetic systems theorists. The section continues with a discussion of the growth of social cognition and self-understanding.

Children's interaction with peers and others in their ever-widening social world is the subject of the next section. Although the peer group often is a supportive, positive influence on children, some children are rejected by their peers or become the victims of bullying.

The next section explores the problems and challenges often experienced by school-age children in our society, including living in a family that is angry, impoverished, or unstable, or experiencing parental divorce. The chapter closes with a discussion of the ways in which children cope with stressful situations.

NOTE: Answer guidelines for all Chapter 13 questions begin on page 201.

Guided Study

The text chapter should be studied one section at a time. Before you read, preview each section by skimming it, noting headings and boldface items. Then read the appropriate section objectives from the following outline. Keep these objectives in mind and, as you read the chapter section, search for the information that will enable you to meet each objective. Once you have finished a section, write out answers for its objectives.

An Expanding Social World (pp. 355–357)

1. Identify the common themes or emphases of different theoretical views of the psychosocial development of school-age children.

2. Define social cognition, and explain how children's theory of mind and emotional understanding evolve during middle childhood.

The Peer Group (pp. 357–366)

3. Discuss the importance of peer groups, providing examples of how school-age children develop their own subculture and explaining the importance of this development.

4. (In Person) Describe the development of self-understanding during middle childhood and its implications for children's self-esteem.

Coping with Problems (pp. 366–375)

8. Identify five essential ways in which functiona families nurture school-age children, and contras the styles of open and closed families.

5. Discuss how friendship circles change during the school years.

9. (A Life-Span View) Discuss the impact of divorc on the psychosocial development of the schoo age child.

6. Discuss the plight of two types of rejected children.

10. Identify the variables that influence the impact c stresses on schoolchildren.

7. (text and Research Report) Discuss the special problems of bullies and their victims, and describe possible ways of helping such children.

11. (Changing Policy) Discuss the impact of povert and homelessness on the development of schoo age children.

12. Discuss several factors that seem especiall important in helping children to cope with stres

Chapter Review

When you have finished reading the chapter, work through the material that follows to review it. Complete the sentences and answer the questions. As you proceed, evaluate your performance for each section by consulting the answers on page 201. Do not continue with the next section until you understand each answer. If you need to, review or reread the appropriate section in the textbook before continuing.

An Expanding Social World (pp. 355–357)

1. Freud describes middle childhood as the period of _____ , when emotional drives are _____ , psychosexual needs are _____ , and unconscious conflicts are _____ .

2. According to Erikson, the crisis of middle childhood is _____

   _____ _____ .

3. Developmentalists influenced by learning theory are more concerned with children's _____ of new cognitive abilities; those influenced by the cognitive perspective focus on _____ ; and the sociocultural perspective emphasizes

   _____ _____ .

Briefly describe the epigenetic systems perspective on the school-age child's new independence.

4. School-age children advance in their understanding of other people and groups; that is, they advance in _____

   _____ . At this time, the preschooler's one-step theory of mind begins to evolve into a complex, _____ view of others.

5. In the beginning of the school years children often explain their actions by focusing on the immediate _____ ; a few years later, they more readily relate their actions to their

   _____ and _____

   _____ .

6. In experiments on children's social cognition, older children are more likely to understand the _____ and origin of various behaviors.

7. Another example of children's advancing social cognition is that, as compared with younger children, older children are more likely to focus on _____ (physical characteristics/personality traits) when asked to describe other children.

8. During the school years, children are able to mentally _____ themselves to keep from getting bored, and they can mask or _____ inborn tendencies. As a result of their new social cognition, children can better manage their own _____ .

The Peer Group (pp. 357–366)

9. A peer group is defined as _____

   _____ .

10. (In Person) As their self-understanding sharpens, children gradually become _____ (more/less) self-critical, and their self-esteem _____ (rises/dips). One reason is that they more often evaluate themselves through _____ _____ . As they mature, children are also _____ (more/less) likely to feel personally to blame for their shortcomings.

11. Although working parents tend to worry about their children's after-school supervision, children tend to be more concerned about breakdowns in their _____ _____ and their parents' _____

    _____ .

12. Some social scientists call the peer group's subculture the _____

    _____ _____ , highlighting the distinctions between children's groups and the general culture.

Identify several distinguishing features of this subculture.

13. Having a personal friend is _____ (more/less) important to children than acceptance by the peer group.

14. Friendships during middle childhood become more _____ and _____ . As a result, older children_____ (change/do not change) friends as often and find it _____ (easier/harder) to make new friends.

15. Middle schoolers tend to choose best friends whose _____ , _____ , and _____ are similar to their own. Generally, having a best friend who is not the same _____ or _____ correlates with being _____ by one's classmates.

16. Friendship groups typically become _____ (larger/smaller) and _____ (more/less) rigid during the school years. This trend _____ (is/is not) followed by both sexes.

17. In their friendship networks, boys tend to emphasize group _____ and _____ , while girls form _____ and more _____ networks.

18. Children who are actively rejected tend to be either _____-_____ or _____-_____ . Children in the latter group are typically _____ , anxious, and unhappy; low in _____ ; and particularly vulnerable to_____ . Those in the former group tend to be _____ and immature in their _____ _____ . As rejected children get

older, their problems _____ (diminish/get worse).

Give an example of the immaturity of rejected children.

19. A key aspect in the definition of bullying is that harmful attacks are _____ .

20. One factor in bullying is that both boys and girls are restricted by overly rigid _____ _____ , that encourage boys to _____ if they are victimized, while girls are expected _____ _____ .

21. (text and Research Report) Bullying during middle childhood _____ (is/is not) universal. An effective intervention in controlling bullying is to change the _____ _____ within the school so that bully-victim cycles are not allowed to persist.

Describe the effects of bullying on children.

22. Contrary to the public perception, bullies usually are not _____ or _____ at the peak of their bullying.

23. Children who regularly victimize other children often become _____ later on.

Coping with Problems (pp. 366–375)

24. Between ages 7 and 11 the overall frequency of various psychological problems _____ (increases/decreases), while the number of evident competencies _____ (increases/decreases).

5. Two factors that combine to buffer school-age children against the stresses they encounter are the development of _____ _____ and an expanding _____ _____ .

6. *Family function* refers to how well the family _____ _____ .

7. A functional family nurtures school-age children by meeting their basic _____ , by encouraging _____ , fostering the development of _____ , nurturing peer _____ , and by providing _____ and _____ .

8. Families with an _____ style encourage contributions from every family member; in those with a _____ style, one parent, usually the _____ , sets strict guidelines and rules.

9. Family structure is defined as the _____ _____ .

0. Children can thrive _____ (only in certain family structures/in almost any family structure).

. (A Life-Span View) The disruption surrounding divorce almost always adversely affects children for at least _____ . Children younger than age _____ and older than _____ seem to cope better overall. Divorce may be hardest of all on children at the _____ of middle childhood

. (A Life-Span View) Divorce jeopardizes both the _____ and _____ of a well-functioning family.

entify several circumstances under which divorce ay not harm the children.

33. (A Life-Span View) Custody means having _____ responsibility for children. Although _____ _____ is theoretically the best decision following a divorce, in practice this often is not the case. Developmental research reveals that _____ (mothers/fathers/neither parent) tend(s) to function better as the custodial parent.

(A Life-Span View) Give several reasons that children whose fathers have custody may fare better than children whose mothers have custody.

34. The impact of a given stress on a child (such as divorce) depends on three factors:

a. _____

b. _____

c. _____

35. (Changing Policy) On the whole, homeless children are even more disadvantaged than their peers of equal SES, with the result that many suffer from a loss of faith in life's possibilities and _____ _____ .

36. One reason that competence can compensate for life stresses is that if children feel confident, their _____ benefits, and they are better able to put the rest of their life in perspective. This explains why older children tend to be _____ (more/less) vulnerable to life stresses than are children who are just beginning middle childhood.

37. Another element that helps children deal with problems is the _____ _____ they receive.

38. A child who is at risk because of poor parenting, difficult temperament, or poverty _____ (probably will/probably won't) still be at risk as an adolescent.

39. During middle childhood, there are typically _____ (fewer/more) sources of social support. This can be obtained from grand-parents or siblings, for example, or from _____ and _____ . In addition, _____ can also be psy-chologically protective for children in difficult cir-cumstances.

40. Most children _____ (do/do not) have an idyllic childhood. Such a childhood _____ (is/is not) necessary for healthy development.

Progress Test 1

Multiple-Choice Questions

Circle your answers to the following questions and check them with the answers on page 202. If your answer is incorrect, read the explanation for why it is incorrect and then consult the appropriate pages of the text (in parentheses following the correct answer).

1. Social cognition is defined as:
   a. a person's awareness and understanding of human personality, motives, emotions, and interactions.
   b. the ability to form friendships easily.
   c. a person's skill in persuading others to go along with his or her wishes.
   d. the ability to learn by watching another person.

2. A common thread running through the five major developmental theories is that cultures through-out history have selected age 6 as the time for:
   a. a period of latency.
   b. the emergence of a theory of mind.
   c. more independence and responsibility.
   d. intellectual curiosity.

3. The best strategy for helping children who are at risk of developing serious psychological prob-lems because of multiple stresses would be to:
   a. obtain assistance from a psychiatrist.
   b. increase the child's competencies or social supports.
   c. change the household situation.
   d. reduce the peer group's influence.

4. Considering different family styles, which would be best for a child?
   a. an open family in which every member con-tributes

b. a closed family in which strict guidelines and rules are set
c. a flexible family style that balances the fami-ly's nurturance and the child's need for inde-pendence.
d. none of the above.

5. Compared with preschoolers, older children are more likely to blame:
   a. failure on bad luck.
   b. teachers and other authority figures.
   c. their parents for their problems.
   d. themselves for their shortcomings.

6. As rejected children get older:
   a. their problems often get worse.
   b. their problems usually decrease.
   c. their friendship circles typically become larger.
   d. the importance of the peer group to their self-esteem grows weaker.

7. Compared with average or popular children, rejected children tend to be:
   a. brighter and more competitive.
   b. affluent and "stuck-up."
   c. economically disadvantaged.
   d. socially immature.

8. Compared to middle school girls, middle school boys are more likely to emphasize _____ their friendship networks.
   a. fewer but closer friends
   b. group identity and loyalty
   c. having one, and only one, best friend on whom they depend
   d. friendships with others who are not the same age or sex

9. (A Life-Span View) Divorce may not be harmful to the child if the:
   a. family income remains stable.
   b. mother has custody of the children.
   c. father does not interfere with the mother's caregiving.
   d. the parents of the child's friends are also divorced.

10. Older schoolchildren tend to be _____ vulner-able to the stresses of life than children who are just beginning middle childhood because they _____ .
    a. more; tend to overpersonalize their problems
    b. less; have better developed coping skills
    c. more; are more likely to compare their well-being with that of their peers
    d. less; are less egocentric

1. Between the ages of 7 and 11, the overall frequency of various psychological problems:
   a. increases in both boys and girls.
   b. decreases in both boys and girls.
   c. increases in boys and decreases in girls.
   d. decreases in boys and increases in girls.

2. Bullying during middle childhood:
   a. occurs only in certain cultures.
   b. is more common in rural schools than in urban schools.
   c. seems to be universal.
   d. is rarely a major problem, since other children usually intervene to prevent it from getting out of hand.

3. During the school years, children become _____ selective about their friends, and their friendship groups become _____ .
   a. less; larger   c. more; larger
   b. less; smaller   d. more; smaller

4. Which of the following was *not* identified as a pivotal issue in determining whether divorce or some other problem will adversely affect a child during the school years?
   a. how many other stresses the child is already experiencing
   b. how many protective buffers are in place
   c. how much the stress affects the child's daily life
   d. the specific structure of the child's family

5. Erikson's crisis of the school years is that of:
   a. industry versus inferiority.
   b. acceptance versus rejection.
   c. initiative versus guilt.
   d. male versus female.

True or False Items

Write T (*true*) or F (*false*) on the line in front of each statement.

_____ 1. (In Person) As they evaluate themselves according to increasingly complex self-theories, school-age children typically experience a rise in self-esteem.

_____ 2. During middle childhood, acceptance by the peer group is valued more than having a close friend.

_____ 3. (Changing Policy) Children from low-income homes often have lower self-esteem.

_____ 4. In the majority of divorce cases in which the mother is the custodial parent, the father maintains a close, long-term relationship with the children.

_____ 5. Divorce almost always adversely affects the children for at least a year or two.

_____ 6. The quality of family interaction seems to be a more powerful predictor of children's development than the actual structure of the family.

_____ 7. Most withdrawn-rejected children are unaware of their social isolation.

_____ 8. Children of low socioeconomic status are more likely than other children to have difficulty mastering the normal skills of middle childhood.

_____ 9. Most aggressive-rejected children are unaware of their social isolation.

_____ 10. School-age children are less able than younger children to cope with chronic stresses.

_____ 11. The problems of most rejected children nearly always disappear by adolescence.

_____ 12. Friendships become more selective and exclusive as children grow older.

Progress Test 2

Progress Test 2 should be completed during a final chapter review. Answer the following questions after you thoroughly understand the correct answers for the Chapter Review and Progress Test 1.

Multiple-Choice Questions

1. Children who are categorized as _____ are particularly vulnerable to bullying.
   a. aggressive-rejected
   b. passive-aggressive
   c. withdrawn-rejected
   d. passive-rejected

2. The main reason for the special vocabulary, dress codes, and behaviors that flourish within the society of children is that they:
   a. lead to clubs and gang behavior.
   b. are unknown to or unapproved by adults.
   c. imitate adult-organized society.
   d. provide an alternative to useful work in society.

3. In the area of social cognition, developmentalists are impressed by the school-age child's increasing ability to:
   a. identify and take into account other people's viewpoints.
   b. develop an increasingly wide network of friends.
   c. relate to the opposite sex.
   d. resist social models.

4. The school-age child's greater understanding of emotions is best illustrated by:
   a. an increased tendency to take everything personally.
   b. more widespread generosity and sharing.
   c. the ability to see through the insincere behavior of others.
   d. a refusal to express unfelt emotions.

5. (In Person) Typically, children in middle childhood experience a decrease in self-esteem as a result of:
   a. a wavering self-theory.
   b. increased awareness of personal shortcomings and failures.
   c. rejection by peers.
   d. difficulties with members of the opposite sex.

6. A 10-year-old's sense of self-esteem is most strongly influenced by his or her:
   a. peers.   c. mother.
   b. siblings.   d. father.

7. Which of the following most accurately describes how friendships change during the school years?
   a. Friendships become more casual and less intense.
   b. Older children demand less of their friends.
   c. Older children change friends more often.
   d. Close friendships increasingly involve members of the same sex, ethnicity, and socioeconomic status.

8. Which of the following is an accurate statement about school-age bullies?
   a. They are unapologetic about their aggressive behavior.
   b. They usually have friends who abet, fear, and admire them.
   c. Their popularity fades over the years.
   d. All of the above are accurate statements.

9. (A Life-Span View) The most effective intervention to prevent bullying in the school is to:
   a. change the social climate through community-wide and classroom education.
   b. target one victimized child at a time.
   c. target each bully as an individual.
   d. focus on improving the academic skills of all children in the school.

10. When 4- to 10-year-old children were shown pictures and asked how a mother might respond to child who curses while playing with blocks, th 4-year-olds tended to focus on:
    a. the child's underlying emotions.
    b. the immediate, observable behavior.
    c. the social consequences of the mother' response.
    d. all of the above.

11. Two factors that most often help the child cop well with multiple stresses are social suppo and:
    a. social comparison.
    b. competence in a specific area.
    c. remedial education.
    d. referral to mental health professionals.

12. (In Person) An 8-year-old child who measures he achievements by comparing them to those of he friends is engaging in social:
    a. cognition.   c. reinforcement.
    b. comparison.   d. modeling.

13. Family _____ is more crucial to children' well-being than family _____ is.
    a. structure; SES
    b. SES; stability
    c. stability; SES
    d. functioning; structure

14. According to Freud, the period between ages and 11 when a child's sexual drives are relative quiet is the:
    a. phallic stage.
    b. genital stage.
    c. period of latency.
    d. period of industry versus inferiority.

15. Research studies have found that, as compared children without major stress, children who a forced to cope with one serious ongoing stre (for example, poverty or large family size) are:
    a. more likely to develop serious psychiatr problems.
    b. no more likely to develop problems.
    c. more likely to develop intense, destructiv friendships.
    d. less likely to be accepted by their peer group.

Matching Items

Match each term or concept with its corresponding description or definition.

Terms or Concepts

_____ **1.** learning theory
_____ **2.** social cognition
_____ **3.** social comparison
_____ **4.** cognitive theory
_____ **5.** society of children
_____ **6.** aggressive-rejected
_____ **7.** withdrawn-rejected
_____ **8.** sociocultural theory
_____ **9.** epigenetic systems theory
_____ **10.** open style
_____ **11.** closed style

Descriptions or Definitions

a. focused on the acquisition of new skills
b. the games, vocabulary, dress codes and culture of children
c. an awareness and understanding of others' motives and emotions
d. one parent, usually the father, sets strict guidelines and rules
e. focused on the development of social awareness
f. children who are disliked because of their confrontational nature
g. evaluating one's abilities by measuring them against those of other children
h. focused on the development of self-understanding
i. contributions from every family member are valued
j. children who are disliked because of timid, anxious behavior
k. views middle schoolers' independence as the result of a species need

Thinking Critically About Chapter 13

Answer these questions the day before an exam as a final check on your understanding of the chapter's terms and concepts.

1. As an advocate of the epigenetic systems perspective, Dr. Wayans is most likely to explain a 10-year-old child's new independence as the result of:
a. the repression of psychosexual needs.
b. the acquisition of new skills.
c. greater self-understanding.
d. the child's need to join the wider community and the parents' need to focus on younger children.

2. Dr. Ferris believes that skill mastery is particularly important because children develop views of themselves as either competent or incompetent in skills valued by their culture. Dr. Ferris is evidently working from the perspective of:
a. behaviorism.
b. social learning theory.
c. Erik Erikson's theory of development.
d. Freud's theory of development.

3. Bonnie, who is low achieving, shy, and withdrawn, is rejected by most of her peers. Her teacher, who wants to help Bonnie increase her self-esteem and social acceptance, encourages her parents to:
a. transfer Bonnie to a different school.
b. help their daughter improve her motor skills.
c. help their daughter learn to accept more responsibility for her academic failures.
d. help their daughter improve her skills in relating to peers.

4. Jorge, who has no children of his own, is worried about his 12-year-old niece because she wears unusual clothes and uses vocabulary unknown to him. What should Jorge do?
a. Tell his niece's parents that they need to discipline their daughter more strictly.
b. Convince his niece to find a new group of friends.
c. Recommend that his niece's parents seek professional counseling for their daughter, because such behaviors often are the first signs of a lifelong pattern of antisocial behavior.
d. Jorge need not necessarily be worried because children typically develop their own subculture of speech, dress, and behavior.

5. Compared with her 7-year-old brother Walter, 10-year-old Felicity is more likely to describe their cousin:
   a. in terms of physical attributes.
   b. as feeling exactly the same way she does when they are in the same social situation.
   c. in terms of personality traits.
   d. in terms of their cousin's outward behavior.

6. Seven-year-old Chantal fumes after a friend compliments her new dress, thinking that the comment was intended to be sarcastic. Chantal's reaction is an example of:
   a. egocentrism.
   b. feelings of inferiority.
   c. the distorted thought processes of an emotionally disturbed child.
   d. immature social cognition.

7. In discussing friendship, 9-year-old children, in contrast to younger children, will:
   a. deny that friends are important.
   b. state that they prefer same-sex playmates.
   c. stress the importance of help and emotional support in friendship.
   d. be less choosy about who they call a friend.

8. Children who have serious difficulties in peer relationships during elementary school:
   a. are at a greater risk of having emotional problems later in life.
   b. usually overcome their difficulties in a year or two.
   c. later are more likely to form an intense friendship with one person than children who did not have difficulties earlier on.
   d. do both b. and c.

9. After years of an unhappy marriage, Brad and Diane file for divorce and move 500 miles apart. In ruling on custody for their 7-year-old daughter, the wise judge decides:
   a. joint custody should be awarded, because this arrangement is nearly always the most beneficial for children.
   b. the mother should have custody, because this arrangement is nearly always the most beneficial for children in single-parent homes.
   c. the father should have custody, because this arrangement is nearly always the most beneficial for children in single-parent homes.
   d. to investigate the competency of each parent, because whoever was the more competent and more involved parent before the divorce should continue to be the primary caregiver.

10. (In Person) Of the following children, who is likely to have the lowest overall self-esteem?
    a. Karen, age 5   c. Carl, age 9
    b. David, age 7   d. Cindy, age 10

11. (In Person) Ten-year-old Benjamin is less optimistic and self-confident than his 5-year-old sister. This may be explained in part by the tendency of older children to:
    a. evaluate their abilities by comparing them with their own competencies a year or two earlier.
    b. evaluate their competencies by comparing them with those of others.
    c. be less realistic about their own abilities.
    d. do both b. and c.

12. (Changing Policy) Hilary is 8 years old and has been living with her mother in a shelter for the homeless for the last 2 years. Compared to her peers, it is most likely that she has:
    a. more chronic illnesses.
    b. more friends because of the tight quarters.
    c. developed better coping strategies.
    d. great hopes that the future will be better.

13. Of the following children, who is most likely become a bully?
    a. Karen, who is taller than average
    b. David, who is above average in verbal assertiveness
    c. Carl, who is insecure and lonely
    d. Cindy, who is frequently subjected to physical punishment and verbal criticism at home

14. I am an 8-year-old who frequently is bullied school. If I am like most victims of bullies, I am probably:
    a. obese.
    b. unattractive.
    c. a child who speaks with an accent.
    d. anxious and insecure.

15. Of the following children, who is most likely have one, and only one "best friend"?
    a. 10-year-old Juan
    b. 7-year-old Marcy
    c. 10-year-old Christina
    d. 7-year-old Andrew

Key Terms

Using your own words, write a brief definition or explanation of each of the following terms on a separate piece of paper.

1. industry versus inferiority
2. social cognition
3. peer group
4. social comparison
5. society of children
6. aggressive-rejected children
7. withdrawn-rejected children
8. bullying
9. family structure

ANSWERS

CHAPTER REVIEW

1. latency; quieter; repressed; submerged
2. industry versus inferiority
3. acquisition; self-understanding; social awareness

From an epigenetic systems perspective, the school-age child's independence is the result of the species' need to free parental efforts so that they may be focused on younger children and to accustom school-age children to their peers and the adults in the community.

4. social cognition; multifaceted
5. behavior; implications; possible consequences
6. motivation
7. personality traits
8. distract; alter; emotions
9. a group of individuals of similar age and social status who play, work, and learn together
10. more; dips; social comparison; more
11. peer relationships; fights or alcohol and cigarette use
12. society of children

The society of children typically has special norms, vocabulary, rituals, dress codes, and rules of behavior.

13. more
14. intense; intimate; do not change; harder
15. interests; values; backgrounds; age; sex; rejected
16. smaller; more; is

17. identity; loyalty; smaller; intimate
18. aggressive-rejected; withdrawn-rejected; lonely; self-esteem; bullying; impulsive; social cognition; get worse

Rejected children often misinterpret social situations—considering a compliment to be sarcastic, for example.

19. repeated
20. sex roles; become tough and not to ask for help; not to be physically assertive
21. is; social climate

The effects of bullying can be long-lasting. Bullied children are anxious, depressed, underachieving, and have lower self-esteem and painful memories.

22. insecure; lonely
23. violent criminals
24. decreases; increases
25. social cognition; social world
26. nurtures its children to develop their full potential
27. needs; learning; self-esteem; friendships; harmony; stability
28. open; closed; father
29. legal and genetic relationship between the adults and children in a household
30. in almost any family structure
31. a year or two; 2; 18; beginning or end
32. harmony; stability

Divorce may not harm children if the family income remains stable, if fights between the parents are few, and if caregiving by both parents is as good as or better than it was before the divorce.

33. caregiving; joint custody; neither parent

Children sometimes respond better to a man's authority than to a woman's. In addition, fathers who choose custody are those who are likely to be suited for it, whereas mothers typically have custody whether they prefer it or not. Father-only homes are, on average, more financially secure.

34. a. how many other stresses the child is already experiencing
b. how much these stresses affect the child's daily life
c. how many protective buffers and coping patterns are in place
35. clinical depression
36. self-esteem; less

37. social support

38. probably will

39. more; peers; pets; religion

40. do not; is not

PROGRESS TEST 1

Multiple-Choice Questions

1. a. is the answer. (p. 356)

2. b. is the answer. (p. 356)

3. b. is the answer. (p. 372)

4. c. is the answer. (p. 368)

5. d. is the answer. (pp. 356–357)

 a., b., & c. Compared with preschool children, schoolchildren are more self-critical, and their self-esteem dips, so they blame themselves.

6. a. is the answer. (p. 362)

7. d. is the answer. (p. 362)

8. b. is the answer. (pp. 360)

9. a. is the answer. (p. 370)

10. b. is the answer. (p. 367)

11. b. is the answer. (p. 367)

12. c. is the answer. (p. 364)

 d. In fact, children rarely intervene, unless a best friend is involved.

13. d. is the answer. (p. 360)

14. d. is the answer. (p. 369)

15. a. is the answer. (p. 355)

True or False Items

1. F In fact, just the opposite is true. (p. 358)

2. F In fact, just the opposite is true. (p. 360)

3. T (p. 371)

4. F Only a minority of fathers who do not have custody continue to maintain a close relationship with their children. (p. 370)

5. T (p. 370)

6. T (p. 367)

7. F Because they generally *are* aware of their isolation, withdrawn-rejected children are likely to be anxious and insecure. (p. 361)

8. T (p. 371)

9. T (p. 361)

10. F Because of the coping strategies that school-age children develop, they are better able than younger children to cope with stress. (p. 367)

11. F The problems of rejected children often ge worse as they get older. (p. 362)

12. T (p. 360)

PROGRESS TEST 2

Multiple-Choice Questions

1. c. is the answer. (p. 361)

 a. These are usually bullies.

 b. & d. These are not subcategories of rejecte children.

2. b. is the answer. (p. 359)

3. a. is the answer. (p. 356)

 b. Friendship circles typically become smalle during middle childhood, as children becom more choosy about their friends.

 c. & d. These issues are not discussed in the chap ter.

4. c. is the answer. (p. 357)

5. b. is the answer. (p. 358)

 a. This tends to promote, rather than reduce, sel esteem.

 c. Only 10 percent of schoolchildren experienc this.

 d. This issue becomes more important durin adolescence.

6. a. is the answer. (p. 360)

7. d. is the answer. (p. 360)

 a., b., & c. In fact, just the opposite is true o friendship during the school years.

8. d. is the answer. (p. 366)

9. a. is the answer. (pp. 364–365)

10. b. is the answer. (pp. 356–357)

 a. & c. Only older children, with their developin social cognition, were able to focus on the mo complex issues.

11. b. is the answer. (p. 372)

12. b. is the answer. (p. 358)

13. d. is the answer. (p. 367)

14. c. is the answer. (p. 355)

15. b. is the answer. (p. 369)

 c. & d. The text did not discuss how stress infl ences friendship or peer acceptance.

Matching Items

1. a (p. 356)   **5.** b (p. 359)   **9.** k (p. 356)

2. c (p. 356)   **6.** f (p. 361)   **10.** i (p. 368)

3. g (p. 358)   **7.** j (p. 361)   **11.** d (p. 368)

4. h (p. 356)   **8.** e (p. 356)

THINKING CRITICALLY ABOUT CHAPTER 13

1. **d.** is the answer. (p. 356)

   a. This describes an advocate of Freud's theory of development.

   b. This is the viewpoint of a learning theorist.

   c. This is the viewpoint of a cognitive theorist.

2. **c.** is the answer. The question describes what is, for Erikson, the crisis of middle childhood: industry versus inferiority. (p. 355)

3. **d.** is the answer. (pp. 373–374)

   a. Because it would seem to involve "running away" from her problems, this approach would likely be more harmful than helpful.

   b. Improving motor skills is not a factor considered in the text and probably has little value in raising self-esteem in such situations.

   c. If Bonnie is like most school-age children, she is quite self-critical and already accepts responsibility for her failures.

4. **d.** is the answer. (p. 359)

5. **c.** is the answer. (p. 356)

   a., b., & d. These are more typical of preschoolers.

6. **d.** is the answer. (p. 361)

   a. Egocentrism is self-centered thinking. In this example, Chantal is misinterpreting her friend's comment.

   b. & c. There is no reason to believe that Chantal is suffering from an emotional disturbance or that she is feeling inferior.

7. **c.** is the answer. (p. 360)

8. **a.** is the answer. (p. 362)

9. **d.** is the answer. (p. 370)

10. **d.** is the answer. Self-esteem decreases throughout middle childhood. (p. 358)

11. **b.** is the answer. (p. 358)

    a. & c. These are more typical of preschoolers than school-age children.

12. **a.** is the answer. (p. 371)

    b., c., & d. Just the opposite is true.

13. **d.** is the answer. (p. 366)

    a. & b. It is taller-than-average *boys* and verbally assertive *girls* who are more likely to bully others.

    c. This is a common myth.

14. **d.** is the answer. (p. 366)

    a., b., & c. Contrary to popular belief, victims are no more likely to be fat or homely or to speak with an accent than nonvictims are.

15. **c.** is the answer. (p. 360)

    a. & d. The trend toward fewer but closer friends is more apparent among girls.

    b. At the end of middle childhood, children become more choosy and have fewer friends.

KEY TERMS

1. According to Erikson, the crisis of middle childhood is that of **industry versus inferiority**, in which children try to master many skills and develop views of themselves as either competent or incompetent and inferior. (p. 356)

2. **Social cognition** refers to a person's awareness and understanding of the personalities, motives, emotions, intentions, and interactions of other people and groups. (p. 356)

3. A **peer group** is a group of individuals of roughly the same age and social status who play, work, or learn together. (p. 357)

4. **Social comparison** is the tendency to assess one's abilities, achievements, and social status by measuring them against those of others, especially those of one's peers. (p. 358)

5. Children in middle childhood develop and transmit their own subculture, called the **society of children**, which has its own games, vocabulary, dress codes, and rules of behavior. (p. 359)

6. The peer group shuns **aggressive-rejected children** because they are overly confrontational. (p. 361)

7. **Withdrawn-rejected children** are shunned by the peer group because of their withdrawn and anxious behavior. (p. 361)

8. **Bullying** is the repeated, systematic effort to inflict harm on a child through physical, verbal, or social attack. (p. 362)

9 **Family structure** refers to the legal and genetic relationships that exist between members of a particular family. (p. 368)

CHAPTER 14

Adolescence: Biosocial Development

Chapter Overview

Between the ages of 11 and 20, young people cross the great divide between childhood and adulthood. This crossing encompasses all three domains of development—biosocial, cognitive, and psychosocial. Chapter 14 focuses on the dramatic changes that occur in the biosocial domain, beginning with puberty and the growth spurt. The biosocial metamorphosis of the adolescent is discussed in detail, with emphasis on sexual maturation, nutrition, and the possible problems arising from dissatisfaction with one's appearance.

Although adolescence is, in many ways, a healthy time of life, the text addresses two health hazards that too often affect adolescence: sexual abuse, and the use of alcohol, tobacco, and other drugs.

NOTE: Answer guidelines for all Chapter 14 questions begin on page 216.

Guided Study

The text chapter should be studied one section at a time. Before you read, preview each section by skimming it, noting headings and boldface items. Then read the appropriate section objectives from the following outline. Keep these objectives in mind and, as you read the chapter section, search for the information that will enable you to meet each objective. Once you have finished a section, write out answers for its objectives.

Puberty Begins (pp. 381–386)

1. Outline the biological events of puberty.

2. Discuss the emotional and psychological impact of pubertal hormones.

3. (text and A Life-Span View) Identify several factors that influence the onset of puberty.

The Growth Spurt (pp. 386–390)

4. Describe the growth spurt in both the male and the female adolescent, focusing on changes in body weight and height.

5. Describe the changes in the body's internal organ systems that accompany the growth spurt.

. Discuss the nutritional needs and problems of adolescents.

xual Characteristics (pp. 390–396)

. Discuss the development of the primary sex characteristics in males and females during puberty.

. (In Person) Discuss how adolescents respond to the sexual changes of puberty and how these reactions have changed over the decades.

. Discuss the development of the secondary sex characteristics in males and females during puberty.

. (Research Report) Discuss the adolescent's preoccupation with body image and the problems that sometimes arise in the development of a healthy body image.

Health and Hazards (pp. 396–404)

11. Discuss sexual abuse, noting its prevalence and consequences for development.

12. (text and Changing Policy) Discuss drug use among adolescents today, including its prevalence, its significance for development, and the best methods of prevention.

Chapter Review

When you have finished reading the chapter, work through the material that follows to review it. Complete the sentences and answer the questions. As you proceed, evaluate your performance for each section by consulting the answers on page 216. Do not continue with the next section until you understand each answer. If you need to, review or reread the appropriate section in the textbook before continuing.

Puberty Begins (pp. 381–386)

1. The period of adolescence extends roughly from age _____ to _____ .

   The period of rapid physical growth and sexual maturation that ends childhood and brings the young person to adult size, shape, and sexual potential is called _____ .

   List, in order, the major physical changes of puberty in

   Girls: _____

   _____

   Boys: _____

   _____

2. Puberty begins when a hormonal signal from the
   _____ triggers hormone production
   in the _____
   _____ , which in turn
   triggers increased hormone production by the

   _____ _____
   and by the _____ , which include
   the _____ in males and the
   _____ in females.

3. The hormone _____ causes the
   gonads to dramatically increase production of sex
   hormones, especially _____ in girls
   and _____ in boys. This, in turn,
   triggers the hypothalamus and pituitary to
   increase production of _____ .

4. The increase in the hormone _____
   is dramatic in boys and slight in girls, whereas
   the increase in the hormone _____
   is marked in girls and slight in boys.

5. During puberty, hormonal levels have their greatest emotional impact _____
   (directly/indirectly), via the _____
   _____ of _____
   _____ . That impact is powerfully influenced by the _____ and
   _____ of the adolescent's family, peer group, and culture.

6. Normal children begin to notice pubertal changes
   between the ages of _____ and
   _____ .

7. (A Life-Span View) Children under extreme
   stress grow more _____ , because
   stress reduces the production of _____
   _____ .

8. (A Life-Span View) Longitudinal research suggests that family emotional distance and stress
   may _____ (accelerate/delay) the
   onset of puberty. Animal studies have revealed
   that this phenomenon occurs because stress causes an _____ (increase/decrease) in
   the production of _____ that initiate
   puberty. Despite this relationship, it is likely that
   puberty is triggered by the interaction of
   _____ and _____ factors.

9. The average American girl experiences her first
   menstrual period, called _____ ,
   between ages _____ and
   _____ .

10. Genes are an important factor in the timing of
    menarche, as demonstrated by the fact that
    _____ and _____
    _____ reach menarche
    at very similar ages.

11. The average age of puberty _____
    (varies/does not vary) from nation to nation and
    from ethnic group to ethnic group.

12. Stocky individuals tend to experience puberty
    _____ (earlier/later) than
    those with taller, thinner builds.

13. Menarche seems to be related to the accumulation
    of a certain amount of body _____
    Consequently, female dancers, runners, and other
    athletes menstruate _____
    (earlier/later) than the average girl, whereas
    females who are relatively inactive menstruate
    _____ (earlier/later).

The Growth Spurt (pp. 386–390)

14. The first sign of the growth spurt is increased
    bone _____ , beginning at the tips
    the extremities and working toward the center of
    the body. At the same time, children begin to
    _____ (gain/lose) weight at a rela-
    tively rapid rate.

15. The change in weight that typically occurs
    between 10 and 12 years of age is due primarily
    to the accumulation of body _____
    The amount of weight gain an individual experi-
    ences depends on several factors, including
    _____ , _____ ,
    _____ , and _____ .

16. During the growth spurt , a greater percentage of
    fat is retained by _____ (males/
    females), who naturally have a higher proportion
    of body fat in adulthood. The height spurt that
    soon follows _____ (does/does not
    burn up some of the stored fat.

7. About a year after these height and weight changes occur, a period of _____ increase occurs, causing the pudginess and clumsiness of an earlier age to disappear. In boys, this increase is particularly notable in the _____ body.

8. Overall, between the ages of 10 and 14, the typical girl gains about _____ in weight and _____ in height; between the ages of 12 and 16, the typical boy gains about _____ in height and about _____ in weight.

9. The chronological age for the growth spurt _____ (varies/does not vary) from child to child.

0. As they mature, adolescent girls generally become increasingly _____ (satisfied/dissatisfied) with their bodies while boys become increasingly _____ (satisfied/dissatisfied).

1. One of the last parts of the body to grow into final form is the _____ .

2. The two halves of the body _____ (always/do not always) grow at the same rate.

3. Young people who experience puberty at the same time as their friends tend to view the experience more _____ (positively/negatively) than those who experience it early or late.

4. For girls, _____ (early/late) maturation may be especially troublesome.

5. For boys, _____ (early/late) maturation is usually more difficult.

6. Internal organs also grow during puberty. The _____ increase in size and capacity, the _____ doubles in size, heart rate _____ (increases/decreases), and blood volume _____ (increases/decreases). These changes increase the adolescent's physical _____ .

Explain why the physical demands placed on a teenager, as in athletic training, should not be the same as those for a young adult of similar height and weight.

27. During puberty, one organ system, the _____ system, decreases in size, making teenagers _____ (more/less) susceptible to respiratory ailments.

28. The hormones of puberty also cause many relatively minor physical changes that can have significant emotional impact. These include increased activity in _____ , _____ , and _____ glands.

29. Due to rapid physical growth, the adolescent needs a higher daily intake of _____ , _____ and _____ . Specifically, the typical adolescent needs about 50 percent more of the minerals _____ , _____ , and _____ during the growth spurt.

30. Some middle schoolers resort to self-destructive behaviors, such as inducing _____ or using _____ to control their weight.

31. Because of menstruation, adolescent females also need additional _____ in their diets and are more likely to suffer _____-_____ _____ than any other subgroup of the population.

Sexual Characteristics (pp. 390–396)

32. Changes in _____ _____ _____ involve the sex organs that are directly involved in reproduction.

Describe the major changes in primary sex characteristics that occur in both sexes during puberty.

(Research Report) Identify some common behavior related to adolescents' preoccupation with their body image.

33. In girls, the event that is usually taken to indicate sexual maturity is _____ . In boys, the indicator of reproductive potential is the first ejaculation of seminal fluid containing sperm, which is called _____ .

34. (In Person) Attitudes toward menarche, menstruation, and spermarche _____ (have/have not) changed over the past two decades, so that most young people _____ (do/do not) face these events with anxiety, embarrassment, or guilt.

35. Sexual features other than those associated with reproduction are referred to as _____ _____ _____ .

Describe the major pubertal changes in the secondary sex characteristics of both sexes.

36. Two secondary sex characteristics that are mistakenly considered signs of womanhood and manliness, respectively, are _____ _____ and the growth of _____ . Breasts can be absent completely with no effect on _____ , _____ , or _____ .

37. (Research Report) Adolescents' mental conception of, and attitude toward, their physical appearance is referred to as their _____ _____ .

38. (Research Report) Adolescent girls with more body fat have fewer _____ or _____ than their thinner counterparts. Among adolescent boys, larger bodies correlate with greater _____ .

39. (Research Report) Media images reinforce the cultural ideal that American men should be _____ and _____ and that women should be _____ and _____ .

Health and Hazards (pp. 396–404)

40. The minor illnesses of childhood become _____ (less/more) common during adolescence, because of increased _____ at this age.

41 Any activity in which an adult uses a child for his or her own sexual stimulation or pleasure is considered _____ _____ _____ .

42. The damage done by sexual abuse depends on many factors, including how often it is _____ , how much it distorts _____ - _____ , and how much it impairs normal _____ .

43. Sexualized adult–child interactions may escalate in late childhood or early adolescence, with onset typically between ages _____ and _____ .

44. Adolescents may react to maltreatment in ways that younger children rarely do, with _____ or by _____ .

5. Although _____ (boys/girls) are more often the victims of sexual abuse, the other sex is also often sexually abused. Molested boys often feel _____ and are likely to worry that they are _____ .

6. Although most abusers are _____ (male/female), about 20 percent of sexual abusers are of the other sex.

7. Drug _____ always harms physical and psychological development, whether or not it becomes _____ . Drug _____ may or may not be harmful, depending in part on the _____ of the person and the reason for the drug's use.

8. After a long period of _____ (decline/increase) during the 1980s, drug use by adolescents began to _____ (increase/decrease) in the 1990s.

(Changing Policy) Why do developmentalists urge teens to delay drug experimentation as long as possible?

(Changing Policy) List several measures that have proven to be at least partly effective in postponing and decreasing drug use.

9. (Changing Policy) An important social factor in adolescent drug use is _____ _____ . A study in Scotland found that parents of middle-school children were more worried about _____ _____ than about _____ , _____ , or _____ . These concerns

_____ (matched/did not match) the actual prevalence of these drug use categories in their children.

50. (Changing Policy) In the United States, students who participate in Project D.A.R.E are _____ (less/no more) likely to abstain from drugs during high school than those who do not.

51. (Changing Policy) The likelihood of young people using drugs is also related to their _____ about drugs use, which, in turn, are affected by _____ _____ .

52. (Changing Policy) Antidrug attitudes softened among adolescent Americans during the 1990s, perhaps because each cohort goes through _____ _____ .

53. Tobacco, alcohol, and marijuana may act as _____ _____ , opening the door not only to regular use of multiple drugs but also to other destructive behaviors, such as risky _____ , _____ from school, _____ behavior, poor _____ _____ , and _____ .

54. By decreasing food consumption and the absorption of nutrients, tobacco can limit the adolescent's _____ _____ .

55. Because alcohol loosens _____ and impairs _____ , even moderate use can be destructive in adolescence. Teenagers who drink regularly are more likely to be _____ active, to engage in _____ behaviors, to be excessively absent from _____ , and more likely to ride in a car with a driver who has been _____ .

56. Marijuana _____ (slows/accelerates) thinking processes, particularly those related to _____ and _____ reasoning.

Progress Test 1

Multiple-Choice Questions

Circle your answers to the following questions and check them with the answers on page 217. If your answer is incorrect, read the explanation for why it is incorrect and then consult the appropriate pages of the text (in parentheses following the correct answer).

1. Which of the following most accurately describes the sequence of pubertal development in girls?
   a. breast buds and pubic hair; growth spurt in which fat is deposited on hips and buttocks; first menstrual period; ovulation
   b. growth spurt; breast buds and pubic hair; first menstrual period; ovulation
   c. first menstrual period; breast buds and pubic hair; growth spurt; ovulation
   d. breast buds and pubic hair; growth spurt; ovulation; first menstrual period

2. Although both sexes grow rapidly during adolescence, boys typically begin their accelerated growth about:
   a. a year or two later than girls.
   b. a year earlier than girls.
   c. the time they reach sexual maturity.
   d. the time facial hair appears.

3. The first readily observable sign of the onset of puberty is:
   a. the growth spurt.
   b. the appearance of facial, body, and pubic hair.
   c. a change in the shape of the eyes.
   d. a lengthening of the torso.

4. More than any other group in the population, adolescent girls are likely to have:
   a. asthma.
   b. acne.
   c. iron-deficiency anemia.
   d. testosterone deficiency.

5. More than half of all teenagers do not get enough of which nutrient in their diet?
   a. vitamin C
   b. magnesium
   c. iron
   d. calcium

6. For males, the secondary sex characteristic that usually occurs last is:
   a. breast enlargement.
   b. the appearance of facial hair.
   c. growth of the testes.
   d. the appearance of pubic hair.

7. For girls, the specific event that is taken to indicate fertility is _____ ; for boys, it is _____ .
   a. the growth of breast buds; voice deepening
   b. menarche; spermarche
   c. anovulation; the testosterone surge
   d. the growth spurt; pubic hair

8. The most significant hormonal changes of puberty include an increase of _____ in _____ and an increase of _____ in _____ .
   a. progesterone; boys; estrogen; girls
   b. estrogen; boys; testosterone; girls
   c. progesterone; girls; estrogen; boys
   d. estrogen; girls; testosterone; boys

9. (Research Report) In general, most adolescents are:
   a. overweight.
   b. satisfied with their appearance.
   c. dissatisfied with their appearance.
   d. unaffected by cultural attitudes about beauty.

10. Most developmentalists agree that puberty is triggered:
    a. by biogenetic factors.
    b. by psychosocial factors.
    c. by the interaction of biogenetic and psychosocial factors.
    d. in a manner that is almost completely unpredictable in any specific person.

11. The damage caused by sexual abuse depends on all of the following factors except:
    a. repeated incidence.
    b. the gender of the perpetrator.
    c. distorted adult-child relationships.
    d. impairment of the child's ability to develop normally.

12. Early physical growth and sexual maturation:
    a. tend to be equally difficult for girls and boys.
    b. tend to be more difficult for boys than for girls.
    c. tend to be more difficult for girls than for boys.
    d. are easier for both girls and boys than later maturation.

13. (Research Report) Developmentalists believe that teenagers' concern about their body image:
    a. should simply be ignored by parents as a passing phase.
    b. is a healthy sign that the developing person is beginning to assume responsibility for his or her own health.

c. is a minor issue, since it tends to occur only in a small segment of the peer culture.

d. should not be taken lightly.

. Drug use by adolescents:
a. peaked in the 1970s.
b. peaked in the 1980s.
c. has begun to increase in the 1990s.
d. continues to decline in the 1990s.

. (Changing Policy) A study in Scotland found that the parents of middle-school children were most concerned about their children's use of:
a. illegal drugs.
b. tobacco.
c. glue and other sniffable solvents.
d. alcohol.

ue or False Items

rite T (*true*) or F (*false*) on the line in front of each atement.

_____ 1. More calories are necessary during adolescence than at any other period during the life span.

_____ 2. Less than half of U.S. high school seniors consume the recommended five servings of fruits and vegetables a day.

_____ 3. The first indicator of reproductive potential in males is menarche.

_____ 4. Lung capacity, heart size, and total volume of blood increase significantly during adolescence.

_____ 5. Puberty generally begins sometime between ages 8 and 14.

_____ 6. (Research Report) Girls who mature late and are thinner than average tend to be satisfied with their weight.

_____ 7. (Research Report) The strong emphasis on physical appearance is unique to adolescents and finds little support from teachers, parents, and the larger culture.

_____ 8. Childhood habits of overeating and underexercising usually lessen during adolescence.

_____ 9. Sexual victimization in adolescence is often the continuation of earlier childhood abuse.

_____ 10. Both the sequence and timing of pubertal events vary greatly from one young person to another.

Progress Test 2

Progress Test 2 should be completed during a final chapter review. Answer the following questions after you thoroughly understand the correct answers for the Chapter Review and Progress Test 1.

Multiple-Choice Questions

1. Which of the following is the correct sequence of pubertal events in boys?
   a. growth spurt, pubic hair, facial hair, first ejaculation, lowering of voice
   b. facial hair, pubic hair, first ejaculation, growth spurt; lowering of voice, facial hair
   c. lowering of voice, pubic hair, growth spurt, facial hair, first ejaculation
   d. growth spurt, facial hair, lowering of voice, pubic hair, first ejaculation

2. Which of the following statements about adolescent physical development is *not* true?
   a. Hands and feet generally lengthen before arms and legs.
   b. Facial features usually grow before the head itself reaches adult size and shape.
   c. Oil, sweat, and odor glands become more active.
   d. The lymphoid system increases slightly in size, and the heart increases by nearly half.

3. In puberty, a hormone that increases markedly in girls (and only somewhat in boys) is:
   a. estrogen.   c. androgen.
   b. testosterone.   d. menarche.

4. Among adolescents, nutritional deficiencies in developed countries are frequently the result of:
   a. eating red meat.
   b. poor eating habits.
   c. anovulatory menstruation.
   d. excessive exercise.

5. In females, puberty is typically marked by a(n):
   a. significant widening of the shoulders.
   b. significant widening of the hips.
   c. enlargement of the torso and upper chest.
   d. decrease in the size of the eyes and nose.

6. Nonreproductive sexual characteristics, such as the deepening of the voice and the development of breasts, are called:
   a. gender-typed traits.
   b. primary sex characteristics.
   c. secondary sex characteristics.
   d. pubertal prototypes.

7. Puberty is initiated when hormones are released from the _____ , then from the _____ gland, and then from the adrenal glands and the _____ .

   a. hypothalamus; pituitary; gonads
   b. pituitary; gonads; hypothalamus
   c. gonads; pituitary; hypothalamus
   d. pituitary; hypothalamus; gonads

8. (Changing Policy) In the United States, middle-school students who participate in Project D.A.R.E. are:

   a. less likely to abstain from drugs during high school.
   b. more likely to abstain from drugs during high school.
   c. no more likely to abstain from drugs during high school.
   d. less likely to experiment with gateway drugs but *more* likely to begin using illegal drugs.

9. With regard to appearance, adolescent girls are *most* commonly dissatisfied with:

   a. timing of maturation.   c. weight.
   b. eyes and other facial features.   d. legs.

10. Compared to younger children who are sexually abused, a teenage victim is more likely to:

    a. engage in self-destructive behaviors such as running away.
    b. engage in a counterattack against the perpetrator or society.
    c. do either of the above.
    d. do neither of the above.

11. Individuals who begin to use tobacco, alcohol, or marijuana before the ninth grade are:

    a. typically affluent teenagers who are experiencing an identity crisis.

    b. more likely to have multiple drug-abuse problems later on.
    c. less likely to have alcohol-abuse problems later on.
    d. usually able to resist later peer pressure leading to long-term addiction.

12. Compounding the problem of sexual abuse boys, abused boys:

    a. feel shame at the idea of being weak.
    b. have fewer sources of emotional support.
    c. are more likely to be abused by fathers.
    d. have all of the above problems.

13. Puberty is *most accurately* defined as the period:

    a. of rapid physical growth that occurs during adolescence.
    b. during which sexual maturation is attained.
    c. of rapid physical growth and sexual maturation that ends childhood.
    d. during which adolescents establish identities separate from their parents.

14. Which of the following does *not* typically occur during puberty?

    a. The lungs increase in size and capacity.
    b. The heart's size and rate of beating increase.
    c. Blood volume increases.
    d. The lymphoid system decreases in size.

15. Teenagers' susceptibility to respiratory ailments typically _____ during adolescence, due to a(?) _____ in the size of the lymphoid system.

    a. increases; increase
    b. increases; decrease
    c. decreases; increase
    d. decreases; decrease

Matching Items

Match each term or concept with its corresponding description or definition.

Terms or Concepts

_____ **1.** puberty
_____ **2.** GH
_____ **3.** testosterone
_____ **4.** estrogen
_____ **5.** growth spurt
_____ **6.** primary sex characteristics
_____ **7.** menarche
_____ **8.** spermarche
_____ **9.** secondary sex characteristics
_____ **10.** body image
_____ **11.** drug abuse
_____ **12.** drug addiction

Descriptions or Definitions

a. onset of menstruation
b. period of rapid physical growth and sexual maturation that ends childhood
c. hormone that increases dramatically in boys during puberty
d. hormone that increases steadily during puberty in both sexes
e. dependence on a drug in order to feel at ease
f. hormone that increases dramatically in girls during puberty
g. first sign is increased bone length and density
h. attitude toward one's physical appearance
i. ingestion of a drug to the extent that it impairs the user's well-being
j. physical characteristics not involved in reproduction
k. the sex organs involved in reproduction
l. first ejaculation containing sperm

Thinking Critically About Chapter 14

Answer these questions the day before an exam as a final check on your understanding of the chapter's terms and concepts.

1. (Research Report) Fifteen-year-old Latoya is preoccupied with her "disgusting appearance" and seems depressed most of the time. The best thing her parents could do to help her through this difficult time would be to:
   a. ignore her self-preoccupation because their attention would only reinforce it.
   b. encourage her to "shape up" and not give in to self-pity.
   c. kid her about her appearance in the hope that she will see how silly she is acting.
   d. offer practical advice, such as clothing suggestions, to improve her body image.

2. Thirteen-year-old Rosa, an avid runner and dancer, is worried because most of her friends have begun to menstruate regularly. Her doctor tells her:
   a. that she should have a complete physical exam, because female athletes usually menstruate earlier than average.
   b. not to worry, because female athletes usually menstruate later than average.
   c. that she must stop running immediately, because the absence of menstruation is a sign of a serious health problem.
   d. that the likely cause of her delayed menarche is an inadequate diet.

3. Twelve-year-old Kwan is worried because his twin sister has suddenly grown taller and more physically mature than he. His parents should:
   a. reassure him that the average boy is one or two years behind the average girl in the onset of the growth spurt.
   b. tell him that within a year or less he will grow taller than his sister.
   c. tell him that one member of each fraternal twin pair is always shorter.
   d. encourage him to exercise more to accelerate the onset of his growth spurt.

4. Calvin, the class braggart, boasts that because his beard has begun to grow, he is more virile than his male classmates. Jacob informs him that:
   a. the tendency to grow facial and body hair has nothing to do with virility.
   b. beard growth is determined by heredity.
   c. girls also develop some facial hair and more noticeable hair on their arms and legs, so it is clearly not a sign of masculinity.
   d. all of the above are true.

5. (Research Report) Research comparing the actual and desired body weights of a group of 14- to 18-year-old girls found that:
   a. all wanted to weigh about 12 pounds less.
   b. late-maturing girls wanted to lose more weight than their early-maturing counterparts.
   c. competitive athletes were more satisfied with their body weights than were nonathletes.
   d. Early-maturing girls wanted to lose more weight than their late-maturing counterparts.

6. A 15-year longitudinal study on drug use showed that 18-year-olds labeled "experimenters":
   a. tended to be tense and insecure as 3-year-olds.
   b. were relatively well-adjusted as 3-year-olds.
   c. were more likely to have serious drug- and alcohol-abuse problems later on.
   d. were also likely to experiment with other high-risk behaviors.

7. Regarding the effects of early and late maturation on boys and girls, which of the following is *not* true?
   a. Early maturation is usually easier for boys to manage than it is for girls.
   b. Late maturation is usually easier for girls to manage than it is for boys.
   c. Late-maturing girls may be drawn into involvement with older boys.
   d. Late-maturing boys may not "catch up" physically, or in terms of their self-images, for many years.

8. Wise physical education teachers recommend athletic training to match an adolescent's size of a year or so earlier because:
   a. the growth spurts in weight and height occur before the less visible spurts of muscles and organs.
   b. during puberty, teenagers' lowered immunity makes them more susceptible to respiratory infections.
   c. teenagers are notoriously clumsy and accident-prone.
   d. of all of the above reasons.

9. Twenty-four-year-old Connie, who has a distorted view of sexuality, has gone from one abusive relationship with a man to another. It is likely that Connie:
   a. has been abusing drugs all her life.
   b. was sexually abused as a child.

c. will eventually become a normal, nurturing mother.
   d. had attention-deficit disorder as a child.

10. (Research Report) If she is like most teenagers, 14-year-old Shania's self-esteem is most strongly influenced by her:
   a. academic ability.
   b. success in sports, music, or art.
   c. friendships.
   d. assessment of her appearance.

11. Which of the following adolescents is likely to begin puberty at the earliest age?
   a. Aretha, an African American teenager who hates exercise
   b. Todd, a football player of European ancestry
   c. Kyu, an Asian American honors student
   d. There is too little information to make a prediction.

12. Of the following teenagers, those most likely to be distressed about their physical development are:
   a. late-maturing girls.
   b. late-maturing boys.
   c. early-maturing boys.
   d. girls or boys who masturbate.

13. Thirteen-year-old Kristin seems apathetic and lazy to her parents. You tell them:
   a. that Kristin is showing signs of chronic depression.
   b. that Kristin may be experiencing psychosocial difficulties.
   c. that Kristin has a poor attitude and needs more discipline.
   d. to have Kristin's iron level checked.

14. I am a hormone that rises steadily during puberty in both males and females. What am I?
   a. estrogen   c. GH
   b. testosterone   d. menarche

15. Eleven-year-old Linda, who has just begun to experience the first signs of puberty, laments, "When will the agony of puberty be over?" You tell her that the major events of puberty typically end about _____ after the first visible signs appear.
   a. 6 years   c. 2 years
   b. 3 or 4 years   d. 1 year

Key Terms

Writing Definitions

Using your own words, write a brief definition or explanation of each of the following terms on a separate piece of paper.

1. adolescence
2. puberty
3. gonads
4. menarche
5. growth spurt

6. primary sex characteristics
7. spermarche
8. secondary sex characteristics
9. body image
10. childhood sexual abuse
11. drug abuse
12. drug addiction
13. drug use
14. gateway drugs
15. generational forgetting

Cross Check

After you have written the definitions of the key terms in this chapter, you should complete the crossword puzzle to ensure that you can reverse the process—recognize the term, given the definition.

ACROSS

1. Glands near the kidneys that are stimulated by the pituitary at the beginning of puberty.
7. The first ejaculation of seminal fluid containing sperm.
12. The first menstrual period.
15. The ovaries in girls and the testes or testicles in boys.
17. Gland that stimulates the adrenal glands and the sex glands in response to a signal from the hypothalamus.
18. Event, which begins with an increase in bone length and includes rapid weight gain and organ growth, that is one of the many observable signs of puberty.
19. Ingestion of a drug, regardless of the amount or affect of ingestion.

DOWN

1. The period of biological, cognitive, and psychosocial transition from childhood to adulthood.
2. Organ system, which includes the tonsils and adenoids, that decreases in size at adolescence.
3. Area of the brain that sends the hormonal signal that triggers the biological events of puberty.
4. Widely abused gateway drug that loosens inhibitions and impairs judgment.
5. Dependence on a drug or a behavior in order to feel physically or psychologically at ease.

6. Drugs—usually tobacco, alcohol, and marijuana—whose use increases the risk that a person will later use harder drugs.
8. Ingestion of a drug to the extent that it impairs the user's well-being.
9. Body characteristics that are not directly involved in reproduction but that signify sexual development.
10. Main sex hormone in males.
11. Gateway drug that decreases food consumption, the absorption of nutrients, and fertility.
13. Main sex hormone in females.

14. Period of rapid physical growth and sexual maturation that ends childhood and brings the young person to adult size.

16. Sex organs that are directly involved in reproduction.

ANSWERS

CHAPTER REVIEW

1. 11; 20; puberty

Girls: onset of breast growth, initial appearance of pubic hair, peak growth spurt, widening of the hips, first menstrual period, completion of pubic-hair growth, and final breast development

Boys: initial appearance of pubic hair, growth of the testes, growth of the penis, first ejaculation, peak growth spurt, voice changes, beard development, and completion of pubic-hair growth

2. hypothalamus; pituitary gland; adrenal glands; gonads (sex glands); testes; ovaries

3. GnRH (gonad releasing hormone); estrogen; testosterone; GH (growth hormone)

4. testosterone; estrogen

5. indirectly; psychological impact; visible changes; values; expectations

6. 8; 14

7. slowly; growth hormones

8. accelerate; increase; hormones; biogenetic; psychosocial

9. menarche; 9; 18

10. sisters; monozygotic twins

11. varies

12. earlier

13. fat; later; earlier

14. length; gain

15. fat; gender; heredity; diet; exercise

16. females; does

17. muscle; upper

18. 38 pounds (17 kilograms); 9 5/8 inches (24 centimeters); 10 inches (25 centimeters); 42 pounds (19 kilograms)

19. varies

20. dissatisfied; satisfied

21. head

22. do not always

23. positively

24. early

25. late

26. lungs; heart; decreases; increases; endurance

The fact that the more visible spurts of weight an height precede the less visible ones of the muscl and organs means that athletic training and weigh lifting should be designed to match the young pe son's size of a year or so earlier.

27. lymphoid; less

28. oil; sweat; odor

29. calories; vitamins; minerals; calcium; iron; zinc

30. vomiting; laxatives

31. iron; iron-deficiency anemia

32. primary sex characteristics

Girls: growth of uterus and thickening of the vagin lining

Boys: growth of testes and lengthening of penis; als scrotum enlarges and becomes pendulous

33. menarche; spermarche

34. have; do not

35. secondary sex characteristics

Males grow taller than females and become wider the shoulders than at the hips. Females take on mo fat all over and become wider at the hips, and the breasts begin to develop. About 65 percent of boy experience some temporary breast enlargement. A the larynx grows, the adolescent's voice (especially boys) becomes lower. Head and body hair becom coarser and darker in both sexes. Facial hair (especia ly in boys) begins to grow.

36. breast development; facial and body hair; concep tion; pregnancy; birth

37. body image

Many adolescents spend hours examining themselv in front of the mirror; some exercise or diet wi obsessive intensity.

38. dates; boyfriends; aggression

39. tall; muscular; thin; shapely

40. less; immunity

41. childhood sexual abuse

42. repeated; adult–child relationships; developmen

43. 8; 12

44. self-destruction; counterattacking

45. girls; shame at being weak; homosexual

46. male

47. abuse; addictive; use; maturation

3. decline; increase

Delaying experimentation increases the adolescent's chances of becoming realistically informed about the risks of drug use and of developing the reasoning ability to limit or avoid the use of destructive drugs in dangerous circumstances.

The measures include health education classes that honestly portray the risk of drug use; increased punishment for store owners who sell alcohol or cigarettes to minors; raising the price of alcohol and cigarettes; enforcing drunk-driving laws; and teaching parents how to communicate with teenagers.

9. parental attitudes; illegal drugs; smoking; drinking; solvent sniffing; did not match

10. no more

11. attitudes; national and local policies, and personal experience

12. generational forgetting

13. gateway drugs; sex; alienation; antisocial; physical health; depression

14. growth spurt

15. inhibitions; judgment; sexually; antisocial; school; drinking

16. slows; memory; abstract

PROGRESS TEST 1

Multiple-Choice Questions

1. a. is the answer. (p. 381)

2. a. is the answer. (p. 384)

3. a. is the answer. (p. 386)

4. c. is the answer. This is because each menstrual period depletes some iron from the body. (p. 390)

5. c. is the answer. (p. 389)

6. b. is the answer. (p. 382)

7. b. is the answer. (p. 391)

8. d. is the answer. (p. 383)

9. c. is the answer. (p. 394)

    a. Although some adolescents become overweight, many diet and lose weight in an effort to attain a desired body image.

    d. On the contrary, cultural attitudes about beauty are an extremely influential factor in the formation of a teenager's body image.

10. c. is the answer. (p. 384)

11. b. is the answer. (p. 397)

12. c. is the answer. (p. 388)

13. d. is the answer. For most adolescents, *thinking* that they look terrible makes them feel terrible— even depressed. (p. 375)

14. c. is the answer. (p. 399)

15. a. is the answer. (p. 402)

True or False Items

1. T (p. 389)

2. T (p. 389)

3. F The first indicator of reproductive potential in males is ejaculation of seminal fluid containing sperm (spermarche). Menarche (the first menstrual period) is the first indication of reproductive potential in females. (p. 391)

4. T (p. 388)

5. T (p. 384)

6. F Studies show that the majority of adolescent girls, even those in the thinnest group, want to lose weight. (p. 394)

7. F The strong emphasis on appearance is reflected in the culture as a whole; for example, teachers (and, no doubt, prospective employers) tend to judge people who are physically attractive as being more competent than those who are less attractive. (p. 395)

8. F These habits generally *worsen* during adolescence. (pp. 389–390)

9. T (p. 398)

10. F Although there is great variation in the timing of pubertal events, the sequence is very similar for all young people. (pp. 381–382)

PROGRESS TEST 2

Multiple-Choice Questions

1. b. is the answer. (pp. 381–382)

2. d. is the answer. During adolescence, the lymphoid system *decreases* in size and the heart *doubles* in size. (p. 388)

3. a. is the answer. (p. 383)

    b. Testosterone increases markedly in boys.

    c. Androgen is another name for testosterone.

    d. Menarche is the first menstrual period.

4. b. is the answer. (p. 389)

5. b. is the answer. (p. 385)

    a. The shoulders of males tend to widen during puberty.

    c. The torso typically lengthens during puberty.

d. The eyes and nose *increase* in size during puberty.

6. **c.** is the answer. (p. 391)

   a. Although not a term used in the textbook, a gender-typed trait is one that is typical of one sex but not of the other.

   b. Primary sex characteristics are those involving the reproductive organs.

   d. This is not a term used by developmental psychologists.

7. **a.** is the answer. (p. 382)

8. **c.** is the answer. (pp. 403)

9. **c.** is the answer. (p. 387)

   a. If the timing of maturation differs substantially from that of the peer group, dissatisfaction is likely; however, this is not the most common source of dissatisfaction in teenage girls.

   b. & d. Although teenage girls are more likely than boys to be dissatisfied with certain features, which body parts are troubling varies from girl to girl.

10. **c.** is the answer. (p. 398)

11. **b.** is the answer. (p. 400)

12. **a.** is the answer. (p. 398)

    b. This was not discussed in the text.

    c. This is true of girls.

13. **c.** is the answer. (p. 381)

14. **b.** is the answer. Although the size of the heart increases during puberty, heart rate *decreases*. (p. 388)

15. **d.** is the answer. (p. 389)

Matching Items

1. b (p. 381)   5. g (p. 385)   9. j (p. 391)
2. d (p. 383)   6. k (p. 391)   10. h (p. 394)
3. c (p. 383)   7. a (p. 385)   11. i (p. 398)
4. f (p. 383)   8. l (p. 391)   12. e (p. 398)

THINKING CRITICALLY ABOUT CHAPTER 14

1. **d.** is the answer. (p. 397)

   a., b., & c. These would likely make matters worse.

2. **b.** is the answer. (p. 386)

   a. Because they typically have little body fat, female dancers and athletes menstruate *later* than average.

   c. Delayed maturation in a young dancer or athlete is usually quite normal.

   d. The text does not indicate that the age of menarche varies with diet.

3. **a.** is the answer. (p. 385)

   b. It usually takes longer than one year for a pr pubescent male to catch up with a female wh has begun puberty.

   c. This is not true.

   d. The text does not suggest that exercise has effect on the timing of the growth spurt.

4. **d.** is the answer. (p. 396)

5. **a.** is the answer. (p. 394)

6. **b.** is the answer. (p. 400)

7. **c.** is the answer. It is *early*-maturing girls who a often drawn into involvement with older boy (p. 388)

8. **a.** is the answer. Overuse injuries tend to occ when athletic demands on a young person's boc do not take this muscle and organ growth lag in account. (p. 388)

   b. In fact, teenagers are *less* susceptible to respi tory ailments than younger children.

9. **b.** is the answer. (p. 397)

10. **d.** is the answer. (p. 394)

11. **a.** is the answer. African Americans often beg puberty earlier than Asian Americans or Ame cans of European ancestry. Furthermore, fema who are inactive menstruate earlier than tho who are more active. (p. 386)

12. **b.** is the answer. (p. 388)

    a. Late maturation is typically more difficult f boys than for girls.

    c. Early maturation is generally a positive expe ence for boys.

    d. Adolescent masturbation is no longer t source of guilt or shame that it once was.

13. **d.** Kristin's symptoms are typical of irc deficiency anemia, which is more common teenage girls than in any other age group. (p. 39

14. **c.** is the answer. (p. 383)

    a. Only in girls do estrogen levels rise marked during puberty.

    b. Only in boys do testosterone levels ri markedly during puberty.

    d. Menarche is the first menstrual period.

15. **b.** is the answer. (p. 382)

KEY TERMS

1. **Adolescence** is the period of biological, cogniti and psychosocial transition from childhood adulthood. (p. 381)

2. **Puberty** is the period of rapid physical growth and sexual maturation that ends childhood and brings the young person to adult size, shape, and sexual potential. (p. 381)

3. The **gonads** are the pair of sex glands in humans—the ovaries in girls and the testes or testicles in boys. (p. 382)

4. **Menarche**, which refers to the first menstrual period, is the specific event that is taken to indicate fertility in adolescent girls. (p. 384)

5. The **growth spurt**, which begins with an increase in bone length and density and includes rapid weight gain and organ growth, is one of the many observable signs of puberty. (p. 385)

6. During puberty, changes in the **primary sex characteristics** involve those sex organs that are directly involved in reproduction. (p. 391)

7. **Spermarche**, which refers to the first ejaculation of seminal fluid containing sperm, is the specific event that is taken to indicate fertility in adolescent boys. (p. 391)

8. During puberty, changes in the **secondary sex characteristics** involve parts of the body that are not directly involved in reproduction but that signify sexual development. (p. 391)

9. (Research Report) **Body image** refers to adolescents' mental conception of, and attitude toward, their physical appearance. (p. 395)

10. **Childhood sexual abuse** is any activity in which an adult uses a child for his or her own sexual stimulation or pleasure—even if the use does not involve physical contact. (p. 397)

11. **Drug abuse** is the ingestion of a drug to the extent that it impairs the user's well-being. (p. 398)

12. **Drug addiction** is a person's dependence on a drug or a behavior in order to feel physically or psychologically at ease. (p. 398)

13. **Drug use** is the ingestion of a drug, regardless of the amount or affect of ingestion. (p. 398)

14. **Gateway drugs** are drugs—usually tobacco, alcohol, and marijuana—whose use increases the risk that a person will later use harder drugs. (p. 400)

15. **Generational forgetting** is the tendency of each new generation to ignore lessons (such as the hazards of drug use) learned by the previous cohort. (p. 403)

Cross Check

ACROSS

1. adrenal
7. spermarche
12. menarche
15. gonads
17. pituitary
18. growth spurt
19. drug use

DOWN

1. adolescence
2. lymphoid
3. hypothalamus
4. alcohol
5. drug addiction
6. gateway drugs
8. drug abuse
9. secondary
10. testosterone
11. tobacco
13. estrogen
14. puberty
16. primary

CHAPTER 15

Adolescence: Cognitive Development

Chapter Overview

Chapter 15 begins by describing the cognitive advances of adolescence. With the attainment of formal operational thought, the developing person becomes able to think in an adult way, that is, to be logical, to think in terms of possibilities, to reason scientifically and abstractly.

Not everyone reaches the stage of formal operational thought, however, and even those who do so spend much of their time thinking at less advanced levels. The discussion of adolescent egocentrism supports this generalization in showing that adolescents have difficulty thinking rationally about themselves and their immediate experiences. Adolescent egocentrism makes them see themselves as psychologically unique and more socially significant than they really are.

The second section addresses the question, "What kind of school best fosters adolescent intellectual growth?" Many adolescents enter secondary school feeling less motivated and more vulnerable to self-doubt than they did in elementary school. The rigid behavioral demands and intensified competition of most secondary schools do not, unfortunately, provide a supportive learning environment for adolescents. Schools can be more effectively organized by setting clear, attainable educational goals that are supported by the entire staff.

The chapter concludes with an example of adolescent cognition at work: decision making in the area of sexual behavior. The discussion relates choices made by adolescents to their cognitive abilities and typical shortcomings, and it suggests ways in which adolescents may be helped to make healthy choices.

NOTE: Answer guidelines for all Chapter 15 questions begin on page 230.

Guided Study

The text chapter should be studied one section at a time. Before you read, preview each section by skimming it, noting headings and boldface items. The read the appropriate section objectives from the following outline. Keep these objectives in mind and, a you read the chapter section, search for the information that will enable you to meet each objective. Onc you have finished a section, write out answers for i objectives.

Adolescent Thought (pp. 407–416)

1. Describe advances in thinking during adolescence.

2. Describe evidence of formal operational thinkir during adolescence, and provide examples adolescents' emerging ability to reason dedu tively and inductively.

3. Discuss adolescent egocentrism, and give thr examples of egocentric fantasies or fables.

chools, Learning, and the Adolescent Mind
)p. 416–422)

4. Evaluate the typical secondary school's ability to meet the cognitive needs of the typical adolescent.

5. Discuss the impact of competitive and cooperative learning on the typical adolescent.

dolescent Decision Making (pp. 422–432)

6. Briefly discuss the typical adolescent's inability to make major life decisions.

7. (Changing Policy) Discuss whether part-time employment is advisable for adolescents.

8. Explain how adolescent thinking contributes to adolescent pregnancy and sexually transmitted disease.

9. (text and A Life-Span View) Discuss the need for better sex education in the schools and the role of parents as sex educators.

Chapter Review

When you have finished reading the chapter, work through the material that follows to review it. Complete the sentences and answer the questions. As you proceed, evaluate your performance for each section by consulting the answers on page 230. Do not continue with the next section until you understand each answer. If you need to, review or reread the appropriate section in the textbook before continuing.

Adolescent Thought (pp. 407–416)

1. The basic skills of thinking, learning, and remembering that advance during the school-age years _____ (continue to progress/stabilize) during adolescence.

2. Advances in _____ _____ improve concentration, while a growing _____ _____ and memory skills allow teens to connect new ideas to old ones, and strengthened _____ and _____ help them become better students.

3. Piaget's term for the fourth stage of cognitive development is _____ _____ thought. Other theorists may explain adolescent advances differently, but virtually all theorists agree that adolescent thought _____ (is/is not) qualitatively different from children's thought. For many developmentalists, the single most distinguishing feature of adolescent thought is the capacity to think in terms of _____ . One specific example of this type of thinking is the development of _____ thought.

4. Compared with younger individuals, adolescents have _____ (more/less) difficulty arguing against their personal beliefs and self-interest.

5. During the school years, children make great strides in _____ (inductive/deductive) reasoning.

6. During adolescence, they become more capable of _____ reasoning—that is, they can begin with a general _____ or _____ and draw logical _____ from it. This type of reasoning is a hallmark of formal operational thought.

7. (Research Report) In the developmental progression from inductive to deductive reasoning, some psychologists believe that adults can reach a less _____ stage following the formal operational stage.

8. Piaget devised a number of famous tasks involving _____ principles to study how children of various ages reasoned hypothetically and deductively.

Briefly describe how children reason differently about the "balance-beam" problem at ages 7, 10, and 13.

9. More recent research has shown that the growth of formal reasoning abilities _____ (always occurs/does not always occur) during adolescence and may be _____ (more/less) complete than Piaget and others believed it to be. Each individual's intellect, experience, talents, and interests _____ (do/do not) affect his or her thinking as much as the ability to reason formally. In addition, past _____ and _____ conditions also have an effect. A study of 13- to 15-year-olds in France found about _____ (what proportion?) at the concrete level, _____ a an intermediate level, and _____ a a formal level. Ten years later, these proportions _____ (had/had not) changed.

10. The adolescent's belief that he or she is uniquely significant and that the social world revolves around him or her is a psychological phenomenon called _____ _____ .

11. An adolescent's tendency to feel that he or she is somehow immune to the consequences of dangerous or illegal behavior is expressed in the _____ _____ .

12. An adolescent's tendency to imagine that her or his own life is unique, heroic, or even mythical, and that she or he is destined for great accomplishments, is expressed in the _____ _____ .

13. Adolescents, who believe that they are under constant scrutiny from nearly everyone, create for themselves an _____ _____ . Their acute self-consciousness reveals that young people are often not at ease with the broader _____ _____ .

14. Adolescent egocentrism enables them to reflect more thoughtfully on their lives but often at the cost of great _____ .

Schools, Learning, and the Adolescent Mind (pp. 416–422)

15. The best setting for personal growth, called the optimum _____ – _____ ,

depends on several factors, including

_____

_____ .

6. The emergence of hypothetical, abstract thought makes adolescents _____ (more/less) interested in the opinions of others. At the same time, they are _____ (more/less) vulnerable to criticism than their behaviors imply. Instead of there being a good fit between adolescents' needs and the schools, there is often a _____

_____ .

ite several ways in which educational settings tend ot to be supportive of adolescents' self-confidence.

7. One outcome of the relatively common mismatch between student needs and the school environment is a widespread dip in academic _____ as young people enter middle school.

8. Educational goals _____ (vary/do not vary) by culture. Similarly, the goals of the American education system _____ (have/have not) changed much over the centuries. Ethnic diversity and geographic differences in learning also are widespread and deep. One example is the widespread national variation in the _____ _____ completion rate.

9. One debate concerns the extent to which academic grades should be based solely on individual _____ _____ , with students _____ against each other from best in the class to worst. In such situations, many students, especially _____ and students from _____ back-

grounds, find it psychologically safer not to work very hard.

20. One possible solution to the stress of individual competition is to encourage team projects and discussion groups, which allow students to succeed if they _____ . In this type of learning, the goal is to excel at the _____ , not necessarily to be better than one's classmates.

21. One benefit of cooperative learning is that it often provides students with their first exposure to people of different _____ , _____ , _____ , and _____ backgrounds.

22. Cooperative learning is _____ (more/less) likely to lead to rivalry among various ethnic, religious, and racial groups.

Adolescent Decision Making (pp. 422–432)

23. For most of the big decisions, such as whether and where to go to college or find a job, adolescents _____ (do/do not) play a major role in choosing.

24. (Changing Policy) Attitudes regarding after-school jobs _____ (vary/do not vary) from country to country.

25. (Changing Policy) In some nations, such as _____ , almost no adolescent is employed or even does significant chores at home. In many _____ countries, many older adolescents have jobs as part of their school curriculum. Most parents in the United States _____ (approve/do not approve) of youth employment.

26. (Changing Policy) Perhaps because many of today's jobs for adolescents are not _____ , research finds that when adolescents are employed more than _____ hours a week, their grades suffer. As adults, those who were employed extensively as teenagers are more likely to use _____ and to feel _____ (more/less) connected to their families.

27. Generally, research reveals that adolescent beliefs, values, and reasoning processes _____ (do/do not) significantly affect their sexual behavior.

28. Diseases that are spread by sexual contact are called _____ _____ diseases. Among these are _____ _____ . Sexually active adolescents also risk exposure to the _____ virus.

29. Teenagers today have _____ (more/fewer) pregnancies than adults in their 20s and _____ (more/fewer) than teenagers did 35 years ago.

30. A major factor in the teen birth problem is that in 1960, most teenage mothers _____ (were/were not) married, _____ (wanted/did not want) their babies, and expected to be _____ . Today, most teenage mothers _____ (are/are not) married, and most _____ (wanted/did not want) to become pregnant.

Describe the likely consequences to all concerned of an American adolescent giving birth.

31. Most young people _____ (believe/do not believe) sex should occur within the context of a committed, loving relationship. This attitude _____ (varies/does not vary) from country to country.

32. Unfortunately, for many adolescents, high-risk behaviors are a proven way to _____ _____ .

33. Ignorance about sex and unavailability of contraception _____ (do/do not) explain the high rates of adolescent pregnancy and STDs.

34. Knowing facts about sex has so little effect on adolescent sexual behavior, because they find it difficult to envision all the _____ _____ ; instead, they focus on _____ considerations or difficulties.

35. The first step in encouraging adolescents to make more rational decisions about their sexuality requires adults to be more _____ in *their* thinking about adolescent sexuality.

36. Many school systems are revising their sex education programs to make them more _____ and focused on _____ _____ .

37. (A Life-Span View) Most parents _____ (are/are not) adequate sex educators for their children. One reason is that many parents are too _____ in beginning to discuss sexual issues.

38. (A Life-Span View) One study found that mothers who were more religious, and more disapproving of teen sex, were _____ (less/more) likely to know when their children were sexually active.

39. In the United States, the teenage birth rate _____ (increased/declined) between 1991 and 1997. At the same time, condom use among _____ (males/females/both sexes) has _____ (increased/decreased). This latter change parallels a change in _____ and _____ _____ .

Progress Test 1

Multiple-Choice Questions

Circle your answers to the following questions and check them with the answers on page 231. If your answer is incorrect, read the explanation for why it is incorrect and then consult the appropriate pages of the text (in parentheses following the correct answer).

1. Many psychologists consider the distinguishing feature of adolescent thought to be the ability to think in terms of:
   a. moral issues.
   b. concrete operations.
   c. possibility, not just reality.
   d. logical principles.

2. Piaget's last stage of cognitive development is:
   a. formal operational thought.
   b. concrete operational thought.
   c. universal ethical principles.
   d. symbolic thought.

3. Advances in metamemory and metacognition deepen adolescents' abilities in:
   a. studying.
   b. the invincibility fable.
   c. the personal fable.
   d. adolescent egocentrism.

4. The adolescent who takes risks and feels immune to the laws of mortality is showing evidence of the:
   a. invincibility fable.   c. imaginary audience.
   b. personal fable.   d. death instinct.

5. Imaginary audiences, invincibility fables, and personal fables are expressions of adolescent:
   a. morality.   c. decision making.
   b. thinking games.   d. egocentrism.

6. The typical adolescent is:
   a. tough-minded.
   b. indifferent to public opinion.
   c. self-absorbed and hypersensitive to criticism.
   d. all of the above.

7. When adolescents enter secondary school, many:
   a. experience a drop in their academic self-confidence.
   b. are less motivated than they were in elementary school.
   c. are less conscientious than they were in elementary school.
   d. experience all of the above.

8. Over the past century, the goals of education in the United States have:
   a. not substantially changed.
   b. shifted from an emphasis on vocational training to scientific understanding.
   c. shifted from an emphasis on scientific understanding to vocational training.
   d. come more in line with the rest of the developed world.

9. Thinking that begins with a general premise and then draws logical conclusions from it is called:
   a. inductive reasoning.
   b. deductive reasoning.
   c. "the game of thinking."
   d. hypothetical reasoning.

10. Serious reflection on important issues is a wrenching process for many adolescents because of their newfound ability to reason:
    a. inductively.   c. hypothetically.
    b. deductively.   d. symbolically.

11. The main reason for high rates of STDs and pregnancy during adolescence is cognitive immaturity, as evidenced by:
    a. the decline of the "good girl" morality.
    b. increased sexual activity.
    c. the inability to think logically about the consequences of sexual activity.
    d. a lack of information about sexual matters.

12. Many adolescents seem to believe that *their* lovemaking will not lead to pregnancy. This belief is an expression of the:
    a. personal fable.   c. imaginary audience.
    b. invincibility fable.   d. "game of thinking."

13. (Changing Policy) A parent in which of the following countries is *least* likely to approve of her daughter's request to take a part-time job after school?
    a. the United States   c. Great Britain
    b. Germany   d. Japan

14. Many school systems have revised their sex education classes to be:
    a. more practical and focused on social interaction.
    b. based on scare tactics designed to discourage sexual activity.
    c. more dependent upon bringing the parents into the education process.
    d. changed in all of the above ways.

15. To estimate the risk of a behavior, such as unprotected sexual intercourse, it is most important that the adolescent be able to think clearly about:
    a. universal ethical principles.
    b. personal beliefs and self-interest.
    c. probability.
    d. peer pressure.

True or False Items

Write T (*true*) or F (*false*) on the line in front of each statement.

_____ 1. Until young adulthood, most people do not make major decisions on their own.

_____ 2. Adolescents are generally better able than 8-year-olds to recognize the validity of arguments that clash with their own beliefs.

_____ 3. Everyone attains the stage of formal operational thought by adulthood.

_____ 4. Most adolescents who engage in risky behavior are unaware of the consequences of their actions.

_____ 5. Adolescents often create an imaginary audience as they envision how others will react to their appearance and behavior.

_____ 6. Most developmentalists feel that competition in the classroom is a healthy cognitive influence on adolescents.

_____ 7. Most teenagers believe that sex should occur only within the context of a committed, loving relationship.

_____ 8. Inductive reasoning is a hallmark of formal operational thought.

_____ 9. Adolescents are the group with the highest rates of the most prevalent sexually transmitted diseases (STDs).

_____ 10. (A Life-Span View) Most sex education occurs outside the home.

Progress Test 2

Progress Test 2 should be completed during a final chapter review. Answer the following questions after you thoroughly understand the correct answers for the Chapter Review and Progress Test 1.

Multiple-Choice Questions

1. Adolescents who fall prey to the invincibility fable may be more likely to:
   a. engage in risky behaviors.
   b. suffer from depression.
   c. have low self-esteem.
   d. drop out of school.

2. Thinking that extrapolates from a specific experience to form a general premise is called:
   a. inductive reasoning.
   b. deductive reasoning.
   c. "the game of thinking."
   d. hypothetical reasoning.

3. Regarding formal operational thought:
   a. it is not always accomplished during adolescence.
   b. it is more likely to be demonstrated in certain domains than in others.
   c. whether it is demonstrated depends in part on an individual's experiences, talents, and interests.
   d. all of the above are true.

4. When young people overestimate their significance to others, they are displaying:
   a. concrete operational thought.
   b. adolescent egocentrism.
   c. a lack of cognitive growth.
   d. immoral development.

5. The personal fable refers to adolescents imagining that:
   a. they are immune to the dangers of risky behaviors.
   b. they are always being scrutinized by others.
   c. their own lives are unique, heroic, or even mythical.
   d. the world revolves around their actions.

6. The typical secondary school environment:
   a. has more rigid behavioral demands than the average elementary school.
   b. does not meet the cognitive needs of the typical adolescent.
   c. emphasizes competition.
   d. is described by all of the above.

7. As compared to elementary schools, most secondary schools exhibit all of the following *except*:
   a. a more flexible approach to education.
   b. intensified competition.
   c. more punitive grading practices.
   d. less individualized attention.

8. A study of 13- to 15-year-old French school children found that:
   a. the proportion of children testing at the formal operational level remained constant over a 10-year period.
   b. the proportion of children testing at the formal operational level changed substantially over a 10-year period.

c. adolescent girls were more likely than boys to have achieved formal operational thinking.

d. adolescent boys were more likely than girls to have achieved formal operational thinking.

9. (Changing Policy) Research has shown that adolescents who work at after-school jobs more than 20 hours per week:

a. are more likely to use drugs as adults.

b. have lower grades.

c. tend to feel less connected to their families.

d. have all of the above characteristics.

10. Educational settings that emphasize individual competition:

a. may be destructive to adolescent development if not used properly.

b. tend to be the most effective in educating students.

c. are more effective in large schools than in small schools.

d. have proven very effective in educating minority students.

11. One of the hallmarks of formal operational thought is:

a. egocentrism.   c. symbolic thinking.

b. deductive thinking.   d. all of the above.

12. In explaining adolescent advances in thinking, sociocultural theorists emphasize:

a. the accumulated improvement in specific skills.

b. mental advances resulting from the transition from primary school to secondary school.

c. the completion of the myelination process in cortical neurons.

d. advances in metacognition.

13. Although, on balance, teenagers display mature decision-making analysis and good choices in most areas, this is not the case in matters of sexual activity, especially if the teen:

a. is well educated.

b. has friends involved in similar activities.

c. is under age 16.

d. is able to draw support from caring adults.

14. Evidence that revised sex education programs are working comes from the fact that _____ is (are) declining.

a. the birth rate among teenagers

b. the percentage of sexually active teenagers

c. the use of condoms among teenagers

d. all of the above

15. To avoid a volatile mismatch, a school should:

a. focus on cooperative rather than competitive learning.

b. base grading on individual test performance.

c. establish the same goals for every student.

d. vary its settings and approach according to children's developmental stages, strengths, and learning styles.

Matching Items

Match each term or concept with its corresponding description or definition.

Terms or Concepts

_____ **1.** invincibility fable
_____ **2.** imaginary audience
_____ **3.** person–environment fit
_____ **4.** hypothetical thought
_____ **5.** deductive reasoning
_____ **6.** inductive reasoning
_____ **7.** formal operational thought
_____ **8.** personal fable
_____ **9.** STD
_____ **10.** volatile mismatch
_____ **11.** adolescent egocentrism

Descriptions or Definitions

a. the tendency of adolescents to focus on themselves to the exclusion of others

b. adolescents feel immune to the consequences of dangerous behavior

c. adolescents feel destined for fame and fortune

d. the idea held by many adolescents that others are intensely interested in them, especially in their appearance and behavior

e. the match or mismatch between an adolescent's needs and the educational setting

f. a disease spread by sexual contact

g. reasoning about propositions that may or may not reflect reality

h. the last stage of cognitive development, according to Piaget

i. thinking that moves from premise to conclusion

j. thinking that moves from a specific experience to a general premise

k. a clash between a teenager's needs and the structure and functioning of his or her school

Thinking Critically About Chapter 15

Answer these questions the day before an exam as a final check on your understanding of the chapter's terms and concepts.

1. A 13-year-old can create and solve logical problems on the computer but is not usually reasonable, mature, or consistent in his or her thinking when it comes to people and social relationships. This supports the finding that:
   a. some children reach the stage of formal operational thought earlier than others.
   b. the stage of formal operational thought is not attained by age 13.
   c. formal operational thinking may be demonstrated in certain domains and not in other domains.
   d. older adolescents and adults often do poorly on standard tests of formal operational thought.

2. (Research Report) An experimenter hides a ball in her hand and says, "Either the ball in my hand is red or it is not red." Most preadolescent children say:
   a. the statement is true.
   b. the statement is false.
   c. they cannot tell if the statement is true or false.
   d. they do not understand what the experimenter means.

3. Fourteen-year-old Monica is very idealistic and often develops crushes on people she doesn't even know. This reflects her newly developed cognitive ability to:
   a. deal simultaneously with two sides of an issue.
   b. take another person's viewpoint.
   c. imagine possible worlds and people.
   d. see herself as others see her.

4. Which of the following is the *best* example of a personal fable?
   a. Adriana imagines that she is destined for a life of fame and fortune.
   b. Ben makes up stories about his experiences to impress his friends.
   c. Kalil questions his religious beliefs when they seem to offer little help for a problem he faces.
   d. Julio believes that every girl he meets is attracted to him.

5. Which of the following is the *best* example of the adolescent's ability to think hypothetically?

   a. Twelve-year-old Stanley feels that people are always watching him.

   b. Fourteen-year-old Mindy engages in many risky behaviors, reasoning that "nothing bad will happen to me."

   c. Fifteen-year-old Philip feels that no one understands his problems.

   d. Thirteen-year-old Josh delights in finding logical flaws in virtually everything his teachers and parents say.

6. Frustrated because of the dating curfew her parents have set, Melinda exclaims, "You just don't know how it feels to be in love!" Melinda's thinking demonstrates:

   a. the invincibility fable.

   b. the personal fable.

   c. the imaginary audience.

   d. adolescent egocentrism.

7. Compared to her 13-year-old brother, 17-year-old Yolanda is likely to:

   a. be more critical about herself.

   b. be more egocentric.

   c. have less confidence in her abilities.

   d. be more capable of reasoning hypothetically.

8. Nathan's fear that his friends will ridicule him because of a pimple that has appeared on his nose reflects a preoccupation with:

   a. his personal fable.

   b. the invincibility fable.

   c. an imaginary audience.

   d. preconventional reasoning.

9. Thirteen-year-old Malcolm, who lately is very sensitive to the criticism of others, feels significantly less motivated and capable than when he was in elementary school. Malcolm is probably:

   a. experiencing a sense of vulnerability that is common in adolescents.

   b. a lower-track student.

   c. a student in a school that emphasizes cooperation.

   d. all of the above.

10. A high school principal who wished to increase the interest level and achievement of minority and female students would be well advised to:

   a. create classroom environments that are not based on competitive grading procedures.

   b. encourage greater use of standardized testing in the elementary schools that feed students to the high school.

   c. separate students into academic tracks based on achievement.

   d. do all of the above.

11. (Changing Policy) Seventy-year-old Artemis can't understand why his daughter doesn't want her teenage son to work after school. "In my day," he says, "we learned responsibility and a useful trade by working throughout high school." You wisely point out that:

   a. most after-school jobs for teens today are not very meaningful.

   b. after-school employment tends to have a more negative impact on boys than girls.

   c. attitudes are changing; today, most American parents see adolescent employment as a waste of time.

   d. teens in most European countries almost never work after school.

12. Who is the *least* likely to display mature decision making?

   a. Brenda, an outgoing 17-year-old art student

   b. Fifteen-year-old Kenny, who has few adults in whom he confides

   c. Monique, a well-educated 15-year-old

   d. Damon, an 18-year-old high school graduate who lives alone

13. After hearing that an unusually aggressive child has been in full-time day care since he was 1 year old, 16-year-old Keenan concludes that nonparental care leads to behavior problems. Keenan's conclusion is an example of:

   a. inductive reasoning.

   b. deductive reasoning.

   c. hypothetical thinking.

   d. adolescent egocentrism.

14. Cindy, a sexually active teenager who does not practice contraception, is likely to think that:

   a. having a child might not be so bad.

   b. it is unlikely that she will become pregnant after just one episode.

   c. she is less likely to become pregnant, or contract a STD, than others are.

   d. all of the above are true.

15. Dr. Malone, who wants to improve the effectiveness of her adolescent sex-education class, would be well advised to:

 a. focus on the biological facts of reproduction and disease, because teenage misinformation is largely responsible for the high rates of unwanted pregnancy and STDs.

 b. personalize the instruction, in order to make the possible consequences of sexual activity more immediate to students.

 c. teach boys and girls in separate classes, so that discussion can be more frank and open.

 d. use all of the above strategies.

Key Terms

Using your own words, write a brief definition or explanation of each of the following terms on a separate piece of paper.

 1. formal operational thought
 2. hypothetical thought
 3. inductive reasoning
 4. deductive reasoning
 5. adolescent egocentrism
 6. invincibility fable
 7. personal fable
 8. imaginary audience
 9. person-environment fit
 10. volatile mismatch
 11. sexually transmitted diseases (STDs)

ANSWERS

CHAPTER REVIEW

 1. continue to progress
 2. selective attention; knowledge base; metamemory; metacognition
 3. formal operational; is; possibilities; hypothetical
 4. less
 5. inductive
 6. deductive; premise; theory; conclusions
 7. absolutist
 8. scientific

Preschoolers have no understanding of how to solve the problem. By age 7, children understand balancing the weights but don't know that distance from the center is also a factor. By age 10, they understand the concepts but are unable to coordinate them. By age 13 or 14, they are able to solve the problem.

 9. does not always occur; less; do; education; historical; one-third; one-third; one-third; had
 10. adolescent egocentrism
 11. invincibility fable
 12. personal fable
 13. imaginary audience; social world
 14. self-criticism
 15. person–environment fit; the individual's developmental stage, cognitive strengths, and learning style as well as the traditions, educational objectives, and future needs of the society
 16. more; more; volatile mismatch

Compared to elementary schools, most secondary schools have more rigid behavioral demands, intensified competition, more punitive grading practices, as well as less individualized attention and procedures.

 17. achievement
 18. vary; have; high school
 19. test performance; ranked; girls; minority
 20. cooperate; task
 21. economic; ethnic; religious; racial
 22. less
 23. do not
 24. vary
 25. Japan; European; approve
 26. meaningful; 15; drugs; less
 27. do
 28. sexually transmitted; gonorrhea, genital herpes, syphilis, and chlamydia; HIV
 29. fewer; fewer
 30. were; wanted; full-time homemakers; are not; do not want

For the mother, the consequences include interference with education and social, personal, and vocational growth; for the couple if they marry, greater risk of abuse, abandonment, or divorce; for the child, greater risk of prenatal and birth complications, of lower academic achievement, and, at adolescence, of drug abuse, delinquency, dropping out of school, and early parenthood.

 31. believe; does not vary
 32. gain status, bond with friends, and free emotions at least for the moment

33. do not

34. possible alternatives (or consequences); immediate

35. rational

36. practical; social interaction

37. are not; late

38. less

39. declined; both sexes; increased; attitudes; sexual communication

PROGRESS TEST 1

Multiple-Choice Questions

1. **c.** is the answer. (p. 408)

   a. Although moral reasoning becomes much deeper during adolescence, it is not limited to this stage of development.

   b. & d. Concrete operational thought, which *is* logical, is the distinguishing feature of childhood thinking.

2. **a.** is the answer. (p. 407)

   b. In Piaget's theory, this stage precedes formal operational thought.

   c. & d. These are not stages in Piaget's theory.

3. **a.** is the answer. (p. 407)

   b., c., & d. These are examples of limited reasoning ability during adolescence.

4. **a.** is the answer. (p. 413)

   b. This refers to adolescents' tendency to imagine their own lives as unique, heroic, or even mythical.

   c. This refers to adolescents' tendency to fantasize about how others will react to their appearance and behavior.

   d. This is a concept in Freud's theory.

5. **d.** is the answer. These thought processes are manifestations of adolescents' tendency to see themselves as being much more central and important to the social scene than they really are. (p. 413)

6. **c.** is the answer. (p. 407)

7. **d.** is the answer. (pp. 416–417)

8. **b.** is the answer. (p. 418)

   d. Educational goals vary widely from nation to nation.

9. **b.** is the answer. (pp. 409–410)

   a. Inductive reasoning moves from specific facts to a general conclusion.

   b. & c. The "game of thinking," which is an example of hypothetical reasoning, involves the ability to think creatively about possibilities.

10. **c.** is the answer. (p. 409)

11. **c.** is the answer. (p. 428)

    a. The text does not suggest that declining moral standards are responsible for the increased rate of STDs.

    b. Although this may be true, in itself it is not necessarily a result of adolescent cognitive immaturity.

    d. Various studies have found that merely understanding the facts of sexuality does not correlate with more responsible and cautious sexual behavior.

12. **b.** is the answer. (pp. 413, 428)

    a. This refers to adolescents' tendency to imagine their own lives as unique, heroic, or even mythical.

    c. This refers to adolescents' tendency to fantasize about how others will react to their appearance and behavior.

    d. This is the adolescent ability to suspend knowledge of reality in order to think playfully about possibilities.

13. **d.** is the answer. Japanese adolescents almost never work after school. (p. 423)

    a. American parents generally approve of adolescent employment.

    b. & c. Jobs are an important part of the school curriculum in many European countries.

14. **a.** is the answer. (p. 429)

    b. Scare tactics were often a central feature of earlier sex education classes.

    c. Generally speaking, parents are not effective sex educators.

15. **c.** is the answer. (p. 428)

True or False Items

1. T (p. 422)

2. T (pp. 408–409)

3. F Some people never reach the stage of formal operational thought. (p. 412)

4. F Adolescents are aware of the fact, but they fail to think through the possible consequences. (pp. 427–428)

5. T (p. 415)

6. F In such competitive situations, many students find it easier and psychologically safer not to try,

thereby avoiding the potential gains and pains of both success and failure. (p. 419)

7. T (p. 426)

8. F Deductive reasoning is a hallmark of formal operational thought. (pp. 409–410)

9. T (p. 425)

10. T (p. 431)

PROGRESS TEST 2

Multiple-Choice Questions

1. **a.** is the answer. (p. 413)

b., c., & d. The invincibility fable leads some teens to believe that they are immune to the dangers of risky behaviors; it is not necessarily linked to depression, low self-esteem, or the likelihood that an individual will drop out of school.

2. **a.** is the answer. (p. 409)

b. Deductive reasoning begins with a general premise and then draws logical conclusions from it.

c. & d. The "game of thinking," which is an example of hypothetical reasoning, involves the ability to think creatively about possibilities.

3. **d.** is the answer. (p. 412)

4. **b.** is the answer. (p. 413)

5. **c.** is the answer. (p. 413)

a. This describes the invincibility fable.

b. This describes the imaginary audience.

d. This describes adolescent egocentrism in general.

6. **d.** is the answer. (p. 417)

7. **a.** is the answer. (p. 417)

8. **b.** is the answer. (p. 413)

c. & d. This study did not report a gender difference in the proportion of children who attained formal thinking.

9. **d.** is the answer. (p. 423)

10. **a.** is the answer. (p. 419)

11. **b.** is the answer. (pp. 409–410)

12. **b.** is the answer. (p. 408)

a. & d. These are more likely to be emphasized by information-processing theorists.

c. This reflects the biological perspective on development.

13. **c.** is the answer. (p. 428)

14. **a.** is the answer. (pp. 431–432)

b. & c. These are on the rise.

15. **d.** is the answer. (p. 417)

Matching Items

1. b (p. 413)	**5.** i (p. 409)	**9.** f (p. 425)
2. d (p. 415)	**6.** j (p. 409)	**10.** k (p. 417)
3. e (p. 416)	**7.** h (p. 408)	**11.** a (p. 413)
4. g (p. 408)	**8.** c (p. 413)	

THINKING CRITICALLY ABOUT CHAPTER 15

1. **c.** is the answer. (p. 412)

2. **c.** is the answer. Although this statement is logically verifiable, preadolescents who lack formal operational thought cannot prove or disprove it. (p. 411)

3. **c.** is the answer. (p. 408)

4. **a.** is the answer. (p. 413)

b. & d. These behaviors are more indicative of a preoccupation with the imaginary audience.

c. Kalil's questioning attitude is a normal adolescent tendency that helps foster moral reasoning.

5. **d.** is the answer. (p. 409)

a. This is an example of the imaginary audience.

b. This is an example of the invincibility fable.

c. This is an example of adolescent egocentrism.

6. **d.** is the answer. (p. 413)

7. **d.** is the answer. (pp. 408–409)

8. **c.** is the answer. (p. 415)

a. In this fable adolescents see themselves destined for fame and fortune.

b. In this fable young people feel that they are somehow immune to the consequences of common dangers.

d. This is a stage of moral reasoning in Kohlberg's theory.

9. **a.** is the answer. (pp. 416–417)

10. **a.** is the answer. (pp. 419–420)

11. **a.** is the answer. (p. 423)

b. There is no evidence of a gender difference in the impact of employment on adolescents.

c. & d. In fact, just the opposite are true.

12. **b.** is the answer. Mature decision making is least likely to be displayed by adolescents who are under age 16, who have less education, and who have few adults to talk with. (p. 428)

13. a. is the answer. (p. 409)

 b. Keenan is reasoning from the specific to the general, rather than vice versa.

 c. Keenan is thinking about an actual observation, rather than a hypothetical possibility.

 d. Keenan's reasoning is focused outside himself, rather than being self-centered.

14. d. is the answer. (p. 428)

15. b. is the answer. (p. 429)

KEY TERMS

1. In Piaget's theory, the last stage of cognitive development, which arises from a combination of maturation and experience, is called **formal operational thought**. A hallmark of formal operational thinking is the capacity for hypothetical, logical, and abstract thought. (p. 408)

2. **Hypothetical thought** involves reasoning about propositions and possibilities that may or may not reflect reality. (p. 408)

3. **Inductive reasoning** is thinking that moves from one or more specific experiences to a general conclusion. (p. 409)

4. **Deductive reasoning** is thinking that moves from the general to the specific, or from a premise to a logical conclusion. (p. 409)

5. **Adolescent egocentrism** refers to the tendency of adolescents to see themselves as much more socially significant than they actually are. (p. 413)

6. Adolescents who experience the **invincibility fable** feel that they are immune to the dangers of risky behaviors. (p. 413)

7. Another example of adolescent egocentrism is the **personal fable**, through which adolescents imagine their own lives as unique, heroic, or even mythical. (p. 413)

 Memory aid: A *fable* is a mythical story.

8. Adolescents often create an **imaginary audience** for themselves, as they assume that others are as intensely interested in them as they themselves are. (p. 415)

9. The term **person–environment fit** refers to the best setting for personal growth, as in the optimum educational setting. (p. 416)

10. When teenagers' individual needs do not match the size, routine, and structure of their schools, a **volatile mismatch** may occur. (p. 417)

11. **Sexually transmitted diseases (STDs)** include all diseases that are spread by sexual contact. (p. 425)

CHAPTER 16

Adolescence: Psychosocial Development

Chapter Overview

Chapter 16 focuses on the adolescent's psychosocial development, particularly the formation of identity, that is required for the attainment of adult status and maturity. The influences of family, friends, and society on this development are examined in some detail. Suicide—one of the most perplexing problems of adolescence—is then explored. The special problems posed by adolescent lawbreaking are discussed, and suggestions for alleviating or treating these problems are given. The chapter concludes with the message that although no other period of life is characterized by so many changes in the three domains of development, for most young people the teenage years are happy ones. Furthermore, serious problems in adolescence do not necessarily lead to lifelong problems.

NOTE: Answer guidelines for all Chapter 16 questions begin on page 244.

Guided Study

The text chapter should be studied one section at a time. Before you read, preview each section by skimming it, noting headings and boldface items. Then read the appropriate section objectives from the following outline. Keep these objectives in mind and, as you read the chapter section, search for the information that will enable you to meet each objective. Once you have finished a section, write out answers for its objectives.

The Self and Identity (pp. 435–439, 440)

1. Describe the development of identity during adolescence.

2. Describe the four major identity statuses, and give an example of each.

3. (In Person) Discuss the problems of identity formation encountered by minority adolescents.

Family and Friends (pp. 439–449)

4. Discuss parental influence on identity formation, including the effect of parent–adolescent conflict and other aspects of family functioning.

5. Discuss the constructive functions of peer relationships and close friendships during adolescence and the unique challenges faced by immigrants.

6. (text and Research Report) Discuss the the development of male–female relationships during adolescence, including the challenges faced by gay and lesbian adolescents.

dolescent Suicide (pp. 450–453)

7. (text and A Life-Span View) Discuss adolescent suicide, noting its incidence and prevalence, contributing factors, warning signs, and gender and national variations.

reaking the Law (pp. 454–457)

8. (text and Changing Policy) Discuss delinquency among adolescents today, noting its prevalence, significance for later development, and best approaches for prevention or treatment.

Conclusion (pp. 457–458)

9. Discuss the theme of this text as demonstrated by adolescent development.

Chapter Review

When you have finished reading the chapter, work through the material that follows to review it. Complete the sentences and answer the questions. As you proceed, evaluate your performance for each section by consulting the answers on page 244. Do not continue with the next section until you understand each answer. If you need to, review or reread the appropriate section in the textbook before continuing.

The Self and Identity (pp. 435–439, 440)

1. The momentous changes that occur during the teen years challenge adolescents to find their own

    _____ .

2. According to Erikson, the challenge of adolescence is _____ _____

    _____ _____ .

3. The ultimate goal of adolescence is to establish a new identity that involves both repudiation and assimilation of childhood values; this is called

    _____ _____ .

4. The young person who prematurely accepts earlier roles and parental values without exploring alternatives or truly forging a unique identity is experiencing identity _____ .

5. An adolescent who adopts an identity that is the opposite of the one he or she is expected to adopt has taken on a _____

    _____ .

6. The young person who has few commitments to goals or values and is apathetic about defining his or her identity is experiencing

    _____ _____ .

7. A time-out period during which a young person experiments with different identities, postponing important choices, is called an identity _____ .

8. Adolescents who have _____ _____ and those who have prematurely _____ tend to have a strong sense of ethnic identification. Those who have _____ tend to be high in prejudice, while those who are _____ _____ tend to be relatively low in prejudice.

9. The process of identity formation can take _____ or longer.

10. The surrounding culture can aid identity formation in two ways: by providing _____ and by providing _____ _____ and _____ that ease the transition from childhood to adulthood.

11. In a culture where most people hold the same moral, political, religious, and sexual values, identity is _____ (easier/more difficult) to achieve.

12. (In Person) For minority-group members, identity achievement is often _____ (more/less) difficult than it is for other adolescents. This may cause them to embrace a _____ identity or, as is more often the case, to _____ on identity prematurely.

Family and Friends (pp. 439–449)

13. People who focus on differences between the younger and older generations speak of a _____ _____ . An exception occurs when the parents grow up in a very different _____ and _____ .

14. The idea that family members in different developmental stages have a natural tendency to see the family in different ways is called the _____ _____ .

15. Parent–adolescent conflict is most common in _____ (early/late) adolescence and

is particularly notable with _____ (mothers/fathers) and their _____ (early/late)-maturing _____ (sons/daughters). This conflict often involves _____ , which refers to repeated, petty arguments about daily habits.

16. Among Chinese, Korean, and Mexican American teens, conflict tends to arise in _____ (early/late) adolescence possibly due the fact that these cultures encourage _____ in their children and emphasize family _____ .

17. Four other elements of family functioning that have been heavily researched include _____ , _____ , _____ , and _____ .

18. In terms of family control, a powerful deterrent to delinquency, risky sex, and drug abuse is _____ _____ . Too much interference, however, may contribute to adolescent _____ .

19. Overall, parent–teen relations in all family types and nations, and among children of both sexes, are typically _____ . If there is conflict, it is more likely to center on details like the adolescent's _____ _____ rather than on _____ .

20. According to B. Bradford Brown, during adolescence the peer group serves four important functions.

   a. _____

   b. _____
      _____

   c. _____
      _____

   d. _____

21. The largely constructive role of peers runs counter to the notion of _____ _____ . Social pressure to conform _____ (falls/rises) dramatically in early adolescence, until about age

_____ , when it begins to
_____ (fall/rise).

22. For many immigrant families, the normal strain between the generations extends over a _____ (shorter/longer) period of time, because adolescents' physical and cognitive drives mature _____ (before/after) they would in traditional societies. This creates a severe _____ _____ in many minority families.

Outline the course of ethnic identity achievement in young Asian Americans.

23. Usually, the first sign of heterosexual attraction is a seeming _____ of members of the other sex. The pace at which adolescents "warm up" to the other sex _____ (is similar/varies) from culture to culture.

24. Another factor that affects heterosexual attraction is the _____ of puberty. Adolescents who mature _____ (early/on time/late) generally are the first to reach out to the other sex. Other factors include _____ , _____ , _____ , and the availability of someone in a setting that allows sexual interaction.

(Research Report) Briefly outline the four-stage progression of heterosexual involvement.

25. (Research Report) Cultural patterns _____ (affect/do not affect) the

_____ of these stages, but the basic _____ seems to be based on _____ factors.

26. (Research Report) For gay and lesbian adolescents, added complications usually _____ (slow down/speed up) romantic attachments. In cultures that are _____ , many young men and women with homosexual or lesbian feelings may _____ their feelings, or try to _____ or _____ them.

Adolescent Suicide (pp. 450–454)

27. Adolescents under age 20 are _____ (more/less) likely to kill themselves than adults are.

28. Thinking about committing suicide, called _____ _____ , is _____ (common/relatively rare) among high school students.

29. Research from around the world indicates that depression _____ (increases/decreases) at puberty, especially among _____ (males/females).

30. Most suicide attempts in adolescence _____ (do/do not) result in death. A deliberate act of self-destruction that does not result in death is called a _____ .

31. List five factors that affect whether thinking about suicide leads to a self-destructive act or to death.

a. _____

b. _____

c. _____

d. _____

e. _____

32. (A Life-Span View) The rate of suicide is higher for adolescent _____ (males/females). The rate of parasuicide is higher for _____ (males/females).

33. (A Life-Span View) Around the world, cultural differences in the rates of suicidal ideation and completion _____ (are/are not) apparent.

34. (A Life-Span View) When a town or school sentimentalizes the "tragic end" of a teen suicide, the publicity can trigger _____

_____ .

(A Life-Span View) List several factors that correlate with suicide ideation and completion at any age.

(Table 16.4) Briefly describe ethnic differences in suicide rates in the United States.

35. Suicide rates in North America have _____ (risen/fallen) since 1960. This is due in part to less parental _____ and greater adolescent access to

_____ , _____ , and

_____ .

Breaking the Law (pp. 454–457)

36. Arrests are far more likely to occur during the

_____ _____

of life than during any other time period. Although statistics indicate that the

_____ (incidence/prevalence) of arrests is highest among this age group, they do not reveal how widespread, or

_____ , lawbreaking is among this age group.

37. If all acts of "juvenile delinquency" are included, the prevalence of adolescent crime is

_____ (less/greater) than official records report.

Briefly describe data on gender and ethnic differences in adolescent arrests.

38. (Changing Policy) Experts find it useful to distinguish _____-_____ offenders, whose criminal activity stops by age 21, from _____-_____

_____ offenders, who become career criminals.

39. (Changing Policy) Developmentalists have found that it _____ (is/is not) currently possible to distinguish children who actually will become career criminals.

40. (Changing Policy) Adolescents who later become career criminals are among the first of their cohort to _____

_____ .

They also are among the least involved in _____ activities, and tend to be _____ in preschool and elementary school. At an even earlier age, they show signs of _____ _____ , such as being slow in _____ development, being _____ , or having poor _____ control.

41. (Changing Policy) For most delinquents, residential incarceration in a prison or reform school usually _____ (is/is not) the best solution.

(Changing Policy) List several background factors that increase a child's risk of later becoming a career criminal.

42. Research from several nations has shown that a major risk factor for becoming a violent criminal is _____ .

43. The victims of adolescent crime tend to be _____ (teenagers/adults).

Conclusion: (pp. 457–458)

44. For most young people, the teenage years overall are _____ (happy/unhappy) ones.

45. Adolescents who have one serious problem _____ (often have/do not usually have) others.

46. In most cases adolescent problems stem from earlier developmental events such as

_____ .

Progress Test 1

Multiple-Choice Questions

Circle your answers to the following questions and check them with the answers on page 245. If your answer is incorrect, read the explanation for why it is incorrect and then consult the appropriate pages of the text (in parentheses following the correct answer).

1. According to Erikson, the primary task of adolescence is that of establishing:
   a. basic trust.
   b. an identity.
   c. intimacy.
   d. integrity.

2. According to developmentalists who study identity formation, foreclosure involves:
   a. accepting an identity prematurely, without exploration.
   b. taking time off from school, work, and other commitments.
   c. opposing parental values.
   d. failing to commit oneself to a vocational goal.

3. When adolescents adopt an identity that is the opposite of the one they are expected to adopt, they are considered to be taking on a:
   a. foreclosed identity.
   b. diffused identity.
   c. negative identity.
   d. reverse identity.

4. The main sources of emotional support for most young people who are establishing independence from their parents are:
   a. older adolescents of the opposite sex.
   b. older siblings.
   c. teachers.
   d. peer groups.

5. (In Person) For members of minority ethnic groups, identity achievement may be particularly complicated because:
   a. their cultural ideal clashes with the Western emphasis on adolescent self-determination.
   b. peers, themselves torn by similar conflicts, can be very critical.
   c. parents and other relatives tend to emphasize ethnicity and expect teens to honor their roots.
   d. of all of the above reasons.

6. In a crime-ridden neighborhood, parents can protect their adolescents by keeping close watch over activities, friends, and so on. This practice is called:
   a. generational stake.   c. peer screening.
   b. foreclosure.   d. parental monitoring.

7. Conflict between adolescent girls and their mothers is most likely to involve:
   a. bickering over hair, neatness, and other daily habits.
   b. political, religious, and moral issues.
   c. peer relationships and friendships.
   d. relationships with boys.

8. If there is a "generation gap," it is likely to occur in _____ adolescence and to center on issues of _____ .
   a. early; morality   c. early; self-control
   b. late; self-discipline   d. late; politics

9. (In Person) Because of the conflict between their ethnic background and the larger culture, minority adolescents will *most often*:
   a. reject the traditional values of both their ethnic culture and the majority culture.
   b. foreclose on identity prematurely.
   c. declare a moratorium.
   d. experience identity diffusion.

10. (Changing Policy) In the long run, the most effective programs for preventing juvenile delinquency would include all of the following *except*:
    a. helping parents discipline in an authoritative manner.
    b. strengthening the schools.
    c. increasing the police presence in the area.
    d. shoring up neighborhood networks.

11. If the vast majority of cases of a certain crime are committed by a small number of repeat offenders, this would indicate that the crime's:
    a. incidence is less than its prevalence.
    b. incidence is greater than its prevalence.
    c. incidence and prevalence are about equal.
    d. incidence and prevalence are impossible to calculate.

12. Compared with normal adolescents, suicidal adolescents are:
    a. more concerned about the future.
    b. academically average students.
    c. rejected by their peers.
    d. less likely to have attempted suicide.

13. The early signs of life-course-persistent offenders include all of the following *except*:
    a. signs of brain damage early in life.
    b. antisocial school behavior.
    c. delayed sexual intimacy.
    d. use of alcohol and tobacco at an early age.

14. (A Life-Span View) Regarding gender differences in self-destructive acts, the rate of parasuicide is _____ and the rate of suicide is _____ .
    a. higher in males; higher in females
    b. higher in females; higher in males
    c. the same in males and females; higher in males
    d. the same in males and females; higher in females

15. Conflict between parents and adolescent offspring is:
    a. most likely to involve fathers and their early-maturing offspring.
    b. more frequent in single-parent homes.
    c. more likely between early-maturing daughters and their mothers.
    d. likely in all of the above situations.

True or False Items

Write T (*true*) or F (*false*) on the line in front of each statement.

_____ 1. In cultures where everyone's values are similar and social change is slight, identity is relatively easy to achieve.

_____ 2. Most adolescents have political views and educational values that are markedly different from those of their parents.

_____ 3. Peer pressure is inherently destructive to the adolescent seeking an identity.

_____ 4. For most adolescents, group socializing and dating precede the establishment of true intimacy with one member of the opposite sex.

_____ 5. Worldwide, arrests are more likely to occur during the second decade of life than at any other time.

_____ 6. Most adolescent self-destructive acts are a response to an immediate and specific psychological blow.

_____ 7. The majority of adolescents report that they have at some time engaged in law-breaking that might have led to arrest.

_____ 8. In finding themselves, teens try to find an identity that is stable, consistent, and mature.

_____ 9. Adolescents who have foreclosed their identities generally have a weak sense of ethnic identification.

_____ 10. Increased accessibility of guns is a factor in the increased rate of youth suicide in the United States.

Progress Test 2

Progress Test 2 should be completed during a final chapter review. Answer the following questions after you thoroughly understand the correct answers for the Chapter Review and Progress Test 1.

Multiple-Choice Questions

1. (Changing Policy) The best way to limit adolescent lawbreaking in general would be to:
    a. strengthen the family, school, and community fabric.
    b. increase the number of police officers in the community.
    c. improve the criminal justice system.
    d. establish rehabilitative facilities for law breakers.

2. (A Life-Span View) Which of the following was not identified as a factor in adolescent suicide and ideation?
   a. chronic depression
   b. loneliness
   c. homosexuality.
   d. minor law-breaking.

3. Parent–teen conflict among Chinese, Korean, and Mexican American families often surfaces late in adolescence because these cultures:
   a. emphasize family closeness.
   b. value authoritarian parenting.
   c. encourage autonomy in children.
   d. do all of the above.

4. If the various cases of a certain crime are committed by many different offenders, this would indicate that the crime's:
   a. incidence is less than its prevalence.
   b. incidence is greater than its prevalence.
   c. incidence and prevalence are about equal.
   d. incidence and prevalence are impossible to calculate.

5. Thinking about committing suicide is called:
   a. cluster suicide.
   b. parasuicide.
   c. suicidal ideation.
   d. fratracide.

6. (Research Report) Which of the following is *not* true regarding peer relationships among gay and lesbian adolescents?
   a. Romantic attachments are usually slower to develop.
   b. In homophobic cultures, many gay teens try to conceal their homosexual feelings by becoming heterosexually involved.
   c. Many girls who will later identify themselves as lesbians are oblivious to these sexual urges as teens.
   d. In many cases, a lesbian girl's best friend is a boy, who is more at ease with her sexuality than another girl might be.

7. The adolescent experiencing identity diffusion is typically:
   a. very apathetic.
   b. experimenting with alternative identities without trying to settle on any one.
   c. willing to accept parental values wholesale, without exploring alternatives.
   d. one who rebels against all forms of authority.

8. Adolescents help each other in many ways, including:
   a. identity formation.   c. social skills.
   b. independence.   d. all of the above.

9. Crime statistics show that during adolescence:
   a. males and females are equally likely to be arrested.
   b. males are more likely to be arrested than females.
   c. females are more likely to be arrested than males.
   d. males commit more crimes than females but are less likely to be arrested.

10. Which of the following is the most common problem behavior among adolescents?
    a. pregnancy
    b. daily use of illegal drugs
    c. minor lawbreaking
    d. attempts at suicide

11. A time-out period during which a young person experiments with different identities, postponing important choices, is called a(n):
    a. identity foreclosure.   c. identity diffusion.
    b. negative identity.   d. identity moratorium.

12. When adolescents' political, religious, educational, and vocational opinions are compared with their parents', the so-called "generation gap" is:
    a. much smaller than when the younger and older generations are compared overall.
    b. much wider than when the younger and older generations are compared overall.
    c. wider between parents and sons than between parents and daughters.
    d. wider between parents and daughters than between parents and sons.

13. Identity achievement is easiest in a culture in which:
    a. diversity in moral and political beliefs is appreciated and encouraged.
    b. social change is rapid.
    c. both a. and b. are true.
    d. everyone holds the same values and social change is slow.

14. Parent–teen conflict tends to center on issues related to:
    a. politics and religion.
    b. education.
    c. vacations.
    d. daily details, such as musical tastes.

15. According to a review of studies from various nations, suicidal ideation is:

    a. not as common among high school students as is popularly believed.

    b. more common among males than females.

    c. more common among females than among males.

    d. so common among high school students that it might be considered normal.

Matching Items

Match each term or concept with its corresponding description or definition.

Terms or Concepts

_____ **1.** identity
_____ **2.** identity achievement
_____ **3.** foreclosure
_____ **4.** negative identity
_____ **5.** identity diffusion
_____ **6.** identity moratorium
_____ **7.** generation gap
_____ **8.** generational stake
_____ **9.** parental monitoring
_____ **10.** parasuicide
_____ **11.** cluster suicide

Descriptions or Definitions

a. premature identity formation

b. a group of suicides that occur in the same community, school, or time period

c. the adolescent has few commitments to goals or values

d. differences between the younger and older generations

e. self-destructive act that does not result in death

f. awareness of where children are and what they are doing

g. an individual's self-definition

h. a time-out period during which adolescents experiment with alternative identities

i. the adolescent establishes his or her own goals and values

j. family members in different developmental stages see the family in different ways

k. an identity opposite of the one an adolescent expected to adopt

Thinking Critically About Chapter 16

Answer these questions the day before an exam as a final check on your understanding of the chapter's terms and concepts.

1. From childhood, Sharon thought she wanted to follow in her mother's footsteps and be a homemaker. Now, at age 40 with a home and family, she admits to herself that what she really wanted to be was a medical researcher. Erik Erikson would probably say that Sharon:

    a. adopted a negative identity when she was a child.

    b. experienced identity foreclosure at an early age.

    c. never progressed beyond the obvious identity diffusion she experienced as a child.

    d. took a moratorium from identity formation.

2. Fifteen-year-old David is rebelling against his devoutly religious parents by taking drugs, stealing, and engaging in other antisocial behavior. Evidently, David has:

    a. foreclosed on his identity.

    b. declared an identity moratorium.

    c. adopted a negative identity.

    d. experienced identity diffusion.

3. Fourteen-year-old Sean, who is fiercely proud of his Irish heritage, is prejudiced against members of several other ethnic groups. It is likely that, in forming his identity, Sean:

    a. attained identity achievement.

    b. foreclosed on his identity.

    c. declared a lengthy moratorium.

    d. experienced identity diffusion.

4. (In Person) In 1957, 6-year-old Raisel and her parents emigrated from Poland to the United States. Compared with her parents, who grew up in a culture in which virtually everyone held the same religious, moral, political, and sexual values, Raisel is likely to have:
   a. an easier time achieving her own unique identity.
   b. a more difficult time forging her identity.
   c. a greater span of time in which to forge her own identity.
   d. a shorter span of time in which to forge her identity.

5. An adolescent exaggerates the importance of differences in her values and those of her parents. Her parents see these differences as smaller and less important. This phenomenon is called the:
   a. generation gap.   c. family enigma.
   b. generational stake.   d. parental imperative.

6. In our society, the most obvious examples of institutionalized moratoria on identity formation are:
   a. the Boy Scouts and the Girl Scouts.
   b. college and the peacetime military.
   c. marriage and divorce.
   d. bar mitzvahs and baptisms.

7. First-time parents Norma and Norman are worried that, during adolescence, their healthy parental influence will be undone as their children are encouraged by peers to become sexually promiscuous, drug-addicted, or delinquent. Their wise neighbor, who is a developmental psychologist, tells them that:
   a. during adolescence, peers are generally more likely to complement the influence of parents than they are to pull their friends in the opposite direction.
   b. research suggests that peers provide a negative influence in every major task of adolescence.
   c. only through authoritarian parenting can parents give children the skills they need to resist peer pressure.
   d. unless their children show early signs of learning difficulties or antisocial behavior, parental monitoring is unnecessary.

8. Which of the following statements would a 13-year-old girl be most likely to make?
   a. "Boys are a sort of disease."
   b. "Boys are stupid although important to us."
   c. "Boys hate you if you're ugly and brainy."
   d. "Boys are a pleasant change from girls."

9. In forming an identity, the young person seeks to make meaningful connections with his or her past. This seeking is described by Erikson as an unconscious striving for:
   a. individual uniqueness.
   b. peer-group membership.
   c. continuity of experience.
   d. vocational identity.

10. Rosaria is an adolescent in an immigrant family. In response to the conflict between the peer-group emphasis on adolescent freedom and the values of her family's culture, Rosaria is most likely to:
    a. rebel against her family, possibly leaving home.
    b. join a delinquent group.
    c. give in to parental control.
    d. ask to live with her grandparents.

11. Statistically, the person *least* likely to commit a crime is a(n):
    a. African American or Latino adolescent.
    b. middle-class white male.
    c. white adolescent of any socioeconomic background.
    d. Asian American.

12. (Changing Policy) Ray was among the first of his friends to have sex, drink alcohol, and smoke cigarettes. These attributes, together with his having been hyperactive and having poor emotional control, would suggest that Ray is at high risk of:
    a. becoming an adolescent-limited offender.
    b. becoming a life-course persistent offender.
    c. developing an antisocial personality.
    d. foreclosing his identity prematurely.

13. Carl is a typical 16-year-old adolescent who has no special problems. It is likely that Carl has:
    a. contemplated suicide.
    b. engaged in some minor illegal act.
    c. struggled with "who he is."
    d. done all of the above.

14. Statistically, who of the following is *most* likely to commit suicide?
    a. Micah, an African American female
    b. Yan, an Asian American male
    c. James, a Native American male
    d. Alison, a European American female

15. (A Life-Span View) Coming home from work, Malcolm hears a radio announcement warning parents to be alert for possible cluster suicide signs in their teenage children. What might have precipitated such an announcement?
    a. government statistics that suicide is on the rise in the 1990s
    b. the highly publicized suicide of a famous rock singer
    c. the recent crash of an airliner, killing all on board
    d. any of the above

Key Terms

Using your own words, write a brief definition or explanation of each of the following terms on a separate piece of paper.

1. identity
2. identity versus role confusion
3. identity achievement
4. foreclosure
5. negative identity
6. identity diffusion
7. identity moratorium
8. generation gap
9. generational stake
10. bickering
11. parental monitoring
12. peer pressure
13. suicidal ideation
14. parasuicide
15. cluster suicide
16. incidence
17. prevalence
18. adolescent-limited offender
19. life-course-persistent offender

ANSWERS
CHAPTER REVIEW

1. identity
2. identity versus role confusion
3. identity achievement
4. foreclosure
5. negative identity
6. identity diffusion
7. moratorium
8. achieved identity; foreclosed; foreclosed; identity achievers
9. 10 years
10. values; social structures; customs
11. easier
12. more; negative; foreclose
13. generation gap; time; place
14. generational stake
15. early; mothers; early; daughters; bickering
16. late; dependency; closeness
17. communication; support; connectiveness; control
18. parental monitoring; depression
19. supportive; musical tastes, domestic neatness sleeping habits; world politics or moral issues
20. a. a source of information and a self-help group
    b. a source of support for the adolescent who is adjusting to changes in the social ecology of adolescence
    c. a kind of mirror in which to check one's reflection
    d. a sounding board for exploring and defining one's values and aspirations
21. peer pressure; rises; 14; fall
22. longer; before; generation gap

The sequence begins with foreclosure on traditional values, continues with rejection of tradition in favor of mainstream values, is followed by a moratorium and culminates in identity achievement by connecting with other young Asian Americans.

23. dislike; varies
24. biology; early; culture; peers; parents

The progression begins with groups of same-sex friends. Next, a loose, public association of a girl's group and a boy's group forms. Then, a smaller, heterosexual group forms from the more advanced members of the larger association. Finally, more intimate heterosexual couples peel off.

25. affect; timing; sequence; biological

26. slow down; homophobic; deny; change; conceal

27. less

28. suicidal ideation; common

29. increases; females

30. do not; parasuicide

31. **a.** the availability of lethal methods

    b. the extent of parental supervision

    c. the use of alcohol and other drugs

    d. gender

    e. the attitudes about suicide held by the adolescent's family, friends, and culture

32. males; females

33. are

34. cluster suicides

At any age, these include chronic depression, death of a close friend, drug abuse, loneliness, social rejection, and homosexuality.

Native American males have the highest rates, followed by European American males, Asian American males, African American males, and Hispanic American males.

35. risen; supervision; alcohol, drugs; guns

36. second decade; incidence; prevalent

37. greater

Boys are three times as likely to be arrested as girls, and African American youth are three times as likely to be arrested as European Americans, who are three times as likely to be arrested as Asian Americans.

38. adolescent-limited; life-course persistent

39. is

40. have sex, drink alcohol, and smoke cigarettes; school; antisocial; brain damage; language; hyperactive; emotional

41. is not

Children who have been abused or neglected, who have few friends, who are early substance users, or who are bullies are at higher risk.

42. being a victim of violence

43. teenagers

44. happy

45. often have

46. genetic vulnerability, prenatal insults, family disruptions, childhood discord, learning difficulties, aggressive or withdrawn behavior in elementary school, inadequate community intervention

PROGRESS TEST 1

Multiple-Choice Questions

1. **b.** is the answer. (p. 435)

    a. According to Erikson, this is the crisis of infancy.

    c. & d. In Erikson's theory, these crises occur later in life.

2. **a.** is the answer. (p. 436)

    b. This describes an identity moratorium.

    c. This describes a negative identity.

    d. This describes identity diffusion.

3. **c.** is the answer. (p. 437)

4. **d.** is the answer. (pp. 443–444)

5. **d.** is the answer. (p. 440)

6. **d.** is the answer. (p. 442)

    a. The generational stake refers to differences in how family members from different generations view the family.

    b. Foreclosure refers to the premature establishment of identity.

    c. Peer screening is an aspect of parental monitoring, but it was not specifically discussed in the text.

7. **a.** is the answer. (p. 441)

8. **c.** is the answer. (pp. 440–441)

9. **b.** is the answer. (p. 440)

    a. This occurs in some cases, but not in *most* cases.

    c. Moratorium is a time-out in identity formation in order to allow the adolescent to try out alternative identities. It is generally not a solution in such cases.

    d. Young people who experience identity diffusion are often apathetic, which is not the case here.

10. **c.** is the answer. (p. 457)

11. **b.** is the answer. Incidence is how often a particular circumstance (such as lawbreaking) occurs; prevalence is how widespread the circumstance is. A crime that is committed by only a few repeat offenders is not very prevalent in the population. (p. 455)

12. **c.** is the answer. (p. 453)

13. **c.** is the answer. Most life-course persistent offenders are among the earliest of their cohort to have sex. (p. 456)

14. **b.** is the answer. (p. 452)

15. **c.** is the answer. (p. 441)

    a. In fact, parent-child conflict is more likely to involve mothers and their early-maturing offspring.

    b. The text did not compare the rate of conflict in two-parent and single-parent homes.

True or False Items

1. T (p. 438)

2. F Parent–teen conflicts center on day-to-day details, not on politics or moral issues. (p. 443)

3. F Just the opposite is true. (p. 445)

4. T (p. 448)

5. T (p. 454)

6. F Most self-destructive acts stem from many earlier developmental events. (p. 458)

7. T (p. 455)

8. T (p. 437)

9. F Just the opposite is true. (p. 436)

10. T (pp. 452)

PROGRESS TEST 2

Multiple-Choice Questions

1. **a.** is the answer. (p. 456)

2. **d.** is the answer. (p. 453)

3. **a.** is the answer. For this reason, autonomy in their offspring tends to be delayed. (p. 442)

4. **c.** is the answer. (p. 455)

    a. This answer would have been correct if the question had stated, "If the majority of cases of a crime are committed by a small number of repeat offenders."

    b. Because it is simply the total number of cases of an event or circumstance (such as a crime), incidence cannot be less than prevalence.

5. **c.** is the answer. (p. 451)

6. **d.** is the answer. Lesbian adolescents find it easier to establish strong friendships with same-sex heterosexual peers than homosexual teenage boys do. (p. 449)

7. **a.** is the answer. (p. 436)

    b. This describes an adolescent undergoing an identity moratorium.

    c. This describes identity foreclosure.

    d. This describes an adolescent who is adopting a negative identity.

8. **d.** is the answer. (p. 444)

9. **b.** is the answer. (p. 455)

10. **c.** is the answer. (p. 455)

11. **d.** is the answer. (p. 437)

    a. Identity foreclosure occurs when the adolescent prematurely adopts an identity, without fully exploring alternatives.

    b. Adolescents who adopt an identity that is opposite to the one they are expected to develop have taken on a negative identity.

    c. Identity diffusion occurs when the adolescent is apathetic and has few commitments to goals or values.

12. **a.** is the answer. (p. 440)

    c. & d. The text does not suggest that the size of the generation gap varies with the offspring's sex.

13. **d.** is the answer. (p. 436)

14. **d.** is the answer. (p. 441)

    a., b., & c. In fact, on these issues parents and teenagers tend to show substantial *agreement*.

15. **d.** is the answer. (p. 450)

Matching Items

1. g (p. 436)
2. i (p. 436)
3. a (p. 436)
4. k (p. 436)
5. c (p. 436)
6. h (p. 437)
7. d (p. 440)
8. j (p. 441)
9. f (p. 442)
10. e (p. 451)
11. b (p. 453)

THINKING CRITICALLY ABOUT CHAPTER 16

1. **b.** is the answer. Apparently, Sharon never explored alternatives or truly forged a unique personal identity. (p. 436)

    a. Individuals who rebel by adopting an identity that is the opposite of the one they are expected to adopt have taken on a negative identity.

    c. Individuals who experience identity diffusion have few commitments to goals or values. This was not Sharon's problem.

d. Had she taken a moratorium on identity formation, Sharon would have experimented with alternative identities and perhaps would have chosen that of a medical researcher.

c. is the answer. (p. 436)

b. is the answer. (p. 436)

a. Identity achievers often have a strong sense of ethnic identification, but usually are low in prejudice.

c. & d. The text does not present research that links ethnic pride and prejudice with either identity diffusion or moratorium.

b. is the answer. Minority adolescents struggle with finding the right balance between transcending their background and becoming immersed in it. (p. 440)

c. & d. The text does not suggest that the amount of time adolescents have to forge their identities varies from one ethnic group to another or has changed over historical time.

b. is the answer. (p. 441)

a. The generation gap refers to actual differences in attitudes and values between the younger and older generations. This example is concerned with how large these differences are perceived to be.

c. & d. These terms are not used in the text in discussing family conflict.

b. is the answer. (p. 437)

a. is the answer. (pp. 445)

b. In fact, just the opposite is true.

c. Developmentalists recommend authoritative, rather than authoritarian, parenting.

d. Parental monitoring is important for all adolescents.

b. is the answer. (p. 447)

c. is the answer. (p. 437)

c. is the answer. Adolescent girls in immigrant families are most likely to docilely live at home until an early marriage. (p. 446)

a. & b. Boys are most likely to do these things.

d. This may be the parents' response to problems with their children.

d. is the answer. (p. 455)

b. is the answer. (p. 456)

d. is the answer. (pp. 435, 450, 455)

c. is the answer. (p. 454)

b. is the answer. (pp. 452–453)

a., c., & d. Cluster suicides occur when the suicide of a well-known person leads others to attempt suicide.

KEY TERMS

1. **Identity**, as used by Erikson, refers to a person's self-definition as a separate individual in terms of roles, attitudes, beliefs, and aspirations. (p. 435).

2. Erikson's term for the psychosocial crisis of adolescence, **identity versus role confusion**, refers to adolescents' need to combine their self-understanding and social roles into a coherent identity. (p. 435)

3. In Erikson's theory, **identity achievement** occurs when adolescents attain their new identity by establishing their own goals and values and abandoning some of those set by their parents and culture and accepting others. (p. 436)

4. In identity **foreclosure**, according to Erikson, the adolescent forms an identity prematurely, accepting earlier roles and parental values wholesale, without truly forging a unique personal identity. (p. 436)

5. Adolescents who take on a **negative identity**, according to Erikson, adopt an identity that is the opposite of the one they are expected to adopt. (p. 436)

6. Adolescents who experience **identity diffusion**, according to Erikson, have few commitments to goals or values and are often apathetic about trying to find an identity. (p. 436)

7. According to Erikson, in the process of finding a mature identity, many young people seem to declare an **identity moratorium**, a kind of time-out during which they experiment with alternative identities without trying to settle on any one. (p. 437)

8. The **generation gap** refers to the alleged distance between generations in values, behaviors, and knowledge. (p. 440)

9. The **generational stake** refers to the tendency of each family member, because of that person's different developmental stage, to see the family in a certain way. (p. 441)

10. **Bickering** refers to the repeated, petty arguing that typically occurs in early adolescence about common, daily life activities. (p. 441)

11. **Parental monitoring** is parental watchfulness about where one's child is and what he or she is doing, and with whom. (p. 442)

12. **Peer pressure** refers to the social pressure to conform to one's friends in behavior, dress, and attitude. It may be positive or negative in its effects. (p. 445)

13. **Suicidal ideation** refers to thinking about committing suicide, usually with some serious emotional and intellectual overtones. (p. 450)

14. **Parasuicide** is a deliberate act of self-destruction that does not result in death. (p. 451)

15. A **cluster suicide** refers to a series of suicides or suicide attempts that are precipitated by one initial suicide, usually that of a famous person or a well-known peer. (p. 453)

16. **Incidence** is how often a particular circumstan (such as lawbreaking) occurs. (p. 455)

17. **Prevalence** is how widespread a particu behavior or circumstance is. (p. 455)

18. **Adolescent-limited offenders** are juvenile del quents, whose criminal activity stops by age (p. 456)

19. **Life-course-persistent offenders** are adolesce lawbreakers who later become career crimina (p. 456)

Early Adulthood: Biosocial Development

hapter Overview

 this chapter we encounter the developing person in e prime of life. Early adulthood is the best time for rd physical labor—because strength is at a peak— d for reproduction—because overall health is good d fertility is high. However, with the attainment of ll maturity, a new aspect of physical development mes into play—that is, decline. Chapter 17 takes a ok at how people perceive changes that occur as the dy ages as well as how decisions they make regard g lifestyle affect the course of their overall develop ent.

The chapter begins with a description of the owth, strength, and health of the individual during lulthood, as well as both visible age-related anges, such as wrinkling, and less obvious changes, ch as declines in the efficiency of the body's sys ms. Sexual-reproductive health, a matter of great ncern to young adults, is discussed in the next sec n, with particular attention paid to trends in sexual sponsiveness during adulthood and fertility prob ms that may develop. The final section looks at ree problems that are more prevalent during young lulthood than at any other period of the life span: ug abuse, compulsive eating and destructive diet g, and violence.

OTE: Answer guidelines for all Chapter 17 ques ns begin on page 260.

uided Study

e text chapter should be studied one section at a ne. Before you read, preview each section by skim ing it, noting headings and boldface items. Then ad the appropriate section objectives from the fol wing outline. Keep these objectives in mind and, as u read the chapter section, search for the informa n that will enable you to meet each objective. Once u have finished a section, write out answers for its jectives.

Growth, Strength, and Health (pp. 465–471)

1. Describe the changes in growth, strength, and overall health that occur during early adulthood.

2. Describe age-related changes in physical appear ance that become noticeable by the late 20s.

3. Discuss changes in the efficiency of various body functions, focusing on the significance of these changes for the individual.

4. (A Life-Span View) Identify age-related trends in the sexual responsiveness of both men and women during the decades from 20 to 40.

8. (text and Changing Policy) Identify the potentially harmful effects of repeated dieting.

9. Describe the typical victims of anorexia nervo[sa] and bulimia nervosa, and discuss possible expl[a]nations for these disorders.

The Sexual-Reproductive System (pp. 471–476)

5. Discuss changing attitudes toward contraception from adolescence to young adulthood.

10. Explain how restrictive stereotypes of "masc[u]line" behavior may be related to the self-destru[c]tive behaviors of many young Americans.

6. (text and In Person) Describe the main causes of infertility in men and women, and list several techniques used to treat this problem, noting some of the issues raised by the techniques.

11. (text and Research Report) Discuss the facto[rs] that may determine whether a young male adu[lt] will suffer a violent death.

Three Health Problems (pp. 476–486)

7. Discuss the causes and consequences of drug abuse during early adulthood.

Chapter Review

When you have finished reading the chapter, work through the material that follows to review it. Complete the sentences and answer the questions. As you proceed, evaluate your performance for each section by consulting the answers on page 260. Do not continue with the next section until you understand each answer. If you need to, review or reread the appropriate section in the textbook before continuing.

1. The early 20s are the best years for

_____

_____ .

(three categories) .

Growth, Strength, and Health (pp. 465–471)

2. Girls usually reach their maximum height by age _____ , and boys by age

_____ .

3. Growth in _____ and increases in _____ continue into the 20s.

4. Physical strength reaches a peak at about age _____ and then decreases.

5. Medical attention in early adulthood is more often necessitated by _____ than by illness.

6. Of the fatal diseases, _____ is the leading killer of adults under age 75, with fewer than 1 in 10,000 being adults between _____ and _____ years of age.

7. When overall growth stops, _____ , or age-related decline, begins.

8. The earliest signs of aging include wrinkles, caused by loss of _____ in facial skin, and the first _____ _____ , caused by a loss of pigment-producing cells in the head.

9. The kidneys begin to lose their efficiency at about age _____ , declining about _____ percent per decade.

10. Lung efficiency, as measured by _____ _____ ,

decreases about _____ percent per decade beginning in the 20s.

11. Notable decline occurs in the ability of the eye's _____ to focus on _____ (near/far) objects. At about age _____ this decline reaches the point where it is labeled _____ , and reading glasses are needed.

12. Many of the body's functions serve to maintain _____ ; that is, they keep physiological functioning in a state of balance. The older a person is, the _____ (less time/longer) it takes for these adjustments to occur. This makes it more difficult for older bodies to adapt to, and recover from,

_____ _____ .

13. (A Life-Span View) Male and female bodies _____ (do/do not) follow a similar sequence of sexual activation at every age.

14. (A Life-Span View) The sequence of sexual activation begins with _____ , followed by _____ _____ , release through _____ , followed by _____ and _____ .

15. (A Life-Span View) During the early years of manhood, sexual excitement, which includes

_____

_____

and _____

_____ , can

occur very quickly and frequently. As men grow older, they often need stimulation that is more _____ or _____ to initiate sexual excitement.

16. (A Life-Span View) Age-related trends in sexual responsiveness _____ (are/are not) as clear-cut for women. As they mature from adolescence toward middle adulthood, women become more likely to experience

_____ .

(A Life-Span View) State several possible reasons for this age-related trend in women.

17. For most of us, our bodies, if adequately maintained, are capable of functioning quite well until we are at least age _____ . The declines of aging primarily affect our

_____ _____ , which is

defined as _____

_____ .

18. The muscles of the body _____ (do/do not) have the equivalent of an organ reserve.

19. The average maximum heart rate

_____ (declines/remains

stable/increases) with age. Resting heart rate

_____ (declines/remains

stable/increases) with age.

Briefly explain why most of the age-related biological changes that occur during the first decades of adulthood are of little consequence to the individual.

20. Age-related biological changes *are* particularly noticeable in professional _____ and serious weekend players.

21. Performance in sports that demand vigorous _____ motor skills peaks in the 20s; in those that demand _____ motor skills, in the _____ . An important factor in the impact of aging on athletic perfor-

mance, however, is the individual's

_____ .

The Sexual-Reproductive System (pp. 471–476)

22. In both sexes, sexual responsiveness, sexual preference, and sexual orientation vary for many reasons, including _____

_____ , _____

_____ , and _____

_____ as well as _____

_____ .

23. In early adulthood, sexual activity increases in both _____ and _____ . Moreover, individuals are more likely to be in _____ relationships, which partly explains why the use of _____ increases and _____ decreases over the years of early adulthood.

24. Most women can still bear a first child as late as age _____ , and most men can father a child _____ .

25. About _____ percent of all married couples experience infertility, which is defined a _____ . Age is _____ (often/rarely) a contributing factor to this problem.

26. The most common fertility problem in men lies i the _____ _____ of sperm or in the sperm's poor swimming ability, or _____ .

27. Sperm grow in the _____ over a period of _____ .

List several factors that can alter normal sperm development.

The above factors can also affect fertility in women. Two additional conditions that can contribute to female infertility are being _____ or _____ .

The most common fertility problem in women is difficulty with _____ . Most women find that ovulation becomes _____ (more/less) regular as middle age approaches. Older women take _____ (longer/less time) to conceive, and they are more likely to give birth to _____ when they do.

The other common fertility problem for women is blocked _____ _____ , often caused by _____ _____ _____ that was not treated promptly. Sexually transmitted diseases, such as _____ , can cause such infections.

A woman who has trouble conceiving may have _____ , a condition in which fragments of the _____ _____ block the reproductive tract. This disorder is most common after age _____ .

A final cause of female infertility is _____ problems that prevent _____ .

Most physicians recommend that women begin their childbearing before age _____ and would-be fathers before age _____ .

Many infertility problems can also be overcome by modern medical techniques, such as _____ to open blocked genital ducts or Fallopian tubes, or the use of _____ to stimulate ovulation. Another possibility is _____ _____ _____ , in which ova are fertilized outside the ovaries. The success rate of this technique is about one baby in _____ attempts. Two variations of this technique, _____ and _____ , involve inserting either sperm and unfertilized _____ or _____ into the Fallopian tube.

35. (In Person) These alternative paths to reproduction raise profound _____ and _____ questions. Another issue is the _____ _____ _____ of alternative conception.

36. (In Person) About _____ of all infertile couples who remain untreated eventually have a baby, and about _____ of the couples who are treated never do.

Three Health Problems (pp. 476–486)

37. Three problems that are more prevalent in early adulthood are _____ _____ , _____ _____ , and _____ .

38. When the absence of a drug in a person's system causes physiological or psychological craving, _____ _____ is apparent.

39. The late teens and early 20s are the time of heaviest _____ and _____ consumption. The greatest use of other drugs, such as _____ , occurs at about age _____ .

40. In general, young adults are _____ (more likely/no more likely) to be addicts than are adolescence or older adults.

41. Women use drugs _____ (less often than/as often as/more often than) men do.

42. The temperament of those most likely to misuse drugs includes attraction to _____ , intolerance of _____ , and vulnerability to _____ . How powerfully these characteristics affect an individual is influenced by both _____ and early _____ _____ .

43. State four reasons for the high rate of drug use and abuse in the first years of adulthood.

   a. _____

   b. _____

   c. _____

   d. _____

44. Drug abuse and addiction generally
_____ (increase/ decrease) from age
_____ to _____ .

45. Compared to others their age, young adult drug
users are more likely to _____

_____ .

46. Many scientists believe that each person has a
certain _____ for his or her weight.
List the factors that can affect this point.

47. To measure whether a person is too fat or too
thin, clinicians calculate his or her

_____ _____

_____ , defined as the ratio of
_____ (in kilograms) divided by
_____ (in meters squared).

48. (text and Changing Policy) The tendency to maintain body weight at a healthy level can be undermined by _____ _____ and
specifics of the social context, such as the notion
that an ideal body is _____-
_____ . The subset of the population
that is most susceptible to this notion is women in
the _____ _____ (which
country?) of _____ ancestry.

49. (Changing Policy) One survey of North American
dieters found that those who were

_____ , well-_____ , and
_____ were the ones most likely to
diet. The same survey reported that the average
women during early adulthood would like to
weigh _____ pounds less, and the
average man about _____ pounds
more.

50. (Changing Policy) Women who attempt to reach
a target weight that is substantially below their
set point generally _____ (do/do not)
eventually regain it.

51. (Changing Policy) Crash dieting can result in

_____ _____ ,

_____ _____ , and
_____ to disease. As the dangers of
eating disorders have become more widely
known, women in the United States aged 20 to
_____ (are/are not) becoming less
likely to be too thin. At the same time, the number of women who are obese has _____
(increased/decreased).

52. Dieting may also trigger physiological changes
that lead to an eating disorder such as

_____ , an affliction
characterized by _____ , or the
_____ (more/less) common disorder
_____ _____ , which
involves successive bouts of binge eating followed by purging through vomiting or massive
doses of laxatives.

53. Binge-purge eating can cause a wide range of
health problems, including damage to the

_____ _____

and _____ _____
from the strain of electrolyte imbalance. A group
that is at particular risk for eating disorders is

_____ _____ .

Briefly summarize how each of the major theories
of development views eating disorders.

Psychoanalytic theory

Learning theory

Cognitive theory

sciocultural theory

epigenetic systems theory

. Stereotypes about "manly" behavior may lead to a problem that afflicts mostly young men—that is, behavior that leads to _____ _____ .

. Many experts believe that _____ _____ are at the root of masculine violence. These values, however, can change, as evidenced by the decline in automobile crash rates involving young drunk men in response to the activism of groups such as _____ and _____ .

. Some experts believe that aggression is the result of an "explosive combination" of high _____ and dashed _____ . A blow to the individual's _____ is more likely to result in violence when the individual is under the influence of _____ ; when there is a _____ present; and when the individual lacks _____ .

. (Research Report) The extent of masculine violence, as reflected in rates of _____ , _____ (varies/does not vary) from culture to culture.

. (Research Report) A contextual factor frequently cited for the high rates of homicide among young American men is the availability of _____ . Research _____ (confirms/does not confirm) that the presence of a gun often transforms non-lethal aggressive impulses into deadly ones.

59. (Research Report) The leading cause of death for young African-American and Latino men is _____ , while among European-American men, _____ are the number one cause.

Progress Test 1

Multiple-Choice Questions

Circle your answers to the following questions and check them with the answers on page 261. If your answer is incorrect, read the explanation for why it is incorrect and then consult the appropriate pages of the text (in parentheses following the correct answer).

1. Senescence refers to:
   a. a loss of efficiency in the body's regulatory systems.
   b. age-related decline.
   c. decreased physical strength.
   d. vulnerability to disease.

2. When do noticeable increases in height stop?
   a. at about the same age in men and women
   b. at an earlier age in women than in men
   c. at an earlier age in men than in women
   d. There is such diversity in physiological development that it is impossible to generalize regarding this issue.

3. A difference between men and women during early adulthood is that men have:
   a. a higher percentage of body fat.
   b. lower metabolism.
   c. proportionately more muscle.
   d. greater organ reserve.

4. The majority of young adults rate their own health as:
   a. very good or excellent.
   b. average or fair.
   c. poor.
   d. worse than it was during adolescence.

5. The automatic adjustment of the body's systems to keep physiological functions in a state of equilibrium, even during heavy exertion, is called:
   a. organ reserve.   c. stress.
   b. homeostasis.   d. muscle capacity.

6. Which of the following temperamental characteristics was *not* identified as being typical of drug
   abusers?
   a. attraction to excitement
   b. intolerance of frustration
   c. extroversion
   d. vulnerability to depression

7. (A Life-Span View) As men grow older:
   a. they often need more direct stimulation to ini-
      tiate sexual excitement.
   b. a longer time elapses between the beginning
      of sexual excitement and full erection.
   c. a longer time elapses between orgasm and the
      end of the refractory period.
   d. all of the above occur.

8. It is estimated that infertility affects:
   a. at least half of all married couples in which
      the woman is in her early 30s.
   b. men more than women.
   c. about one-third of all married couples.
   d. about 15 percent of all married couples.

9. Sperm develop in the testes over a period of:
   a. one month.
   b. four days.
   c. seventy-four days.
   d. one year.

10. Endometriosis is:
    a. a sexually transmitted disease.
    b. lack of ovulation or irregular ovulation in an
       older woman.
    c. a disease characterized by the presence of
       uterine tissue on the surface of the ovaries or
       the Fallopian tubes.
    d. a condition that invariably results from pelvic
       inflammatory disease.

11. In vitro fertilization is a solution for infertility
    that is caused by:
    a. endometriosis.
    b. low sperm count.
    c. low sperm count or ovulatory problems.
    d. PID.

12. A 50-year-old woman can expect to retain what
    percentage of her strength at age 20?
    a. 25
    b. 50
    c. 75
    d. 90

13. According to epigenetic systems theory, eati
    disorders such as anorexia nervosa are more con
    mon in young women who are genetically su
    ceptible to:
    a. depression.
    b. alcohol abuse.
    c. obesity.
    d. suicide.

14. (Research Report) The leading cause of dea
    among young adult African-American men is:
    a. cancer.
    b. homicide.
    c. fatal accidents.
    d. suicide.

15. Which of the following was *not* suggested as
    reason for the high rate of drug use and abuse
    the first years of adulthood?
    a. Young adults often have friends who u
       drugs.
    b. Young adults are trying to imitate their pa
       ents' behavior.
    c. Young adults may use drugs as a way
       relieving job or educational stress.
    d. Young adults often fear social rejection.

True or False Items

Write T (*true*) or F (*false*) on the line in front of ea
statement.

_____ 1. Conditioned older athletes can perfor
              much   better   than   uncondition
              younger persons.
_____ 2. Few adults actually use all the musc
              capacity that they could develop duri
              young adulthood.
_____ 3. The older a person is, the longer it tak
              for his or her blood glucose level
              return to normal after heavy exertion.
_____ 4. (A Life-Span View) Age-related tren
              in sexual responsiveness are similar f
              men and women.
_____ 5. African-Americans use drugs mc
              often during early adulthood than
              whites or Hispanics.
_____ 6. Compared with a woman in her 20s,
              40-year-old woman is more likely
              have cycles with no ovulation ar
              cycles in which several ova are release
_____ 7. Most physicians recommend th
              women who want to have childr
              begin childbearing by age 35.
_____ 8. College women and male athletes are
              particular risk for eating disorders.

_____ 9. A healthy BMI is somewhere between 19 and 25.

_____ 10. (Research Report) Homicide is the leading cause of death for young American men of all ethnic groups.

Progress Test 2

Progress Test 2 should be completed during a final chapter review. Answer the following questions after you thoroughly understand the correct answers for the Chapter Review and Progress Test 1.

Multiple-Choice Questions

1. The early 20s are the peak years for:
   a. hard physical work.
   b. problem-free reproduction.
   c. athletic performance.
   d. all of the above.

2. Of the fatal diseases, _____ is the leading cause of death in young adults.
   a. heart disease
   b. cancer
   c. diabetes
   d. multiple sclerosis

3. The first sign of aging that is likely to be noticed by a man around age 30 is:
   a. reduced organ reserve.
   b. diminishing physical strength.
   c. failure of homeostatic mechanisms during heavy exertion.
   d. graying or thinning of the hair.

4. The efficiency of the lungs:
   a. remains stable throughout the 20s.
   b. begins to decline during the 20s.
   c. begins to decline during the 30s.
   d. declines significantly at about age 30.

5. Normally, the average resting heart rate for both men and women:
   a. declines noticeably during the 30s.
   b. declines much faster than does the average maximum heart rate.
   c. reaches a peak at about age 30.
   d. remains stable until late adulthood.

6. (A Life-Span View) As they mature from adolescence through early adulthood, women become more likely to experience orgasm during love-making in part because:
   a. the woman's responses occur earlier because of increased experience.
   b. with experience, both partners are more likely to focus on aspects of love-making that intensify the woman's sexual responses.
   c. they are less concerned about becoming pregnant.
   d. of all of the above reasons.

7. The most common fertility problem in men lies in:
   a. the low number of their sperm.
   b. the sperm's poor motility.
   c. the condition called endometriosis.
   d. both a. and b.

8. PID refers to:
   a. a drug taken to stimulate ovulation.
   b. a sexually transmitted disease.
   c. pelvic inflammatory disease.
   d. fertilization outside the uterus.

9. A technique that involves fertilization of the ovum outside the uterus is referred to as:
   a. endometriosis.
   b. artificial insemination.
   c. in vitro fertilization.
   d. surrogate fertilization.

10. In most cases of infertility, age is:
    a. a relatively unimportant factor.
    b. one factor among many.
    c. the primary factor.
    d. not a factor at all.

11. The typical bulimic patient is a:
    a. college-age woman.
    b. woman who starves herself to the point of emaciation.
    c. woman in her late 40s.
    d. woman who suffers from life-threatening obesity.

12. (Changing Policy) Repeated or extensive weight loss may result in:
    a. nutritional imbalance.
    b. vulnerability to disease.
    c. energy loss.
    d. all of the above.

13. Relative to all other age groups, young adult males are at increased risk for virtually every kind of:
    a. eating disorder.
    b. violence.
    c. acute disease.
    d. chronic disease.

14. The heaviest use of drugs other than alcohol and marijuana in the United States is:
    a. during adolescence.
    b. at about age 23.
    c. during the 30s.
    d. during late adulthood.

15. Researchers have found that athletic performance peaks earliest in sports that require:
    a. fine motor skills.
    b. vigorous gross motor skills.
    c. greater flexibility than physical strength.
    d. extensive conditioning before peak performance is achieved.

Matching Items

Match each definition or description with its corresponding term.

Terms

_____ 1. senescence
_____ 2. homeostasis
_____ 3. organ reserve
_____ 4. infertility
_____ 5. motility
_____ 6. pelvic inflammatory disease (PID)
_____ 7. endometriosis
_____ 8. in vitro fertilization (IVF)
_____ 9. anorexia nervosa
_____ 10. bulimia nervosa

Definitions or Descriptions

a. fertilization of ova outside the body
b. a condition characterizing about 15 percent of a married couples
c. often caused by sexually transmitted diseases
d. extra capacity for responding to stressful events
e. a state of physiological equilibrium
f. an affliction characterized by binge-purge eating
g. age-related decline
h. condition in which fragments of the uterus block the reproductive tract
i. an affliction characterized by self-starvation
j. with age, declines in male sperm

Thinking Critically About Chapter 17

Answer these questions the day before an exam as a final check on your understanding of the chapter's terms and concepts.

1. Your instructor asks you to summarize, in one sentence, the extent and cause of biosocial decline during early adulthood. You wisely respond:
    a. "Any difficulties experienced by young adults in biosocial development are usually related to factors other than aging per se."
    b. "Significant declines in all aspects of physical well-being become apparent by the mid 20s."
    c. "With the attainment of full maturity, development is released from the constraints of heredity."
    d. "The first signs of aging are usually not apparent until middle adulthood."

2. When we are hot, we perspire in order to give off body heat. This is an example of the way our body functions maintain:
    a. senescence.   c. endometriosis.
    b. homeostasis.   d. motility.

3. Due to a decline in organ reserve, 28-year-old Brenda:
    a. has a higher resting heart rate than she did when she was younger.
    b. needs longer to recover from strenuous exercise than she did when she was younger.
    c. has a higher maximum heart rate than her younger sister.
    d. has all of the above.

4. (A Life-Span View) Summarizing the results of cross-sectional research, the lecturer states that "Women's sexual responses are heightened by age." The most likely explanation for the lecturer's statement is that:
    a. in women, sexual sensitivity increases with age.
    b. with age, men's responses slow down, allowing women more time to experience orgasm.
    c. the sample is unrepresentative of the population.
    d. cross-sectional research tends to exaggerate age differences.

(A Life-Span View) If Benny is like most men, as he grows older, he will require:

a. less direct stimulation to become sexually excited.

b. a shorter refractory period following each orgasm.

c. a longer time between erection and ejaculation.

d. all of the above.

Corretta and Vernon Castle have been trying to conceive a baby for more than a year. Because they are both in their 40s, their physician suspects that:

a. Vernon is infertile.

b. Corretta is infertile.

c. neither Vernon nor Corretta is infertile.

d. Vernon and Corretta are equally likely to be infertile.

Twenty-five-year-old Michelle believes that she is infertile. Because she has been sexually active with a number of partners and once had gonorrhea, her doctor suspects she may have:

a. endometriosis.

b. low motility.

c. irregular ovulation.

d. pelvic inflammatory disease.

Sheila dieted for several weeks until she lost ten pounds. Upon returning to a normal diet, she is horrified to find that she has gained some of the weight back. It is likely that Sheila's weight gain was caused by:

a. overconsumption of high-fat foods.

b. too little exercise in her daily routine.

c. her homeostatic mechanism returning to her natural set point.

d. a low body set point.

Of the following, who is most likely to suffer from anorexia nervosa?

a. Bill, a 23-year-old professional football player

b. Florence, a 30-year-old account executive

c. Lynn, a 20-year-old college student

d. Carl, a professional dancer

Twenty-year-old Gwynn, who is nine pounds heavier than the national average for her height and build, should probably:

a. go on a crash diet, since every additional pound of fat is hazardous to her health.

b. gradually reduce her weight to slightly below the national average.

c. realize that because of her high body set point she will be unable to have children.

d. not worry, since this is probably a healthy weight for her body.

11. As a psychoanalyst, Dr. Mendoza is most likely to believe that eating disorders are caused by:

a. the reinforcing effects of fasting, bingeing, and purging.

b. low self-esteem and depression, which act as a stimulus for destructive patterns of eating.

c. unresolved conflicts with parents.

d. the desire of working women to project a strong, self-controlled image.

12. Michael, who is in his mid-20s, is most likely to seek medical attention for:

a. a common cold.

b. a sports- or drug-related injury.

c. a life-threatening chronic illness.

d. infertility.

13. (Changing Policy) Which of the following is an example of a cohort influence on biosocial development during early adulthood?

a. The number of North American women with a BMI below 19 has decreased over the past three decades.

b. Women in the United States of European ancestry are particularly vulnerable to an obsession with thinness.

c. Violent death is far more prevalent among young adult males than among females.

d. Women with a family history of depression have a heightened risk of becoming anorexic.

14. Lucretia, who has a body-mass index of 24, has been trying unsuccessfully to lose ten pounds. It is likely that her difficulty is due to the fact that:

a. she has a glandular disorder.

b. she suffers from bulimia nervosa.

c. her natural weight set point is higher than she would like.

d. her obesity is accompanied by a very low metabolic rate.

15. Nathan has a powerful attraction to excitement, a low tolerance for frustration, and a vulnerability to depression. He also may be vulnerable to:

a. alcoholism.

b. cocaine abuse.

c. most psychoactive drugs.

d. none of the above.

Key Terms

Using your own words, write a brief definition or explanation of each of the following terms on a separate piece of paper.

1. senescence
2. homeostasis
3. organ reserve
4. infertility
5. pelvic inflammatory disease (PID)
6. in vitro fertilization (IVF)
7. drug addiction
8. set point
9. body-mass index (BMI)
10. anorexia nervosa
11. bulimia nervosa

ANSWERS

CHAPTER REVIEW

1. hard physical work, problem-free reproduction, peak athletic performance
2. 16; 18
3. muscle; fat
4. 30
5. injuries
6. cancer; 20; 34
7. senescence
8. elasticity; gray hairs
9. 30; 4
10. vital capacity; 5
11. lens; near; 55; presbyopia
12. homeostasis; longer; physical stress
13. do
14. arousal; peak excitement; orgasm; refraction; recovery
15. faster heartbeat; penile erection; direct (or explicit); prolonged
16. are not; orgasm
    a. The slowing of the man's responses lengthens the sex act, providing the more prolonged stimulation that many women need to reach orgasm.
    b. With experience, both partners may be more likely to recognize and focus on those aspects of love-making that intensify the woman's sexual responses.

c. The culture may teach women that sex is v lent and that they should say no to it. It m take years for women to acknowledge a appreciate their sexuality.

d. According to the ethological perspective, a related increases in sexual passions amc women are the result of the reduced lik hood of reproduction.

17. 70; organ reserve; the extra capacity that ea organ has for responding to unusually stress events or conditions that demand intense or p longed effort

18. do

19. declines; remains stable

The declines of aging primarily affect our org reserve. In the course of normal daily life, adults dom have to call upon this capacity, so the deficit organ reserve generally go unnoticed.

20. athletes

21. gross; fine; 30s; lifestyle

22. innate predispositions; childhood experienc cultural taboos; daily circumstances

23. incidence; prevalence; committed; contracepti abortion

24. 40; at any age

25. 15; being unable to conceive a child after a yea more of intercourse without contraception; ofte

26. low number; motility

27. testes; 74 days

Anything that impairs normal body functioning, su as illness with a high fever, medical therapy invc ing radiation or prescription drugs, exposure to er ronmental toxins, unusual stress, or an episode drug abuse, can affect the number, shape, and mo ty of the sperm.

28. underweight; obese

29. ovulation; less; longer; twins

30. Fallopian tubes; pelvic inflammatory dise (PID); gonorrhea or chlamydia

31. endometriosis; uterine lining; 25

32. uterine; implantation

33. 30; 40

34. surgery; drugs; in vitro fertilization (IVF); fi GIFT; ZIFT; ova; zygotes

35. legal; ethical; economic inequality

36. one-third; one-half

37. drug abuse; destructive dieting; violence

38. drug addiction

. marijuana; alcohol; cocaine; 23

. more

. less often than

. excitement; frustration; depression; genes; family experiences

. **a.** For some young adults, drug abuse is a way of striving for independence from parents.

b. Many abuse drugs in an effort to escape the life stresses that cluster during the 20s.

c. The group activities of young adults, including large parties, concerts, and sports events, often promote drug use.

d. Young adults are the group least likely to be regularly exposed to religious faith and practice.

. increase; 18; 26

. avoid, fail, or drop out of college; lose or quit jobs; be employed below their potential; be involved in transitory, uncommitted sexual relationships; die violently; and suffer from serious eating disorders

. set point

eredity, age, illness, hormones, childhood eating bits, and exercise levels can affect one's set point.

. body-mass index (BMI); weight; height

. cultural norms; fat-free; United States; European

. young; educated; employed; 8; 5

. do

. nutritional imbalance; energy loss; vulnerability; are; increased

. anorexia nervosa; self-starvation; more; bulimia nervosa

. gastrointestinal system; cardiac arrest; college women

ccording to psychoanalytic theory, women with eat-g disorders have a conflict with their mothers, who ovided their first nourishment. According to learn-g theory, disordered eating may set up a mulus–response chain in which self-starvation lieves emotional stress and tension. Cognitive theo-suggests that as women enter the workplace they y to project a strong, self-controlled, "masculine" age. Sociocultural explanations focus on the con-mporary cultural pressures to be model-like in pearance. Epigenetic systems theory suggests that cause self-starvation may cause menstruation to ase and sexual hormones to decrease, girls who are netically susceptible to depression or addiction ay resort to this self-destructive behavior to relieve e pressures to marry and reproduce.

54. violent death

55. social values; MADD; SADD

56. self-esteem; expectations; self-concept; alcohol; weapon; self-restraint

57. homicide; varies

58. firearms; confirms

59. homicide; accidents

PROGRESS TEST 1

Multiple-Choice Questions

1. **b.** is the answer. (p. 466)

a., c., & d. Each of these is a specific example of the more general process of senescence.

2. **b.** is the answer. (p. 465)

3. **c.** is the answer. (p. 465)

a. & b. These are true of women.

d. Men and women do not differ in this characteristic.

4. **a.** is the answer. (p. 465)

5. **b.** is the answer. (p. 467)

a. This is the extra capacity that each organ of the body has for responding to unusually stressful events or conditions that demand intense or prolonged effort.

c. Stress, which is not defined in this chapter, refers to events or situations that tax the body's resources.

d. This simply refers to a muscle's potential for work.

6. **c.** is the answer. (p. 478)

7. **d.** is the answer. (p. 469)

8. **d.** is the answer. (p. 473)

b. Until middle age, infertility is equally likely in women and men.

9. **c.** is the answer. (p. 474)

10. **c.** is the answer. (p. 474)

a. Sexually transmitted diseases can cause infertility by contributing to pelvic inflammatory disease (PID).

b. This is another common fertility problem in women.

d. PID often is a cause of infertility; it is not, however, the same as endometriosis.

11. **c.** is the answer. (p. 475)

12. **d.** is the answer. (p. 468)

13. a. is the answer. Depression and low self-esteem often serve as stimulus triggers for fasting, bingeing, and purging, which may temporarily relieve these states of emotional distress. (p. 482)

14. b. is the answer. (p. 485)

a. Although this is the most common fatal disease in early adulthood, it certainly is not the most common cause of death.

c. This is the leading cause of death for young European-American men.

d. Suicide is much less frequently a cause of death for African-American men, partly because they tend to have extensive family and friendship networks that provide social support.

15. b. is the answer. In fact, just the opposite is true. Young adults may use drugs to express independence from their parents. (p. 478)

True or False Items

1. T (p. 471)
2. T (p. 470)
3. T (p. 468)
4. F Age seems to affect men and women differently with respect to sexual responsiveness—with men becoming less responsive and women, more responsive. (p. 469)
5. F Just the opposite is true. (p. 498)
6. T (p. 474)
7. F Physicians recommend that women begin childbearing by age *30*. (pp. 474–475)
8. T (p. 481)
9. T (p. 480)
10. F Among young European American men, accidents are the number-one cause of death. (p. 485)

PROGRESS TEST 2

Multiple-Choice Questions

1. **d.** is the answer. (p. 465)
2. **b.** is the answer. (p. 466)
3. **d.** is the answer. (p. 467)

   a., b., & c. These often remain unnoticed until middle age.
4. **b.** is the answer. (p. 467)
5. **d.** is the answer. (p. 470)
6. **b.** is the answer. (p. 469)
7. **d.** is the answer. (p. 473)

   c. This is a common fertility problem in women.

8. c. is the answer. (p. 474)

b. Sexually transmitted diseases can cause PID.

d. This describes in vitro fertilization.

9. c. is the answer. (p. 475)

a. Endometriosis is a condition in which fra ments of the uterine lining become implanted a grow on the surface of the ovaries or t Fallopian tubes, blocking the reproductive tract

b. In this technique sperm collected from a m donor are artificially inserted into the uterus.

d. In this technique, fertilization occurs outsi the uterus but it involves another woman w carries the fetus.

10. b. is the answer. (pp. 473–474)

11. a. is the answer. (p. 481)

b. This describes a woman suffering from anore ia nervosa.

c. Eating disorders are much more common younger women.

d. Most women with bulimia nervosa are usua close to normal in weight.

12. d. is the answer. (p. 483)

13. b. is the answer. (p. 483)

a. Eating disorders are more common in wom than men.

c. & d. Disease is relatively rare at this age.

14. b. is the answer. (p. 478)

15. b. is the answer. (p. 471)

Matching Items

1. g (p. 466)
2. e (p. 467)
3. d (p. 468)
4. b (p. 473)
5. j (p. 473)
6. c (p. 474)
7. h (p. 474)
8. a (p. 475)
9. i (p. 481)
10. f (p. 481)

THINKING CRITICALLY ABOUT CHAPTER

1. **a.** is the answer. (p. 466)

b. Physical declines during the 20s are usually little consequence.

c. This is not true nor does it address the instr tor's request.

d. The first signs of aging become apparent at earlier age.

2. **b.** is the answer. (p. 467)

a. This is age-related decline.

c. This is a common fertility problem for wome

d. This refers to the swimming ability of sperm.

3. b. is the answer. (p. 468)

a. Resting heart rate remains stable throughout adulthood.

c. Maximum heart rate declines with age.

4. b. is the answer. (p. 469)

5. c. is the answer. (p. 469)

6. d. is the answer. Infertility becomes increasingly common with advancing age. (p. 473)

7. d. is the answer. (p. 474)

a. In this condition, fragments of the uterine lining become implanted and grow on the surface of the ovaries or the Fallopian tubes, blocking the reproductive tract.

b. This is a common fertility problem in men.

c. Although this may contribute to infertility, Michelle's age and the fact that sexually transmitted diseases can cause PID makes d. the best answer.

8. c. is the answer. (p. 480)

9. c. is the answer. (p. 481)

a. & d. Eating disorders are more common in women than men.

b. Eating disorders are more common in younger women.

10. d. is the answer. (p. 480)

11. c. is the answer. (p. 481)

a. & b. These explanations would more likely be offered by those who emphasize learning theory or cognitive theory.

d. This is a sociocultural explanation of eating disorders.

12. b. is the answer. (p. 465)

13. a. is the answer. (p. 483)

b., c., & d. A cohort is a group of people born about the same time. These examples illustrate possible ethnic (b), gender (c), and genetic (d) influences on biosocial development.

14. c. is the answer. (p. 480)

a. & d. There is no evidence that Lucretia has a glandular disorder or is obese. In fact, a BMI of 24 is well within the normal weight range.

b. There is no evidence that Lucretia is bingeing and purging.

15. c. is the answer. (p. 478)

a. & b. Although these are also correct, they are both psychoactive drugs, making c. the best answer.

KEY TERMS

1. **Senescence** is age-related decline throughout the body. (p. 466)

2. **Homeostasis** refers to the process by which body functions are automatically adjusted to keep our physiological functioning in a state of balance. (p. 467)

3. **Organ reserve** is the extra capacity of each body organ for responding to unusually stressful events or conditions that demand intense or prolonged effort. (p. 468)

4. A couple is said to experience **infertility** if they have been unable to conceive a child after a year or more of intercourse without contraception. (p. 473)

5. **Pelvic inflammatory disease (PID)** is a common fertility problem for women, in which pelvic infections lead to blocked Fallopian tubes. (p. 474)

6. **In vitro fertilization (IVF)** is a technique in which ova are surgically removed from the ovaries and fertilized by sperm in the laboratory. (p. 475)

7. **Drug addiction** is evident in a person when the absence of a drug in his or her body produces the drive to ingest more of the drug. (p. 478)

8. **Set point** is the specific body weight that a person's homeostatic processes strive to maintain. (p. 480)

9. The **body mass index (BMI)** is the ratio of a person's weight in kilograms divided by his or her height in meters squared. (p. 480)

10. **Anorexia nervosa** is an affliction characterized by self-starvation that is most common in high-achieving college-age women. (p. 481)

11. **Bulimia nervosa** is an eating disorder that involves compulsive binge eating followed by purging through vomiting or taking massive doses of laxatives. (p. 481)

18

Early Adulthood: Cognitive Development

Chapter Overview

During the course of adulthood, there are many shifts in cognitive development—in the speed and efficiency with which we process information, in the focus and depth of our cognitive processes, perhaps in the quality, or wisdom, of our thinking. Developmental psychologists use three different approaches in explaining these shifts, with each approach providing insights into the nature of adult cognition. This chapter takes a postformal approach, describing age-related changes in an attempt to uncover patterns or predictable stages.

The chapter begins by describing how adult thinking differs from adolescent thinking. The experiences and challenges of adulthood result in a new, postformal thought, evidenced by dialectical and adaptive thinking—the dynamic, in-the-world cognitive style that adults typically use to solve the problems of daily life.

The second section explores how the events of early adulthood can affect moral development. Of particular interest are Fowler's six stages in the development of faith.

The third section examines the effect of the college experience on cognitive growth; findings here indicate that years of education correlate with virtually every measure of cognition as thinking becomes progressively more flexible and tolerant. A final section discusses the importance of life events, such as parenthood, job promotion, or illness, in triggering cognitive growth during young adulthood.

NOTE: Answer guidelines for all Chapter 18 questions begin on page 273.

Guided Study

The text chapter should be studied one section at a time. Before you read, preview each section by skimming it, noting headings and boldface items. Then read the appropriate section objectives from the fol-

lowing outline. Keep these objectives in mind and, you read the chapter section, search for the inform tion that will enable you to meet each objective. On you have finished a section, write out answers for objectives.

1. Describe three approaches to the study of adu cognition.

Postformal Thought (pp. 490–494)

2. Identify the main characteristics of postform thought, and describe how it differs from form operational thought.

3. (text and Research Report) Explain how emotio ally charged problems differentiate adolesce and adult reasoning.

Define dialectical thought, and give examples of its usefulness.

Draw a conclusion about whether postformal thought represents a separate stage of development.

ult Moral Reasoning (pp. 495–498)

Explain Carol Gilligan's view of how moral reasoning changes during adulthood.

(A Life-Span View) Briefly describe the six stages of faith outlined by James Fowler.

Explain how the Defining Issues Test helps relate moral development to other aspects of adult cognition and life satisfaction.

Cognitive Growth and Higher Education
(pp. 499–506)

9. Discuss the relationship between cognitive growth and higher education.

10. Compare college students today with their counterparts of a decade or two ago.

Cognitive Growth and Life Events (pp. 506–508)

11. (text and In Person) Discuss how life events may trigger new patterns of thinking and result in cognitive growth.

Chapter Review

When you have finished reading the chapter, work through the material that follows to review it. Complete the sentences and answer the questions. As you proceed, evaluate your performance for each section by consulting the answers on page 273. Do not continue with the next section until you understand each answer. If you need to, review or reread the appropriate section in the textbook before continuing.

1. Unlike the relatively "straightforward" cognitive growth of earlier ages, cognitive development during adulthood is _____ and _____ . Developmentalists have used three approaches to explain this development: the _____ approach, the

_____ approach, and the

_____-_____

approach.

Postformal Thought (pp. 490–494)

2. Compared to adolescent thinking, adult thinking
   is more _____ ,
   _____ , and _____ .
   Adults are also less inclined toward the
   "_____ _____
   _____ " as their thinking becomes
   more specialized and experiential.

3. Gisela Labouvie-Vief has noted that one hallmark
   of mature adult thinking is the realization that
   most of life's answers are _____
   rather than _____ .

4. Reasoning that is adapted to the subjective real-
   life contexts to which it is applied is called

   _____ _____ .

5. Developmentalists distinguish between
   _____ thinking, which arises from
   the _____ experiences and
   _____ of an individual, and
   _____ thinking, which follows
   abstract _____ . The latter kind of
   thinking is _____ (more/less) adaptive for schoolchildren, adolescents, and young
   adults than for mature adults.

6. In her research, Labouvie-Vief found that
   although older adults recognize logical premises
   in solving real-life problems, they also explore the
   real-life possibilities and _____
   _____ that might bear on an issue.

7. Other research demonstrates that the difference
   between adolescent and young adult reasoning is
   particularly apparent for problems that are

   _____ _____ .

8. (Research Report) In the Blanchard-Fields study
   of the effect of emotions on reasoning about
   social dilemmas, more mature thinkers scored
   higher because they were better able to take into
   account the _____
   _____ of each party's version of
   events.

9. Some theorists consider _____
   _____ the most advanced form o[f]
   cognition. This thinking recognizes that every
   idea, or _____ , implies an oppos[ite]
   idea, or _____ ; these are then
   forged into a(n) _____ of the two[.]
   This type of thinking fosters a worldview that
   recognizes that most of life's important questio[ns]
   _____ (have/do not have) single,
   unchangeable, correct answers.

10. True dialectic thinkers acknowledge the
    _____ nature of reality *and* the ne[ed]
    to make firm _____ to values the[y]
    realize will change over time.

11. All adults _____ (think/do not
    think) in a postformal manner, and everyone w[ho]
    thinks in a postformal way _____
    (is/is not) also capable of formal operational
    thought. Dialectical thinking is more typical of
    _____-_____ adults
    than of _____ or _____
    adults and is more evident in certain
    _____ than in others. For these re[a]-
    sons, developmentalists _____
    (do/do not) all agree that postformal thought
    represents a distinct stage of cognitive develop[-]
    ment.

Adult Moral Reasoning (pp. 495–498)

12. According to James Rest, one catalyst for pro-
    pelling young adults from a lower moral stage [to]
    a higher one is _____ .

13. Lawrence Kohlberg maintains that in order to [be]
    capable of "truly ethical" reasoning, a person
    must have experienced sustained responsibilit[y]
    for _____

14. Carol Gilligan believes that in matters of mora[l]
    reasoning _____ (males/ females[)]
    tend to be more concerned with the question o[f]
    rights and justice, whereas
    _____ (males/females) are more
    concerned with personal relationships. Gilliga[n]
    also maintains that as people become responsi[ble]
    for the needs of others they begin to construct

principles that are _____
and _____ , because they see that
moral reasoning based chiefly on justice principles is inadequate to solve real-life moral dilemmas.

. (A Life-Span View) The theorist who has outlined
six stages in the development of faith is
_____ . In the space below, identify
and briefly describe each stage.

Stage One: _____

_____

Stage Two: _____

_____

Stage Three: _____

_____

Stage Four: _____

_____

Stage Five: _____

_____

Stage Six: _____

_____

. (A Life-Span View) Although Fowler's stage theory of faith _____ (is/is not) widely
accepted, the idea that religion plays an important role in human development
_____ (is/is not).

. The current approach to research on moral reasoning is based on a series of questions about
moral reasoning called the _____
_____ _____ . In gen-
eral, scores on this test increase with
_____ and with each year of
_____ _____ .

gnitive Growth and Higher Education
p. 499–506)

. Years of education _____ (are/are
not) strongly correlated with most measures of
adult cognition. This relationship is
_____ (stronger/weaker) than that
between socioeconomic status and adult cognition.

19. College education leads people to become more
_____ of other viewpoints.

Briefly outline the year-by-year progression in how
the thinking of college students becomes more flexible and tolerant.

20. William Perry found that the thinking of students, over the course of their college careers,
progressed through _____ levels of
complexity.

21. College seems to make people more accepting of
other viewpoints because it makes people less
_____ by them.

22. Research has shown that the more years of higher
education a person has, the deeper and more
_____ that person's reasoning is
likely to become.

23. Over the past two decades, college students in the
United States have become less concerned about
developing a _____
_____ and more
concerned about _____
_____ .

24. Collegiate populations have become
_____ (more/less) diverse and het-
erogeneous in recent years.

25. Worldwide, college has changed from an activity
of the _____ to one of the
_____ .

26. As colleges have become more diverse, more and
more _____ _____ are

specifically organized for various interest groups. Today's cohort of college students tends to be more suspicious of _____ , _____ , and _____ that have no direct impact on college life.

27. Another cohort difference is that most of today's college students _____ (work/do not work) during their college years, so that cognitive growth depends more on the _____ and less on the _____ than in the past.

List several educational factors that appear to be unrelated to fostering cognitive growth in college students, and several factors that are important.

28. (Changing Policy) Young full-time students living on campus are _____ (more/less) likely to accept cheating than are students who commute. Many students have a _____ (broader/more limited) definition of cheating than professors. For example, many students seem unaware of the rules defining _____ .

29. (Changing Policy) Dr. Berger's analysis of cheating behavior led her to suspect that students may have a different _____ _____ that encourages cheating in order to cope with institutions that penalize those who are _____ _____ and those who are educationally _____ .

Cognitive Growth and Life Events (pp. 506–508)

30. It has been suggested that significant life events such as _____ _____ can trigger new patterns of thinking.

Progress Test 1

Multiple-Choice Questions

Circle your answers to the following questions a[nd] check them with the answers on page 274. If yo[ur] answer is incorrect, read the explanation for why it [is] incorrect and then consult the appropriate pages [in] the text (in parentheses following the correct answe[r]).

1. Differences in the reasoning maturity of adol[es]cents and young adults are most likely to [be] apparent when:
   a. low-SES and high-SES groups are compared[.]
   b. ethnic-minority adolescents and adults a[re] compared.
   c. ethnic-majority adolescents and adults a[re] compared.
   d. emotionally charged issues are involved.

2. Which of the following is *not* one of the ma[jor] approaches to the study of adult cogniti[on] described in the text?
   a. the information-processing approach
   b. the postformal approach
   c. the systems approach
   d. the psychometric approach

3. Compared to adolescent thinking, adult thinki[ng] tends to be:
   a. more personal.   c. more integrative.
   b. more practical.   d. all of the above.

4. Labouvie-Vief has shown that the hallmark [of] adult adaptive thought is the:
   a. ability to engage in dialectical thinking.
   b. reconciliation of both objective and subjecti[ve] approaches to real-life problems.
   c. adoption of conjunctive faith.
   d. all of the above.

5. (A Life-Span View) According to James Fowl[er,] the experience of college often is a springboa[rd] to:
   a. intuitive-projective faith
   b. mythic-literal faith
   c. individual-reflective faith
   d. synthetic-conventional faith

6. Which approach to adult cognitive development focuses on life-span changes in the efficiency of encoding, storage, and retrieval?

   a. postformal
   b. information-processing
   c. psychometric
   d. dialectical

7. Postformal thinking is most useful for solving _____ problems.

   a. science
   c. everyday
   b. mathematics
   d. abstract, logical

8. The term for the kind of thinking that involves the consideration of both poles of an idea and their reconciliation, or synthesis, in a new idea is:

   a. subjective thinking.
   b. postformal thought.
   c. adaptive reasoning.
   d. dialectical thinking.

9. Thesis is to antithesis as _____ is to _____ .

   a. a new idea; an opposing idea
   b. abstract; concrete
   c. concrete; abstract
   d. provisional; absolute

10. Which of the following adjectives best describe(s) cognitive development during adulthood?

   a. multidirectional and multicontextual
   b. linear
   c. steady
   d. tumultuous

11. Which of the following most accurately describes postformal thought?

   a. subjective thinking that arises from the personal experiences and perceptions of the individual
   b. objective reasoning that follows abstract, impersonal logic
   c. a form of logic that combines subjectivity and objectivity
   d. thinking that is rigid, inflexible, and fails to recognize the existence of other potentially valid views

12. The Defining Issues Test is a:

   a. standardized test that measures postformal thinking.
   b. projective test that assesses dialectical reasoning.
   c. series of questions about moral dilemmas.
   d. test that assesses the impact of life events on cognitive growth.

13. According to Carol Gilligan:

   a. in matters of moral reasoning, females tend to be more concerned with the question of rights and justice.
   b. in matters of moral reasoning, males tend to put human needs above principles of justice.
   c. moral reasoning advances during adulthood in response to the more complex moral dilemmas that life poses.
   d. all of the above are true.

14. An important factor in determining whether college students learn to think deeply is:

   a. the particular interactions between students and faculty.
   b. the college's overall religious or secular philosophy.
   c. the college's size.
   d. all of the above.

15. Research has revealed that a typical outcome of college education is that students become:

   a. very liberal politically.
   b. less committed to any particular ideology.
   c. less tolerant of others' views.
   d. more tolerant of others' views.

True or False Items

Write T (*true*) or F (*false*) on the line in front of each statement.

_____ 1. Research shows that the main reason most young adults today attend college is to improve their thinking and reasoning skills.

_____ 2. Adult cognitive growth is more straightforward than that of childhood and adolescence.

_____ 3. Objective, logical thinking is "adaptive" for the school-age child and adolescent who is in the process of categorizing and organizing his or her experiences.

_____ 4. Because they recognize the changing and subjective nature of beliefs and values, dialectical thinkers avoid making personal or intellectual commitments.

_____ 5. Certain kinds of experiences during adulthood—especially those that entail assuming responsibility for others—can propel an individual from one level of moral reasoning to another.

_____ 6. In recent years, the number of college students has risen dramatically, both in residential and in nonresidential colleges.

_____ 7. Postformal thought is less absolute and less abstract than formal thought.

_____ 8. (A Life-Span View) Mythic-literal faith, like other "lower" stages in the development of faith, is not generally found past adolescence.

_____ 9. In predicting an individual's level of cognitive development, it would be more helpful to know that person's educational background than his or her age.

_____ 10. The college student of today is more likely to live at home and attend school on a part-time basis than were the students of the previous generation.

Progress Test 2

Progress Test 2 should be completed during a final chapter review. Answer the following questions after you thoroughly understand the correct answers for the Chapter Review and Progress Test 1.

Multiple-Choice Questions

1. Which approach to adult cognitive development emphasizes the analysis of components of intelligence?
   a. postformal
   b. psychometric
   c. information-processing
   d. all of the above

2. Which approach to adult cognitive development "picks up where Piaget left off"?
   a. psychometric
   b. information-processing
   c. postformal
   d. dialectical

3. As adult thinking becomes more focused on occupational and interpersonal demands, it also becomes less inclined toward:
   a. the game of thinking.
   b. dialectical thought.
   c. adaptive thought.
   d. all of the above.

4. The result of dialectical thinking is a view that:
   a. one's self is an unchanging constant.
   b. few of life's important questions have single, correct answers.
   c. "everything is relative."
   d. all of the above are true.

5. The existence of a fifth, postformal stage of cognitive development during adulthood:
   a. is recognized by most developmentalists.
   b. has very little empirical support.
   c. remains controversial among development researchers.
   d. is widely accepted in women, but not in men.

6. Formal operational thinking is most useful for solving problems that:
   a. involve logical relationships or theoretic possibilities.
   b. require integrative skills.
   c. involve the synthesis of diverse issues.
   d. require seeing perspectives other than one's own.

7. College seems to make people more accepting of other people's attitudes because it:
   a. boosts self-esteem.
   b. makes new ideas less threatening.
   c. promotes extroversion.
   d. does all of the above.

8. The goal of dialectical thinking is forging a(n) _____ from opposing poles of an idea.
   a. thesis
   b. antithesis
   c. synthesis
   d. hypothesis

9. Formal operational thinking is to postformal thinking as _____ is _____ .
   a. psychometric; information-processing
   b. adolescence; adulthood
   c. thesis; antithesis
   d. self-esteem; extroversion

10. Carol Gilligan suggests that during adulthood:
    a. men and women come to recognize the limitations of basing moral reasoning solely on principles of justice.
    b. men and women come to recognize the limitations of basing moral reasoning solely on individual needs.
    c. men and women develop a more reflective, less absolute moral awareness.
    d. all of the above are true.

11. (A Life-Span View) According to James Fowler, individual-reflective faith is marked by:
    a. a willingness to accept contradictions.
    b. a burning need to enunciate universal values.
    c. a literal, wholehearted belief in myths and symbols.
    d. the beginnings of independent questioning of teachers and other figures of authority.

2. (In Person) Research studies have shown that college students who cheat :
   a. are more likely to believe that the purpose of school is to get good grades rather than to learn.
   b. have a much broader definition of cheating than professors do.
   c. usually have the same value system as their professors regarding academic dishonesty.
   d. are more likely to break social and legal rules throughout their lives.

3. (A Life-Span View) According to James Fowler, the simplest stage of faith is the stage of:
   a. universalizing faith.
   b. intuitive-projective faith.
   c. mythic-literal faith.
   d. conventional faith.

4. Many of the problems of adult life are characterized by ambiguity, partial truths, and extenuating circumstances, and therefore are often best solved using _____ thinking.
   a. formal
   b. reintegrative
   c. postformal
   d. executive

5. Research has shown that one effect of college on students is:
   a. a switch from conservative to liberal ideas.
   b. a greater tolerance of political, social, and religious views that differ from their own.
   c. movement from synthetic-conventional faith to individual-reflective faith.
   d. a greater ability to make commitments.

Thinking Critically About Chapter 18

Answer these questions the day before an exam as a final check on your understanding of the chapter's terms and concepts.

1. Concluding her comparison of postformal thinking with Piaget's cognitive stages, Lynn notes that:
   a. not every adult thinks in a postformal manner.
   b. dialectical thinking is more evident in some contexts than in others.
   c. not everyone who thinks in a postformal way is also capable of formal operational thought.
   d. all of the above are true.

2. Carol Gilligan's research suggests that the individual who is most likely to allow the context of personal relationships to wholly determine moral decisions is a:
   a. 20-year-old man.
   b. 20-year-old woman.
   c. 40-year-old woman.
   d. 50-year-old person of either sex.

3. Research suggests that a college sophomore or junior is most likely to have reached a phase in which he or she:
   a. believes that there are clear and perfect truths to be discovered.
   b. questions personal and social values, and even the idea of truth itself.
   c. rejects opposing ideas in the interest of finding one right answer.
   d. accepts a simplistic either/or dualism.

4. (Table 18.1) In his scheme of cognitive and ethical development, Perry describes a position in which the college student says, "I see I am going to have to make my own decisions in an uncertain world with no one to tell me I'm right." This position marks the culmination of a phase of:
   a. either/or dualism.
   b. modified dualism.
   c. relativism.
   d. commitments in relativism.

5. After suffering a heart attack in his 30s, Rob begins to think differently about life and its deeper meaning. This is an example of:
   a. the effect of a mentor on cognitive development.
   b. having reached the reintegrative stage of adult cognition.
   c. a life event that results in cognitive growth.
   d. a biological or age-related change in intelligence.

6. Dr. Polaski studies how thinking during adulthood builds on the earlier formal thinking skills of adolescence. Evidently, Dr. Polaski follows the _____ approach to the study of development.
   a. postformal
   b. psychometric
   c. cognitive
   d. information-processing

7. (A Life-Span View) Jack's uncle believes strongly in God but recognizes that other, equally moral people do not. The openness of his faith places him in which of Fowler's stages?
   a. universalizing faith
   b. conjunctive faith
   c. individual-reflective faith
   d. mythic-literal faith

8. When she was younger, May-Ling believed that "Honesty is always the best policy." She now realizes that although honesty is desirable, it is not *always* the best policy. May-Ling's current thinking is an example of:
   a. formal thought.
   b. dialectical thinking.
   c. mythic-literal thinking.
   d. conjunctive thinking.

9. Who would be the most likely to agree with the statement, "To be truly ethical a person must have the experience of sustained responsibility for the welfare of others"?
   a. Labouvie-Vief   c. Piaget
   b. Kohlberg   d. Fowler

10. Spike is in his third year at a private, religious liberal arts college, while his brother Lee is in his third year at a public, secular community college. In terms of their cognitive growth, what is the most likely outcome?
    a. Spike will more rapidly develop complex critical thinking skills.
    b. Lee will develop greater self-confidence in his abilities since he is studying from the secure base of his home and family.
    c. All other things being equal, Spike and Lee will develop quite similarly.
    d. It is impossible to predict.

11. In concluding her presentation on "The College Student of Today," Coretta states that:
    a. "The number of students in higher education has increased significantly in virtually every country worldwide."
    b. "There are more low-income and ethnic-minority students today than ever before."
    c. "More students choose specific career-based majors rather than a liberal arts education."
    d. all of the above are true.

12. (In Person) The story of Dorothy demonstrates that _____ may trigger cognitive development.
    a. deep religious faith
    b. higher education, even at an advanced age
    c. significant life events
    d. commitment to a career

13. In concluding his paper on postformal thinking, Stanley notes that:
    a. postformal thinking is not the same kind of universal, age-related stage that Piaget described for earlier cognitive growth.
    b. very few adults attain this highest stage of reasoning.
    c. most everyday problems require sensitivity to subjective feelings and therefore do not foster postformal thinking.
    d. all of the above are true.

14. In predicting an individual's level of cognitive development, it would be most helpful to know that person's:
    a. age.
    b. socioeconomic status.
    c. educational background.
    d. history of life challenges.

15. (A Life-Span View) In Fowler's theory, at the highest stages of faith development, people incorporate a powerful vision of compassion for others into their lives. This stage is called:
    a. conjunctive faith.
    b. individual-reflective faith.
    c. synthetic-conventional faith.
    d. universalizing faith.

Key Terms

Writing Definitions

Using your own words, write a brief definition or explanation of each of the following terms on a separate piece of paper.

1. postformal thought
2. dialectical thought
3. thesis
4. antithesis
5. synthesis
6. Defining Issues Test

Cross Check
After you have written the definitions of the key terms in this chapter, you should complete the crossword puzzle to ensure that you can reverse the process—recognize the term, given the definition.

ACROSS

1. Stage of faith in which a person has a powerful vision of compassion, justice, and love that applies to all people.
7. The final stage of dialectical thinking.
8. A proposition or statement of belief.
3. Theorist who believes that as their life experiences expand, both males and females broaden their moral perspectives.
5. Type of thinking that arises from the personal experiences and perceptions of an individual.
6. Moral reasoning theorist who developed the DIT.

DOWN

2. Faith that is magical, illogical, imaginative, and filled with fantasy.
3. Thinking that involves consideration of both poles of an idea simultaneously.
4. Theorist who delineated six stages of faith.
5. Thinking that is suited to solving real-world problems and is less abstract, less absolute, and more integrative and synthetic than formal thought.
6. Test of moral reasoning that consists of a series of questions about moral dilemmas.
9. Approach to adult cognition that analyzes components of intelligence such as those measured by IQ tests.
0. Second stage of dialectical thinking.
1. Thinking that follows abstract, impersonal logic.
2. During early adulthood, the experience that deepens thinking and leads people to become more tolerant of views that differ from their own.
4. Theorist who described the progressive changes in thinking during the college years.

4. postformal thought
5. subjective; personal; perceptions; objective; logic; more
6. contextual circumstances
7. emotionally charged
8. interpretive biases
9. dialectical thought; thesis; antithesis; synthesis; do not have
10. subjective; commitments
11. do not think; is not; middle-aged; younger; older; contexts; do not
12. college
13. the welfare of others
14. males; females; relative; changeable
15. James Fowler

Intuitive-projective faith is magical, illogical, filled with fantasy, and typical of children ages 3 to 7.

Mythic-literal faith, which is typical of middle childhood, is characterized by taking the myths and stories of religion literally.

ANSWERS

CHAPTER REVIEW

1. multidirectional; multicontextual; postformal; psychometric; information-processing
2. personal; practical; integrative; game of thinking
3. provisional; enduring

Synthetic-conventional faith is a nonintellectual acceptance of cultural or religious values in the context of interpersonal relationships.

Individual-reflective faith is characterized by intellectual detachment from the values of culture and the approval of significant others.

Conjunctive faith incorporates both powerful unconscious ideas and rational, conscious values.

Universalizing faith is characterized by a powerful vision of universal compassion, justice, and love that leads people to put their own personal welfare aside in an effort to serve these values.

16. is not; is

17. Defining Issues Test; age; college education

18. are; stronger

19. tolerant

First-year students often believe that there are clear and perfect truths to be found. This phase is followed by a wholesale questioning of values. Finally, after considering opposite ideas, students become committed to certain values, at the same time realizing the need to remain open-minded.

20. nine

21. threatened

22. dialectical

23. meaningful life philosophy; finding a good job

24. more

25. elite; masses

26. student organizations; politicians; governments; philosophies

27. work; classroom; dorm

The unrelated factors include the college's overall philosophy (religious or secular), funding (public or private), and size. The related factors include the particular interactions between students and teachers and among students themselves, peer tutoring, structured group learning, and reflective teaching.

28. more; more limited; plagiarism

29. value system; culturally different; underprepared

30. the birth of a child, the loss of a loved one, a new intimate relationship or the end of an old one, a job promotion or dismissal, being the victim of an attack

PROGRESS TEST 1

Multiple-Choice Questions

1. **d.** is the answer. (pp. 491, 492)

a., b., & c. Socioeconomic status and ethnicity d[o] not predict reasoning maturity.

2. **c.** is the answer. (p. 489)

3. **d.** is the answer (p. 490)

4. **b.** is the answer. (p. 491)

5. **c.** is the answer. (p. 496)

6. **b.** is the answer. (p. 489)

a. This approach emphasizes the emergence of [a] new stage of thinking that builds on the skills [of] formal operational thinking.

c. This approach analyzes the measurable compo[ne]nts of intelligence.

d. This is a type of thinking rather than a[n] approach to the study of cognitive development[.]

7. **c.** is the answer. (p. 490)

a., b., & d. Because of its more analytical natur[e,] formal thinking is most useful for solving the[se] types of problems.

8. **d.** is the answer. (pp. 491–492)

a. Thinking that is subjective relies on person[al] reflection rather than objective observation.

b. Although dialectical thinking *is* characteris[tic] of postformal thought, this question refers speci[f]ically to dialectical thinking.

c. Adaptive reasoning, which also is characteris[tic] of postformal thought, goes beyond mere logic [in] solving problems to also explore real-life com[m]plexities and contextual circumstances.

9. **a.** is the answer (p. 491)

10. **a.** is the answer. (p. 489)

b. & c. Comparatively speaking, linear an[d] steady are *more* descriptive of childhood and ad[o]lescent cognitive development.

11. **b.** is the answer. (p. 490)

12. **d.** is the answer. (p. 498)

13. **c.** is the answer. (p. 495)

a. In Gilligan's theory, this is more true of mal[es] than females.

b. In Gilligan's theory, this is more true [of] females than males.

14. **a.** is the answer. (p. 504)

15. **d.** is the answer. (p. 501)

True or False Items

1. F Most people today attend college primarily [to] secure better jobs. (p. 501)

2. F Adult cognitive growth is multidirectional. ([p.] 489)

3. T (p. 490)

4. F   Dialectical thinkers recognize the need to make commitments to values even though these values will change over time. (p. 493)

5. T (p. 495)

6. F   There are more nonresidential students. (p. 502)

7. T (p. 490)

8. F   Many adults remain in the "lower" stages of faith, which, like "higher" stages, allow for attaining strength and wholeness. (pp. 496–497)

9. T (p. 499)

10. T (p. 502)

PROGRESS TEST 2

Multiple-Choice Questions

1. **b.** is the answer. (p. 489)

    a. This approach emphasizes the possible emergence in adulthood of new stages of thinking that build on the skills of earlier stages.

    c. This approach studies the encoding, storage, and retrieval of information throughout life.

2. **c.** is the answer. (p. 489)

3. **a.** is the answer. (p. 490)

    b. & c. During adulthood, thinking typically becomes more dialectical and adaptive.

4. **b.** is the answer. (p. 493)

    a. & c. On the contrary, a dialectic view recognizes the limitations of extreme relativism and that one's self evolves continuously.

5. **c.** is the answer. (p. 494)

6. **a.** is the answer. (pp. 490–494)

    b., c., & d. Postformal thought is most useful for solving problems such as these.

7. **b.** is the answer. (p. 501)

    a. & c. The impact of college on self-esteem and extroversion were not discussed. Moreover, it is unclear how such an impact would make a person more accepting of others.

8. **c.** is the answer. (pp. 492–493)

    a. A thesis is a new idea.

    b. An antithesis is an idea that opposes a particular thesis.

    d. Hypotheses, which are testable predictions about behavior, are not an aspect of dialectical thinking.

9. **b.** is the answer. (p. 490)

10. **d.** is the answer. (p. 495)

11. **d.** is the answer. (p. 496)

    a. This describes conjunctive faith.

    b. This describes universalizing faith.

    c. This describes mythic-literal faith.

12. **a.** is the answer. (p. 504)

    b. In fact, students who cheat generally have a more limited definition of cheating than their professors do.

    c. The text suggests that students who cheat may have a different value system that encourages cooperation in order to cope with institutions that penalize students who are culturally different or educationally underprepared.

    d. The text does not suggest that students who cheat become lifelong rule breakers.

13. **b.** is the answer. (p. 496)

14. **c.** is the answer. (p. 490)

    a. Formal thinking is best suited to solving problems that require logic and analytical thinking.

    b. & d. These terms are not discussed in the text.

15. **b.** is the answer. (p. 499)

    a. The text does not discuss stability or change in students' political views.

    c. This is James Fowler's stage theory of the development of faith.

    d. This is true but not part of Perry's theory.

THINKING CRITICALLY ABOUT CHAPTER 18

1. **d.** is the answer. (p. 494)

2. **b.** is the answer. (p. 495)

    a. According to Gilligan, males tend to be more concerned with human rights and justice than with human needs and personal relationships, which are more the concern of females.

    c. & d. These answers are incorrect because, according to Gilligan, as people mature and their experience of life expands, they begin to realize that moral reasoning based chiefly on justice principles or on individual needs is inadequate to resolve real-life moral dilemmas.

3. **b.** is the answer. (p. 500)

    a. First-year college students are more likely to believe this is so.

    c. & d. Over the course of their college careers, students become *less* likely to do either of these.

4. **c.** is the answer. (p. 500)

5. **c.** is the answer. (p. 508)

6. **a.** is the answer. (p. 489)

    b. This approach analyzes components of intelligence such as those measured by IQ tests.

    c. Each of these approaches is cognitive in nature.

d. This approach studies the encoding, storage, and retrieval of information throughout life.

7. **b.** is the answer. (pp. 496)

8. **b.** is the answer. May-Ling has formed a synthesis between the thesis that honesty is the best policy and its antithesis. (p. 493)

   a. This is an example of postformal rather than formal thinking.

   c. & d. These are stages in the development of faith as proposed by James Fowler.

9. **b.** is the answer. (p. 495)

   a. & c. Neither Labouvie-Vief nor Piaget focuses on ethics in their theories.

   d. Fowler's theory, which identifies stages in the development of faith, does not emphasize this experience.

10. **c.** is the answer. (p. 504)

11. **d.** is the answer. (p. 502)

12. **c.** is the answer. (pp. 506–507)

13. **a.** is the answer. (p. 494)

    b. Because postformal thinking is typical of adult thought, this is untrue.

    c. It is exactly this sort of problem that *fosters* postformal thinking.

14. **c.** is the answer. (p. 499)

    a. & b. Years of education are more strongly correlated with cognitive development than are age and socioeconomic status.

    d. Although significant life events can trigger cognitive development, the text does not suggest that the relationship between life events and measures of cognition is predictable.

15. **d.** is the answer. (p. 499)

KEY TERMS

Writing Definitions

1. Proposed by some developmentalists as a fifth stage of cognitive development, **postformal thought** is suited to solving real-world problems and is less abstract, less absolute, and more integrative and synthetic than formal thought. (p. 490)

2. **Dialectical thought** is thinking that involves considering both poles of an idea (thesis and antithesis) simultaneously and then forging them into a synthesis. (p. 491)

3. The first stage of dialectical thinking, a **thesis** is a proposition or statement of belief. (p. 491)

4. A statement that contradicts the thesis, an **antithesis** is the second stage of dialectical thinking. (p. 491)

5. The final stage of dialectical thinking, the **synthesis** reconciles thesis and antithesis into a new, more comprehensive level of truth (p. 493)

6. The **Defining Issues Test** is a series of questions about moral dilemmas used to research moral reasoning. (p. 498)

Cross-Check

ACROSS	DOWN
1. universalizing	2. intuitive-projective
7. synthesis	3. dialectical
8. thesis	4. Fowler
13. Gilligan	5. postformal
15. subjective	6. Defining Issues
16. Rest	9. psychometric
	10. antithesis
	11. objective
	12. college
	14. Perry

CHAPTER 19

Early Adulthood: Psychosocial Development

Chapter Overview

[Bi]ologically mature and no longer bound by parental [au]thority, the young adult typically is now free to [ch]oose a particular path of development. Today, the [op]tions are incredibly varied. Not surprisingly, then, [th]e hallmark of psychosocial development during [ea]rly adulthood is diversity. Nevertheless, develop[m]entalists have identified several themes or patterns [th]at help us understand the course of development [b]etween the ages of 20 and 40.

The chapter begins with a discussion of the two [ba]sic psychosocial needs of adulthood, love and [w]ork. No matter what terminology is used, these two [n]eeds are recognized by almost all developmentalists.

The next section addresses the need for intimacy [in] adulthood, focusing on the development of friend[sh]ip, love, and marriage. The impact of divorce on [fa]milies is discussed.

The final section of the chapter is concerned with [ge]nerativity, or the motivation to achieve during [ad]ulthood, highlighting the importance of work and [pa]renthood and addressing the special challenges fac[in]g stepparents, adoptive parents, and foster parents.

[N]OTE: Answer guidelines for all Chapter 19 ques[ti]ons begin on page 289.

[G]uided Study

[Th]e text chapter should be studied one section at a [ti]me. Before you read, preview each section by skim[m]ing it, noting headings and boldface items. Then [re]ad the appropriate section objectives from the fol[lo]wing outline. Keep these objectives in mind and, as [yo]u read the chapter section, search for the informa[ti]on that will enable you to meet each objective. Once [yo]u have finished a section, write out answers for its [ob]jectives.

The Tasks of Adulthood (pp. 511–514)

1. Identify the two basic tasks, or crises, of adulthood, and explain how the viewpoint of most developmentalists regarding adult stages has shifted.

2. Explain how the social clock influences the timing of important events during early adulthood.

Intimacy (pp. 514–528)

3. (text and In Person) Review the developmental course of friendship during adulthood, noting factors that promote friendship and gender differences in friendship patterns.

4. (Research Report) Identify Sternberg's three components of love, and discuss the pattern by which they develop in relationships.

5. Discuss the impact of cohabitation on relationships, and identify three factors that influence marital success.

6. Discuss the impact of social systems on divorce, the reasons for today's rising divorce rate, and the usual impact of divorce on families.

7. (A Life-Span View) Discuss spouse abuse, focusing on its forms, contributing factors, and prevention.

8. Discuss the adjustment problems that accompany divorce, especially those of the custodial parent.

Generativity (pp. 528–539)

9. Discuss the importance of work to the individu and whether the traditional stages of the care cycle are pertinent to today's workers.

10. Identify possible reasons for the variability in t job cycle today and the developmental implic tions for adults just entering the work force.

11. (text and Changing Policy) Discuss the myth challenges, and opportunities of dual-earner far ily life.

12. Focusing on broad themes, describe the stages the family life cycle, noting the rewards and ch lenges of each stage.

13. Discuss the special challenges facing stepparer adoptive parents, and foster parents.

Chapter Review

When you have finished reading the chapter, work through the material that follows to review it. Complete the sentences and answer the questions. As you proceed, evaluate your performance for each section by consulting the answers on page 289. Do not continue with the next section until you understand each answer. If you need to, review or reread the appropriate section in the textbook before continuing.

The Tasks of Adulthood (pp. 511–514)

1. Developmentalists generally agree that two psychosocial needs must be met during adulthood. These are _____ _____ _____ .

2. According to Freud, the healthy adult was one who could _____ and _____ .

3. According to Maslow, the need for _____ and _____ was followed by a need for _____ and _____ .

4. In Erikson's theory, the identity crisis of adolescence is followed in early adulthood by the crisis of _____ _____ _____ , and then later by the crisis of _____ _____ _____ .

5. Today, most social scientists regard adult lives as less _____ and _____ than stage models suggest.

Briefly describe what was in the 1950s the most common pattern of development during the early and middle 20s.

6. Although most developmentalists _____ (take/do not take) a strict stage view of adulthood, they do recognize that development is influenced by the

_____ _____ ,

which is defined as _____

_____ .

7. Internationally, societies in _____ (highly developed/less developed) regions have tended to be quite age-stratified.

8. A prime influence on the social clock is

_____ _____ . The lower a person's SES, the _____ (younger/older) the age at which he or she is expected to leave school, begin work, marry, have children, and so forth.

9. The influence of SES is particularly apparent with regard to the age at which _____ (men/women) are expected to _____ and finish _____ .

10. Women from low-SES backgrounds may feel pressure to marry by age _____ , and most stop childbearing by age _____ , whereas wealthy women may not feel pressure to marry until age _____ or to stop childbearing until age _____ .

Intimacy (pp. 514–528)

11. Two main sources of intimacy in early adulthood are _____ _____ and _____ _____ .

12. As a buffer against stress and a source of positive feelings, _____ are particularly important.

Briefly state why this is so.

13. Young adulthood is the prime time to solidify friendships and make new ones for two reasons:

a. _____
_____ .

b. _____
_____ .

14. Four factors that promote friendship by serving as _____ _____ _____ are:

a. _____
b. _____
c. _____
d. _____

15. When it comes to our close confidants, most of us have two or three basic _____ , and everyone who has those traits is _____ from consideration.

16. During early adulthood _____ (men/women/both men and women) tend to be more satisfied with their _____ _____ than with almost any other part of their lives.

17. (In Person) Gender differences in friendship _____ (are/are not) especially apparent during adulthood. In general, men's friendships are based on _____ _____ and _____ , whereas friendships between women tend to be more _____ and _____ .

Briefly contrast the types of conversations men and women are likely to have with their friends.

18. (In Person) Research has shown that _____ (women/men) are more likely to reveal their weaknesses to friends, whereas _____ (women/men) are more likely to reveal their strengths. Thus, men may view friendship as a means of maintaining a positive _____ , while women regard it as a means of coping with _____ _____ .

19. (In Person) Another gender difference is that men's friendships are more clearly tinged with open _____ .

20. (In Person) List three reasons that men's friendships seem so much less intimate than women's.

a. _____
_____ .

b. _____
_____ .

c. _____
_____ .

Describe some of the opportunities and problems of cross-sex friendships.

21. The typical _____ (female/male) friendship pattern seems to be better in terms of meeting intimacy needs.

22. A woman's tendency to seek mutual loyalty among confidantes may undermine her _____ performance and handicap her _____ . Men who cannot share problems with friends may be handicapped _____ .

23. (Research Report) Robert Sternberg has argued that love has three distinct components: _____ , _____ , and _____ . Sternberg also believes that the emergence and prominence of each component tends to follow a pattern that is _____ (unpredictable/predictable).

24. (Research Report) Early in a relationship _____ intimacy tends to be high, while _____ intimacy is much lower.

25. (Research Report) Relationships grow because _____ _____ intensifies, leading to the gradual establishment and strengthening of _____ .

26. (Research Report) When commitment is added to passion and intimacy, the result is _____ love.

27. (Research Report) With time, _____ tends to fade and _____ tends to stabilize, even as _____ develops.

28. Increasingly common among young adults in many countries is the living pattern called _____ , in which two unrelated adults of the opposite sex live together.

29. Cohabitation _____ (does/does not) seem to benefit the participants. Cohabitants tend to be less _____ , less _____ , and less satisfied with their _____ _____ than married people.

30. An estimated _____ percent of all adults in the United States spend part of adulthood in gay or lesbian partnerships. Homosexual couples _____ (have/do not have) the same relationship problems as heterosexual couples.

31. In the United States today, the proportion of adults who are unmarried is _____ (higher/lower) than in the previous 100 years; only _____ percent of brides are virgins; nearly _____ percent of all first births are to unmarried mothers; and the divorce rate is _____ percent of the marriage rate.

32. Adults in many developed nations spend about _____ of the years between 20 and 40 single.

33. The younger marriage partners are when they first wed, the _____ (more/ less) likely their marriage is to succeed. According to Erikson, this may be because intimacy is hard to establish until _____ is secure.

34. Marriage between people who are similar in age, SES, ethnicity, and the like, called _____ , is _____ (more/less) likely to succeed than marriage that is outside the group, called _____ . Similarity in leisure interests and _____ preferences, called _____ _____ , is particularly important to marital success.

35. A third factor affecting marriage is _____ _____ , the extent to which the partners perceive equality in the relationship. According to _____ theory, marriage is an arrangement in which each person contributes something useful to the other.

36. A final factor that predicts marital satisfaction is the idea that the relationship is a _____ _____ _____ .

37. In the United States, almost one out of every _____ marriages ends in divorce. This rate _____ (varies/does not vary significantly) from country to country. Worldwide, divorce has _____ (increased/decreased/ remained stable) over most of the past 50 years.

38. Many developmentalists believe that spouses today expect _____ (more/less) from each other than spouses in the past did.

39. Most people find the initial impact of divorce to be quite _____ (negative/positive) and adjustment to divorce _____ (more/less) difficult than they expected.

State two reasons why this is so.

40. Another adjustment problem is that the ex-spouses' _____ _____ usually shrinks in the first year after divorce.

41. Newly divorced people are more prone to
_____
_____
_____ .
In most cases, such effects _____ .
(do/do not) eventually dissipate with time.

42. Compared to others, single divorced adults are
_____ (most/least) likely to be very
happy with their lives. The presence of
_____ is a key factor that makes
adjustment to divorce more problematic, particularly for custodial _____ (mothers/
fathers).

43. _____ (Most/Only a minority of)
noncustodial fathers maintain intimate ongoing
relationships with their children.

44. The tendency of many custodial mothers to
express their financial and social frustration by
limiting the father's access to the children
_____ (is/is not necessarily)
destructive. Children do best with an involved,
_____ father who provides
_____ and _____ con-
sistent with the mother's caregiving.

(A Life-Span View) Identify several factors that contribute to spouse abuse.

45. (A Life-Span View) One form of spouse abuse,
_____ _____
_____ , entails outbursts of fighting,
with both partners sometimes becoming
involved. This type of abuse
_____ (usually leads/usually does
not lead) to worse abuse.

46. (A Life-Span View) The second type of abuse,
_____ _____ ,
occurs when one partner, almost always the
_____ , uses a range of methods to

punish and degrade the other. This form of abuse
leads to the _____
_____ syndrome and
_____ (becomes/does not usually
become) more extreme with time.

47. (A Life-Span View) To break the cycle of abuse,
the woman usually requires _____
_____ , which has helped to
_____ (increase/reduce) the incidence of this abuse.

Generativity (pp. 528–539)

48. The motivation to _____ is one of
the strongest of human motives. The observable
expression of this motive _____
(varies/does not vary) significantly from culture
to culture.

49. Even more important to workers than their pay-
check is the opportunity that work provides to
satisfy _____ needs by allowing
them to:

a. _____
_____ .

b. _____
_____ .

c. _____
_____ .

d. _____
_____ .

50. The four traditional stages of the career cycle are
_____ , _____ ,
_____ , and _____ .
This pattern fit the _____-
_____ job market that was typical i
the 1950s. In such a market, low levels of
_____ are needed, and employees
are nearly _____ .

51. Today, the employment scene is very different.
One reason for this is the shift in developing
nations from an economy based on
_____ to one based on
_____ , and in developed nations
from an economy based on
_____ to one based on
_____ and _____ .

2. Among the fastest-growing occupations in the United States are _____ _____ _____ .

3. Today, the work path for individuals is much less _____ and _____ than it once was. In many of today's jobs, although the skills are quite _____ , they may be obsolete tomorrow. This means that people in their 20s should seek educational and vocational settings that foster a variety of _____ and _____ skills.

4. Another reason for the variability in the job cycle is that workers today are more _____ . For example, in developed nations nearly _____ (how much?) the civilian labor force is female. Due to the increased proportion of _____ in the work force, _____ diversity in the work place is also much greater today than in the past.

ate two implications of these trends for young ults just starting out in the work world.

. Many women, members of minorities, and immigrants continue to experience difficulty in breaking through the _____ _____ , an invisible barrier to career advancement.

. In the happiest couples, _____ (one/neither/both) spouse(s) work(s) either very long hours or very few hours.

. Contemporary children generally _____ (suffer/do not suffer) when both parents work outside as well as inside the home.

. Women who are simultaneously wife, mother, and employee _____

(inevitably/do not necessarily) experience the stress of multiple obligations called

_____ _____ .

In fact, among dual-earner families

_____ _____

is more prevalent as two people share obligations.

59. Generally speaking, adults who balance marital, parental, and vocational roles _____ (are/are not) happier and more successful than those who function in only one or two of them.

60. (Changing Policy) Today, family _____—coordinating housework, child care, work schedules, and so on—typically requires a level of planning and mutual agreement that was unnecessary in earlier generations. There _____ (are/are not) signs that today's younger couples are approaching greater equity in hours of domestic work and work outside the home.

61 (Changing Policy) An increasingly common kind of marital inequity occurs when the wife _____ _____ . This can be particularly devastating to men who are _____-_____ workers or men who are _____ .

62. Proportionately, about _____ of all North American adults will become stepparents, adoptive parents, or foster parents at some point in their lives.

63. Strong bonds between parent and child are particularly hard to create when a child has already formed _____ to other caregivers.

64. Because they are legally connected to their children for life, _____ (adoptive/step/foster) parents have an advantage in establishing bonds with their children.

65. Stepchildren, foster children, and adoptive children tend to leave home _____ (at the same age as/earlier than/later than) children living with one or both biological parents.

Progress Test 1

Multiple-Choice Questions

Circle your answers to the following questions and check them with the answers on page 290. If your answer is incorrect, read the explanation for why it is incorrect and then consult the appropriate pages of the text (in parentheses following the correct answer).

1. According to Erik Erikson, the first basic task of adulthood is to establish:
   a. a residence apart from parents.
   b. intimacy with others.
   c. generativity through work or parenthood.
   d. a career commitment.

2. Most social scientists who study adulthood emphasize that:
   a. intimacy and generativity take various forms throughout adulthood.
   b. adult lives are less orderly and predictable than stage models suggest.
   c. each culture has a somewhat different social clock.
   d. all of the above are true.

3. Which of the following was *not* identified as a gateway to attraction?
   a. physical attractiveness
   b. frequent exposure
   c. similarity of attitudes
   d. apparent availability

4. The social circles of ex-spouses usually _____ in the first year following a divorce.
   a. shrink
   b. grow larger
   c. become more fluid
   d. become less fluid

5. In the United States and other Western countries, the lower a person's socioeconomic status:
   a. the younger the age at which the social clock is "set" for many life events.
   b. the older the age at which the social clock is "set" for many life events.
   c. the more variable are the settings for the social clock.
   d. the less likely it is that divorce will occur.

6. According to Erikson, the failure to achieve intimacy during early adulthood is most likely to result in:
   a. generativity.   c. role diffusion.
   b. stagnation.   d. isolation.

7. Regarding friendships, most young adults ten to:
   a. be very satisfied.
   b. be very dissatisfied.
   c. find it difficult to form social networks.
   d. be without close friends.

8. Between ages 20 and 30:
   a. 60 percent of men and 46 percent of wome have never married.
   b. 3 percent of men and women are alread divorced.
   c. the unmarried are in the majority.
   d. all of the above are true.

9. (Research Report) According to Robert Sternber consummate love emerges:
   a. as a direct response to passion.
   b. as a direct response to physical intimacy.
   c. when commitment is added to passion ar intimacy.
   d. during the early years of parenthood.

10. An arrangement in which two unrelated, unma ried adults of the opposite sex live together called:
    a. cross-sex friendship.
    b. a passive-congenial pattern.
    c. cohabitation.
    d. affiliation.

11. Differences in religious customs or rituals a *most* likely to arise in a:
    a. homogamous couple.
    b. heterogamous couple.
    c. cohabiting couple.
    d. very young married couple.

12. Children in dual-earner families:
    a. are slower to develop intellectually.
    b. gain several benefits, including more acti relationships with their fathers.
    c. often experience role overload.
    d. often have weak social skills.

13. The four stages of the traditional career cycle:
    a. are less applicable today than they were in t 1950s.
    b. derive from a time when workers were mc specialized than they are today.
    c. accurately describe all but the least techni of occupations.
    d. fit the job market of today better than the j market of earlier cohorts.

4. Adults who combine the roles of spouse, parent, and employee tend to report:
   a. less overall happiness than other adults.
   b. more overall happiness than other adults.
   c. regrets over parental roles.
   d. problems in career advancement.

5. Compared to adolescents who live with their biological parents, stepchildren, foster children, and adoptive children:
   a. leave home at an older age.
   b. leave home at a younger age.
   c. have fewer developmental problems.
   d. have the same developmental problems.

True or False Items

Write T (*true*) or F (*false*) on the line in front of each statement.

_____ 1. According to Erikson, the adult experiences a crisis of intimacy versus isolation and, after that, a crisis of generativity versus stagnation.

_____ 2. A prime influence on the cultural clock-setting is socioeconomic status.

_____ 3. (Research Report) According to Sternberg, early in a relationship, emotional intimacy is at its highest.

_____ 4. The younger the bride and groom, the more likely their marriage is to succeed.

_____ 5. Single adults who live alone typically experience profound loneliness.

_____ 6. A high level of marital homogamy is extremely rare.

_____ 7. Most divorced fathers manage to fulfill the emotional and financial needs of their children after divorce, even if they do not have custody.

_____ 8. Because of the complexity of the high-tech work world, most young adults can expect to remain at the same job throughout their careers.

_____ 9. (Changing Policy) Abuse is common among unmarried couples living together, whether heterosexual, gay, or lesbian.

_____ 10. Many stepchildren are fiercely loyal to the absent parent.

Progress Test 2

Progress Test 2 should be completed during a final chapter review. Answer the following questions after you thoroughly understand the correct answers for the Chapter Review and Progress Test 1.

Multiple-Choice Questions

1. Erikson theorizes that if generativity is not attained, the adult is most likely to experience:
   a. lack of advancement in his or her career.
   b. infertility or childlessness.
   c. feelings of emptiness and stagnation.
   d. feelings of profound aloneness or isolation.

2. (Changing Policy) Women often stay in a relationship with an abusive husband because:
   a. they believe that this is the norm for marital relationships.
   b. they have been conditioned to accept the abuse.
   c. they are isolated from those who might encourage them to leave.
   d. of both b. and c.

3. (In Person) Which of the following was *not* cited in the text as a reason for men's friendships tending to be much less intimate than women's?
   a. The tendency of boys to be more active and girls more verbal during childhood lays the groundwork for interaction patterns in adulthood.
   b. Intimacy is grounded in mutual vulnerability, a characteristic discouraged in men.
   c. Many men fear their friendships will be associated with homosexuality.
   d. Men tend to be more focused on achievement needs than women.

4. The prime effect of the social clock is to make an individual aware of:
   a. his or her socioeconomic status.
   b. the diversity of psychosocial paths during early adulthood.
   c. the means of fulfilling affiliation and achievement needs.
   d. the "right" or "best" time for assuming adult roles.

5. Today, the economy of developed nations is shifting from a focus on _____ to a focus on _____ .
   a. industry; information
   b. service; information
   c. agriculture; industry
   d. labor; agriculture

6. (In Person) Cross-sex friendships provide several advantages to both men and women, including that they:
   a. allow men to assist women in solving problems.
   b. expand each partner's perspective.
   c. make it acceptable for men and women to engage in good-natured teasing.
   d. allow men and women to develop sexual relationships without the bonds of marriage.

7. (In Person) Whereas men's friendships tend to be based on _____ , friendships between women tend to be based on _____ .
   a. shared confidences; shared interests
   b. cooperation; competition
   c. shared interests; shared confidences
   d. finding support for personal problems; discussion of practical issues

8. (Research Report) According to Robert Sternberg, the three dimensions of love are:
   a. passion, intimacy, and consummate love.
   b. physical intimacy, emotional intimacy, and consummate love.
   c. passion, commitment, and consummate love.
   d. passion, intimacy, and commitment.

9. Research on cohabitation in the United States suggests that:
   a. relatively few young adults ever live with an unrelated partner of the other sex.
   b. adults who are divorced or widowed often cohabit.
   c. adults who cohabit tend to be happier and healthier than married people are.
   d. marriages preceded by cohabitation are less durable.

10. A homogamous marriage is best defined as a marriage between:
    a. people who are physically similar to each other.
    b. people of similar social backgrounds.
    c. people of dissimilar socioeconomic backgrounds.
    d. two caring people of the same sex.

11. The text suggests that the main reason for the rising divorce rate is that today's couples experience:
    a. greater rigidity of sex roles in marriage.
    b. higher expectations about marriage and the marriage partner.
    c. deterioration in their overall communication skills.
    d. increased incidence of drug- and alcohol-related abuse.

12. Today's work force:
    a. is more diverse than in previous years.
    b. should not expect to remain in one career for their entire working lives.
    c. must exhibit a greater sensitivity to cultural differences.
    d. is characterized by all of the above.

13. Over the years of adulthood, people who balance marital, parental, and vocational loads:
    a. inevitably suffer from the stress of role overload.
    b. are far more likely to divorce.
    c. generally are happier than those who function in only one or two of these roles.
    d. Both a. and b.

14. Stepparents, adoptive parents, and foster parents:
    a. experience rewards that go beyond the immediate household.
    b. have basically the same parenting problems as biological parents.
    c. tend to have fewer problems as parents because they typically begin parenthood when the children are older.
    d. typically develop equally secure attachments to their children as do biological parents.

15. Depending on the amount of stress they are under, women who simultaneously serve as mother, wife, and employee may experience:
    a. marital equity.
    b. a glass ceiling.
    c. role overload.
    d. social homogamy.

Matching Items

Match each definition or description with its corresponding term.

Terms

_____ **1.** social clock
_____ **2.** cohabitation
_____ **3.** patriarchal terrorism
_____ **4.** heterogamy
_____ **5.** marital equity
_____ **6.** exchange theory
_____ **7.** social homogamy
_____ **8.** glass ceiling
_____ **9.** homogamy
_____ **10.** common couple violence

Definitions or Descriptions

a. abusive relationship that leads to battered-wife syndrome
b. an invisible barrier to career advancement
c. the similarity with which a couple regard leisure interests and role preferences
d. a marriage between people with dissimilar interests and backgrounds
e. the culturally set timetable at which key life events are deemed appropriate
f. predicts success in marriages in which each partner contributes something useful to the other
g. arrangement in which two unrelated adults of the opposite sex live together
h. the extent to which partners perceive equality in their relationship
i. a marriage between people with similar interests and backgrounds
j. abusive relationship that tends to improve with time

Thinking Critically About Chapter 19

Answer these questions the day before an exam as a final check on your understanding of the chapter's terms and concepts.

1. Jack is in his mid-20s. Compared to his father, who was 25 during the late 1950s, Jack is:
  a. more likely to have settled on a career.
  b. less likely to have settled on a career.
  c. likely to feel more social pressure to make decisions regarding career, marriage, and so forth.
  d. more likely to be concerned with satisfying his need for achievement at a younger age.

2. Marie notes that her parents have been married for 25 years even though each seems somewhat unfulfilled in terms of their relationship. Her friends had a similar relationship and divorced after five years. Given the research on divorce, how might Marie explain the differences?
  a. "My parents are just much more patient with and understanding of each other."
  b. "Couples today expect more of each other."
  c. "My parents feel that they must stay together for financial reasons."
  d. "I can't understand what keeps my parents together."

3. JoniJill and Randy did not anticipate the problems they encountered after their divorce. This is most likely because:
  a. they did not focus on the needs that had been met during their marriage.
  b. emotional entanglements lingered after the divorce.
  c. the conflict engendered by the divorce led to anger and bitterness.
  d. of both a. and b.

4. In order to determine ways to lower the high rate of divorce, Dr. Wilson is conducting research on marital satisfaction and the factors that contribute to it. Which of the following would he consider to be important factors?
  a. homogamy
  b. social homogamy
  c. marital equity
  d. All of the above contribute to marital satisfaction.

5. (Research Report) Rwanda and Rodney have been dating for about a month. Their relationship is most likely characterized by:
  a. strong feelings of commitment.
  b. consummate love.
  c. physical intimacy and feelings of closeness without true emotional intimacy.
  d. all of the above.

6. I am 25 years old. It is most likely that I:
   a. am married.
   b. am divorced.
   c. have never been married.
   d. am divorced and remarried.

7. If asked to explain the high failure rate of marriages between young adults, Erik Erikson would most likely say that:
   a. achievement goals are often more important than intimacy in early adulthood.
   b. intimacy is difficult to establish until identity is formed.
   c. divorce has almost become an expected stage in development.
   d. today's cohort of young adults has higher expectations of marriage than did previous cohorts.

8. Of the following people, who is *least* likely to report being "very happy" with his or her present life?
   a. Drew, who has never married
   b. Leah, who became a widow five years ago
   c. Malcolm, who has been married ten years
   d. Sharice, a single, divorced adult

9. Which of the following employer initiatives would be most likely to increase employee job satisfaction?
   a. offering higher wages
   b. offering improved worker benefits
   c. the opportunity to develop personal skills
   d. All of the above have about the same impact on employee satisfaction.

10. Which of the following would be the *worst* advice for a young adult entering the job market today?
    a. Seek education that fosters a variety of psychosocial and cognitive skills.
    b. Expect that educational requirements for work will shift every few years.
    c. To avoid diluting your skills, concentrate your education on preparing for one specific job.
    d. Be flexible and willing to adjust to the varied pacing and timing of today's jobs.

11. Of the following people, who is the most likely to encounter a glass ceiling in his or her career?
    a. Ben, a middle-aged white social worker
    b. Simone, an African American engineer
    c. Don, an Asian American attorney
    d. Paul, a white banker in his mid-20s

12. As compared to biological parents, which of th following is most likely to be true of stepparents adoptive parents, and foster parents?
    a. They are rarely able to win the love of th child away from the biological parents.
    b. They are more humble, less self-absorbed, an more aware of the problems facing children.
    c. They tend to favor their own children ove adopted, foster, or stepchildren.
    d. They keep their children at home much longe than do biological parents.

13. (Research Report) Arthur and Mabel have bee married for 5 years. According to Sternberg, their relationship is a satisfying one, which of th following best describes their relationship?
    a. They are strongly committed to each other.
    b. They are passionately in love.
    c. They are in the throes of establishing int macy.
    d. They are beginning to wonder why the pas sion has left their relationship.

14. Your brother, who became a stepparent when h married, complains that he can't seem to develo a strong bond with his 9-year-old stepchild. Yo tell him:
    a. strong bonds between parent and child ar particularly hard to create once a child is ol enough to have formed attachments to othe caregivers.
    b. the child is simply immature emotionally an will, with time, warm up considerably.
    c. most stepparents find that they eventuall develop a deeper, more satisfying relationshi with stepchildren than they had ever imag ined.
    d. he should encourage the child to think of hi as the child's biological father.

15. Your sister, who is about to marry, seeks you advice on what makes a happy marriage. Yo should mention that all but which one of the fo lowing factors contribute to marital happiness?
    a. cohabitation before marriage
    b. the degree to which a couple is homogamou or heterogamous
    c. the degree of marital equity
    d. whether identity needs have been met befor marriage

ey Terms

sing your own words, write a brief definition or
xplanation of each of the following terms on a sepa-
te piece of paper.

. intimacy versus isolation

. generativity versus stagnation

. social clock

. gateways to attraction

. cohabitation

. homogamy

. heterogamy

. social homogamy

. common couple violence

. patriarchal terrorism

. glass ceiling

. role overload

. role buffering

NSWERS

HAPTER REVIEW

. affiliation and achievement (affection and instru-
mentality or interdependence and independence
or communion and agency)

. love; work

. love and belonging; success and esteem

. intimacy versus isolation; generativity versus
stagnation

. orderly; predictable

the 1950s, men in their early 20s would finish their
ucation, choose their occupation, marry, buy a
use, and have children. Women would marry and
ve children.

. do not take; social clock; the culturally set
timetable that establishes when various events
and endeavors are appropriate

. highly developed

. socioeconomic status; younger

. women; marry; childbearing

. 18; 30; 30; 40

. close friendship; romantic partnership

. friends

iends choose each other, often for the very qualities
at make them good sources of emotional support.
ey are also a source of self-esteem.

13. a. Most young adults try to postpone the over-
riding commitments of marriage and having
children.

b. Because today's elderly are healthier, few
young adults must provide care for aging
parents.

14. gateways to attraction

a. physical attractiveness

b. availability

c. absence of unwanted traits

d. frequent exposure

15. filters; excluded

16. both men and women; friendship networks

17. are; shared activities; interests; intimate; emotional

Women talk more often about their intimate concerns
and delve deeper into personal and family issues;
men typically talk about external matters such as
sports, politics, or work.

18. women; men; self-concept; problems via shared
fears, sorrows, and disappointments

19. competition

20. a. Intimacy is grounded in mutual vulnerability,
a characteristic discouraged in men.

b. From childhood, boys are inclined to be more
active and girls more verbal.

c. Many men avoid any expression of affection
toward other men because they fear its association with homosexuality.

Cross-sex friendships offer men and women an
opportunity to explore their commonalities, to gain
practical skills traditionally "reserved" for the other
sex, and to expand their perspectives. Because each
sex tends to have its own expectations for friendship,
misunderstandings can occur in cross-sex friendships.
Another hazard is that men are often inclined to try to
sexualize friendships.

21. female

22. job; vocationally; psychologically

23. passion; intimacy; commitment; predictable

24. physical; emotional

25. personal intimacy; commitment

26. consummate

27. passion; intimacy; commitment

28. cohabitation

29. does not; happy; healthy; financial status

30. 2 to 5 percent; have

31. higher; 10; 50; 49

32. half

33. less; identity
34. homogamy; more; heterogamy; role; social homogamy
35. marital equity; exchange
36. work in progress
37. two; varies; increased
38. more
39. negative; more

First, until the divorce, ex-spouses often are unaware of things that *were* going well. Second, even after divorce, emotional dependence between the former partners often is strong.

40. social circle
41. loneliness, disequilibrium, promiscuous sexual behavior, and erratic patterns of eating, sleeping, working, and drug and alcohol use; do
42. least; children; mothers
43. Only a minority of
44. is; authoritative; guidance; discipline

Many factors contribute to spouse abuse, including social pressures that create stress, cultural values that condone violence, personality pathologies, and drug and alcohol addiction.

45. common couple violence; usually does not lead
46. patriarchal terrorism; husband; battered-wife; becomes
47. outside intervention; reduce
48. achieve; varies
49. generativity
    a. develop and use their personal skills or talents
    b. express their creative energy
    c. aid and advise co-workers
    d. contribute to the community
50. exploration; establishment; maintenance; decline (retirement); low-tech; expertise; interchangeable
51. agriculture; industry; industry; information; service;
52. physical or occupational therapist, human service worker, computer engineer, home health caregiver, systems analyst, medical assistant, paralegal, and special-education teacher
53. linear; secure; specific; psychosocial; cognitive
54. diverse; half; immigrants; ethnic

First, it is a mistake to plan on staying in one career forever. Second, to be successful today workers must be sensitive to cultural differences.

55. glass ceiling
56. neither
57. do not suffer
58. do not necessarily; role overload; role buffering
59. are
60. logistics; are
61. earns more, and is more committed to her caree than the husband; blue-collar; immigrants
62. one-third
63. attachments
64. adoptive
65. earlier than

PROGRESS TEST 1

Multiple-Choice Questions

1. **b.** is the answer. (p. 511)
2. **d.** is the answer. (p. 513)
3. **c.** is the answer. (p. 513)
4. **a.** is the answer. (p. 525)
   c. & d. The fluidity of social circles followi divorce was not discussed.
5. **a.** is the answer. (p. 514)
   d. Low SES is actually a risk factor for divorce.
6. **d.** is the answer. (p. 511)
   a. Generativity is a characteristic of the crisis f lowing the intimacy crisis.
   b. Stagnation occurs when generativity needs a not met.
   c. Erikson's theory does not address this issue.
7. **a.** is the answer. (p. 515)
   c. Because they are mobile and tend to have fev commitments, young adults find it relatively ea to form friendships.
   d. Almost never do young adults feel bereft friendship.
8. **d.** is the answer. (p. 521)
9. **c.** is the answer. (p. 519)
   d. Sternberg's theory is not concerned with t stages of parenthood.
10. **c.** is the answer. (p. 519)
11. **b.** is the answer. (p. 522)
    a. By definition, homogamous couples share v ues, background, and the like.
    c. & d. These may or may not be true, dependi on the extent to which such a couple is homo mous.
12. **b.** is the answer. (p. 534)

a. & d. It is a common *myth* that children in dual-earner families suffer neglect.

c. Role overload more often pertains to adults who must balance the roles of parent, spouse, and employee.

3. **a.** is the answer. (p. 529)

b. & d. In fact, just the opposite is true.

c. The traditional career cycle is *more* typical of low-tech occupations.

4. **b.** is the answer. (p. 534)

c. Most parents report that they are pleased that they have had children.

5. **b.** is the answer. (p. 539)

c. & d. The text does not discuss variations in the incidence of developmental problems in the various family structures.

True or False Items

1. T (pp. 511–512)

2. T (p. 514)

3. F   Physical intimacy and feelings of closeness are highest in the earliest stages of a relationship. (p. 518)

4. F   Just the reverse is true. (pp. 521–522)

5. F   Most single adults have a network of supportive friends, and most enjoy their independence. (pp. 517)

6. T (p. 522)

7. F   Most divorced fathers gradually become alienated from their children, and few offer adequate support. (p. 528)

8. F   Most young adults should learn basic skills so that they have the flexibility to move into different jobs. (p. 530)

9. T (p. 526)

10. T (p. 538)

PROGRESS TEST 2

Multiple-Choice Questions

1. **c.** is the answer. (p. 512)

a. Lack of career advancement may prevent generativity.

b. Erikson's theory does not address these issues.

d. Such feelings are related to the need for intimacy rather than generativity.

2. **d.** is the answer. (p. 527)

3. **d.** is the answer. (p. 517)

4. **d.** is the answer. (p. 513)

5. **a.** is the answer. (p. 530)

b. Today, the economies of developed nations focus on *both* service and information.

c. This describes the shift in the economies of poor, undeveloped nations.

6. **b.** is the answer. (p. 517)

a. Men are frustrated that women won't allow them to do this.

c. Women become upset by such teasing.

d. Men may try to make a platonic relationship sexual, women are offended when they do so.

7. **c.** is the answer. (p. 516)

8. **d.** is the answer. (p. 518)

a., b., & c. According to Sternberg, consummate love emerges when commitment is added to passion and intimacy.

9. **b.** is the answer. (p. 520)

a. Slightly more than half of all women aged 25 to 40 in the United States cohabit before their first marriage.

c. In fact, a large study of adults found that cohabitants were much *less* happy and healthy than married people were.

d. No such finding was reported in the text.

10. **b.** is the answer. (p. 522)

a. & d. These characteristics do not pertain to homogamy.

c. This describes a heterogamous marriage.

11. **b.** is the answer. (p. 524)

12. **d.** is the answer. (pp. 530–532)

13. **c.** is the answer. (p. 534)

14. **a.** is the answer. (p. 539)

d. Without the emotional pull of both early contact and genetic connections, close attachments may be difficult to establish.

15. **c.** is the answer. However, role overload may not always be experienced by women serving multiple functions. (p. 534)

a. Just the opposite may be true. She may feel that she is shouldering the burden of responsibility.

b. & d. These may be true but they have nothing to do with her feeling overloaded.

Matching Items

1. e (p. 513)	**5.** h (p. 522)	**9.** i (p. 522)
2. g (p. 519)	**6.** f (pp. 522–523)	**10.** j (p. 526)
3. a (p. 527)	**7.** c (p. 5522)	
4. d (p. 522)	**8.** b (p. 533)	

THINKING CRITICALLY ABOUT CHAPTER 19

1. b. is the answer. (pp. 529–530)

c. & d. The text does not indicate that there are cohort effects in these areas.

2. b. is the answer. (p. 524)

3. d. is the answer. (p. 525)

4. d. is the answer. The most successful relationships are between people of similar backgrounds and similar interests. The partners' perceptions of marital equity are also important. (pp. 522–523)

5. c. is the answer. (p. 518)

a. & b. These feelings emerge more gradually in relationships.

6. c. is the answer. (p. 521)

7. b. is the answer. (pp. 521–522)

a. In Erikson's theory, the crisis of intimacy *precedes* the need to be productive through work.

c. & d. Although these items are true, Erikson's theory does not address these issues.

8. d. is the answer. (p. 526)

9. c. is the answer. (pp. 528–529)

10. c. is the answer. (p. 530)

a., b., & d. These would all be good pieces of advice for new workers today.

11. b. is the answer. (p. 533)

a., c., & d. Women and members of minority groups are more likely to encounter glass ceilings in their careers.

12. b. is the answer. (p. 539)

13. a. is the answer. (p. 519)

14. a. is the answer. (p. 535)

b. Many stepchildren remain fiercely loyal to the absent parent.

c. Most stepparents actually have unrealistically high expectations of the relationship they will establish with their stepchildren.

d. Doing so would only confuse the child and, quite possibly, cause resentment and further alienation.

15. a. is the answer. Cohabitation before marriage does *not* strengthen the relationship. (p. 522)

KEY TERMS

1. According to Erik Erikson, the first crisis of adulhood is **intimacy versus isolation**, whic involves the need to share one's personal life wit someone else or risk profound loneliness. (p. 511

2. In Erikson's theory, the second crisis of adul hood is **generativity versus stagnation**, whic involves the need to be productive in some mear ingful way, usually through work or parenthoo (p. 512)

3. The **social clock** represents the culturally se timetable that establishes when various even and behaviors in life are appropriate and calle for. (p. 513)

4. Gateways to attraction refer to the various qual ties, such as physical attractiveness, availabilit and frequent exposure, that contribute to the fo mation of friendships and intimate relationship (p. 515)

5. Increasingly common among young adults in a industrialized countries is the living patter called **cohabitation**, in which two unrelate adults of the opposite sex live together. (p. 519)

6. Homogamy refers to marriage between peop who are similar in attitudes, socioeconomic bac ground, interests, ethnicity, religion, and the lik (p. 522)

7. Heterogamy refers to marriage between peop who are dissimilar in attitudes, interests, SE religion, ethnic background, and goals. (p. 522)

8. Social homogamy is defined as similarity leisure interests and role preferences. (p. 522)

9. Common couple violence is a form of abuse which one or both partners in a couple engage outbursts of verbal and physical attack. (p. 526)

10. Patriarchal terrorism is the form of spouse abu in which the husband uses violent methods accelerating intensity to isolate, degrade, ar punish the wife. (p. 527)

11. A **glass ceiling** is an invisible barrier to care advancement that is most often encountered k women and minority workers. (p. 533)

12. Role overload refers to the stress of multip obligations that may occur for a parent in a dua earner family. (p. 534)

13. Role buffering is a situation in a dual-earn family in which one role that a parent pla reduces the disappointments that may occur other roles. (p. 534)

20
Middle Adulthood: Biosocial Development

Chapter Overview

This chapter deals with biosocial development during the years from 40 to 60. The first section describes changes in appearance and in the functioning of the sense organs and vital body systems, noting the potential impact of these changes. The next section discusses health-related behaviors of the middle-aged, focusing on smoking, drinking, eating habits, and exercise. The third section identifies variations in health related to ethnicity and gender, pointing out that, overall, middle-aged persons are healthier today than in earlier cohorts. The chapter concludes with a discussion of the changes in the sexual-reproductive system that occur during middle adulthood and shows why most individuals find these changes less troubling than they were led to expect them to be.

NOTE: Answer guidelines for all Chapter 20 questions begin on page 304.

Guided Study

The text chapter should be studied one section at a time. Before you read, preview each section by skimming it, noting headings and boldface items. Then read the appropriate section objectives from the following outline. Keep these objectives in mind and, as you read the chapter section, search for the information that will enable you to meet each objective. Once you have finished a section, write out answers for its objectives.

Normal Changes in Middle Adulthood (pp. 545–550)

1. (text and In Person) Identify the typical physical changes of middle adulthood and discuss their impact.

2. Describe how the functions of the sense organs and vital body systems change during middle adulthood.

Health Habits over the Years (pp. 550–555)

3. (text and Research Report) Describe the relationship between certain lifestyle factors—smoking, alcohol use, nutrition, weight, and exercise—and health.

Variations in Health (pp. 555–563)

4. Differentiate four measures of health, and explain the concept of quality-adjusted life years.

5. Explain how variations in health are related to ethnicity.

6. (Changing Policy) Explain why group differences in health are often misattributed to genes and ancestry.

7. Cite sex differences in mortality and morbidity rates and several ways in which these differences have been exacerbated by the medical community.

The Sexual-Reproductive System (pp. 563–568)

8. Identify the typical changes that occur in the sexual-reproductive system during middle adulthood.

9. (A Life-Span View) Discuss historical changes in the psychological impact of menopause, and explain what researchers mean by "male menopause."

10. Identify age-related changes in sexual expression.

Chapter Review

When you have finished reading the chapter, wor' through the material that follows to review i' Complete the sentences and answer the questions. A you proceed, evaluate your performance for each sec tion by consulting the answers on page 304. Do no continue with the next section until you understan each answer. If you need to, review or reread th appropriate section in the textbook before continuing

Normal Changes in Middle Adulthood (pp. 545–550)

1. Some of the normal changes in appearance that occur during middle adulthood include

   _____

   _____

   _____

2. With the exception of excessive

   _____ _____ ,

   the physical changes that typically occur during middle adulthood usually _____
   (do/do not) have significant health consequence

3. The physical changes of middle adulthood may have a substantial impact on a person's

   _____ ; this is particularly true for

   _____ (men/women).

4. (In Person) The overall impact of aging on the individual depends in large measure on the indi-vidual's _____ toward growing old

5. Age-related deficits in the sense organs are most obvious in _____ and

   _____ .

6. Compared to women, who begin to show hearin deficits at around age _____ , men begin to show some deficits by age

_____ . The rate of hearing loss is faster in _____ (women/men).

7. Most losses in hearing during middle adulthood are the result of the interaction of _____ and _____ .

8. Age-related hearing loss is the result of prolonged exposure to_____ .

9. With normal aging, the ability to hear differences in _____ _____ declines faster than the ability to understand _____ .

10. Speech-related hearing losses are first apparent for _____-(high/low) frequency sounds.

11. After puberty, _____ affects focusing much more than age does. Due to the fact that the _____ of their eyes are too _____ (flat/curved), people who need glasses before age 20 tend simply to be _____ (nearsighted/farsighted/astigmatic). In contrast, older adults tend to be _____ , due to the fact that the _____ of their eyes become _____ (too curved/flatter). A 50-percent decrease in the _____ of the lens results in many older adults wearing _____ .

12. Other aspects of vision that decline steadily with age are _____ _____ , _____-_____ _____ , _____ _____ , and _____ _____ . These changes are particularly likely to become apparent by age _____ .

13. Serious accidents are much more common in late _____ or late _____ than in middle adulthood, when most people are sufficiently _____ to compensate for minor visual losses.

14. A more serious vision problem is the disease _____ , a hardening of the eyeball caused by an increase of _____ within the eyeball. By age _____ , this disease is the leading cause of _____ . The incidence of this disease is especially high among those of _____ descent.

15. Systemic declines in the efficiency and the organ reserve of the _____ , _____ , and _____ _____ make middle-aged people _____ (more/less) vulnerable to disease. Declines are also evident in the _____ system, resulting in an increased risk of _____ diseases such as _____ _____ and _____ .

16. Thanks to better _____ _____ and _____ , the overall death rate among the middle-aged is _____ what it was sixty years ago, especially for the two leading causes of death in this age group: _____ _____ and _____ . The overall health of middle-aged adults _____ (varies/does not vary) significantly from one nation to another.

Health Habits over the Years (pp. 550–555)

17. For most conditions and diseases, it is a person's _____ _____ over the years that have the greatest influence on delaying and preventing physiological decline.

18. (Research Report) Cigarette-smoking is a known risk factor for most serious diseases, including _____ .

19. (Research Report) All smoking diseases are _____- and _____-sensitive. Although smoking rates have dropped in North America, rates in most _____ nations and _____ nations have not. These statistics highlight the importance of

_____ and _____ ,
rather than _____ in smoking.

20. Some studies find that adults who drink moder-
ately may live longer, possibly because alcohol
increases the blood's supply of
_____ , a protein that helps reduce
the amount of _____ in the body.
Another possible explanation of the relationship
between moderate drinking and longevity is that
moderate drinking may reduce
_____ and aid
_____ .

21. Alcohol dependence and abuse are most common
at about age _____ .

List some of the damaging effects of heavy drinking
on the body.

22. Worldwide, alcohol is a leading factor in the
_____ _____
_____ , which is a measure that
combines indicators of premature
_____ and _____
worldwide.

23. Specific foods probably _____
(can/cannot) prevent, or cause, major health
problems. Nevertheless, research _does_ support the
health benefits of avoiding too much
_____ and including sufficient
amounts of _____ in one's diet.

24. Adults in industrialized countries typically consume _____ percent of their calories
as fat. The National Cancer Institute recommends
that adults increase their consumption of fiber to
no more than _____ grams per day
and reduce their consumption of fat to less than
_____ percent.

25. High-fiber diets lower a person's risk of several
forms of _____ , particularly that of
the _____ .

26. Overweight, defined as _____
_____ , is present in
_____ (how many?) middle-aged
residents of the United States. Obesity, defined a
_____
is a risk factor for _____
_____ , _____ , and
_____ , and a contributing factor f
_____ , the most common disabilit
for older adults.

27. Throughout much of the world, the percentage
people who are overweight or obese is
_____ (less than/greater
than/about the same as) that of previous generations. Many experts believe that being slightly
overweight _____ (increases/does
not increase) a person's risk of disease, disabilit
or death.

28. Women are more likely to be depressed if they
are _____ (overweight/under-
weight), while men are more likely to be
depressed if they are _____ (over-
weight/underweight)

29. Between ages 20 and 50, a person's metabolism
_____ (slows/increases) by about
third, which means that middle-aged people ne
to eat _____ (more/less) simply to
maintain their weight.

30. Even more important to health than eating less
during middle age is _____ more.
People who are active _____
(do/do not) have lower rates of serious illness
and death than inactive people. Exercise also
reduces the ratio of body _____ to
body _____ . An additional advan
tage is enhanced _____ functionin
due to improved circulation to the
_____ .

List some of the health benefits of regular exercise.

Variations in Health (pp. 555–563)

1. Individuals who are relatively well-educated, financially secure, and living in or near cities tend to live _____ (shorter/longer) lives and have _____ (more/ fewer) chronic illnesses or disabilities.

2. In the United States, people living in the _____ and _____ are healthier than those in the _____ and _____ . The reasons for such differences include variations in

_____

_____ .

3. Perhaps the most solid indicator of health of given age groups is the rate of _____ , or death.

4. A more comprehensive measure of health is _____ , defined as _____ of all kinds; it can be sudden, or _____ , or it can be _____ , extending over a long time period.

5. To truly portray quality of life, we need to measure _____ , which refers to a person's inability to perform basic activities, and _____ , which refers to how healthy and energetic a person feels.

6. In terms of quality of life, _____ is probably the most important measure of health.

7. The concept of _____-_____ _____ _____ indicates how many years of full vitality are lost as a result of a particular disease or disability.

8. Between the ages of 45 and 55, the chance of dying is twice as high for _____ , and only half as high for _____ , as it is for European Americans. In between are the mortality rates for _____ and _____ .

_____ . Self-reported health status, morbidity, and disability _____ (do/do not) follow the same ethnic patterns as does mortality.

39. In all minority groups, the illness and death rates among recent immigrants are _____ (higher/lower) than among long-time U.S. residents.

State several possible explanations for this difference.

40. (Changing Policy) Categorizing people in racial terms may mistakenly cause people to conclude that _____ and ancestral _____ are the main explanations for group differences in health. In addition to these, other factors in group differences in health are _____ and _____ , as well as the pressures and opportunities provided by the larger society

41. (Changing Policy) The racial difference in the death rates of black and white Americans is greatest during the early _____ (what decade?), when U.S. blacks are _____ (how many?) times as likely to die as whites. Genetic predispositions and ancestry probably _____ (explain/do not explain) this pattern. Extrinsic factors, particularly _____ and _____ , are especially harmful between _____ and age 65.

42. (Changing Policy) Recent studies have also found that rates of _____

_____ among adults of West African ancestry rose as adults grew up farther away from rural Africa. Another study found that the _____ of breast cancer in middle-aged African American women is less than in European American women, but their rate of _____ from the disease is higher. This, too, demonstrates that ethnic health differences are influenced less by genes than by factors related to _____ , _____ , and _____ .

43. Compared to middle-aged women, middle-aged men are _____ as likely to die of any cause and three times as likely to die of _____ _____ . Not until age _____ are the rates equivalent.

44. Beginning in middle age, women have higher _____ and _____ rates than men. Contributing to the gender difference in mortality is the fact that men are more likely to _____ , _____ , be _____ , repress _____ , and ignore their _____ _____ .

45. Contributing to the gender difference in morbidity and disability is the tendency of the medical community to focus on treating _____ _____ rather than _____ _____ , and on preventing _____ rather than avoiding _____ . This has meant that more research money is dedicated to studying diseases that are more common in _____ (men/women).

The Sexual-Reproductive System (pp. 563–568)

46. At an average age of _____ , a woman reaches _____ , as ovulation and menstruation stop and the production of the hormones _____ , _____ , and _____ drops considerably.

47. All the various biological and psychological changes that precede menopause are referred to as the _____ . The first symptom is typically shorter _____ _____ , followed by variations in the timing of her _____ . Symptoms such as hot flashes and flushes and cold sweats are caused by _____ _____ , that is, a temporary disrup-

tion in the body mechanisms that maintain body temperature.

48. Two other serious changes caused by reduced levels of _____ are loss of bone _____ , which can lead to the thin and brittle bones that accompany _____ , and an increase of arterial _____ that can set the stage for _____ _____ .

49. Whether natural menopause is troubling depends, in part, on factors in the _____ context, such as _____ values and prevailing _____ views.

50. In the United States, approximately _____ percent of women going through natural menopause and _____ percent going through surgically induced menopause experience symptoms sufficiently difficult that they require _____ _____ _____ , or HRT.

51. Continued use of HRT beyond menopause has been shown to reduce the risk of _____ _____ disease, _____ fractures, and _____ disease. The long-term consequences of HRT, however, are not yet known.

(A Life-Span View) Briefly explain why menopause more often welcomed by women today than in the past.

52. (A Life-Span View) Physiologically, men _____ (do/do not) experience anything like the female climacteric. Although the average levels of testosterone decline gradually, if at all, with age, they can dip if a man becomes _____ _____ or unusually worried.

53. Frequency of intercourse and orgasm usually _____ (declines/increases/ remains unchanged) during middle age.

54. During middle adulthood, sexual stimulation takes _____ (longer/less time) and needs to be _____ (more/ less) direct than earlier in life.

55. Most middle-aged men report that they _____ (are/are not) satisfied with their sex life. The physical changes that follow menopause generally _____ (impair/need not impair) sexual relationships.

Progress Test 1

Multiple-Choice Questions

Circle your answers to the following questions and check them with the answers on page 305. If your answer is incorrect, read the explanation for why it is incorrect and then consult the appropriate pages of the text (in parentheses following the correct answer).

1. During the years from 40 to 60, the average adult:
a. becomes proportionally slimmer.
b. gains about 5 pounds per year.
c. gains about 1 pound per year.
d. is more likely to be noticeably overweight.

2. (In Person) The overall impact of aging depends *largely* on the individual's:
a. general physical health.
b. genetic predisposition toward disease.
c. attitudes about aging.
d. health habits and lifestyle.

3. Age-related deficits in speech-related hearing are most noticeable for:
a. high-frequency sounds.
b. low-frequency sounds.
c. mid-range-frequency sounds.
d. rapid conversation.

4. Compared to the acuity problems of younger adults, which tend to be confined to _____ , those of older adults also tend to include _____ .
a. farsightedness; nearsightedness
b. farsightedness; nearsightedness and decreasing depth perception
c. astigmatism; farsightedness
d. nearsightedness; farsightedness and decreasing depth perception

5. Characterized by an increase in fluid within the eyeball, this eye disease is the leading cause of blindness by age 70. It is called:
a. myopia.   c. cataracts.
b. astigmatism.   d. glaucoma.

6. At midlife, individuals who _____ tend to live longer and have fewer chronic illnesses or disabilities.
a. are relatively well educated
b. are financially secure
c. live in or near cities
d. are or do all of the above

7. The term that refers to diseases of all kinds is:
a. mortality.   c. disability.
b. morbidity.   d. vitality.

8. On average, women reach menopause at age:
a. 39.   c. 46.
b. 42.   d. 51.

9. In explaining ethnic variations in health and illness during middle age, _____ factors are more important than_____ factors.
a. genetic; social and psychological
b. social and psychological; genetic
c. intrinsic; cultural
d. cultural; extrinsic

10. In middle age, _____ rates are higher for men than for women, whereas _____ rates are higher for women than men.
a. mortality; morbidity
b. morbidity; mortality
c. vitality; disability
d. disability; vitality

11. The leading cause of mortality in both sexes is:
a. lung cancer.   c. heart disease.
b. accidents.   d. stroke.

12. The concept that indicates how many years of full physical, intellectual, and social health are lost to a particular physical disease or disability is:
    a. vitality
    b. disability
    c. morbidity
    d. quality-adjusted life years.

13. (A Life-Span View) Today, decisions regarding childbearing are made to a large extent on the basis of:
    a. age.
    b. religion.
    c. education level.
    d. financial situation.

14. (Research Report) Which of the following is true of all smoking diseases?
    a. They are a natural result of smoking for ten years or more, whether or not the person eventually quit.
    b. They are related to dosage of nicotine taken in and to length of time the person has smoked.
    c. They are all incurable.
    d. They are all based on the psychological addiction to tobacco.

15. The first symptom of the climacteric is usually:
    a. shorter menstrual cycles.
    b. a drop in the production of progesterone.
    c. increased variation in the timing of ovulation.
    d. weight gain.

True or False Items

Write T (*true*) or F (*false*) on the line in front of each statement.

_____ 1. The mortality rate of middle-aged European Americans is higher than that of middle-aged African Americans.

_____ 2. During middle age, back muscles, connecting tissues, and bones lose strength.

_____ 3. Approximately half of all middle-aged Americans are obese.

_____ 4. Moderate users of alcohol are more likely than teetotalers to have heart attacks.

_____ 5. Those who exercise regularly have lower rates of serious illness than do sedentary people.

_____ 6. Middle-aged adults are less likely to improve their health habits than are members of any other age group.

_____ 7. During middle adulthood, sexual responses slow down, particularly in men.

_____ 8. The climacteric refers specifically to the psychological changes that accompany menopause.

_____ 9. (A Life-Span View) Despite popular reference to it, there is no "male menopause."

_____ 10. (A Life-Span View) A woman's culture, expectations, and attitude, more than biology, determine her psychological reaction to menopause.

Progress Test 2

Progress Test 2 should be completed during a final chapter review. Answer the following questions after you thoroughly understand the correct answers for the Chapter Review and Progress Test 1.

Multiple-Choice Questions

1. For most people, the normal changes in appearance that occur during middle age have the greatest impact on their:
   a. physical strength.   c. cardiovascular reserve
   b. flexibility.   d. self-image.

2. Age-related deficits in the sense organs are most obvious in:
   a. taste and touch.   c. smell and balance.
   b. vision and hearing. d. balance and hearing

3. After puberty, visual acuity is influenced more by _____ than by _____ .
   a. heredity; age
   b. age; heredity
   c. overall health; heredity
   d. heredity; overall health

4. People are more vulnerable to disease during middle adulthood because:
   a. they exercise beyond their capacity.
   b. they tend to have poorer health habits.
   c. their vital body systems decline in efficiency.
   d. of all of the above reasons.

5. Overall, the death rate of people between ages 4 and 60 is about _____ what it wa fifty years ago.
   a. one-and-a-half times   c. one-third
   b. twice   d. one-half

6. (Changing Policy) The impact of racial prejudice on health during middle age is illustrated by the fact that:

a. the mortality rate of black men aged 25 to 44 living in segregated neighborhoods is four times that of black men who live in mostly white neighborhoods.

b. socioeconomic status is positively correlated with morbidity rates.

c. socioeconomic status is negatively correlated with morbidity rates.

d. the mortality rate from breast cancer in middle-aged African American women is 46 percent higher than in European American women.

7. To be a true index of health, morbidity rates must be refined in terms of which of the following health measure(s)?

a. mortality rate

b. disability and mortality rates

c. vitality

d. disability and vitality

8. The term "male menopause" was probably coined to refer to:

a. the sudden dip in testosterone that sometimes occurs in men who have been sexually inactive.

b. age-related declines in fertility among men.

c. men suffering from erectile dysfunction.

d. age-related declines in testosterone levels in middle-aged men.

9. The mortality rates of women and men become equivalent at age:

a. 65.   c. 80.

b. 70.   d. 85.

10. What is one reason that middle-aged women have higher morbidity rates than men in the same age group?

a. Traditionally, less research money has been dedicated to problems more likely to affect women than men, but unlikely to lead to sudden death.

b. Because women traditionally have less muscular strength than men, their morbidity is higher.

c. There simply are more middle-aged women than men living.

d. All of the above are true.

11. Which of the following was *not* suggested as an explanation for variations in health among recent immigrants and long-time U.S. residents?

a. Hardier individuals tend to emigrate.

b. Immigrants who are more assimilated tend to have healthier lifestyles.

c. Recent immigrants tend to be more optimistic.

d. Recent immigrants have stronger family support.

12. Which of the following is *not* true regarding alcohol consumption?

a. Alcohol decreases the blood's supply of high-density lipoprotein.

b. Alcohol dependence is more common in middle adulthood.

c. Alcohol is implicated in about half of all accidents, suicides, and homicides.

d. Alcohol abuse is the main cause of cirrhosis of the liver.

13. Which of the following diets has been associated with increased risk of certain cancers?

a. low-fat diet

b. low-fat, high-protein diet

c. high-fat, high-fiber diet

d. high-fat, low-fiber diet

14. Which of the following is true of sexual expressiveness in middle age?

a. Menopause impairs a woman's sexual relationship.

b. Men's frequency of ejaculation increases until approximately age 55.

c. Signs of arousal in a woman are as obvious as they were at age 20.

d. Although their responses slow down, men express satisfaction with their sex life.

15. Which of the following is *not* true of hormone replacement therapy (HRT)?

a. HRT increases the risk of Alzheimer's disease.

b. Long-term HRT reduces the risk of coronary heart disease.

c. Only a small percentage of women going through natural menopause experience symptoms sufficiently difficult that they require HRT.

d. HRT typically includes both estrogen and progesterone.

Matching Items

Match each definition or description with its corresponding term.

Terms

_____ 1. mortality
_____ 2. morbidity
_____ 3. vitality
_____ 4. glaucoma
_____ 5. menopause
_____ 6. climacteric
_____ 7. global disease burden
_____ 8. HRT
_____ 9. osteoporosis
_____ 10. disability
_____ 11. quality-adjusted life years

Definitions or Descriptions

a. disease of all kinds
b. a measure that combines indicators of prematu
   death and disability
c. the leading cause of blindness by age 70
d. often prescribed to treat the symptoms
   menopause
e. a condition of thin and brittle bones
f. death; as a measure of health, it usually refers
   the number of deaths each year per thousar
   individuals
g. the cessation of ovulation and menstruation
h. more important to quality of life than any oth
   measure of health
i. the various biological and psychological chang
   that precede menopause
j. the inability to perform normal activities
k. concept that indicates how many years of fu
   vitality are lost to a particular disease

Thinking Critically About Chapter 20

Answer these questions the day before an exam as a final check on your understanding of the chapter's terms and concepts.

1. Which of the following types of exercise would be most beneficial in promoting general health and reducing risk of disease?
   a. sprinting 100 yards in 12 seconds
   b. lifting weights three times a week
   c. playing three sets of tennis twice a week
   d. cycling regularly at an intensity that raises the heart rate to 75 percent of its maximum

2. Mr. Johnson has experienced more frequent colds and bouts of flu since he became 45 years old. His increased susceptibility to illness is likely due to:
   a. a reduction in the effectiveness of his immune system.
   b. an increase in immune-system activity to compensate for other age-related declines.
   c. a decrease in the level of testosterone circulating in his bloodstream.
   d. an increase in the level of testosterone circulating in his bloodstream.

3. Fifty-five-year-old Dewey is concerned becau sexual stimulation seems to take longer a needs to be more direct than earlier. As a frier you should tell him:
   a. "You should see a therapist. It is not normal.
   b. "See a doctor if your 'sexual prowess' doesr improve soon. You may have some under ing physical problem."
   c. "Don't worry. This is normal for middle-ag men."
   d. "You're too old to have sex, so just give it uf

4. The mortality rates of the following ethr groups, in order from highest to lowest, are:
   a. Asian Americans; African Americans; European Americans.
   b. African Americans; Asian Americans; European Americans.
   c. African Americans; European Americans; Asian Americans.
   d. European Americans; African Americans; Asian Americans.

5. Which of the following is true regarding changes in vision during middle age?
   a. They lead to serious accidents such as falls.
   b. They lead to nighttime car accidents due to the blindness caused by oncoming headlights.
   c. They make it harder to focus on small print for several hours.
   d. They do both a. and b.

6. In the United States, people who live in the _____ tend to be healthier than those who live in the _____ .
   a. East; West
   b. West and Midwest; South and Middle Atlantic
   c. South; North
   d. Northeast; Northwest

7. Forty-five-year-old Val is the same weight she has been since college and continues to eat the same types and amounts of food she has always eaten. In order to maintain her weight through middle age, Val should:
   a. continue to eat the same amounts and types of foods.
   b. reduce her caloric intake.
   c. eat more foods high in LDL.
   d. reduce her intake of foods high in HDL.

8. (A Life-Span View) One hundred years ago, the psychological impact of menopause on women was probably:
   a. about the same as it is today.
   b. less than it is today.
   c. greater than it is today.
   d. determined more by expectations and culture than it is today.

9. (A Life-Span View) Which of the following *most* accurately describes research findings regarding psychological adjustment to menopause?
   a. Older women tend to have very negative attitudes about menopause.
   b. Both younger and older women tend to have very negative attitudes about menopause.
   c. Menopause tends to be a more negative experience in countries other than the United States.
   d. Most women find menopause more welcome than regretted.

10. Rodney, a 45-year-old African American store manager, has been experiencing some problems with his vision lately. His optometrist should probably:
    a. reassure Rodney that everyone's vision begins to deteriorate rapidly after age 40.
    b. give Rodney a glaucoma test.
    c. reduce the strength of Rodney's lenses so that his eye muscles will be strengthened.
    d. do all of the above.

11. Fifty-year-old Beth has a college degree and a good job and lives near Seattle, Washington. Compared to her sister, who dropped out of high school and is struggling to survive on a dairy farm in rural Wisconsin, Beth is most likely to:
    a. live longer.
    b. have fewer chronic illnesses.
    c. have fewer disabilities.
    d. do or have all of the above.

12. Morbidity is to mortality as _____ is to _____ .
    a. disease; death
    b. death; disease
    c. inability to perform normal daily activities; disease
    d. disease; subjective feeling of being healthy

13. Your middle-aged father is more likely to suffer from rheumatoid arthritis than you are because:
    a. rheumatoid arthritis is an autoimmune disease.
    b. with age, the immune system is more likely to mistake body cells as foreign invaders and attack them.
    c. the immune system begins to decline during middle age.
    d. of both a. & b.
    e. of a., b., & c.

14. Concluding her presentation on body weight and health, Lynn states that:
    a. "Research consistently shows that 'you can't be too thin.'"
    b. "Animal research demonstrates that it is better to be a little overweight than underweight."
    c. "Even being slightly overweight increases the risk of virtually every cause of disease."
    d. "As long as metabolism remains normal, being overweight is not a health problem."

15. Compared to his identical twin brother, 48-year-old Andy has lower blood pressure, better circulation, a lower ratio of body fat to body weight, and higher HDL in his blood. The most probable explanation for these differences is that Andy:

   a. doesn't smoke.
   b. eats a high-fiber diet.
   c. engages in regular aerobic exercise.
   d. does all of the above.

Key Terms

Using your own words, write a brief definition or explanation of each of the following terms on a separate piece of paper.

1. glaucoma
2. autoimmune diseases
3. global disease burden
4. mortality
5. morbidity
6. disability
7. vitality
8. quality-adjusted life years (QALYs)
9. menopause
10. climacteric
11. osteoporosis
12. hormone replacement therapy (HRT)

ANSWERS

CHAPTER REVIEW

1. hair turns gray and thins; skin becomes drier and more wrinkled; pockets of fat settle on the upper arms, buttocks, and eyelids; back muscles, connecting tissues, and bones lose strength, causing some individuals to become shorter; many become noticeably overweight
2. weight gain; do not
3. self-image; women
4. attitude
5. hearing; vision
6. 50; 30; men
7. age; genes
8. noise
9. pure tones; conversation
10. high
11. heredity; corneas; curved; nearsighted; farsighted; corneas; flatter; elasticity; bifocals

12. depth perception; eye-muscle resilience; color sensitivity; dark adaptation; 50
13. adolescence; adulthood; cautious
14. glaucoma; fluid; 70; blindness; African-Americans
15. lungs; heart; digestive system; more; immune; autoimmune; rheumatoid arthritis; lupus
16. health habits; disease prevention; half; heart disease; cancer; varies
17. health habits
18. cancer of the lung, bladder, kidney, mouth, and stomach, as well as heart disease, stroke, pneumonia, and emphysema
19. dose; duration; European; developing; culture; cohort; genes
20. HDL (high-density lipoprotein); LDL (low-density lipoprotein); tension; digestion
21. 40

Heavy drinking is the main cause of cirrhosis of the liver; it also stresses the heart and stomach, destroys brain cells, hastens calcium loss, decreases fertility and is a risk factor for many forms of cancer.

22. global disease burden; death; disability
23. cannot; fat; fiber
24. 40; 30; 30
25. cancer; colon
26. a BMI of 25 or higher; two of every three; a BMI of 30 or higher; heart disease; diabetes; stroke; arthritis
27. greater than; increases
28. overweight; underweight
29. slows; less
30. exercising; do; fat; weight; cognitive; brain

Regular aerobic exercise increases heart and lung capacity, lowers blood pressure, increases HDL in the blood, reduces the ratio of body fat to body weight, and enhances cognitive functioning. It also sometimes helps reduce depression and hostility.

31. longer; fewer
32. West; Midwest; South; Middle Atlantic; the quality of the environment and health care, as well as genetic, dietary, religious, socioeconomic, medical, and cultural patterns
33. mortality
34. morbidity; disease; acute; chronic
35. disability; vitality
36. vitality
37. quality-adjusted life years (QALYs)

38. African Americans; Asian Americans; Native Americans; Hispanic Americans; do

39. lower

One reason is that people who emigrate tend to be hardier. Another is health habits, which tend to be healthier in those less assimilated, particularly with regard to alcohol use, exercise, and diet. Recent immigrants also tend to be more optimistic, and have stronger family communication and support.

40. genes; culture; education; SES

41. 40s; three; do not explain; prejudice; poverty; adolescence

42. hypertension (high blood pressure); incidence; mortality; education; income; racism

43. twice; heart disease; 85

44. morbidity; disability; smoke; drink; overweight; emotions; medical symptoms

45. acute illnesses; chronic conditions; death; disability; men

46. 51; menopause; estrogen; progesterone; testosterone

47. climacteric; menstrual cycles; period; vasomotor instability

48. estrogen; calcium; osteoporosis; fat; coronary heart disease

49. social; cultural; medical

50. 10; 90; hormone replacement therapy

51. coronary artery; hip; Alzheimer's

Traditionally, the more children a couple had, the more fortunate they were considered to be. The impact of the loss of fertility was therefore much more significant. Today, the end of childbearing is determined less by age than by personal factors such as financial situation. Thus, as the time when sexual activity is no longer accompanied by fear of pregnancy, menopause is more often welcomed than regretted.

52. do not; sexually inactive

53. declines

54. longer; more

55. are; need not impair

PROGRESS TEST 1

Multiple-Choice Questions

1. d. is the answer. (p. 545)

b. & c. Weight gain varies substantially from person to person.

2. c. is the answer. (p. 546)

3. a. is the answer. (p. 547)

4. d. is the answer. (p. 548)

5. d. is the answer. (p. 548)

a. This is the technical name for nearsightedness.

b. & c. Although not discussed in the text, these are serious, but usually correctable, eye conditions.

6. d. is the answer. (p. 555)

7. b. is the answer. (p. 556)

a. This is the overall death rate.

c. This refers to a person's inability to perform activities that most others can.

d. This refers to how physically, intellectually, and socially healthy an individual feels.

8. d. is the answer. (p. 563)

9. b. is the answer. (p. 560)

c. & d. Genes and culture *are* intrinsic and extrinsic factors, respectively.

10. a. is the answer. (pp. 561–562)

11. c. is the answer. (pp. 561–562)

12. d. is the answer. (p. 557)

a. Vitality is a measure of how healthy and energetic a person feels.

b. Disability measures only the inability to perform basic activities.

c. Morbidity refers only to the rate of disease.

13. d. is the answer. (p. 566)

14. b. is the answer. (p. 551)

15. a. is the answer. (p. 564)

True or False Items

1. F   The death rate for African Americans is twice that of European Americans. (p. 558)

2. T (p. 545)

3. F   Approximately two of every three are overweight, and 2 percent of men and 1 percent of women are obese. (p. 553)

4. F   Moderate use of alcohol is associated with reduced risk of heart attacks. (p. 552)

5. T (p. 554)

6. F   Middle-aged adults are much more likely to improve their health habits than younger adults. (p. 550)

7. T (p. 566)

8. F   The climacteric refers to both the physiological and the psychological changes that accompany menopause. (p. 564)

9. T (p. 566)

10. T (p. 566)

PROGRESS TEST 2

Multiple-Choice Questions

1. **d.** is the answer. (p. 545)

a., b., & c. For the most part, the normal physical changes of middle adulthood have no significant health consequences.

2. **b.** is the answer. (p. 545)

3. **a.** is the answer. (p. 548)

c. & d. Although overall health is an important factor in all aspects of aging, the text does not compare the relative influences of overall health and heredity on visual acuity.

4. **c.** is the answer. (p. 549)

a. If anything, people exercise under their capacity.

b. In fact, the middle-aged often have better health habits.

5. **d.** is the answer. (p. 550)

6. **a.** is the answer. (p. 561)

b. & c. Although socioeconomic status is *negatively* correlated with morbidity rates, this is probably the result of other factors, such as limited access to health care.

d. Although this is true, the text does not suggest that this is the result of racial prejudice.

7. **d.** is the answer. (p. 556)

8. **a.** is the answer. (p. 566)

b. Most men continue to produce sperm throughout adulthood and are, therefore, theoretically fertile indefinitely.

c. This disorder was not discussed.

d. For men, there is no sudden drop in hormone levels during middle adulthood.

9. **d.** is the answer. (pp. 561–562)

10. **a.** is the answer. (p. 562)

11. **b.** is the answer. Recent immigrants, who are *less* assimilated, tend to have healthier lifestyles. (p. 559)

12. **a.** is the answer. Alcohol *increases* the blood's supply of HDL, which is one possible reason that adults who drink in moderation may live longer than "teetotalers." (p. 552)

13. **d.** is the answer. (pp. 552–553)

14. **d.** is the answer. (p. 567)

15. **a.** is the answer. In fact, HRT has been demon-strated to *reduce* the risk of Alzheimer's disease (p. 565)

Matching Items

1. f (p. 556)   **5.** g (p. 563)   **9.** e (p. 564)

2. a (p. 556)   **6.** i (p. 564)   **10.** j (p. 556)

3. h (p. 557)   **7.** b (p. 552)   **11.** k (p. 557)

4. c (p. 548)   **8.** d (p. 565)

THINKING CRITICALLY ABOUT CHAPTER 2(

1. **d.** is the answer. (p. 554)

a., b., & c. These forms of exercise will not pro-duce the beneficial effects of regular aerobic exer-cise.

2. **a.** is the answer. Although declines in th immune system begin in adolescence, they ar not evident until middle adulthood, when recov ery from all types of illness takes longer. (p. 549

3. **c.** is the answer. (p. 566)

4. **c.** is the answer. (p. 558)

5. **c.** is the answer. (p. 548)

a. & b. These are more common in early or la adulthood. Although middle-aged people d have trouble with blindness from oncomin headlights, they cope quite well with this prob lem.

6. **b.** is the answer. (p. 555)

7. **b.** is the answer. (p. 554)

a. As Val ages, her metabolism will slow dow so she should reduce her caloric intake.

c. & d. Just the opposite is true. She shoul decrease her intake of foods high in LDL an increase her intake of foods high in HDL.

8. **c.** is the answer. At that point in history, the mo children a couple had, the more fortunate the were considered to be. (p. 566)

9. **d.** is the answer. (p. 566)

a., b., & c. The text does not indicate that att tudes toward menopause vary with age, or th its experience varies from country to country.

10. **b.** is the answer. The incidence of glaucoma especially high among African American (p. 548)

a. Age-related changes in vision are particularl likely to become apparent after age *50*.

c. This probably would not help Rodney at all.

11. **d.** is the answer. People who are relatively we educated, financially secure, and live in or nea cities tend to receive all of these benefits. (p. 555)

2. a. is the answer. (p. 556)

b. This answer would be correct if the statement were "Mortality is to morbidity."

c. This answer would be correct if the statement were "Disability is to morbidity."

d. This answer would be correct if the statement were "Morbidity is to vitality."

3. d. is the answer. (p. 549)

c. & e. The immune system actually begins to decline during adolescence.

4. c. is the answer. (p. 553)

a. At least one longitudinal study found that death was as likely to occur among those who were 10 percent underweight as among those who were 30 percent overweight.

b. Animal research demonstrates just the opposite.

d. Metabolic rate influences the likelihood of being overweight, but does not counteract its health consequences.

5. c. is the answer. (p. 554)

a. & b. Although both of these behaviors promote health, only regular aerobic exercise produces *all* the health benefits that Andy is experiencing.

KEY TERMS

Glaucoma, an eye disease characterized by a hardening of the eyeball due to an increase of fluid within it, becomes increasingly common after age 40 and is the leading cause of blindness by age 70. (p. 548)

Autoimmune diseases are illnesses that occur when the immune system malfunctions, reacting to the person's own body cells as if they were foreign invaders. (p. 549)

3. Global disease burden is a measure that combines indicators of premature death with indicators of disability; it can be calculated for the entire world. (p. 552)

4. Mortality means death. As a measure of health, it usually refers to the number of deaths each year per thousand individuals. (p. 556)

5. Morbidity means disease. As a measure of health, it refers to the rate of diseases of all kinds, which can be sudden and severe (acute) or extend over a long time period (chronic). (p. 556)

6. Disability refers to a person's inability to perform activities that most others can. (p. 556)

7. Vitality refers to how healthy and energetic—physically, intellectually, and socially—an individual actually feels. (p. 557)

8. Quality-adjusted life years (QALYs) is the concept that indicates how many years of full vitality an individual loses due to a particular disease or disability. (p. 557)

9. At **menopause**, ovulation and menstruation stop and the production of the hormone estrogen drops. (p. 563)

10. The **climacteric** refers to all the various biological and psychological changes that accompany menopause. (p. 564)

11. Osteoporosis is a condition of porous and brittle bones leading to increased fractures and frailty in old age for which women who are thin, Caucasian, and postmenopausal are at increased risk. (p. 564)

12. Hormone replacement therapy (HRT) is intended to help relieve menopausal symptoms, especially in women who experience an abrupt drop in hormone level because their ovaries are surgically removed. (p. 565)

CHAPTER 21

Middle Adulthood: Cognitive Development

Chapter Overview

The way psychologists conceptualize intelligence has changed considerably in recent years. Chapter 21 begins by examining the contemporary view of intelligence, which emphasizes it's multidimensional nature. Most experts now believe that there are several distinct intelligences rather than a single general entity.

The chapter then examines the multidirectional nature of intelligence, noting that some abilities (such as short-term memory) decline with age, while others (such as vocabulary) generally increase. This section includes a discussion of the debate over whether cognitive abilities inevitably decline during adulthood, or may possibly remain stable or even increase.

The next section focuses on the fact that intelligence is characterized more by interindividual variation than by consistency from person to person. Each person's cognitive development occurs in a unique context influenced by variations in genes, life experiences, and cohort effects.

A final section discusses the cognitive expertise that often comes with experience, pointing out the ways in which expert thinking differs from that of the novice. Expert thinking is more specialized, flexible, and intuitive and is guided by more and better problem-solving strategies.

The chapter concludes with the message that during middle adulthood individual differences are much more critical in determining the course of cognitive development than is chronological age alone.

NOTE: Answer guidelines for all Chapter 21 questions begin on page 318.

Guided Study

The text chapter should be studied one section at a time. Before you read, preview each section by skimming it, noting headings and boldface items. Then read the appropriate section objectives from the following outline. Keep these objectives in mind and, as you read the chapter section, search for the information that will enable you to meet each objective. Once you have finished a section, write out answers for objectives.

Multidimensional Intelligence: Not One, But Man (pp. 571–578)

1. Distinguish between fluid and crystallized intelligence, and explain how each is affected by age.

2. Differentiate the three fundamental forms intelligence described by Robert Sternberg, and discuss how each tends to vary over the life span.

3. (Research Report) Explain the concept of selecti optimization with compensation.

4. Outline Howard Gardner's theory of intelligence, noting the impact of genes, culture, and aging on the various dimensions of intelligence.

Plastic Intellectual Change (pp. 584–588)

8. Discuss the plasticity of intelligence.

9. Describe how the cognitive processes of experts differ from those of novices.

Multidimensional Intelligence: Not Just increase or decrease (pp. 578–579, 580–581)

5. Discuss the multidirectionality of intelligence.

6. (A Life-Span View) Briefly trace the history of the controversy regarding adult intelligence, including the findings of cross-sectional and longitudinal research and how cross-sequential research compensates for their shortcomings.

Contextual Intelligence: Where You Are and Where You Were (pp. 579, 582–584)

7. (text and In Person) Explain how and why context and cohort affect intellectual development during adulthood.

Chapter Review

When you have finished reading the chapter, work through the material that follows to review it. Complete the sentences and answer the questions. As you proceed, evaluate your performance for each section by consulting the answers on page 318. Do not continue with the next section until you understand each answer. If you need to, review or reread the appropriate section in the textbook before continuing.

Multidimensional Intelligence: Not One, But Many? (pp. 571–578)

1. Historically, psychologists have thought of intelligence as _____ (a single entity/several distinct abilities).

2. A leading theoretician, _____ , argued that there is such a thing as general intelligence, which he called _____ .

3. In the 1960s, researchers _____ and _____ differentiated two aspects of intelligence, which they called _____ and _____ intelligence.

4. As its name implies, _____ intelligence is flexible reasoning used to draw inferences and understand relations between concepts. This type of intelligence is also made up of

basic mental abilities, including

_____ _____ ,

_____ _____ , and

_____ _____

_____ .

5. The accumulation of facts, information, and knowledge that comes with education and experience with a particular culture is referred to as _____ intelligence.

6. During adulthood, _____ intelligence declines markedly, along with related abilities such as _____ _____ and _____-_____ _____ . However, if a person's intelligence is simply measured by one _____ score, this decline is temporarily disguised by a(n) _____ (increase/decrease) in _____ intelligence.

7. Originally, psychologists thought that _____ intelligence was primarily genetic and that _____ intelligence was primarily learned. Today, most psychologists think that this distinction _____ (is/is not) valid.

8. Research reveals that _____ intelligence continues to expand throughout most of adulthood.

9. In the WAIS, total IQ is an average of two types of intelligence: _____ , which remains in the _____ range throughout adulthood, and _____ , which drops an average of _____ points during adulthood.

10. The theorist who has proposed that intelligence is composed of three fundamental aspects is _____ . The _____ aspect consists of mental processes fostering efficient learning, remembering, and thinking. This type of thinking is particularly valued at

_____

(what stage of life?).

11. The _____ aspect enables the person to be flexible and innovative when dealing with new situations. This type of thinking is always _____ rather than

_____ , meaning that such thinkers frequently find _____ solutions to problems rather than relying on the one that has always been considered correct. Different cultures value this type of thinking in some _____ more than others.

12. The _____ aspect concerns the ability to adapt to the contextual demands of a given situation. This type of thinking is particularly useful for managing the conflicting personalities in a _____ or _____ .

13. Most adults believe that practical intelligence _____ (increases/decreases/is stable) with age.

14. (Research Report) Researchers such as Paul Baltes have found that people devise alternative strategies to compensate for age-related declines in ability. He calls this _____

_____ _____

_____ .

15. The researcher who believes that there are eight distinct intelligences is _____ . Evidence from brain-damaged people _____ (supports/does not support) the multidimensional view of intelligence.

16. The value placed on different dimensions of intellectual ability _____ (varies/ does not vary) from culture to culture _____ (and/but not) from one stage of life to another.

Briefly explain why, according to the multidimensional view of intelligence, so few middle-aged adults do any regular exercise or engage in sports.

Multidirectional Intelligence: Not Just Increase Decrease (pp. 578–579, 580–581)

17. The multiple dimensions of intelligence can follow different trajectories with age; that is, they are _____ . Some, such as

_____-_____

_____ , generally fall steadily,

whereas others, such as _____ , generally rise. Other abilities, such as _____ _____ , might rise, fall, and rise again, depending on how much they are used in daily life.

8. (A Life-Span View) For most of the twentieth century, psychologists were convinced that intelligence peaks during _____ and then gradually declines.

9. (A Life-Span View) During the 1950s, Nancy Bayley and Melita Oden found that on several tests of concept mastery, the scores of gifted individuals _____ (increased/ decreased/remained unchanged) between ages 20 and 50.

0. (A Life-Span View) Follow-up research by Bayley demonstrated a general _____ (increase/ decrease) in intellectual functioning from childhood through young adulthood. This developmental trend was true for _____ (most/a few) of the subtests of the _____ _____ _____ _____ .

1. (A Life-Span View) Bayley's study is an example of a _____ (cross-sectional/longitudinal) research design. Earlier studies relied on _____ (cross-sectional/longitudinal) research designs.

A Life-Span View) Briefly explain why cross-sectional research can sometimes yield a misleading picture f adult development.

2. (A Life-Span View) Cite three reasons that longitudinal findings may be misleading.

a. _____

b. _____

c. _____

3. (A Life-Span View) One of the first researchers to recognize the problems of cross-sectional and lon-

gitudinal studies of intelligence was _____ .

24. (A Life-Span View) Schaie developed a new research technique combining cross-sectional and longitudinal approaches, called _____-_____ research. (A Life-Span View) Briefly explain this type of research design.

25. (A Life-Span View) Using this design, Schaie found that on five _____ _____ _____ , most people improved throughout most of adulthood. The results of this research are known collectively as the _____ _____ _____ .

26. (A Life-Span View) Schaie's research on adult changes in intelligence reveals an increase in cognitive abilities from age _____ until the late _____ , except for _____ _____ , which begins to shift slightly downward by age_ _____ .

Contextual Intelligence: Where You Are and Where You Were (pp. 579, 582–584)

27. Genetic makeup and each individual's unique experiences contribute to the _____ variation that is the basis for the variety of patterns of adult cognitive development. One source of variation that has been largely overlooked is variations in these experiences during _____ that are related to changes in _____ and _____ responsibilities. Other sources are variations in _____ level, _____ , _____ , _____ , and _____ status.

28. The importance of context in the multidirectional nature of intelligence highlights the specifics of each person's _____ .

29. Schaie's research on cohort differences in cognitive growth found that more recently born cohorts outperformed earlier cohorts on two abilities: _____ _____ and _____ _____ . This improvement in recent cohorts is also reflected in scores on _____ tests. Two likely explanations for this are years of _____ and teachers who encouraged students to think for themselves. Changes in _____ _____ are a likely explanation for the improved arithmetic scores of recent cohorts.

Plastic Intellectual Change (pp. 584–588)

30. Intellectual abilities are characterized by their _____ , which means that abilities can become enhanced or diminished, depending on how, when, and why a person uses them. This characteristic _____ (declines somewhat/does not decline) with increasing age. A critical factor in whether proficiency in a particular area can be improved is _____ .

31. Some developmentalists believe that as we age, we develop specialized competencies, or _____ , in activities that are important to us.

32. There are several differences between experts and novices. First, novices tend to rely more on _____ (formal/informal) procedures and rules to guide them, whereas experts rely more on their _____ _____ and the immediate _____ to guide them. This makes the actions of experts more _____ and less _____ .

33. Second, many elements of expert performance become _____ , almost instinctive, which enables experts to process information more quickly and efficiently.

34. A third difference is that experts have more and better _____ for accomplishing a particular task.

35. A final difference is that experts are more _____ .

36. In developing their abilities, experts point to the importance of _____ , usually at least _____ (how long?) before their full potential is achieved. This highlights the importance of _____ in the development of expertise.

37. Research studies indicate that expertise is quite _____ (general/specific), and that practice and specialization _____ (can/cannot) always overcome the effects of age.

38. A conclusion of this chapter is that in middle adulthood _____ _____ are more critical in determining the course of cognitive development than is age alone.

39. (Changing Policy) The fact that intelligence rises and falls with _____ and _____ means that age generally _____ (is/is not) the reason older workers are less able to do a job.

40. (Changing Policy) For the cohort that grew up during the _____ _____ retirement and leisure activities often were viewed with _____ (dread/eager anticipation).

41. (Changing Policy) A longitudinal study of 7,000 college seniors found that those who engaged in more extracurricular activities had grade point averages that were _____ (lower/as good as or better) than those of students who avoided all such activities.

Progress Test 1

Multiple-Choice Questions

Circle your answers to the following questions and check them with the answers on page 318. If your answer is incorrect, read the explanation for why it

correct and then consult the appropriate pages of
the text (in parentheses following the correct answer).

Multiple-Choice Questions

1. (A Life-Span View) Most of the evidence for an
age-related decline in intelligence came from:
   a. cross-sectional research.
   b. longitudinal research.
   c. cross-sequential research.
   d. random sampling.

2. (A Life-Span View) The major flaw in cross-sectional research is the virtual impossibility of:
   a. selecting subjects who are similar in every
aspect except age.
   b. tracking all subjects over a number of years.
   c. finding volunteers with high IQs.
   d. testing concept mastery.

3. (A Life-Span View) Because of the limitations of
other research methods, K. Warner Schaie developed a new research design based on:
   a. observer-participant methods.
   b. in-depth questionnaires.
   c. personal interviews.
   d. both cross-sectional and longitudinal
methods.

4. Why don't traditional intelligence tests reveal
age-related declines in processing speed and
short-term memory during adulthood?
   a. They measure only fluid intelligence.
   b. They measure only crystallized intelligence.
   c. They separate verbal and non-verbal IQ
scores, obscuring these declines.
   d. They yield a single IQ score, allowing adulthood increases in crystallized intelligence to
mask these declines.

5. Which of the following is most likely to *decrease*
with age?
   a. vocabulary
   b. accumulated facts
   c. speed of thinking
   d. practical intelligence

6. The basic mental abilities that go into learning
and understanding any subject have been classified as:
   a. crystallized intelligence.
   b. plastic intelligence.
   c. fluid intelligence.
   d. rote memory.

7. Some psychologists contend that intelligence consists of fluid intelligence, which _____ during
adulthood, and crystallized intelligence, which
_____ .
   a. remains stable; declines
   b. declines; remains stable
   c. increases; declines
   d. declines; increases

8. Charles Spearman argued for the existence of a
single general intelligence factor, which he
referred to as:
   a. *g*.
   b. practical intelligence.
   c. analytic intelligence.
   d. creative intelligence.

9. The plasticity of adult intellectual abilities refers
primarily to the effects of:
   a. fluid intelligence.
   b. experience.
   c. genetic inheritance.
   d. crystallized intelligence.

10. The shift from conscious, deliberate processing of
information to a more unconscious, effortless performance requires:
   a. automatic responding.
   b. subliminal execution.
   c. plasticity.
   d. encoding.

11. Concerning expertise, which of the following is
true?
   a. In performing tasks, experts tend to be more
set in their ways, preferring to use strategies
that have worked in the past.
   b. The reasoning of experts is usually more formal, disciplined, and stereotyped than that of
the novice.
   c. In performing tasks, experts tend to be more
flexible and to enjoy experimentation more
than novices do.
   d. Experts often have difficulty adjusting to situations that are exceptions to the rule.

12. Because each person is genetically unique and
has unique life experiences, _____ during middle adulthood is (are) more important in determining intellectual development than _____ .
   a. cohort differences; interindividual variation
   b. interindividual variation; cohort differences
   c. nature; nurture
   d. interindividual variation; age

13. (A Life-Span View) Which of the following describes the results of Nancy Bayley's follow-up study of members of the Berkeley Growth Study?

    a. Most subjects reached a plateau in intellectual functioning at age 21.

    b. The typical person at age 36 improved on two of ten subtests of the Wechsler Adult Intelligence Scale: Picture Completion and Arithmetic.

    c. The typical person at age 36 was still improving on the most important subtests of the intelligence scale.

    d. No conclusions could be reached because the sample of subjects was not representative.

14. Which of the following is *not* one of the general conclusions of research about intellectual changes during adulthood?

    a. In general, most intellectual abilities increase or remain stable throughout early and middle adulthood until the 60s.

    b. Cohort differences have a powerful influence on intellectual differences in adulthood.

    c. Intellectual functioning is affected by educational background.

    d. Intelligence becomes less specialized with increasing age.

15. The psychologist who has proposed that intelligence is composed of analytic, creative, and practical aspects is:

    a. Charles Spearman.   c. Robert Sternberg.
    b. Howard Gardner.   d. K. Warner Schaie.

True or False Items

Write T (*true*) or F (*false*) on the line in front of each statement.

_____ 1. Verbal IQ falls markedly over the course of adulthood.

_____ 2. A person's IQ is unaffected by years of schooling.

_____ 3. (A Life-Span View) To date, cross-sectional research has shown a gradual increase in intellectual ability.

_____ 4. (A Life-Span View) Longitudinal research usually shows that intelligence in most abilities increases throughout early and middle adulthood.

_____ 5. By age 60, most people decline in even the most basic cognitive abilities.

_____ 6. IQ scores have shown a steady upward drift over most of the twentieth century.

_____ 7. (A Life-Span View) All people reach intellectual peak in adolescence.

_____ 8. Historically, most psychologists ha considered intelligence to be compris of several distinct abilities.

_____ 9. Today, most researchers studying cc nitive abilities believe that intelligen is multidimensional.

_____ 10. Compared to novices, experts tend to more intuitive and less stereotyped their work performance.

Progress Test 2

Progress Test 2 should be completed during a fi chapter review. Answer the following questions af you thoroughly understand the correct answers the Chapter Review and Progress Test 1.

Multiple-Choice Questions

1. The debate over the status of adult intellige focuses on the question of its inevitable decli and on:

    a. pharmacological deterrents to that decline.

    b. the accompanying decline in moral reasonin

    c. its possible continuing growth.

    d. the validity of longitudinal versus person observation research.

2. Which of the following generational differen emerged in Schaie's studies of intelligence?

    a. Recent cohorts of young adults were better math than those who were young in previc decades.

    b. Recent cohorts of young adults were better reasoning ability, but worse at math, th those who were young in previous decades.

    c. Recent cohorts of young adults were better all intellectual abilities than those who w young in previous decades.

    d. Recent cohorts of young adults were worse all intellectual abilities than those who w young in previous decades.

3. The accumulation of facts that comes about w education and experience has been classified as

    a. crystallized intelligence.

    b. plastic intelligence.

    c. fluid intelligence.

    d. rote memory.

4. According to the text, the current view of intelligence recognizes all of the following characteristics *except*:

a. multidimensionality.
b. plasticity.
c. interindividual variation.
d. *g*.

5. Thinking that is more intuitive, flexible, specialized, and automatic is characteristic of:

a. fluid intelligence.
b. crystallized intelligence.
c. expertise.
d. plasticity.

6. The _____ nature of intelligence was attested to by Howard Gardner, who proposed the existence of eight different intelligences.

a. multidirectional   c. plastic
b. multidimensional   d. practical

7. The _____ nature of intelligence refers to the fact that each intellectual ability may rise, fall, or remain stable, according to its own unique developmental trajectory.

a. multidirectional   c. plastic
b. multidimensional   d. practical

8. At the present stage of research in adult cognition, which of the following statements has the most research support?

a. Intellectual abilities inevitably decline from adolescence onward.
b. Each person's cognitive development occurs in a unique context influenced by variations in genes, life experiences, and cohort effects.
c. Some 90 percent of adults tested in cross-sectional studies show no decline in intellectual abilities until age 40.
d. Intelligence becomes crystallized for most adults between ages 32 and 41.

9. Research on expertise indicates that during adulthood, intelligence:

a. increases in most primary mental abilities.
b. increases in specific areas of interest to the person.
c. increases only in those areas associated with the individual's career.
d. shows a uniform decline in all areas.

10. Research indicates that during adulthood declines occur in:

a. crystallized intelligence.
b. fluid intelligence.
c. both crystallized and fluid intelligence.
d. neither crystallized nor fluid intelligence.

11. Fluid intelligence is based on all of the following *except*:

a. short-term memory.   c. speed of thinking.
b. abstract thinking.   d. general knowledge.

12. In recent years, researchers are more likely than before to consider intelligence as:

a. a single entity.
b. primarily determined by heredity.
c. entirely the product of learning.
d. made up of several abilities.

13. (A Life-Span View) One of the drawbacks of longitudinal studies of intelligence is that:

a. they are especially prone to the distortion of cohort effects.
b. people who are retested may show improved performance as a result of practice.
c. the biases of the experimenter are more likely to distort the results than is true of other research methods.
d. all of the above are true.

14. To a developmentalist, an *expert* is a person who:

a. is extraordinarily gifted at a particular task.
b. is significantly better at a task than people who have not put time and effort into performing that task.
c. scores at the ninetieth percentile or better on a test of achievement.
d. is none of the above.

15. One reason for the variety in patterns in adult intelligence is that during adulthood:

a. intelligence is fairly stable in some areas.
b. intelligence increases in some areas.
c. intelligence decreases in some areas.
d. people develop specialized competencies in activities that are personally meaningful.

Matching Items

Match each definition or description with its corresponding term.

Terms

_____ **1.** fluid intelligence
_____ **2.** crystallized intelligence
_____ **3.** multidimensional
_____ **4.** multidirectional
_____ **5.** interindividual variation
_____ **6.** plasticity
_____ **7.** practical intelligence
_____ **8.** expertise

Definitions or Descriptions

a. intellectual skills used in everyday problem sol-
   ing
b. individual differences caused by heredity ar
   experience
c. intelligence is made up of several different abi
   ties
d. specialized competence
e. flexible reasoning used to draw inferences
f. intellectual flexibility
g. cognitive abilities can follow different trajectori
   with age
h. the accumulation of facts, information, ar
   knowledge

Thinking Critically About Chapter 21

Answer these questions the day before an exam as a final check on your understanding of the chapter's terms and concepts.

1. In identifying the multiple aspects of intelligence, Gardner explains that:
   a. intelligence appears in three fundamental forms.
   b. a general intelligence can be inferred from these various abilities.
   c. each intelligence has its own neurological network in a particular section of the brain.
   d. fluid intelligence declines with age, while crystallized intelligence increases.

2. In Sternberg's theory, which aspect of intelligence is most similar to the abilities comprising fluid intelligence?
   a. analytic
   b. creative
   c. practical
   d. None of the above is part of Sternberg's theory.

3. Concerning the acquisition of fluid and crystallized intelligence, most experts agree that:
   a. both fluid and crystallized intelligence are primarily determined by heredity.
   b. both fluid and crystallized intelligence are primarily acquired through learning.
   c. fluid intelligence is primarily genetic, whereas crystallized intelligence is primarily learned.
   d. the nature-nurture distinction is invalid.

4. Regarding the multidirectionality of intelligenc which of the following statements has the mc empirical support?
   a. Most intellectual abilities remain stable wi age.
   b. Most intellectual abilities decline with age.
   c. Each intellectual ability may increase, c crease, or remain stable with age.
   d. There is a single mental capacity underlyir all intellectual skills, and this capacity m rise or fall with age.

5. Compared to novice chess players, chess exper most likely:
   a. have superior long-term memory.
   b. have superior short-term memory.
   c. are very disciplined in their play, stickir closely to formal rules for responding to ce tain moves their opponents might make.
   d. are quite flexible in their play, relying on the years of practice and accumulated experienc

6. A psychologist has found that the mathematic ability of adults born in the 1920s is significant different from that of those born in the 1950s. Sł suspects that this difference is a reflection of tł different educational emphases of the two histo cal periods. This is an example of:
   a. longitudinal research. **c.** a cohort effect.
   b. sequential research.   **d.** all of the above.

7. Sharetta knows more about her field of specialization now at age 45 than she did at age 35. This increase is most likely due to:
   a. an increase in crystallized intelligence.
   b. an increase in fluid intelligence.
   c. increases in both fluid and crystallized intelligence.
   d. a cohort difference.

8. (A Life-Span View) A contemporary developmental psychologist is most likely to *disagree* with the statement that:
   a. many people show increases in intelligence during middle adulthood.
   b. for many behaviors, the responses of older adults are slower than those of younger adults.
   c. intelligence peaks during adolescence and declines thereafter.
   d. intelligence is multidimensional and multidirectional.

9. (A Life-Span View) Regarding their accuracy in measuring adult intellectual decline, cross-sectional research is to longitudinal research as _____ is to _____ .
   a. underestimate; overestimate
   b. overestimate; underestimate
   c. accurate; inaccurate
   d. inaccurate; accurate

10. (A Life-Span View) Dr. Hatfield wants to analyze the possible effects of retesting, cohort differences, and aging on adult changes in intelligence. Which research method should she use?
   a. cross-sectional   c. cross-sequential
   b. longitudinal   d. case study

11. Joseph has remained associated with interesting and creative people throughout his life. In contrast, James has become increasingly isolated as he has aged. Given these lifestyle differences, which aspect of intelligence will be most affected in Joseph and James?
   a. fluid intelligence
   b. crystallized intelligence
   c. overall IQ
   d. It is impossible to predict how their intelligence will be affected.

12. When Merle retired from teaching, he had great difficulty adjusting to the changes in his lifestyle. Robert Sternberg would probably say that Merle was somewhat lacking in which aspect of his intelligence?
   a. analytic   c. practical
   b. creative   d. plasticity

13. Following her presentation on "Contemporary Thinking About Adult Intelligence," Sonia is asked to summarize the current state of the debate over the course of intelligence throughout adulthood. Her response is:
   a. "Intelligence increases throughout most of adulthood."
   b. "Following its peak in adolescence, intelligence declines throughout adulthood."
   c. "The recognition of adult cognition as multidimensional, multidirectional, variable, and plastic has defused this debate."
   d. "The issue remains controversial; some researchers maintain that intelligence increases during adulthood, while others contend that it decreases."

14. Compared to her 20-year-old daughter, 40-year-old Lynda is likely to perform better on measures of what type of intelligence?
   a. fluid
   b. practical
   c. analytic
   d. none of the above

15. Most developmentalists would agree with which of the following statements?
   a. Faster thinking is deeper thinking.
   b. Slower thinking is deeper thinking.
   c. Speed of thinking is a critical element of fluid intelligence.
   d. Speed of thinking is a critical element of crystallized intelligence.

Key Terms

Using your own words, write a brief definition or explanation of each of the following terms on a separate piece of paper.

1. general intelligence (*g*)
2. fluid intelligence
3. crystallized intelligence
4. practical intelligence
5. plasticity
6. expertise
7. expert

ANSWERS

CHAPTER REVIEW

1. a single entity
2. Charles Spearman; *g*
3. Cattell; Horn; fluid; crystallized
4. fluid; inductive reasoning; abstract thinking; speed of thinking
5. crystallized
6. fluid; processing speed; short-term memory; IQ; increase; crystallized
7. fluid; crystallized; is not
8. crystallized
9. verbal; average; performance; 25
10. Robert Sternberg; analytic; the beginning of adulthood
11. creative; divergent; convergent; unusual; domains
12. practical; family; organization
13. increases
14. selective optimization with compensation
15. Howard Gardner; supports
16. varies; and

Kinesthetic ability is much less valued by middle-aged adults than by those who are younger. For this reason, older adults in cultures that emphasize competitive, strength-based sports for the young are less likely to value (or practice) any kinesthetic skills than their counterparts in cultures that value activities older adults can do.

17. multidirectional; short-term memory; vocabulary; mathematical reasoning
18. adolescence
19. increased
20. increase; most; Wechsler Adult Intelligence Scale
21. longitudinal; cross-sectional

Cross-sectional research may be misleading not only because it is impossible to select adults who are similar to each other in every important aspect except age, but also because each age group has its own unique history of life experiences.

22. **a.** People who are retested several times may improve their performance simply as a result of practice.
    b. because people may drop out of lengthy longitudinal studies, the remaining subjects may be a self-selected sample.
    c. Longitudinal research takes a long time.
23. Schaie
24. cross-sequential

In this approach, each time the original group of subjects is retested a new group is added and tested at each age interval.

25. primary mental abilities; Seattle Longitudinal Study
26. 20; 50s; number ability; 40
27. interindividual; adulthood; family; career; education; income, health, personality; marital
28. cohort
29. verbal memory; inductive reasoning; IQ; education; teaching strategy
30. plasticity; declines somewhat; education
31. expertise
32. formal; accumulated experience; context; intuitive; stereotyped
33. automatic
34. strategies
35. flexible (or creative)
36. practice; 10 years; motivation
37. specific; cannot
38. individual differences
39. training; experience; is not
40. Great Depression; dread
41. as good as or better

PROGRESS TEST 1

Multiple-Choice Questions

1. **a.** is the answer. (p. 580)
   b. Although results from this type of research may also be misleading, longitudinal studies often demonstrate age-related *increases* in intelligence.

c. Cross-sequential research is the technique devised by K. Warner Schaie that combines the strengths of the cross-sectional and longitudinal methods.

d. Random sampling refers to the selection of subjects for a research study.

a. is the answer. (p. 580)

b. This is a problem in longitudinal research.

c. & d. Neither of these is particularly troublesome in cross-sectional research.

d. is the answer. (p. 581)

a., b., & c. Cross-sequential research as described in this chapter is based on *objective* intelligence testing.

d. is the answer. (p. 573)

a. & b. Traditional IQ tests measure both fluid and crystallized intelligence.

c. is the answer. (p. 573)

a., b., & d. These often increase with age.

c. is the answer. (p. 572)

a. Crystallized intelligence is the accumulation of facts and knowledge that comes with education and experience.

b. Although intelligence is characterized by plasticity, "plastic intelligence" is not discussed as a specific type of intelligence.

d. Rote memory is memory that is based on the conscious repetition of to-be-remembered information.

d. is the answer. (p. 573)

a. is the answer. (p. 571)

b. Practical intelligence refers to the intellectual skills used in everyday problem solving.

c. & d. These are two aspects of intelligence identified in Robert Sternberg's theory.

b. is the answer. Life experiences give intelligence its flexibility and account for the variety of patterns of adult cognitive development. (p. 584)

a. is the answer. (p. 586)

b. This was not discussed in the chapter.

c. Plasticity refers to the flexible nature of intelligence.

d. Encoding refers to the placing of information into memory.

c. is the answer. (p. 586)

a., b., & d. These are more typical of *novices* than experts.

d. is the answer. (p. 579)

a. & b. Cohort differences are a source of interindividual variation.

c. The text does not discuss the relative impact of nature and nurture on intelligence during adulthood.

13. **c.** is the answer. (p. 580)

b. In fact, these were the only two subtests on which performance did *not* improve.

d. No such criticism was made of Bayley's study.

14. **d.** is the answer. In fact, intelligence often becomes *more specialized* with age. (p. 587)

15. **c.** is the answer. (p. 574)

a. Charles Spearman proposed the existence of an underlying general intelligence, which he called *g*.

b. Howard Gardner proposed that intelligence consists of eight autonomous abilities.

d. K. Warner Schaie was one of the first researchers to recognize the potentially distorting cohort effects on cross-sectional research.

True or False Items

1. F   Verbal IQ declines minimally from the early 20s to the early 70s. (p. 574)

2. F   Intellectual functioning as measured by IQ tests is powerfully influenced by years of schooling. (p. 583)

3. F   Cross-sectional research shows a decline in intellectual ability. (p. 580)

4. T (p. 580)

5. F   Many adults show intellectual improvement over most of adulthood, with no decline, even by age 60. (p. 579)

6. T (p. 583)

7. F   There is agreement that intelligence does *not* peak in adolescence and decline thereafter. (p. 580)

8. F   Historically, psychologists have conceived of intelligence as a single entity. (p. 571)

9. T (pp. 571–572)

10. T (p. 586)

PROGRESS TEST 2

Multiple-Choice Questions

1. **c.** is the answer. (p. 579)

2. **b.** is the answer. (pp. 583–584)

3. **a.** is the answer. (p. 572)

b. Although intelligence is characterized by plasticity, "plastic intelligence" is not discussed as a specific type of intelligence.

c. Fluid intelligence consists of the basic abilities that go into the understanding of any subject.

d. Rote memory is based on the conscious repetition of to-be-remembered information.

4. d. is the answer. This is Charles Spearman's term for his idea of a general intelligence, in which intelligence is a single entity. (p. 571)

5. c. is the answer. (pp. 585–586)

6. b. is the answer. (p. 578)

7. a. is the answer. (pp. 578–579)

b. This refers to the fact that intelligence consists of multiple abilities.

c. This characteristic suggests that intelligence can be molded in many ways.

d. Practical intelligence refers to the skills used in everyday problem solving.

8. b. is the answer. (p. 579, 583)

a. There is agreement that intelligence does *not* peak during adolescence.

c. Cross-sectional research usually provides evidence of *declining* ability throughout adulthood.

d. Crystallized intelligence refers to the accumulation of knowledge with experience; intelligence does not "crystallize" at any specific age.

9. b. is the answer. (p. 587)

10. b. is the answer. (p. 573)

a., c., & d. Crystallized intelligence typically *increases* during adulthood.

11. d. is the answer. This is an aspect of crystallized intelligence. (p. 572)

12. d. is the answer. (pp. 571–572)

a. Contemporary researchers emphasize the multidimensional nature of intelligence.

b. & c. Contemporary researchers see intelligence as the product of both heredity and learning.

13. b. is the answer. (p. 580)

a. This is a drawback of cross-sectional research.

c. Longitudinal studies are no more sensitive to experimenter bias than other research methods.

14. b. is the answer. (p. 585)

15. d. is the answer. (p. 584)

Matching Items

1. e (p. 572)
2. h (p. 572)
3. c (pp. 571–572)
4. g (p. 578)
5. b (p. 579)
6. f (p. 584)
7. a (p. 575)
8. d (p. 584)

THINKING CRITICALLY ABOUT CHAPTER 2

1. c. is the answer. (p. 578)

a. This is Sternberg's theory.

b. This refers to Spearman's view of a *g* factor.

d. While this is true, it is not part of Gardne theory.

2. a. is the answer. This aspect consists of men processes fostering efficient learning, rememb ing, and thinking. (p. 574)

b. This aspect enables the person to accommoda successfully to changes in the environment.

c. This aspect concerns the extent to which int lectual functions are applied to situations that familiar or novel in a person's history.

3. d. is the answer. This is so in part because t acquisition of crystallized intelligence is affect by the quality of fluid intelligence. (p. 573)

4. c. is the answer. (pp. 578–579)

5. d. is the answer. (p. 586)

b. & d. The text does not suggest that expe have special memory abilities.

c. This describes the performance of novice rath than experts.

6. c. is the answer. (p. 583)

a. & b. From the information given, it is impos ble to determine which research method the ps chologist used.

7. a. is the answer. (p. 572)

b. & c. According to the research, fluid inte gence declines markedly during adulthood.

d. Cohort effects refer to generational differen in life experiences.

8. c. is the answer. (p. 580)

9. b. is the answer. (p. 580)

c. & d. Both cross-sectional and longitudi research are potentially misleading.

10. c. is the answer. (p. 581)

a. & b. Schaie developed the cross-sequen research method to overcome the drawbacks the cross-sectional and longitudinal metho which were susceptible to cohort and retesti effects, respectively.

d. A case study focuses on a single subject a therefore could provide no information on coh effects.

11. b. is the answer. Because the maintenance of cr tallized intelligence depends partly on how it used, the consequences of remaining socia involved or of being socially isolated beco increasingly apparent in adulthood. (p. 574)

2. b. is the answer. Creative intelligence enables the person to accommodate successfully to changes in the environment, such as those accompanying retirement. (pp. 573–574)

a. This aspect of intelligence consists of mental processes that foster efficient learning, remembering, and thinking.

c. This aspect of intelligence concerns the extent to which intellectual functions are applied to situations that are familiar or novel in a person's history.

d. Plasticity refers to the flexible nature of intelligence; it is not an aspect of Sternberg's theory.

3. c. is the answer. (p. 571)

4. b. is the answer. (p. 575)

5. c. is the answer. (p. 572)

KEY TERMS

1. General intelligence (*g*) is the idea that intelligence is one basic trait, underlying all cognitive abilities, according to Spearman. (p. 571)

2. Fluid intelligence is made up of those basic mental abilities—inductive reasoning, abstract think-

ing, speed of processing, and the like—required for understanding any subject matter. (p. 572)

3. Crystallized intelligence is the accumulation of facts, information, and knowledge that comes with education and experience within a particular culture. (p. 573)

4. A new approach to adult intelligence—the study of **practical intelligence**—focuses on the intellectual skills used in everyday problem solving. (p. 575)

5. Intelligence is characterized by **plasticity**, meaning that abilities can become enhanced or diminished, depending on how, when, and why a person uses them. (p. 584)

6. A hallmark of adulthood is the development of **expertise**, or specialized competencies, in activities that are personally meaningful to us. (p. 584)

7. According to developmentalists, an **expert** is someone who is notably more skilled and knowledgeable about a specific intellectual topic or practical ability than the average person is. (p. 585)

CHAPTER 22

Middle Adulthood: Psychosocial Development

Chapter Overview

Chapter 22 is concerned with midlife, commonly believed to be a time of crisis and transition, when self-doubt, reevaluation of career goals, changes in family responsibilities, and a growing awareness of one's mortality lead to turmoil. The chapter first examines the changes that occur at midlife, showing that although middle adulthood may have its share of pressures and stress, a crisis is not inevitable.

The next section examines the question of whether there is stability of personality throughout adulthood, identifying five basic clusters of personality traits that remain fairly stable throughout adulthood. One personality trend that does occur during middle age, as gender roles become less rigid, is the tendency of both sexes to take on characteristics typically reserved for the opposite sex.

The third section depicts the changing dynamics between middle-aged adults and their adult children and aging parents, showing why the various demands of the younger and older generations have led the middle-aged to be called the "sandwich generation." Changes in the marital relationship are also examined.

The final section of the chapter examines the evolution of work in the individual's life during middle adulthood. As many women and men begin to balance their work lives with parenthood and other concerns, many engage in a scaling back of their effort in the workplace.

NOTE: Answer guidelines for all Chapter 22 questions begin on page 334.

Guided Study

The text chapter should be studied one section at a time. Before you read, preview each section by skimming it, noting headings and boldface items. Then read the appropriate section objectives from the following outline. Keep these objectives in mind and, as you read the chapter section, search for the information that will enable you to meet each objective. Once you have finished a section, write out answers for i objectives.

Changes During Middle Age (pp. 591–592, 593)

1. Discuss the changes that normally occur durir middle age, including whether midlife inevitably a time of crisis.

2. (A Life-Span View) Explain why middle-age adults are considered the "sandwich generation.

Personality Throughout Adulthood (pp. 592, 594–59

3. Describe the Big Five clusters of personality trai and discuss reasons for their relative stabili during adulthood.

4. (text and In Person) Explain the concept of an ecological niche, noting how it interacts with personality.

5. Explain the tendency toward gender role convergence during middle age.

Family Dynamics in Middle Adulthood (pp. 598–606)

6. Characterize the relationship between middle-aged adults and the older and younger generations.

7. Differentiate three patterns of grandparent–grandchild relationships, and discuss historical trends in their prevalence.

8. (Research Report) Discuss the reasons for and value of grandparents becoming surrogate parents.

9. Discuss how and why marital relationships tend to change during middle adulthood.

10. (text and Changing Policy) Discuss the impact of divorce and remarriage during middle adulthood, including reasons for the high divorce rate among the remarried, and describe the dilemma faced by middle-aged women in the "marriage market."

Work (pp. 606–609)

11. Describe how the balance among work, family, and self often shifts during middle adulthood.

Chapter Review

When you have finished reading the chapter, work through the material that follows to review it. Complete the sentences and answer the questions. As you proceed, evaluate your performance for each section by consulting the answers on page 334. Do not continue with the next section until you understand each answer. If you need to, review or reread the appropriate section in the textbook before continuing.

Changes During Middle Age (pp. 591–592, 593)

1. At about age _____ , people reach a point called _____ , which ushers in _____ _____ , which lasts until about age _____ .

2. Midlife is popularly thought of as a period of
_____ .

List several sources of upheaval that may make middle age a troubling time.

3. At this time, some adults reassess the balance between _____ and
_____ .

4. In recent years, the demands placed on middle-aged adults by the younger and older generations have _____ (increased/ decreased), so that this group is referred to as the
_____ _____ .

5. (A Life-Span View) Approximately
_____ (what proportion?) of middle-aged adults who have grown children find at least one of them still living with them. This is especially likely when the parents are in
_____ _____ and when the children are _____
_____ .

6. (A Life-Span View) Middle-aged _____
(men/women) are especially likely to be called on to provide elder care. Those who are particularly likely to feel unfairly burdened with elder care are _____-_____-
_____ . An added stress occurs when the adult children who are living with their parents have _____
_____ .

7. (A Life-Span View) Although having many
_____ to fill might make some middle-aged adults feel_____ , it may also increase their _____
_____ .

8. (A Life-Span View) Although it has long been assumed that middle-aged women were
_____ , research has revealed that this is less likely to be the case if the roles are
_____ to the woman, her
_____ are satisfying, and if the
_____ requirements are not overwhelming.

9. (A Life-Span View) State three reasons why overwhelming demands are unusual in middle age.

a. _____

b. _____

c. _____

10. The notion of a midlife crisis _____
(is/is not) accepted by most developmentalists as an inevitable event during middle age.

11. How people react to middle age has more to do with their overall _____
_____ than it has to do with calendar milestones.

Personality Throughout Adulthood (pp. 592, 594–597)

12. The major source of developmental continuity during adulthood is the stability of
_____ .

13. List and briefly describe the Big Five personality factors.

a. _____
_____

b. _____
_____

c. _____
_____

d. _____
_____

e. _____
_____

14. Whether a person ranks high or low in each of the Big Five is determined by the interacting influences of _____ , _____
early _____-_____ ,
and the experiences and choices made at a younger age. By age _____ , the Big Five usually become quite stable. This stability results not only from _____ but also from the fact that by this age most people have settled into an _____
_____ .

15. (In Person) By age _____ , those high in _____ have likely found mates who share their _____ .

Adults who are high in _____ are likely to choose a vocation that draws on their general _____ .

[r]aw several other comparisons of the ecological [ni]ches carved out by adults who are high in extrover[si]on, and those who are high in neuroticism.

Certain traits such as _____ toward others and _____ about oneself show marked individual patterns.

Most adults settle into a niche that reinforces their basic _____ .

The cumulative experiences of living a life often lead to _____-_____ and greater _____ with age.

In many cultures, gender roles _____ (loosen/become more rigid) during middle age. Some researchers even believe that there is a _____ _____ of personality traits, as women become more _____ , while men become more able to openly express _____ or _____ .

One reason for gender-role shifts during middle age is that reduced levels of _____ _____ may free men and women to express previously suppressed traits.

The psychoanalyst who believed that everyone has both a masculine and feminine side is _____ . According to this theory, middle-aged adults begin to explore the _____ _____ of their personality.

Longitudinal research suggests a _____ explanation for gender convergence in personality. The current cohort of middle-aged adults is _____ (more/less) marked in their convergence of sex roles because sex roles today are _____ (more/less) sharply defined than in the past.

Family Dynamics in Middle Adulthood (pp. 598–606)

23. Being the "generation in the middle," middle-aged adults are the _____ _____ of their families. This role is sometimes ignored because_____ is often confused with _____ , the latter defined as _____ _____ .

24. American families today are _____ (more/less) likely to consist of several generations living under the same roof.

25. Because of their role in maintaining the links between the generations, middle-aged adults become the _____ . This role tends to be filled most often by _____ (women/men).

26. The relationship between most middle-aged adults and their parents tends to _____ (improve/worsen) with time. One reason is that, as adult children mature, they develop a more _____ view of the relationship as a whole.

Briefly explain why this is especially true *today*.

27. Three generations of a family living under one roof is more common among _____ and_____ Americans.

28. Whether or not middle-aged adults and their parents live together depends mostly on _____ , which is the belief that _____ .

29. Most middle-aged adults _____ (maintain/do not maintain) close relationships with their children.

30. Two out of every three Americans become a _____ during middle adulthood. Most react quite _____ (positively/negatively) to the occurrence of this event.

31. Grandparent–grandchild relationships take one of three forms: _____ , _____ , or _____ . A century ago, most American grandparents adopted a _____ role. The _____ pattern, which was prevalent among grandparents for most of the twentieth century, is rare today among those who

_____ .

32. Most contemporary grandparents seek the _____ role as they strive for the love and respect of their grandchildren while maintaining their own _____ .

33. Some of the diversity in grandparent–grandchild relationships today results from differences in _____ , _____ traditions, and_____

_____ . Another factor is the _____ _____ of the three generations.

34. The grandparent–grandchild bond tends to be closer if the grandchild is relatively _____ , if the parent is the

_____ ,

and if the grandparent is

_____ .

35. The trend toward relatively uninvolved grandparenting in middle age is particularly unfortunate in_____ and _____ groups, in which grandparents traditionally transmit the _____ ,

_____ , _____ , and _____ of the community.

36. (Research Report) Grandparents who take over the work of raising their children's children are referred to as _____

_____ . This role is more common when parents are _____

_____ .

37. (Research Report) Grandparents are most likely to provide surrogate care for children who need _____ _____ , such as infants who are _____-

_____ or _____ . If the

relationship is the result of a legal decision that the parents were _____ or _____ , it becomes

_____ _____ .

38. (Research Report) More than one in _____ (how many?) grandparents witnesses the divorce of their adult child. As a result, the parents of the _____ ex-spouse are often shut out of their grandchildren's lives.

39. For the majority of middle-aged adults, their most intimate relationship is with their _____ . For a growing minority, however, intimacy is achieved through _____ with a partner.

40. Throughout adulthood, the family relationship most closely linked to personal happiness, health and companionship is _____ .

41 After the first decade or so, marital happiness tends to gradually _____ (increase/decrease).

List several possible reasons for this finding.

42. Divorce in middle adulthood is typically _____ (more/less) difficult than divorce in early adulthood.

43. Most divorced people remarry, on average, within _____ years of being divorced.

State several of the benefits that remarriage m bring to middle-aged adults.

44. Compared with people in first marriages, remarried people are _____ (more/less) likely to describe their marriage as either very happy or quite unhappy.

tate two possible explanations for the divorce rate mong remarried couples.

5. (Changing Policy) Middle-aged _____ (women/men) are disadvantaged when it comes to finding a marriage partner for three reasons:

a. _____

b. _____

c. _____

/ork (pp. 606–609)

5. Job security usually _____ (increases/decreases) during middle adulthood. During middle adulthood, the percentage of adults who work _____ (varies/does not significantly vary) by gender and _____ (varies/does not significantly vary) with whether the individual has children.

7. During middle adulthood there is often a shift in the balance among _____ , _____ , and _____ .

8. During _____ adulthood, the combined demands of the workplace and the individual's own aspirations for promotion often create _____ .

9. During the _____ stage of marriage, women and men with children often engage in a _____ _____ of their employment effort in order to combine work and _____ .

iefly describe three different scaling-back strategies.

1. Some middle-aged workers assume the position of a _____ as they help an inexperienced worker "learn the ropes."

Progress Test 1

Multiple-Choice Questions

Circle your answers to the following questions and check them with the answers on page 335. If your answer is incorrect, read the explanation for why it is incorrect and then consult the appropriate pages of the text (in parentheses following the correct answer).

1. The most important factor in how a person adjusts to middle age is his or her:
   a. gender.
   b. developmental history.
   c. age.
   d. race.

2. The Big Five personality factors are:
   a. emotional stability, openness, introversion, sociability, locus of control.
   b. neuroticism, extroversion, openness, emotional stability, sensitivity.
   c. extroversion, agreeableness, conscientiousness, neuroticism, openness.
   d. neuroticism, gregariousness, extroversion, impulsiveness, openness.

3. Concerning the prevalence of midlife crises, which of the following statements has the *greatest* empirical support?
   a. Virtually all men, and most women, experience a midlife crisis.
   b. Virtually all men, and about 50 percent of women, experience a midlife crisis.
   c. Women are more likely to experience a midlife crisis than are men.
   d. Few contemporary developmentalists believe that the midlife crisis is a common experience.

4. Middle-age shifts in personality often reflect:
   a. the particular traits that are valued within the culture at that time.
   b. rebellion against earlier life choices.
   c. the tightening of gender roles.
   d. all of the above.

5. During middle age, gender roles tend to:
   a. become more distinct.
   b. reflect patterns established during early adulthood.
   c. converge.
   d. be unpredictable.

6. Middle-aged adults who are pressed on one side by adult children and on the other by aging parents are:
   a. said to be in the sandwich generation.
   b. especially likely to suffer burnout.
   c. especially likely to suffer alienation.
   d. all of the above.

7. Which of the following statements *best* describes the relationship of most middle-aged adults to their aging parents?
   a. The relationship tends to improve with time.
   b. During middle adulthood, the relationship tends to deteriorate.
   c. For women, but not men, the relationship tends to improve with time.
   d. The relationship usually remains as good or as bad as it was in the past.

8. In families, middle-aged adults tend to function as the _____ , celebrating family achievements, keeping the family together, and staying in touch with distant relatives.
   a. sandwich generation
   b. nuclear bond
   c. intergenerational gatekeepers
   d. kinkeepers

9. Which of the following is *not* one of the basic forms of grandparent–grandchild relationships?
   a. autonomous   c. companionate
   b. involved   d. remote

10. During middle adulthood, *scaling back* refers to the tendency of both men and women to:
    a. limit their involvement in activities that take away from their careers.
    b. deliberately put less than full effort into their work.
    c. pull away from their spouses as they reevaluate their life's accomplishments.
    d. explore the "shadow sides" of their personalities.

11. Most grandparents today strive to establish a(n) _____ relationship with their grandchildren.
    a. autonomous   c. companionate
    b. involved   d. remote

12. Concerning the degree of stability of personality traits, which of the following statements has the greatest research support?
    a. There is little evidence that personality traits remain stable during adulthood.

b. In women, but less so in men, there is notab continuity in many personality characteristic

c. In men, but less so in women, there is notab continuity in many personality characteristic

d. In both men and women, there is notable con tinuity in many personality characteristics.

13. People who exhibit the personality dimension _____ tend to be outgoing, active, an assertive.
    a. extroversion   c. conscientiousness
    b. agreeableness   d. neuroticism

14. According to Jung's theory of personality:
    a. as men and women get older, gender roli become more distinct.
    b. to some extent, everyone has both a masculin and a feminine side to his or her character.
    c. the recent blurring of gender roles is makir adjustment to midlife more difficult for bo men and women.
    d. gender roles are most distinct during chile hood.

15. Which of the following personality traits was *n* identified in the text as tending to remain stabi throughout adulthood?
    a. neuroticism   c. openness
    b. introversion   d. conscientiousness

True or False Items

Write T (*true*) or F (*false*) on the line in front of ea statement.

_____ 1. At least 75 percent of American m experience a significant midlife cris between ages 38 and 43.

_____ 2. Better than age as a predictor whether a midlife crisis will occur is a individual's developmental history.

_____ 3. By age 30, an individual's basic perso ality traits become stable.

_____ 4. The current cohort of middle-age adults is notable for the marked conve gence of their sex roles.

_____ 5. The extended family is typical of mo ern societies, such as those in Nor America today.

_____ 6. Today's parents are less likely to mai tain close relationships with their adu children.

_____ 7. After the first 10 years, marital happ ness is more likely to increase than decrease.

_____ 8. Remarried people generally report more extreme levels of happiness or unhappiness than people in first marriages.

_____ 9. As adults mature, personality tends to improve.

_____ 10. There is no evidence that the stability of personality traits is influenced by heredity.

Progress Test 2

Progress Test 2 should be completed during a final chapter review. Answer the following questions after you thoroughly understand the correct answers for the Chapter Review and Progress Test 1.

Multiple-Choice Questions

1. Society recognizes *midlife* as occurring at about age _____ and *middle age* as lasting until about age _____ .
   a. 45; 60
   b. 40; 60
   c. 45; 65
   d. 40; 65

2. By what age have most people settled into a particular ecological niche?
   a. 20
   b. 25
   c. 30
   d. 40

3. Which of the following factors play a role in whether grandparents will become surrogate parents?
   a. Both parents are full-time college students.
   b. The child is a rebellious school-age boy.
   c. One parent is busy establishing a career and the other does not want to assume the burden of raising a child.
   d. The parents are too old to care for a child.

4. (text and In Person) Which of the following is true regarding the ecological niche of a middle-aged adult?
   a. It is determined by the person's characteristic traits.
   b. It depends almost entirely on the person's life experiences.
   c. It is shaped by and might interact with his or her personality traits.
   d. It limits the extent to which the person can change during adulthood.

5. Whether a person ranks high or low in each of the Big Five personality factors is determined by:
   a. heredity.
   b. temperament.
   c. his or her lifestyle.
   d. the interaction of genes, culture, and early experiences.

6. Regarding the strength of the contemporary family bond, most developmentalists believe that:
   a. family links are considerably weaker in the typical contemporary American family than in earlier decades.
   b. family links are considerably weaker in the typical contemporary American family than in other cultures.
   c. both a. and b. are true.
   d. despite the fact that extended families are less common, family links are not weaker today.

7. Which of the following statements *best* describes the relationship of most middle-aged adults to their adult children?
   a. The relationship tends to improve with time.
   b. During middle adulthood, the relationship tends to deteriorate.
   c. For women, but not men, the relationship tends to improve with time.
   d. The relationship usually remains as good or as bad as it was in the past.

8. Which of the following statements explains why couples are particularly likely to report an increase in marital satisfaction during middle adulthood?
   a. Marital satisfaction is closely tied to financial security, which tends to improve during middle adulthood.
   b. The successful launching of children is a source of great pride and happiness.
   c. There often is improvement in marital equity during this period.
   d. For all of the above reasons, couples are likely to report improvement in their marriages during middle adulthood.

9. Middle-aged men and women may feel freer to express previously suppressed traits because of:
   a. reduced levels of sex hormones.
   b. less restrictive cultural roles.
   c. historical trends in gender roles.
   d. all of the above reasons.

10. Which of the following is *not* true concerning marriage during middle adulthood?
    a. Divorce at this time is more difficult than divorce in early adulthood.
    b. Most middle-aged divorced adults remarry within 5 years.
    c. Remarriages break up more often than first marriages.
    d. Remarried people report higher average levels of happiness than people in first marriages.

11. Which of the following was *not* cited as a factor in the great diversity of grandparent–grandchild relationships today?
    a. ethnic traditions
    b. the health of the older generation
    c. the developmental stage of the grandchild
    d. the developmental stage of the grandparent

12. Which of the following personality traits tends to remain stable throughout adulthood?
    a. agreeableness   c. openness
    b. neuroticism   d. all of the above

13. The trend toward relatively uninvolved grandparenting in middle age:
    a. provides more independence for each generation.
    b. diminishes the sense of generational continuity.

c. is particularly unfortunate in immigran groups, in which grandparents traditionally are responsible for passing on values, traditions, and customs.
    d. does all of the above.

14. Of the following, which is a biosocial explanation offered in the text for the tendency of both men and women to move toward more similar gender roles during middle age?
    a. Sex hormones decline during this period.
    b. Life experiences lead to a loosening of traditional gender roles.
    c. Both sexes have a "shadow side" to their personality that emerges at midlife.
    d. The physical changes of this time, including decreased functioning of most vital systems lead to a reassessment of the purpose of life.

15. Concerning developmental changes in personality traits, the text notes that:
    a. there are no significant changes in personality as people move through middle adulthood.
    b. because women are more likely than men to experience an abrupt transition in their roles their personalities are more likely to change.
    c. experience often leads to self-improvement and greater generativity.
    d. b. and c. are true.

Matching Items

Match each definition or description with its corresponding term.

Terms

_____ 1. companionate
_____ 2. kinkeepers
_____ 3. sandwich generation
_____ 4. surrogate parents
_____ 5. remote
_____ 6. extroversion
_____ 7. agreeableness
_____ 8. conscientiousness
_____ 9. neuroticism
_____ 10. openness
_____ 11. involved

Definitions or Descriptions

a. tendency to be outgoing
b. grandparent-grandchild relationship sought by most grandparents today
c. tendency to be imaginative
d. type of grandparenting common a century ago
e. tendency to be organized
f. those who focus more on the family
g. tendency to be helpful
h. type of grandparenting common throughout most of the twentieth century
i. those pressured by the needs of the older and younger generations
j. tendency to be moody
k. role grandparents may be called on to play when parents are poor, young, or newly divorced

Thinking Critically About Chapter 22

Answer these questions the day before an exam as a final check on your understanding of the chapter's terms and concepts.

Forty-five-year-old Ken, who has been single-mindedly climbing the career ladder, now feels that he has no more opportunity for advancement and that he has neglected his family and made many wrong decisions in charting his life's course. Ken's feelings are probably signs of:

a. normal development during middle age.
b. an unsuccessful passage through early adulthood.
c. neuroticism.
d. his being in the sandwich generation.

For her class presentation, Christine plans to discuss the Big Five personality factors. Which of the following is *not* a factor that Christine will discuss?

a. extroversion   c. independence
b. openness   d. agreeableness

It has long been assumed that, for biological reasons, I will inevitably experience a midlife crisis. I am:

a. a middle-aged man.
b. a middle-aged woman.

c. either a middle-age man or a middle-aged woman.
d. neither a. nor b.

4. Ben and Karen, both 35 years old, have been married 10 years and have two small children. Since the couple is still in the "establishment" stage of their marriage, it is likely that:

a. one spouse will work full time while the other works part time.
b. both will work full-time, one at a higher-paying job and one at a lower-paying "career."
c. they will take turns, with one working full speed while the other does most of the housework and child care.
d. They will follow any one of the above "scaling back" strategies.

5. Compared to when they were younger, middle-aged Sarah is likely to become more _____ , while middle-aged Donald becomes more _____ .

a. introverted; extroverted
b. assertive; emotionally expressive
c. disappointed with life; satisfied with life
d. extroverted; introverted

6. The parents of Rebecca and her middle-aged twin, Josh, have become frail and unable to care for themselves. It is likely that:
   a. Rebecca and Josh will play equal roles as caregivers for their parents.
   b. Rebecca will play a larger role in caring for their parents.
   c. Josh will play a larger role in caring for their parents.
   d. If Rebecca and Josh are well educated, their parents will be placed in a professional caregiving facility.

7. During middle adulthood a person's overall happiness:
   a. tends to decrease.
   b. strongly correlates with his or her marital happiness.
   c. tends to increase.
   d. is most strongly related to his or her career satisfaction.

8. Ben and Nancy have been married for 10 years. Although they are very happy, Nancy worries that with time this happiness will decrease. Research would suggest that Nancy's fear:
   a. may or may not be reasonable, depending on whether she and her husband are experiencing a midlife crisis.
   b. is reasonable, since marital discord is most common in couples who have been married 10 years or more.
   c. is unfounded, since after the first 10 years or so, the longer a couple has been married, the happier they tend to be.
   d. is probably a sign of neuroticism.

9. Of the following, the best example of a "cohort bridge" is:
   a. 25-year-old Karen, who is caring for her frail grandfather.
   b. 50-year-old Jack, who describes his relationship with his granddaughter as "autonomous."
   c. 45-year-old Danielle, who is explaining her daughter's taste in music to her own mother.
   d. 60-year-old Leonard, who sends money each month to his daughter and son-in-law.

10. Fifty-year-old Kenneth remarried this year following his divorce 3 years ago. It is likely that Kenneth will:
    a. become healthier.
    b. become more social.
    c. have improved relationships with his children.

d. experience all of the above.
e. experience none of the above.

11. Both of Brenda's marriages ended in divorce. Which of the following was *not* suggested in the text as a reason remarriages break up more often than first marriages?
    a. Some people are temperamentally prone to divorce.
    b. Remarried people are more likely to describe their marriages as either very happy or quite unhappy, with less middle ground.
    c. People generally feel less commitment in second marriages.
    d. For some people, divorce is less troublesome than having to accept a mate as he or she is.

12. Lilly enjoys her grandchildren on her own terms, visiting when she chooses and not interfering with their upbringing. Lilly's grandparenting style would best be described as:
    a. remote.   c. companionate.
    b. involved.   d. autonomous.

13. (A Life-Span View) After a painful phone call with her unhappy middle-aged mother, your college roommate confides her fear that she will not be able to handle the burdens of children, career, and caring for her aging parents. Your response is that:
    a. she's right to worry, since middle-aged women who juggle these roles simultaneously almost always feel unfairly overburdened.
    b. her mother's unhappiness is a warning sign that she herself may be genetically prone toward developing a midlife crisis.
    c. Both a. and b. are true.
    d. If these roles are important to her, if her relationships are satisfying, and if the time demands are not overwhelming, filling these roles is likely to be a source of satisfaction.

14. All his life, Bill has been a worrier, often suffering from bouts of anxiety and depression. Which personality cluster best describes these traits?
    a. neuroticism   c. openness
    b. extroversion   d. conscientiousness

15. Jan and her sister Sue have experienced similar frequent changes in careers, residences, and spouses. Jan has found these upheavals much less stressful than Sue and so is probably characterized by which of the following personality traits?
    a. agreeableness   c. openness
    b. conscientiousness d. extroversion

Key Terms

Writing Definitions

Using your own words, write a brief definition or explanation of each of the following terms on a separate piece of paper.

1. middle age
2. sandwich generation
3. midlife crisis
4. Big Five

5. ecological niche
6. gender crossover
7. kinkeepers
8. familism
9. remote grandparent
10. involved grandparent
11. companionate grandparent
12. surrogate parents
13. mentor

Cross Check

After you have written the definitions of the key terms in this chapter, you should complete the crossword puzzle to ensure that you can reverse the process—recognize the term, given the definition.

ACROSS

3. The belief that family members should be close and supportive of one another.
5. Clusters of personality traits that remain quite stable throughout adulthood.
9. Grandparents who enjoy involvement with their grandchildren on their own terms while maintaining their autonomy and living separately.
11. Because they are often squeezed by the needs of the younger and older generations, middle-aged adults are often referred to as the _____ generation.
12. The years between ages 40 and 65.
15. A guide or teacher who helps an inexperienced person.
16. Grandparents who live in or nearby their grandchildren's household and who are actively involved in their day-to-day lives.
16. The extent to which a person is anxious, moody, and self-punishing.

DOWN

1. A person who celebrates family achievements, gathers the family together, and keeps in touch with family members who have moved away.
2. A period of unusual anxiety and radical reexamination that is widely associated with middle age.
4. Tendency of many middle-aged workers to begin to balance their work lives with other concerns.

5. The extent to which a person is outgoing, assertive, and active.
7. The lifestyle and social context into which adults settle that are compatible with their individual personality needs and interests.
8. The extent to which a person is organized, deliberate, and conforming.
10. The extent to which a person is kind, helpful, and easygoing.
14. Distant grandparents who are honored, respected, and obeyed by the younger generations.

ANSWERS

CHAPTER REVIEW

1. 40; midlife; middle age; 65

2. crisis

People become aware that they are beginning to grow old and often must make adjustments in their parental roles and achievement goals. For many adults, midlife is also a time to reexamine earlier choices regarding intimacy and generativity.

3. work; family

4. increased; sandwich generation

5. half; good health; financially needy

6. women; daughters-in-law; serious disabilities

7. roles; squeezed; life satisfaction

8. overburdened; important; relationships; time

9. a. Adult children's independence reduces their burden.

b. Disabled adults usually require less care than when they were children.

c. Major caregiving of the very oldest is often borne by other older adults.

10. is not

11. developmental history

12. personality

13. a. extroversion: outgoing, assertive

b. agreeableness: kind, helpful

c. conscientiousness: organized, conforming

d. neuroticism: anxious, moody

e. openness: imaginative, curious

14. genes; culture; child rearing; 30; genes; ecological niche

15. 30; extroversion; outgoingness; neuroticism; apprehensiveness

Extroverts often have established a busy social life and their jobs, recreational activities, and other details of their lives foster social contact. By contrast, adults who are high in neuroticism expect the worst from life and may alienate those around them. They also may be fearful of taking a new job and become stuck in a cycle of self-pity and unhappiness.

16. warmth; confidence

17. temperament

18. self-improvement; generativity

19. loosen; gender crossover; assertive; tenderness; sadness

20. sex hormones

21. Carl Jung; shadow side

22. historical; less; less

23. cohort bridges; family; household; people wh eat and sleep together in the same dwelling

24. less

25. kinkeepers; women

26. improve; balanced

Most of today's elderly are healthy, active, and inde pendent, giving them and their grown children measure of freedom and privacy that enhances th relationship between them.

27. Hispanic; Asian

28. familism; family members should be close an supportive of one another

29. maintain

30. grandparent; positively

31. remote; involved; companionate; remot involved; were born in the United States

32. companionate; independence (autonomy)

33. personality; ethnic; national background; deve opmental stage

34. young; first sibling to have children; neither to young nor too old

35. immigrant; minority; values; beliefs; languag customs

36. surrogate parents; poor, young, unemploye drug- or alcohol-addicted, single, or new divorced

37. intensive involvement; drug-affected; rebelliou abusive; neglectful; kinship care

38. three; noncustodial

39. spouse; cohabitation

40. marriage

41. increase

Families at this stage typically have greater financ security and have met the goal of raising a family. addition, disputes over equity in domestic work ar other issues of parenting generally subside. A thi reason is that many couples have more time for ea other.

42. more

43. 5

Divorced women typically become financially mo secure, and divorced men typically become healthi and more social once they have a new partner. F men, it also improves their relationship with o spring.

44. more

The high divorce rate of the remarried may be due the fact that some people are temperamentally pro to divorce.

15. women

   a. Middle-aged men tend to marry younger women.

   b. Men die at younger ages.

   c. Few marriages take place between a younger man and an older woman.

16. increases; does not significantly vary; does not significantly vary

17. work, family; self

18. early; workaholics

19. establishment; scaling back; parenthood

One spouse may choose to work part time. Or, both partners may work full time, one at a "job" to earn money and the other at a lower-paying "career." In another scaling-back strategy, the partners take turns pursuing work and domestic and child care.

20. mentor

PROGRESS TEST 1

Multiple-Choice Questions

1. **b.** is the answer. (p. 592)

2. **c.** is the answer. (p. 594)

3. **d.** is the answer. (p. 592)

   a. & b. Recent studies have shown that the prevalence of the midlife crisis has been greatly exaggerated.

   c. The text does not suggest a gender difference in terms of the midlife crisis.

4. **a.** is the answer. (p. 596)

   b. This answer reflects the notion of a midlife crisis—a much rarer event than is popularly believed.

   c. Gender roles tend to loosen in middle adulthood.

5. **c.** is the answer. (pp. 596–597)

   a. Gender roles become *less* distinct during middle adulthood.

   b. Gender roles often are most distinct during early adulthood, after which they tend to loosen.

   d. Although there *is* diversity from individual to individual, gender-role shifts during middle adulthood are nevertheless predictable.

6. **a.** is the answer. (p. 592)

   b. & c. These are job-related problems.

7. **a.** is the answer. (p. 599)

   c. The relationship improves for both men and women.

   d. Because most of today's elderly are healthy, active, and independent, this gives them and

their grown children a measure of freedom and privacy that enhances the relationship between them.

8. **d.** is the answer. (p. 598)

   a. This term describes middle-aged women *and* men, who are pressured by the needs of both the younger and older generations.

   b. & c. These terms are not used in the text.

9. **a.** is the answer. (pp. 600–601)

10. **b.** is the answer. (p. 608)

11. **c.** is the answer. (p. 601)

   a. This is not one of the basic patterns of grandparenting.

   b. This pattern was common for most of the twentieth century.

   d. This pattern was common a century ago.

12. **d.** is the answer. (p. 594)

13. **a.** is the answer. (p. 594)

   b. This is the tendency to be kind and helpful.

   c. This is the tendency to be organized, deliberate, and conforming.

   d. This is the tendency to be anxious, moody, and self-punishing.

14. **b.** is the answer. (p. 597)

   a. Jung's theory states just the opposite.

   c. If anything, the loosening of gender roles would make adjustment easier.

   d. According to Jung, gender roles are most distinct during adolescence and early adulthood, when pressures to attract the other sex and the "parental imperative" are highest.

15. **b.** is the answer. (p. 594)

True or False Items

1. F Studies have found that crises at midlife are not inevitable. (p. 592)

2. T (p. 592)

3. T (p. 594)

4. F In fact, the current cohort is *less* marked in their convergence of sex roles because male and female roles are already less sharply defined than before. (p. 597)

5. F The extended family is typical of traditional societies, but not those in North America. (p. 598)

6. F Just the opposite is true. (p. 600)

7. T (p. 603)

8. T (p. 605)

9. T (p. 596)

10. F The stability of personality is at least partly attributable to heredity. (p. 594)

PROGRESS TEST 2

Multiple-Choice Questions

1. b. is the answer. (p. 591)

2. c. is the answer. (p. 594)

3. b. is the answer. Grandparents are most likely to act as surrogate parents if the parents are poor, young, unemployed, drug or alcohol addicted, single or newly divorced or if the child needs intensive involvement or is rebellious (as in b.). (p. 604)

4. c. is the answer. (pp. 594–595)

5. d. is the answer. (p. 594)

6. d. is the answer. (p. 598)

7. a. is the answer. (p. 600)

  c. The relationship improves for both men and women.

  d. It generally improves, especially if the children have emerged from adolescence successfully. Because most of today's elderly are healthy, active, and independent, this gives them and their grown children a measure of freedom and privacy that enhances the relationship between them.

8. d. is the answer. (p. 603)

9. d. is the answer. (p. 597)

10. d. is the answer. (p. 605)

11. b. is the answer. (p. 602)

12. d. is the answer. (p. 594)

13. d. is the answer. (p. 602)

14. a. is the answer. (p. 597)

  b. This explanation is *not* biosocial.

  c. This explanation, offered by Carl Jung, is also *not* biosocial.

  d. This explanation, although biosocial, was not offered in the text.

15. c. is the answer. (p. 596)

Matching Items

1. b (p. 601)   **5.** d (p. 600)   **9.** j (p. 594)
2. f (p. 598)   **6.** a (p. 594)   **10.** c (p. 594)
3. i (p. 592)   **7.** g (p. 594)   **11.** h (p. 601)
4. k (p. 602)   **8.** e (p. 594)

THINKING CRITICALLY ABOUT CHAPTER 22

1. a. is the answer. (p. 591)

  b. & c. Ken's feelings are common in middle-aged male workers, and not necessarily indicative of neuroticism.

  d. The sandwich generation refers to middle-aged adults being squeezed by the needs of the younger and older generations.

2. c. is the answer. (p. 594)

3. d. is the answer. Researchers have found no evidence that a midlife crisis is inevitable in middle adulthood. (p. 592)

4. a. is the answer. (p. 608)

5. b. is the answer. This is an example of the convergence of gender roles during middle adulthood. (p. 597)

  a. & d. Extroversion is a relatively *stable* personality trait. Moreover, there is no gender difference in the developmental trajectory of this trait.

  c. There is no gender difference in life satisfaction at any age.

6. b. is the answer. Because women tend to be kinkeepers, Rebecca is likely to play a larger role than her brother. (pp. 598–599)

  d. The relationship of education to care of frail parents is not discussed in the text.

7. b. is the answer. (p. 603)

8. c. is the answer. (p. 603)

  a. Marital satisfaction can be an important buffer against midlife stress.

  d. There is no reason to believe Nancy's concern is abnormal, or neurotic.

9. c. is the answer. Only in this example is a member of one generation drawing together, or bridging, members of the younger and older generations. (p. 598)

10. d. is the answer. (p. 605)

11. c. is the answer. (p. 605)

12. c. is the answer. (p. 601)

  a. Remote grandparents are more distant from their grandchildren than Lilly is.

  b. Involved grandparents are more active than Lilly in the day-to-day life of their grandchildren.

  d. This is not one of the basic patterns of grandparenting.

13. d. is the answer. (p. 593)

a. is the answer. (p. 594)

b. This is the tendency to be outgoing.

c. This is the tendency to be imaginative and curious.

d. This is the tendency to be organized, deliberate, and conforming.

c. is the answer. Openness to new experiences might make these life experiences less threatening. (p. 604)

EY TERMS

Midlife ushers in **middle age**, which lasts until about age 65. (p. 591)

Middle-aged adults are commonly referred to as the **sandwich generation** because they are often squeezed by the needs of the younger and older generations. (p. 592)

The **midlife crisis** is a period of unusual anxiety, radical reexamination, and sudden transformation that is widely associated with middle age. (p. 592)

The **Big Five** are clusters of personality traits that remain quite stable throughout adulthood. (p. 594)

Ecological niche refers to the lifestyle and social context adults settle into that are compatible with their individual personality needs and interests. (p. 594)

Gender crossover is the idea that each sex takes on the other sex's roles and traits in later life. (p. 596)

Because women tend to focus more on family than men do, they are the **kinkeepers**, the people who celebrate family achievements, gather the family together, and keep in touch with family members who have moved away. (p. 598)

8. **Familism** is the idea that family members should support each other because family unity is more important than individual freedom and success. (p. 599)

9. **Remote grandparents** are distant but esteemed elders, who are honored, respected, and obeyed by the younger generations. (p. 600)

10. **Involved grandparents** live in or nearby the grandchildren's household and are actively involved in their day-to-day lives. (p. 601)

11. **Companionate grandparents** enjoy involvement with grandchildren on their own terms while maintaining their autonomy and living separately. (p. 601)

12. Grandparents who take over the work, cost, and worry of raising their grandchildren due to their children's extreme social problems are called **surrogate parents**. (p. 602)

13. A **mentor** is a guide or teacher who helps an inexperienced person. (p. 609)

Cross-Check

ACROSS	DOWN
3. familism	1. kinkeeper
6. Big Five	2. midlife crisis
9. companionate	4. scaling back
11. sandwich	5. extroversion
12. middle age	7. ecological niche
13. mentor	8. conscientiousness
15. involved	10. agreeableness
16. neuroticism	14. remote

CHAPTER 23

Late Adulthood: Biosocial Development

Chapter Overview

Chapter 23 covers biosocial development during late adulthood, discussing the myths and reality of this final stage of the life span. In a society such as ours, which glorifies youth, there is a tendency to exaggerate the physical decline brought on by aging. In fact, the changes that occur during the later years are largely a continuation of those that began earlier in adulthood, and the vast majority of the elderly consider themselves to be in good health.

Nonetheless, the aging process is characterized by various changes in appearance, by an increased incidence of impaired vision and hearing, and by declines in the major body systems. These are all changes to which the individual must adjust. In addition, the incidence of chronic diseases increases significantly with age.

Several theories have been advanced to explain the aging process. The most useful of these focus on cellular malfunctions, declining immune function, and our genetic makeup. However, environment and lifestyle factors also play a role, as is apparent from studies of those who live a long life.

NOTE: Answer guidelines for all Chapter 23 questions begin on page 351.

Guided Study

The text chapter should be studied one section at a time. Before you read, preview each section by skimming it, noting headings and boldface items. Then read the appropriate section objectives from the following outline. Keep these objectives in mind and, as you read the chapter section, search for the information that will enable you to meet each objective. Once you have finished a section, write out answers for its objectives.

Ageism (pp. 616–620)

1. Define ageism, and identify two reasons for changing views about old age.

2. (A Life-Span View) Describe ongoing changes in the age distribution of the American population.

3. Distinguish among three categories of the aged, and explain the current state of the dependency ratio.

338

Primary Aging (pp. 620–627)

4. (text and In Person) Differentiate between primary and secondary aging, and list several characteristic effects of aging on the individual's appearance, noting how the aged see themselves.

5. Describe age-related problems in vision and hearing.

6. (text and Research Report) Discuss the adjustments older adults may have to make in various areas of life in order to maintain optimal functioning.

Secondary Aging (pp. 627–632)

7. Identify several reasons that the incidence of chronic disease increases significantly with age, and explain the concept of compression of morbidity.

Causes of Senescence (pp. 632–638)

8. Outline the wear-and-tear and cellular accidents theories of aging.

9. Explain how the immune system functions, and describe age-related changes in its functioning.

10. Explain senescence from an epigenetic systems theory perspective.

11. Discuss the role of genetics in aging, and explain what the Hayflick limit is and how it supports the idea of a genetic clock.

Can Aging Be Stopped? (pp. 638–644)

12. Identify lifestyle characteristics associated with the healthy, long-lived adult.

13. (Changing Policy) Discuss nutritional and exercise needs during late adulthood, and suggest how these might best be met.

Chapter Review

When you have finished reading the chapter, work through the material that follows to review it. Complete the sentences and answer the questions. As you proceed, evaluate your performance for each section by consulting the answers on page 351. Do not continue with the next section until you understand each answer. If you need to, review or reread the appropriate section in the textbook before continuing.

Ageism (pp. 616–620)

1. The prejudice that people tend to feel about older people is called _____ .

2. The cultural bias that labels teenagers as irresponsible and trouble-prone and older people as senile and rigid _____ (is/is not) weakening.

3. The scientific study of aging is called _____ .

4. The study of populations and the social statistics associated with them is called _____ .

5. (A Life-Span View) In the past, when populations were sorted according to age, the resulting picture was a(n) _____ , with the youngest and _____ (smallest/largest) group at the bottom and the oldest and

_____ (smallest/largest) group at the top.

(A Life-Span View) List two reasons for this picture.

a. _____

_____

b. _____

_____

6. (A Life-Span View) Today, because of

_____ _____

_____ and increased

_____ , the shape of the population is becoming closer to a(n)

_____ .

7. (A Life-Span View) The fastest-growing segment of the population is people age

_____ and older.

8. (A Life-Span View) The shape of the demographic pyramid _____ (varies/is the same) throughout the world.

_____ (What country?) has the longest average life span and the lowest

_____ _____ of all nations with large populations.

9. (A Life-Span View) As birth rates fall, young adults tend to _____ (accelerate/postpone) life transitions, such as completing their education. In the United States, the average age of retirement has _____ (increased/decreased) in recent years.

10. The ratio of self-sufficient, productive adults to dependent children and elderly adults is called the _____ _____ . Because of the declining _____ rate and the small size of the cohort just entering _____ _____ , this ratio is _____ (lower/higher) than has been for a century.

List several possible benefits and problems that will result from the increasing number of older people.

11. Approximately _____ percent of the elderly live in nursing homes.

12. Older adults who are healthy, relatively well-off financially, and integrated into the lives of their families and society are classified as

    _____-_____ .

13. Older adults who suffer major physical, mental, or social losses are classified as

    _____-_____ . The

    _____-_____ are

    dependent on others for almost everything; they are _____ (the majority/a small minority) of those over age 65.

Primary Aging (pp. 620–627)

4. Developmentalists distinguish between the irreversible changes that occur with time, called

    _____ _____ ,

    and _____ _____ ,

    which refers to changes caused by particular

    _____ or _____ . This latter category of age-related changes

    _____ (is/is not) inevitable with the passage of time.

5. Every body system experiences a gradual reduction in _____ and

    _____ _____ with age.

6. As people age, the skin becomes

    _____ , _____ , and

    _____ (more/less) elastic, which produces wrinkling and makes blood vessels and pockets of fat more visible. Dark patches of skin known as _____

    _____ also become visible.

7. Most older people are more than

    _____ shorter than they were in early adulthood, because their

    _____ have settled closer together.

8. With age, body fat tends to collect more in the

    _____ and _____

    _____ than in the arms, legs, and upper face.

19. Body weight is often _____ (higher/lower) in late adulthood, particularly in

    _____ (men/women), who have

    more _____ and less body

    _____ than the other sex.

20. Another reason for the change in body weight is the loss of bone _____ that causes bones to become more porous and fragile.

21. (In Person) Changes in appearance can have serious _____ and _____ consequences. When older-looking people are treated in a stereotyped way—such as by using _____-they may feel (and become) less competent.

22. More than _____ (what proportion?) of those older than 80 have one of the three major eye diseases of the elderly. The first of these, _____ , involves a thickening of the _____ of the eye. The second,

    _____ , involves the

    _____ of the eyeball because of a buildup of _____ within the eye. The disease _____

    _____ _____

    involves deterioration of the _____ .

23. The leading cause of legal blindness among the elderly is _____

    _____ _____ .

24. Age-related hearing loss, or _____ , affects about _____ percent of those aged 65 and older. Some elderly persons experience a buzzing or ringing in the ears called _____ . The only treatment for this condition is _____ .

25. Because hearing aids are regarded as a symbol of agedness, less than _____ percent of the elderly use them.

26. Four hearing losses associated with aging are:

    a. _____

    b. _____

    c. _____

    d. _____

27. Sometimes younger adults automatically lapse into _____ when they talk to older adults.

Describe this form of speech.

28. The examples of the young-old, old-old, and oldest-old indicate that aging may be

_____ , _____ , or

_____ .

29. Optimal aging requires _____

_____ to body changes, not

_____ _____ . To have

the most beneficial impact, _____

interventions and _____ changes

should take place during usual aging—typically

during _____ or _____

adulthood.

30. Two statistics that indicate that many elderly people understand the importance of active adjustment to aging are:

   a. _____

   b. _____

31. Scientists _____ (agree/do not agree) on how much sleep people need. A frequent sleep complaint among older adults is _____ , which is often treated by prescription _____ drugs.

Explain why this medical intervention may be particularly harmful in late adulthood.

32. Frequent waking during the night becomes more common during late adulthood because the decrease in the brain's _____

_____ with advancing age means sleep is not as deep and _____ are not as long.

33. (Research Report) Many gerontologists now recommend _____ , rather than pharmacological solutions, to treat insomnia in the elderly. In one study, elderly volunteers in the _____ (experimental/control) group received four weekly sessions of sleep education and counseling, while volunteers in the _____ (experimental/control) group received no treatment. In this study, the independent variable was the _____ and _____ , and the dependent variable was _____ _____ .

(Research Report) Briefly summarize the results of this study.

Secondary Aging (pp. 627–632)

34. It _____ (is/is not) inevitable that aging brings on disease.

35. In a recent survey, most older adults reported that their health limited their activities _____ (very little/a great deal).

36. The incidence of chronic diseases _____ (increases/does not increase) with age. However, whether a person becomes ill depends less on age than on _____ factors, past _____ , current _____ and _____ habits, and _____ factors such as social support.

. Give two reasons for the increased incidence of chronic diseases.

a. _____

_____

b. _____

_____

. Older people take _____ (less/more) time to recover from illnesses and are _____ (less/more) likely to die of them.

. A goal of many researchers is a limiting of the time any person spends ill, that is, a(n)

_____ _____

_____ .

uses of Senescence (pp. 632–638)

. The oldest theory of aging is the

_____-_____-

_____ theory, which compares the human body to a(n) _____ . Overall, this analogy _____ (is a good one/doesn't hold up).

. A more promising theory suggests that some occurrence in the _____ themselves, such as the accumulation of accidents that occur during _____ _____ , causes aging. According to this theory, toxic environmental agents and the normal process of _____ repair result in _____ that damage the instructions for creating new cells.

Another aspect of the cellular theory of aging is that metabolic processes can cause electrons to separate from their atoms, resulting in atoms called _____ _____ _____ that scramble DNA molecules or produce errors in cell maintenance and repair.

Free radical damage _____ (is/is not) inevitable, and may be slowed by certain _____ that nullify the effects of free radicals. These include vitamins _____ , _____ , and _____ , and the mineral _____ .

44. The body's self-healing processes include a gene called _____ , which causes a flawed cell to stop_____ . Women may be protected against heart disease by the hormone _____ . Postponing or limiting childbearing may _____ (extend/shorten) a woman's life.

45. The "attack" cells of the immune system include the _____ from the bone marrow, which create _____ that attack invading _____ and _____ , and the _____ from the _____ gland, which produce substances that attack any kind of infected cells.

46. The first notable change in the immune system involves the _____

_____ , which begins to shrink during _____ . Over the course of adulthood the power, production, and efficiency of T- and B-cells _____ (increases/decreases/remains constant).

47. Additional support for the immune theory of aging comes from research on AIDS, or

_____ _____

_____ _____ , which is caused by_____ , or

_____ _____

_____ .

48. Individuals with stronger immune systems tend to live _____ (longer/shorter) lives than their contemporaries. This has led some researchers to conclude that the _____ of the immune system is *the* cause of aging.

49. Females tend to have _____ (weaker/stronger) immune systems than males, as well as _____ (smaller/larger) thymus glands. However, as a result, women are more vulnerable to _____ diseases such as rheumatoid arthritis.

50. Some theorists believe that, rather than being a mistake, aging is incorporated into the _____ plans of all species.

51. The oldest age to which members of a species can live, called the _____ _____ _____ , which in humans is approximately 120 years, is quite different from _____ _____ _____ , which is defined as _____ _____ _____ _____ .

52. Life expectancy varies according to _____ , _____ , and _____ factors that affect frequency of _____ in childhood, adolescence, or middle age. In the United States today, average life expectancy at birth was about _____ for men and _____ for women. In 1900, in developed nations, the average life expectancy was about age _____ .

Briefly state two possible explanations for senescence according to epigenetic systems theory.

53. According to another theory of senescence, DNA acts as a genetic _____ , switching on genes that promote aging at a genetically predetermined age. Support for this theory comes from several diseases that involve premature signs of aging and early death, including _____ _____ and the rare disease _____ .

54. When human cells are allowed to replicate outside the body, the cells stop replicating at a certain point, referred to as the _____ _____ . Cells from people with diseases characterized by accelerated aging replicate _____ (more/fewer) times before dying.

Can Aging Be Stopped? (pp. 638–644)

55. Researchers have been able to extend the life of some animal species by reducing their _____ .

56. Most scientists believe that aging occurs at the level of the _____ , with _____ at least partly responsible. Except in the case of rare diseases, aging probab _____ (is/is not) directly controlle by one or several particular genes. This means that human aging probably can't be slowed wit a specific _____ or via _____ _____ .

57. The availability of universal health care has resulted in a steady increase in average life expectancy in _____ (which country?). Conversely, the average life span has bee reduced in _____ , where _____ , _____ , and other epigenetic factors have recently increased and in several nations of _____ , where _____ kills young adults wl would have survived a generation ago.

58. (Changing Policy) Vitamin and mineral needs _____ (increase/decrease) with ag However, calorie requirements _____ (increase/decrease) by abo _____ percent from those of early and middle adulthood. During late adulthood, diet that is _____ and healthy is even more important than earlier.

59. (Changing Policy) Getting enough nutrients is more problematic for the aged than for younge adults primarily because the senses of _____ and _____ diminish with age.

List three external factors that make getting enou nutrients more difficult for some older adults.

a. _____

b. _____

c. _____

0. (Changing Policy) Many of the elderly also take

_____ that affect nutritional

requirements.

1. (Changing Policy) For the very old, regular exer-

cise _____ (is/is not) beneficial.

Describe the most beneficial type and frequency of

exercise for older adults.

2. (Changing Policy) The gap between research,

public policy, and practice is revealed by the fact

that less than _____ percent of those

over age 50 currently eat a _____

_____ or use _____

_____ to build their muscles.

3. The places famous for long-lived people are in

_____ , _____

regions where pollution is minimized.

Furthermore, in these places, tradition ensures

that the elderly are _____ and play

an important social role. Because of the absence

of _____ , some

researchers believe the people in these regions are

lying about their true age.

List four characteristics shared by long-lived people

these regions.

a. _____

b. _____

c. _____

d. _____

Progress Test 1

Multiple-Choice Questions

Circle your answers to the following questions and
check them with the answers on page 353. If your
answer is incorrect, read the explanation for why it is
incorrect and then consult the appropriate pages of
the text (in parentheses following the correct answer).

1. Ageism is:
   a. the study of aging and the aged.
   b. prejudice or discrimination against older peo-
      ple.
   c. the genetic disease that causes children to age
      prematurely.
   d. the view of aging that the body and its parts
      deteriorate with use.

2. (A Life-Span View) The U.S. demographic pyramid is becoming a square because of:
   a. increasing birth rates and life spans.
   b. decreasing birth rates and life spans.
   c. decreasing birth rates and increasing life
      spans.
   d. rapid population growth.

3. Primary aging refers to the:
   a. changes that are caused by illness.
   b. changes that can be reversed or prevented.
   c. irreversible changes that occur with time.
   d. changes that are caused by poor health habits.

4. Auditory losses with age are more serious than
   visual losses because:
   a. they affect a far larger segment of America's
      elderly population.
   b. they are more difficult for doctors to diagnose
      than are visual losses.
   c. hearing aids, in contrast to glasses, are ineffec-
      tive as a corrective measure.
   d. those who suffer from them are less likely to
      take the necessary corrective steps.

5. Which disease involves the hardening of the eyeball due to the buildup of fluid?
   a. cataracts
   b. glaucoma
   c. senile macular degeneration
   d. myopia

6. Factors that explain the increased incidence of
   chronic diseases during late adulthood include all
   of the following *except*:
   a. increased hypochondria.
   b. accumulated risk factors.
   c. decreased efficiency of body systems.
   d. diminished immunity.

7. A direct result of damage to cellular DNA is:
   a. errors in the reproduction of cells.
   b. an increase in the formation of free radicals.
   c. decreased efficiency of the immune system.
   d. the occurrence of a disease called progeria.

8. Which theory explains aging as due in part to mutations in the cell structure?
   a. wear and tear
   b. immune system deficiency
   c. cellular accidents
   d. genetic clock

9. According to the theory of a genetic clock, aging:
   a. is actually directed by the genes.
   b. occurs as a result of damage to the genes.
   c. occurs as a result of hormonal abnormalities.
   d. can be reversed through environmental changes.

10. Laboratory research on the reproduction of cells cultured from humans and animals has found that:
    a. cell division cannot occur outside the organism.
    b. the number of cell divisions was the same regardless of the species of the donor.
    c. the number of cell divisions was different depending on the age of the donor.
    d. under the ideal conditions of the laboratory, cell division can continue indefinitely.

11. Presbycusis refers to age-related:
    a. hearing losses.
    b. decreases in ability of the eyes to focus on distant objects.
    c. changes in metabolism.
    d. changes in brain activity during sleep.

12. Highly unstable atoms that have unpaired electrons and cause damage to other molecules in body cells are called:
    a. B-cells.   c. free radicals.
    b. T-cells.   d. both a. and b.

13. In triggering our first maturational changes and then the aging process, our genetic makeup is in effect acting as a(n):
    a. immune system.
    b. cellular accident.
    c. demographic pyramid.
    d. genetic clock.

14. Age-related changes in the immune system include all of the following *except*:
    a. shrinkage of the thymus gland.
    b. loss of T-cells.

c. reduced efficiency in repairing damage from B-cells.
   d. reduced efficiency of antibodies.

15. Women are more likely than men to:
    a. have stronger immune systems.
    b. have smaller thymus glands.
    c. be immune to autoimmune diseases such as rheumatoid arthritis.
    d. have all of the above traits.

True or False Items

Write T (*true*) or F (*false*) on the line in front of each statement.

_____ 1. Younger adults tend to underestimate the proportion of the elderly that are institutionalized.

_____ 2. People with stronger immune systems tend to live longer than their contemporaries.

_____ 3. Because of demographic changes, the majority of America"s elderly population is now predominantly "old-old" rather than "young-old."

_____ 4. Gerontologists focus on distinguishing aging in terms of the quality of aging, that is, in terms of young-old versus old-old.

_____ 5. Although the thymus gland shrinks with age, the efficiency of the immune system is not affected.

_____ 6. The immune system helps to control the effects of cellular damage.

_____ 7. A decline in the number of free radicals may accelerate the aging process.

_____ 8. Although average life expectancy is increasing, maximum life span has remained unchanged.

_____ 9. (Changing Policy) In view of changed nutritional needs during late adulthood, nutritionists generally recommend that the elderly supplement their diet with large doses of vitamins.

_____ 10. The importance of lifestyle factors contributing to longevity is underscored by studies of the long-lived.

Progress Test 2

Progress Test 2 should be completed during a final chapter review. Answer the following questions after you thoroughly understand the correct answers for the Chapter Review and Progress Test 1.

Multiple-Choice Questions

1. People tend to view late adulthood more negatively than is actually the case because:
   a. they are afraid of their own impending death.
   b. of the tendency to categorize and judge people on the basis of a single characteristic.
   c. of actual experiences with older people.
   d. they were taught to do so from an early age by their parents.

2. (A Life-Span View) An important demographic change in America is that:
   a. ageism is beginning to diminish.
   b. population growth has virtually ceased.
   c. the median age is falling.
   d. the number of older people in the population is increasing.

3. Changes in appearance during late adulthood include all of the following *except* a:
   a. slight reduction in height.
   b. significant increase in weight.
   c. redistribution of body fat.
   d. marked wrinkling of the skin.

4. Heart disease and cancer are:
   a. caused by aging.
   b. genetic diseases.
   c. examples of secondary aging.
   d. all of the above.

5. As a result of the _____ birth rate, the population dependency ratio is _____ than it was at the turn of the twentieth century.
   a. increasing; higher
   b. increasing; lower
   c. decreasing; higher
   d. decreasing; lower

6. Regarding the body's self-healing processes, which of the following is not true?
   a. The hormone estrogen may offer women some protection against heart disease.
   b. Given a healthy lifestyle, cellular errors accumulate slowly, causing little harm.
   c. Aging makes cellular repair mechanisms less efficient.
   d. Women who postpone childbirth have less efficient cellular repair mechanisms.

7. Researchers have discovered a gene called P53 that:
   a. responds to DNA damage by causing flawed cells to stop duplicating.
   b. accelerates the pace of aging by increasing the number of cell errors.
   c. causes increased production of three enzymes involved in the destruction of oxygen free radicals.
   d. has all of the above effects.

8. The oldest age to which a human can live is ultimately limited by:
   a. cellular accidents.
   b. the maximum life span.
   c. the average life expectancy.
   d. the Hayflick limit.

9. The disease called progeria, in which aging occurs prematurely in children, provides support for explanations of aging that focus on:
   a. wear and tear.
   b. cellular accidents.
   c. cross-linkage.
   d. a genetic clock.

10. Senile macular degeneration is:
    a. the leading cause of deafness among the elderly.
    b. an eye disease in which the retina deteriorates.
    c. experienced as a ringing or rhythmic buzzing in the ears.
    d. experienced by one-third of those older than 74.

11. In studies of three regions of the world known for the longevity of their inhabitants, the long-lived showed all of the following characteristics *except*:
    a. their diets were moderate.
    b. they were spared from doing any kind of work.
    c. they interacted frequently with family members, friends, and neighbors.
    d. they engaged in some form of exercise on a daily basis.

12. In defending itself against internal and external invaders, the immune system relies on two kinds of "attack" cells: _____, manufactured in the bone marrow, and _____, manufactured by the thymus gland.
    a. B-cells; T-cells
    b. T-cells; B-cells
    c. free radicals; T-cells
    d. B-cells; free radicals

13. The view of aging that the body and its parts deteriorate with use and with accumulated exposure to environmental stresses is known as the _____ theory.

 a. programmed senescence
 b. genetic clock
 c. cellular accidents
 d. wear-and-tear

14. The statistical study of population and population trends is called:

 a. gerontology.   c. ageism.
 b. demography.   d. senescence.

15. In humans, average life expectancy varies according to all of the following *except*:

 a. historical factors.
 b. ethnic factors.
 c. cultural factors.
 d. socioeconomic factors.

Matching Items

Match each term or concept with its corresponding description or definition.

Terms or Concepts

_____ **1.** young-old
_____ **2.** old-old
_____ **3.** glaucoma
_____ **4.** cataracts
_____ **5.** B-cells
_____ **6.** T-cells
_____ **7.** compression of morbidity
_____ **8.** oxygen free radicals
_____ **9.** Hayflick limit
_____ **10.** primary aging
_____ **11.** secondary aging

Descriptions or Definitions

 a. the universal changes that occur as we grow older
 b. limiting the time a person is ill
 c. the number of times a cell replicates before dying
 d. unstable atoms with unpaired electrons that damage cells
 e. attack infected cells and strengthen other aspects of the immune system's functioning
 f. the majority of the elderly
 g. thickening of the lens of the eye
 h. the minority of the elderly
 i. create antibodies that attack bacteria and viruses
 j. age-related changes that are caused by health habits, genes, and other conditions
 k. hardening of the eyeball due to the buildup of fluid

Thinking Critically About Chapter 23

Answer these questions the day before an exam as a final check on your understanding of the chapter's terms and concepts.

 1. Which of the following is *most* likely to be a result of ageism?

 a. the participation of the elderly in community activities
 b. laws requiring workers to retire by a certain age
 c. an increase in multigenerational families
 d. greater interest in the study of gerontology

 2. Loretta majored in psychology at the local university. Because she wanted to serve her community, she applied to a local agency to study the effect of aging on the elderly. Loretta is a:

 a. developmental psychologist.
 b. behaviorist.
 c. gerontologist.
 d. demographer.

 3. An 85-year-old man enjoys good health and actively participates in family and community activities. This person is best described as being:

 a. ageist.   c. old-old.
 b. young-old.   d. a gerontologist.

(A Life-Span View) Concluding her presentation on demographic trends in the United States, Marisa states that, "By the year 2030:
a. there will be more people aged 60 and older than below age 30."
b. there will be more people aged 30 to 59 than below age 30."
c. there will be more people below age 30 than above age 60."
d. the American population will be divided roughly into thirds—one-third below age 30, one-third aged 30 to 59, and one-third aged 60 and older."

Renne has to spend time at a nursing facility because of a broken kneecap. Although the facility contains a large dining room for residents, she prefers to eat alone in her room. The *most* likely reason for this is:
a. her failed hearing.
b. that she has digestive problems and does not want anyone to know.
c. she does not want to be with other old people.
d. all of the above.

(Changing Policy) Given the changes and needs of late adulthood, an older person should probably:
a. avoid most forms of exercise.
b. follow a regular but slower-paced program of exercise.
c. exercise for longer periods than younger adults.
d. focus on swimming and water exercises.

In summarizing research evidence concerning the causes of aging, you should state that:
a. "Errors in cellular duplication cannot explain primary aging."
b. "Impairments of the immune system are closely involved in aging."
c. "Aging is simply a mistake; species are not genetically programmed to die."
d. a., b., and c. are equally accurate.

A flu that younger adults readily recover from can prove fatal to older adults. The main reason for this is that older adults:
a. are often reluctant to consult doctors.
b. have a greater genetic predisposition to the flu.
c. have diminished immunity.
d. are often weakened by inadequate nutrition.

9. The wear-and-tear theory might be best suited to explain:
a. the overall process of aging.
b. the wrinkling of the skin that is characteristic of older adults.
c. the arm and shoulder problems of a veteran baseball pitcher.
d. the process of cell replacement by which minor cuts are healed.

10. (Changing Policy) With regard to nutrition, most elderly should probably be advised to:
a. take large doses of vitamins and, especially, antioxidants.
b. eat foods that are high in calories.
c. consume a varied and healthy diet.
d. eat large meals but eat less often.

11. (Changing Policy) Charlotte wants to make sure her elderly grandmother has every nutritional advantage to keep her mind healthy. She should suggest that her grandmother:
a. increase her intake of vitamins and minerals and decrease her caloric intake.
b. decrease her intake of vitamins and minerals and increase her caloric intake.
c. increase the amount of medication she takes and decrease her fluid intake.
d. decrease the amount of medication she takes and increase her fluid intake.

12. Researchers have been able to extend the lives of animals by all of the following means *except*:
a. selective breeding.
b. using chemicals to alter defective P53 genes.
c. reducing their diet.
d. boosting the vitamin, mineral, and protein content of the diet.

13. Mary and Charlie are both 50. As they advance through adulthood, it is likely that:
a. Charlie will be healthier than Mary.
b. until late adulthood, Charlie is more likely to suffer a chronic disease.
c. Mary's immune responses will be weaker.
d. all of the above are true.

14. Because age is not an accurate predictor of dependency, some gerontologists prefer to use the term _____ to refer to the *young-old*, and the term _____ to refer to the *oldest-old*.
a. optimal aging; usual aging
b. usual aging; impaired aging
c. impaired aging; optimal aging
d. optimal aging; impaired aging

15. In concluding her presentation on human longevity, Katrina states that:

   a. current average life expectancy is about twice what it was at the turn of the century.

   b. current maximum life span is about twice what it was at the turn of the century.

   c. both average life expectancy and maximum life span have increased since the turn of the century.

   d. although maximum life span has not increased, average life expectancy has, because infants are less likely to die.

Key Terms

Writing Definitions

Using your own words, write a brief definition or explanation of each of the following terms on a separate piece of paper.

   1. ageism

   2. gerontology

   3. demography

   4. dependency ratio

   5. young-old

   6. old-old

   7. oldest-old

   8. primary aging

   9. secondary aging

   10. cataracts

   11. glaucoma

   12. senile macular degeneration

   13. presbycusis

   14. elderspeak

   15. compression of morbidity

   16. wear-and-tear theory

   17. oxygen free radicals

   18. antioxidants

   19. B-cells

   20. T-cells

   21. maximum life span

   22. average life expectancy

   23. genetic clock

   24. Hayflick limit

ross Check

fter you have written the defini-
ons of the key terms in this chap-
r, you should complete the
rossword puzzle to ensure that
ou can reverse the process—rec-
gnize the term, given the defini-
on.

CROSS

1. Compounds such as vitamins E and C that nullify the effects of oxygen free radicals.
5. Maximum number of years that a particular species is genetically programmed to live.
6. Eye disease that can destroy vision, caused by the hardening of the eyeball due to the buildup of fluid.
8. The study of old age.
5. The universal and irreversible physical changes that occur as people get older is referred to as _____ aging.
7. Theory of aging that the parts of the human body deterio-rate with use as well as due to accumulated exposure to pol-lution and radiation, inade-quate nutrition, disease, and various other stresses.
8. Older people who suffer severe physical, mental, or social problems in later life.

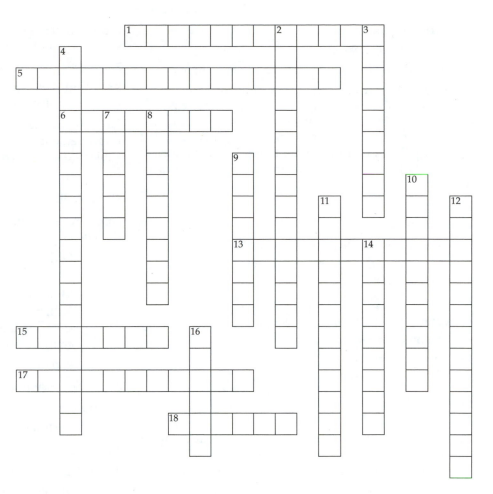

16. Immune system cells that are manufactured in the bone marrow and create antibodies that attack specific invading bacteria and viruses.

OWN

2. Ratio of self-sufficient, productive adults to children and the elderly.
3. The changes that occur with age that are caused by health habits, genes, and other influences that vary from person to person are referred to as _____ aging.
4. Highly unstable atoms with unpaired electrons that are capable of reacting with other molecules in the cell, tearing them apart and possibly accelerating aging.
7. Prejudice against older people.
8. Common eye disease involving the thickening of the lens that, left untreated, can distort vision.
9. Elderly people who are healthy and vigorous.
10. The study of populations and social statistics associat-ed with these populations.
11. Theory of aging that the regulatory mechanism in the cells' DNA controls cellular processes and "times" aging and the moment of death.
12. Maximum number of times that cells cultured from humans and animals divide before dying.
14. Elderly adults who are dependent on others for almost everything.

ANSWERS

CHAPTER REVIEW

1. ageism
2. is
3. gerontology
4. demography
5. pyramid; largest; smallest

   a. Each generation of young adults gave birth to more than enough children to replace them-selves.

   b. A sizable number of each cohort died before advancing to the next higher section of the pyramid.

6. falling birth rates; longevity; square
7. 75

8. varies; Japan; birth rate

9. postpone; decreased

10. dependency ratio; birth; late adulthood; higher

Some experts warn of new social problems, such as increased expenses for medical care and decreased concern for the quality of education for children. Fortunately, in several European nations, this has led to social policies that benefit all the generations, such as publicly funded health care and continuing education.

11. 5

12. young-old

13. old-old; oldest-old; a small minority

14. primary aging; secondary aging; conditions; illnesses; is not

15. capacity; organ reserve

16. dryer; thinner; less; age spots

17. one inch; vertebrae

18. torso; lower face

19. lower; men; muscle; fat

20. calcium

21. social; psychological; elderspeak

22. one-third; cataracts; lens; glaucoma; hardening; fluid; senile macular degeneration; retina

23. senile macular degeneration

24. presbycusis; 40; tinnitus; surgery

25. 10

26. a. difficulty in detecting where a sound is coming from

    b. difficulty in deciphering electronically transmitted speech

    c. difficulty in noticing high-frequency sounds

    d. mishearing conversation

27. elderspeak

Like babytalk, elderspeak uses simple and short sentences, exaggerated emphasis, slower talk, higher pitch, and repetition.

28. optimal, usual; impaired

29. active adjustment; passive acceptance; medical; lifestyle; early; middle

30. a. The aged are less likely to be victims of crime than are younger adults.

    b. The elderly are less likely to be the driver in a serious auto accident.

31. do not agree; insomnia; narcotic

These drugs may mask age-related physiological problems for which sleep disturbances are a symptom, not a cause. In addition, prescription doses are often too strong for an older person, causing confusion, depression, or impaired cognition.

32. electrical activity; dreams

33. cognitive; experimental; control; education counseling; sleep patterns

Subjects in the experimental groups showed more improvement in their sleep patterns than the control subjects did.

34. is not

35. very little

36. increases; genetic; lifestyle; eating; exercise; psychosocial

37. a. Older people are more likely to have accumulated several risk factors for chronic diseases.

    b. Many of the biological changes that occur with aging reduce the efficiency of the body's systems, making the older person more susceptible to disease.

38. more; more

39. compression of morbidity

40. wear-and-tear; machine; doesn't hold up

41. cells; cell reproduction; DNA; mutations

42. oxygen free radicals

43. is; antioxidants; A; C; E; selenium

44. P53; duplicating; estrogen; extend

45. B-cells; antibodies; bacteria; viruses; T-cells; thymus

46. thymus gland; adolescence; decreases

47. acquired immune deficiency syndrome; HIV; human immunodeficiency virus

48. longer; decline

49. stronger; larger; autoimmune

50. genetic

51. maximum life span; average life expectancy; the number of years the average newborn of a particular species is likely to live

52. historical; cultural; socioeconomic; death; 74; 8; 50

One explanation is that since reproduction is essential for the survival of our species, it was genetically important for deaths to occur either very early in life or after childbearing and child rearing. Another is that genetic abnormalities usually cause the organism to die long before parenthood, thus ensuring that those genes are not passed on.

53. clock; Down syndrome; progeria

54. Hayflick limit; fewer

55. diet

56. cell; genes; is not; vitamin; genetic engineering

57. Sweden; Russia; pollution, stress; Africa; AIDS

58. decrease; decrease; 10; varied

59. smell; taste

    a. poverty

    b. living alone

    c. dental problems

60. drugs

61. is

Activities that involve continuous rhythmic movement three or four times a week for at least half an hour are more beneficial than those that require sudden, strenuous effort. In addition, strength training to stave off age-related muscle loss is highly recommended for older adults.

62. 1; restricted diet; resistance training

63. rural; mountainous; respected; verifiable birth or marriage records

    a. Diet is moderate, consisting mostly of fresh vegetables.

    b. Work continues throughout life.

    c. Families and community are important.

    d. Exercise and relaxation are part of the daily routine.

PROGRESS TEST 1

Multiple-Choice Questions

1. **b.** is the answer. (p. 616)

    a. This is gerontology.

    c. This is progeria.

    d. This is the wear-and-tear theory.

2. **c.** is the answer. (p. 618)

3. **c.** is the answer. (p. 620)

    a., b., & d. These are examples of secondary aging.

4. **d.** is the answer. (p. 624)

    a. Visual and auditory losses affect about the same number of aged persons.

    b. & c. Hearing losses are no more difficult to detect, or to correct, than vision losses.

5. **b.** is the answer. (p. 623)

    a. Cataracts are caused by a thickening of the lens.

    c. This disease involves deterioration of the retina.

    d. Myopia, which was not discussed in this chapter, is nearsightedness.

6. **a.** is the answer. (pp. 629–630)

7. **a.** is the answer. (p. 633)

    b. In fact, free radicals damage DNA, rather than vice versa.

    c. The immune system compensates for, but is not directly affected by, damage to cellular DNA.

    d. This genetic disease occurs too infrequently to be considered a *direct* result of damage to cellular DNA.

8. **c.** is the answer. (pp. 633)

9. **a.** is the answer. (p. 638)

    b. & c. According to the genetic clock theory, time, rather than genetic damage or hormonal abnormalities, regulates the aging process.

    d. The genetic clock theory makes no provision for environmental alteration of the genetic mechanisms of aging.

10. **c.** is the answer. (pp. 638)

11. **a.** is the answer. (p. 623)

12. **c.** is the answer. (p. 634)

    a. & b. These are the "attack" cells of the immune system.

13. **d.** is the answer. (p. 638)

    a. This is the body's system for defending itself against bacteria and other "invaders."

    b. This is the theory that aging is caused by mutations in the cell structure or in the normal course of DNA repair.

    c. This is a metaphor for the distribution of age groups, with the largest and youngest group at the bottom, and the smallest and oldest group at the top.

14. **c.** is the answer. B-cells create antibodies that *repair* rather than damage cells. (p. 635)

15. **a.** is the answer. (p. 635)

    b. & c. Women have *larger* thymus glands than men. They are also *more* susceptible to autoimmune diseases.

True or False Items

1. F   The proportion tends to be overestimated, not underestimated. (p. 619)

2. T (p. 635)

3. F   Although our population is aging, the terms *old-old* and *young-old* refer to degree of physical and social well-being, not to age. (p. 620)

4. T (p. 620)

5. F   The shrinking of the thymus gland contributes to diminished immunity. (p. 635)

6. T (p. 635)

7. F   Inasmuch as free radicals damage DNA and other molecules, it is their *presence* that may contribute to aging. (p. 634)

8. T (p. 637)

9. F   Research has shown that large doses of vitamins may be harmful. (p. 640)

10. T (p. 643)

PROGRESS TEST 2

Multiple-Choice Questions

1. **b.** is the answer. (p. 616)

2. **d.** is the answer. (p. 618)

   a. Ageism is prejudice, not a demographic change.

   b. Although birth rates have fallen, population growth has not ceased.

   c. Actually, with the "squaring of the pyramid," the median age is rising.

3. **b.** is the answer. Weight often decreases during late adulthood. (p. 621)

4. **c.** is the answer. (pp. 620, 630)

   a. & b. Over time, the interaction of accumulating risk factors with age-related weakening of the heart and relevant genetic weaknesses makes the elderly increasingly vulnerable to heart disease.

5. **c.** is the answer. (p. 619)

6. **d.** is the answer. The text does not discuss the impact of age of childbearing on a woman's cell repair mechanisms. However, it does present evidence that women who postpone or limit childbearing may *extend* life. (p. 634)

7. **a.** is the answer. (p. 634)

8. **b.** is the answer. (p. 636)

   a. This is a theory of aging.

   c. This statistic refers to the number of years the average newborn of a particular species is likely to live.

   d. This is the number of times a cultured cell replicates before dying.

9. **d.** is the answer. (p. 638)

a. & b. Progeria is a genetic disease; it is no caused by the wearing out of the body or by cellular mutations.

c. This explanation for aging was not discussed.

10. **b.** is the answer. (p. 623)

    a. Senile macular degeneration is an *eye* disease.

    c. This describes tinnitis.

    d. Senile macular degeneration affects one in si of those older than 74.

11. **b.** is the answer. In fact, just the opposite is true (p. 643)

12. **a.** is the answer. (p. 635)

13. **d.** is the answer. (p. 632)

    a. & b. According to these theories, aging i genetically predetermined.

    c. This theory attributes aging and disease to th accumulation of cellular errors.

14. **b.** is the answer. (p. 617)

    a. This is the study of old age.

    c. This is prejudice against the elderly.

    d. This is the weakening and decline of the body that occurs with age.

15. **b.** is the answer. (p. 637)

Matching Items

1. f (p. 620)   5. i (pp. 634–635)   9. c (p. 638)
2. h (p. 620)   6. e (p. 635)   10. a (p. 620)
3. k (p. 623)   7. b (p. 631)   11. j (p. 620)
4. g (p. 623)   8. d (p. 634)

THINKING CRITICALLY ABOUT CHAPTER 2:

1. **b.** is the answer. (pp. 616–617)

2. **c.** is the answer. (p. 617)

   a. Although Loretta is probably a developmenta psychologist, that category is too broad to be cor rect.

   b. Behaviorism describes her approach to study ing, not what she is studying.

   d. Demographics is the study of populations.

3. **b.** is the answer. (p. 620)

   a. An ageist is a person who is prejudiced agains the elderly.

   c. People who are "old-old" have social, physica and mental problems that hamper their success ful aging.

   d. A gerontologist is a person who studies aging.

4. **d.** is the answer. (p. 618)

5. **a.** is the answer. Most older adults suffer from

hearing loss, and this often makes them more likely to want to remain socially isolated. (pp. 624–625)

b. & c. There is no indication that she has digestive problems or that she does not want to associate with other older people.

b. is the answer. (p. 640)

c. & d. Older adults need not exercise longer, nor should their exercise be limited to water activities.

b. is the answer. (p. 635)

a. Errors in cellular duplication *do*, in part, explain primary aging.

c. For each species there *does* seem to be a genetically programmed maximum life span.

c. is the answer. (p. 635)

a. In fact, older adults are more likely to consult doctors.

b. There is no evidence that this is true.

d. Most older adults are adequately nourished.

c. is the answer. In this example, excessive use of the muscles of the arm and shoulder has contributed to their "wearing out." (p. 632)

c. is the answer. (p. 640)

a. Large doses of vitamins can be harmful.

b. Older adults need fewer calories to maintain body weight.

d. This is an unhealthy dietary regimen.

d. is the answer. (p. 640)

d. is the answer. Although nutrition *is* important to overall health at any age, the text does not suggest that specific nutrients can extend life. (pp. 638–639)

b. is the answer. (pp. 629–630)

a. At that age, women tend to be healthier than men.

c. Throughout life, women generally have *stronger* immune systems than men.

d. is the answer. (pp. 620)

d. is the answer. (p. 637)

a. Current average life expectancy is twenty-eight years more than it was at the turn of the century.

b. & c. Maximum life span has not changed since the turn of the century.

KEY TERMS

Ageism is prejudice against older people. (p. 616)

2. **Gerontology** is the study of old age. (p. 617)

3. **Demography** is the study of populations and social statistics associated with these populations. (p. 617)

4. The **dependency ratio** is the ratio of self-sufficient, productive adults to children and elderly adults. (p. 619)

5. Most of America's elderly can be classified as **young-old**, meaning that they are "healthy and vigorous, relatively well-off financially, well integrated into the lives of their families and communities, and politically active." (p. 620)

6. Older people who are classified as **old-old** are those who suffer severe physical, mental, or social problems in later life. (p. 620)

7. Elderly adults who are classified as **oldest-old** are dependent on others for almost everything. (p. 620)

8. **Primary aging** refers to the universal and irreversible physical changes that occur as people get older. (p. 620)

9. **Secondary aging** refers to changes that are more common as people age but are caused by health habits, genes, and other influences that vary from person to person. (p. 620)

10. **Cataracts** are a common eye disease involving the thickening of the lens of the eye that, left untreated, can distort vision. (p. 623)

11. **Glaucoma** is an eye disease that can destroy vision; it is caused by the hardening of the eyeball due to the buildup of fluid. (p. 623)

12. The leading cause of legal blindness in the elderly, **senile macular degeneration** involves deterioration of the retina. (p. 623)

13. **Presbycusis** is age-related loss of hearing. (p. 623)

14. **Elderspeak** is a babyish way of speaking to older adults, using simple sentences, higher pitch, and repetition. (p. 624)

15. Researchers who are interested in improving the health of the elderly focus on a **compression of morbidity**, that is, a limiting of the time any person spends ill. (p. 631)

16. According to the **wear-and-tear theory** of aging, the parts of the human body deteriorate with use as well as with accumulated exposure to pollution and radiation, inadequate nutrition, disease, and various other stresses. (p. 632)

17. **Oxygen free radicals** are highly unstable atoms with unpaired electrons that are capable of reacting with other molecules in the cell, tearing them apart and possibly accelerating aging. (p. 634)

18. **Antioxidants** are compounds such as vitamins E and C that nullify the effects of oxygen free radicals. (p. 634)

19. **B-cells** are immune system cells that are manufactured in the bone marrow and create antibodies that attack specific invading bacteria and viruses. (pp. 634–635)

    Memory aid: The *B*-cells come from the *b*one marrow and attack *b*acteria.

20. **T-cells** are immune system cells that are manufactured in the thymus and produce substances that attack infected cells of the body. (p. 635)

21. The **maximum life span** is the maximum number of years that a particular species is genetically programmed to live. For humans, the maximum life span is approximately 120 years. (p. 636)

22. **Average life expectancy** is the number of years the average newborn of a particular species is likely to live. (p. 637)

23. According to one theory of aging, our genetic makeup acts, in effect, as a **genetic clock**, trigger-

ing hormonal changes in the brain, regulating c lular processes, and "timing" aging and t moment of death. (p. 638)

24. The **Hayflick limit** is the maximum number times that cells cultured from humans and a mals divide before dying. (p. 638)

Cross-Check

ACROSS	DOWN
1. antioxidants	2. dependency ratio
5. maximum life span	3. secondary
6. glaucoma	4. oxygen free radicals
13. gerontology	7. ageism
15. primary	8. cataracts
17. wear-and-tear	9. young-old
18. old-old	10. demography
	11. genetic clock
	12. Hayflick limit
	14. oldest-old
	16. B-cells

CHAPTER 24

Late Adulthood: Cognitive Development

Chapter Overview

This chapter describes the changes in cognitive functioning associated with late adulthood. The first section reviews the parts of the information-processing system, providing experimental evidence that suggests declines in both the information-processing and the problem-solving abilities of older adults. The second section describes neurological and other reasons for this decline.

Nonetheless, as the third section points out, real-life conditions provide older adults with ample opportunity to compensate for the pattern of decline observed in the laboratory. It appears that, for most people, cognitive functioning in daily life remains essentially unimpaired.

The main exception to the generally positive picture of cognitive functioning during late adulthood is dementia, the subject of the fourth section. This pathological loss of intellectual ability can be caused by a variety of diseases and circumstances; risk factors, treatment, and prognosis differ accordingly.

The final section of the chapter makes it clear that cognitive changes during late adulthood are by no means restricted to declines in intellectual functioning. For many individuals, late adulthood is a time of great aesthetic, creative, philosophical, and spiritual growth.

NOTE: Answer guidelines for all Chapter 24 questions begin on page 370.

Guided Study

The text chapter should be studied one section at a time. Before you read, preview each section by skimming it, noting headings and boldface items. Then read the appropriate section objectives from the following outline. Keep these objectives in mind and, as you read the chapter section, search for the information that will enable you to meet each objective. Once you have finished a section, write out answers for its objectives.

Changes in Information Processing
(pp. 647–653)

1. Summarize the laboratory findings regarding changes in the sensitivity of the sensory register and the capacity of working memory during late adulthood.

2. Summarize the laboratory findings regarding changes in the older adult's ability to access the knowledge base and to use control processes efficiently.

3. (A Life-Span View) Describe research methods for assessing long-term memory in older adults.

Reasons for Age-Related Change (pp. 653–657)

4. Suggest several reasons, other than the aging process itself, that might contribute to age-related declines in cognitive functioning.

5. Describe age-related changes in the brain's size, weight, number of cells, and speed of processing.

Cognition in Daily Life (pp. 657–662)

6. (Research Report) Characterize and explain discrepancies between how the elderly perform on memory and problem-solving tasks in the laboratory, on the one hand, and in daily life, on the other.

7. Summarize and critique the findings of studies showing that special training can reduce the intellectual declines associated with aging.

8. (text and Changing Policy) Discuss the impact of nursing homes on the practical competencies of older adults, and whether age-related declines in memory and processing speed are inevitable.

Dementia (pp. 662–670)

9. Identify the two most common forms of dement and discuss the differences between them.

10. Identify and describe other organic causes dementia as well as causes of reversible deme tia.

New Cognitive Development in Later Life (pp. 670–674)

11. (text and In Person) Discuss the claims of deve opmentalists regarding the possibility of positi cognitive development during late adulthoo and cite several areas of life in which such deve opment may occur.

Chapter Review

When you have finished reading the chapter, wo through the material that follows to review Complete the sentences and answer the questions. / you proceed, evaluate your performance for each se tion by consulting the answers on page 370. Do n continue with the next section until you understar each answer. If you need to, review or reread th appropriate section in the textbook before continuin

1. Adult cognitive development becomes even mo _____ than before, meaning that some abilities increase, others wane, and some remain stable. It is also more complex and _____ than during early and midd adulthood.

Changes in Information Processing (pp. 647–653)

2. In Schaie's longitudinal study, older adults began to show significant declines on the five "primary mental abilities": _____

_____ , _____

_____ , _____

_____ , _____

_____ , and _____

_____ .

3. Variability in intellectual ability tends to be _____ (less/greater) in later life.

4. The _____ _____ stores incoming sensory information for a split second after it is received. Research suggests that senescence _____ (has no impact on/causes small declines in) the sensitivity and power of the sensory register.

5. Age-related changes in the sensory register _____ (can/cannot) easily be compensated for.

6. In order for sensory information to be registered, it must cross the _____ _____ . Due to sensory-system declines, some older people _____ (can/cannot) register certain information.

7. Research has found that differences in the subjects' _____ and _____ acuity accounted for half the variance in their _____ scores.

8. Because declines in sensory _____ can be much larger than declines in the sensory register, some experts believe that sensory function may be a fundamental index of _____ _____ .

9. Once information is perceived, it must be placed in _____ _____ .

10. Working memory has two interrelated functions: to temporarily _____ information and then to _____ it. Compared to younger adults, older adults seem to have _____ (smaller/larger/about the same) working-memory capacity.

11. Older adults are particularly likely to experience difficulty when they are asked to remember several items of information while _____ them in complex ways. This is especially true if the new information is mixed with material that is _____ . In general, increasing the number of things an adult must _____ to, or must _____ , reduces performance even more in late adulthood than earlier.

12. Of all the aspects of information processing, _____ _____ is the component that shows the most substantial declines with age.

13. The _____ _____ consists of one's storehouse of information held in _____-_____ memory. This storehouse is far from perfect, since _____ _____ and _____ _____ allow most of this material to be forgotten.

14. Research on memory reveals that _____ (short-term/ long-term/both short- and long-term/neither short- nor long-term) memory is (are) diminished in older adults.

15. Memory takes two forms: _____ memory is "automatic" memory involving _____ , _____ responses, _____ procedures, and the _____ . This type of memory is _____ (more/less) vulnerable to age-related deficits than is _____ memory. This latter type of memory involves _____ , _____ , _____ , and the like, most of which was _____ (consciously/unconsciously) learned.

16. As people get older, differences in implicit- and explicit-memory might be reflected in their remembering how to _____ a particular task but not being as able to _____ its actions.

17. (A Life-Span View) Definitive research assessing long-term memory is difficult because it is hard to verify _____ _____.
For adults of any age, events that occurred between ages _____ and _____ are remembered better than earlier or later events. A common memory error is _____ _____ , not remembering who or what was the source of a specific piece of information.

18. (A Life-Span View) One solution to the assessment problem has been to make _____-_____ comparisons of people's memories of public events or facts. Another has been to probe memory of _____ learning.

19. (A Life-Span View) Overall, how much of their knowledge base is available to older adults seems to depend less on _____ _____ and more on _____ _____ .

20. The _____ _____ of human information processing function in an executive role and include _____ mechanisms, _____ strategies, _____ _____ , and _____ _____ . Older adults tend to use _____ (simpler and less efficient/more complex but less efficient/about the same) control processes as younger adults.

21. Older adults are more likely to rely on prior _____ , general _____ , and _____ _____ .

22. A significant part of the explanation for memory difficulties in the aged may be inadequate _____ _____ .

Reasons for Age-Related Changes (pp. 653–657)

23. Declines in cognitive functioning may be due to the primary aging process and result from _____ and _____

changes. Declines may also be associated with secondary factors, including disparaging _____ , diminished opportunities for _____ , and difficulty with the methods psychologists use to _____ cognition.

24. Stereotyping is most harmful to an individual who _____ the prejudice and reacts with _____ .

25. Older adults may _____ (overestimate/underestimate) their memory skills when they were younger; consequently, they tend to _____ (overestimate/underestimate) their current memory losses. As a result of this misperception, older adults may lose _____ in their memory.

26. The impact of ageist stereotypes on cognitive functioning is revealed in a study in which the memory gap between old and young _____ (deaf/hearing) _____ (Chinese/American) students was twice as great as that for _____ (deaf/hearing) _____ (Chinese/American) students and five times as great as that for _____ .

27. Laboratory tests of memory may put older persons at a disadvantage because they generally use _____ material, which reduces motivation in older adults. Also, they are constructed to minimize spontaneous _____ , or the use of one item to recall another. Many tests also focus on abstract _____ memory, but in so doing, exclude _____ and _____ memory, as well as any benefit that a large _____ might provide.

28. Laboratory experiments also do not reflect differences in _____ and _____ , causing many older adults to question their purpose.

By the end of adulthood, the brain has lost at least _____ percent of its weight and _____ percent of its overall volume. Much of this loss is due to the death of _____ at an increasing rate after about age _____ .

The age-related changes that have the greatest impact on cognitive declines are related to the brain's _____ processes, which become _____ with age beginning in the late _____ . This can be traced to reduced production of _____ , including _____ , _____ , _____ , and _____ . It is also due to reductions in the volume of _____ _____ , the speed of the _____ _____ _____ , and the activation of various parts of the cortex.

According to some experts, the slowing of brain processes means that thinking becomes _____ , _____ , and _____ with advancing age. One way to compensate for this change is to provide older adults with more _____ to analyze information.

Intellectual ability _____ (is/is not) directly related to the brain's size, weight, or number of cells.

When brain cells die, existing cells _____ (take over/do not take over) their function. Throughout adulthood, _____ continue to grow from each neuron, allowing connections among surviving neurons to become more extensive.

Scientists have recently discovered that _____ cells in the brains of humans can generate new neurons and that there is less brain shrinkage in the _____ _____ than in lower portions of the brain.

gnition in Daily Life (pp. 657–662)

To an older adult, one of the most salient changes associated with aging is _____

_____ , particularly _____ failure.

36. Most older adults _____ (do/ do not) consider memory problems a significant handicap in daily life.

37. Research has shown that problem solving in daily life _____ (is/is not) less impaired with age than problem solving in a laboratory setting. In general, the less _____ the circumstances, the better an older person remembers.

38. (Research Report) Efforts to improve memory in older adults by teaching them memory techniques such as the _____ _____ _____ are not always effective.

State four general conclusions regarding age-related changes in memory and cognition.

a. _____

b. _____

c. _____

d. _____

39. In problem-solving tasks, older adults tend to be _____ (slower/faster) to abandon old strategies

40. A hallmark of successful aging is "_____ _____ _____ _____ ," or the capability to compensate for age-related declines in intellectual functioning.

State several methods older adults use to compensate for intellectual declines associated with aging.

41. Through regular _____ adults may be able to halt or even reverse the slowing of thinking processes that accompanies aging.

In addition, _____ _____ can help by stimulating _____ to develop new connections. It is also possible to slow brain deterioration with low-fat diets that reduce _____ , by consumption of _____ such as vitamin _____ , by replacement of _____ in women, and the use of _____ steroids as well as _____ and _____ .

42. Four factors that have a direct impact on thinking during adulthood are _____ functioning, _____ _____ , past _____ , and the individual's sense of _____ .

43. (Changing Policy) Because many nursing homes reinforce _____ , _____ , and _____ behaviors in residents, they may not foster the kinds of practical competencies that are experienced by older adults who live independently. Research has shown that giving patients the freedom to make mistakes in order to preserve their health—an approach called _____ _____ _____—may slow the more rapid decline observed in traditional nursing homes.

Dementia (pp. 662–670)

44. Although pathological loss of intellectual ability in elderly people is often referred to as _____ , a more precise term for this loss is _____ , which is defined as _____ .

45. Traditionally, when dementia occurred before age _____ , it was called _____ _____ ; when it occurred after this age, it was called _____ _____ . This age-based distinction is arbitrary, however, because the same _____ may occur at any age.

46. Dementia, which can be caused by more than 70 diseases and circumstances, has several general

symptoms, including _____ _____ .

47. The most common form of dementia is _____ _____ . This disorder is characterized by abnormalities the _____ _____ , called _____ and _____ , that destroy normal brain functioning.

48. Plaques are formed _____ (inside/outside) the brain cells from a protein called _____ ; tangles are masses (protein found _____ (inside/outside) the cells. Plaques and tangles usually begin in the _____ of the brain.

49. Physiologically, the brain damage that accompanies this disease _____ (does/does not) vary with the age of the victim.

50. When Alzheimer's disease appears in _____ (middle/late) adulthood, which is quite _____ (common/rare), it usually progresses _____ (less/more) quickly, reaching the last phase within _____ years. such cases, the disease is caused by one of sever _____ abnormalities.

51. With age, Alzheimer's disease becomes _____ (more/no more/less) common, affecting about one in every _____ adults over age 65 and about 1 in every _____ over age 85.

52. About _____ (what proportion?) (the population inherits the gene _____ , which increases the risk of Alzheimer's disease. Up to _____ percent inherit the protective _____ allele of the same gene, which may dissipate th _____ that cause the formation of plaques. More than _____ (what proportion?) of all adults have neither the prote tive nor the destructive gene.

53. The first stage of Alzheimer's disease is marked by _____ about recent events. Mo

people _____ (recognize/do not recognize) that they have a memory problem during this stage, which is often indistinguishable from the normal decline in _____ memory called _____ _____ _____ .

. In the second stage, there are noticeable deficits in the person's _____ and _____-_____ _____ . The third stage begins when memory loss becomes dangerous and _____ because the person can no longer manage _____ _____ _____ . People in the fourth stage require _____-_____ _____ . In the fifth stage, people become completely _____ and do not respond with any action or emotion at all. In general, death comes _____ (how many years?) after stage one.

. There _____ (is/is not) a cure for Alzheimer's disease. One promising treatment is the use of _____ _____ _____ to delay the disease in women. Other approaches aim to slow the buildup of the protein _____ or use _____ therapy to teach victims and caregivers ways to make the disease less devastating.

. The second major type of dementia is _____-_____ _____ . This condition occurs because a temporary obstruction of the _____ _____ , called a(n) _____ , prevents a sufficient supply of blood from reaching the brain. This causes destruction of brain tissue, commonly called a(n) _____ .

. The underlying cause of MID is systemic _____ , which is common in people who have problems with their _____ systems, including those with _____ _____ ,

_____ , tingling or _____ in their extremities, and _____ . Measures to improve circulation, such as _____ , or to control hypertension and diabetes through _____ and _____ , can help to prevent or control the progress of MID.

58. Unlike the person with Alzheimer's disease, the person with MID shows a _____ (gradual/sudden) drop in intellectual functioning. The prognosis for a person with MID is generally quite _____ (good/poor).

59. Another form of dementia, called _____ _____ , originates in brain areas that do not directly involve thinking and memory. These dementias, which cause a progressive loss of _____ control, include _____ disease, _____ disease, and _____ _____ .

60. The best known of these dementias is _____ _____ , which produces muscle tremors or rigidity. This disease is related to the degeneration of neurons that produce the neurotransmitter _____ . Among the factors implicated as contributors to this disease are _____ _____ and certain _____ .

61. Another organic cause of dementia is _____ disease, which involves atrophy of the _____ and _____ lobes of the brain. The symptoms of this disease include _____ changes such as the loss of _____ skills and _____ .

62. Many AIDS and syphilis patients develop a brain _____ that causes dementia.

63. Chronic alcoholism can lead to _____ syndrome, the chief symptom of which is severely impaired _____-_____ _____ .

64. Oftentimes the elderly are thought to be suffering from brain disease when, in fact, their symptoms are caused by some other factor such as

_____ , _____

_____ , _____

_____ , or _____ .

65. Symptoms of dementia can result from drug _____ that occur when a person is taking several different medications. This problem is made worse by the fact that many of the drugs prescribed to older adults can, by themselves, slow down _____

_____ .

66. In general, psychological illnesses such as schizophrenia are _____ (more/less) common in the elderly than in younger adults. Approximately _____ percent of the elderly who are diagnosed as demented are actually experiencing psychological illness.

67. At some time during their later years, _____ (many/a small percentage of) older adults experience symptoms of depression. Generally speaking, depression _____ (is/is not) very treatable in late adulthood.

68. One consequence of untreated depression among the elderly is that the rate of _____ is higher for those over age _____ than for any other group.

69. In most cases, the precipitating event for suicide is a(n) _____ _____ , with _____ and _____ being the most common such events. A related cause is _____ , particularly _____ or diseases that affect the _____ .

New Cognitive Development in Later Life
(pp. 670–674)

70. According to Erik Erikson, older adults are more interested in _____

_____

than younger adults and, as the "social witness-

es" to life, are more aware of the _____ of the generations.

71. According to Abraham Maslow, older adults are more likely to achieve _____ .

72. (In Person) Many people become more apprecia-tive of _____ and _____

_____ as they get older.

73. Many people also become more _____ and _____ than when they were younger.

74. One form of this attempt to put life into perspec-tive is called the _____

_____ , in which the older person connects his or her own life with the future.

75. The reflectivity of old age may explain why pro-fessional productivity in the fields of _____ and _____ peaks in the 60s and 70s.

76. One of the most positive attributes commonly associated with older people is _____ , which Baltes defines as expert knowledge in the _____ _____ of life.

List five features that distinguish wisdom from oth-er forms of human understanding.

Progress Test 1

Multiple-Choice Questions

Circle your answers to the following questions and check them with the answers on page 371. If your answer is incorrect, read the explanation for why it is incorrect and then consult the appropriate pages of the text (in parentheses following the correct answer).

1. The information-processing component that is concerned with the temporary storage of incoming sensory information is:
   a. working memory.
   b. long-term memory.
   c. the knowledge base.
   d. the sensory register.

2. Older adults tend to have the greatest difficulty picking up sensory stimuli that are:
   a. very loud or bright.
   b. ambiguous or of low intensity.
   c. abstract or meaningless.
   d. all of the above.

3. The two basic functions of working memory are:
   a. storage that enables conscious use and processing of information.
   b. temporary storage and processing of sensory stimuli.
   c. automatic memories and retrieval of learned memories.
   d. permanent storage and retrieval of information.

4. Memory for skills is called:
   a. explicit memory.
   b. declarative memory.
   c. episodic memory.
   d. implicit memory.

5. Strategies to retain and retrieve information in the knowledge base are part of which basic component of information processing?
   a. sensory register
   b. working memory
   c. control processes
   d. explicit memory

6. The plaques and tangles that accompany Alzheimer's disease usually begin in the:
   a. temporal lobe.
   b. frontal lobe.
   c. hippocampus.
   d. cerebral cortex.

7. Secondary aging factors that may explain some declines in cognitive functioning include:
   a. fewer opportunities for learning in old age.
   b. disparaging self-perceptions of cognitive abilities.
   c. difficulty with traditional methods of measuring cognitive functioning.
   d. all of the above.

8. (Changing Policy) Research showing that special training can remediate age-related cognitive declines must be interpreted cautiously because:
   a. it generally has involved relatively healthy and independent adults rather than those who are in poor health.

   b. there is evidence that intellectual plasticity increases with age.
   c. the studies are few in number and are based on very small sample sizes.
   d. of all of the above reasons.

9. Which of the following is a characteristic of laboratory experiments that inhibits the older adult's memory abilities?
   a. practice
   b. priming
   c. motivation
   d. time limitations

10. Dementia refers to:
    a. pathological loss of intellectual functioning.
    b. the increasing forgetfulness that sometimes accompanies the aging process.
    c. abnormal behavior associated with mental illness and with advanced stages of alcoholism.
    d. a genetic disorder that doesn't become overtly manifested until late adulthood.

11. Which of the following diseases does *not* belong with the others?
    a. Huntington's disease
    b. Parkinson's disease
    c. multiple sclerosis
    d. multi-infarct dementia

12. Alzheimer's disease is characterized by:
    a. a proliferation of plaques and tangles in the cerebral cortex.
    b. a destruction of brain tissue as a result of strokes.
    c. rigidity and tremor of the muscles.
    d. an excess of fluid pressing on the brain.

13. Multi-infarct dementia and Alzheimer's disease differ in their progression in that:
    a. multi-infarct dementia never progresses beyond the first stage.
    b. multi-infarct dementia is marked by sudden drops and temporary improvements, whereas decline in Alzheimer's disease is steady.
    c. multi-infarct dementia leads to rapid deterioration and death, whereas Alzheimer's disease may progress over a period of years.
    d. the progression of Alzheimer's disease may be halted or slowed, whereas the progression of multi-infarct dementia is irreversible.

14. Medication has been associated with symptoms of dementia in the elderly for all of the following reasons *except*:
    a. standard drug dosages are often too strong for the elderly.
    b. the elderly tend to become psychologically dependent upon drugs.
    c. drugs sometimes have the side effect of slowing mental processes.
    d. the intermixing of drugs can sometimes have detrimental effects on cognitive functioning.

15. The primary purpose of the life review is to:
    a. enhance one's spirituality.
    b. produce an autobiography.
    c. give advice to younger generations.
    d. put one's life into perspective.

True or False Items

Write T (*true*) or F (*false*) on the line in front of each statement.

_____ 1. As long as their vision and hearing remain unimpaired, older adults are no less efficient than younger adults at inputting information.

_____ 2. Changes in the sensory register are a major contributor to declines in information processing.

_____ 3. Intellectual ability is directly related to the brain's size, weight, and number of cells.

_____ 4. A majority of the elderly feel frustrated and hampered by memory loss in their daily lives.

_____ 5. In studies of problem solving in real-life contexts, the scores of older adults were better than those of younger adults.

_____ 6 The majority of cases of dementia are organically caused.

_____ 7. Alzheimer's disease is partly genetic.

_____ 8. When brain cells die, existing cells may take over their functions.

_____ 9. Late adulthood is often associated with a narrowing of interests and an exclusive focus on the self.

_____ 10. According to Maslow, self-actualization is actually more likely to be reached during late adulthood.

Progress Test 2

Progress Test 2 should be completed during a final chapter review. Answer the following questions after you thoroughly understand the correct answers for the Chapter Review and Progress Test 1.

Multiple-Choice Questions

1. Research suggests that aging results in:
   a. increased sensitivity of the sensory register.
   b. a significant decrease in the sensitivity of the sensory register that cannot usually be compensated for.
   c. a small decrease in the sensory register's sensitivity that can usually be compensated for.
   d. no noticeable changes in the sensory register.

2. Which of the following most accurately characterizes age-related changes in working memory?
   a. Both storage capacity and processing efficiency decline.
   b. Storage capacity declines while processing efficiency remains stable.
   c. Storage capacity remains stable while processing efficiency declines.
   d. Both storage capacity and processing efficiency remain stable.

3. Information remembered for years or decades is stored in:
   a. sensory register.   c. long-term memory.
   b. working memory.   d. short-term memory.

4. Conscious memory for words, data, and concepts is called _____ memory.
   a. sensory
   b. implicit
   c. explicit
   d. knowledge base

5. In general, with increasing age the control processes used to remember new information:
   a. become more efficient.
   b. become more complex.
   c. become more intertwined.
   d. become simpler and less efficient.

6. Which type of memory is most vulnerable to age-related deficits?
   a. sensory register
   b. implicit memory
   c. explicit memory
   d. knowledge base

7. Regarding the role of genes in Alzheimer's disease, which of the following is *not* true?
   a. Some people inherit a gene that increases their risk of developing the disease.
   b. Some people inherit a gene that lowers their risk of developing the disease.
   c. Most people inherit either the protective or the destructive gene.
   d. Alzheimer's disease is a multifaceted disease that involves multiple genetic and environmental factors.

8. One study tested memory in different age groups by requiring younger and older adults to remember to make telephone calls at a certain time. It was found that:
   a. older adults did worse than younger adults because their memories were not as good.
   b. older adults did better than younger adults because they were able to trust their memories.
   c. older adults did better than younger adults because they didn't trust their memories and therefore used various reminders.
   d. older adults did worse than younger adults because they were less accustomed to having to do things at a certain time.

9. Laboratory studies of memory in late adulthood fail to take into account the effects of:
   a. the knowledge base of older adults.
   b. practice, priming, and enhanced motivation.
   c. the explicit memory that is central to the functioning of older adults.
   d. the ability of older adults to rely on their long-term memories.

10. Dementia:
   a. is more likely to occur among the aged.
   b. has no relationship to age.
   c. cannot occur before the age of 60.
   d. is an inevitable occurrence during late adulthood.

11. The most common form of dementia is:
   a. Alzheimer's disease.
   b. multi-infarct dementia.
   c. Parkinson's disease.
   d. alcoholism and depression.

12. Organic causes of dementia include all of the following *except*:
   a. Parkinson's disease.   c. brain tumors.
   b. Down syndrome.   d. leukemia.

13. The psychological illness most likely to be misdiagnosed as dementia is:
   a. schizophrenia.   c. personality disorder.
   b. depression.   d. phobic disorders.

14. On balance, it can be concluded that positive cognitive development during late adulthood:
   a. occurs only for a small minority of individuals.
   b. leads to thought processes that are more appropriate to the final stage of life.
   c. makes older adults far less pragmatic than younger adults.
   d. is impossible in view of increasing deficits in cognitive functioning.

15. A key factor underlying the older adult's cognitive developments in the realms of aesthetics, philosophy, and spiritualism may be:
   a. the realization that one's life is drawing to a close.
   b. the despair associated with a sense of isolation from the community.
   c. the need to leave one's mark on history.
   d. a growing indifference to the outside world.

Matching Items

Match each definition or description with its corresponding term.

Terms

_____ 1. sensory register
_____ 2. working memory
_____ 3. knowledge base
_____ 4. control processes
_____ 5. subcortical dementias
_____ 6. dementia
_____ 7. Alzheimer's disease
_____ 8. multi-infarct dementia (MID)
_____ 9. Parkinson's disease
_____ 10. source amnesia
_____ 11. life review

Definitions or Descriptions

a. the inability to remember the origins of a specific piece of information
b. temporarily stores information for conscious processing
c. strategies for retaining and retrieving information
d. severely impaired thinking, memory, or problem solving ability
e. stores incoming sensory information for a split second
f. caused by a temporary obstruction of the blood vessels
g. stores information for several minutes to several decades
h. caused by a degeneration of neurons that produce dopamine
i. putting one's life into perspective
j. characterized by plaques and tangles in the cerebral cortex
k. brain disorders that do not directly involve thinking and memory

Thinking Critically About Chapter 24

Answer these questions the day before an exam as a final check on your understanding of the chapter's terms and concepts.

1. Leland's parents are in their 70s, and he wants to do something to ensure that their cognitive abilities remain sharp for years to come. As a friend, what would you encourage Leland to suggest that his parents do?
   a. They should take long walks several times a week.
   b. They should spend time reading and doing crossword puzzles.
   c. They should go to a neurologist for regular checkups.
   d. They should do a. and b.

2. An example of priming is:
   a. trying to remember an author's name by remembering the titles of various books he or she has written.
   b. trying to solve a problem more efficiently by thinking of how to shorten the number of steps involved.
   c. writing down a telephone number to be sure you won't forget it.
   d. asking a friend to call and remind you about the time of a meeting that you'll both be attending.

3. (A Life-Span View) Although 75-year-old Sharonda remembers a relative once telling her that her ancestors were royalty in their native country, she can't recall which relative it was. Like many older adults, Sharonda is evidently displaying signs of:
   a. multi-infarct dementia.
   b. Pick's disease.
   c. subcortical dementia.
   d. source amnesia.

4. Depression among the elderly is a serious problem because:
   a. rates of depression are far higher for the elderly than for younger adults.
   b. in late adulthood depression becomes extremely difficult to treat.
   c. depression in the elderly often goes untreated, contributing to a higher rate of suicide than for any other age group.
   d. organic forms of dementia cause depression.

5. Given the nature of cognitive development, a profession in which an individual's greatest achievements are particularly likely to occur during late adulthood is:

a. medicine.
c. mathematics.
b. philosophy.
d. administration.

6. Developmentalists believe that older people's tendency to reminisce:

a. represents an unhealthy preoccupation with the self and the past.
b. is an underlying cause of age segregation.
c. is a necessary and healthy process.
d. is a result of a heightened aesthetic sense.

7. A patient has the following symptoms: atrophy of frontal and temporal lobes, loss of social skills, personality change, and loss of memory. The patient is probably suffering from:

a. Alzheimer's disease.
b. Pick's disease.
c. Huntington's disease.
d. Parkinson's disease.

8. Because of deficits in the sensory register, older people may tend to:

a. forget the names of people and places.
b. be distracted by irrelevant stimuli.
c. miss details in a dimly lit room.
d. reminisce at length about the past.

9. Holding material in your mind for a minute or two requires which type of memory?

a. short-term memory
c. long-term memory
b. explicit memory
d. sensory register

10. Marisa's presentation on "Reversing the Age-Related Slowdown in Thinking" includes all of the following points *except*:

a. regular exercise.
b. avoiding the use of anti-inflammatory drugs.
c. cognitive stimulation.
d. consumption of antioxidants.

11. Which type of material would 72-year-old Jessica probably have the greatest difficulty remembering?

a. the dates of birth of family members
b. a short series of numbers she has just heard
c. the first house she lived in
d. technical terms from her field of expertise prior to retirement

12. Sixty-five-year-old Lena is becoming more reflective and philosophical as she grows older. A developmental psychologist would probably say that Lena:

a. had unhappy experiences as a younger adult.
b. is demonstrating a normal, age-related tendency toward interiority.
c. will probably become introverted and reclusive as she gets older.
d. feels that her life has been a failure.

13. Concerning the public's fear of Alzheimer's disease, which of the following is true?

a. A serious loss of memory, such as that occurring in people with Alzheimer's disease, can be expected by most people once they reach their 60s.
b. Of people 65 to 75, at most 5 percent of the population is affected by conditions such as Alzheimer's disease.
c. Alzheimer's disease is much more common today than it was 50 years ago.
d. Alzheimer's disease is less common today than it was 50 years ago.

14. At the present stage of research into cognitive development during late adulthood, which of the following statements has the greatest support?

a. There is uniform decline in all stages of memory during late adulthood.
b. Long-term memory shows the greatest decline with age.
c. Working memory shows the greatest decline with age.
d. The decline in memory may be the result of the failure to use effective encoding and retrieval strategies.

15. Lately, Wayne's father, who is 73, harps on the fact that he forgets small things such as where he put the house keys and has trouble eating and sleeping. The family doctor diagnoses Wayne's father as:

a. being in the early stages of Alzheimer's disease.
b. being in the later stages of Alzheimer's disease.
c. suffering from senile dementia.
d. possibly suffering from depression.

Key Terms

1. explicit memory
2. implicit memory
3. control processes
4. source amnesia
5. priming
6. dementia
7. Alzheimer's disease
8. multi-infarct dementia (MID)
9. subcortical dementias
10. Parkinson's disease
11. life review
12. wisdom

ANSWERS

CHAPTER REVIEW

1. multidirectional; multicontextual
2. verbal meaning; spatial orientation; inductive reasoning; number ability; word fluency
3. greater
4. sensory register; causes small declines in
5. can
6. sensory threshold; cannot
7. visual; auditory; cognitive
8. acuity; cognitive aging
9. working memory
10. store; process; smaller
11. analyzing; distracting; attend; ignore
12. working memory
13. knowledge base; long-term; selective attention; selective memory
14. both short- and long-term
15. implicit; habits; emotional; routine; senses; less; explicit; words; data; concepts; consciously
16. perform; describe
17. personal recollections; 10; 30; source amnesia
18. cross-sectional; high school
19. how long ago information was learned; how well it was learned
20. control processes; storage; retrieval; selective attention; logical analysis; simpler and less efficient

21. knowledge; principles; rules of thumb
22. control processes
23. neurophysiological; biological; self-perceptions; learning; measure
24. internalizes; helplessness, self-doubt, or misplaced anger
25. overestimate; overestimate; confidence
26. hearing; American; deaf; American; Chinese
27. meaningless; priming; explicit; implicit; contextual; knowledge base
28. context; motivation
29. 5; 10; neurons; 60
30. communication; slower; 50s; neurotransmitters; dopamine; glucamate; acetylcholine; serotonin; neural fluid; cerebral blood flow
31. slower; simpler; shallower; time
32. is not
33. take over; dendrites
34. stem; cerebral cortex
35. cognitive decline; memory
36. do not
37. is; artificial
38. method of loci
    a. Mental processes slow down with age.
    b. The elderly do show memory declines.
    c. The elderly are less likely to use memory strategies.
    d. Memory in late adulthood is not as weak as anticipated.
39. slower
40. selective optimization with compensation

Older adults compensate by using mnemonic devices and written reminders, by allowing additional time for problem solving, by repeating instructions that might be confusing, and by focusing on meaningful tasks and ignoring those that are irrelevant.

41. exercise; cognitive stimulation; dendrites; atherosclerosis; antioxidants; E; estrogen; anti-inflammatory; aspirin; ibuprofen
42. pulmonary; physical exercise; education; control
43. passive; dependent; predictable; therapeutic risk taking
44. senility; dementia; severely impaired judgment, memory, or problem-solving ability
45. 60; presenile dementia; senile dementia (or senile psychosis); symptoms
46. severe memory loss, rambling conversation and language lapses, confusion about place and time

inability to function socially or professionally, and changes in personality

7. Alzheimer's disease; cerebral cortex; plaques; tangles

8. outside; B-amyloid; inside; hippocampus

9. does not

0. middle; rare; more; 3 to 5; genetic

1. more; 100; 5

2. one-fifth; apoE4; 10; apoE2; proteins; half

3. absentmindedness; recognize; explicit; benign senescent forgetfulness

4. concentration; short-term memory; debilitating; basic daily needs; full-time care; mute; 10 to 15

5. is not; estrogen replacement therapy; APP; group and family

6. multi-infarct dementia; blood vessels; infarct; stroke (or ministroke)

7. arteriosclerosis; circulatory; heart disease; hypertension; numbness; diabetes; exercise; diet; drugs

. sudden; poor

9. subcortical dementia; motor; Parkinson's; Huntington's; multiple sclerosis

0. Parkinson's disease; dopamine; genetic vulnerability; viruses

1. Pick's; frontal; temporal; personality; social; motivation

2. infection

3. Korsakoff's; short-term memory

4. medication; alcohol abuse; mental illness; depression

5. interactions; mental processes

6. less; 10

7. many; is

8. suicide; 60

9. social loss; retirement; widowhood; illness; cancer; brain

0. arts, children, and the whole of human experience; interdependence

1. self-actualization

2. nature; aesthetic experiences

3. reflective; philosophical

4. life review

5. history; philosophy

6. wisdom; fundamental pragmatics

isdom is unspecialized and concerns all of human perience; entails practical and procedural knowlge; defines a contextual approach to life problems; cepts uncertainty in defining and solving life's oblems; and recognizes individual differences in lues, goals, and priorities.

PROGRESS TEST 1

Multiple-Choice Questions

1. **d.** is the answer. (p. 648)

   a. Working memory deals with mental, rather than sensory, activity.

   b. & c. Long-term memory, which is a subcomponent of the knowledge base, includes information that is stored for several minutes to several years.

2. **b.** is the answer. (p. 648)

3. **a.** is the answer. (p. 648)

   b. These are the functions of the sensory register.

   c. This refers to long-term memory's processing of implicit and explicit memories, respectively.

   d. This is the function of long-term memory.

4. **d.** is the answer. (p. 650)

   a. & b. Explicit memory is memory of facts and experiences, which is why it is often called declarative memory.

   c. This type of memory, which is a type of explicit memory, was not discussed.

5. **c.** is the answer. (p. 651)

6. **d.** is the answer. (p. 663)

7. **d.** is the answer. (p. 653)

8. **a.** is the answer. (p. 661)

   b. Plasticity tends to *decrease* with age.

   c. The text did not mention this as a limitation of such studies.

9. **d.** is the answer. (p. 655)

10. **a.** is the answer. (p. 662)

11. **d.** is the answer. Each of the other answers is an example of subcortical dementia. (pp. 666–667)

12. **a.** is the answer. (p. 663)

    b. This describes multi-infarct dementia.

    c. This describes Parkinson's disease.

    d. This was not given in the text as a cause of dementia.

13. **b.** is the answer. (p. 667)

    a. Because multiple infarcts typically occur, the disease *is* progressive in nature.

    c. The text does not suggest that MID necessarily leads to quick death.

    d. At present, Alzheimer's disease is untreatable.

14. **b.** is the answer. (p. 668)

15. **d.** is the answer. (p. 670)

True or False Items

1. F   The slowing of perceptual processes and decreases in attention associated with aging are also

likely to affect efficiency of input. (pp. 648–649)

2. F   If they do in fact occur, changes in the sensory register are too insignificant to seriously affect information processing. (p. 648)

3. F   These affect intellectual activity only in cases of extreme malformation, damage, or disease. (p. 657)

4. F   Most older adults perceive some memory loss but do not feel that it affects their daily functioning. (p. 657)

5. T (p. 658)

6. T (pp. 662–668)

7. T   (p. 663)

8. T (p. 657)

9. F   Interests often broaden during late adulthood, and there is by no means exclusive focus on the self. (p. 670)

10. T (p. 670)

PROGRESS TEST 2

Multiple-Choice Questions

1. **c.** is the answer. (p. 648)

2. **a.** is the answer. (p. 649)

3. **c.** is the answer. (p. 649)

    a. The sensory register stores information for a split second.

    b. Working memory stores information briefly.

    d. Short-term memory is another name for working memory.

4. **c.** is the answer. (p. 650)

    a. Sensory memory, or the sensory register, stores incoming sensory information for only a split second.

    b. This is unconscious, automatic memory for skills.

    c. Explicit memory *is* only one part of the knowledge base. Another part—implicit memory—is unconscious memory for skills.

5. **d.** is the answer. (p. 651)

6. **c.** is the answer. (p. 650)

    a. & b. Age-related deficits in these types of memory are minimal.

    d. Although explicit memory *is* part of the knowledge base, another part—implicit memory—shows minimal age-related deficits.

7. **c.** is the answer. More than half of all people inherit *neither* the protective nor the destructive gene. (p. 663)

8. **c.** is the answer. (p. 658)

9. **b.** is the answer. Laboratory experiments test explicit memory, not implicit memory. (p. 655)

10. **a.** is the answer. Although age is not the key factor, it is true that dementia is more likely to occur in older adults. (p. 662)

11. **a.** is the answer. (p. 662)

    b. MID is responsible for about 15 percent of all dementia.

    c. & d. Compared to Alzheimer's disease, which accounts for about 70 percent of all dementia, these account for a much lower percentage.

12. **d.** is the answer. (pp. 662–668)

13. **b.** is the answer. (p. 669)

    a. & c. These psychological illnesses are less common in the elderly than in younger adults, and less common than depression among the elderly.

    d. This disorder was not discussed in association with dementia.

14. **b.** is the answer. (pp. 670–672)

    a. & d. Positive cognitive development is *typical* of older adults.

    c. Pragmatism is one characteristic of wisdom, an attribute commonly associated with older people.

15. **a.** is the answer. (p. 670)

    b. & c. Although these may be true of some older adults, they are not necessarily a *key* factor in cognitive development during late adulthood.

    d. In fact, older adults are typically *more* concerned with the whole of human experience.

Matching Items

1. e (p. 648)	5. k (p. 667)	9. h (p. 667)
2. b (p. 648)	6. d (p. 662)	10. a (p. 652)
3. g (p. 649)	7. j (p. 663)	11. i (p. 670)
4. c (p. 651)	8. f (p. 666)	

THINKING CRITICALLY ABOUT CHAPTER 24

1. **d.** is the answer. While c. might be something they should do, the most important things are for them to get exercise and maintain activities that promote cognitive stimulation. (p. 660)

2. **a.** is the answer. (p. 655)

    b., c., & d. These are examples of control processes that facilitate problem solving (b.) and retrieval (c. & d.).

3. **d.** is the answer. (p. 652)

a., b. & c. Sharonda's inability to recall the source of this information is a common form of forgetfulness among older adults; it is not necessarily a sign of dementia.

4. **c.** is the answer. (p. 669)

a. In general, psychological illnesses are less common in the elderly than in younger adults.

b. Depression is quite treatable at any age.

d. Symptoms of *depression* are often mistaken as signs of *dementia*.

5. **b.** is the answer. (p. 672)

6. **c.** is the answer. (p. 672)

d. This would lead to a greater appreciation of nature and art, but not necessarily to a tendency to reminisce.

7. **b.** is the answer. (p. 668)

8. **c.** is the answer. (p. 648)

a. & d. The sensory register is concerned with noticing sensory events rather than with memory.

b. Age-related deficits in the sensory register are most likely for ambiguous or weak stimuli.

9. **a.** is the answer. (p. 648)

b. Explicit memory involves words, data, concepts, and the like. It is *a part of* long-term memory.

c. Long-term memory includes information remembered for years or decades.

d. The sensory register stores information for a split second.

10. **b.** is the answer. In fact, *use* of anti-inflammatory drugs may help sustain cognitive functioning in old age. (pp. 660, 662)

11. **b.** is the answer. Older individuals are particularly likely to experience difficulty holding new information in mind, particularly when it is essentially meaningless. (p. 655)

a., c., & d. These are examples of long-term memory, which declines very little with age.

12. **b.** is the answer. (p. 672)

13. **b.** is the answer. (p. 663)

c. & d. The text does not indicate the existence of cohort effects in the incidence of Alzheimer's disease.

14. **d.** is the answer. (pp. 651–652)

a. Some aspects of information processing, such as long-term memory, show less decline with age than others, such as working memory.

b. & c. The text does not indicate that one particular subcomponent of memory shows the *greatest* decline.

15. **d.** is the answer. (pp. 669)

a., b., & c. The symptoms Wayne's father is experiencing are those of depression, which is often misdiagnosed as dementia in the elderly.

KEY TERMS

1. **Explicit memory** is memory of consciously learned words, data, and concepts. This type of memory is more vulnerable to age-related decline than implicit memory. (p. 650)

2. **Implicit memory** is unconscious or automatic memory involving habits, emotional responses, routine procedures, and the senses. (p. 650)

3. Memory **control processes**, which include strategies for retaining information in the knowledge base, retrieval strategies for reaccessing information, selective attention, and rules or strategies that aid problem solving, tend to become simpler and less efficient with age. (p. 651)

4. **Source amnesia** is the inability to remember the origins of a specific fact, idea, or conversation. (p. 652)

5. **Priming** is the use of an event or clue to make it easier to remember another one. (p. 655)

6. **Dementia** is severely impaired judgment, memory, or problem-solving ability. (p. 662)

7. **Alzheimer's disease**, a progressive disorder that is the most common form of dementia, is characterized by plaques and tangles in the cerebral cortex that destroy normal brain functioning. (p. 663)

8. **Multi-infarct dementia (MID)**, which accounts for about 15 percent of all dementia, occurs because an infarct, or temporary obstruction of the blood vessels (often called a stroke), prevents a sufficient supply of blood from reaching an area of the brain. (p. 666)

9. **Subcortical dementias** such as Parkinson's disease, Huntington's disease, and multiple sclerosis cause a progressive loss of motor control which initially does not directly involve thinking or memory. (p. 667)

10. **Parkinson's disease**, which produces dementia as well as muscle rigidity or tremors, is related to the degeneration of neurons that produce dopamine. (p. 667)

11. In the **life review**, an older person attempts to put his or her life into perspective by recalling and recounting various aspects of life to members of the younger generations. (p. 670)

12. As used in this context, **wisdom** refers to exper knowledge in the fundamental pragmatics of life (p. 673)

25

Late Adulthood: Psychosocial Development

Chapter Overview

Ageism distorts popular perceptions of the later years with negative stereotypes. Certain psychosocial changes are common during this stage of the life span —retirement, the death of a spouse, and failing health —yet people respond to these experiences in vastly different ways.

Individual experiences may help to explain the fact that theories of psychosocial aging, discussed in the first section of the chapter, are often diametrically opposed. The second section of the chapter focuses on the challenges to generativity that accompany late adulthood, such as finding new sources of achievement once derived from work. In the third section, the importance of marriage, friends, neighbors, and family in providing social support is discussed, as are the different experiences of married and single older adults. The final section focuses on the frail elderly— the minority of older adults, often poor and/or ill, who require extensive care.

NOTE: Answer guidelines for all Chapter 25 questions begin on page 387.

Guided Study

The text chapter should be studied one section at a time. Before you read, preview each section by skimming it, noting headings and boldface items. Then read the appropriate section objectives from the following outline. Keep these objectives in mind and, as you read the chapter section, search for the information that will enable you to meet each objective. Once you have finished a section, write out answers for its objectives.

Theories of Late Adulthood (pp. 677–684)

1. Explain the central premises of self-theories of psychosocial development during late adulthood.

2. Discuss Erikson's stage of integrity versus despair and the process of achieving integrity in old age.

3. Identify and describe the stratification theories of psychosocial development during late adulthood.

4. Discuss dynamic theories of late adulthood.

Keeping Active (pp. 684–690)

5. Discuss the impact of retirement on the individual and the factors that influence adjustment to this event.

6. List and discuss several alternative sources of achievement during late adulthood.

7. (Changing Policy) Explain how the economic circumstances of the elderly have changed in recent years, and discuss the issue of generational equity.

The Social Convoy (pp. 690–697)

8. Describe the components of the social convoy, and explain this convoy's increasing importance during late adulthood.

9. Discuss how, and why, marriage relationships tend to change as people grow old.

10. Discuss the impact of being old and single (never-married, divorced, or widowed) on both women and men.

11. (text and In Person) Discuss friendships and sibling relationships among older people.

12. Discuss the relationship between the generations as it exists today, and identify several reasons for the current pattern of detachment.

The Frail Elderly (pp. 698–705)

13. Describe the frail elderly, and explain why their number is growing.

14. (text and A Life-Span View) Identify and discuss four factors that may protect the elderly from frailty.

5. Discuss alternative care arrangements for the frail elderly, identifying some of the potential advantages and disadvantages of each.

6. (Research Report) Describe the typical case of elder abuse.

Chapter Review

When you have finished reading the chapter, work through the material that follows to review it. Complete the sentences and answer the questions. As you proceed, evaluate your performance for each section by consulting the answers on page 387. Do not continue with the next section until you understand each answer. If you need to, review or reread the appropriate section in the textbook before continuing.

Theories of Late Adulthood (pp. 677–684)

1. Theories of psychosocial development in late adulthood include _____ theories, _____ theories, and _____ theories.

2. _____ theories emphasize the active part that individuals play in their own psychosocial development.

3. The most comprehensive theory is that of _____ _____ , who called life's final crisis _____ versus _____ .

4. Another version of self theory suggests that the search for _____ is lifelong. This idea originates in Erikson's crisis of _____ versus _____ .

5. Partly as a result of changes in _____ , _____ , and _____ ,

maintaining identity during late adulthood is particularly challenging. In the strategy _____ _____ , new experiences are incorporated unchanged. This strategy involves _____ reality in order to maintain self-esteem.

6. The opposite strategy is _____ _____ , in which people adapt to new experiences by changing their self-concept. This process can be painful, since it may cause people to doubt their _____ and _____ , leading to what Erikson called _____ .

7. Paul Baltes emphasizes _____ _____ _____ , which is the idea that individuals set their own _____ , assess their own _____ , and then figure out how to accomplish what they want to achieve despite the _____ and _____ of life.

8. People who have a strong sense of _____ believe that they can master any situation life presents, including aging.

9. Self theories have recently received strong support from research in the field of _____ _____ , which has shown that various life events seem to be at least as much affected by _____ as by life circumstances. Studies of twins have found that genetic influences often _____ (weaken/become more apparent) later in life.

10. Theorists who emphasize _____ maintain that _____ forces limit individual _____ and direct life at every stage. One form of this theory focuses on _____ _____ , reflecting how industrialized nations segregate the oldest generation.

11. According to _____ theory, in old age the individual and society mutually with-

draw from each other. This theory is _____ (controversial among/ almost universally accepted by) gerontologists.

12. The opposite idea is expressed in _____ theory, which holds that older adults remain socially active. According to this theory, if older adults do disengage, they do so as a result of _____ .

13. The dominant view is that the more _____ the elderly play, the greater their _____ _____ and the longer their lives.

14. The most recent view of age stratification is that disengagement theory and activity theory are too _____ . According to this view, older adults become more _____ in their social contacts.

15. Another stratification theory, which draws attention to the values underlying the gender divisions promoted by society, is _____ theory. According to this theory, _____ policies and _____ values make later life particularly burdensome for women.

16. Currently in the United States, women make up nearly _____ (what proportion?) of the population over age 65 and nearly three-fourths of the elderly who are _____ .

17. According to the _____ _____ theory, race is a _____ _____ , and racism and racial discrimination shape the experiences and attitudes of both racial _____ and racial _____ .

18. Some theorists believe that stratification theory unfairly stigmatizes _____ and _____ groups. They point out that compared to European Americans, elderly _____ and _____ Americans are more often nurtured by _____ families. As a result of this _____ , fewer are put in nursing homes. Similarly, elderly women are less likely to be _____ and _____

than elderly men because they tend to be _____ and _____ .

19. An important concept in age stratification theory is that _____ shifts often change the meaning of gender and ethnicity.

20. According to _____ theory, each person's life is an active, changing, self-propelled process occurring within ever-changing _____ contexts.

21. According to _____ theory, people experience the changes of late adulthood in much the same way they did earlier in life. Thus, the so-called _____ _____ personality traits are maintained throughout old age.

22. The dynamic viewpoint stresses that the entire _____ _____ works toward _____ , even as elements of _____ _____ change.

23. Self theories echo _____ theories in the importance they place on childhood _____ and _____ . Social stratification theories apply many concepts from _____ theory. And the stress on dynamic change is an extension of _____ _____ theory.

Keeping Active (pp. 684–690)

24. Today, retirement is a much more varied experience than _____ theory suggests.

25. Mandatory retirement is _____ (legal/illegal) in many countries. Today, adults are retiring at _____ (a younger age than/about the same age as) in the past.

26. Early retirement is often the result of _____ _____ . A second problem faced by retirees is whether their _____ will last.

27. Between 1980 and 1997 the percentage of Americans over age 65 living in poverty _____ (increased/remained stable/decreased). Compared to other groups, _____ and _____ continue to have higher poverty rates, although their situation has improved.

8. Many of the elderly use the time they once spent earning a living to pursue _____ interests.

9. The eagerness of the elderly to pursue educational interests is exemplified by the rapid growth of _____ , a program in which older people live on college campuses and take special classes.

0. Compared to younger adults, older adults are _____ (more/less) likely to feel a strong obligation to serve their community.

1. Although the political activism of the older generation causes some younger adults to voice concerns regarding _____ _____ , the idea that the elderly are narrowly focused on their self-interest is unfair.

2. The major United States organization affecting the elderly is the _____ .

3. (Changing Policy) Ironically, while the financial circumstances of the American elderly have improved in recent years, other age groups, notably _____ , have grown poorer. More than one American child in five now lives below the poverty line. This has led to calls for _____ _____ , defined as _____ _____ .

4. (Changing Policy) Because _____ is at the heart of intergenerational relationships, it is unfair and counterproductive to blame the elderly for the financial plight of the younger generations.

5. Many older adults stay busy by maintaining their _____ and _____ . This reflects the desire of most elderly people to _____ (relocate when they retire/age in place). One result of this is that many of the elderly live _____ .

e Social Convoy (pp. 690–697)

. The phrase _____ _____ highlights the fact that the life course is traveled in the company of others.

37. Most elderly Americans _____ (are/are not) married, and they tend to be _____ , _____ , and _____ than those who never married or who are divorced or widowed.

38. The best predictor of the nature of a marriage in its later stages is _____ _____ .

Give two possible reasons that marriages may improve with time.

39. Poor health generally has a _____ (major/minor) impact on the marital relationship.

40. The death of a mate usually means not only the loss of a close friend and lover but also a lower _____ , less _____ , a(n) _____ social circle, and disrupted _____ _____ .

41. In general, living without a spouse is somewhat easier for _____ (widows/widowers).

State several reasons for this being so.

42. Only about _____ percent of those currently over age 65 in the United States have never married. A large portion of these are _____ and _____ , many of whom have long-time _____ and _____ networks.

43. Divorce is very _____ (rare/common) in late life. As a group, older divorced

_____ (men/women) tend to fare better.

Briefly explain this gender difference.

44. A study of loneliness found that adults without partners _____ (were/were not) lonelier than adults with partners, and that divorced or widowed adults _____ (were/were not) lonelier than never-married adults. The loneliest of all were _____ _____ . The least lonely were _____ _____ .

45. Older people's satisfaction with life is more strongly correlated to contact with _____ than to contact with younger members of their own family.

46. Compared to men, women tend to have _____ (larger/smaller) social circles, including _____ and a close _____ (male/female) friend who is not related.

47. (In Person) Although bonds between siblings often _____ (intensify/weaken) in late adulthood, rivalries that began in childhood _____ (may/may not) continue throughout life.

48. Because more people are living longer, more older people are part of _____ families than at any time in history. Sometimes, this takes the form of a _____ family, in which there are more _____ than in the past but with only a few members in each generation.

49. While intergenerational relationships are clearly important to both generations, they also are likely to include _____ and

_____ . The _____– _____ relationship is an example of this.

The Frail Elderly (pp. 698–705)

50. Elderly people who are physically infirm, very ill, or cognitively impaired are called the _____ _____ .

51. The crucial sign of frailty is an inability to perform the _____ _____ , which comprise five tasks: _____ , _____ , _____ , _____ , and _____ .

52. Actions that require some intellectual competence and forethought are classified as _____ _____ . These include such things as _____ _____ .

53. The number of frail elderly is _____ (increasing/decreasing). One reason for this trend is that the fastest-growing segment of the American population is people aged _____ and older. As more people reach old age, the absolute numbers of frail individuals will _____ (increase/decrease). A second reason is that medical care now _____ . A third is that health care emphasizes _____ _____ more than _____ _____ . The result has been an increasing _____ (morbidity/ mortality) rate, even as _____ (morbidity/mortality) rates fall. A final reason is that adequate nutrition, safe housing, and other preventive measures often don't reach those who _____ .

54. Long life _____ (does/does not) inevitably include years of frailty. Nor does being _____ , or a member of a _____ , or being _____ . One of the best defenses

against frailty is an active drive for

_____ , _____ , and

_____ . The dynamic systems perspective also reminds us that some people enter
late adulthood with protective

_____ in place. These include

_____ .

5. (A Life-Span View) Many elderly persons never
become frail because of four protective factors:

_____ , _____

_____ , _____

_____ , and _____

_____ .

6. In caring for the frail elderly, cultures such as that
of _____ (which country?) stress the
obligation of children to their parents, rather than
of the elderly caring for each another, as in

_____ .

State three reasons that caregivers may feel
unfairly burdened and resentful.

a. _____

_____

b. _____

_____

c. _____

_____

7. An especially helpful form of caregiver support is
_____ , in which
a professional caregiver takes over to give the
family caregiver a break.

8. (Research Report) Most cases of elder maltreatment _____ (involve/do not
involve) family members.

9. Many older Americans and their relatives feel
that _____ _____
should be avoided at all costs.

Progress Test 1

Multiple-Choice Questions

Circle your answers to the following questions and
check them with the answers on page 388. If your
answer is incorrect, read the explanation for why it is
incorrect and then consult the appropriate pages of
the text (in parentheses following the correct answer).

1. According to disengagement theory, during late
adulthood people tend to:
   a. become less role-centered and more passive.
   b. have regrets about how they have lived their
lives.
   c. become involved in a range of new activities.
   d. exaggerate lifelong personality traits.

2. (Changing Policy) Regarding generational equity,
which of the following is implicit in a life-span
perspective?
   a. The current distribution of benefits is particularly imbalanced for racial minorities.
   b. The outlay of public funds for health care is
weighted toward preventive medicine in
childhood and adolescence.
   c. As a group, the elderly are wealthier than any
other age group.
   d. Each age and cohort has its own particular
and legitimate economic needs that other generations might fail to appreciate.

3. Elderhostel is:
   a. a special type of nursing home in which the
patients are given control over their activities.
   b. a theory of psychosocial development advo-
cating that the elderly can help each other.
   c. an agency that allows older people of the
opposite sex to live together unencumbered
by marriage vows.
   d. a program in which older people live on college campuses and take special classes.

4. Longitudinal studies of monozygotic and dizygotic twins have recently found evidence that:
   a. genetic influences weaken as life experiences
accumulate.
   b. strongly supports disengagement theory.
   c. some traits seem even more apparent in late
adulthood than earlier.
   d. all of the above are true.

5. A former pilot, Eileen has always been proud of her 20/20 vision. Although to the younger members of her family it is obvious that her vision is beginning to fail, Eileen denies that she is having any difficulty and claims that she could still fly an airplane if she wanted to. An identity theorist would probably say that Eileen's distortion of reality is an example of:
   a. identity assimilation.
   b. identity accommodation.
   c. selective optimization.
   d. disengagement.

6. In general, older people are:
   a. more likely to retire at a later age.
   b. likely to retire for health-related reasons.
   c. likely to retire simply because they want to.
   d. more likely to retire at their employers' request.

7. The idea that individuals set their own goals, assess their abilities, and figure out how to accomplish what they want to achieve during late adulthood is referred to as:
   a. disengagement.
   b. selective optimization with compensation.
   c. dynamic life-course development.
   d. age stratification.

8. After retirement, the elderly are likely to:
   a. get a part-time job.
   b. become politically involved.
   c. do volunteer work because they feel a particular commitment to their community.
   d. do any of the above.

9. Which of the following theories does *not* belong with the others?
   a. disengagement theory
   b. feminist theory
   c. critical race theory
   d. continuity theory

10. Which of the following is most true of the relationship between the generations today?
    a. Because parents and children often live at a distance from each other, they are not close.
    b. Older adults prefer not to interfere in their children's lives.
    c. Younger adults are eager to live their own lives and do not want to care for their parents.
    d. The generations tend to see and help each other frequently.

11. (In Person) The importance of longstanding friendships is reflected in which of the following?
    a. the intensification of friendly bonds between in-laws
    b. the mother–daughter relationship becoming more like one between two friends
    c. the intensification of friendly bonds between siblings
    d. a change in the husband–wife relationship to one of friendship

12. In general, during late adulthood the *fewest* problems are experienced by individuals who:
    a. are married.
    b. have always been single.
    c. have long been divorced.
    d. are widowed.

13. Which of the following is true of adjustment to the death of a spouse?
    a. It is easier for men in all respects.
    b. It is initially easier for men but over the long term it is easier for women.
    c. It is emotionally easier for women but financially easier for men.
    d. It is determined primarily by individual personality traits, and therefore shows very few sex differences.

14. According to dynamic theories:
    a. self-integrity is maintained throughout life.
    b. adults make choices and interpret reality in such a way as to express themselves as fully as possible.
    c. people organize themselves according to their particular characteristics and circumstances.
    d. each person's life is largely a self-propelled process, occurring within ever-changing social contexts.

15. Which of the following most accurately expresses the most recent view of developmentalists regarding stratification by age?
    a. Aging makes a person's social sphere increasingly narrow.
    b. Disengagement is always the result of ageism.
    c. Most older adults become more selective in their social contacts.
    d. Older adults need even more social activity to be happy than they did earlier in life.

True or False Items

Write T (*true*) or F (*false*) on the line in front of each statement.

_____ 1. Behavioral geneticists claim that all aspects of the self are entirely genetic.

_____ 2. As one of the most disruptive experiences in the life span, widowhood tends to have similar effects on men and women.

_____ 3. Theories that stress dynamic change are an extension of epigenetic systems theory.

_____ 4. (In Person) In late adulthood, relationships between siblings tend to improve.

_____ 5. Older adults do not understand the social concerns of younger age groups.

_____ 6. Most developmentalists support the central premise of disengagement theory.

_____ 7. About one-third of the elderly are involved in structured volunteer work.

_____ 8. Most older people suffer significantly from a lack of close friendships.

_____ 9. Nearly one in two older adults makes a long-distance move after retirement.

_____ 10. Loneliness during late adulthood is greater for individuals who were never married than for any other group.

Progress Test 2

Progress Test 2 should be completed during a final chapter review. Answer the following questions after you thoroughly understand the correct answers for the Chapter Review and Progress Test 1.

Multiple-Choice Questions

1. Critics of disengagement theory point out that:
   a. older people want to substitute new involvements for the roles they lose with retirement.
   b. disengagement usually is not voluntary on the part of the individual.
   c. disengagement often leads to greater life satisfaction for older adults.
   d. disengagement is more common at earlier stages in the life cycle.

2. A beanpole family is one that consists of:
   a. fewer generations with fewer members than in the past.
   b. fewer generations with more members than in the past.
   c. more generations than in the past but with only a few members in each generation.
   d. more generations with more members than in the past.

3. According to continuity theory, during late adulthood people:
   a. become less role-centered.
   b. become more passive.
   c. become involved in a range of new activities.
   d. cope with challenges in much the same way they did earlier in life.

4. Developmentalists who believe that stratification theory unfairly stigmatizes women and minority groups point out that:
   a. European Americans are more likely than African Americans to be placed in nursing homes.
   b. elderly women are less likely than men to be lonely and depressed.
   c. multigenerational families and churches often nurture Hispanic Americans.
   d. all of the above are true.

5. (Changing Policy) Since Michael Harrington wrote *The Other America* in 1962:
   a. Social Security has been extended to more people.
   b. a range of medical and social benefits are being provided to the aged.
   c. the proportion of the elderly below the poverty line has been reduced.
   d. all of the above have been accomplished.

6. (A Life-Span View) Protective factors that act as buffers for the elderly include:
   a. personality and social setting.
   b. financial resources and age.
   c. attitude and social network.
   d. none of the above.

7. The major United States organization affecting the elderly is:
   a. Elderhostel.
   b. the American Association of Retired Persons.
   c. Foster Grandparents.
   d. Service Corps of Retired Executives.

8. Developmentalists fear that because younger African Americans are less dependent on family and church, they may experience greater social isolation in late adulthood than did earlier generations. If this does in fact occur, it would most directly:
   a. provide support for disengagement theory.
   b. be an example of how a cohort shift can change the meaning of ethnicity.
   c. illustrate the process of selective optimization with compensation.
   d. support activity theory.

9. Which of the following would *not* be included as an instrumental activity of daily life?
   a. grocery shopping   c. making phone calls
   b. paying bills   d. taking a walk

10. One of the most important factors contributing to life satisfaction for older adults appears to be:
    a. contact with friends.
    b. contact with younger family members.
    c. the number of new experiences to which they are exposed.
    d. continuity in the daily routine.

11. Research studies of loneliness among elderly adults have reported each of the following results *except*:
    a. elderly women tend to be lonelier than men.
    b. adults without partners were lonelier than adults with partners.
    c. divorced adults were lonelier than never-married adults.
    d. widowed adults were lonelier than never-married adults.

12. In general, the longer a couple has been married, the more likely they are to:
    a. be happier with each other.
    b. have frequent, minor disagreements.
    c. feel the relationship is not equitable.
    d. do all of the above.

13. Adjustment to divorce in late adulthood tends to be:
    a. equally easy for men and women.
    b. easier for women.
    c. easier for men.
    d. initially easier for women, but over the long term easier for men.

14. Which of the following is *not* a major factor contributing to an increase in the number of frail elderly?
    a. an increase in average life expectancy
    b. a research focus on acute, rather than chronic illnesses
    c. inadequate expenditures on social services
    d. a lack of facilities in many areas to care for the elderly

15. According to Erikson, achieving integrity during late adulthood above all involves:
    a. the ability to perceive one's own life as worthwhile.
    b. being open to new influences and experiences.
    c. treating other people with respect.
    d. developing a consistent and yet varied daily routine.

Matching Items

Match each definition or description with its corresponding term.

Terms

_____ 1. disengagement theory
_____ 2. self theories
_____ 3. continuity theory
_____ 4. generational equity
_____ 5. activity theory
_____ 6. stratification theories
_____ 7. activities of daily life (ADLs)
_____ 8. instrumental activities of daily life (IADLs)
_____ 9. dynamic theories
_____ 10. Elderhostel

Definitions or Descriptions

a. theories such as Erik Erikson's that emphasize self-actualization
b. an educational program for the elderly
c. eating, bathing, toileting, walking, and dressing
d. theory that a person's life is an active, largely self-propelled process that occurs within ever-changing social contexts.
e. theory that people become less role-centered as they age
f. actions that require intellectual competence and forethought
g. equal contributions from, and fair benefits for, each age cohort
h. theories such as feminist theory and critical race theory that focus on the limitations on life choices created by social forces
i. theory that elderly people become socially withdrawn only involuntarily
j. theory that each person copes with late adulthood in the same way he or she did earlier in life

Thinking Critically About Chapter 25

Answer these questions the day before an exam as a final check on your understanding of the chapter's terms and concepts.

1. Which of the following statements *most* accurately describes psychosocial development in late adulthood?
   a. Many leading gerontologists believe that people become more alike as they get older.
   b. Older adults generally fit into one of two distinct personality types.
   c. Many gerontologists believe that the diversity of personalities and patterns is especially pronounced among the elderly.
   d. Few changes in psychosocial development occur after middle adulthood.

2. An advocate of which of the following theories would be most likely to agree with the statement, "Because of their more passive style of interaction, older people are less likely to be chosen for new roles"?
   a. disengagement   c. self
   b. continuity   d. dynamic

3. An advocate for feminist theory would point out that:
   a. since most social structures and economic policies have been established by men, women's needs are devalued.
   b. women in the United States make up the majority of the elderly and the elderly poor.
   c. many elderly women are expected to care for frail relatives even if it strains their own health.
   d. all of the above are true.

4. Professor Martin states that "membership in certain groups can place the elderly at risk for a number of dangers." Professor Martin evidently is an advocate of which theory of psychosocial development?
   a. self theories   c. dynamic
   b. social stratification   d. continuity

5. When they retire, most older adults:
   a. immediately feel more satisfied with their new way of life.
   b. adjust well to retirement and even improve in health and happiness.
   c. have serious, long-term difficulties adjusting to retirement.
   d. disengage from other roles and activities as well.

6. The one *most* likely to agree with the statement, "Older adults have an obligation to help others and serve the community," is:
   a. a middle-aged adult.   c. an older man.
   b. an older woman.   d. an older adult.

7. An elderly man with dementia is most likely to be cared for by his spouse in _____ and by his children in _____ .
   a. Korea; the United States
   b. the United States; Korea
   c. Japan; Sweden
   d. Sweden; Japan

8. (Research Report) Research indicates that the primary perpetrators of elder abuse are:
   a. professional caregivers.
   b. mean-spirited strangers.
   c. another relative.
   d. middle-aged children.

9. Which of the following best describes the relationship between the elderly and younger generations?
   a. If children move, the elderly will also move in order to continue to be near them.
   b. The elderly enjoy social contact with the younger generation and particularly enjoy having long visits from their grandchildren.
   c. Assistance typically flows from the older generation to their children.
   d. The relationship between mothers and daughters improves with age, with conflict decreasing substantially.

10. Of the following older adults, who is most likely to be involved in a large network of intimate friendships?
    a. William, a 65-year-old who never married
    b. Darrel, a 60-year-old widower
    c. Florence, a 63-year-old widow
    d. Kay, a 66-year-old married woman

11. Following a heated disagreement over family responsibilities, Sidney's grandson stormed away shouting "Why should I listen to you?" Afterward, Sidney is filled with despair and feels that all his years of work to build a strong family were wasted. An identity theorist would probably say that Sidney is demonstrating:
    a. identity assimilation.
    b. identity accommodation.
    c. selective optimization.
    d. a healthy identity that is firm but flexible.

12. Claudine is the primary caregiver for her elderly parents. The amount of stress she feels in this role depends above all on:
    a. how frail her parents are.
    b. her subjective interpretation of the support she receives from others.
    c. her relationship to her parents prior to their becoming frail.
    d. her overall financial situation.

13. Wilma's elderly mother needs help in taking care of the instrumental activities of daily life. Such activities would include which of the following?
    a. bathing
    b. eating
    c. paying bills
    d. all of the above

14. In concluding her presentation on the frail elderly, Janet notes that "the number of frail elderly is currently _____ than the number who are active, financially stable, and capable; however, the frail elderly are _____ in absolute number."
    a. greater; decreasing
    b. less; increasing
    c. greater; increasing
    d. less; decreasing

15. Jack, who is 73, looks back on his life with a sense of pride and contentment; Eleanor feels unhappy with her life and that it is "too late to start over." In Erikson's terminology, Jack is experiencing _____ , while Eleanor is experiencing _____ .
    a. generativity; stagnation
    b. identity; emptiness
    c. integrity; despair
    d. completion; termination

Key Terms

Using your own words, write a brief definition or explanation of each of the following terms on a separate piece of paper.

1. self theories
2. stratification theories
3. disengagement theory
4. activity theory
5. dynamic theories
6. continuity theory
7. Elderhostel

8. social convoy

9. frail elderly

10. activities of daily life (ADLs)

11. instrumental activities of daily life (IADLs)

2. respite care

ANSWERS

CHAPTER REVIEW

1. self; stratification; dynamic

2. Self

3. Erik Erikson; integrity; despair

4. identity; identity; role confusion

5. appearance; health; employment; identity assimilation; distorting

6. identity accommodation; values; beliefs; despair

7. selective optimization with compensation; goals; abilities; limitations; declines

8. self-efficacy

9. behavioral genetics; genes; become more apparent

10. stratification; social; choice; age stratification

11. disengagement; controversial among

12. activity; ageism

13. roles; life satisfaction

14. extreme; selective

15. feminist; social; cultural

16. two-thirds; poor

17. critical race; social construct; minorities; majorities

18. women; minority; African; Hispanic; multigenerational; familism; lonely; depressed; caregivers; kinkeepers

19. cohort

20. dynamic; social

21. continuity; Big Five

22. social system; continuity; individual lives

23. psychoanalytic; self-concept; identity; sociocultural; epigenetic systems

24. disengagement

25. illegal; a younger age than

26. failing health; money

27. decreased; minorities; widows

28. educational

29. Elderhostel

30. more

31. generational equity

32. American Association of Retired Persons (AARP)

33. children; generational equity; equal contributions from, and fair benefits for, each generation

34. interdependence

35. home; yard; age in place; alone

36. social convoy

37. are; healthier; wealthier; happier

38. its nature early on

One reason may be traced to the effects of their children, who were a prime source of conflict when they were younger but are now a source of pleasure. Another is that all the shared contextual factors tend to change both partners in similar ways, bringing them closer together in personality, perspectives, and values.

39. minor

40. income; status; broken; daily routines

41. widows

One reason is that elderly women often expect to outlive their husbands and have anticipated this event. Another is that in most communities widows can get help from support groups. A third is that many elderly men were dependent on their wives to perform the basic tasks of daily living.

42. 4.4; gays; lesbians; companions; social

43. rare; women

For divorced older women life is likely to improve with age, especially if they have successfully raised children or succeeded in a career against all odds. Because women are usually the kinkeepers, many former husbands find themselves isolated from children, grandchildren, and old friends.

44. were; were; men currently without a partner who had lost two or more wives through death or divorce; wives still in their first marriage

45. friends

46. larger; relatives; female

47. intensify; may

48. multigenerational; beanpole; generations

49. tension; conflict; mother–daughter

50. frail elderly

51. activities of daily life (ADLs); eating; bathing; toileting; dressing; transferring from a bed to a chair

52. instrumental activities of daily life (IADLs); shopping, paying bills, driving a car, taking medications, and keeping appointments

53. increasing; 85; increase; prolongs life; death post-ponement; life enhancement; morbidity; mortality; need them the most

54. does not; female; minority; poor; autonomy; control; independence; buffers; family members and friends, past education and continued educational opportunity, pensions, good health habits

55. attitude; social network; physical setting; financial resources

56. Korea; the United States
   a. If one relative is doing the caregiving, other family members tend to feel relief rather than an obligation to help.
   b. Care-receivers and caregivers often disagree about the nature and extent of care that is needed.
   c. Services designed for caregivers are difficult to obtain from social agencies.

57. respite care

58. involve

59. nursing homes

PROGRESS TEST 1

Multiple-Choice Questions

1. **a.** is the answer. (p. 680)
   b. This answer depicts a person struggling with Erikson's crisis of integrity versus despair.
   c. This answer describes activity theory.
   d. Disengagement theory does not address this issue.

2. **d.** is the answer. (p. 691)
   a. Some people believe this, but it is not advocated by life-span developmentalists.
   b. Just the opposite is true.
   c. Although some of the elderly are among the richest, most are in the middle-income bracket.

3. **d.** is the answer. (p. 686)

4. **c.** is the answer. (p. 679)
   a. Such studies have found that genetic influences do not weaken with age.
   b. This research provides support for self theories rather than disengagement theory.

5. **a.** is the answer. (pp. 678)
   b. Accommodating people adapt to new experiences (such as failing vision) by changing their self-concept.
   c. People who selectively optimize are more realistic in assessing their abilities than Eileen evidently is.

   d. There is no sign that Eileen is disengaging, or withdrawing from her social relationships.

6. **c.** is the answer. (p. 685)
   a. & b. Workers are retiring earlier than in the past, and not always for health-related reasons.
   d. Mandatory retirement is illegal in many nations.

7. **b.** is the answer. (p. 679)
   a. This is the idea that the elderly withdraw from society as they get older.
   c. This is the theory that each person's life is a self-propelled process occurring within ever changing social contexts.
   d. According to this theory, the oldest generation is segregated from the rest of society.

8. **d.** is the answer. Contrary to earlier views that retirement was not a happy time, researchers now know that the elderly are generally happy and productive, spending their time in various activities. (pp. 686–689)

9. **d.** is the answer. Each of the other theories can be categorized as a stratification theory. (pp. 680–683)

10. **d.** is the answer. (p. 697)

11. **c.** is the answer. (p. 696)
    a., b., & d. These may occur in some cases, but they are not discussed in the text.

12. **a.** is the answer. (p. 692)

13. **c.** is the answer. (p. 693)

14. **d.** is the answer. (p. 683)
    a. This expresses continuity theory.
    b. This expresses self theory.
    c. This expresses stratification theory.

15. **c.** is the answer. (p. 681)
    a. This is the central idea behind disengagement theory.
    b., & d. These ideas are expressions of activity theory.

True or False Items

1. F They claim only a third to a half of the variation in characteristics is genetic. (p. 680)

2. F Women tend to be more prepared and have more friends to sympathize with them. Men, who tend to depend on their wives for basic needs and emotional support, find it hard to turn to others for help. (p. 693)

3. T (p. 684)

4. T (p. 696)

5. F In fact, older adults are willing to vote against the interests of their own group if a greater good is at stake. (p. 689)

6. F In fact, disengagement theory has *few* serious defenders. (pp. 680–681)

7. T (p. 687)

8. F Most older adults have at least one close friend and, as compared with younger adults, are less likely to feel a need for more friendships. (p. 695)

9. F A minority of older adults moves to another state. (p. 689)

10. F If anything, loneliness tends to be less in never-married older adults. (p. 694)

PROGRESS TEST 2

Multiple-Choice Questions

1. **a.** is the answer. (pp. 684–685)

   b. If disengagement were *not* voluntary, this would not be a choice of the elderly.

   c. & d. Neither of these answers is true, nor a criticism of disengagement theory.

2. **c.** is the answer. (p. 695)

3. **d.** is the answer. (p. 683)

   a. & b. These answers describe disengagement theory.

   c. This answer pertains to activity theory.

4. **d.** is the answer. (p. 682)

5. **d.** is the answer. (p. 690)

6. **c.** is the answer. (p. 701)

7. **b.** is the answer. (p. 688)

   a. Elderhostel is an educational program for older adults.

   c. & d. These service organizations affect a much smaller percentage of the elderly.

8. **b.** is the answer. (p. 683)

   a. & d. This finding does not bear directly on either theory of late adulthood.

   c. Selective optimization is an example of *successful* coping with the losses of late adulthood, which would seem to run counter to feelings of social isolation.

9. **d.** is the answer. (p. 698)

10. **a.** is the answer. (p. 695)

    b., c., & d. The importance of these factors varies from one older adult to another.

11. **a.** is the answer. (p. 694)

12. **a.** is the answer. (p. 692)

    b. & c. The longer a couple has been married, the *less* likely they are to have frequent disagreements or feel that the relationship is not equitable.

13. **b.** is the answer. (p. 694)

14. **c.** is the answer. Many nations spend substantial money on services for the elderly. (pp. 699–700)

    a. As more people reach old age, the absolute numbers of frail individuals will increase.

    b. Such research neglects the study of diseases that are nonfatal, yet disabling.

    d. Services are relatively scarce in rural areas, where a large number of elderly people reside.

15. **a.** is the answer. (p. 677)

Matching Items

1. e (p. 680)
2. a (p. 677)
3. j (p. 683)
4. g (p. 690)
5. i (p. 681)
6. h (p. 680)
7. c (p. 698)
8. f (p. 698)
9. d (p. 683)
10. b (p. 686)

THINKING CRITICALLY ABOUT CHAPTER 25

1. **c.** is the answer. (p. 677)

2. **a.** is the answer. (p. 680)

   b. Continuity theory, a type of dynamic theory, maintains that older adults cope with aging in much the same ways as when they were younger.

   c. Self theories emphasize the quest for self-actualization.

   d. Dynamic theories emphasize that life is a self-propelled, ever-changing process within an ever-changing social context.

3. **d.** is the answer. (pp. 681–682)

4. **b.** is the answer. "Groups" are the social "strata" that this theory focuses on. (p. 680)

   a. & c. These theories emphasize the efforts of the individual to reach his or her full potential (self theories) by interpreting experiences in the face of ever-changing social contexts (dynamic theories, of which continuity theory is one [d.]).

5. **b.** is the answer. (pp. 685–686)

   a. Retirement almost always requires some period of adjustment.

   d. There is much evidence that *conflicts* with disengagement theory.

6. **d.** is the answer. (p. 687)

a. Middle-aged adults tend to be more focused on individual and family needs.

b. & c. The text does not suggest that there is a gender difference in older adults' sense of obligation to serve others.

7. **b.** is the answer. (p. 702)

c. & d. The text does not compare care for the frail elderly in these countries.

8. **d.** is the answer. (p. 704)

9. **c.** is the answer. (p. 697)

a. Even if children move, their parents prefer to stay in their homes.

b. Although the elderly enjoy social contact with the younger generations, they prefer shorter visits.

d. Tension and conflict continues throughout life in mother–daughter relationships.

10. **c.** is the answer. (p. 693)

a. & b. At every age, women have larger social circles and more intimate relationships with their friends than men.

d. Widows tend to be more involved in friendship networks than married women.

11. **b.** is the answer. (p. 678)

a. People who assimilate are *unlikely* to doubt their values or beliefs.

c. Selective optimization, which has no direct bearing on Sidney's response, refers to adults who structure their lives so that they can do what they want despite the physical and cognitive losses of late adulthood.

d. On the contrary, Sidney's self-doubt is an unhealthy sign of crumbling too easily in the face of this circumstance.

12. **b.** is the answer. (p. 703)

13. **c.** is the answer. (p. 698)

a. & b. These are examples of "activities of daily life."

14. **b.** is the answer. (p. 699)

15. **c.** is the answer. (p. 677)

a. This is not the crisis of late adulthood in Erikson's theory.

b. & d. These are not crises in Erikson's theory.

KEY TERMS

1. **Self theories** such as Erik Erikson's theory focus on how adults make choices, confront problems, and interpret reality in such a way as to express themselves as fully as possible. (p. 677)

2. **Stratification theories** emphasize that social forces limit individual choices and affect the ability to function. (p. 680)

3. According to **disengagement theory**, aging results in social withdrawal and passivity. (p. 680)

4. **Activity theory** is the view that older people remain active in a variety of social spheres and become withdrawn only unwillingly. (p. 681)

5. According to **dynamic theories**, each person's life is an active, largely self-propelled process that occurs within ever-changing social contexts. (p. 683)

6. According to the **continuity theory** of aging, each person copes with late adulthood in much the same way that he or she coped with earlier periods of life. (p. 683)

7. **Elderhostel** is a program in which older adults live on college campuses and take special classes. (p. 686)

8. The **social convoy** is the network of people with whom we establish meaningful relationships as we travel through life. (p. 690)

9. The **frail elderly** are the minority of older adults who are physically infirm, very ill, or cognitively impaired. (p. 698)

10. In determining frailty, gerontologists often refer to the **activities of daily life (ADLs)**, which comprise five tasks: eating, bathing, toileting, dressing, and transferring from a bed to a chair. (p. 698)

11. The **instrumental activities of daily life (IADLs)** are actions that require some intellectual competence and forethought, such as shopping for food, paying bills, and taking medication. (p. 698)

12. **Respite care** is an arrangement in which a professional caregiver takes over to give a family caregiver a break from caring for a frail elderly person. (p. 703)

EPILOGUE

Death and Dying

Epilogue Overview

Death marks the close of the life span—a close individuals must come to terms with both for themselves and their loved ones. Indeed, an understanding and acceptance of death is crucial if life is to be lived to the fullest.

The first section focuses on the dying person's emotions, noting that the meanings of death, and the reactions that death prompts, vary from individual to individual. Although the concept of an unvarying sequence of stages among the dying is not universally accepted, the pioneering work of Elisabeth Kübler-Ross was instrumental in revealing the emotional turmoil of terminally ill patients and the importance of honest communication.

The next section deals with how dying patients and their families plan for death and with the controversial issue of whether and when we should hasten the death of a loved one. The section also discusses hospice and other forms of palliative care designed to help the terminally ill patient to die "a good death."

A third section explores the social context of dying, noting that perceptions of death vary markedly according to their historical and cultural context.

The final section deals with changing expressions of bereavement and how people can be aided in the process of recovery.

NOTE: Answer guidelines for all Epilogue questions begin on page 399.

Guided Study

The text Epilogue should be studied one section at a time. Before you read, preview each section by skimming it, noting headings and boldface items. Then read the appropriate section objectives from the following outline. Keep these objectives in mind and, as you read the Epilogue section, search for the information that will enable you to meet each objective. Once you have finished a section, write out answers for its objectives.

The Dying Person's Emotions (pp. 709–710, 711)

1. Identify Kübler-Ross's stages of dying, and discuss these stages in light of more recent research.

2. (A Life-Span View) Discuss age-related differences in the conceptualization of and emotional reactions to death.

Deciding How to Die (pp. 710–714, 715)

3. Discuss the steps that patients, family members, and medical personnel can take to plan for a swift, pain-free, and dignified death.

4. (Changing Policy) Explain the concept of palliative care, focusing on the advantages and disadvantages of hospices.

5. (text and Research Report) Discuss issues surrounding assisted suicide and active euthanasia, noting the Dutch experience with legislation regarding assisted dying.

The Social Context of Dying (pp. 714, 716–721)

6. Describe some cultural and religious variations in how death is viewed and treated.

7. Describe recent changes in the mourning process, and suggest steps that can be taken in helping someone to recover from bereavement.

Epilogue Review

When you have finished reading the Epilogue, wor through the material that follows to review Complete the sentences and answer the questions. A you proceed, evaluate your performance for each se tion by consulting the answers on page 399. Do n continue with the next section until you understar each answer. If you need to, review or reread tl appropriate section in the textbook before continuinɡ

The Dying Person's Emotions (pp. 709–710, 711)

1. A major factor in our understanding of the gamı of emotional reactions among the dying was the pioneering work of _____ Her research led her to propose that the dying g through _____ (how many?) emotional stages. .

2. In order, the stages of dying are

_____ , _____ ,

_____ , _____ , and

_____ .

3. The final stage _____ (is/is not) a happy stage; it is a stage in which the person is

_____

4. Other researchers typically _____ (have/have not) found the same five stages of dying occurring in sequence.

5. In her interviews with the dying, Kübler-Ross quickly discovered the importance of _____ (concealing/not concealing information about their condition.

6. (A Life-Span View) The age of the dying person _____ (does/does not) significantl affect his or her emotional response to death.

(A Life-Span View) Briefly describe the typical rea tions of the following individuals to their ov impending death:

a young child: _____

_____

an adolescent: _____

_____

a young adult: _____

_____

middle-aged adult: _____

_____

older adult: _____

_____

(A Life-Span View) The emotional response to death also depends on the age of the _____ . Little children, for example, are often_____ that the dying person _____ them. Generally speaking, deaths that are expected _____ (are/are not) easier to cope with because they permit _____ _____ . A common emotion in mourners of every age is

_____ .

ciding How to Die (pp. 710–714, 715)

Many adults hope to die _____ , with little _____ and great

_____ .

Because of modern medical techniques, a swift and peaceful death is _____ (more/less) difficult to ensure today than in the past.

Adults often die in pain, largely because analgesic medicines are _____ because of a fear of causing _____ . Pain is particularly likely for the _____-_____ patients in _____

_____ .

There is a growing consensus, both in _____ and in _____ practice, that the ultimate authority regarding what measures are to be used in terminal cases should be the _____ .

Some people make a _____ _____ to indicate what medical intervention they want if they become incapable of expressing those wishes. To avoid complications, each person should also designate a _____ , someone who can make decisions for them on the spot if needed.

Proxies _____ (do/do not) guarantee a problem-free death. One problem is that

_____ members may disagree with the proxy; another is that more than _____ (how much?) the time proxy directives are ignored during emergencies.

14. Usually, if a patient prefers to die naturally, the order _____ _____ _____ is placed on that person's hospital chart. A situation in which medication relieves pain and hastens death is called

_____ _____ .

Together, DNR orders and pain medication are a form of _____ _____ .

15. Generally speaking, _____ (most/few) doctors and nurses are trained to handle the psychological demands of palliative care. The institution called the _____ provides this type of care to terminally ill patients.

16. (Changing Policy) The hospice was conceived in response to the _____ of the typical hospital death.

17. (Changing Policy) Hospice patients are assigned a _____ _____ _____ , who is present much of the time and is responsible for some of the routine care.

18. (Changing Policy) The hospice concept _____ (does/does not) solve all the problems of dying.

(Changing Policy) State several criticisms of hospice care.

19. (Changing Policy) There are _____ (few/many) hospices for children. In the United States, about _____ percent of all deaths occur with hospice care.

20. Two other factors that help to determine whether or not a person will have a good death are

_____ values and _____ practices.

21. Especially controversial are issues concerning
_____-_____
_____ , in which a doctor provides the means for a person to end his or her life, and
_____ , in which someone intentionally acts to terminate the life of a suffering person.

22. (Research Report) In 1993, the _____ legislature passed a law guaranteeing that doctors would not be prosecuted for assisting suicide if they followed several guidelines.

23. (Research Report) In the United States, the state of _____ has allowed physician-assisted suicide since 1998. Since that time, concerns that physician-assisted suicide might be used more often with minorities, the poor, and the disabled _____ (have/have not) been proven to be well-founded.

The Social Context of Dying (pp. 714, 716–721)

24. Through the study of death we have learned that perceptions of death are _____ (variable/the same) in all cultures.

25. In most _____ traditions, elders take on an important new status through death.

26. In many _____ nations, death affirms faith in Allah and caring for the dying is a holy reminder of mortality.

27. Among Buddhists, disease and death are inevitable sufferings, which may bring _____ . Among _____ and _____ , helping the dying to relinquish their ties to this world and prepare for the next is considered an obligation for the immediate family.

28. Preparations for death are not emphasized in the _____ tradition because hope for _____ should never be extinguished.

29. Many _____ believe that death is the beginning of eternity in _____

or _____ , and thus welcome or fear it.

30. The study of death reveals that _____ often has more influence on variations in death practices than _____ does. Customs of _____ also vary tremendously.

31. Two themes that emerge in cultural variations of death practices are:
a. _____
b. _____

32. In recent times, mourning has become more _____ , less _____ , and less _____ . Younger generations are likely to prefer _____ _____ , while older generations prefer _____ _____ . One result of trends is that those who have lost a loved one are more likely to experience _____ _____ and _____ _____ than in the past.

33. List two steps that others can follow to help a bereaved person.
a. _____
b. _____

34. A frequent theme of those who work with the bereaved is the value of a(n) _____ _____ .

35 (In Person) Particularly among younger people, grieving is sometimes aided today by an _____ _____ to the dead.

Progress Test 1

Circle your answers to the following questions an check them with the answers on page 399. If yo answer is incorrect, read the explanation for why it incorrect and then consult the appropriate pages the text (in parentheses following the correct answer

ltiple-Choice Questions

Kübler-Ross found that doctors often chose not to inform terminally ill patients of their condition and sometimes concealed the information from families as well. Such an approach would tend to:
a. minimize possibilities for grief.
b. increase feelings of isolation and sorrow.
c. discourage the family from retaining memories of the deceased.
d. maximize possibilities for passive euthanasia.

(A Life-Span View) Medical advances have meant that death today is more often:
a. far less painful for the dying individual.
b. emotionally far less painful for the bereaved.
c. a solitary, lengthy, and painful experience.
d. predictable, and therefore a less traumatic experience.

Kübler-Ross's stages of dying are, in order:
a. anger, denial, bargaining, depression, acceptance.
b. depression, anger, denial, bargaining, acceptance.
c. denial, anger, bargaining, depression, acceptance.
d. bargaining, denial, anger, acceptance, depression.

(text and A Life-Span View) Recent research regarding the emotions of terminally ill patients has found that:
a. all patients reach the stage of acceptance.
b. emotional stages generally follow one another in an orderly sequence.
c. age has an important effect on emotions.
d. most experience depression.

Most adults hope that they will die:
a. with little pain.
b. with dignity.
c. swiftly.
d. in all of the above ways..

A pain-free death is least likely to be experienced by:
a. the oldest-old patients in nursing homes.
b. hospice patients.
c. children dying of cancer.
d. patients who fail to make a living will.

7. *Hospice* is best defined as:
a. a document that indicates what kind of medical intervention a terminally ill person wants.
b. mercifully allowing a person to die by. not doing something that might extend life.
c. an alternative to hospital care for the terminally ill.
d. providing a person with the means to end his or her life.

8. Palliative care refers to:
a. heroic measures to save a life.
b. conservative medical care to treat an illness.
c. efforts to relieve pain and suffering.
d. allowing a terminally ill patient to die naturally.

9. A situation in which, at a patient's request, another person acts to terminate his or her life is called:
a. involuntary euthanasia
b. voluntary euthanasia
c. a physician-assisted suicide
d. DNR

10. Which of the following is a normal response in the bereavement process?
a. experiencing powerful emotions
b. culturally diverse emotions
c. a lengthy period of grief
d. All of the above are normal responses.

11. A "double effect" in medicine refers to a situation in which:
a. the effects of one drug on a patient interact with those of another drug.
b. medication relieves pain and has a secondary effect of hastening death.
c. family members disagree with a terminally ill patient's proxy.
d. medical personnel ignore the wishes of a terminally ill patient and his or her proxy.

12. (Changing Policy) Criticisms made against hospices include all of the following *except*:
a. the number of patients served is limited.
b. in some cases a life is being ended that might have been prolonged.
c. burnout and the rapid growth of hospices might limit the number of competent hospice workers.
d. the patient is needlessly isolated from family and friends.

True or False Items

Write T (*true*) or F (*false*) on the line in front of each statement.

_____ 1. The terminally ill generally want to know about and discuss their condition.

_____ 2. Subsequent research has confirmed the accuracy of Kübler-Ross's findings regarding the five stages of dying.

_____ 3. Modern life-prolonging medical technologies have tended to make dying a pain-free, dignified death more difficult and less likely to occur.

_____ 4. Following the death of a loved one, the bereaved can best ensure their psychological health and well-being by increasing their social contacts and the number of activities in which they are involved.

_____ 5. To help a bereaved person, one should ignore the person's depression.

_____ 6. (Changing Policy) Researchers agree that the hospice is beneficial to the dying person and his or her family.

_____ 7. Physician-assisted suicide and voluntary euthanasia are legal almost everywhere in the world.

_____ 8. (Changing Policy) Hospices administer pain-killing medication but do not make use of artificial life-support systems.

_____ 9. In the long run, the bereavement process may have a beneficial effect on the individual.

_____ 10. (Changing Policy) There is general consensus that hospice care is a good alternative to hospital care for the dying.

Progress Test 2

Progress Test 2 should be completed during a final review of the Epilogue. Answer the following questions after you thoroughly understand the correct answers for the Epilogue Review and Progress Test 1.

Multiple-Choice Questions

1. Kübler-Ross's primary contribution was to:
   a. open the first hospice, thus initiating the hospice movement.
   b. show how the emotions of the dying occur in a series of clear-cut stages.
   c. demonstrate that varied and contradictory emotions are normal among the terminally ill.
   d. show the correlation between people's conceptualization of death and their developmental stage.

2. In recent times, mourning has become all of th[e] following *except*:
   a. more private.
   b. less emotional.
   c. more likely to lead to social isolation.
   d. more religious.

3. (Changing Policy) Which of the following is *not* [a] limitation of hospices?
   a. Most insurance plans will not pay for hospi[ce] care unless the patient has been diagnosed [as] terminally ill.
   b. Hospice care can be very expensive.
   c. Almost no hospices serve children.
   d. The dying typically do not receive skille[d] medical care.

4. Legal experts and medical personnel increasing[ly] agree that the ultimate authority in deciding ho[w] a terminal patient is treated should be:
   a. the patient's physician.
   b. the legal system.
   c. the patient's family members.
   d. the patient.

5. Younger generations tend to prefer _____ an[d] older generations tend to prefer _____ .
   a. burial after a traditional funeral; burial after [a] traditional funeral
   b. a small memorial service after cremation; [a] small memorial service after cremation
   c. burial after a traditional funeral; a sma[ll] memorial service after cremation
   d. a small memorial service after cremation; bur[i]al after a traditional funeral

6. Recent research reveals that Kübler-Ross's stag[es] of dying:
   a. occur in sequence in virtually all terminally [ill] patients.
   b. do not occur in hospice residents.
   c. are typical only in Western cultures.
   d. make feelings about death seem much mo[re] predictable and universal than they actual[ly] are.

7. Today, it may be more difficult for the termina[lly] ill to die a swift, dignified, and pain-free dea[th] because:
   a. modern medicine can sustain life beyond i[ts] time.
   b. many doctors view death as an enemy to [be] fended off at all costs.
   c. the dying often are in discomfort or outrig[ht] pain because analgesic medications are unde[r] prescribed.
   d. of all of the above reasons.

Living wills are an attempt to:

a. make sure that passive euthanasia will not be used in individual cases.

b. specify the extent of medical treatment desired in the event of terminal illness.

c. specify conditions for the use of active euthanasia.

d. ensure that death will occur at home rather than in a hospital.

Many _____ welcome or fear death because they believe it is the beginning of eternity in heaven or hell.

a. Buddhists

b. Muslims

c. Christians

d. Jews

(text and Changing Policy) The hospice made acceptable three basic principles regarding death and dying, including all of the following *except* that:

a. an interdisciplinary team can provide the best care for any sick person.

b. death is a family affair.

c. the dying person should be left alone to reconcile his or her feelings about life.

d. palliative care is a worthy medical goal.

11. To develop the greatest understanding of variations in mourning practices, a person would do best to focus on:

a. the age and gender of terminally ill patients.

b. religious differences among the bereaved.

c. cultural differences among the bereaved.

d. whether the death permitted anticipatory grief reactions among the bereaved.

12. Healing after the death of a loved one is most difficult when:

a. the death is a long, protracted one.

b. the bereaved is not allowed to mourn in the way or she wishes.

c. a period of grief has already elapsed.

d. there are no other mourners.

tching Items

tch each term or concept with its corresponding cription or definition.

ns or Concepts

_____ 1. DNR

_____ 2. hospice

_____ 3. living will

_____ 4. voluntary euthanasia

_____ 5. double effect

_____ 6. physician-assisted suicide

_____ 7. palliative care

_____ 8. lay primary caregiver

_____ 9. anticipatory grief

Definitions or Descriptions

a. hospice treatment that relieves suffering and safeguards dignity

b. an alternative to hospital care for the terminally ill

c. hospital chart order to allow a terminally ill patient to die naturally

d. a document expressing a person's wishes for treatment should he or she become terminally ill and incapable of making such decisions

e. providing the means for a terminally ill patient to end his or her life

f. family member who coordinates hospice care for a patient

g. reduces shock and eases the acceptance of a loved one's death

h. intentionally taking an action to end the life of a terminally ill patient

i. situation in which a pain-relieving drug also hastens the death of a terminally ill patient

Thinking Critically About the Epilogue

Answer these questions the day before an exam as a final check on your understanding of the chapter's terms and concepts.

1. Among my people, elders take on an important new status through death as they join the ancestors who watch over our entire village. I am:
   a. African.
   b. Muslim.
   c. Hindu.
   d. Native American.

2. Among my people, family members have an obligation to help the dying to relinquish their ties to this world and prepare for the next. I am:
   a. African.
   b. Muslim.
   c. Hindu.
   d. Native American.

3. The terminally ill patient who promises to live a better life if spared from dying is probably in which of Kübler-Ross's stages?
   a. denial
   b. anger
   c. depression
   d. bargaining

4. The terminally ill patient who is convinced his laboratory tests must be wrong is probably in which of Kübler-Ross's stages?
   a. denial
   b. anger
   c. depression
   d. bargaining

5. (A Life-Span View) A terminally ill adolescent is likely to:
   a. fear death primarily because it means being separated from family members.
   b. become upset about his or her appearance.
   c. become absorbed with learning the facts about his or her illness.
   d. be angry at the idea that, just as life is about to begin, it must end.

6. (A Life-Span View) Roger, who is middle-aged, is terminally ill. He is most likely to need:
   a. constant companionship.
   b. detailed information about the "mechanics" of dying.
   c. counseling to help overcome his anger at having his life cut short.
   d. reassurance that others will take over his obligations and responsibilities.

7. Dr. Welby writes the orders DNR (do not resuscitate) on her patient's chart. Evidently the patient has requested:
   a. a living will.
   b. hospice care.
   c. voluntary euthanasia.
   d. an assisted suicide.

8. Seeing his terminally ill father without hope and in excruciating pain, Carl agreed to provide the means for him to end his life. This is an example of:
   a. passive euthanasia.
   b. voluntary euthanasia.
   c. an assisted suicide.
   d. an act that became legal in most countries 1993.

9. The doctor who injects a terminally ill patient with a lethal drug is practicing:
   a. passive euthanasia.
   b. active euthanasia.
   c. an assisted suicide.
   d. an act that became legal in most countries 1993.

10. Summarizing her presentation on the process mourning, Rita states that most developmentalists view mourning as:
   a. an unnecessary and emotionally crippling process.
   b. a disruptive force in development.
   c. a necessary and healthy process.
   d. important for some, but not all, individuals.

11. Which of the following statements would probably be the most helpful to a grieving person?
   a. "Why don't you get out more and get back into the swing of things?"
   b. "You're tough; bear up!"
   c. "If you need someone to talk to, call me any time."
   d. "It must have been his or her time to die."

12. Dr. Robinson is about to counsel her first terminally ill patient and his family. Research suggests that her most helpful strategy would be to:
   a. keep most of the facts from both the patient and his family in order not to upset them.
   b. be truthful to the patient but not his family.
   c. be truthful to the family only, and swear them to secrecy.
   d. honestly inform both the patient and his family.

...ey Terms

...ing your own words, write a brief definition or ...planation of each of the following terms on a sepa-...e piece of paper.

living will

double effect

palliative care

hospice

physician-assisted suicide

voluntary euthanasia

...NSWERS

...PILOGUE REVIEW

Elisabeth Kübler-Ross; five

denial; anger; bargaining; depression; acceptance

is not; almost void of feelings

have not

not concealing

does

...*ung children*, who may not understand the concept ...death, are usually upset because it suggests being ...parated from those they love.

...cause they tend to focus on the quality of present ..., *adolescents* may primarily be concerned with the ...ect of their condition on their appearance and ...ial relationships.

...*ung adults* often feel rage and depression at the idea ...t, just as life is about to begin in earnest, it must ...d.

...*middle-aged adults*, death is an interruption of ...portant obligations and responsibilities.

...*older adult*'s feelings about dying depend on the ...ticular situation. If one's spouse has already died, ...example, acceptance of death is comparatively ...y.

mourner; angry; abandoned; are; anticipatory grief; fear of isolation and pain

swiftly; pain; dignity

more

underprescribed; addiction; oldest-old; nursing homes

law; hospital; individual who must undergo those treatments

12. living will; proxy

13. do not; family; half

14. DNR (do not resuscitate); double effect; palliative care

15. few; hospice

16. dehumanization

17. lay primary caregiver

18. does not

The fact that hospice patients must be diagnosed as terminally ill and give up all hope of recovery severely limits the number of participants. Patients and their families must accept this diagnosis, agreeing that life or a cure is virtually impossible. Also, hospice care is expensive and therefore not available to everyone. Finally, hospices are much better prepared to meet the needs of young adult patients with cancer than older patients with combinations of illnesses.

19. few; 17

20. cultural; community

21. physician-assisted suicide; voluntary euthanasia

22. Dutch

23. Oregon; have not

24. variable

25. African

26. Muslim

27. enlightenment; Hindus; Sikhs

28. Jewish; life

29. Christians; heaven; hell

30. culture; religion; mourning

31. a. Religious and spiritual concerns often reemerge.

    b. Returning to one's roots is a common urge.

32. private; emotional; religious; small memorial services after cremation; burial after a traditional funeral; social isolation; physical illness

33. a. Be aware that powerful, complicated, and culturally diverse emotions are likely.

    b. Understand that bereavement is often a lengthy process.

34. intimate, caring relationship

35. electronic letter

PROGRESS TEST 1

Multiple-Choice Questions

1. **b.** is the answer. (p. 710)

2. **c.** is the answer. (p. 711)

3. **c.** is the answer. (p. 709)

4. **c.** is the answer. (pp. 709, 711)

5. **d.** is the answer. (p. 710)

6. **a.** is the answer. (p. 710)

7. **c.** is the answer. (p. 712)

   a. This is a living will.

   b. & d. These are forms of euthanasia.

8. **c.** is the answer. (p. 712)

9. **b.** is the answer. (p. 714)

   a. There is no such thing as involuntary euthanasia.

   c. In this situation, a doctor provides the means for a *patient* to end his or her own life.

   d. DNR, or *do not resuscitate*, refers to a situation in which medical personnel allow a terminally ill person who has experienced severe pain to die naturally.

10. **d.** is the answer. (pp. 718–719)

11. **b.** is the answer. (p. 712)

12. **d.** is the answer. A central feature of hospices is that the dying are *not* isolated from loved ones, as they might be in a hospital. (p. 713)

True or False Items

1. T (p. 710)

2. F Later research has not confirmed Kübler-Ross's findings that the emotions of an individual faced with death occur in orderly stages. (pp. 709–710)

3. T (p. 710)

4. F The psychological well-being of the bereaved depends above all on their being able to openly express their grief. (p. 719)

5. F   A friend should listen, sympathize, and not ignore the mourner's pain. (p. 719)

6. F   Hospices have significant benefits, but some people are critical of them in part because they deny hope to the dying and because they are expensive. (p. 713)

7. F   These practices are *illegal* throughout most of the world. (p. 714)

8. T (p. 713)

9. T (p. 720)

10. F   Hospice care remains a controversial subject. (p. 713)

PROGRESS TEST 2

Multiple-Choice Questions

1. **c.** is the answer. (pp. 709–710)

2. **d.** is the answer. In recent times, mourning ha become less religious than formerly. (p. 718)

3. **d.** is the answer. Hospices generally *do* provic patients with skilled medical care. (p. 713)

4. **d.** is the answer. (p. 710)

5. **d.** is the answer. (p. 718)

6. **d.** is the answer. (p. 709)

   b. & c. There is no evidence that hospice resident experience different emotional stages than othe who are dying, or that these stages are a produ of Western culture.

7. **d.** is the answer. (p. 710)

8. **b.** is the answer. (p. 710)

9. **c.** is the answer. (p. 716)

10. **c.** is the answer. (pp. 712–713)

11. **c.** is the answer. (p. 716)

    a. Age *is* an important factor in both mournir and the dying person's emotions; gender, howe er was not discussed as a source of variation dying practices.

    b. Culture often has more influence on variatio in death practices than religion does.

    d. Anticipatory grief primarily influences the ea with which the bereaved are able to accept t loss of their loved one.

12. **b.** is the answer. (p. 718)

    a. & c. In such situations, death is expected ar generally easier to bear.

    d. This issue was not discussed.

Matching Items

1. c (p. 712)	5. i (p. 712)	9. g (p. 711)
2. b (p. 712)	6. e (p. 714)	
3. d (p. 710)	7. a (p. 712)	
4. h (p. 714)	8. f (p. 713)	

THINKING CRITICALLY ABOUT THE EPILOGUE

1. **a.** is the answer. (p. 714)

   b. The text notes that in many Muslim natior death serves to affirm faith in Allah.

   d. The text does not discuss the way in whic Native Americans conceptualize death.

2. **c.** is the answer. (p. 716)

3. **d.** is the answer. (p. 709)

a. People in this stage refuse to believe that their condition is terminal.

b. In this stage, the dying person directs anger at others for his or her condition.

c. In this stage, the dying person mourns his or her own impending death.

a. is the answer. (p. 709)

b. is the answer. (p. 711)

d. is the answer. (p. 711)

b. is the answer. (p. 712, 714)

a. A living will is a document expressing how a person wishes to be cared for should he or she become terminally ill.

c. This is when a person *intentionally acts* to end another's life.

d. In this situation, a person provides the means for another to take his or her own life.

b. is the answer. (p. 714)

b. is the answer. (p. 714)

c. is the answer. (p. 719)

c. is the answer. (p. 719)

a., b., & d. These statements discourage the bereaved person from mourning.

d. is the answer. (p. 710)

KEY TERMS

1. A **living will** is a document that specifies what medical intervention a person wants if he or she becomes incapable of expressing those wishes. (p. 710)

2. A **double effect** is a situation in which medication has the intended effect of relieving a dying person's pain and the secondary effect of hastening death. (p. 712)

3. **Palliative care**, such as that provided in a hospice, is care that relieves suffering while safeguarding the person's dignity. (p. 712)

4. A **hospice** is an institution in which terminally ill patients receive palliative care. (p. 712)

5. A **physician-assisted suicide** is one in which a doctor provides the means for a person to end his or her life. (p. 714)

6. **Voluntary euthanasia** is when at a patient's request, someone intentionally acts to terminate his or her life. (p. 714)

More About Research Methods

Appendix B Overview

The first section describes three ways of gathering information about development: library research, observational learning, and case studies. The second section discusses the various ways in which developmentalists ensure that their studies are valid.

NOTE: Answer guidelines for all Appendix B questions begin on page 405.

Guided Study

Appendix B should be studied one section at a time. Before you read, preview each section by skimming it, noting headings and boldface items. Then read the appropriate section objectives from the following outline. Keep these objectives in mind and, as you read the appendix section, search for the information that will enable you to meet each objective. Once you have finished a section, write out answers for its objectives.

Learning More (pp. B-1–B-3)

   1. Identify several helpful resources for conducting library research on development, and state four guidelines for systematic observation.

   2. Differentiate the four research methods that a[re] used in case-study research.

Ways to Make Research More Valid (pp. B-4–B-6)

   3. Describe the six techniques used by psychologis[ts] to ensure the validity of their research.

Appendix B Review

When you have finished reading Appendix B, wo[rk] through the material that follows to review [it.] Complete the sentences and answer the questions. [As] you proceed, evaluate your performance for each se[c-] tion by consulting the answers on page 405. Do n[ot] continue with the next section until you understa[nd] each answer. If you need to, review or reread t[he] appropriate section in the textbook before continuin[g.]

Learning More (pp. B-1–B-3)

   1. Two collections of abstracts that review current articles from developmental journals are

   _____ and

   _____ .

Two journals that cover development in all three domains are _____ and _____ .

A good way to deepen your understanding of development is by conducting systematic _____ of children around you. The observational profile described by the text author consists of the following four items:

a. _____

b. _____

c. _____

d. _____

A research method that is more elaborate and detailed than an observational study is called a

_____ _____ .

This method begins with _____

_____ , in which the researcher unobtrusively records everything the child does and that others do with the child. From these data, researchers often calculate the

_____ _____

_____ spent in various activities and the _____ of various behaviors. The next step in case study research is a period of _____ _____ that lasts for at least _____ (how long?). Following this, the researcher generally will _____ the child's caregiver, with the goal of learning the child's _____ , especially of any _____ , _____ or _____ ; the child's _____ _____ ; the child's _____ _____ ; and a description of the child's _____ and _____ .

Finally, specific _____ are used to assess the child's abilities.

ys to Make Research More Valid (pp. B-4–B-6)

To make statements about people in general, called a _____ , scientists study a group of research _____ , called a

_____ .

10. An important factor in selecting this group is

_____ _____ ; that is, the group must be large enough to ensure that the results are not distorted by a few

_____ _____ .

11. When a sample is typical of the group under study—in gender, ethnic background, and other important variables—the sample is called a(n) "_____ _____ ."

12. When the person carrying out research is unaware of the purpose of the research, that person is said to be in a state of _____ .

13. Researchers use _____

_____ to define variables in terms of specific, observable behavior that can be measured precisely.

14. To test a hypothesis, researchers often compare a(n) _____ _____ , which receives some special treatment called the _____ _____ , with a(n) _____ _____ , which does not. To test the possible effects of this treatment, the two groups are compared in terms of some _____ _____ .

Progress Test

Circle your answers to the following questions and check them with the answers on page 405. If your answer is incorrect, read the explanation for why it is incorrect and then consult the appropriate pages of the text (in parentheses following the correct answer).

1. A valuable collection of abstracts that review current articles from a variety of developmental journals is:
   a. *Psycscan: Developmental Psychology.*
   b. *Child Development Abstracts.*
   c. *Developmental Psychology.*
   d. a. and b.
   e. a., b., & c.

2. Two journals that publish research on all three domains of development are:
   a. *The Developmentalist* and *Child Psychology*.
   b. *Developmental Psychology* and *Child Development*.
   c. *Developmental Science* and *Aging*.
   d. *Child Psychology* and *The Developmentalist*.

3. Which of the following is *not* a recommended guideline for conducting a systematic observation of a child?
   a. Ask the child's age before beginning the observation.
   b. Write down everything that the child does or says.
   c. Interpret what you observed.
   d. Describe the specific child.

4. The research method in which one child is observed closely over time is called:
   a. naturalistic observation.
   b. informal interaction.
   c. a case study.
   d. an experiment.

5. Watching a child unobtrusively while recording everything the child does and that others do with the child describes:
   a. naturalistic observation.
   b. informal interaction.
   c. a case study.
   d. an experiment.

6. Which of the following is the correct sequence of steps in the structured case study described in the text?
   a. interview caregiver; informal interaction; naturalistic observation; test the child
   b. informal interaction; interview caregiver; naturalistic observation; test the child
   c. test the child; interview caregiver; informal interaction; naturalistic observation
   d. naturalistic observation; informal interaction; interview caregiver; test the child

7. Following a period of observation, researchers often summarize their data by calculating:
   a. the independent and dependent variables.
   b. the percentage of time spent in various activities and the frequency of various behaviors.
   c. the size of the sample.
   d. the extent of "blindness" in the research study.

8. The entire group of people about whom a scientist wants to learn is called the:
   a. reference group.
   b. sample.
   c. representative sample.
   d. population.

9. A researcher's conclusions after conducting study are not valid because a few extreme cases distorted the results. In designing this study, researcher evidently failed to pay attention to importance of:
   a. sample size.
   b. "blindness."
   c. representativeness.
   d. all of the above.

10. Rachel made a study of students' opinions about different psychology professors. She took great care to survey equal numbers of male and female students, students who received high grades and students who received low grades, and members of various minorities. Clearly, Rachel wished ensure that data were obtained from a:
    a. population.
    b. "blind" sample.
    c. control group.
    d. representative sample.

11. A person who gathers data in a state of "blindness" is one who:
    a. is unaware of the purpose of the research.
    b. is allowing his or her personal beliefs to influence the results.
    c. has failed to establish operational definition for the variables under investigation.
    d. is basing the study on an unrepresentative sample of the population.

12. Which of the following is an example of a good operational definition of a dependent variable?
    a. walking
    b. aggression
    c. 30 minutes of daily exercise
    d. taking steps without support

13. The control group in an experiment:
    a. receives the treatment of interest.
    b. does not receive the treatment of interest.
    c. is always drawn from a population different from the experimental group.
    d. must be larger in size than the experimental group.

For a psychologist's generalizations to be valid, the sample must be representative of the population under study. The sample must also be:

a. significant.
b. all the same age.
c. large enough.
d. none of the above.

The particular individuals who are studied in a specific research project are called the:

a. independent variables.
b. dependent variables.
c. subjects.
d. population.

y Terms

ing your own words, write a brief definition or lanation of each of the following terms on a sepa- e piece of paper.

population

subjects

sample

sample size

representative sample

blindness

experimental group

control group

NSWERS

PENDIX B REVIEW

Psycscan: Developmental Psychology; Child Development Abstracts and Bibliography

Developmental Psychology; Child Development

observations

A description of the physical and social context.

A description of the specific child who is the focus of the observation.

A detailed transcript of everything the child does or says in three minutes.

An interpretation of the observed behavior.

case study

naturalistic observation; percentage of time; frequency

informal interaction; half an hour

7. interview; history; illnesses; stresses; problems; daily routine; current problems; character; personality

8. tests

9. population; subjects; sample

10. sample size; extreme cases

11. representative sample

12. blindness

13. operational definitions

14. experimental group; independent variable; control group; dependent variable

PROGRESS TEST

1. **d.** is the answer. (p. B-1)

2. **b.** is the answer. (p. B-2)

3. **a.** is the answer. (p. B-2)

4. **c.** is the answer. (p. B-3)

   a. Although case studies often involve naturalistic observation, *groups* of individuals can also be the subjects of this research method.

   b. Observation does not involve direct interaction with subjects.

   d. Experiments involve directly manipulating an independent variable.

5. **a.** is the answer. (p. B-3)

   b. Unobtrusive observations are, by their very nature, *not* a form of interaction.

   c. Case studies are not limited to the use of naturalistic observation.

   d. Experiments involve directly manipulating an independent variable.

6. **d.** is the answer. (p. B-3)

7. **b.** is the answer. (p. B-3)

   a. The variables *in an experiment* are operationally defined, not calculated.

   c. Samples are used in experiments to represent the complete population of subjects under study.

   d. "Blindness" refers to whether the person gathering the data in an experiment is aware of the purpose of the study.

8. **d.** is the answer. (p. B-4)

   a. This is not a term used in scientific research.

   b. & c. Samples are subsets of the larger populations from which they are drawn.

9. **a.** is the answer. (p. B-4)

   b. "Blindness" has no relevance here.

c. Although it is true that a distorted sample is unrepresentative, the issue concerns the small number of extreme cases—a dead giveaway to sample size.

10. **d.** is the answer. Rachel has gone to great lengths to make sure that her student sample is typical of the entire population of students who takes psychology courses. (p. B4)

11. **a.** is the answer. (p. B5)

12. **d.** is the answer. (p. B5)

a., b., & c. Each of these definitions is too ambiguous to qualify as an operational definition.

13. **b.** is the answer. (p. B5)

a. This describes the experimental group.

c. The control group must be similar to the experimental group (and therefore drawn from the same population).

d. The control group is usually the same size as the experimental group.

14. **c.** is the answer. (p. B4)

15. **c.** is the answer. (p. B4)

a. These are the factors that a researcher manipulates in an experiment.

b. These are the outcomes that a researcher measures in an experiment.

d. It is almost always impossible to include every member of a population in an experiment.

KEY TERMS

1. The **population** is the entire group of individuals who are of particular concern in a scientific study. (p. B-4)

2. **Subjects** are the people who are studied in a research project. (p. B-4)

3. A **sample** is a subset of individuals who are drawn from a specific population. (p. B-4)

4. **Sample size** refers to the number of subjects in a specific sample. (p. B-4)

5. A **representative sample** is a group of research subjects who accurately reflect key characteristics of the population being studied. (p. B-4)

6. **Blindness** is the situation in which a person who is collecting the data in a research project is deliberately kept unaware of the purpose of the study in order to avoid unintentionally influencing the results. (p. B-5)

7. The **experimental group** in an experiment is the group of subjects who experience the condition or treatment (independent variable) under investigation. (p. B-5)

8. The **control group** in an experiment is the comparison group of subjects who are comparable to those in the experimental group in every relevant way except that they do not experience the independent variable. (p. B-5)